PROCLAMATION:

Aids for Interpreting the Lessons of the Church Year

✠ ADVENT ✠ CHRISTMAS

SERIES B

Thor Hall
and
James L. Price

FORTRESS PRESS Philadelphia, Pennsylvania

Table of Contents

Library of Congress Catalog Card Number 74-24899

ISBN 0-8006-4071-3

Second printing 1976

5975G76 Printed in U.S.A. 1-4071

General Preface

Proclamation: Aids for Interpreting the Lessons of the Church Year is a series of twenty-six books designed to help clergymen carry out their preaching ministry. It offers exegetical interpretations of the lessons for each Sunday and many of the festivals of the church year, plus homiletical ideas and insights.

The basic thrust of the series is ecumenical. In recent years the Episcopal church, the Roman Catholic church, the United Church of Christ, the Christian Church (Disciples of Christ), the United Methodist Church, the Lutheran and Presbyterian churches, and also the Consultation on Church Union have adopted lectionaries that are based on a common three-year system of lessons for the Sundays and festivals of the church year. *Proclamation* grows out of this development, and authors have been chosen from all of these traditions. Some of the contributors are parish pastors; others are teachers, both of biblical interpretation and of homiletics. Ecumenical interchange has been encouraged by putting two persons from different traditions to work on a single volume, one with the primary responsibility for exegesis and the other for homiletical interpretation.

Despite the high percentage of agreement between the traditions, both in the festivals that are celebrated and the lessons that are appointed to be read on a given day, there are still areas of divergence. Frequently the authors of individual volumes have tried to take into account the various textual traditions, but in some cases this has proved to be impossible; in such cases we have felt constrained to limit the material to the Lutheran readings.

The preacher who is looking for "canned sermons" in these books will be disappointed. These books are one step removed from the pulpit: they explain what the lessons are saying and suggest ways of relating this biblical message to the contemporary situation. As such they are springboards for creative thought as well as for faithful proclamation of the word.

This volume of *Proclamation* has been prepared by Thor Hall and James L. Price. Dr. Hall was the editor and homiletician for the volume, and Dr. Price was the exegete. Dr. Hall is a native of Norway and a graduate of the University of Oslo and the Scandinavian Methodist Seminary in Gothenburg, Sweden. He served as pastor and as Executive Secretary of the Youth Department of the Methodist Church in Norway before coming to the United States in 1957 to engage in graduate study at Duke University, Durham, N. C. He holds the Ph.D. degree from Duke University and served on the Duke faculty from 1962-1972. Dr. Hall was named Distinguished Professor of Religious Studies at the University of Tennessee at Chattanooga in 1972. He is the author of numerous books and articles. One previous book, *The Future Shape of Preaching* (1971), was published with Fortress Press. Dr. Hall is an ordained minister of the United Methodist Church. Dr. Price, the exegete, is a graduate of Washington and Lee University (B.A.), Union Theological Seminary, Richmond, Va. (B.D.), and Princeton Theological Seminary (Th.M.). His graduate work was interrupted by a three year term as naval chaplain during World War II. After the war Dr. Price taught philosophy and religion for two years at Washington and Lee University and then continued his studies at Cambridge University, from which he received the Ph.D. degree. He joined the Duke faculty in 1952 and is now Professor of Religion there. His field of specialization is New Testament history and theology. He plays an active role in several learned societies and has contributed articles and essays to various scholarly publications. His major work is *Interpreting the New Testament* (New York: Holt, Rinehart & Winston, 1961; 2nd ed., 1971). Dr. Price is an ordained minister in the Presbyterian Church in the U.S.

Introduction

Advent and Christmas open the church year. Consisting of six Sundays and two special festivals, this liturgical octave represents one of the most tightly structured seasons in the ecclesiastical calendar. It takes us step by step from the most serious awareness of the absence of God to the most overwhelming experience of his presence.

The eight chapters in this little book are designed to help preachers relate to each of these steps. The assumption is that each unit, each individual festival, plays a unique role in the ongoing life of the Christian community. We have sought to define that role and keep our exegetical and homiletical reflections relevant to it. In the process we have occasionaily felt constrained by the lectionary. But it has also challenged us to greater concentration and depth where the natural inclination was to hurry on. In the end we must confess to an increased respect for the wisdom of church traditions set forth in the lectionary.

One difficulty in guiding the church through Advent is the tendency to shift the focus back and forth from pre-Christian messianic expectations, to present hopes, to futuristic considerations. We have sought to avoid any dissipation of the Advent observance by holding all of these dimensions together at each stage of the way. Our own focus, for which we have found support in the lectionary itself, has been on the successive stages in the process of preparation, and primarily the attitudes which are appropriate for each stage. With this we hope to have provided perspectives that are relevant to every dimension of Advent, whether historical, existential, or apocalyptic.

It would be interesting, in a cooperative endeavor such as this, involving both exegetical and homiletical interpretations, to reflect on the relationship between the two perspectives. Our readers will find that "exegesis" and "homiletical interpretation" occasionally overlap. This is clearly a consequence of the new consensus which is developing among biblical scholars and systematic theologians, namely, the emphasis on the theological character of the Bible and the biblical character of theology. We have made only vague attempts to avoid such overlap, and only for the purpose of saving space. In other contexts our readers will find that the exegesis has a more historical-critical orientation while the homiletical interpretation is more concerned with contemporary application. Throughout, we think, the two perspectives complement and supplement each other.

The various churches' lectionaries do not differ significantly for the Advent sequence. Minor variations occur in the Christmas and post-Christmas listings, and as space has allowed reference has been made to these alternate readings. On no occasion do we have no reference to any of the texts listed in an alternate lectionary. This book should therefore be equally useful to all denominations whose lectionaries are listed.

An apology is in order. Being limited to 64 printed pages, and having eight units to consider, we have naturally been restricted as to the extent of our treatment of each text. We have endeavored to be specific enough to help preachers in the process of preparing sermons, but we have not been able to go into every detail as we would have wanted to discuss them. We can only hope to have said enough to provide useful perspectives and suggest possible avenues for further exploration and reflection. That should be a satisfying function for this book.

Thor Hall

The First Sunday in Advent

Lutheran	*Roman Catholic*	*Episcopal*	*Pres./UCC/Chr.*	*Methodist/COCU*
Isa. 63:16b–17; 64:1–8	Isa. 63:16b–17; 64:3b–8	Isa. 63:16b–64:8	Isa. 63:16–64:4	Isa. 63:16–64:8
1 Cor. 1:3–9	1 Cor. 1:3–9	1 Cor. 1:3–9	1 Cor. 1:3–9	Cor. 1:3–9
Mark 13:33–37	Mark 13:33–37	Mark 13:33–37	Mark 13:32–37	Mark 13:32–37

EXEGESIS

The lessons for the First Sunday in Advent represent three quite different forms of discourse, forms suited to the various situations which occasioned them: from the OT, a prophet's psalm of lamentation on behalf of a despondent people; from the NT, first, an apostle's thanksgiving typical of those introducing letters to his churches, and, second, a pair of parables from the Gospel, similar to several others spoken by Jesus concerning the kingdom of God. All three passages raise an urgent question: when God confronts man in historic acts of judgment and salvation—as surely he shall, revealing himself in unpredictable ways—how will it be with his people?

First Lesson: Isa. 63:16b–17; 64:1–8. Part of a psalm of lamentation, this passage epitomizes its content and moods. The whole poem, 63:7–64:12, is the lament and intercessory prayer of a community spoken by a prophet. Interpretation of the passage calls for information concerning its author and the situation to which he addresses himself. Our knowledge of such matters is, however, somewhat limited.

The first major sections of the book of Isaiah present the work of two quite distinctive prophetic figures. Chaps. 1–39 contain oracles of "Isaiah son of Amoz," a dynamic prophet whose ministry in Jerusalem spanned the latter half of the eighth century B.C. and the early years of the seventh. Chaps. 40–55 contain the words of an anonymous prophet who ministered to the captives of Judah in Babylon in the sixth century. "Second Isaiah," as he is commonly called, was certainly influenced by the first Isaiah's vision of God and understanding of the prophet's calling. He sought to apply the earlier prophet's message to changed circumstances, as well as to discern the "new things" God was presently accomplishing through his "servant," Israel.

The last division of the book, chaps. 56–66, preserves the messages of another or, more probably, several anonymous prophets directed to the people of Judea after their return from Babylonian exile during a period from around 540–500 B.C., or later. Like their predecessor in Babylon, these men were linked closely with the tradition of the original Isaiah. They extended his influence into a third century. Preserving thus the words of the prophet Isaiah and those of his successors, the book of Isaiah "witnesses not only to great men in crisis moments of Israel's history; it reveals also how rich was the continuity of faith of those who . . . were the bearers of the tradition and the maintainers of its truth."[1]

There are some clues in this psalm of lamentation to the historical situation it presupposes. Jerusalem is desolate; its temple destroyed, 64:10 f.; also 63:18. The tragedies of 586 B.C. may appear to lie in the recent past, but this lament voices the despondency of those returning to rebuild Zion more than a half century later (cf. Haggai). The prophet of the exile had faced a despondent people too, crushed by the disasters they had experienced, but he proclaimed to them that God himself was soon to accomplish a new exodus for his people, more marvelous than their deliverance from Egypt (e.g., 43:18–21; 46:11–13; 49:14 ff.). This prophet, however, shares his people's pessimism and malaise. Like his predecessor he can celebrate God's redemptive acts in Israel's history, but he views them as long past. How he yearns to announce a new theophany! But to him imminent salvation seems problematic. One senses in this poem an uneasy impatience resulting from hope long deferred, as though God's anger must be restrained, his will to save stirred up.

There is an unrelieved tension in the theology of this prophet and his people. On the one hand, the thought of God's intervention threatens further judgments. What will happen to those who wait for him but who can lay claim to no merit? The dreaded answer inhibited many from invoking God's presence. They felt that they had experienced too much judgment, too little mercy. Was God himself to blame? "O Lord, why dost thou make us err from thy ways and harden our heart, so that we fear thee not?" (63:17; also 63:15; 64:7). On the other hand the prophet declares that since God is the Father of Israel—and this people the work of his hand—he cannot reject them although he punishes them. There are limits to his will to judge this people according to their deserts; he imposes self-restraint when wroth. Because of these convictions prophet and people can cry: "O that thou wouldst rend the heavens and come down" (64:1).

The crux of the theological dilemma posed in this lamentation is its assertion that God's coming brings benediction only to the righteous: "Thou meetest him that joyfully works righteousness, those that remember thee in thy ways . . . in our sins we have been a long time, and shall we be saved?" (64:5).

Second Lesson: 1 Cor. 1:3–9. Paul adopts a common literary convention in writing to his young churches, appending to his salutations a thanksgiving for those to whom he writes. In this lesson the apostle thanks God for the Corinthian Christians upon whom so many divine gifts have been bestowed. As in other letters, Paul here associates the reality of the Spirit's gifts with the (final) revealing of Christ and with the Christian's reception of his final inheritance. For Paul, the Spirit's manifestations

1. P. Ackroyd, "Isaiah," *Interpreter's One-Volume Commentary* (New York/Nashville: Abingdon, 1971), p. 330.

served as a kind of pledge or down payment of that inheritance (1 Cor. 2:9–10; 2 Cor. 1:19–22; cf. Rom. 5:5; 8:11, 14–17, 23).

Paul's many sharp rebukes of the Corinthian Christians have led some readers to wonder whether the apostle's thanksgiving is the permissible hyperbole of polite speech. His commendations seem to need serious qualifications. Notice that Paul refers only to gifts of speech and knowledge, gifts which many Corinthians were either prizing too highly or else abusing. (See a discussion of these two gifts, in reverse order: 1 Cor. 8:1–11:1 and 12:1–14:40.) Is there irony then in this passage? Probably not. Paul makes positive, theological use of the thanksgiving form, and his assurances here find support in other of his writings. He salutes those who are called into fellowship with God's Son as persons consecrated in their calling. God's grace is thus revealed to undeserving men as a power overcoming sin (cf. Rom. 5:18–21; 6:22 f.).

The agonizing dilemma of the prophet of the sixth century B.C. is resolved in this "gospel"—God comes not to call the righteous, but sinners. Those who have experienced his salvation invoke the name of the Lord Jesus not with foreboding but with joy. They wait expectantly for *further* revelations and for the coming of his "Day."

The indicatives of Paul's gospel usually carry moral imperatives. Even in this thanksgiving one may feel the force of exhortation: "In every way you are enriched . . . you are not lacking any spiritual gift . . . you are called into the fellowship, to share in the life of his [God's] Son" (vv. 5, 7, 9 NEB). See 1:10; also 12:7: "To each is given the manifestation of the Spirit *for the common good*" (cf. Rom 12:4–8).

Gospel: Mark 13:33–37. Among those things Jesus taught his disciples concerning the future is the appeal for ever-present watchfulness. So in the lesson from the Gospel, his answer to the question "When" is a summons to be ready at any time. The pair of parables at the close of Mark 13 underscores this exhortation: "And what I say to you, I say to everyone: 'Keep awake'" (13:37 NEB). In giving shape to this apocalyptic discourse Mark affirms that authentic Christian watchfulness is not holding to the belief that the end will come soon or in plotting its signs, but rather a constant attention to proclaiming the church's gospel in that indeterminate time-span before the end. The lesson is exhortation; it discourages speculation.

Mark 13 is commonly held to be a composition drawn from several sources. Some sayings attributed here to Jesus appear in other contexts in Matthew and Luke (e.g., cf. vv. 9–13 and Matt. 10:17–21; or v. 21 and Luke 17:23). Moreover, words of Jesus concerning imminent events in Judea, vv. 14–20, are not clearly related here, or at other places in the Gospels, to signs heralding the end, vv. 24–27, 5–13. Uncertainties remain concerning the precise references of "in those days," v. 24, or "when you see these things taking place," v. 29. Mark probably drew upon a collection of Jesus' sayings which had been extended and applied to conditions in the early church by others. These traditions had fostered the hope of Jesus' imminent coming by presenting a table of premonitory signs. Yet by emphasizing Jesus' exhortation ("and what I say to you, I say to all"), Mark deliberately cools this apocalyptic ardor and summons his readers to their missionary task, calling upon them to grasp any opportunity for witness bearing, since the time of the end is unpredictable.

Although one may detect stages in the formation of this gospel tradition, Mark, and the compilers of his sources, were warranted in attributing the whole to Jesus. By his words and deeds the church's Lord radically altered the OT visions of God's coming to men. By confronting men now in Christ God gathers his people into fellowship with him. And when he comes in the future, in his own time and way, he will appear as the glorified Son of man.

HOMILETICAL INTERPRETATION

The message of Advent is anticipation. The preacher should make sure that he understands the inner dynamics of anticipation and structures his Advent sermons so as to bring his congregation to experience the season's peculiar qualities of attitude and thought and action.

The pericopes for Advent I are well suited both for the exploration and the expression of this special mood. The writers—prophet, apostle, evangelist, all three—are looking toward the future, yet they are also conscious of the present, and their perspective is informed by what they know of the past. They are confident that the future is in God's hands and that God will act decisively in his own time and in his own way. All three base their confidence on the steadfastness of the love which God has revealed in all that he has done in the past. And each one is concerned to relate this hope and this trust to the present situation of their readers and the current conditions of life. Thus, all three texts selected for this day invite us, at the opening of the liturgical year, to look at the present status of things from the double perspective of a believing Janus—with a backward and a forward look informing our attitude and thought and action. This double orientation is perhaps the very essence of anticipation.

The legitimacy of this kind of homiletical reapplication of the textual perspective to our own time and place is guaranteed by the authority of our writers and is integral to the role of the preacher. Each of these writers proclaimed—as each of us must—a kerygma that comes out of the past, that concerns the future, and is relevant to the present. The prophetic writer did this by reaffirming the message of the original Isaiah and of Second Isaiah in the context of the postexilic crisis. But his own existence was clearly the crucible in which his predecessor's kerygma became a present message. Paul and Mark wrote the same way, as preachers burdened with the task of reinterpreting the Christian kerygma for their own situation and that of their readers.

We shall return to the question of their relevance in a minute. But first, look again at these texts—and now for the purpose of discovering the deeper dynamic of anticipation which is at work within them.

The lamentation of the postexilic prophet (Isa. 63:16b-17; 64:1–8) seems depressingly pessimistic, quite inconsistent with the happy predictions of his predecessor, Second Isaiah of the exile. That earlier prophet had the time-compressing, foreshortening perspective of the true seer. He could envision God's mighty deliverance coming soon. His form of anticipation gave him a foretaste of the future in the present—anticipation meant leaping ahead and living with a consciousness anchored in the new age beyond the present time. Not so for the writer of our text. His vision could not soar freely, disregarding his own and his people's historicity. His was a more timid, chastened spirit, tied in with the times and the troubles of his contemporaries. Yet, there was anticipation in his spirit also—not as though he had made a spiritual jet flight across several time zones, arriving at the same hour as he took off, bur rather as though he were plodding steadily through the dreary desert below, sorely conscious that the end was not yet in sight, still trustful that one day he would see it. His was a realistic type of anticipation, a faith not so much in the form of a leap beyond as a leap within—not so keenly aware of God's presence as of his absence. There is a peculiar courage and strength in this sort of attitude. Preachers would do well to study it and identify with it, especially during Advent, and particularly in our time.

The Pauline text (1 Cor. 1:3–9) adds another dimension to the concept of anticipation—a characteristic Christian perspective which ought not to be minimized in our Advent observance. The Christian community exists, suggests Paul, between two advents: it was established in that first advent, the revelation of God's grace through Jesus, the Christ who came in the form of a servant; it will be fulfilled in a second advent, the revelation of Jesus Christ as Lord and King. It is this second advent, "the day of our Lord Jesus Christ," which is on Paul's mind as he describes the Corinthian church as "waiting." There is clearly something more to come, and this gives the Christian's existence a "not yet" quality which cannot fully be comprehended within the "already" of present faith. As Justin Martyr expressed it, "The prophet foretold two comings of Christ—one, which has already happened, as that of a dishonored and passible man, and the second, when as has been foretold he will come from heaven in glory with his angelic host" (*The First Apology*).

The annual Advent season thus gives the church an opportunity to anticipate the second advent as well as to recollect the memory of the first. The season in fact evokes a picture of the full drama of salvation and the church's place within it. The faithful community looks back to the time before it was even a community—when its members were "separated from Christ," "strangers to the covenant's promise," "without God and without hope in the world" (Eph. 2:11–12)—recapitulating by way of liturgy its situation prior to that dramatic passage from death to life, from darkness into the light. That recollection forms the backdrop for the festival of the incarnation which is to come at Christmas. But the church also looks forward, from the vantage point of its present interim, to the day of fulfillment, the final phase of the drama. With real anticipation, not only liturgical recapitulation, Christians live an ongoing life of faith, always open to what God has promised to do, always trustful because, as Paul says, "God is faithful." Once again we have identified an attitude which preachers ought to cultivate during Advent. We are members of a community which is oriented in two directions–in retrospect of a first coming which established our faith, and in prospect of a second coming which will complete it.

A third aspect of the attitude of anticipation comes before us in the Markan text (13:33–37), namely, the element of urgency, even immediacy, which characterizes the eschatology of the Christian community. Mark's short apocalypse offers a direct refutation of all speculative, futuristic types of apocalypticism, those forms of anticipation which are intent on answering questions of what and when and where. Mark's perspective does not allow for any such projections or any relaxing of the present eschatological tension. For him the hour is now. Anticipation means staying awake, being alert and watchful at each moment. There is no logic by which the tension of the moment can be reduced; to have faith means simply to stay faithful at each moment. God's *kairos* is not linked with the *chronos*; it is not scheduled at a certain point in time. God works according to his own will, and his will is free at all times. This gives the attitude of anticipation an urgency far more immediate than any speculative apocalypticism can ever evoke. It makes Advent into a symbol of the Christian's total life style, not just a mood he experiences at a certain time of the year.

We can now return to the question of the relevance of these dimensions of our texts to our present situation. Most of us are quite aware by now of the moral, spiritual, and intellectual crises through which we are passing. The loss of moral compass, spiritual integrity, and intellectual confidence, all part of our existence here and now, calls for an Advent observance of extraordinary depth and more than usual religious sensitivity.

The postexilic prophet may well help us handle the contemporary malaise with greater honesty and realism. There are theologians of hope among us, prophets in the Second-Isaiah tradition who orient their thought to the future and to the future's impact on the present. But that message is perhaps too optimistic, too easy for many. There are those among us also who are more like the lamenting postexilic poet, speaking of the absence (if not the death) of God and describing the church's task as "the unveiling of religious meaning in the darkness of God's absence" (Altizer). Both groups may have a word of God for our times, but perhaps preachers need to take more seriously the despairing spirits among us. Our OT text can help us to do just that.

No Christian will be permanently despairing, however. Paul can help us here. The contemporary Christian needs to see both that there has been one decisive coming and that there will be another. That is the situation in which we are set. Such is the true nature of faith. The believer has seen enough to know that the world is not forsaken by God. Something unique has happened which has turned his spirit from despair to trust—Paul calls it "the grace of God given you in Christ Jesus." On the basis of what he has seen, the Christian has the assurance that he is not alone in the world. He is enriched and sustained by a faithful God. And when the great advent is over, the fulfillment will come—the consummation of God's own purpose, in heaven and on earth. Such is the Christian's hope.

When will that be? Mark's answer is relevant here—he refuses the question. He does not quench expectation; he turns it into present activity. The thing to do is to live responsibly in the interim, to work in the world, wherever one has been put in charge, each on his own job. One's work is not a diversion, a pastime. It is an integral part of the total drama of salvation, that part which the master has charged each of his servants to do. That is the Christian way to anticipate the coming fulfillment. That is the way to live in Advent.

The Second Sunday in Advent

Lutheran	*Roman Catholic*	*Episcopal*	*Pres./UCC/Chr.*	*Methodist/COCU*
Isa. 40:1–11	Isa. 40:1–5, 9–11	Isa. 40:1–5, 9–11	Isa. 40:1–5, 9–11	Isa. 40:1–11
2 Pet. 3:8–14	2 Pet. 3:8–14	2 Pet. 3:8–14	2 Pet. 3:8–14	2 Pet. 3:8–14
Mark 1:1–8	Mark 1:1–8	Mark 1:1–8	Mark 1:1–8	Mark 1:1–8

EXEGESIS

First Lesson: Isa. 40:1–11. The OT lesson is the initial poem in the collection of prophecies attributed to Second Isaiah, chaps. 40–55, often called the Book of Consolation. This poem announces the triumphal march of God through the wilderness to Jerusalem and the cities of Judah. Thus the way is being prepared for the return of his people who are in bondage. See also 41:17–20; 43:1–44:8. By his power the Holy One of Israel will accomplish a mighty deliverance of his chosen people: shepherding his flock, leading them forward, and carrying their weak to their own land. The prophet hears the voice of God renewing his covenant with Israel ("my people," "your God"), assuring them that their term of hard servitude is at an end, that a full or even double measure of punishment for their sins has been received.

It is significant for an understanding of this prophet's message to note that while he was confident that God was ready to redeem Israel, he views Israel's exile as God's just judgment (Isa. 42:24–25; 43:22–28; 48:1 ff.). The contrast between the prophet's perception of God's readiness to save all mankind and of man's inconstancy and frailty is sharply expressed. "Man is no more enduring reality than grass; the only enduring reality is his experience of the word of God."[1] Man can neither frustrate nor annul that word—that is to say, *the word and the deed it accomplishes.* God's word of promise must "stand forever."

And what of that promise, which seemed at the time so far from reality? Jews in Babylon were released by Cyrus the Persian to rebuild the cities of Judah, but recovery was slow and the results disappointing. Yet the vision of the new Jerusalem lived on through a long period of political and economic depression (as several of the OT readings for Advent confirm). And so did this prophet's faith in the power and will of God to repossess the scattered people of his creation and to win a victory which should reveal the glory of the Lord to all. Later Jewish seers and mystics added to this prophetic legacy of the restored community the promise of the renewal of nature and even of the entire universe. Indeed, this breathtaking upheaval was proclaimed by one of the prophets in Isaiah's succession. (See 65:17 ff., and 66:22–23.) Thus the image of the "new Jerusalem" gained a vitality to which no earth-bound reality could do justice, and the renewal of the earth by the word of the Lord was perceived to be more than its restoration. With the discovery of the Dead Sea Scrolls we now know that a Jewish sectarian group had established a community in the wilderness a few decades before Jesus' ministry, in the belief that by studying the law of Moses which God had commanded, and through radical obedience, they were preparing "the way of the Lord." By this means Isaiah's prophecy and God's promise would be realized. Early Christians, according to our Gospel lesson for today, saw this scripture fulfilled in a different way, in the coming of John the Baptist, but only as his prophetic ministry was linked to that of Jesus who is Christ, the Son of God, the tender "shepherd" destined by God to reveal the divine glory (Isa. 40:11; cf. John 10:11–16; 17:1–5).

Second Lesson: 2 Pet. 3:8–14. Apocalypticism flourished in Jewish communities in the period of Christian origins encouraging both political revolution and quietistic withdrawal from the world. In either case the images of the new Jerusalem always contained more than was ever present in the old city or seemed possible as human achievement. God's intervention would be required, and it was imminently expected. Jewish disciples of Jesus found this way of thinking ready at hand to express the radical newness of the gospel and the glorious hope it inspired. In the theology of the early church the marvelous advent of God as judge and savior—the coming of the prophets' day of the Lord—was envisioned as the coming of Christ. In the mother tongue of Jesus and of the earliest Christians there were no words for "return" or "coming again." The term "second coming" is not found in the NT (it is used by Justin Martyr writing in the second century). Jesus' future coming is portrayed in the canonical books as his "*parousia*," a Greek term ordinarily used to describe

1. J.L. McKenzie, *Second Isaiah* (New York: Doubleday, 1968), p. 18.

the coming to a community of an emperor or royal dignitary, for whose appearance elaborate preparations would be made. Thus the future manifestation of Christ "in power and great glory"–his *parousia* (literally, his regal "presence") among men–was sharply contrasted with his previous presence in lowliness and obscurity, the Messiah despised and rejected.

The writer of the epistle from which today's Second Lesson is taken, for reasons one can only conjecture, took as a pseudonym "Simon Peter." According to common belief this letter was written in the early decades of the second century, and is the latest book in the NT. The writer reaffirms, for his generation, the faith of Paul and the early church in the *parousia* of Christ. In the face of his antagonists' denials, he could have argued from traditional Jewish apocalyptic that the presence of "scoffers" in the church signaled the imminence of the last days. Instead, like Jesus and Paul, he stressed the unpredictability and suddenness of the end (v. 10). Drawing upon Ps. 90:4 as scriptural authority, he declares that God's time is not to be confused with man's reckoning. But unlike some Jewish and other Christian apocalyptists he does not believe that God will foreshorten the time or the agonies traditionally associated with the end (cf. Mark 13:19–20). Rather, he teaches that God mercifully delays the *parousia* in order to give everyone opportunity for repentance (v. 9). This also is in agreement with the Pauline perspective (Rom. 2:3–5; cf. 1 Tim. 2:4).

One aspect of this lesson may create special difficulties for modern Christians. In his attempt to rebut the scoffers, the writer of 2 Peter argues that just as the earth was once destroyed by water, it will finally be destroyed by fire. Employed here is an ancient Persian (and later Stoic) theory of a final world conflagration. Jewish and Christian apocalypses are known to have subscribed to this speculative idea (see Zech. 1:18; 3:8; Sybl. Or. IV. 172–182). This notion persisted into the period of the church fathers as is shown in the Shepherd of Hermas (4.3.3) and in Justin Martyr's *Apology* (I.20). The writer of 2 Peter, however, sees, beyond this disintegration of the universe, the fulfillment of a promise of divine re-creation, described as "a new heaven and a new earth in which righteousness dwells."

The NT witness for the most part seems to discourage speculation of this sort, very largely due, we may believe, to our Lord's lack of curiosity about such matters or his reticence to probe into them. In the OT an Oriental myth of a great desolating flood was exploited to give expression to Israel's faith in the sovereignty and justice of God. In this passage a cardinal teaching of the NT concerning the coming of the day of the Lord is expressed in the currently popular imagery of world conflagration. On the basis of his biblical religion our writer opted for this theory rejecting his opponents' claim that the world was immutable or eternal. The faithful acceptance of the apostolic proclamation that God is the sovereign Lord of creation, and that Christ's *parousia* is grounded upon his enduring word, does not necessitate literal interpretation of this cosmological imagery.

Gospel: Mark 1:1–8. "Here begins the good news about Jesus Christ the Son of God"—this is the title for the earliest extant compilation of the traditions concerning Jesus in narrative form. Mark employs the term "good news," as Paul did, to refer to both the content of the Christian proclamation and the act of preaching. The good news *is* Christ (8:35; 10:29). From the beginning of his story, Mark's interest is to show that the good news is being sent forth into all the world. First the Baptist, then Jesus (1:14), then the twelve disciples of the risen Lord (13:10), proclaim the arrival of God's time of salvation, the beginning of the new age foretold by Israel's prophets. Mark's interest is not limited to the life of a Jewish Messiah recently the victim of a violent death; he proclaims the risen Christ—Jesus the Son of God—who is every reader's contemporary and who is re-presented to men in the telling of his story.

With this beginning Mark closely associates two OT passages, one drawn from the First Lesson for today. The linking of these prophetic testimonies, Mal. 3:1 and Isa. 40:3, probably preceded Mark's use of them. Although the texts are referred directly to John's mission, briefly described in vv. 4–8, they function as a preface to the whole Gospel as the fulfillment of God's dealings with Israel.[1] The church's adaptation of the Isaiah passage (cf. Mark 1:3 and Isa. 40:3) clearly reveals that John was considered the forerunner, the prophet ordained by God to prepare the way for the Messiah's coming. Isaiah had foretold the coming of God, not of a messiah. Isa. 40:3 was thus applicable to the Baptist only on the assumption that the risen Christ is now "Lord." As the revealer of the glory of God Jesus claims the homage of all men. See the early Christian hymn, Phil. 2:5–11; cf. John 1:14, 18.

The lesson from Isaiah proclaims that when God comes to save his people he decrees that their iniquities are pardoned (40:2). Mark reports that John proclaimed "a baptism in token of repentance, for the forgiveness of sins" (v. 4 NEB). Like the prophet of the exile, who pleaded with his people to return to God, John called those who flocked to hear him to "repent" (lit. to turn around) in expectation of the coming judgment, to radically redirect their lives. Mark clearly writes to those who live in the time for a worldwide proclamation of the forgiveness of sins, the time for repentance and especially for witness to the good news about the Christ who has come, who continues to come, and who will come at the close of the age.

HOMILETICAL INTERPRETATION

The texts for Advent II all focus on preparation. The anticipation which characterizes the message of Advent is here expressed in terms of activity—not *any* activity, not the usual busyness of the Advent season, but an appropriate process which means one is preparing to receive that which is to be given and respond to what is about to take place.

1. Eduard Schweizer, *The Good News According to Mark* (Richmond: John Knox, 1970), p. 29.

The three texts come, of course, out of different traditions, but there is a remarkable unanimity of emphasis among them. The prophet of the exile, the pseudonymous author of 2 Peter, and Mark the evangelist, all consider the kind of self-awareness which characterizes the anticipation of the events to come. The promised coming is announced by each one. It is the presupposition for everything they say. It is described both as a saving and a judging event; it has the quality of an unearned blessing and the character of a moral test. All three writers emphasize that God's coming is his own free, unqualified act. But all three emphasize also that since God is initiating such remarkable events there are certain concomitant responses which people ought to make.

We should be sure to understand their emphases correctly. At no point do these writers say that the divine act is conditioned on or qualified by any human activity. Their emphasis on the moral test involved is never moralistic, and their interpretation of the event itself never legalistic. The moral test is the *result* of the promise, never the precondition for its fulfillment. The blessed gift always precedes the moral test. Advent is not something that occurs because we have met the requirements and prepared correctly; rather, we are to prepare ourselves to receive and experience that which God has already announced that he will do, regardless. Preparation, then, is our response to the promise, not the condition for its fulfillment.

It is important to understand the genius of this point of view. Much preaching during Advent is dangerously close to misrepresenting the biblical message. Not a few among us reverse the factors and proclaim that God's coming is a result of proper preparation. Not only during Advent do we twist things this way. We often preach as if repentance precedes grace and grace is the consequence of faith. But this is a misunderstanding of the nature of grace and a misrepresentation of the relationship between God and us.

We shall attempt to sketch the relevance of these texts for our own situation in a moment. In the meantime, what sort of preparation are these writers talking about?

Second-Isaiah focuses on heralding the good news and accepting it in humility. 2 Peter talks of a cataclysmic "day of the Lord" and urges his readers to consider what sort of persons they ought to be while waiting. Mark's prologue ties together the announcement of the coming salvation/judgment with the response of humble confession and serious repentance, all in reference to John the Baptizer, "the voice in the wilderness." Taken together, these pericopes give us a series of biblical answers to Paul Gerhardt's moving Advent question:

> O how shall I receive thee,
> How greet thee, Lord, aright?

(Service Book and Hymnal of the Lutheran Church in America [1958], hymn #11.)

The prophet makes a clear announcement of the tone and content of the message he has been authorized to proclaim (Isa. 40:1–2). His message is a word from God, its tone is comfort, and its content is deliverance for the people and the return of God's favor. What beautiful words of consolation and healing are piled up in this opening statement by the unknown prophet of the exile! Characteristically, his message is all in the indicative mood; wherever imperative formulations occur ("comfort my people," "speak tenderly to Jerusalem," "cry to her," "lift up your voice with strength"), they grow from the same kerygmatic roots. Even the command, "prepare in the wilderness the way of the Lord," is enclosed in the proclamation "every valley shall be lifted up and every mountain and hill be made low" (vv. 3–4). The picture is clear: God will do a new thing ("the Lord God comes with might," v. 10); the people should be alerted to what they will see ("behold your God," v. 9). Their own existence may be ever so precarious ("all flesh is as grass," v. 6); God's promises are still secure ("the word of our God will stand for ever," v. 8). All that is needed now is to get ready to receive the mighty deliverance which God is prepared to accomplish. Clearly, there is a word here for our time also!

In contrast, the text from 2 Peter 3:8–14 seems at first glance so closely tied in with the first century and the radical apocalypticism which flourished in the Jewish community and among the early Christian churches as to be virtually incapable of homiletical use today. The followers of Jesus found this way of thinking close at hand as a way of expressing the radicality and the cosmic impact of the gospel—especially when they wanted to proclaim the marvelous hope which the revelation of Christ inspired, namely, the expectation of his *parousia*, his coming in glory and power. On closer examination, however, one will find the writer's perspective remarkably relevant to the exposition of that process of preparation which is part of the Advent attitude. Though the language is apocalyptic, the text is quite free of the speculative form of apocalypticism (see exegesis, above). Also, the passage is utterly free from the type of passive quietism which came to characterize some early Christians (as for example the Thessalonians). The writer's emphasis is on the reliability of the promised fulfillment ("the Lord is not slow about his promise," v. 9a); the inclusiveness of God's desire to save ("not wishing that any should perish, but that all should reach repentance," v. 9b); the radical renewal which the *parousia* brings ("the earth and the works that are upon it will be burned up," "but according to his promise we wait for new heavens and a new earth in which righteousness dwells," v. 10, 13); and the serious challenge that all this presents to the believer ("what sort of persons ought you to be in lives of holiness and godliness," v. 11). This last point is most significant. The writer describes the proper attitude as "*waiting for and hastening* the coming of the day of the Lord," (v. 12). That is a suggestive image of the type of attitude which characterizes the Christian's Advent preparation.

The preaching of John the Baptizer, as reported by Mark (1:2–8), makes that same image somewhat more specific. As the exegetical notes above indicated, this may in fact be the main function of the story within the plan of composition of Mark's Gospel. It is surely the reason for selecting the story as text for Advent II. John announced the coming of the one "mightier than I" (v. 7) and proceeded, as charged, to "prepare the way" and "make his paths straight." This he did by preaching "a baptism of repentance for the forgiveness of sins" (v. 4). As noted in the exegesis, Mark describes John's preaching as having a more decidedly evangelical tone than that which is expressed in Matthew's story (see 3:1–12). Nevertheless, the proper preparation in anticipation of the coming one is the same in both stories: honest confession; an act of cleansing, signifying serious repentance; and complete openness toward the greater spiritual realities which lie ahead. Thus we learn from "the voice in the wilderness" how we ought to encounter and embrace the one who came, who comes, and who shall come.

Now, let us return to the question of the contemporary meaning of these texts. We are all concerned with the mindless superficiality and the soulless materialism of our Advent season. To limit the scope of these texts to whatever they say about preparing for Christmas, however, would be to apply a similar kind of superficiality to the Bible itself. These passages express something central to the gospel and touch the very essence of our existence as men and women. That is why we need to listen long and well to what word is spoken to us through these texts.

Second Isaiah's word of liberation addresses all oppressed people, and yet it is different from the political theologies of our day. Contemporary liberation theology tends to express itself more in the imperative than the indicative mood. It is at times nothing more than revolutionary exhortation or political ideology, and for many, that word does not touch the heart of the problem of oppressed people. Second Isaiah may help us here. He takes the frailty of man seriously, and thus has a word especially for the helpless. But he takes God's redemptive activity equally seriously. He proclaims liberation as God's own strange procession through the desert of our history and thus raises the possibility that the social and political relandscaping which is now occurring among us could be interpreted as God's own work, the beginnings of God's "straight highway" in this world.

2 Peter adds another important note at this point: the emphasis on the radicality of God's redemptive work and the responsibility of those who wait and work toward it to live a style of life that corresponds to that new world of righteousness which they are expecting. Theologians in the past have talked about the Christian life style as an "interim ethic." In one sense that may be descriptive, but it is important to understand that for the Christian, life in the interim is informed by the quality of that which is to come. As the writer of 2 Peter says, "Therefore, beloved, since you wait for these (new heavens and a new earth), be zealous to be found in him without spot or blemish, and at peace" (v. 14).

This, then, is the way to prepare the future: to put the past behind and to reorient oneself to that which is to come. This is precisely what the Markan text also says when it draws the picture of John, "the voice," calling the people—the whole world—to confession of sins and repentance. To be prepared for him who will cleanse all things, one must humbly submit oneself to this cleansing process. "I baptize you with water," he says; "*he* will baptize you with the Holy Spirit" (v. 8).

The Third Sunday in Advent

Lutheran	*Roman Catholic*	*Episcopal*	*Pres./UCC/Chr.*	*Methodist/COCU*
Isa. 61:1–3, 10–11	Isa. 61:1–2a, 10–11	Isa. 61:1–3, 10–11	Isa. 61:1–4, 8–11	Isa. 61:1–4, 8–11
1 Thess. 5:16–24	1 Thess. 5:16–24	I Thess. 5:16–24	1 Thess. 5:16–24	1 Thess. 5:16–24
John 1:6–8, 19–28	John 1:6–8, 19–28	John 1:6–8, 19–28	John 1:6–8, 19–28	John 1:6–8, 19–28

EXEGESIS

First Lesson: Isa. 61:1–3, 10–11. The OT lesson for the Third Sunday in Advent may have been a set passage in Jesus' day. According to Luke 4, when our Lord entered the Nazareth synagogue on a Sabbath he was handed the Isaiah scroll. From it he read the opening lines of this lesson. Having done so he said, to everyone's astonishment: "Today this scripture has been fulfilled in your hearing!"

What occasioned the composition of Isaiah 61? According to many scholars this poem belongs to a collection composed by several prophets who ministered to those Jews in Jerusalem and Judea who had returned from Babylonian captivity in the latter half of the sixth century. Their message had been influenced decisively by the oracles of Isaiah and those of his great successor in the period of exile, especially the poems of the latter celebrating the coming glories of Zion (Isa. 51:1–52:12; see the exegesis of the First Lesson [Isa. 40:1–11] for Advent I). The anonymous prophet who wrote today's lesson certainly thought of himself as carrying forward the commission of Second Isaiah—his opening lines reveal a prophetic consciousness echoing Isaiah 40. It is indeed possible that this prophet believed that he was fulfilling the mission of the Servant, at least in regard to heralding the arrival of the salvation promised to Zion. He was called to bring the good news of liberation and comfort to the distressed postexilic community. The relief that was forthcoming would not only lift their minds and spirits; their cities, which still bore the marks of desolation, were to be rebuilt; their lost wealth and glory were to be abundantly compensated.

The promises relating to Jerusalem's material prosperity are omitted from this Sunday's lesson, but in order to understand the prophet's message and Zion's glad response in vv. 10–11, one should not overlook vv. 4–9. Second Isaiah had been convinced that all mankind should see the salvation of God in and through Israel's restoration. This theme is taken up by his successors. At first sight the notions of Gentile servitude and reparations seem reprehensible, reflecting wishful thinking or chauvinism, or both. The emphasis falls, however, on the future mission of Israel to other peoples, either that of the whole nation or, more probably, that of a redeemed and faithful remnant within Israel. Other poems in the third division of the Book of Isaiah (56–66) affirm a significant role for Gentiles in the new and open city of Jerusalem. The first poem envisages non-Jews coming to worship at Zion (56:6–7) and, in the last chapter of the book, we read that Gentiles are to serve as priests and Levites (66:18–21). If, as we suppose, these passages were written in postexilic Judea they are all the more remarkable. According to other writings from this period, laws concerning purity of blood and cultic practices were rigorously enforced and fostered a narrow exclusivism. Among these anonymous prophets who sought to keep alive Isaiah's vision of the transcendent Lord of creation, there arose the clear conviction that "the difference between Israelites and Gentiles must disappear in the fullness of Israel."[1]

In vv. 8 and 9 the God of Israel declares his purpose of salvation. The response of Zion is a jubilant cry (vv. 10–11). "Salvation" and "righteousness" are parallel conceptions in Second Isaiah, referring to God's saving acts whereby he overcomes the wrongs men suffer and commit. So here, Zion celebrates God's saving acts by means of which God will manifest his glory in Israel and bring forth the praise of all the nations.

What then is Israel's glory? Her faithful response and her righteousness of life. One common theme among the latter prophets of the Isaiah tradition is that God demands of his people moral excellence. In the absence of this righteousness the day of salvation is delayed; to hasten this day the prophets labored to raise among this people "oaks of righteousness," a planting of the Lord (cf. Isa. 60:21b).

Second Lesson: 1 Thess. 5:16–24. The Second Lesson for today consists of a few of the admonitions written by the apostle Paul as he closes his First Letter to the Thessalonians, the earliest correspondence in the Pauline corpus (A.D. 50 and 51). The writing is chiefly concerned with two issues arising from Paul's teaching concerning the *parousia* of Christ. Two questions voiced the anxiety of the largely non-Jewish membership in this congregation in northern Greece: will Christians who die before Christ's coming forfeit their salvation? and, when will Christ appear in glory to gather his own?

The first question called for careful instruction, not merely for comfort of the bereaved. Appealing to "a word of the Lord," Paul assures his readers that just as Jesus died and rose again, "even so, through Jesus, God will bring with him those who have fallen asleep." Moreover, those who are alive at the *parousia* will have no precedence over those who died holding the faith (see 4:13–18).

1. J.L. McKenzie, *Second Isaiah* (New York: Doubleday, 1968), p. 68.

Concerning the time of the *parousia* Paul recalls his teaching among the Thessalonians. Christ's coming will be sudden, perhaps when least expected, "like a thief in the night," or like the onset of an expectant mother's labor pains (see 5:2–3). Such uncertainty should not give rise to fears. For, writes Paul, "God has not destined us for wrath, but to obtain salvation through our Lord Jesus Christ." In this context Paul stresses a cardinal truth: the Christian is called to live each day as though it were the last. Each day is the day of the Lord and as "sons of the day" Christians are called to a life of sobriety, of moral earnestness. Note his reference to faith, love, and hope (5:8; 1:3; cf. 1 Cor. 13).

Ethical instruction prefaces and concludes Paul's discussion of these theological issues relating to the Christian hope. As here, so in his later letters, Paul makes the affirmation of Christ's *parousia* the occasion for a serious call to the devout life.

The dicta "do not quench the Spirit, do not despise prophesying" may relate to some particular abuses in this church. Paul deals with the extraordinary gifts of speaking in tongues and prophesying in his Corinthian letters (see especially, 1 Cor. 12–14). In this church they were valued inordinately, leading to individualism and pride. But Paul never considered it his prerogative to stifle the activity of the Holy Spirit.

The benediction, vv. 23–24, may be compared with a previous one in 1 Thess. 3:11–13. Both emphasize that Christian growth is a continuous process requiring vigilance and constancy. But the possibilities for moral development and self-discipline are not the ground of Paul's confidence; rather "he who calls you is faithful and he will do it."

Gospel: John 1:6–8, 19–28. Martyrdom often increases the stature of a great man; he is thereby thrust into the limelight of history and admirers put forth claims which he would not have made for himself. This seems to have been what happened to John the Baptist, put to death by Herod Antipas early in the third decade of the first century. When the Fourth Gospel was written, around A.D. 100, some disciples of the Baptist were casting him in the role of one or more of the great figures expected at the close of the age. Luke's Gospel, written more than a decade earlier, reports that before his death some were questioning "whether perhaps John were the Christ" (3:15). In the Book of Acts we read of some of John's disciples in Ephesus (19:1–7). Post-canonical writings reveal that a cult of John the Baptist persisted for some time.

The Gospel for last Sunday, Mark 1, showed that the writer of the most primitive tradition concerning Jesus' ministry had little interest in John's personal achievements. As the forerunner of Christ John was significant. The latest of the four Gospels gives more attention to John's person, but only to emphasize more strongly than the others that his importance consisted solely in his having been a witness to Jesus.

For more than two hundred years the prophet Isaiah and his successors proclaimed the coming of the day of salvation as the appearance of a great light from God. See the following passages from all three divisions of the book: Isa. 9:2; 42:6; 60:12. In the prologue to John's Gospel "the voice in the wilderness" proclaims the coming of this light (vv. 6–8); "the real light which gives light to every man was coming into the world" in the person of Jesus, the eternal word of God (cf. John 3:19; 5:35–36; 8:12; 9:5).

Today's lesson reports two interrogations of John on the first of three days during which John's witness to Jesus is elaborated (see 1:29, 35). Most important is John's disclaimer of messiahship. Somewhat surprising is his rejection of the role of Elijah (Mal. 3:1; 4:5). The church, according to Mark, had identified John as the Elijah who was to come. This was probably on the basis of Jesus' estimate of John, (see Matt. 11:1–6; Luke 7:18–23). The three early Gospels report that John lacked an awareness of the full significance of Jesus. As long as this uncertainty existed John's role in relation to traditional messianic figures remained in doubt. Those who acclaimed Jesus as Messiah believed that the Baptist was to Jesus what, in Jewish messianism, Elijah was to the coming of the day of the Lord.

Documents belonging to the two centuries before Christ testify that Jews looked for the coming of a prophet "like Moses." Deut. 18:15 inspired this hope. The sectarians living at Qumran were taught to adhere closely to the laws of Moses until a prophet would come to interpret their true meaning. He would be one of three persons sent by God to usher in the final time of salvation (1QS 9:10–11; CD 6:10–11, 20:1; see also 1 Macc. 4:41–50; 14:41.) In today's lesson the Baptist denies that he is this prophet like Moses. He is only the voice "crying in the wilderness, make straight the way of the Lord" (a shortened form of Isa. 40:3).

In Jewish apocalyptic there was a notion that when the messiah came he would be hidden until his sudden manifestation to all (e.g., Justin Martyr, *Dialogue with Trypho* 8:4). The Fourth Gospel reports that John the Baptist held this view. But the reference here to the greater one, standing unknown in the midst of his people, is something more than historical reminiscence of the Baptist's testimony. John's Gospel teaches that no one comes to recognize Jesus for what he is without the help of God (see 1:31, 33; 3:27; 6:37, 41–45, etc.).

HOMILETICAL INTERPRETATION

The texts for Advent III may well be taken as invitations to celebration. There is a note of immediate expectancy in them, or readiness, and of excitement. They are well chosen as background for preaching the message of Advent, especially as we come closer to Christmas itself.

As we suggested above, in preaching the Advent message we should make sure that we focus on the peculiar qualities of attitude and thought and action which are related to anticipation and preparation, delving deeply into the experience of waiting before we go on to the celebration of fulfillment. The pericopes for Advent III at first glance seem to contradict this point—they lead us right to the threshold of the events which we wait for, "the coming" to which Advent looks forward. Yet, on closer examination, the texts before us go no further than the threshold. They serve, in fact, only to intensify our anticipation and give clear focus to our preparations. These writers, each in his own way and each in his own context, give expression to the special kind of mood which belongs to those who have high hopes and expectations which are soon to be fulfilled. The prophet poetically, the apostle with both exhortation and benediction, and the evangelist by way of theological historiography, all bring their readers—and us—to the last stage of waiting, to the point where the fulfillment is immediately ahead and the first signs of its coming are already evident. In the imagery of a traditional Christmas, the door is about to be opened.

It is of course difficult first to bring the liturgy and the message of Advent to this high pitch of expectancy and then attempt to hold everything without rushing ahead to the proclamation of the events to come. Most of us have problems in limiting ourselves to the preliminary dimensions of the Christmas story. But there is much to be gained by trying. The celebration ahead will be much more meaningful if it is set against the background of waiting. Waiting is more meaningful than we normally think.

More meaningful? How? Are there perhaps things we should learn about life and faith at this last moment before the dramatic events which we anticipate will take place, things we would miss if we rush impatiently ahead? Our texts give clues for answering such questions, perspectives which are relevant to our life and thought in all seasons of advent.

The postexilic prophet whose message is recorded in Isa. 61:1–3, 10–11 makes the dramatic announcement that he has been authorized (anointed) and sent "to bring good news to the lowly." The passage is a beautiful program declaration with a distinct evangelical tone. As the exegesis above indicates, the passage resembles closely the hopeful words of Second Isaiah, and they were also claimed by Jesus as he began his own ministry at the synagogue in Nazareth. Chosen as part of the pericopes for Advent III, the passage sets the scene for interpreting the coming event as a radically new thing, as a redemptive act of God on behalf of all who suffer and are downtrodden. We should note that the day of the Lord is not here announced as a reward for the righteous or a dread for sinners. It is described, instead, as a free act of God's unqualified goodness whereby he raises the weak up in strength and makes sinners righteous by his own power. It is in the light of that kind of declaration that the prophet announces that he is ready to celebrate. "I will greatly rejoice in the Lord," he says. We should note this also. He does not proceed to celebrate his own announcement; it is the coming events that will make his gospel significant. Thus the prophet has made clear that it is in the nature of the Advent attitude first to make sure that the true character of the coming event is understood, then to prepare to celebrate it. We shall look at the implications of this for our own life and thought in a moment.

A second clue to the meaning of this last stage of Advent preparation is contained in the text of the Second Lesson (1 Thess. 5:16–24). The above exegesis has set the passage within its historical and contextual frame. The advent considered here is of course the anticipation of the *parousia*, the "second coming," and Paul is anxious to have his readers keep from rushing impatiently ahead. There is something that needs to happen to them before the dramatic fulfillment of their expectations takes place, something "God through Jesus Christ wants you to do," he says. By analyzing the text one finds that it has to do with human relationships ("try to treat one another with kindness"), with the relationship to God ("always be joyful, never give up praying"), as well as with the understanding of life ("thank God whatever happens"). And deeper yet, Paul suggests that the final stage of preparation has to do with what we are, with the level of consecration, the spiritual soundness and moral irreproachability we have reached "when our Lord Jesus Christ comes." Waiting, then, has a purpose. It is productive. Moreover, God is at work among us, even during Advent. As Paul says, "He who calls you can be relied on, and he will do this."

The third of our texts (John 1:6–8, 19–28) makes a corollary point, though in a different manner, by describing the last stage of the preparation for Jesus' ministry—that represented by the testimony of John the Baptizer. Once again, the exegesis above has provided the textual and historical context. As explained there, the story is theologically motivated, intended to show that John was simply the forerunner, a testimony to the light, but not the light itself. From the standpoint of our perspective here, there is a clue in this pericope relative to the last stage of advent preparation. Says John, "I am only baptizing with water, but someone is standing among you of whom you do not know; he is to come after me . . ." The point is this: Essential to our preparation for the coming events is the awareness that the things to come are far greater than the signs that have so far appeared. We should try to understand this well, for we easily think that the fulfillment to come is continuous with our preparations in the present. John says, not so; what *I* have said has as much to do with what *he* will do as water has with fire!

Let us lift our eyes for a moment from the texts themselves and focus on the clues they provide us in reference to our own observance of Advent. We have said that they can intensify our anticipation and give clear focus to our preparations, expressing the special kind of mood which characterizes the last phase of waiting.

The prophet's point is important. Advent is not merely to look forward with open-ended anticipation, with the empty stare of a person who doesn't know what to expect. Advent is more specifically to be prepared for the shape and meaning of things to come. It is precisely the recognition that the coming events represent a radically new redemptive initiative of God on behalf of suppressed and suffering people that will give intensity to our anticipation and spark the desire to celebrate. This should be our approach in every dimension of Advent. The first coming of Christ clearly means that God has chosen to identify himself with the poor and humble. The continuing coming of Christ in our history is similarly marked by concern for the suffering. And in the final coming, when Christ will draw all men to himself, those who have gone through tribulation will be brought closest to his throne. Those of us who have not yet learned this point have no understanding of the good news–they have not yet learned their Advent lesson.

The apostle can also teach us something of what this last stage of Advent means. It is not to forget oneself and disregard one's relationships and involvements in the present, thinking solely of the future and postponing–even suspending–the concerns of life in the world. Rather, Advent is to strive to be and to act so as to be found in harmony with the nature of things to come. It is to be prepared to step into the future, and according to Paul the best preparation for the future is to live in the quality of that future life here and now. This emphasis could, of course, easily deteriorate into sheer moralism, but the apostle shows himself a master of that tendency. Advent, the time of waiting, is itself a time of grace. God, who calls us into the future can be relied on to work his will among us even here and now. Thus, to observe Advent is to be transformed into the character of coming events.

The evangelist adds significantly to this point when he stresses that the things to come are far greater than we can ever see or think while waiting. Nothing or no one that appears during any of our advents is worthy so much as to undo the shoes of the one who is coming. That is the implication of John's self-appraisal. That ought also to be the estimation we make of all our Advent preparations. When we reach that understanding of our present experiences, our anticipation of the coming fulfillment will be so much more intense. We may think that we know what God will be doing, but our vision is blurred, we see only as in a mirror, not even half has yet been told. When he comes, as he will, John says, you'll see something else!

And with that, the Advent spirit has been brought to its absolutely highest pitch of expectation.

The Fourth Sunday in Advent

Lutheran	*Roman Catholic*	*Episcopal*	*Pres./UCC/Chr.*	*Methodist/COCU*
2 Sam. 7:(1–7) 8–11, 16	2 Sam. 7:1–5, 8b–11, 16	2 Sam. 7:1–5, 8b–11, 16	2 Sam. 7:8–16	2 Sam. 7:1–5, 7–16
Rom. 16:25–27	Rom. 16:25–27	Rom. 16:25–27	Rom. 16:25–27	Rom. 16:25–27
Luke 1:26–38	Luke 1:26–38	Luke 1:26–38	Luke 1:26–38	Luke 1:26–38

EXEGESIS

First Lesson: 2 Sam. 7: (1–7) 8–11, 16. With the establishment of the dynasty of King David a millennium before Jesus' birth, the belief arose that a ruler of the kingdom of Judah would become the anointed one (messiah) enthroned by God as the savior of his people. This messianic prophecy is given in today's lesson from the OT. The text probably reflects a late elaboration of God's promise to David. In its present form it may echo Psalm 89. But its core preserves the original source. David had in mind to build an appropriate house (temple) for God. But Nathan objects; God will establish an enduring house (dynasty) for David (cf. Ps. 132; also 1 Chron. 17). The heart of the original promise is personal, being an assurance to David that his descendants would rule God's people, that eventually his kingdom would be made sure for all time. For the Christian church this ancient oracle reached fulfillment in Jesus, in his resurrection, but also in the signs of his nativity.

For a better understanding of the Second Lesson and Gospel the pre-Christian development of this particular theme in Jewish messianism should be recalled. Some of the "royal psalms" belong to the period when the Davidic dynasty held sway over Judah. At the coronation of descendants of David, or on other state occasions presided over by these kings, psalms such as the following would be recited: Psalms 2, 35, 72 and 110. References in them to divine sonship reflect a traditional homage paid to oriental monarchs by their courts. But worldwide sovereignty was ascribed to the Davidic kings in the hope that there might be achieved under the incumbent that enduring prosperity and victory promised to his illustrious ancestor.

Oracles in the Book of Isaiah represent a further development. The eighth century prophet saw the evils of the kings on David's throne and prophesied God's judgments against them. Yet he remained confident that God's promise would not fail. Isa. 7:10–17 and 9:1–7 announce the birth of a great heir to David's throne, ostensibly in the prophet's time (ca. 735 B.C.). This infant's birth would be a sign that God was with his people still, raising up a worthy scion of the house of David. These passages surely describe the justice and peace of an ideal state, rather than present conditions approximating it (cf. Mic. 5:1–6; Jer. 23:5, 30:9). Isaiah 11 is another oracle declared by the prophet of Jerusalem, or possibly by one of his successors. In it is portrayed a future even more remote from present reality; indeed conditions of the realm are described as a return to the halcyon days of Eden.

The Babylonian exile brought an abrupt end to the Davidic dynasty and to such idealizations. Israel's royal messianism underwent reappraisal. No longer could hopes be pinned on Judah's next king; God's promise was related to the indefinite future. In the postexilic period the belief in the coming of a messiah was firmly established but, at the same time, a great variety of pictures describing the nature of his coming and reign emerged. Alongside visions of a Davidic messiah were those of the coming of an anointed priest or a prophet like Moses, or both, or all three. The functions and relationships of these various saviors remain unclear, particularly in the apocalyptic portrayals of the age to come. Yet, one may conclude, hope for the coming of a Davidic messiah persisted as a dominant aspect of Israel's eschatology. The Davidic ideal of a savior-king was often associated with political or even imperial objectives but, since David's son would be the agent of God's salvation, his rule would result in the universal reign of God and usher in the final age of righteousness and peace. (Psalms of Solomon 17, 18). A scrap of an ancient scroll, found recently in one of the caves near the ruins of an Essene settlement by the Dead Sea, is proof that shortly before Jesus' birth 2 Samuel 7 was still treasured by pious Jews and voiced their hope. The faithful few who withdrew into the wilderness to "prepare the way of the Lord" were convinced that God would soon fulfill his promise to David, and that they would enjoy that final blessedness which their savior-king would bestow.[1]

Second Lesson: Rom. 16:25–27. This Pauline benediction is missing at the end of some Greek manuscripts of the Letter to the Romans; in others it is found at the conclusion of chap. 14; in one manuscript after chap. 15. From this evidence some persons have judged that the benediction was appended by an early copyist. Moreover, the idea that the gospel revealed "a divine secret *kept in silence* for long ages" is not found elsewhere in Paul's letters. This presence in Romans of a formulation of Christian doctrine by another should be seen, perhaps, along with other passages in the letter not originally composed by Paul. In the salutation, Paul very probably cites a traditional creed of the early church, 1:3–4. Paul had not had previous contacts with this Roman congregation, yet he was confident that his readers would join him in subscribing to this common confession concerning Christ.

Paul was often forced to take an independent position and in the course of his missions developed a distinctive theology. Nevertheless he remained certain that his gospel differed in no essentials from that preached by those who were apostles before him. (Gal. 1:17; 2:6; 1 Cor. 15:1–11). Interpreters of Paul's letters have found numerous places where the apostle seems to be elaborating a traditional creed or hymn, relating his own expositions to a common faith. We may conclude that just as Paul found inspiration in statements of the faith composed by earlier Christians, so Paul's letters later inspired others to draw upon his theology in formulating their statements of doctrine or in voicing their praise. Rom. 16:25–27 may be an example of the latter.

Our interest falls upon two complementary assertions in this Pauline benediction as an Advent lesson. The fact that a long-held secret or mystery "is now disclosed" is the paramount emphasis; but the importance of "the prophetic scriptures" in grasping the meaning of this disclosed mystery is an essential corollary. In this lesson prophecy and gospel are related in a special way. On the one hand, the idea is excluded that Israel's prophets had perceived this future *as historical event.* While

1. J.M. Allegro, "Fragments of a Qumran Scroll of Eschatological Midrashim," *Journal of Biblical Literature* 77 (1958): 350–354.

God's purpose included the coming of the prophets and the historical crises which their messages provoked, *only* when the Christ had come in the person of Jesus was the divine secret disclosed. On the other hand, once the Christ had come the true meaning of his life, death, and resurrection, and his future reign, needed to be interpreted by means of the "prophetic scriptures." In short, God's promised salvation and its surprising fulfillment belong together and derive their true significance from this relation. Especially during the Advent season Christian worship reaffirms this.

The earliest Christians found in the OT lesson for today a basic text in interpreting the gospel. Modern Christians seldom appeal to it. 2 Samuel 7 is left aside in favor of more "spiritual" messianic figures. Jesus, it may be urged, surely disclaimed the political or nationalistic ambitions associated with Nathan's oracle. The fact remains, however, that this testimony to Christ figures prominently in the NT, namely in proclamations concerning his resurrection and in the annunciation of his birth.

Paul begins his Letter to the Romans commending to his readers the gospel he is called to proclaim, a gospel promised through the prophets: Jesus, the son of David in his human descent, by his resurrection declared the Son of God in power, his whole being determined by the Holy Spirit. As the traditional ending of Romans makes clear, this early Christian creed describes a fulfillment which no prophetic scriptures, considered apart, could have possibly disclosed. Yet in order to proclaim the mystery of Christ, appeal was made to OT passages, in this instance to 2 Samuel 7, supported by other scriptures which promised an eventual exaltation by God of a Davidic savior-king who would own God as Father, and who would be owned by God as his Son (cf. Acts 2:24–36; 13:32–39; Heb. 1:5; 5:5).

Gospel: Luke 1:26–38. When the messenger of God announces to Mary the birth of Jesus he proclaims that her child will be called "the Son of the Most High," that God will give him "the throne of his father David," so that he is king forever. This message is at once a repetition of the prophecy of Nathan and, as noted above, an anticipation of the apostolic proclamation of Jesus' resurrection. As in the Acts, so at the beginning of his Gospel, Luke declares that the messiahship of Jesus is confirmed in this dual sonship. The promise made to the future son of David is about to be fulfilled in the birth of the Christ child. Thus Gabriel reaffirms the oracle of Nathan: Mary, betrothed to a member of "the house of David," is to bear a son (cf. Luke 1:27, 21; 2 Sam. 7:12). Jesus, however, is also to be called the Son of God, as promised in 2 Sam. 7:14 (Luke 1:32, 34).

We noted above that this Christmas story of the annunciation anticipates the Easter message. This is not only confirmed by the old creed in Rom. 1:3–4 and the preaching of Peter and of Paul in Acts (chaps. 2 and 13); Luke's story of the nativity discloses its origin in Christian worship. Each episode serves as a testimony of those who have been moved to praise and glorify God for the gift of his Son. It seems certain that those who compiled these traditions, and those who heard them read, already knew the story of Jesus Christ who had been designated Son of God in power by his resurrection from the dead.[2]

The whole of Luke's nativity tradition is prophetic. This appears most clearly in the two annunciations, the Magnificat, the Benedictus, and the prophecies of Simeon and Anna. But as in the OT's witness of faith, deriving from Nathan's oracle, so in this NT witness to Gabriel's word, the content of prophecy was shaped by later experience—in this instance, by knowledge of its fulfillment. The mystery of the incarnation of the Son of God, first powerfully disclosed in the resurrection of the crucified Jesus, was hidden in this infant's lowly origin, in the unexpected, humanly-improbable miracle of Christmas (see Luke 1:35, 37).

To Luke and to his first readers this story of the annunciation to Mary (and the related episodes) served as a paradigm: How were they to prepare for Christ's coming, his new advents, his final coming? In hearing this Christmas lesson, early Christians—as later ones—may have been moved with Elizabeth to say of Mary: "Blessed are you among women . . .!" But the story itself only reports that Mary had found favor with God; that she was simply ready to hear and obey the word of promise (Luke 1:28–30, 38). The grace of God to Mary, and Mary's faithful response, epitomize the situation and the mood of every Advent: God visits those in whom he is well-pleased, offering them the blessing of his peace; Mary personifies pure receptivity to the Holy Spirit, in her fear and trembling and in her instant readiness to let the word of God have its way.

HOMILETICAL INTERPRETATION

The main motif of the texts for Advent IV is "annunciation," or the announcement that now the events we have anticipated and waited for are beginning to take place. Everything we have been considering up to now is preparation. From this moment on the fulfillment is beginning to take shape. The wheels are set in motion, God is doing a new thing, and it is for us only to stand in awe and wonder of it all!

Once more, it is appropriate to point out that the texts selected, representing three different historical contexts, show a remarkable unanimity of perspective. The story of God's promise to David, the Pauline benediction at the end of Romans, and the evangelist's story of the annunciation to Mary—all three proclaim a divine initiative which is all the more wonderful because it is so typically God-like, so clearly an expression of God's own will to save, and so strangely unqualified by human contributions as to be received only as a gift, as the unfolding of a secret plan that is God's own doing from beginning to end. In all three passages the individuals involved—every man, we—are simply observers, recipients. In this drama, God is the lead actor, everyone else is acted upon. In the grammar of revelation, God is the subject of every sentence, his works the predicate, and we simply the objects of his favor. That is why, also, in all

2. P. Minear, "The Interpreter and the Nativity Stories," *Theology Today* 5 (1950-51): 363 ff.

three passages those who are the recipients of annunciation express their response by way of humble glorification of God, in a magnificat or a gloria which focuses simply and solely on the greatness and the goodness of God.

This point should be emphasized both as an appropriate prologue to Advent IV and as prolegomena to the proclamation of the Christmas gospel, if not the NT message as a whole. If there is a need to argue that Christian preaching is essentially kerygmatic and that every facet of the Christian message has its roots deep in the proclamation of God's mighty acts, Advent IV and the Christmas story surely provide the key to that argument. And if preachers need a criterion by which to test the authenticity of their preaching, let them test themselves on their proclamation of God's mighty acts on this day and in this season of the liturgical year! Why do so many of us find it difficult to preach at Christmas? Could it be that we have lost sight of the evangelical and theocentric quality of the Christmas story and try to make up for it by way of sheer moralism, cultural nostalgia, or pure sentimentalism—weak bases for preaching any time, but especially at the high festivals of the church year?

Let us see if we can catch the *euangellion* in our texts before we seek to identify what its meaning might be for us and for those who are to hear us on this Sunday.

The exegesis above has given us a view of the immediate textual background and the larger historical setting of the passage from 2 Sam. 7:8–11, 16. As pointed out there, the promise to David has tremendous importance both for Jewish messianism and for the Christology of the early church. In the context of our concerns here I am primarily interested in the personal and theological dimensions of the story. There is a gospel in it, and with a delightful twist of irony, a gospel with a smile, if you will.

Look at David, comfortable after years of political struggle, safe in his own house, and now concerned that the ark of God still dwells under tent curtains in the tabernacle. He wanted to celebrate his new-found security by building God a house, and Nathan at first thought it a good idea. But overnight, in Nathan's mind, things were turned around. He was urged to go to David and ask, "Should *you* build *me* a house to dwell in?" What follows is a beautiful recitation of God's past works on behalf of David ("I took you from the pasture," "I have been with you wherever you have gone"), and a projection of the same providential care in the future ("I will make for you a great name," "I will appoint a place for my people Israel"). And then the summation, in direct response to David's ambitions: "The Lord declares that *he* will make *you* a house."

There is a meaningful shift in the meaning of "house," here, but more significant is the clear shift of focus from David to God, from human plans to divine initiative. That is precisely the kind of thing that happens between Advent and Christmas, between anticipation and fulfillment, between the time of preparation and the annunciation of the events themselves. The meaning of the annunciation may well be summed up in the statement, "Now you stand aside and see what I am about to do!" Hearing it causes a complete transformation of perspective.

In David's case, the shift caused an immediate reappraisal—a prayer in fact, so closely parallel to the humble magnificat of Mary that one is surprised that the lectionary does not include it (vv. 18–29). Overwhelmed, David "sits down before the Lord" and says, "Who am I my Lord God, that thou hast brought me this far?" And now, these new things—promises concerning the house of thy servant for a long time to come! What am I to say, except that it is "according to thine own heart that thou hast brought about all this greatness"—"thou art great," "thou art God," "thy name be magnified."

We shall leave the OT text, returning to its implications for us in a moment. In the meantime, we should be sure to catch the flavor of the benediction inserted at the end of Romans (16:25–27). As the exegesis indicates, this formulation may have been introduced at that point by some later copyist or editor. It nevertheless represents an essentially Pauline perspective and ties in well with Paul's introductory salutation to the Roman Christians. One point in the passage is that the Christ-event must be seen as related to the promises of old. More importantly it points out how overwhelmingly new the Christ-event is.

The text refers to "the secret kept back for long ages but now revealed" (v. 25). The secret, in Pauline contexts, is not so much a gnostic insight reserved for a few as a more inclusive truth revealed to the many! The reference to "you," that is the Roman Christians, being strengthened "by my gospel," and to "all nations" having the secret made known to them according to God's command, may well be intended as a reminder of Paul's special message and mission. The phrase "to bring about obedience to the faith" (v. 26) parallels closely the reference in the opening salutation to Paul's apostleship "among the gentiles" (1:5). The entire benediction, then, makes the same point which is explicated in greater detail in the Letter to the Ephesians, where the writer celebrates the extraordinary new truth which has been made known in Christ, namely, God's mysterious plan "to unite all things in him," heaven and earth, Jews and Gentiles (cf. Eph. 1:9–14). The secret of Christ, which has not been known before, is that "the gentiles are fellow heirs, members of the same body, and partakers of the promise of Jesus Christ through the gospel" (Eph. 3:4–6).

Paul consistently claimed that this is the true meaning of Christ's appearance—his whole ministry was built on it. Peter also, in defending the baptism of Cornelius before the circumcision party at Jerusalem, explained how he learned the secret for himself: God had shown him something radically new about his relationship to mankind (Acts 11:1–18). And James, at the apostolic council at Jerusalem, shows that the secret was already made known to the prophets (Acts 15:13–18). James and Peter thus acquiesced to the new inclusiveness of the gospel ("Who was I that I could withstand God," Acts 11:17). Paul, on the other hand, positively celebrated it, and the benediction (whether Paul's or someone else's) ending the Letter to the Romans, sums it all up in a short but eloquent gloria: "To the only wise God be glory for evermore through Jesus Christ!" (16:27).

Let us take a quick look at our third text, the annunciation to Mary (Luke 1:26–38). Again we are focusing on the personal and theological dimension of the story. Its message is the same as that of the narrative from 2 Samuel. No picture is more unimaginable than the visit of the archangel to young Mary of Nazareth in Galilee. It was as if the highest of the heavens touched the very lowest of the earth. That in itself is a symbolic expression of the inexplicable wonder of what was about to take place. When Mary heard the greeting, "Hail, O favored one," she wondered, the story says, what sort of greeting this might be. But the annunciation itself was stranger yet: She was to be a mother, and her son was to be the bearer of the Davidic line in whom the promises of old were to be fulfilled! Numbed, but not so much as to be unaware of the fact that the normal human qualifications were missing ("I have no husband"), Mary was told that when God moves to do his work he is not dependent on earthly preconditions ("With God nothing is impossible"). Virgin birth, if that is what we have here, is thus primarily a *theological* symbol; it points to the radical theocentricity of the events announced. So the shift we observed earlier occurred once more: from man to God, and now also from biological impossibility to transcendent truth. In catching the meaning of this truth, Mary declared herself willing to be God's "handmaid," whichever way God might otherwise decide to use her ("Let it be to me according to thy word"). Later, looking back, she could find no better way to express herself than in a humble magnificat, a prayer in which there was no room for herself, only for the recitation of God's great works, now, toward her personally, as in the past for the people of Israel (cf. 1:46–55).

We have examined certain personal and theological accents in the texts for Advent IV. Is there any room for an annunciation in *our own* celebration of Advent? What might it mean for *us* to hear it? These are questions of homiletical application.

Perhaps we should look at ourselves in the light of David's experience. The fact is that we are often more concerned with what *we* intend to do for God than we are with what *he* is doing with and for us. We think of this as responsible Christian living, but lose sight of the fact that responsibility presupposes responsiveness, which presupposes *that* to which we respond responsively, namely, God's prior work initiated long before we were even responsive. Annunciation straightens all this out. It declares what God is about to do and causes us to stand in awe, marveling at the complete freedom with which he relates to what we do and who we are. Advent IV should mean at least that much to us.

The Second Lesson adds a significant note to this contemporary application of the annunciation motif. We are living at a time when an emphasis on the inclusiveness and universality of the gospel is needed, but when the church is reluctant to leave its own exclusiveness and parochialism behind. The mystery of Christ's coming is still a secret to many. People are still unwilling to recognize that in Christ there is no Jew or Gentile, no insider or outsider, no sacred or secular, no conservative or radical. God's will, announced in Christ's coming, is to unite all things in him, and Christ accomplishes that by reaching out to all men, regardless. Those who see it will also celebrate it. They will glorify him who opened all doors and broke down all walls of separation, and they will become new men among their fellow men because of it. Advent IV ought to lead us toward that sort of development.

Finally, we should perhaps dare to affirm that Mary, "the handmaid of the Lord," ought to be a model for us. She is an appropriate image of faithful response to annunciation. We have heard the announcements of what God intends to do in our world, and we tend to answer by asking "How can this be?" Skeptically or fearfully, we focus on preconditions we consider necessary, and seeing none we doubt the announcement. Mary learned that God works in mysterious ways, and believing that, she decided to "let it be." So can we. There are many virgin areas of existence where God would bring fulfillment into being if we would only serve as his handmaids. Perhaps Advent IV could be summed up for us as the annunciation for Mary: "Let it be with me according to thy word."

The Nativity of Our Lord, Christmas Day

Lutheran	*Roman Catholic*	*Episcopal*	*Pres./UCC/Chr.*	*Methodist/COCU*
Isa. 62:10–12	Isa. 62:11–12	Isa. 62:10–12	Isa. 62:6–12	Isa. 62:6–12
Titus 3:4–7	Titus 3:4–7	Titus 3:4–7	Col. 1:15–20	Titus 3:4–7
Luke 2:1–20	Luke 2:15–20	Luke 2:15b–20	Matt. 1:18–25	Luke 2:15–20

EXEGESIS

First Lesson: Isa. 62:6–12. During the sixth and early fifth centuries before Christ, prophets of Judea in Isaiah's succession persisted in heralding the coming glories of the city of God. Prospects for the recovery of Jerusalem seemed grim but these prophets trusted in the promises of God. The OT reading for Christmas Day is taken from the collection of "Zion poems" assembled at the close of the Book of Isaiah. Several lessons in this Advent season are drawn from them.

Two images in Isaiah 62 are found in a companion poem from the same period, Isaiah 60: Jerusalem's restoration is depicted as the lighting of a brilliant lamp attracting other nations from afar; and new names are bestowed by God upon the city to mark the radical reversal of its fortune.

(See the exegesis of the First Lesson [Isa. 61:10–62:3] for the Second Sunday after Christmas.) But the vision of the glorious highway directed toward Jerusalem and prepared for the coming of the Lord, which climaxes Isaiah 62, links this poem with an older one attributed to the original Isaiah, and also to another written by Second Isaiah in the exile years (cf. 62:10–12 with Isa. 35:8–10 and 40:3–5; note the quotation from Isa. 40:10 in 62:11).

What distinguishes this Zion poem from the others, however, is its impressive dual theme: this prophet's confidence in God's imminent coming as savior calls him to a vocation of unceasing witness and intercession. The opening lines sound a note which resounds in the voices of the watchmen on Jerusalem's walls who invoke God's deliverance by their constant, prayerful vigilance.

The coming salvation is first described as a condition of material prosperity: eschatological Israel shall reap the rewards of honest labor and praise the Lord of the harvest. But the poem ends on a more elevated theme.

We noted above that the vision of God marching across the Judean wilderness in triumphal procession to Zion fired the imagination of Israel's later prophets. This image might have conjured up a theophany of God's return to his holy place, the second temple; or a vision of the nation's restoration to independence and power under a mighty king. But the symbolism of the holy highway stirred deeper, older memories than the establishment of the Davidic dynasty or the glory of Solomon's temple. It evoked the memory of Israel's deliverance from Egyptian bondage, "by the right hand" and "mighty arm" of God, and the long trek through wastelands to Canaan supported by divine providence. (cf. Isa. 62:8 and Exod. 6:6; 15:6, 12; Deut. 4:34; 7:19; also Isa. 51:9–11; 63:12). Associated with this image of deliverance was the commandment of the holy God claiming holiness for his covenant people (Deut. 7:6; also Exod. 19:4–6). Eschatological Israel, this prophet declares, "shall be called 'the holy people, the redeemed of the Lord,' " v. 12a. The poem summons its readers to pray without ceasing for the realization of this noble destiny, to the end that God's power may reclaim his "forsaken" city, and that it may truly become "a praise in the earth," vv. 12b, 7.

Second Lesson: Titus 3:4–7. The Second Lesson for Christmas Day proclaims the fulfillment of this hope of the prophets for eschatological Israel. The writer of the brief letter to Titus declares that "when the goodness and loving kindness of God our Savior appeared, he saved us . . ." For this Christian writer, however, God's salvation was not conceived of locally, as the transformation of Zion; the more expansive hope of the prophets in Isaiah's succession comes into view: "For the grace of God has dawned upon the world with healing *for all mankind* . . . ," (2:11 NEB). Nevertheless, for this writer, as for the prophets, the formation in history of a holy people is a necessary consequence and summons of this redemption. Jesus offered himself—in life and in death—"to redeem us from all iniquity and to purify for himself a people of his own who are zealous for good deeds" (2:11–14; see also 3:8, 14).

The heavy emphasis upon "good deeds" is one of several features of this letter which have led many persons to doubt that Paul wrote it. But whether this Titus was addressed by Paul some sixty years or so after the birth of Jesus, or by "a Paulinist" near the turn of the century, the lesson for today proclaims a conviction close to the heart of the great apostle to the Gentiles: "He saved us, not because of deeds done by us in righteousness, but in virtue of his own mercy . . . so that we might be justified by his grace and become heirs in hope of eternal life" (e.g., Rom. 5:1–11; 6:22–23). In Pauline Christianity the saving proclamation is God's fulfilled word, "promised ages ago," and now manifested in history "at the proper time" in the epiphany (appearing) of his son Jesus Christ (cf. Titus 1:2–3; Gal. 4:4–7; Rom. 1:1–3). Moreover, the powerful cleansing and transforming work of the Holy Spirit in human life is a consequence of hearing this proclamation with faith (cf. Titus 3:5b; Gal. 3:1–5). And finally from Paul's perspective, the historic event, Jesus Christ, is always viewed as pointing to a future coming of the Lord, expressed by our writer as "the appearing of the glory of our great God and Savior Jesus Christ" (cf. Titus 2:13; 1 Cor. 1:4–9).

It is important to note that those who are "heirs in hope of eternal life" are not encouraged because of their "regeneration" into the illusion of cheap grace. Neither can they imagine themselves as living some form of spiritual life which frees them from the concrete moral obligations growing out of life in the church and in the world. Christian existence, in the historical situation between the two advents of Christ, is an existence under grace. And "by it," this epistle declares, "we are disciplined to renounce godless ways and worldly desires, and to live a life of temperance, honesty and godliness *in the present age* . . ." (2:11–12 NEB).

Gospel: Luke 2:1–20. Luke's narrative of Christ's nativity is interlarded with hymns in praise of "the Lord God of Israel"—the Magnificat, Benedictus, and others. In an alternative lection for Christmas Day from Colossians, we read a magnificent hymn in praise of Christ, Col. 1:15–20. The fact that it is Jesus who is the subject of this hymn—a man who so shortly before its composition first saw the light of day cradled in an animal's feeding trough, and who was cut down in the prime of his manhood by an ignominious execution—is remarkable indeed. How does one explain the origin of this faith which ascribes to the boy born in Bethlehem the preeminent role in man's creation (vv. 15–17) and redemption (vv. 18–20)?

Beyond doubt the event which gave rise to this amazing Christology was the cross and its sequel, the resurrection. According to a very early creed cited above, Jesus, a man descended from David, had been designated "Son of God in power by his resurrection from the dead" (Rom. 1:3–4; cf. the exegesis of the Second Lesson [Rom. 16:25–27] for Advent IV).

Reflection upon this belief led the apostles not only to think forward towards the future manifestation in glory of the Lord Christ—"the first-born from the dead" (cf. Col. 1:18; 1 Cor. 15:20, 23; Acts 26:33; Rev. 1:5)—but also to think backwards, to speak of his origin. Matthew and Luke proclaim that from the moment of his conception in Mary's womb Jesus was already the Messiah, the Son of God (Matt. 1:20–23; Luke 1:30–35).[1] In Colossians, as in another Pauline epistle, hymns of praise affirm Jesus' preexistent glory and preeminence (cf. Phil. 2:6–7). Originally these two Christologies may have developed apart, but in second century Christian writings belief in the preexistence of the Son of God is related to the gospel Christologies; the virginal birth of Jesus (Matt./Luke) is the coming into history of the preexistent Word (John; cf. Heb. 1:2).

The evangelist who wrote the Gospel narrative of Christ's nativity (Luke 2:1 ff.) delighted in contrasting the supposed anonymity of lowly folk with the obvious recognition given the high and mighty. Caesars, governors, petty kings, high priests—who order the lives of "the poor"—have their place in history. But "the word of the Lord came to John the son of Zechariah in the wilderness" (3:1–2), and Mary laid in "a manger" her holy child, "the son of God," "because there was no place for them in the inn" (2:1–7; 1:35b; see also Luke 6:20–26; 14; 16:19–31, etc.).

The question is raised: who were the men of the first century who left the deepest impress upon human history? Caesar Augustus or Jesus; Tiberius Caesar or John the Baptist?

Some shepherds are called to Bethlehem to celebrate the birth of the Christ child. These night-watchers were far removed from the centers of power and influence in their day. Such a pastoral scene may seem to cast an aura of romanticism, even of unreality, over the Christmas story. But to such lowly folk, we are told, "the angel of the Lord appeared"—an ancient Semitic way of expressing the reality of God revealing himself to men (cf. Exod. 3:2, 4). In the world of Jesus' day men commonly believed in the existence of invisible powers, of intermediate beings between God and men. In contemporary apocalyptic writings, good angels (as well as evil ones) received names, not to invest them with "personality," but to emphasize their roles as revealers and interpreters of God's historic acts of judgment and of salvation. It must not be supposed that Luke's angels are introduced into the narrative for their artistic effect; their presence here—announcing and hymning the birth of Jesus—reveals the faith of the evangelist. Just as God (and God alone) could raise up a man to be the world's savior (1:26–38), only God could reveal the presence of his unique gift, the Son of his love, in "a babe wrapped in swaddling cloths and lying in a manger" (2:10–12).

1. Does Luke's report that Mary gave birth to her "first-born son" call attention to his uniqueness and preeminence, to the beginning of the fulfillment of God's promised salvation, and not only to the fact that Jesus became the first of Mary's children? Cf. Col. 1:15, 18.

Here, as often in scripture, God is proclaimed as opposing the proud and arrogant, and as giving grace to the humble (e.g., Ps. 3:34; 1 Pet. 5:5). But as the shepherds hastened to act upon their conviction that God had marvelously condescended to them in their work-a-day world, so all the humble upon whom God chooses to confer his grace must move out of the shadows of their anonymity and publish abroad their conviction "concerning this child." Who knows who may be "filled with wonder" when the witness of mere shepherds heralds "the good news of a great joy"?

> "Glory to God in the highest heaven,
> and on earth his peace for men on whom his
> favor rests."
>
> Luke 2:14 NEB

HOMILETICAL INTERPRETATION

This is the day—"the day the Lord has made"—the day of fulfillment, to which anticipation, preparation, waiting, and annunciation have pointed. For the preacher, it should be the greatest day in the liturgical year, a day of proclamation, of unapologetic celebration of the marvelous plan of salvation which God has unveiled in the world.

There is a double dialectic in the message of this day, however. Combined in it are both grandness and humility, glory and simplicity. This is to show that salvation is entirely God's doing, while we are simply the recipients, the beneficiaries of God's gift. It also makes clear that when salvation appears, it comes in humble earthly form, and its unveiling is easily missed because of the heavy incognito in which it appears.

The sermon on Christmas Day ought to contain all these elements: the consciousness of our own need of salvation; the awareness of the grandness of God's redemptive love; the excitement of seeing God in action within human history; and the recognition that what we actually see is so earthly and human, even like the humblest among us. This will correct two prevalent errors often contained in Christmas sermons, one that is evident in the traditional exposition of the phrase "in the fullness of time," another that is expressed in the tendency to glorify the birth narratives and romanticize the manger scene. The first comes to view when we argue that the redemptive events finally came to fulfillment because all the conditions were right, or when we seek to prove that God could not have chosen a better time or a better place. As if all the developments of history—social, political, cultural, intellectual, and religious—came together to form a perfectly obvious asterisk by the name of Nazareth in Galilee or Bethlehem in Judea! What nonsense! What a well-meaning misrepresentation of the gospel itself, robbing it of one of its most remarkable features, namely, the unlikeliness of the whole event! And the second error is not much better: Think of the silly artistic pictures of the holy family, dressed in silks and velvets, surrounded by shepherds fresh from the shower, animals spruced for the show, polished woodwork, blended color-schemes, and angels pink and plump like the well-fed offspring of European nobility! We ought not to perpetuate this sort of unreality. The message for today is that God has brought his saving work down to earth, into history—and that not at the apex of things but at its lowest point, in humility.

It is not difficult to exegete this theme from the texts selected for today. It is there in the postexilic poem from the Isaiah tradition, in the short passage from the pastoral epistle to Titus, and in the birth narrative of Luke—the central text for every Christmas celebration. But it comes in slightly different nuances in the three different contexts, and that adds to the depth and breadth of its significance.

Look again at the Isaiah poem (62:6–12). The unknown prophet is aware of the crushing realities of life in Jerusalem; he refers to the city as "forsaken" and "desolate" (v. 4). No internal strength can be summoned to form the basis for recovery, and yet the prophet envisions the city as "a crown of beauty," "a royal diadem in the hand of your God" (v. 3). This will be so, the prophet says, because "the Lord has sworn by his right hand and his mighty arm" to "establish Jerusalem and make it a praise in the earth" (vv. 8, 7). In the meantime the city can do no more than post watchmen on the walls, to keep God reminded of his promises and the people prepared for the coming salvation (vv. 6, 11).

I mentioned a double dialectic of grandness and humility, glory and simplicity, all pointing to the unlikeliness of the proclamation that salvation is coming this way, at this point in time. This poem contains that dialectic in full measure. A forsaken city is told that it shall be called "sought out" (v. 12). That is like the last becoming first, the smallest the greatest, and lowest the uppermost! But it is the way God has always done his work, as Paul describes it in a different context:

> "He chose what is foolish in the world to shame the wise, God chose what is weak in the world to shame the strong, God chose what is low and despised in the world, even things that are not, to bring to nothing things that are, so that no human being might boast in the presence of God." (1 Cor. 1: 27–29)

The Christmas theme we are focusing on here is an old theme, then, and as characteristic of the OT as of the New. It is a beautiful word, a comforting message, but it is not likely to be understood by those who put their faith in what they can see and lose confidence when God's grand designs are wrapped in history's swaddling clothes. The political observer is not likely to see a city "sought out" rising from the rubble of a ravaged Jerusalem; only the seer looks again in light of God's promises and says, "Behold, your salvation comes!" The world's wise men will always look for the promised king at the palace, but the wisest ones are those who are not put off by a revelation in a manger cradle!

Our second text, the passage from the Epistle to Titus (3:4–7), utilizes the same dialectic of grandness and humility, glory and simplicity, but applies it to the personal, existential dimension and makes it a theological principle of the first order. In the context of a series of moral and ecclesiastical exhortations, the writer reminds his reader of the background from which he and his pastoral flock have come:

> "We ourselves were once foolish, disobedient, led astray, slaves to various passions and pleasures, passing our days in malice and envy, hated by men and hating one another." (v. 3)

That, in a nutshell, is worldly life, isn't it? Not much basis for hope, grandness, or glory there! "But," he says,

> "when the goodness and loving kindness of God our Savior appeared, he saved us, not because of deeds done by us in righteousness, but in virtue of his own mercy . . . , so that we might be justified by his grace and become heirs in hope of eternal life." (vv. 4–5a, 7)

Justification by grace, the Pauline family crest, is here invoked as basis for Christian self-understanding and as background for Christian morality and ecclesiastical life style. Selected as a Christmas text it symbolizes the tight consistency of the Christian kerygma; from the proclamation of incarnation, to the atonement, and to the final consummation, the message is always the same: not because of our deeds, our status, or our capabilities are we saved and given a future, but because of God's grand grace. Or as this writer puts it:

> "by the washing of regeneration and renewal in the Holy Spirit, which he poured out upon us richly through Jesus Christ our Savior." (vv. 5b–6)

Grandness and humility—God's grandness and our humility—that is the structure of the Christian message and of Christian existence. It is not surprising, then, that the Christmas story itself, our third text for today (Luke 2:1–20), is structured on the same model. Here glory and simplicity are combined in such a way as to make simplicity glorious and glory simple.

Look at the story again, and especially at the contrasts built into it: Here is an imperial decree—and a simple man from Nazareth, with a pregnant fiancee, complying. Here is the Davidic house and line—but without room in the city of David. Here are shepherds, keeping lonely watch in the field—and angels bringing them the first announcement of the messianic fulfillment. Here is the proclamation of the Savior, Christ, the Lord—and the sign, a baby, swathed in cloth bands, cradled in a manger. Here is an angel chorus—and a pilgrimage to a stable; shepherds observing a baby—and making known the marvels which had been revealed concerning this child; a mother pondering a great future for her son—in full view of the humble circumstances of his birth. Enlarge the perspective a little, and you see wise men following a star—and ending up at a stable; a king—trembling at the thought of a baby boy; and a young mother giving name to her first-born—and calling him Jesus, Joshua, "Yahweh will save."

What a story, and what a preposterous faith it proclaims! Could anything be more unlikely? It is not only the cross, but the cradle also, that represents "a stumbling block to Jews and folly to gentiles" (1 Cor. 1:23). The natural reaction is to ask, like Nathanael, "Can anything good come out of Nazareth?" (John 1:46). Yet that is precisely what the gospel says:

Here, in these circumstances, God has unveiled his glory; here, in the form of man, salvation has been revealed to men!

Unveiled? Revealed? Strange words to use about something so simple, so common, so human. As preachers we must be sure to acknowledge this strangeness. It is only by recognizing the incognito character of salvation history that we can preach the gospel with historical realism and proclaim the faith faithfully. Moreover, it is only by allowing the humility and simplicity of these events to stand unretouched that we can say what the Christmas story itself actually says: that the Word has become flesh, God is made man, heaven has come down to earth, eternity has invaded time. It's all highly unlikely, and to look at it with the eye of an observer is to wonder where the evidence is—isn't it all just another birth, just another promising baby, just another aspiring mother? Our eyes say yes, but the gospel claims that the event isn't at all exhausted in the act of observation. History never is. It must be looked at again, from the perspective of faith, and then suddenly the events take on a different meaning, a depth and a height that can only be described as transcendent, a significance and truth that can only be called revelation.

And that is not only the way to understand the Christmas story. The dialectic of humility and grandness, simplicity and glory, is equally the perspective by which we live as Christians in the here and now. For the incarnation of the Word is continuing; God constantly encounters us in the form of men (and women); heaven is never very far from our earth; and eternity is always present in time. To celebrate Christmas is thus only partly to look back and recollect a first, unique salvation history; it is much more than that. It is to catch such a view of what God did then—and of the peculiar dialectic of how he did it—as can serve us as framework for understanding what God does now, in our world, presently.

There is an application to the Christmas sermon, then, namely, the task of showing that salvation history continues. Our three texts for Christmas Day can thus become texts for every day. There are perspectives in them which can teach the man of faith to see God's fulfillment take shape in the midst of desolation, justification take hold in the context of human twistedness, and salvation reveal itself among the humble of the earth. On Christmas Day we look to God and see a baby in a manger; that enables us every day to look to the earth's little ones and see God.

The First Sunday after Christmas

Lutheran	*Roman Catholic*	*Episcopal*	*Pres./UCC/Chr.*	*Methodist/COCU*
Isa. 45:22–25	Sir 3:3–7, 14–17a	Isa. 60:13–21	Jer. 31:10–13	Jer. 31:10–13
Col. 3:12–21	Col. 3:12–21	Gal. 4:4–7	Heb. 2:10–18	Heb. 2:10–18
Luke 2:25–38	Luke 2:22–40	John 1:1–18	Luke 2:25–35	Luke 2:22–40

EXEGESIS

First Lesson: Isa. 45:22–25. Prophecies by two of the great men in Isaiah's succession (the other, Isa. 60:13–21) and a third written in the book of Jeremiah (Jer. 31:10–13), are among the readings variously appointed for the First Sunday after Christmas. All three prophecies describe the well-being of people whom God visits with his salvation. Not only are their miserable fortunes reversed, but conditions of their restoration are described in awe-inspiring eschatological imagery.

In the magnificent poem of Second Isaiah (45:14–25) two themes are joined: the absolute uniqueness of God the creator and savior of men (vv. 14–15, 18, 21); and the unity of all mankind in a confession of the sole sovereignty of God (vv. 14, 22–24). In this poem "the prophet reaches a breadth of vision not attained in earlier writings of the Old Testament."[1]

It is indeed remarkable that a Hebrew prophet of the sixth century B.C. could represent particular nations, from the most remote regions known to Israelites, professing that there is no deity but the God who appears "hidden" among a defeated and captive people who are no longer a nation! (v. 15). One is reminded of another incongruous vision–this one associated with Jesus' nativity–the coming of wise men or magi from far-off Mesopotamia prostrating themselves before an infant Israelite as before a world sovereign (Matt. 2:1 ff.). However, the prophet of the Babylonian exile, like the early Christian evangelists, declared that God's saving revelations are not reserved for a particular people nor for persons susceptible to divination or the occult, but are given to the human race (v. 19). When the world's savior was born he was hidden in lowliness, but there sounded forth the "good news of a great joy which shall come to all the people" (Luke 2:10; Matt. 2:5–6).

In the Hebrew prophet's poem God's appeal reaches a climax in the invitation: "Turn unto me and be saved all the ends of the earth!" (v. 20). While all other gods are wholly impotent–being no gods–the true God revealed in and through Israel has the intention and the power to save all mankind. The earth was not created that it might become a "chaos" (note vv. 18–19); God has confirmed by an oath his purpose to save not only Israel but all the nations: "From my mouth has gone forth in righteousness a word," saith the Lord, a word "which shall not return" or be recalled (v. 23; cf. Isa. 55:10–11).

1. J.L. McKenzie, *Second Isaiah* (New York: Doubleday, 1968), p. 82.

"Righteousness" in Second Isaiah does not usually refer to a quality of the divine nature, but rather to a saving act within history whereby God establishes his rightful claim over his creatures and overcomes the wrongs they suffer and commit. Paul the apostle declared that "when the time had fully come" God revealed this "righteousness" in the gospel of his Son Jesus Christ, as an incomparable "power for salvation to everyone who has faith, to the Jew first and also the Greek" (Rom. 1:16–18; 3:21). The final line of Isaiah's poem, v. 25, affirms that Israel's ultimate "triumph and glory" is her witness to the universal Lord (cf. Isa. 49:6).

Advent readings have contained the words of other anonymous prophets who also held aloft the radiant light of Second Isaiah, celebrating in Jerusalem, years later, the unfulfilled glories of their city's restoration. Isa. 60:13–21, as well as Isaiah 62, and also Jer. 31:10–13, may echo Zion poems written by the exiled prophet in the Isaiah tradition (interlarded with the Servant songs in the book of Isaiah, chaps. 49–55). The theme of these poems is an advent theme: Zion is called to reflect the light and joy of God's revealed glory, illuminating a dark and saddened world (Luke 1:76–79; 2:8–11; cf. 2 Cor. 4:6; Phil. 2:14–16; 1 Pet. 2:9-10). Isaiah of Jerusalem had spoken of a deep darkness overshadowing the land before the birth of the messianic prince (Isa. 9:1). Did postexilic prophets envision the fulfillment of this hope of the original Isaiah, and later of Jeremiah, in their own time? Some aspects of their description of Zion's renewal are traditional: nations coming from afar to worship the Lord, bringing the scattered Israelites and pouring wealth into a joyful Jerusalem; the city and the temple rebuilt and beautified by the contributions of many nations. But the conclusion of Isaiah 60 images a radically new and transformed city of God. In the same way, the Christian seer, exiled on Patmos, brooded upon this transcendent image and, reflecting upon the hope which had come to men with the coming of Christ, dreamed of a "new Jerusalem coming down out of heaven" (Revelation 21). In his vision the city had no temple—"for its temple is the Lord God the Almighty and the Lamb" (Rev. 21:2-4; cf. Isa. 60:7, 13). Other "former things" were also passed away. Thus Isaiah's vision of Zion illuminated by an unearthly light, and attracting kings who bring their glory into it, provides the inspiration for a Christian's *sursum corda*: through the eyes of faith one views the new Jerusalem which is to come, having "no need of sun or moon to shine upon it, for the glory of the Lord is its light, and its lamp is the Lamb. By its light shall the nations walk . . ." (Rev. 21:23–25; cf. Isa. 60:19–22).

Second Lesson: Col. 3:12–21. It is fitting that a lesson for the First Sunday after Christmas be taken from this book which views the Christian's life as "an inheritance of the saints in light." The apostle proclaims that God has indeed "delivered us from the dominion of darkness and transferred us to the kingdom of his beloved Son, in whom we have redemption, the forgiveness of sins" (Col. 1:12–14). A reading from this letter, appointed for some churches earlier in Advent, describes the preeminence of Christ (1:15–20); the lesson for today describes the traits of those persons who belong to him (3:12–21).

Several religions in late antiquity employed the imagery of the "putting off" and "putting on" of clothing with reference to their initiatory rites. Probably in this passage Christian baptism is implied. But these admonitions do not apply to a single occasion; they demand that the Christian actualize in daily obedience that human possibility which opens before him in baptism. Just as "the old nature with its practices" must be divested (vv. 5–9), so too must the new nature be renewed, until it conforms to the will of the Creator (vv. 9–11). Christ's rule, which is now inaugurated in the gathering together of persons of diverse cultures into his church, moves towards the ultimate goal when "Christ is all and in all" (v. 11).

Five spiritual endowments are enumerated in our lesson, closely corresponding to two previous lists of vices (five in each) which must disappear (vv. 5, 8). "In this list, the accent is not placed on a certain disposition, but on the action through which the new man reveals his identity. To be sure, were it only out of his own resources, he would be incapable of such actions. He owes his new capabilities to the election, sanctification, and love which God has imparted to him. All of the five terms that describe the new man's conduct are used in other passages to designate acts of God or of Christ"; here they "show how a Christian should deal with his fellow men."[2]

The forebearance and forgiveness of Christ are singled out as providing indicators of the direction and the motive for Christian conduct. But above all else the Christian is required to "put on love" (cf. 1 Cor. 13:13; Rom. 12:18, 10). "The peace of Christ" (v. 15a) refers to the peace which Christ brings (Luke 2:14, 29–32; John 14:27), as well as the peace to which the fellow members of Christ's body are summoned (cf. Rom. 5:1). The thanksgiving enjoined in v. 15b is expressed by an attentive listening to the gospel and in the psalms sung by the church to glorify God. In summary, the complete life of believers is to be dedicated to Christ as Lord in obedience (vv. 16–17; cf. 1 Cor. 10:31; Rom. 12:1; 14:5–6).

The lesson ends with instruction to wives and husbands, children and parents. Tables like this one, describing the moral obligations which members of the household have to one another, were common in pagan and Jewish literature of the Hellenistic Age. (See especially the First Lesson appointed for today in the Roman Catholic lectionary from Sir. 3:3–7, 14–17a.) The apostle took over this conventional mode of ethical instruction, as did the authors of other letters. Their distinction as Christian teaching lies not so much in the actual admonitions as in their consequences and in the motives adduced to enforce them (cf. 1 Pet. 2:13 ff.; Eph. 5:22–6:9; Titus 2:1–10, etc.). Non-Christian parallels often assume

2. E. Lohse, *Colossians and Philemon* (Philadelphia: Fortress Press, 1971) pp. 146–47.

that superior members in the household have all the rights, the inferior ones only duties. The early Christian tables stress a reciprocity of obligation. Of greater significance, however, is the unique sanction supplied in the repetitious phrase "in the Lord" (vv. 18, 20; also 22–24). These injunctions express what peoples in ancient societies considered fitting and proper in wife/husband and parent/child relationships. It is a difficult but necessary task to distinguish what is historically conditioned from what is essential in the ethical imperatives of the Bible, and to relate the latter to the different, but also contingent, situations of today. Particular ideas regarding family structures and relationships may be only conventions which cannot be taken as immutable Christian formulae. But what is timeless is the mandate that obedience to Christ find concrete expression in these interpersonal relations.

Gospel: Luke 2:22–40. To the Galatians Paul wrote: "When the time had fully come God sent forth his Son, born of woman, born under the law [of Moses], to redeem those who were under the law . . ." (Gal. 4:4–5a). If Christ's pre-existence is implied in this proclamation, his birth, which is twice mentioned, places particular emphasis upon the historical existence of God's Son. With exemplary Jewish piety, the holy family are presented by Luke as "performing everything according to the law of the Lord" (2:22, 24, 27b, 39). Mary's ceremonial purification (Lev. 12:2–8) and the presentation of the infant Jesus in the Jerusalem temple (Exod. 13:1–16; Num. 18:16?) become the setting for awesome prophecies concerning the destinies of this child and his mother.

When Jesus' parents made their "offering of the poor," the aged Simeon received them, and taking Jesus in his arms for blessing, began speaking of him in a language which led Mary and Joseph to marvel. In this baby's face Simeon saw the bringer of God's salvation. Thus his words concerning the "consolation" of Israel, as one might expect, echo prophecies in the Isaiah tradition, several of which have been among our Advent readings (2:32; cf. Isa. 40:1; 42:6; 49:6; 52:10; 60:1–3). Simeon is now ready to die in peace having seen the Lord's glory (cf. 2 Cor. 4:6).

The oracle concerning the fall and rising of many in Israel is predictive of the radically opposite attitudes of persons to the presence in history of the Messiah: compare 1 Pet. 2:4–8 and Rom. 9:30–33 with Isa. 28:16; 8:14–15; and Acts 3:22–23 with Deut. 18:15–19. The cryptic word concerning Mary's wounded heart, presently resigned but questioning, foretells the sorrow that will be hers when this divine mystery in which she is called to participate, brings her innocent son to willing acceptance of a violent death for man's redemption (Luke 1:29; 2:19, 50–51; cf. 1 Cor. 2:7–13).

The feminine counterpart of the aged Simeon is the prophetess Anna (2:39–40). Attention is focused upon her long life, like Simeon's lived in longing for "the redemption of Jerusalem." This old widow exemplifies true piety which is not discouraged through long years of faithful service, deferred hope, and unanswered prayers. Unto such God's grace is shown in revealing the presence of Christ. This last of the paired episodes in Luke's nativity narrative emphasizes a theme which runs through them all: the revelation of God in the person of Jesus is the marvelous fulfillment of his covenanted promises to Israel, his unimaginable response to his people's undaunted trust and prayers.

HOMILETICAL INTERPRETATION

No sooner have we completed our celebration of Christmas, the festival of the fulfillment of God's promised salvation, before the church proceeds to develop its consequences. In the pericopes selected for the First Sunday after Christmas, we are being led toward a significant broadening of the Christmas theme—not backward to a repetition of themes already covered in the texts for Christmas Day, but forward to considerations that will make Christmas more meaningful, more significant yet.

This is not always understood. Liturgically speaking, this Sunday is somewhat problematic; it has the character of an aftermath about it. Many preachers feel that they have already exhausted the Christmas theme during Advent; they have wrung out the last drops of inspiration from the Christmas message on Christmas Day, and now they don't quite know what to do, except to repeat it one more time, or else forget about the ecclesiastical calendar altogether and go to the secular one instead, preaching on some civil theme related to the old and the new year.

But the ecclesiastical pericopes are selected on purpose, and the liturgical year has a meaningful design. The First Sunday after Christmas is given a series of texts that point to a broad spectrum of consequences which are integral to the Christian message of salvation, some that relate to theology, some that have to do with Christian life style, and some that focus on christological devotion and Christian piety. It is all set within the same kerygmatic context; we are still within the realm of "the coming," and all the texts are directly related to the dramatic promise and fulfillment which we celebrate at Advent and Christmas: the revelation of salvation. But today we are being asked to focus on certain significant extensions in the meaning of these events, inward and outward. What we see, in fact, is the beginning of a distinctly Christian theology, Christian ethic, and Christian piety.

The first text, Isa. 45:22–25 has already been set in context by the above exegesis. As mentioned there, this poem by the great prophet of the exile expresses a breadth of vision not previously reached by OT authors. That vision clearly points ahead to a universalism which is more characteristic of the NT than of the Old—so much so that the church has found it possible to utilize this text as an expression of the universal implications of the Christ-event. In the context of the Christian liturgy the text becomes in fact a Christocentric text, proclaiming something that the church considers vitally important in its explication of the meaning of Christ's coming.

What is it? Two things, set over-against one another in a dialectic tension which becomes part of the very structure of the Christian message and therefore of Christian theology, namely, universality and singularity. Both themes are clear in the text: God's appeal is addressed to "all the ends of the earth" (v. 22), not only to "all the offspring of Israel" (v. 24). At the same time it is made clear that God's call is for a radical conversion and singular commitment: "Turn to me and be saved" (v. 22), "To me every knee shall bow, every tongue shall swear" (v. 23), "Only in the Lord . . . are righteousness and strength" (v. 24). Such emphases are so characteristic of the Christian perspective that one will have no difficulty finding precisely the same dialectic expressed at crucial points in the NT itself (for example, the Great Commission, Matt. 28:18–20; the Kenotic Hymn, Phil. 2:5–11; and the Little Bible, John 3:16).

It is clear that the double emphasis on universality and singularity causes tension, even conflict, within Christian preaching and theology. Our natural inclination is to soften the dialectic, either by toning down the difference between the two emphases, or by emphasizing one to the exclusion of the other. None of this will work, however. One cannot for long talk about God's universal gift of salvation without confronting the question of the relationship between general and special revelation. No matter how much one attempts to generalize the concept of revelation, the incarnation will always be there to challenge us with its singularity. But by the same token, it is impossible to talk about that unique, once-for-all revelation without also testifying to its openness, its inclusiveness, its "ecumenicity" (its being directed at the whole inhabited world).

We are touching a crucial aspect of the gospel here. In its follow-up of Christmas, the church has desired that both these points shall be made clear—as they are in a pair of basic sayings attributed to Jesus: "When I am lifted up from the earth, I will draw all men to myself"; "No one can come to me unless the Father who sent me draws him" (John 12:32; 6:44). The sermon on this First Sunday after Christmas ought to resound with the same double note: The one who has come among us makes a gift and a claim that are addressed to all men; both the gift and the claim are universal! Here, in this unique event, God has given us a sign: his will to save is inclusive! To see the sign and understand its meaning is to confess that here and nowhere else is salvation manifested in its fullness!

Let us leave the *theological* extension of the Christmas message for now and look at the *ethical* consequences of it as these are developed in our second text, Col. 3:12–21. Again we see how the Christmas message is broadened and made basic to the Christian conception of things—in this case, to self-understanding, life style and behavior. The perspective is summed up in the following statement:

> "Whatever you do, in word or deed, do everything in the name of the Lord Jesus, giving thanks to God the Father through him." (v. 17)

Here is the definitive statement of the Christocentric life style. The Christian life takes shape in the constant awareness of the Lordship of Christ, which means obedience to his word ("Let the word of Christ dwell in you richly," v. 16), openness to his indwelling ("Let the peace of Christ rule in your hearts," v. 15), and conformity to his spirit ("As the Lord has forgiven you, so you also must forgive," v. 13). More specifically, the Christian community will live the life of a "chosen" people, characterized by "compassion, kindness, lowliness, meekness, and patience" (v. 12), and above all by "love, which binds everything together in perfect harmony" (v. 14). And in, with, and through it all, the Christian life style expresses itself in "thankfulness"; three times the apostle includes this admonition (vv. 15–17). It is obviously the central motivation for everything the believer is and does.

We have here put our finger on the essence of Christian morality—and that within a few days of having celebrated the incarnation! Obviously the kerygma and the didache aren't all that far apart after all; the proclamation of salvation does not lead to "quietism" or "antinomianism" (passive unconcern about the things of the world or the quality of one's actions). On the contrary, having seen what God has done, the believer is immediately encouraged to "put on" a life style that corresponds to the new situation in which he is set ("As the Lord . . . so you . . .," vv. 12–13). There is no tension here between "the law" and "the gospel," no discrepancy between theological proclamation and ethical teaching. They are closely integrated, united as two sides of the same message, one showing what God does on his own initiative, out of his own unmerited, unqualified desire to save; the other pointing to what the believer does in response, as an expression of the gratitude which he feels because of the overwhelming goodness of God towards him.

Once more we are touching a fundamental aspect of the gospel. In the aftermath of Christmas, the church has been eager to have the point made clear: Gift and gratitude belong together, receptivity and responsibility are one. This, in fact, defines the structure of all apostolic exhortation; every imperative is anchored in an indicative, Christian ethic is an ethic of response. (Cf. Col. 1:3–23.) The Christian life style is therefore a very appropriate theme for the First Sunday after Christmas; it points to a broader dimension in the meaning of Christ's coming—the establishment of God's kingdom, his rule, in the hearts of men. No one celebrates Christmas right except he gives serious attention to what it means to live "as is fitting in the Lord" (v. 18).

When we proceed to the third of our texts, Luke 2:22–40, we find still another extension of the Christmas message—this in the direction of personal devotion and spiritual commitment. The author of Luke's Gospel seems to have desired to put this theme in such close proximity to the story of Christ's coming that he hurries on to describe the testimony of the two aged believers in the temple, Simeon and Anna, and in the process to make a couple of points that are fundamental to the understanding of Christian piety.

The first and most obvious one is that only those who have the eye of faith shall see these humble, ordinary events take on the meaning of revelation and fulfillment. It is difficult to say whether the writer of Luke considered his stories of Simeon and Anna as "proofs" for the messianic claims of the Christ child. It is possible that he did, but since these stories have their focus in the personal piety and spiritual sensitivity of the persons involved, it is more likely that he intended simply to emphasize the quality of faith and clarity of perspective which are needed to grasp the deeper meaning of these particular historical events. At any rate any viable homiletical interpretation of the stories of Simeon and Anna must include the fact that these were devout worshipers, people "looking for the consolation of Israel" (v. 25). They were both deeply involved in the messianic expectations that ran as a broad stream through the contemporary Jewish community. Simeon had been told "by the Holy Spirit that he would not see death before he had seen the Lord's Christ" (v. 26); Anna "did not depart from the temple, worshiping with fasting and prayer night and day" (v. 37). So they were spiritually conditioned, and had the clarity of vision to see in the poor child being brought up to the temple from the provinces the fulfillment of their messianic hopes.

That says much about the essential role of piety in the confrontation with the Christ child. In one sense it is the key to the entire experience—to understanding the salvation-historical meaning of the whole event.

But the stories of Simeon and Anna say more. A second aspect, equally basic to Christian piety, is the absolute finality of commitment which characterizes their response and their testimony. Simeon makes the most beautiful statement of this imaginable:

> "Lord, now lettest thou thy servant depart in peace, according to thy word; for mine eyes have seen thy salvation which thou hast prepared in the presence of all peoples. . . ." (vv. 29–31)

And Anna, in her own way, "gave thanks to God, and spoke of him to all who were looking for the redemption of Jerusalem" (v. 38).

The texts for the First Sunday after Christmas have thus been brought full circle: Christian piety is the source of both thankfulness and of commitment! In the faithful response to the Christ-event lie the roots of both the Christian life style and the christological claims to universality and uniqueness. Christian theology and Christian ethic are thus grounded in Christian piety. They are the extensions of the meaning of this child's birth, as seen by the faithful soul, outwardly toward the whole world, and inwardly in the shaping of our life. The central text for this Sunday might therefore well be: "For mine eyes have seen thy salvation!"

The Name of Jesus (January 1)

Lutheran	*Roman Catholic*	*Episcopal*
Num. 6:22–27	Num. 6:22–27	Isa. 9:2–4a, 6–7
Rom. 1:1–7	Rom. 1:1–7	Rom. 1:1–7
Luke 2:21	Luke 2:16–21	Luke 2:15–21

EXEGESIS

First Lesson: Num. 6:22–27. When the books of the NT were being written, any man who had heard of "Jesus" might have known that a Jew from Nazareth who bore that common name had been crucified by the Roman governor, Pontius Pilate, earlier in the century. But for Christians—and Christians only—"Jesus" referred to a living reality, to the one acclaimed the Son of God in power . . . by his resurrection from the dead. In our treatment of the Advent lessons we noted that in two of the Gospel narratives "Jesus" was the name given by God to Mary's baby before he was born (Luke 1:31; Matt. 1:20–21). Without diminishing the importance of this prophetic sign, one may say that it was clearly of greater moment to the evangelists that "Jesus" now designated the risen Lord. Their purpose in writing the Gospels was that "*in his name* [the name of the Lord Jesus], repentance and forgiveness of sins should be proclaimed to all nations" (Luke 24:44–48; cf. Matt. 28:16–20; John 20:30–31; also Rom. 1:3–4; Acts 4:10–12). Before those who believed in Jesus as "Christ" and "Lord" came to use generally the name given them by others ("Christians"), they were sometimes identified as "those who call upon the name of the Lord Jesus Christ" (e.g., 1 Cor. 1; 2; Acts 2:21). By the apostle, Jesus' followers were exhorted to do everything—"in word or deed"—"in the name of the Lord Jesus, giving thanks to God the Father through him" (Col. 1:2). An early hymn proclaimed that God had "highly exalted him and bestowed on him the name which is above every name, that at the name of Jesus every knee should bow . . ." (Phil. 2:6–11; cf. Eph. 2:15–23).

The prominence given to "the name of Jesus" in the NT, and the meaning of this phrase in its various contexts are the legacy of Israel. Among ancient Semites a name signified more than mere identification, a means of distinguishing one person from others. One's name signified the nature or character of its bearer and declared, as by oracle, one's future destiny or representative historical role (Gen. 32:24–30; also 25:19–26; Isa. 8:1–4; Hos. 1:4–9, etc.). Particularly in the case of a deity the name was believed to be substantially a part of the name-bearer's being or powers. To manifest the deity's name was to make known the divine nature or will, or to establish the deity's presence in some numinous sense (e.g., Exod. 3:13–15; Deut. 12:1–5, 10–11; Ezek. 43:7 [LXX]). The OT lesson which contains the so-called "Aaronic benediction" exhibits one feature of this complex usage of the divine name in the scriptures; another is illustrated in the alternative lection from the prophecy of Isa. 9:2–4, 6–7.

The traditional prayer of the priests, recorded in Numbers 6, ostensibly implores God's blessing upon Israel. Yet in summary it is stated that this act intends more than this, for when the priests say this blessing "they put my name upon the people of Israel, and I will bless them," says the Lord (v. 27). It would seem that in this thrice-repeated name of God (YHWH) the covenant with Israel was reaffirmed. On the one hand, the invocation of the name of God acknowledged the supreme gift and claim of his self-revelation and presence; on the other hand, by this priestly mediation the people placed themselves under the authority, protection, and mercy of God (cf. Sir. 50:20–24; Ps. 67:1–2).

In the discovery of a "manual of discipline" among the Dead Sea Scrolls, evidence was provided that the traditional Aaronic benediction was given an eschatological application by a Jewish sect shortly before the period of Christian origins. We read that those who were to be received into this congregation of "the elect" celebrated with the sectarian priests God's "merciful grace to Israel" and also heard a recitation by the priests "of the iniquities of the children of Israel . . . during the dominion of Satan." Following a corporate confession of sin by the initiates, and their acceptance of divine judgment, we read that the priests blessed all the men of "the covenant" casting their "lot" with God, saying:

> "MAY HE BLESS THEE with all good and KEEP THEE from all evil, and ILLUMINE thy heart with insight into the things of life [or life-giving wisdom], and GRACE thee with knowledge of things eternal, and LIFT UP HIS GRACIOUS COUNTENANCE TOWARDS THEE to GRANT THEE PEACE everlasting." 1QS i,9 – ii,11.[1]

Early Christian writings, reflecting the belief that Jesus had become the historic and eschatological manifestation of the divine name, reflect also a messianic understanding of the special benefactions for which Israel petitioned God in this traditional blessing. Under the inspiration of the Holy Spirit, Christians confessed that "Jesus is Lord" (1 Cor. 12:3); that "in Christ" God the Father had blessed his people "with every spiritual blessing in the heavenly places," and "lavished" upon them "the riches of his grace" (Eph. 1:3–7); that "in the face of Jesus Christ" God's "glory" had shone to illumine the faithful (2 Cor. 4:6); and that "the peace of God which passes all understanding" was given to "keep their hearts and minds in Christ Jesus" (Phil. 4:7; John 14:27). In place of the Aaronic blessing one often reads in the NT the apostolic benediction: "Grace to you and peace from God our Father and the Lord Jesus Christ" (Rom. 1:7, 1 Cor. 1:3; Gal. 1:3; cf. 1 Pet. 1:2; Rev. 1:4–5, etc.).

During Advent our attention was drawn repeatedly to visions of Isaiah and of his successors depicting the fulfillment of the promise of a Davidic

1. T. H. Gaster, *The Dead Sea Scriptures in English Translation* (New York: Doubleday, 1956), p. 40.

Savior-King as the coming of a great light. (See the exegesis of the Gospel [John 1:6–8, 19–28] for Advent III.) An alternative reading from the OT for today (Isa. 9:2–4a, 6–7) turns again to one of these prophecies and focuses upon the names by which the prophet characterizes this last representative of David's royal line (vv. 6–7; cf. 2 Sam. 7:14; Ps. 2:7). Perhaps these titles were given to each Davidic monarch upon his succession to the throne in the vain hope that in his person he would realize these ideals. But no king of Judah ever did. Christians believe that the Christ child became the one who realized them, in his ministry and in his death and resurrection. In these events he established his just and eternal reign. And so today they confess him by these names, and believe that "of the increase of his government and of his peace there will be no end."

Second Lesson: Rom. 1:1–7. "Through Jesus Christ our Lord," Paul declared, he had "received grace and apostleship to bring about the obedience of faith *for the sake of his name* among all the nations . . ." (v. 5). Reference has been made to the common view that Paul drew upon a traditional creed in this salutation which begins his letter to the Romans (vv. 3–4). "The Gospel of God," believed by both writer and readers, concerned Jesus Christ, the one who was promised beforehand in the prophetic scriptures and who is now confessed in the church by the names "Son of David" and "Son of God." (See the exegesis of the Second Lesson [Rom. 16:25–27] for Advent IV and the Gospel [Luke 2:1–20] for Christmas Day.) For Paul, however, the designation of Jesus as "Lord" was especially significant. This was that "name which is above every name," bestowed upon Jesus by God as a consequence of his obedience unto death (Phil. 2:6–11; Rom. 5:19–21; Eph. 2:15–23).

The reference in this passage of the phrase "for the sake of his name" is not immediately clear. Does Paul simply refer here, as elsewhere, to his having received his apostolic commission from the Lord Jesus and therefore declare that his authority is grounded in this fact enabling him to preach the Gospel, in Christ's behalf, to the Gentiles? (Rom. 1:5 NEB; 1:1; cf. Gal. 1:1, 11–12). It is probable that in his choice of words Paul meant to assert this, but also to convey something more than this. The fact that Paul had been "set apart" by the Lord himself may have evoked the thought that as the bearer of the holy name "Lord," Jesus claims the allegiance of all nations, that the extension of the good news concerning the Jewish Messiah to include all men is a direct consequence of the elevation of the Messiah Jesus to the rank of *Lord* (cf. Gal. 1:15–16). Israel's witness to the salvation of God among the nations was intended to bring honor to the divine name, or, as we might say, credibility to the revealed truth concerning God's being and purpose. This was not always the result, and "for his name's sake" God acted both in judgment and to save (Pss. 23:1–3; 66:1–4; 79:8–10a; Isa. 42:1–4—Matt. 12:15–21; cf. Ps. 106:7–8; Ezek. 20:6 ff.; Isa. 52:5—Rom. 2:23–24). The witness of the Lord's apostle, and "the obedience of faith" on the part of those receiving the "gospel concerning God's Son," has now the specific purpose of commending his saving revelation—"for the sake of his name"—to all mankind (Rom. 1:16–17; 3:21–26).

Gospel: Luke 2:15–21. According to Luke's nativity narrative the shepherds knew not the personal name of the baby whom they found lying in a manger. But that which was told them "concerning this child" gave them cause for "glorifying and praising God": "to you is born this day in the city of David a Savior, who is Christ the Lord" (vv. 10–11; 16–17; 20). Because Mary's baby was to become the savior, he was to be named "Jesus" (YHWH is salvation: or YHWH saves, or will save); because of Jesus' willing obedience, God was to "highly exalt" him and "bestow" on him the ineffable name "Lord."

By the time Luke compiled his story the term "Messiah" (anointed = Christos) had become, through Christian usage, a personal name: Jesus Christ, or Christ Jesus. In some non-Jewish circles the term savior had come to stand for the Jewish Messiah, the agent of divine redemption (cf. John 4:25–30; 40–42). Thus we conclude that Luke's account penetrates prophetically to the substance of "the good news" announced by the Christmas messengers of God. These two titles "Savior" and "Lord" epitomize the historic consequences of that holy birth; the Bringer of Salvation is destined to become the Lord of the Whole Earth!

The reader of Luke's narrative is not led, however, by the evangelist's reflection of these later developments, to leave the scene of a particular history. "At the end of eight days," we read, when Mary's baby "was circumcised, he was called Jesus . . ." (v. 21a). By notice of this ordinary act of pious Jewish parents, Luke once again demonstrates a truth affirmed by Paul, that when "God sent forth his Son" he was, indeed, "born of woman, born under the law . . ." (Gal. 4:4; Gen. 17:9–14). But this ordinary event—the giving of a common name to a male Jewish infant on the occasion of his circumcision—is linked, in this witness, to the extraordinary origin of this child. The name by which he is called was "the name given by the angel before he was conceived in the womb" (v. 21b; cf. Matt. 1:21). Was there ever a more fitting name given to a baby? Once upon a time "Jesus" revealed, and throughout all time "our Lord" will accomplish, *God's purpose to save* all the peoples of the earth.

HOMILETICAL INTERPRETATION

The liturgical festival of the Name of Jesus, scheduled according to tradition one week after Christmas Day, is perhaps one of the most obscure festivals of the ecclesiastical year. Most Protestant churches ignore it. If Christian services are held on New Year's Day at all, other things are on people's minds, primarily those that have to do with the secular calendar, New Year's resolutions and the like.

But the church's primary liturgical task is to celebrate the Christian kerygma. Although there are understandable reasons why the particular facet of the church's proclamation which tradition associates with this festival has been displaced by other more immediate homiletical concerns, preachers ought to take seriously their kerygmatic responsibilities and not allow secondary or secular themes to substitute for the systematic development of the Christian message. If in the octave of Advent and Christmas feasts the proclamation surrounding the "name of Jesus" is missing, the full meaning of the Christmas message is not heard or understood; and in so far as that is the case the theological self-consciousness of a congregation will be lacking and the full maturation of faith hindered.

It is of course true that the theme for this day is not altogether absent from contemporary preaching. Most evangelical Christians are well aware of it; the name of Jesus is for many the central theme both of Christian devotion and Christian thought. Often, however, this emphasis falls prey to purely magical and superstitious notions because the theme is for a large part torn out of its proper historical and theological setting—that setting which the church's lectionary intends to remind us of. The recovery of a proper festival of the Name of Jesus is therefore an important endeavor, and one in which evangelical and liturgical churches can all play a part.

The two first texts chosen for this day are representative of central emphases in the OT and the New, with the third text, that from the Gospel of Luke, for all its unpretentiousness marking the dramatic turning point on the road between the two covenants. The OT text describes the origins of the Aaronic benediction—the naming of the people of Israel with the name of God. The Second Lesson contains an early form of the apostolic benediction and refers to the emergence of the Son, Jesus Christ, as Lord and manifestor of God's grace and power, in whose name all nations shall be named the people of God. And the Gospel text—a single verse describing how Mary's son obtained the name of Jesus, Joshua, "the Lord will save"—sums up the message for this day, pointing to both the unbroken continuity of the two traditions and the radical difference between them. In this manner the church's lectionary brings the believing community face to face with its most crucial task, that of defining its own identity, its own name. The first Christian church had to undertake that task early, both in relation to its Jewish background and the Hellenistic cultural context; the church in its contemporary situation is called upon to recapitulate by way of the lectionary this crucial stage in the development of the Christian faith. The question we are urged to raise is this: In whose name shall we live? By whose name are we called? The church's answer—preposterous to any Jew and foolish to any Greek—is the name of Jesus.

Let us take a closer look at the three texts from this perspective. When the Aaronic benediction was authorized, according to our first text (Num. 6:22–27), the prescription was explicit:

> "Thus you shall bless the people of Israel . . . so shall they put my name upon the people of Israel, and I will bless them."

The name is the Lord's ("The Lord bless you and keep you, the Lord make his face to shine upon you and be gracious to you, the Lord lift up his countenance upon you and give you peace"). Blessing, grace and peace—all is given in and with the name of God.

We should make sure that we understand this biblical emphasis on "the name". (Cf. "Name," *Interpreter's Dictionary of the Bible.*) The word itself is rooted in conceptions of essential identity: to name is to brand or mark something or someone. One's name is thus identical with one's existence. It is an expression of one's innermost being. To be given someone's name or to be called by someone's name is to be claimed by the owner of that name or considered as belonging to that someone. One is under the authority of the one by whose name one is named, and one is under the protection of the one whose name one bears. To speak or act in someone's name is to act as the representative of that someone and to participate in his character and his authority. To behave or act in a way that is contrary to the character of the one whose name one bears is to bring dishonor to the name, to profane its meaning, and lose one's identity.

Thus, to have the Lord's name put on us is an awesome thing. It determines who we are and whose we are. It defines our being and character as it describes our situation and our context. The repetitive pronouncement of the Aaronic benediction over the people of Israel was to be an ongoing reminder to each and everyone in that community that their identity, their blessings, and their responsibilities, were consequences of their being named by God. They were his people.

The same intention lies behind the apostolic practice of pronouncing benedictions at the beginning and closing of each letter; it was their way of constantly reminding the church of its identity and character. In the Letter to the Romans, Paul or some Pauline successor works into the text two separate benedictions taken over from other sources. One stands at the beginning of the letter, our second text for today (Rom. 1:1–7); the other at the end (cf. above, Advent IV, Second Lesson [Rom. 16:25–27]). The opening passage of his letter is in fact so similar in form and content to the passage in which the Aaronic benediction was authorized as to suggest that it may be intended as the Christian counterpart of that fundamental naming ceremony. This seems to be the reason for the combination of the two texts in today's lectionary.

The apostolic writer refers specifically to Jesus and confesses him as Christ and Lord. The name of Jesus is basic to his own apostolic calling ("to bring about obedience to the faith for the sake of his name among all the nations," v. 5) as well as to the life of every believer ("who are called to belong to Jesus Christ," v. 6). Thus there is still a name to be "put on" the people of God—but now not only the people of Israel, but on all nations, and now no longer the general name of God, "the Lord," but the name of "Jesus Christ, our Lord." The change is significant, so much so that the benediction which overarches the faithful community must itself be given a new formulation: "Grace to you and peace from God our Father and the Lord Jesus Christ" (v. 7). This is one of the earliest forms of the apostolic benediction, and it confesses boldly that blessing, grace, and peace are now given in and with the name of Jesus the Christ.

The festival of the Name of Jesus thus marks both the continuity which exists between the old and the new covenant and the radical transition between them. This point can find no clearer expression than the picture provided in our Gospel text (Luke 2:21). The child just born, in whose coming the church finds the fulfillment of ancient promises—a faith attested to by the angelic messengers and affirmed by the most sensitive of believers (cf. Simeon and Anna, First Sunday after Christmas, Gospel [Luke 2:25–38])—this child is now brought under the law through the ancient ritual of circumcision and given a name that has deep roots in the Jewish traditions. But in that very process a claim is made on behalf of this child which is unique, which cannot be made on behalf of anyone else. He is called Jesus, Joshua, "the Lord will save." Here, for the first and only time, so the church says, that name is truly appropriate and meaningful. Of all the children of Israel who are "born of a woman, born under the law" (Gal. 4:4), this one is different. His coming signifies the end of the old order and the breaking in of a new age. As the Gospel of John has it, "The law was given through Moses; grace and truth came through Jesus Christ" (John 1:17).

It is this conviction, the faith that Jesus is the Christ, that characterizes the Christian community and gives it its identity. It is precisely this conviction which sets the church apart from other religious communities—from the Jews who do not believe that he is the fulfillment of God's promises and therefore look for another, and from those who believe that fulfillment may come with every child and who therefore cannot accept his uniqueness. The festival of the Name of Jesus thus brings us face to face with the most essential feature in the Christian message: the claim that salvation is singular, that it is manifested in Jesus and no one else. As Peter is reported to have said before the rulers of the temple:

> "There is salvation in no one else, for there is no other name under heaven given among men by which we must be saved." (Acts 4: 12)

The bold claim on behalf of Jesus is of course also the most offensive feature in the Christian message, and the church has often had trouble with it. We need only refer to the problems involved in defining the relationship between Christian faith and the other world religions or in clarifying the issues surrounding the interaction of historicity and universality (Lessing's famous question). There is no doubt that tough intellectual questions arise whenever one religion claims absoluteness or when a single historical person is given universal significance. Regardless of how we otherwise approach these issues, however, if the church is to take seriously the message of this day it must continue to proclaim as its own conviction the truth of the ancient hymn: God has

> "bestowed on him the name which is above every name, so that at the name of Jesus every knee should bow, in heaven and on earth and under the earth, and every tongue confess that Jesus Christ is Lord, to the glory of God the Father." (Phil. 2: 9–11)

In summary, nothing is more characteristic of the Christian than to believe in the name of Jesus (John 1:12; 2:23; 3:18; 1 John 3:23; 5:13). We are baptized in his name (Matt. 28:19; Acts 2:38; 8:16; 10:48; 19:5). We are urged to meet together in his name (Matt. 18:20), pray in his name (John 14:14; 15:16; 16:23–24), receive others in his name (Luke 9:48), and do mighty works in his name (Mark 16:17)—including preaching, teaching, and healing in his name (Luke 24:47; Acts 3:16; 4:17–18; 5:28, 40). The Christian must also be ready to be persecuted for the name's sake (Matt. 10:22; Mark 13:13; Luke 21:12, 17; Acts 9:16; 21:13). In fact, there is no better statement of the commitment we are to make than that which Peter gave on the day of Pentecost:

> "Repent, and be baptized every one of you in the name of Jesus Christ for the forgiveness of your sins; and you shall receive the gift of the Holy Spirit." (Acts 2: 38)

And that is also the message of the festival of the Name of Jesus.

The Second Sunday after Christmas

Lutheran	*Roman Catholic*	*Episcopal*	*Pres./UCC/Chr.*	*Methodist/COCU*
Isa. 61:10–62:3	Sir. 24:1–4, 12–16	Isa. 61:10–62:3	Isa. 60:1–5	Isa. 61:10–62:3
Eph. 1:3–6, 15–18	Eph. 1:3–6, 15–18	Eph. 1:3–6, 15–18	Rev. 21:22–22:2	Rev. 21:22–22:2
John 1:1–18	John 1:1–18	Matt. 2:13–15, 19–23 *or* Luke 2:41–52	Luke 2:21–24	John 1:1–18

EXEGESIS

First Lesson: Isa. 61:10 (11)–62:3 (4–5). With this reading from the OT we return to a "Zion poem" written by one of the later prophets in Isaiah's succession. (See above, the exegesis of the First Lesson [Isa. 61:1–3, 10–11] for Advent III.) The poem is an antiphonal piece beginning with words of the prophet (vv. 1–7). Then follows an utterance of God (vv. 8–9). In conclusion Zion's glad response is depicted (vv. 10–11). Isaiah 62 is a companion poem in which the prophet again speaks, picking up themes and symbolism introduced in the afore-cited response of the people. Prophetic words of reassurance are supported by a divine oath concerning the future of Jerusalem (62:8–9).

Isaiah 61 describes the mission of the prophet and of the citizens of Jerusalem as being that of faithful witnesses to the arrival of God's salvation. This hapless, helpless remnant of Judah is told that God will heal their brokenness and restore their ravaged land. And, as a result, they will be called to fulfill their role on behalf of the Gentiles—represented here as a priestly mediation. Israel shall be supported in her task by the labors and wealth of other nations (vv. 5–7).

The joy in Jerusalem upon hearing these words of promise is described in the sensuous imagery of a wedded couple's connubial bliss (v. 10). The festive garments of "salvation" and "righteousness," with which the couple are clothed, symbolize, however, the saving acts of God whereby he vindicates his holy purpose in history and the people he has chosen to serve it (vv. 8–9; see Luke 1:46–55, and the promises made by God to Abraham, e.g., Gen. 12:2, 18:18). The horticultural image joined to this nuptial one is probably not a random mixing of metaphors. V. 11 seems to echo Isa. 45:8. But it is noteworthy that the prophet employs an image used by the original Isaiah (also by Jeremiah) as a figure of the Davidic messianic prince (Isa. 11:1; Jer. 23:5; cf. Zech. 3:8). The figure of the "bride" of the Messiah, symbolizing the "new Jerusalem" in John's apocalypse (Rev. 21:2, 9), is a metamorphosis of these juxtaposed images refashioned by the hope which was based on the death and resurrection of Jesus the Christ, and prompted by an experience of the Lord's faithful love for his church (cf. Eph. 5:21–33; 2 Cor. 11:2).

An alternative lection for today, Isa. 60:1–5, is a fragment of another Zion poem from the same prophetic circle and period. Jerusalem's restoration is here described in a prominent Isaianic figure as the flooding of an existing "thick darkness" with God's marvelous light. The scattered children of Israel, and all the nations of the earth, are attracted to the resplendent city wherein God's glory is revealed. In proclaiming the gospel of the incarnation in the early church, Christians were drawn to this magnificent imagery, as we shall see in the Gospel lesson for today. And still our hearts "thrill and rejoice" when Isaiah's emotion-laden lines, which are so full of promise, are read in the setting of Christian worship.

Second Lesson: Eph. 1:3–6; 15–18. The Second Lesson for today contains excerpts of the "benediction" (1:3–14) and "thanksgiving" (1:15–23) which begin the letter to the Ephesians. The traditional assignment of this letter to the apostle Paul is questioned by an impressive number of modern scholars. One reason for this doubt is that the initial, lengthy, and complex sentence after the address (vv. 3–14!) represents a departure from Paul's typical epistolary style. A more serious objection arises from the different uses made by the writer of key Pauline terms and concepts. But whether written by Paul or a later disciple, the great majority of interpreters agree that the Letter to the Ephesians is an impressive statement of Paul's understanding of the Christian gospel. Its main themes are enunciated in the beautiful introduction from which this reading is taken.

The closest parallel in the NT to "the great benediction" in Ephesians is the so-called Benedictus (Luke 1:68–79; cf. 1 Peter 1:3 ff.; Jewish parallels have been noted, e.g., Tobit 13:1 ff., 1 Macc. 4:30–33, 1QS xi 2–8, etc.). The unusual phrase, "spiritual blessing in the heavenly places," does not imply "a timeless, otherworldly, abstract blessing." Rather it refers to "that decision, action and revelation" of God in Christ, which was "culminated" and "sealed" when the Holy Spirit was given to both Jews and Gentiles (1:13–14; 4:30). This plentiful divine blessing is revealed therefore *in* history, and the reference to "the heavenly places" affirms rather than renders doubtful this interpretation. In the thought of this writer, "divine blessing in the heavenlies" is not limited to "an invisible sphere," but "exerts its influence upon life, history and conduct on earth."[1]

Vv. 4–6 may introduce a quotation from an early Christian hymn or confession, a not uncommon feature of Pauline letters. Its theme is reminiscent of a pervasive one in the Johannine books, summarily expressed in the reciprocal truth: "We love because he first loved us" (1 John 4:19, also 10–11; John 13:34–35). The Second Lesson appointed for Christmas Day placed a similar emphasis on the distinctively Christian life style, which is grounded in God's prevenient love and grace in sending his Son to be the savior of the world (cf. Eph. 1:4b; Titus 2:11–14). But among the NT writings only Paul speaks explicitly of God's purpose in Christ as being the "adoption of sons," and consequently of believers as "heirs" (Rom. 8:14–17, 22; Gal. 4:4–7). Noteworthy too in this benediction is the Pauline emphasis upon God's principal purpose in blessing mankind, i.e., "so that the glory of his grace be praised. . . ." (v. 6a [M. Barth's trans.]; also Eph. 1:12, 14; 3:20–21; 5:19–20; cf. 1 Cor. 10:31; Rom. 15:6). Perhaps one may see an anticipation of this idea in the poem, Isaiah 62, part of which was read today. In it the people of Zion are identified not only as those who render God praise; God's purpose is to establish them as "a praise in the earth" (cf. Eph. 1:5; Isa. 62:7; see also Isa. 43:18–21: "the people whom I formed for myself *that they might declare my praise*").

As noted above, the Second Lesson for today also excerpts a part of the Pauline "thanksgiving" in the Ephesian letter (1:15–23). A prayer perennially offered by man, surrounded as he is by dark, impenetrable mysteries, is that God will illumine or enlighten him. The intercession offered by the writer of Ephesians is a Christian's plea for further enlightenment (vv. 16–18). The remembrance of Christ, and the experience of his blessing, not only quickens hope in men's hearts; such realities make them aware of the promised "riches of his glorious inheritance," which are only partially understood and appreciated. A fitting prayer at the close of the Christmas season would be this intercession. Substance may be given to this prayer, and encouragement to make it one's own, if one reflects upon the resources in Christ which are declared in the confession of faith following this intercession in vv. 19–23.

For comment on the vision of "the new Jerusalem" in the Revelation to John, 21:22—22:2, an alternative lection for today, and on the relation of this imagery to Isaiah's prophecies, see the exegesis of the First Lesson (Isa. 45:22–25 and Isa. 60:13–21) for the First Sunday after Christmas.

1. M. Barth, *Ephesians* (New York: Doubleday, 1974), pp. 101-103.

Gospel: John 1:1–18. The Fourth Gospel, as is well known, contains no nativity narrative, no "Christmas story" such as one finds in Luke's Gospel. Yet John's stately prologue proclaims the coming of the Christ, and provides a profound theological setting for interpreting this historic event. New "names" are given to Jesus in the introduction to this Gospel: the "Logos (or Word) of God"; "the (true) light of men" in whom was "life"; "the only Son of the Father." A question, unresolved among interpreters of John, is this: At what point does the evangelist introduce the ministry of Jesus? At v. 4, or at v. 9 (following the testimony of John the Baptist), or at v. 14? If one assumes that in the prologue the proclamation of the gospel of Christ followed (as usual) upon the announcement of his coming by John, the forerunner of the Messiah, then v. 9 may mark the introduction of the historic ministry of Jesus, and vv. 10–13 summarize the mixed reception to his words and work among men and the fateful consequences thereof. V. 14 would then begin a confessional statement by those "who received him, who believed in his name":

> "And the word was made flesh and dwelt among *us*, full of grace and truth; *we have beheld his glory*, glory as of the only Son from the Father . . . *And from his fullness have we all received, grace upon grace. . . .*" vv. 14 (15) 16.)

Because of the poetic and strophic character of John's prologue, ending with this corporate confession of faith, many persons have thought that John 1:1–18 is another example of the use by a NT writer of a traditional creed or hymn. It is likely that we have here an original adaptation of a hymn in praise of Christ, sung by a community which preserved those traditions concerning Jesus which underlie the Fourth Gospel, and whose witness is found in four other NT writings associated with the disciple John (1, 2, 3 John; Revelation; see also 1 John 1:1–4).

What did it mean for the early Christians to say of Christ, "We have beheld his glory"? On the one hand, since God's glory—his true being and nature—was revealed in the man Jesus, it remained undeniably an earth-bound vision (as Paul said, "we walk by faith, not by sight," 2 Cor. 5:7; cf. 1 Cor. 13:12). Yet, on the other hand, in the Gospel's story of Christ's coming in the "flesh," the glory of God kept breaking through his words and deeds, opening the eyes of the blind and bringing life to the dying (this too Paul affirmed, "and we all with unveiled face, beholding the glory of the Lord, *are being changed* into his likeness . . . ," 2 Cor. 3:18).

In the movement of the Christian Year from Advent to Easter and beyond, the eyes of faith are still being opened and new life imparted through this divine paradox and mystery: "No one has ever seen God; but God's only Son, he who is nearest to the Father's heart, he has made him known" (v. 18 NEB; cf. John 17:3).

HOMILETICAL INTERPRETATION

We are now on the "continental divide" between Christmastide and the Epiphany season—the Second Sunday after Christmas being celebrated only if it comes before January 6, which is the Day of Epiphany. Whenever the calendar provides us a Second Sunday after Christmas we are invited by the lectionary to spend one more day developing a still deeper comprehension of the meaning of Christmas, by joining in the sort of enthusiastic kerygmatic extension of the Christmas message which emerged within the first Christian community as it grew to greater theological self-consciousness.

Once more it is important for the preacher to have a clear conception of what the day is all about. In a sense it is the quality of our sermonizing in this post-Christmas season that gives evidence of our grasp of the Christmas message itself. The aftermath of Christmas ought not to be characterized by our letting the gift lie unused or showing that we do not really care about it—with our getting along as if nothing new has happened at all. The lectionary guides us to a series of texts which express in the most imaginative language the kinds of superstructures which earlier believers utilized in projecting the deeper meaning of that "coming" which they had just observed. The three texts, the Zion poem from the postexilic Isaiah tradition, the great benediction from the letter to the Ephesians, and the prologue to the Gospel of John, all give free rein to a faith that soars to new heights of excitement and delves into greater depths of comprehension.

Advent, as we have emphasized above, is premised on anticipation, preparation, and waiting. Longing, yearning, and postponement—these are the true moods and attitudes of Advent. When Isa. 61:10–11 was included in the lectionary for Advent III, it was the futuristic note in the text that was at the forefront. When this same text reappears in the lesson for today, it must be interpreted in retrospect to the fulfillment which has now appeared, thus expressing the present desire of believers to "rejoice in the Lord" and "exult in (their) God." In one sense we are now, finally, at the point where our Christmas celebration reaches its absolute emotional pitch.

Characteristic of the Zion poems, as the above exegesis indicates, is the richness of imagery through which the prophet expresses his people's response to the message of redemption. From a variety of life contexts, all of them marked by celebration and joy, the prophet picks up images of festivity. Two in particular preoccupy him, namely, the wedding feast and the renewal of nature in spring—both occasions of overwhelming emotional excitement. We see the bridegroom "decking himself with a garland" and the bride "adorning herself with her jewels" (v. 10). Images and application intertwine as the poet describes being "clothed with the garments of salvation" and "covered with the robe of righteousness." We see the earth "bringing forth its shoots" and gardens "causing what is sown to spring up" (v. 11), and we are immediately told that likewise "God will cause righteousness and praise to spring forth before all nations." Magnificent—that's the word—magnificent is all that the Lord God does, and the prophet who sees it cannot and "will not keep silent" about it (62:1). He will sing out about it until the meaning of it "goes forth as brightness," "as a burning torch."

Obviously, the prophet is attempting to say what his words can hardly express. He is overwhelmed with the awareness of it all, and he rejoices, playing with words, exulting in images which are more like ejaculations of a freed spirit. We ought not to be surprised at this—or at the next step that may occur, namely, the complete explosion of all normalized language and the shattering of its fragments in an emotional fireworks of glossolalia. Ecstasy is not an unknown experience among those that have discovered the magnitude of the gospel. Normally, of course, we do not feel things that strongly. Many among us have closed ourselves to any notion of celebration—concepts like "the dancing God" or "the feast of fools" are repulsive to us simply because they go beyond the cool rationality of our institutional religiosity. But there is still the possibility of a heart-warming breakthrough to the fullness of the spirit, to the overwhelming awareness of what has really taken place in and with the events which we have observed and acknowledged. And perhaps the level of exultation which we experience now is a direct corollary to the level of intensity with which we went through Advent.

Our second text, Eph. 1:3–6, 15–16, part of the so-called great benediction which introduces that letter, represents another such expansive attempt at articulating something of the magnificence of the Christmas message. The intent of the passage, in today's language, would perhaps be expressed like this: "Think of it, man, and it'll blow your mind!" If not exactly so, it will at least stretch one's imagination. It shows how the community of faith refashioned the ancient kerygma of the mighty works of God and gave them a Christocentric focus. And it shows how the church took the humble events of Jesus' birth and death and wove them into the fabric of God's own universal plan of salvation, not on the periphery, as an afterthought, but as the central motif around which the entire pattern is organized.

The language itself is stirring: God is now "the God and Father of our Lord Jesus Christ" (v. 3); "in Christ" he has "blessed us with every spiritual blessing"; he "chose us in him before the foundation of the world" (v. 4); "destined us in love to be his sons through Jesus Christ" (v. 5); "bestowed (lavished) his glorious grace on us in the beloved" (vv. 6, 7); in whom we have "redemption," "forgiveness of our trespasses" (v. 7), even knowledge of "the mystery of his will" (v. 9), namely, his "plan for the fullness of time, to unite all things in him, things in heaven and things on earth" (v. 10). See what a sweeping Christology this is, encompassing all of history, from beginning to end! Read it out loud and you must marvel at the glory of it all. And then discover what the heart is already looking for—the way to respond, the apostolic model, which is life "for the praise of his glory" (vv. 12, 14), "holy and blameless before him" (v. 4).

The consideration of such dizzying heights and such awesome depths is not of course the type of fare we usually provide for our contemporary congregations. But why not, on this Second Sunday after Christmas, help them catch a glimpse of these "meatier" things? They need to be taught that the gospel is not a Sunday School story whose meaning is exhausted in the mere hearing of it. There is more here than meets the eye. Perhaps the way to go about it is to emulate the epistle writer—first to let them hear and see, and then pray that they may "have the eyes of their hearts enlightened" so that they may know "what are the riches of his glorious inheritance in the saints" (v. 18).

The third text for this Sunday, the prologue to the Gospel of John (1:1–18), extends this perspective even further. It displays a Christology of such expansive scope and sweep as to obliterate the distinction between time and eternity, history and transcendence. Fact and mythology are mixed together in such a way as to tie Christmas with creation, Christ child with the Logos, and birth with incarnation. There is talk of "the beginning"; of "life" and "light"; of "coming into the world"; of being "in the world" as one "unknown"; of those who "receive," who "believe in his name"; of "fullness of grace and truth"; of "glory," "glory as of the only Son from the Father"; of "grace upon grace"; of "the only Son, who is in the bosom of the Father," and who "has made him known."

What a fantastic superstructure that has here been built on the birth of a baby boy in a Bethlehem barn! Yet it is quite in line with the growing Christology of the first and second generations of Christians. The same structure is in fact evident in several NT contexts, and for the most part in the form of liturgical fragments—hymns, prayers, benedictions—which have been incorporated by NT writers at points where the gospel of Christ is to be summarized or celebrated (cf. Phil. 2:6–11; Col. 1:15–20; 1 Pet. 3:18–19, 22; 1 Tim. 3:16; Eph. 2:14–16; Heb. 1:3). It is a cyclical structure, beginning with Christ's preexistence, his coexistence with God, and continuing with his voluntary subjection to earthly existence, in the form of man, even in suffering and death, in complete identification with our human lot. But his death is not the end. There is a return phase in the cycle—Christ's elevation to power and Lordship through his resurrection, ascension, and re-enthronement at the right hand of God the Father. There is also a second turn in the cycle, a second coming and a final consummation. We call it the "kenotic cycle." It is clearly inspired by the Hellenistic logos mythology and represents a high water mark of NT reflection on the meaning of the Christ-event.

We would do well to make it a point on this Sunday to remind our congregations of the liturgical, imaginative, poetic, and celebrative nature of this language. During long centuries of heavily philosophical dogmatism, whether orthodox or rationalistic, the incarnation drama has often been reduced to metaphysical and speculative notions concerning the "substance" of the Son, his "nature" and "being," his ontological relationship to the Father, and much else of the same sort. That is in the character of "scholastic" theology, it seems. But the church ought not to allow its kerygmatic and liturgical imagination to be captured in such stale objectifications—not on this day, at any rate. For the texts for today are all the expression of the heart's excitement at seeing the Christmas story set in the context of salvation history, within the continuum of God's mighty works from the beginning to the consummation. What the church does is to claim that this whole history has a Christocentric orientation, and it celebrates that claim with unabashed emotion and fanciful imagery. To understand this right we must feel it, and to feel it we must let ourselves go!

The church shall move on to the Epiphany season next—to the celebration of the light that goes forth from God through Christ to all men, to the whole world, universally. But before we enter that phase of the liturgical year, this Second Sunday after Christmas has given us an opportunity to celebrate the light that shines into our own hearts through faith in Christ, our Savior and Lord. For before entering Epiphany, the church needs to know what Paul meant when he said,

> "It is the God who said, 'Let light shine out of darkness,' who has shone in our hearts to give the light of the knowledge of the glory of God in the face of Christ." (2 Cor. 4: 6)

That knowledge is the proper climax to the Christmas season.

PROCLAMATION:

Aids for Interpreting the Lessons of the Church Year

EPIPHANY

C. Fitzsimons Allison
and
Werner H. Kelber

PROCLAMATION:

Aids for Interpreting the Lessons of the Church Year

EPIPHANY

SERIES B

C. Fitzsimons Allison
and
Werner H. Kelber

FORTRESS PRESS Philadelphia, Pennsylvania

Library of Congress Catalog Card Number 74-24900

ISBN 0-8006-4072-1

Second printing 1976

5976G76 Printed in U.S.A. 1-4072

General Preface

Proclamation: Aids for Interpreting the Lessons of the Church Year is a series of twenty-six books designed to help clergymen carry out their preaching ministry. It offers exegetical interpretations of the lessons for each Sunday and many of the festivals of the church year, plus homiletical ideas and insights.

The basic thrust of the series is ecumenical. In recent years the Episcopal church, the Roman Catholic church, the United Church of Christ, the Christian Church (Disciples of Christ), the United Methodist Church, the Lutheran and Presbyterian churches, and also the Consultation on Church Union have adopted lectionaries that are based on a common three-year system of lessons for the Sundays and festivals of the church year. *Proclamation* grows out of this development, and authors have been chosen from all of these traditions. Some of the contributors are parish pastors; others are teachers, both of biblical interpretation and of homiletics. Ecumenical interchange has been encouraged by putting two persons from different traditions to work on a single volume, one with the primary responsibility for exegesis and the other for homiletical interpretation.

Despite the high percentage of agreement between the traditions, both in the festivals that are celebrated and the lessons that are appointed to be read on a given day, there are still areas of divergence. Frequently the authors of individual volumes have tried to take into account the various textual traditions, but in some cases this has proved to be impossible; in such cases we have felt constrained to limit the material to the Lutheran readings.

The preacher who is looking for "canned sermons" in these books will be disappointed. These books are one step removed from the pulpit: they explain what the lessons are saying and suggest ways of relating this biblical message to the contemporary situation. As such they are springboards for creative thought as well as for faithful proclamation of the word.

The authors of this *Epiphany–Series B* volume of *Proclamation* are C. FitzSimons Allison and Werner H. Kelber. Professor Allison, the homiletician, is a graduate of the University of the South (B.A.), Virginia Theological Seminary (B.D.), and Oxford University (D.Phil.). From 1956-67 he was Associate Professor of Church History, School of Theology, University of the South, Sewanee, Tenn. Since 1967 he has been

Professor of Church History, Virginia Theological Seminary, Alexandria, Va. He is the author of three books: *Fear, Love and Worship* (Seabury Press, 1962), *The Rise of Moralism: The Proclamation of the Gospel from Hooker to Baxter* (S.P.C.K. and Seabury Press, 1966), and *Guilt, Anger and God* (Seabury Press, 1972). He has lectured extensively at lay and clergy conferences, and in 1965 he served as the preacher on the Episcopal series of the Protestant Hour. Professor Kelber, the exegete, received his Ph.D. in 1970 from the University of Chicago. From 1970-73 he taught at the University of Dayton, Ohio. He is presently Assistant Professor of New Testament, Department of Religious Studies, Rice University, Houston, Texas. His study of the Gospel of Mark, *The Kingdom in Mark*, was published by Fortress Press in 1974.

Table of Contents

The Epiphany of Our Lord

Lutheran	*Roman Catholic*	*Episcopal*	*Pres./UCC/Chr.*	*Methodist/COCU*
Isa. 60:1-6	Isa. 60:1-6	Isa. 60:1-6	Isa. 60:1-6	Isa. 60:1-6
Eph. 3:2-12	Eph. 3:2-3a, 5-6	Eph. 3:1-12	Eph. 3:1-6	Eph. 3:1-12
Matt. 2:1-12	Matt. 2:1-12	Matt. 2:1-12	Matt. 2:1-12	Matt. 2:1-12

EXEGESIS

First Lesson: Isa. 60:1-6. This passage is part of the theology of Trito-Isaiah (chaps. 55-66), an anonymous author who reformulated the exilic message of Deutero-Isaiah (chaps. 40-55) for a postexilic situation. In 538 B.C. the Persian king Cyrus had issued an edict ordering the Babylonian Jews to return to their homeland and to rebuild the temple in Jerusalem (cf. Ezra 6:1-5). But this second exodus did not fully meet the high expectations aroused by Deutero-Isaiah (cf. 40:3-5, 9-11). The economic situation in the homeland was oppressive, and work on the temple was stalled by apathy and voices of discontent. Trito-Isaiah addresses himself to the exiles who have returned from Babylon to find their hopes frustrated by the realities of the Promised Land.

In Isa. 60:1-6 (which is properly concluded by v. 7) two major themes are developed: the epiphany of Yahweh and the pilgrimage of the nations. Generally, the two themes fall into vv. 1-3 and 4-6 (and 7). The imperative openings of each section are in the second person singular; the addressee is Zion-Jerusalem, home of the exiles. Jerusalem is to rise from hopelessness, because the coming of Yahweh will transform her into a place of light. The warlike features of older epiphanies (Judg. 5:4-5; Ps. 18:7-15) are absent; the focus is the light motif. Just as the sun rises in a blaze of fire, so will the epiphany of Yahweh fill Zion with light. With the rest of the world covered in darkness, Zion's magnetic force on the nations pulls them toward her light (v. 3). V. 4a, a literal adoption of Isa. 49:18a, introduces a description of the pilgrimage of the foreign nations. The five place names in vv. 6-7 indicate the universal nature of this journey to Jerusalem. Among the gifts delivered by the nations are first of all the sons and daughters of Israel (vv. 4b, 9b). The Jews of the dispersion will arrive in the company of the Gentiles (v. 4b literally reads: "your sons they bring them from far"). Other offerings by land and by sea are the nations' wealth and possessions (vv. 5-7).

Trito-Isaiah theologizes on a universal scale. Jerusalem's "covenant with death" (28:15) is canceled and the dispersing movement away from the center will be reversed. All the Jews of the diaspora (not merely the Babylonian exiles), and "the full number of the Gentiles" (cf. Rom. 11:25) will enter into voluntary service for the kingdom of God. This is the promise of a new future for the returned exiles.

Second Lesson: Eph. 3:2-12. Ephesians is not so much a letter, i.e., a dispatch occasioned by the specific needs of a local church, as it is an epistle, i.e., a deliberate theological treatise dealing with the nature of the universal church. The author is a Paulinist, who, steeped in Paul's theology and writing under his name, at the same time moves beyond the thinking of his teacher. This epistle is often considered the most "ecumenical" of the NT documents, because its central theme is unity.

In Eph. 3:2-12 the author dwells on the mystery of Christ. The concept of mystery contains both hiddenness and revelation. The mystery had been hidden in God since creation (v. 9), and therefore removed from the grasp of all previous generations. It has now been revealed to Christian apostles and prophets. Although Paul is the least among these apostolic founders (v. 8), the mystery was also revealed to him at his conversion (v. 3 is probably a reference to the Damascus incident). The author conceives of apostles and prophets as the recipients of revelatory insights into the mystery of Christ. By implication, this sets them apart from Christians who learn of the mystery through the medium of the apostles' message. This "holiness" of the apostles is a subtle, but significant development beyond Paul, whose emphasis was more on the interdependence of all Christians (1 Corinthians 12), and less on the privileged role of one type of Christian. The mystery, most clearly spelled out in v. 6 and reminiscent of Rom. 11:25, concerns the participation of the Gentiles in the body of the church. The Gentiles' exclusion from "the commonwealth of Israel" (2:12) is to be corrected by their integration into the body. Jew and Gentile are to be joined together in the fullness of Christ who is embodied in the church. The Christian apostles are commissioned to proclaim that there is a divine plan operative in history to unite all in Christ.

This revelation of the mystery of unity defines the destiny of both man and the powers of the universe. The heavenly powers have separated man from God, depriving the former of access to the latter. This is the religious drama underlying v. 10. The church by its exemplary existence in unity will inform these heavenly powers of the collapse of the wall of separation. As a result, the unity achieves cosmic dimensions with Christ "filling all in all" (1:23).

Gospel: Matt. 2:1-12. The theme of the Matthean infancy narrative (chaps. 1 and 2) is the identity of Jesus: who is he and where does he come from? After his Davidic designation has been traced through the genealogy (1:1-17), and his name revealed by an angel (1:18-25), Matthew's story of the visit of the wise men designates the birthplace of Jesus.

Matt. 2:1-12 might properly be called a placement story, because it establishes Jesus' geographic origin. Bethlehem, disclosed at the outset (v. 1) and confirmed by the Jewish leaders (v. 5), is sanctioned by prophetic authority (v. 6). We encounter in v. 6 Matthew's practice of firmly anchoring all crucial aspects of Jesus in the Holy Scripture (cf. 1:23; 2:15, 18). Jesus takes the place of David in whose city he was born (cf. 1 Sam. 17:12, 15; 20:6). The formula quotation 2:6 is a composite, combining Mic. 5:2 with 2 Sam. 5:2b. From 2 Sam. 5:2b comes the statement that Jesus "will shepherd my people Israel." This supplement to the Bethlehem quotation proper carries additional weight. Born in David's city, Jesus is the royal shepherd sent to Israel, the people of God. The place determines his mission.

Despite Matthew's deliberate utilization of OT passages, his Jesus is not in all respects discernible as the fulfiller of Scripture. One should not lose sight of the fact that Matthew supports a Jesus who does not live up to the expectations of those in charge of Scripture. While the Matthean Jesus is indeed appointed Davidic shepherd over his people, his mission is primarily directed toward "the lost sheep of the house of Israel" (15:24; 10:6). Those physically handicapped, the women, and ultimately the Gentiles will make up the mixed community of this unorthodox Davidic shepherd. It is Jesus' unconventional fulfillment of Scripture which causes tension and in the end brings the cross.

This tension is already manifest in 2:1-12. The revelation of the place provokes a conflict between "Herod the king" and "all of Jerusalem" (v. 3) on the one hand, and the "king of the Jews" (v. 2) on the other. From the outset a counterstructure evolves in opposition to the structure of Jesus' life. His place is in danger. But Herod the Great holds no lasting power over Jesus. The wise men, even though appointed to wrongdoing, fail to become an instrument of evil. The wise men, representatives of the unusual and universal following of Jesus, find his place, worship the child, and return to their own land.

HOMILETICAL INTERPRETATION

Isaiah, Ephesians, and Matthew, here combined, focus the light of the Epiphany season with their respective themes. The prophet discloses the light to be wider than Israel and to include the Gentiles. Ephesians declares that the Gentiles "should be fellow heirs, and of the same body" and that this unity will disclose the eternal purpose of God. Matthew relates the fulfilling of this purpose in the visit of the wise men who have been drawn by the light of the star.

The modern wise men in W. H. Auden's "Christmas Oratorio" indicate how they, too, are drawn by that star "Onto that Glassy Mountain . . . where knowledge but increases vertigo . . ." The scientist, the historian, and the social scientist are led to exclaim respectively: "to discover how to be truthful now . . .," "to discover how to be living now," and "to discover how to be loving now . . .," and finally all together "to discover how to be human now is the reason we follow this star."

This modern adaptation of the Christmas story (by one of the greatest Christian poets of modern times) is an endless and unparalleled source of insight and wisdom. The issues of apologetics, secularism, ecumenicity, mission, and unity are particularly appropriate topics for Epiphany. Like ancient Israel the contemporary church needs continually to be reminded that it does not exist for itself. The mission of the church is an inescapable theme for the season and from the lessons.

"The church exists by mission as fire by burning" has been a motto of theologians of missions. In spite of growing cultural isolation and diminishing confidence within brand name denominations in Europe and the United States, the theological truths remain the same. As Johannes Blauw asserts: "The Church of Jesus Christ has the right, solely as a missionary Church, to call herself 'Church' at all."[1] The churches in the "third world" are showing the truth of this teaching as they manifest, especially in Africa, unprecedented vitality and growth.

Conventional idolatries of race, clan, and nation grow as cultural accretions on the hull of the ship of faith, thereby slowing its grace. They are scraped off as that ship endures the culture shock of crossing radical frontiers. The Light that is the light of the nations is hid by the encrustation of minutiae, inflated to irrelevant proportions, which are effective only in hiding the Light from those who are entrusted with its care but who are too timid and afraid to give it away. Hence, in the very action of the mission the church finds and refines itself anew.

The author of Ephesians knows himself to be the messenger of this mission, this new reality in Christ. The contemporary preacher, sharing with Paul the preaching entrusted to him, declares what had been unknown and now has been revealed. Ansolino in Hemingway's *For Whom the Bell Tolls* speaks of the darkness enclosing modern men: "We do not have God here anymore, neither his Son nor the Holy Ghost." Preaching the mystery is always needed everywhere. It not only passes across the boundaries of Israel and the world of the Gentiles but across the boundaries of the words of men. Even the principalities and powers in heavenly

1. *The Missionary Nature of the Church* (New York: McGraw Hill, 1962), p. 129.

places are informed by this new unity and community (=the ecumenical community, consisting of Jews and non-Jews) of the manifold wisdom of God (Eph. 3:10).

W. A. Visser't Hooft accurately pointed out that there was no theological justification for the plural of the word church. It is one faith, one baptism, one Lord, and one holy folk. We sing the words of "Onward Christian Soldiers" with little recognition of the scandal we are perpetrating by our continued unhappy divisions. "We are not divided, all one body we; one in hope and doctrine, one in charity." In the lessons, in theology, and in history the mission and the unity are one. As we declare the message, we participate in the mission, we become one in the common task, and the eternal purpose "purposed in Christ Jesus" is disclosed.

This exhilarating and promised purpose could lead the preacher, using the passage from Isaiah, to a very thorny but important issue. This third portion of Isaiah addresses itself to the exiles who have returned from Babylon to find their hopes frustrated by the realities of the Promised Land. The realities were in stark contrast to the vision given them by Deutero-Isaiah of their homeland and their new temple in Jerusalem. This discrepancy between the vision and the reality, between the ideal and the actual, between hope and history is among the most poignant agonies people always face.

One wise clergyman has observed that it takes a layman of unusually strong faith to survive the frustration and despair so often resulting from an inside knowledge of sin in the institutional church. Clergy themselves are often tempted to a subtle anti-clericalism, not knowing that a comparable situation exists in hospitals, universities, city halls, and business offices. Jobs, marriages, adulthood, and retirement have aspects that are like the Jews' disappointment on their return to Jerusalem when the Promised Land did not fit the hopes kindled in Babylon. In fact all life seems adumbrated by the hopes and frustrations of moving from Babylon to Jerusalem or from Egypt to the Promised Land.

F. W. Robertson preached one of his greatest sermons on this subject. It is entitled, "The Illusiveness of Life."[2] Two points are covered by the sections "The Deception of Life's Promise" and "The Meaning of That Deception." He points out that on one level the children of Israel were deceived by the promise of a "land flowing with milk and honey," that Abraham was deceived by the promise of inheriting the land. He, together with Isaac and Jacob, wandered in the land of promise "as in a *strange* country" and these "all in faith, not having received the promises . . ." (Heb. 11).

On another level, the meaning of that deception is that the promise is

2. F. W. Robertson, *Sermons*, 3rd series (London: Kegan Paul, 1886), pp. 77-89.

tailored to our present condition, while the subsequent disappointment causes us to look higher and live more deeply. Hebrews again shows that Abraham, Isaac, and Jacob dwelt in tents, as sojourners, because they sought a "city which hath foundations, whose builder and maker is God." Though they "died not having received the promises, but having seen them afar off . . . (they) were persuaded . . . that they were strangers and pilgrims on earth," knowing their homeland to be a heavenly one. The greatest disappointments seem to come with the greatest expectations. But in this case the meaning of the disappointment is not despair but a deeper and more mature vision. Robertson shows that God has no Canaan for his home, no milk and honey for animal appetites, "for the city which hath foundations is built in the soul of man. He in whom Godlike character dwells has all the universe for his own . . . 'All things,' saith the apostle, 'are yours; whether life or death, or things present or things to come; if ye be Christ's, then are ye Abraham's seed, and heirs according to the promise.' "

Nothing seems to remind us more of our condition as "strangers and pilgrims" on earth than our dreams. This present age especially needs to consider the part dreams play in Scripture. In this lesson from Matthew the wise men are "warned of God in a dream." In Genesis God came to Abimelech (20:3), Laban (31:10), Joseph (37:5), and Pharaoh (41:25) in dreams. In Numbers (12:6) God tells that he "will speak unto him in a dream." In Judges (7:15) Gideon heard of the dream of one of his men. In the NT the angel appeared unto Joseph in a dream and even Pilate's wife "suffered many things in a dream" because of Jesus.

Men's dreams are often unsettling and assumed by the age to be no more than autogenic. But in the light of these lessons the Epiphany season, and the example of Joseph and the wise men we may consider anew the unsettling aspect of dreams in the light of the "meaning of that deception," and as a means by which the gracious God "appears to" us.

The Baptism of Our Lord
The First Sunday after Epiphany

Lutheran	*Roman Catholic*	*Episcopal*	*Pres./UCC/Chr.*	*Methodist/COCU*
Isa. 42:1-7	Isa. 42:1-4, 6-7	Isa. 42:1-7	Isa. 61:1-4	Isa. 42:1-7
Acts 10:34-38	Acts 10:34-38	Acts 10:34-38	Acts 11:4-18	Acts 10:34-38
Mark 1:4-11	Mark 1:6b-11	Mark 1:7-11	Mark 1:4-11	Mark 1:4-11

EXEGESIS

First Lesson: Isa. 42:1-7. In the wake of the Babylonian conquest and destruction of Jerusalem in 587 B.C., the military and intellectual elite of the city was deported to Babylon on the Euphrates. Among the exiles was the author of chaps. 40-55 of Isaiah, generally referred to as Deutero-Isaiah. Speaking to a people who had lost home and political identity, he adapts the theology of Isaiah to the new condition of exile.

Isa. 42:1-9 is the first of the four so-called Servant Songs, all of which are found in Deutero-Isaiah (49:1-6; 50:4-11; 52:13–53:12). The protagonist of these poems is a mysterious Servant of Yahweh. Scholars have given him various identities: an unknown individual, the prophet Deutero-Isaiah himself, the king, or the people collectively. At present many scholars prefer the collective identity (cf. Isa. 41:8). The language of the Songs is unmistakably messianic, e.g., much of what is said about the Servant could likewise have been said about the king. By the same token, the designation "Servant" was commonly applied to the king in ancient Near Eastern cultures.

Our first Song falls into two parts. The first part (vv. 1-4) depicts the Servant's official commission, and the second part (vv. 5-7 plus 8 and 9), a section formerly not part of this Song, outlines his universal mission. The speaker throughout is Yahweh, the God of creation (v. 5). In full possession of and guided by the Spirit of Yahweh, the Servant will impart justice to the nations (v. 1b). This propagation of justice is the most conspicuous assignment entrusted to him. Broadly speaking, justice (*mispat*: vv. 1b, 3b, 4a) indicates the divinely willed order of life which will prevail over disorder and chaos. The specific meaning of justice is spelled out in vv. 3 and 7. V. 3 does not speak of the suffering of the Servant, but of the Servant's compassion for the suffering people. Above all, justice entails an active concern for the oppressed. Through the assignment of the Servant the poor of the earth will recognize that their day has come. Quietly and without public fanfare the Servant will execute his mission (v. 2), which will produce nothing short of a covenant with the people of Israel and salvation for the nations (v. 6).

After the collapse of Israel's kingship Deutero-Isaiah reformulates salvation along the line of royal ideology. If one accepts the Servant's collective identity, it is the people themselves who will receive and implement the messianic promises.

Second Lesson: Acts 10:34-38. These verses form the opening words of Peter's sermon to the household of Cornelius in Caesarea. Peter is the dominant figure in the first half of Acts (chaps. 1-12), and Paul becomes the hero in the second part (chaps. 13-28). The career of both men is marked by frequent sermons, the famous speeches in Acts, which have been the object of scholarly debates. A generation ago it was argued that these speeches contain the pattern of the earliest Christian kerygma (C.H. Dodd, M. Dibelius), but recently they were identified as Lukan compositions (U. Wilckens). By and large, the speeches in Acts may well be understood as summaries of Lukan theology.

Peter's speech in Caesarea (10:34-43) appears in the context of the conversion of Cornelius (chap. 10). The latter is a watershed event because it signals the breakthrough toward the Gentiles; Cornelius is the first Gentile to be won for Christianity. Peter's speech tips the balance in favor of the Gentiles, resulting in the bestowal of the Spirit (10:44-45) and the Gentiles' baptism (10:47-48).

The introductory verses 34-35 appeal to the Gentile audience. The inclusion of the Gentiles is founded in the impartiality of God (v. 34). Fear of God and ethical conduct are the presuppositions for Christian membership (v. 35). Godfearers were Gentiles who sympathized with the Jewish religion, without fully submitting to its instructions. Cornelius himself had been such a Godfearer (10:22). The emphasis on doing good works is symptomatic of Lukan ethics (Luke 6:46-49; 19:11-27; Acts 20:35). V. 36 traces the origin and destiny of the gospel word. Originally intended for Israel, the gospel's limited appeal was transcended by its own object, Jesus the Lord. That Jesus is the Prince of Peace is a Lukan theme (Luke 2:14; 7:50; 9:54-55; 10:5; 19:38). Born in the year of the census and Zealotic violence, Jesus came to travel the way of peace (Luke 1:79). V. 37 traces the gospel's progress from John's baptism through Galilee to Judea. From there the gospel is to move through Samaria into the Gentile world and as far as Rome. V. 38 introduces the message proper of the gospel. The earthly Jesus, anointed at baptism, lived a life in Spirit and power; healings and exorcisms have confirmed God's presence with him. Peter preaches Jesus the benefactor whose ethical powers overcome the mortality of man. As such Jesus becomes a paradigm of Gentile existence in the world.

Gospel: Mark 1:4-11. Our passage is part of the Markan prologue (1:1-13). John, preparer of the way (1:1-3), announces and baptizes Jesus (1:4-11). Equipped with the Spirit in baptism, Jesus is driven by this Spirit into the confrontation with Satan (1:12-13). From this he emerges ready to embark upon his public career which opens with the proclamation of the gospel of the kingdom (1:14-15).

In the story of the appearance of John the Baptist (vv. 4-8) a desert tradition and a river tradition collide. According to v. 4 John operates in the wilderness, whereas in v. 5 he baptizes in the river Jordan. But "men do not go out to the wilderness to be baptized, but to the Jordan" (W. Marxsen). The phrase "in the wilderness" in v. 4 grows directly out of the preceding OT quotation of v. 3. John fulfills the precursor prophecy; he is the "one crying in the wilderness." Specifically, he is Elijah who was expected to herald the Day of the Lord (Mal. 4:5). His outward appearance (v. 6) is that of Elijah (cf. 2 Kings 1:8). His baptism constitutes an initiatory rite preparing the people for the gathering into the kingdom of God. John is the forerunner not merely in a temporal sense, but also paradigmatically. Although qualitatively different from Jesus (vv. 7-8), he is the model of what is to come. Causing a mass movement away from Jerusalem and out of Judea (v. 5), he anticipates the profoundly unsettling effects the irruption of the kingdom will have upon people. In the end, both John and Jesus will be "delivered up" (cf. 1:14 with 9:31 and 10:33).

The baptismal account (vv. 9-11) further explains Jesus' identity. The Son of God (1:1), whose identity is confirmed by the heavenly voice (v. 11), comes from Nazareth in Galilee (v. 9). In Mark's view Jesus is the Nazarene (1:9, 24; 10:47; 14:67; 16:6) who proclaims the kingdom in Galilee, dissociates himself from Jerusalem, and leads the way back to Galilee (14:28; 16:7). Mark does not report a Bethlehem tradition. His Jesus is from Galilee, not the fulfiller of the Bethlehem prophecy.

When Jesus rises from the water, he alone witnesses the heavens opened (v. 10). Accordingly, the heavenly voice addresses itself to Jesus personally (v. 11). The descent of the Spirit is not witnessed by John. It is an intimate affair between God and Jesus. From the moment of baptism Jesus is the Son of God, fully recognized, however, only by the Roman centurion (15:39).

HOMILETICAL INTERPRETATION

Whatever the identity of the "Servant" in these "Servant Passages" the preacher is certainly justified in applying them to the present ecclesia, the contemporary people of this covenant called to be "a light of the Gentiles." The expectation of the triumph of justice over disorder and chaos is proclaimed in Isaiah and something of its content is described as the prophet spells out what this justice means. To "fear God and to work righteousness" is the essence of Christian membership in the body according to this passage from Acts. The baptism of Christ indicates the fulfillment and personification of Isaiah's vision of justice and the personal content of the story related in Acts.

One of the themes that tie the lessons together is that of law-gospel. The justice of God that is the hope of Second Isaiah and the justice of God incarnate in Christ both lead to and through suffering to completion and fulfillment. The weight of this justice breaks all self-righteous attempts to carry it. The resulting suffering refines and expands the hope and the vision. In Acts, the boundary of Jewishness is broken by the weight of the *kerygma*, the story of God who is the God of all. The Gentile, like Cornelius, is included as the object of God's reconciling the world unto himself in Christ Jesus. This passage in the middle of the Book of Acts marks the transition from a local to a universal call.

It must be noticed that the weight of the law, the vision of justice, and the demand for righteousness are not diminished by Christ but heightened. The world knows, even better than conventional church people, the corrosive effects of religious and ethical demands. Theodore Reik, Sigmund Freud, Erich Fromm, and many other perceptive observers of human hurt have faulted Christianity because it makes too severe demands upon the self-esteem of an individual. It cannot be denied that Isaiah disclosed an even loftier vision of the people's vocation than what they had before inferred; and Jesus did not diminish the aescetic and prophetic demand of John the Baptist but moved it further into the center of men's hearts demanding more not less.

These times seem particularly eager to resolve the religious and cultural exactions by reducing their weight, lowering the demand, easing the obligation, and palliating the discrepancy between what we are and what we are to become. The world tells us that to have such a vision of righteousness by which we are judged, as that of Isaiah or especially that of Jesus Christ, is to enhance our guilt, lower our self-esteem, and trigger all the self-damaging dynamics of ill health. Better, they say, to lower the demands to realistic levels of human expectation which are, in some conceivable way, attainable.

Yet this unattainable and perfect vision is that shown in Isaiah ("He will not fail . . . till he sets judgment upon earth and we are called in righteousness"), preached in Acts ("Those who work righteousness are accepted by God"), and personified by Jesus as shown in Mark. What the world does not know is that a religion based on any "realistic" level of human expectation is a religion of self-righteousness. We are by the very impossible weight of God's law unable ever to have our dignity and identity based upon our self-righteousness. All self-righteous pretentions and idolatrous horizons are torn down and demolished by an honest and unflinching facing of the law. As the people of Israel are led through their history the narrow horizon of Yahweh as a tribal deity is wiped away. Especially here in Isaiah we see that the suffering endured in exile has produced wider dimensions of the original vision.

What the world does not know is that the unadulterated law leads to the gospel. As C. H. Dodd and others have taught: the law is a guard, guide, and schoolmaster that leads us to Christ. The weight of the law brings us to our knees, and we are now bereft of any self-righteousness that will fulfill the vision and empty of any arrogance that separates us from God's (and human) love. Sigmund Freud assumed the essential content of Christianity to be merely a lofty ideal (heightened super-ego material, in his terms) and people were already under more severe demands than they could fulfill from the ethical standards of a high civilization. He knew as Paul taught that "the strength of sin is the law" (1 Cor. 15:56). But he did not know the rest of the Pauline teaching: "For by grace you are saved by faith; and that not of yourselves: it is the gift of God: not of works, lest any man should boast" (Eph. 2:8-9).

It must be admitted, however, that much of what the world hears in the name of Christianity is merely law and it is quite understandable that a religion merely of law must be reduced to allow people breathing room. Hence, the new permissiveness increasingly pervades the world and the church. Those who fight such a trend only in the name of the law are unaware that such a strategy increases rather than prevents the lowering of the standards. After many years at the College of Preachers, listening to the sermons lay people heard from their clergy, Dr. Theodore Wedel reported sadly that too few had any *kerygmatic* context; the majority were an unrelieved recitation of the law's demands, whether personal or social in its dimension. One only has to consider what the word "preach" means to modern ears to realize how rarely the *kerygma*, which was preached in the early church and recorded in the Book of Acts, is being heard today. It is as though, with the domestication of the church, preaching is largely confined to Romans 12 ("I beseech you therefore brethren . . .") without opening up, unpacking, or explaining all that is implied in the "therefore." What Paul has shown in the preceding eleven chapters enables his listener to do what he exhorts in chapter 12. It is not enough for the preacher to be correct in his exhortation, he must also so declare the gospel that it enables the listener to do God's service.

The strategy then for the preacher is clear. The law in all its awesome demand for righteousness must not be lowered, nor adulterated, nor thought to be fulfilled by new idolatrous limits. Isaiah's vision of justice vanquishing over disorder and chaos, Acts' insistence that God is no respecter of persons but accepts all who work righteousness, and the fulfillment of both in the person Jesus baptized by John is not to be diminished, qualified, and tailored to fit the weaknesses, sins, and imperfections of a congregation. As impotent as the law is to enable sinners to fulfill it, the law is still "holy, just, and good" (Rom. 7:12). The effective preacher shows how the very inability to obey the law opens new horizons, as with Israel and the early church; purges arrogance, self-righteousness, and self-pity; and brings the hearers a wider hope, a nobler vision, and a deeper serenity in the gospel.

Tactics are always best left to the person on the scene. The strategy should in no way be so confining that the law must always be pushed to the point of the listeners' despair before the gospel is declared. George Whitefield realized this when he preached to Jonathan Edwards' congregation; skipping his usual prior use of law for conviction of sin, he moved immediately with that congregation into the good news of forgiveness. It might be that some today are unable even to hear the law until they first are made aware of the gospel foundation upon which the demand can be borne.

The Second Sunday after Epiphany

Lutheran	*Roman Catholic*	*Episcopal*	*Pres./UCC/Chr.*	*Methodist/COC*
1 Sam. 3:1-10	1 Sam. 3:3b-10, 19	Isa. 3:1-10	1 Sam. 3:1-10	1 Sam. 3:1-10
1 Cor. 6:12-20	1 Cor. 6:13c-15a, 17-20	1 Cor. 6:13b-20	1 Cor. 6:12-20	1 Cor. 6:12-20
John 1:43-51	John 1:35-42	John 1:43-51	John 1:35-42	John 1:35-42

EXEGESIS

First Lesson: 1 Sam. 3:1-10. The First Book of Samuel presents a complex portrait of the man of Ramah: a Nazirite by virtue of his mother's vow (1:11), a judge (7:6, 15-17), a prophet (3:20), head of a guild of ecstatic prophets (19:20), priest (2:18; 7:9), and leader of the monarchic movement (10:1, 20-25; 16:1-13). This man of God served to unite the different religious interests of Israel. On a pilgrimage to the temple of Shiloh his mother Hannah, stricken with barrenness, had prayed to Yahweh for a son, and her prayer was heard (1:3-18). In fulfillment of a vow she entrusted Samuel, this son of prayer, to Eli, chief priest of the temple at Shiloh (1:21-28). Under Eli's supervision Samuel received training in the service of the priesthood (2:11, 18-20, 26; 3:1). The young priest's rise at Shiloh coincided with the decline of the house of Eli. The temple had been corrupted by the misconduct of Eli's sons (2:12-17), and Samuel himself is to pronounce Yahweh's judgment over the house of Eli (3:11-14). There is, however, no specific statement that Samuel was to be Eli's successor (1 Sam. 2:35 does not necessarily point to Samuel).

It was because of the priestly corruption at Shiloh that Yahweh had withheld revelations from the sanctuary (v. 1). The dimness of Eli's eyes (v. 2) is mentioned to explain Samuel's behavior. Samuel assumes that he is called to render service to a helpless Eli. The statement concerning the burning lamp (v. 3) indicates that night had not given way to dawn. The ark (v. 3) was the same cultic object which David transferred to Jerusalem (2 Sam. 6:12-19) and Solomon worshipped in his temple (2 Sam. 8:1-11). It was the throne of divine presence from which proceeded the call to Samuel. The threefold call of Yahweh (vv. 4-9) heightens the drama toward the climactic moment of revelation (v. 10). The divine presence is intimated in reserved language: "Yahweh came and stood" (v. 10).

1 Sam. 3:1-10 suggests that the temple is the traditional place of revelation. It was not unusual for priests to be prophets. Samuel "was established as a prophet of Yahweh" (v. 20) by perceiving the voice of Yahweh for the first time (cf. v. 7) and by delivering its message. Yahweh's revelation occurs by hearing, rather than in dreams or visions; it reaches Samuel awake. The revealed information is designed to make history (vv. 11-14).

Second Lesson: 1 Cor. 6:12-20. The Corinthian Christians drew drastic consequences from the Christ event. Christ, they believed, had saved them—no strings attached. As a result they were free and no longer subject to the conditions of the old world. Christ had rescued them from bodily captivity and historical confinement. Their speaking in tongues signified the language of the Spirit and the vocabulary of the new being. This is also why they engaged in sexual excesses. They confess Christ in a life of total freedom. They are believing Christians who act in good faith, and not immoral pagans who succumb to the titillations of the world. In 1 Cor. 6:12-20 Paul does not attack immorality as a lapse of virtue, but libertinism as a religious conviction.

"All things are lawful for me" (v. 12a) was the Corinthians' motto used to legitimize unlimited freedom in all matters, including sexuality. While in principle acknowledging the Corinthian freedom slogan (v. 12c), Paul qualifies the notion that salvation equals total freedom on seven points. First, the communal principle: "not all things are helpful" (v. 12b). Helpful (*sympheron*) is what benefits the communal whole. In Pauline ethics the profit of the individual is less important than the common good (cf. 1 Cor. 7:35; 10:33; 12:7). Second, the principle of constructive realism: "I will not be enslaved by anything" (v. 12c). The uninhibited exercise of freedom undercuts its very foundation, causing new forms of slavery. Third, the eschatological principle: "God . . . will raise us up by his power" (v. 14). The Corinthians live in spiritual intoxication and consider the body the worthless part of man. For Paul man *is* body destined to be resurrected. The eschaton makes its claim upon the present conduct of the body. Fourth, the christological principle: "your bodies are members of Christ" (v. 15). Membership in the body of Christ precludes intercourse with prostitutes (vv. 15-17). Fifth, the anthropological principle: "the immoral man sins against his own body" (v. 18). Licentiousness leads to self-destruction. Sixth, the pneumatological principle: "your body is a temple of the Holy Spirit" (v. 19). Both the community (3:16) and the individual are the locus of the Spirit. Seventh, the soteriological principle: "you were bought with a price" (v. 20). Freedom is to be used in responsible gratitude toward the Lord.

Paul rejects sexual libertinism. But he does so not by downgrading the body and moralizing on the temptations of the flesh, but by restoring the damaged reputation of the body.

Gospel: John 1:43-51. Presumably Jesus is still in Bethany beyond the Jordan (1:28) when he decides to go to Galilee (v. 43a). After Andrew (v. 40) and Simon Peter (v. 41), Philip is the third disciple to be "found" by Jesus. Philip in turn recruits Nathanael (v. 45). Cana in Galilee, Nathanael's home town (21:2), is also the goal of Jesus' journey (2:1 ff.). Philip's pronouncement that Jesus is "son of Joseph" (v. 45c; cf. 6:42) reflects the Jewish custom of identifying a man by reference to his father. For Philip Jesus' Nazarene origin is in fulfillment of the OT (v. 45b). But Nathanael objects (v. 46a) with: "Nazareth! Can anything good come from there?" This is the classic protest against the Galilean identity of the Messiah (cf. 7:52). The heart of the matter is the obscurity and unmessianic status of Jesus' birthplace. Nazareth was an insignificant village in Lower Galilee; it is never mentioned in the OT, the Talmud, the Midrash, or Josephus! Nathanael's willingness to accept Philip's invitation earns him Jesus' praise (v. 47). He is a symbol of Israel at her best, sincere and dedicated to God. Jesus knows the character of Nathanael (cf. 10:14), and Nathanael expresses surprise at his knowledge (v. 48a). Jesus' reference to the fig tree (v. 48b) assumes that he had "seen" Nathanael earlier under a fig tree studying the Scripture in search for the truth. Overwhelmed by Jesus' omniscience Nathanael confesses him as Son of God and King of Israel (v. 49). But Jesus discounts his confession (v. 50a). Faith based solely on the miraculous is unacceptable. Greater things are promised (v. 50b), and Jesus reveals himself enigmatically as Son of man.

V. 51, a notoriously difficult saying, is the first of a total of twelve Son of man occurrences in John. The traditional interpretation argues for the motif of unity: Jesus is the point of contact between heaven and earth (thus R. Bultmann, R. E. Brown, etc.). Recently W. Meeks interpreted v. 51 in terms of alienation and foreignness: Jesus is the stranger par excellence.

The Johannine structure of thought develops along a spiral path. Philip pronounces Jesus the Messiah of Nazareth. Nathanael reacts sceptically. Next comes Nathanael's confession of Jesus as Son of God and King of Israel. This in turn meets with Jesus' scepticism. Jesus is all that—and more. In touch with the heavenly world, he is the Son of man from above who has entered into the hostile world below.

HOMILETICAL INTERPRETATION

The call of Samuel and the call of Philip and Nathanael are contained in two of our lessons. Samuel is born into a time of the emptiness of revelation. The call of God had been withheld from the sanctuary due to the corruption in the house of Eli. When there is no call of God it is a barren time for any vocation; all occupations tend to be only jobs empty of meaning, of purpose, of joy. Perhaps Samuel's birth to Hannah in her barrenness is meant to be symbolic of the barrenness of a time when God's revelation is no more heard in the land.

Certainly modern times reflect this time of Eli when for much of the culture God is not only silent but dead. Harry McPherson, writing in the *Washington Post*, laments these times as having "many Indians but no chiefs." In all branches of the culture—in the armed forces, politics, arts, education, the church—there seems to be a paralysis of leadership. In Samuel's time this was due to corruption which had provoked God to withhold his revelation, his call. Samuel, himself a miracle from Hannah's barrenness, brings to his vocation both the prophetic and priestly strain.

This combination of priestly and cultic with prophetic and tribal perhaps accounts for Samuel's ambivalence toward kingship. Murray Newman's *The People of the Covenant* fills in for us the dire military and political threat the Philistines were to Israel in Samuel's time. One tradition found the monarchy quite congenial and kingship the answer to their present dilemma. The other tradition saw kingship from a more primitive perspective and thought that it would threaten the purity of covenant relationship with Yahweh. Although Samuel marks the end of the house of Eli he maintains the older traditions of Israel and combines them just in time to save Israel from devastation by the Philistines. The revelation comes to Samuel in the primitive and dramatic threefold call to the ear, the primary organ of the Elohist tradition. The call comes to Israel through Samuel who is the answer to Hannah's prayer to be delivered from her barrenness. Thus, the personal and social implications of the call are neither separated nor divided.

Amos warns of a famine, not a famine of bread and water but a "famine of hearing the words of the Lord" (Amos 8:11). It was such a time for Hannah and Israel. And it was prayer, arising out of the distress of this famine, that was answered by Samuel's birth. Then Yahweh gave not only Samuel to Hannah but also revelation and vocation to Israel. So today in our famine of "hearing the words of the Lord" the prayers of those distressed by their barrenness in job and life are given the call of God, "Follow me." These were the two simple words of Jesus to these disciples: "Follow me." All Christian disciples learn their vocation from these words. The traditional baptismal vow of Christians is to follow Jesus as Lord and Savior.

It is said that every preacher should have some diagnostic understanding of his times. Why now is there what Eugene Ionesco calls "metaphysical emptiness"? Why now this state that W. B. Yeats described as one in which "the best lack all conviction and the worst are full of passionate intensity"? St. Paul asks, "And how shall they preach except they be sent?" (Rom. 10:15), and then answers his own question: "So then faith cometh by hearing, and hearing by the word of God" (Rom. 10:17). The word of God came to Samuel by hearing. Why did it not come before? We are told it was because of the corruption in the house of Eli. Thus, the silence of God can be seen as his wrath.

The corruption in Corinth to which Paul addresses himself in this passage from 1 Corinthians has deeper roots than a mere lapse of virtue. It is not mere quaint metaphor that relates fornication and adultery throughout the OT to unfaithfulness and idolatry. Sex is often concerned with much more than sex: dignity, reassurance, revenge, identity, and meaning. The films by Fellini and Bergman vividly illustrate the religious dimension of sexual search. The OT is much more apt and relevant to our times than many suppose when it shows the crucial tension between a god of nature and the God of history, between the fertility cults and the worship of Yahweh. So much conventional understanding of Christianity sees sexual behavior as only a matter of character and morality. Actually Paul claims that sexual abberations and immorality are symptoms of much deeper religious distortions. In Rom. 1:19-32 he discloses the link between ceasing to worship God and the resulting sexual corruption. Some critics have suggested that Ingmar Bergman's trilogy, "Through a Glass Darkly," "Winter Night," and "Silence," is a commentary on this passage from Romans, which sees the loss of faith, fornication, incest, lesbianism, suicide, and god as a "creeping thing" as the judgment of God. William

Burroughs, in an article in *The Atlantic*, reports that his motive in writing about sexual depravity was to contribute to the growing body of literature that makes every conceivable corruption as explicit as possible thereby diminishing what can be felt as shameful. W. H. Auden prays for those who think "knowledge of the flesh can take the guilt of being born away" or that "simultaneous passions make one eternal chastity."[1]

The Corinthian situation to which Paul in this lesson addresses himself is a bit different from common pagan immorality. Although the Corinthian Christians doubtless retain a spillover from the notorious cultural reputation their city had earned as a capital of licentiousness in that part of the Empire, they are now Christians who are justifying such behavior on the grounds of "freedom." Our exegete has underlined the seven arguments that Paul marshals against this sexual antinomianism. Our contemporary situations certainly cry out for some sane and helpful word from the preacher in regard to similar conditions, and the preacher could do a lot worse than flesh out and illustrate the seven points Paul made.

One common theme must not be overlooked. Paul discloses a view, a way to see flesh and spirit and God that enables his hearers to be truly free. He knows that fussing at a fat man will not keep him from gluttony, neither will exhortation to purity keep people from immorality. Certainly the crucial matter to straighten out immediately is what Paul means by "flesh." The "carnal spirit" that seems common to the seventeen "works of the flesh" enumerated in Gal. 5:19-21 is a much wider and more subtle matter than anything connoted in the mind of modern man by the word "flesh." The denigration of the body, which is the reputed view of the Jansenist and the Puritan, is no effective antidote to sexual immorality. We can see in the example of the Corinthians that it was precisely this distorted and dishonorable attitude toward the body that provided the excuse for their licentiousness. If the body doesn't count and we are now really "spiritual," it doesn't matter what the body does. This view was perpetuated in church history by the Manichaeans who were often at the same time radically ascetic and licentious, whose "freedom" was deduced by just such a failure to honor and appreciate the holiness and dignity of the body.

True freedom in matters of service and morality is a result of response to God's call. "If you continue in my word, then are ye my disciples indeed; and ye shall know the truth and the truth shall make you free" (John 8:31-32). Like Philip and Nathanael all disciples will be free as they respond to his call, "Follow me," and that truth will make men free.

1. W. H. Auden, *Collected Works* (New York: Random House, 1945), p. 426.

The Third Sunday after Epiphany

Lutheran	*Roman Catholic*	*Episcopal*	*Pres./UCC/Chr.*	*Methodist/COC*
Jon. 3:1-5, 10	Jon. 3:1-5, 10	Jon. 3:1-5, 10	Jon. 3:1-5, 10	Jon. 3:1-5, 10
1 Cor. 7:29-31	1 Cor. 7:29-31	1 Cor. 7:17-23	1 Cor. 7:29-31	1 Cor. 7:29-31
Mark 1:14-20	Mark 1:14-20	Mark 1:14-20	Mark 1:14-22	Mark 1:14-20

EXEGESIS

First Lesson: Jon. 3:1-5, 10. Unlike all other prophetic writings of the OT, the Book of Jonah is not a collection of sayings by the prophet, but a story about him. Jonah, the book's antihero, seeks to evade Yahweh's command to change the wicked ways of the Assyrian capital Nineveh. He flees on a ship, has himself thrown overboard in order to placate the tempestuous sea, and is swallowed by a great fish. Three days later he is vomited out upon dry land. After this experience Jonah carries out Yahweh's command, and thus contributes to the rescue of the Ninevites. Resentful of a God who is "slow to anger, and abounding in steadfast love" (4:2), the prophet goes into a sullen retreat. But Yahweh demonstrates to him that his pity for Nineveh was justified.

Our passage (3:1-5, 10) reports Yahweh's renewed command after the fish episode and Jonah's prophetic appearance at Nineveh. This time Jonah promptly obeys Yahweh. That the message would be the same as before is understood (3:4; 1:2). The description of the city reads: "Nineveh was a great city to God" (v. 3b), i.e., in the eyes of God it represented the Gentile nations. Jonah proceeds to the center of Nineveh (v. 4a) and makes his proclamation of judgment. Nothing but the bare fact of the coming disaster is announced. While Jonah is conscious only of retribution (cf. 4:2), Yahweh is using the threat of judgment as motivation for repentance. Vv. 6-9 narrate the fasting of the king of Nineveh, of his people, and the animals. This massive repentance arouses the mercy of Yahweh, and he decides to spare the city (v. 10).

The Book of Jonah is influenced by the universalist, humanistic ideas of postexilic wisdom theology. Yahweh's mercy is not meant for Israel exclusively. It can be granted to the people and even the animals (3:7; 4:11) of a hated foreign city (Nahum 3:1-7), if this city turns from violence and corruption to Yahweh. Jonah represents the kind of particularism that would restrict Yahweh's mercy to Israel. The God Jonah fears is "the God of heaven, who made the sea and the dry land" (1:9); in relation to other nations he is but the God of judgment. God tries to teach Jonah that the presupposition of salvation is repentance, rather than national origin. Jonah is truly a prophet of judgment, but he functions in the service of a God of universal mercy.

Second Lesson: 1 Cor. 7:29-31. In chap. 7 of 1 Corinthians Paul deals with the issues of marriage, divorce, and celibacy. He writes in response to questions asked by Corinthians (7:1), although the theological stance of these Christians is not fully clear. It is widely assumed that Paul encounters two basic trends in Corinth: the libertinists who consider unlimited sexual freedom a sign of salvation (1 Cor. 5:1-2; 6:12-20), and an ascetically inclined group which regards sexual intercourse as sinful. This latter group possibly influenced Paul's writing of chap. 7. Ultimately, both directions express contempt for the body and discredit it as a creation of God.

Despite certain ascetic leanings on the part of Paul himself, the purpose of chap. 7 is not to recommend asceticism as a way of life, but to define the freedom of the individual (vv. 7, 17, 24) in a passing world. Salvation does not require a change in social status (v. 20), because no position is endowed with more grace than another (v. 7b). Therefore the unmarried should stay single, although this should not be made a rule either (vv. 8-9). Likewise, the married ought not to seek separation (vv. 10-11, 27a), although divorce is not unthinkable (v. 11a), despite the Lord's prohibition (v. 10).

The eschatological argument begins with v. 26. The "impending distress" indicates the anxiety of the end time. In the last analysis, it is for apocalyptic reasons that the *status quo* is to be maintained. Those who now choose marriage will get themselves most severely entangled in the crisis of the world (v. 28). Vv. 29-31 sum up the nature of Christian life under the force of eschatology. Because time is foreshortened (v. 29a) the believer is no longer to involve himself in the structure and struggle of the old world. Detached from all earthly conditions, he is to live "as if not," because "this world in its basic structure is (already) in the process of perishing" (v. 31b). In themselves vv. 29-31 could have been spoken by a Stoic, and yet Paul does not counsel withdrawal from the world into the inner self, but perseverance in one's place. Nor does he recommend abstinence from worldly goods because such are evil. The goods are relativized, but not debased. In the literal sense, Pauline ethics is time-conditioned. Under the pressure of the end time, Paul discovers the transience of all goods. *Sub specie aeternitatis* everything loses its earthly glamor. No change is needed, for total change is expected.

Gospel: Mark 1:14-20. The Jesus of "Nazareth in Galilee" (1:9) emerges from his wilderness confrontation (1:12-13) and enters Galilee to make it the place of his first public proclamation (1:14-15). His arrival follows on the heels of John's exit. The Galilean manifesto is called "the gospel of God," and its major concern is "the kingdom of God" (v. 15a). The principal identity of the Markan Jesus is that of proclaimer and bearer of the kingdom. All aspects of his career must be viewed in light of his programmatic kingdom announcement. The latter is divided into kergyma (v. 15a) and parenesis (v. 15b). Scholarly opinions differ with regard to the status of the kingdom: has it actually arrived, or is it merely at hand? Most interpreters opt for the nearness of the kingdom, but the eschatological force of the kerygma is such that arrival and presence could well be the meaning of Jesus' gospel. Repentance and faith, the parenesis, do not necessarily constitute acts of preparation for the kingdom. Rather they might indicate the direct consequences ensuing from the arrival of the kingdom. A radical break with one's former mode of living and confidence in view of the eschatological happening—these are the demands imposed upon people who live in the wake of the irruption of the kingdom.

Immediately following the announcement of the kingdom the evangelist reports the enlistment of four men into the service of discipleship (1:16-20). Discipleship is one of the pivotal topics in Mark. If it is the kingdom which is of concern to the Markan Jesus, then the call of the disciples accords it a communal dimension. The kingdom consists of people, but in the curious sense of dislodging them from their native habitat. Following Jesus requires a break with past life. But discipleship is not an end in itself. Jesus' call: "I will make you to become fishers of men" (v. 17b) entails a program which points to the future. Throughout his ministry Jesus will instruct the disciples with the aim of making them fishers of men. Primarily through exorcisms, healings, and teaching (6:7, 13, 30) are they to continue the legacy of Jesus. The gospel's reader who learns of the vocation of these men looks upon them as the founding figures of the kingdom. In their vocation he recognizes his own origin and vocation. He can follow Jesus if he continues the work in and for the kingdom of God on earth.

HOMILETICAL INTERPRETATION

Among the themes contained in these lessons is the continuing Epiphany theme of the worldwide mission of the church. Jonah's resistance to the mission and God's disclosure of his universal claim and love dramatize this theme. The short passage from Corinthians gives us a look at all present life through the perspective of the end and imminent judgment. Mark tells of the proclamation of the kingdom and its relation to repentance, belief, and the calling of the disciples. If one focuses on the theme of repentance it is important to undergird the common assumption concerning the chronology of repentance and forgiveness with some vehicle of grace that enables repentance.

In Jonah it is judgment. The judgment of Yahweh pursues Jonah on the sea and in the fish until he consents to preach this judgment to Nineveh. The judgment breaks the bondage of Jonah's idolatrous fixation on what he insists are the limits of Yahweh's grace and thus enables Jonah to repent and to preach. The judgment he proclaims against the city evokes repentance by the people, fasting by all from king to beasts, and repentance even of Yahweh, who changes his mind and spares the city. It is an awkward theme for tidy minds to have almighty God repent. It seems to involve the most primitive aspects of anthropomorphism. However, what is said of democracy can be said even more aptly of anthropomorphic symbols of God: "Democracy is the worst form of government, except for all the alternatives." So all the alternatives to human analogies for God are worse than the human ones. That God is some "force," "primal cause," or "creating principle" contains far more reductionist and dehumanizing connotations than "Father." In both Old and New Testaments we have portraits of God whose will and action are changed by prayer and repentance. Charles Simeon's response to the charge of being unsystematic in presenting God's treatment of men and salvation was that he "refused to be more systematic than the scripture." It is a good rule for preachers of any day.

The repentance in Mark's account also comes after judgment and even before "belief" (1:13). But here the content of judgment is the kingdom of God. "The time is fulfilled and the kingdom of God is at hand." This judgment becomes the occasion and leverage for repentance and belief. There is strong psychological evidence that people cannot repent by mere exercise of their wills. There must be some judgment, some tragedy, some dying, some new hopes, or some word that makes it possible for one to repent, to have one's mind changed. In the Episcopal *Book of Common Prayer* there is profound wisdom in the absolutions in Morning and Evening Prayer that include petitions to be granted "true repentance" after the declaration of absolution. Provision is made here for the ambiguity in human wills known to every perceptive pastor. Forgiveness and mercy are inaccessible without repentance but the truest repentance is the grateful response to forgiveness and mercy. Hence, as Christians our lives are characterized by the symbiotic and mutual relationship between repentance and forgiveness. The prodigal son's repentance was not finished, but begun, in the pig-pen. One characteristic common to all saints is their deepening repentance as their sense of God's mercies widens.

Regardless of the differences among scholars concerning the emphasis upon the "realized" kingdom, the preacher should be confident that it is eminent, immanent, and imminent. Any emphasis on one that excludes the others is false to the data and to the experience of the faithful. The kingdom is eminent: it is higher, loftier, and of greater priority than any other allegiance. Its claim is first, over that of nation, church, parents, spouse, or job. Thus, the kingdom always comes in judgment on lesser priorities and even duties and obligations. The hard saying about being not worthy of the kingdom without "leaving" or even "hating" all lesser claims illustrates the absolute demand of the eminence of the kingdom. Even Israel (e.g., Jonah's experience) cannot see itself as coterminous with the kingdom. The attempt to equate the church with the kingdom is to forget the lesson of Jonah and to create a new idolatry that reduces all prophetic self-criticism of the church to disloyalty. The eminence of the kingdom brooks no higher loyalties and no fidelity to any lesser end is finally acceptable. The eminent kingdom is the test of idolatry.

The immanence of the kingdom on the other hand is realized already. Wherever demons are cast out and people healed in the name of Christ the kingdom "has come upon you." The other side to the denial that Israel or the church can be equated with the kingdom is that they cannot be separated either. Although the kingdom of God is always judging the holy folk, the church is the indwelling locus of the kingdom in history. After hearing a long lecture by a young historian cataloguing distortions and faithlessness of the church, A. T. Mollegen, when asked what he thought, replied, "But the lecturer forgets that it is the only church we have." However inadequate the people of Israel were, it was the only Israel we had. There is a certain subtle arrogance in being so critical of the church in one's vision of purity and perfection that it becomes a barrier to the commitment, loyalty, and love of the church in history. The immanent kingdom is inevitably involved in institutions "far gone from original righteousness" and any individual whose dignity is too pure to be compromised by the ambiguities in the church, already possesses a purity "too good for this world" but does not belong to the eminent kingdom either. The immanent kingdom is the test of humility and courage.

The imminent kingdom shares attributes of the other two aspects but brings the final eschatological judgment to bear on each moment of history. The hard sayings mentioned above and the passage of Paul in Corinthians can only be seen gracefully in the perspective of the imminent kingdom. Because history is in the hands of God, and no one knows the "hour when the bridegroom cometh," we must all live now aided by the perspective of the end. This view helps hinge our hearts and wills to the solid foundation of the kingdom by which we can swing through all threats, tragedies, and suffering. The imminent kingdom is the last word. This is reassuring in tragedy but disconcerting to self-righteousness. Has anyone ever said (or felt), "If it's the last thing I ever do, I'll get revenge!"? If so, it is a prayer for hell. We have seen the last word in Christ. "Vengeance is mine saith the Lord." The demands of the imminent kingdom dig their foundations deeper than our marriages, families, and nations. "Meats for the belly, and the belly for meats: but God shall destroy both it and them," Paul declares in 1 Corinthians 6. In our passage from chap. 7 he is not speaking of the immanent kingdom but he is speaking of the imminent kingdom that prepares us for inevitable loss and gives us the final perspective by which to look at such good things as sex and marriage, "for the fashion of this world passeth away." The imminent kingdom is the test of the ultimate commitment.

". . . and they left their father Zebedee in the ship . . ." This poignant remark points to one of the costs of discipleship, the imminent and eminent dimensions of the kingdom place all other relationships and duties in subordinate positions. That this cost is no stoic ideal but good news, even "an easy yoke," needs to be proclaimed as desperately as any aspect of the gospel. C. S. Lewis's treatment of *storge*, the domestic and filial affections and loyalties appropriate in a family, is a superb help in showing how a good thing (domestic loyalty) can be bad.[1] It is from the demonic aspects of *storge* that we are rescued by *agape*. So much conventional Christianity is understood to be no more than domestication. This end of harnessing all drives and aims to the family is a source of much unnecessary strife and misunderstanding. The simple but subtle point, that because something is good it does not mean it is good enough, needs to be made. The total demand of the kingdom and *agape* sets us free from trying to reduce redemption to mere domestic harmony. The latter is a by-product of the total and mutual commitment to that Family that transcends the limitations of all earthly families.

The Fourth Sunday after Epiphany

theran	*Roman Catholic*	*Episcopal*	*Pres./UCC/Chr.*	*Methodist/COCU*
ut. 18:15-20	Deut. 18:15-20	Deut. 18:15-20	Deut. 18:15-22	Deut. 18:15-22
or. 8:1-13	1 Cor. 7:32-35	1 Cor. 8:1b-13	1 Cor. 7:32-35	1 Cor. 7:32-35
rk 1:21-28	Mark 1:21-28	Mark 1:21-28	Mark 1:21-28	Mark 1:21-28

EXEGESIS

First Lesson: Deut. 18:15-20. The Book of Deuteronomy is not solely a legal code, but rather a mixture of laws, parenesis, covenant obligations,

1. C. S. Lewis, *The Four Loves* (New York: Harcourt Brace, 1960).

blessings and curses, as well as promises. In its final version the book presents "a compendium and summary of the whole law and wisdom of the people of Israel" (Luther). Deuteronomy is often linked up with the reform movement undertaken by King Josiah (640-609 B.C.) in Judah (cf. 2 Kings 22-23). Although the document may in some measure have been instrumental in Josiah's reforms, large parts of it appear to be of northern origin. It is safe to say, however, that the Deuteronomist, the final redactor of the individual units of material, addressed his theology to the Israel of the monarchic period.

While speaking to the people of the seventh century, Deuteronomy purports to be a speech of Moses. It is presented in the guise of Moses' farewell speech delivered in Moab forty years after the exodus and before entering the Promised Land (1:1-5). By redacting older traditions, the Deuteronomist uses Moses, figure of the distant past, as Yahweh's mouthpiece to discuss the issues of a people who are centuries removed from exodus and occupation.

Deut. 18:15-20 is situated in the broader context of a thematic treatment of prophecy (18:9-22). Following a prohibition of all forms of divination and sorcery (vv. 9-14), a prophet like Moses is announced who is to replace the perverters of prophecy (vv. 15-20); a criterion is added which serves to discriminate between true and false prophets (vv. 21-22).

The promised prophet (vv. 15, 18) will mediate between Yahweh and the people in the manner and power of Moses. In lieu of a specific ordinance from Yahweh, the Deuteronomist resorts to a scriptural argument (vv. 16-18). The old Sinai tradition reveals Israel's wish to be spared the immediacy of Yahweh's presence (Deut. 5:22-27). Yahweh honored this request by instituting the role of mediating prophet. This prophetic institution is not necessarily to be understood as a futuristic, messianic promise. It could just as well have served to confirm the office of the prophet for Israel. The passage explains how Yahweh through Moses provided for the institution of prophecy. Yahweh anticipated and sanctioned the existence of prophecy in Israel. The integrity of the office requires the people's obedience (v. 19) as well as the prophet's loyalty to Yahweh (v. 20). Both Qumran and early Christians, recognizing the futuristic proclivity of Deut. 18:15-20, interpreted the prophetic promise messianically (cf. 4 Q Testimonia 5-8; Acts 3:22-23; 7:37).

Second Lesson: 1 Cor. 8:1-13. The issue of "food offered to idols" (v. 1a) transports us into the Hellenistic world of mystery cults and sacrificial rites. Many religious ceremonies involved animal sacrifices. Part of the meat was burnt on the altar, and part of it was either sold on the market or offered at banquets. By and large the Corinthians had no scruples about eating this latter meat. Paul reveals the theoretical basis of their practice in vv. 1 and 4; in each case the clause "we know that" introduces a religious confession current at Corinth. "All of us possess knowledge" entails the conviction that "there is no God but one," for which reason "an idol has no real existence." The radical application of monotheism produces a sense of superior knowledge which shatters the Hellenistic universe of gods. The issue of eating meat sacrificed to a god is thus rendered obsolete.

Paul rejects the Corinthians' enlightened disavowal of the existence of gods (v. 5). Supernatural powers do indeed exist (as for Pauline demonology, cf. 10:19-22). But for the believer in God the creator and Jesus Christ the mediator of creation (v. 6) these gods have lost all power over man. They can still be effective, however, for people who do not possess full knowledge yet (v. 7a). If knowledge of salvation results in slighting these "weaker" people, it is deficient and lacking in perception (v. 2). Granted the iconoclastic force of the Christ event (v. 8), the newly acquired knowledge ought not to be made a rule and used against people. This type of knowledge "puffs up" (v. 1b), i.e., it becomes an end in itself at the expense of those who do not fully know. "Love" is the Pauline corrective against the Corinthian theology of superior knowledge and unadulterated freedom (cf. chap. 13). The essence of love is the "upbuilding" (v. 1b) of, or concern for, the weaker brother. Out of consideration for people who still have strong feelings about sacrificial meat, all should abstain (vv. 7-13). For if one's outlook is still dominated by belief in gods, the eating of meat offered to gods will breed feelings of guilt and anxiety. What is freedom for some might thus be the cause of bondage for others.

Pauline ethics does not imply the carrying out of a principle for the sake of consistency. Rather it suggests concession to the weaker ones, even if they do not act in full faith.

Gospel: Mark 1:21-28. Jesus' first public action after the calling of the four disciples (1:16-20) is an exorcism. As he enters the synagogue of Capernaum, he finds himself engaged in a confrontation with hostile forces. The overriding motif of Mark 1:21-28 is a power struggle.

At the outset Jesus' teaching is strongly emphasized (vv. 21-22; cf. v. 27). Although its content is not articulated, it is characterized as a teaching in authority (v. 22b), in opposition to scribal expertise (v. 22b), and of absolute novelty (v. 27c). Resting on the power and commission of God, Jesus' message spells out a radical alternative to the present ordering of life. This new set of priorities which Jesus introduces at Capernaum is inseparable from his programmatic kingdom message (1:14-15). It is by means of teaching and exorcising (as well as healing) that he institutes the rule of God on earth.

Provoked by Jesus' words of authority a man possessed by an unclean spirit screams aloud: "Have you come to destroy us?" (v. 24c). The evil spirit properly recognizes the power and purpose of Jesus' mission. Jesus is both the man from Nazareth (v. 24b) and the Holy One of God (v. 24d) who came to overthrow not merely a single proponent of evil, but the demonic power structure itself. In response to the spirit's pained confession Jesus "rebukes" him (v. 25a). The rendering of *epitimao* with "rebuke" or "reproach" is, however, inadequate. This verb, a technical term in exorcism language, connotes an aggressive act to wrest the power away from an opponent (cf. 8:32-33). Jesus divests the evil spirit of his authority and deprives him of his base of power (v. 25). The defeat of the spirit is signalled by the man's convulsion and a loud cry at the moment of exit (v. 26). The audience is perplexed and yet senses the eschatological dimension of the event (v. 27). Jesus' fame spreads throughout Galilee (v. 28).

Jesus' exorcism at Capernaum causes a clash between the kingdom of God and the kingdom of Satan. Fundamental to the event is the struggle of two kingdoms. By the power of his new word Jesus challenges a conventional order of life and crushes the powers of darkness. Out of the confrontation with Satan's subordinate, the unclean spirit, God's kingdom becomes a reality on earth. In the process of this power struggle Jesus' identity is revealed—out of the mouth of the enemy. It is the Spirit-filled Son who overcomes the evil spirit.

HOMILETICAL INTERPRETATION

The material in Deuteronomy promising a prophet follows, and is in contrast to, the castigation of all forms of witchcraft and divination. The Second Lesson is Paul's advice concerning eating meat sacrificed to idols. It contains his assumption that although the idols are nothing, supernatural powers of evil do exist. Mark launches Jesus' ministry almost immediately with an exorcism of an unclean spirit. It has been difficult for modern minds to grasp biblical assumptions concerning the sinister existence of evil forces. Histories of witchcraft abound with such phrases as "until the end of the 17th century" referring to some practices of magic and superstition practiced in the West. Those of us who are the products of the 18th century Enlightenment, 19th century industry, and 20th century technology have perhaps only recently begun to take seriously the weird things that have been largely banished to the edge of civilized man's consciousness.

Joseph Addison's famous hymn "The Spacious Firmament on High" (1712), based on Psalm 19, is a beautiful example of high confidence in the basically rational nature of the universe. This remarkable, and historically unique, confidence is at least partially the product of the revelation of God the *Logos*. The early church reinterpreted the Deuteronomic prophecy to mean Christ, the superstition banishing "Lord of Creation," and passed this confidence in regard to nature on to Addison so that indeed this prophet did historically banish, if not obliterate, the sorcery, divination, and witchcraft that had survived so many centuries in Christendom. Addison's faith, and that faith alone, enabled him to write:

> In reason's ear they all rejoice
> And utter forth a glorious voice;
> For ever singing as they shine,
> "The hand that made us is divine." [1]

We did, however, pay an expensive price for that confident assumption of the essential rationality of man and nature that characterized so much, if not all, of the eighteenth century. The price was a deism that ceased to ask the questions to which revelation is an answer and left us unprepared for the irrational aspects of both man and nature. The contemporary preacher is facing a situation somewhat new for western culture in the revival of sorcery, divination, witchcraft, and other "abominations to the Lord" that the prophet was to replace in Deuteronomy. It has come as something of a surprise to some to discover, as one clergyman put it, "All the spirits ain't the Holy Spirit." Discernment of spirits is one of the much needed gifts.

Jesus' discernment and exorcism of the unclean spirit provide some guidelines for a sermon focused on this issue. On the one hand, to ignore or deny a realm of unseen spirits, good and evil, is to be unbiblical and to make the eighteenth century mistake all over again. On the other hand, to relinquish the *Logos*-given skepticism toward superstition or the confidence in the Holy Spirit as that by which we can make sense of nature and human nature is to slip back into the weird world of superstition, darkness, and death. The promise made in Deuteronomy to raise up a prophet for us is finally completed in Christ.

The theological arguments concerning the *filioque* clause are complex indeed but one of the quite practical points in favor of the clause is that we discern the spirits by the Christ. It is he by whom the spirits are measured. The two natures of Christ could be helpful guidelines in the preacher's approach to the apparently accelerating growth and influence of exotic sects and strange groups. The fullness of his humanity condemns any solution to the problem of being human that destroys anything human. "Grace never destroys nature." Redemption is not destruction but a fulfillment. The fullness of his divinity saves us from any self-help, self-righteous religious solutions. This was no hero who tried harder, who

1. *The Hymnal* (New York: Oxford University Press, 1940), no. 309.

was a more clever scribe, who had insights "before his time." This was "God in Christ reconciling the world unto himself." God who is invisible is known by the "express image of his person." By Christ we not only know what it means to be truly human, but also what kind of God we have.

The issue of meat offered to idols in the Corinthian selection would seem at first glance to be an obsolete question. Few congregations in the West find themselves in a dilemma similar to that of the Corinthians but it does raise the more general question of how far a Christian may participate in activities of a non-Christian culture. Many feasts today are dedicated to ends so incompatible with Christianity that the question of whether a Christian is free to participate in them inevitably arises. There are activities, groups, and clubs that a strong Christian could enter but his presence there might be injurious to the faith of other Christians. The priority of the obligation of love and consideration of others, over one's own rights and liberty that Paul sets for the Corinthians, would seem to apply to a present day Christian's choice in an increasingly secularized culture.

One of the stories about St. Francis is that he and several companions obligated themselves to a fast for a long period of time. One of the members found it particularly arduous, so much so that Francis heard his brother's stomach rumbling in protest all night. Realizing it was not given to his brother to be able to endure the fast and not wishing for him to be cut off in humiliation from the group, Francis broke his own vow and ate with the brother. Francis himself was free to maintain his fast but following Paul's priorities in this passage, concerning meat sacrificial to idols, he followed not his own liberty but refrained from continuing his fast for the sake of the love of a weaker brother.

The dramatic account of the exorcism should not obscure the prior and equally important theme of Jesus' teaching. The Scripture is strangely silent about the content of that teaching. It was concerned about the kingdom and relied heavily on Scriptures, and he taught as "one that had authority, and not as the scribes." Before he is discerned to be the Messiah, the promised prophet of Deuteronomy has begun to be realized by the whole long line of prophets of Israel and completed in Christ. Both the law and the prophets function to prevent Israel from slipping into witchcraft and nature worship. St. Clement's Church in Alexandria, Virginia, has a startling entrance. On one side is a mural depicting Moses and the law and on the other side the great prophets disclosing men's inability to obey the law while both sides funnel the worshipers into the church under the arms of the cross. Here is an artistic and architectural depiction of the OT experience and its relation to the New. It illustrates the connection between our lessons from Deuteronomy and Mark.

The Fifth Sunday after Epiphany

utheran	*Roman Catholic*	*Episcopal*	*Pres./UCC/Chr.*	*Methodist/COCU*
eph. 3:14-20	Job 7:1-4, 6-7	Zeph. 3:14-20	Job 7:1-7	Job 7:1-7
Cor. 9:16-23	1 Cor. 9:16-19, 22-23	1 Cor. 9:16-23 22-23	1 Cor. 9:16-19,	1 Cor. 9:16-23
ark 1:29-39	Mark 1:29-39	Mark 1:29-39	Mark 1:29-39	Mark 1:29-39

EXEGESIS

First Lesson: Zeph. 3:14-20. The prophet Zephaniah proclaimed the word of Yahweh during the reign of King Josiah (640-609 B.C.; cf. 1:1) in Jerusalem. The book is a collection of sayings; some go back to Zephaniah himself, others are later additions. The major theme emerging from the prophet's message is the Day of Yahweh. On this great and terrible day Yahweh will consume the whole earth (1:14-18; 2:2; 3:8). Zephaniah more than any other OT prophet is a man of judgment, who offers but a glimpse of the deliverance of a righteous remnant (2:3, 7). Our passage (3:14-20) comprises a late addition which may reflect a postexilic situation. It balances Zephaniah's gloomy outlook for the future: the Day of Doom is to be followed by the Day of Deliverance.

The epilogue (3:14-20) addresses Jerusalem which is to become the center of a renewed Israel. The people of the city are invited to sing an ode of joy, because the national enemy, executioner of divine judgment, will be removed. (V. 15a is phrased in the prophetic perfect; the event, though still in the future, is described as having already occurred.) Yahweh will establish himself as King amidst his people (v. 15b; cf. v. 17a). Faith in the kingship of Yahweh, while not universally popular in Israel, was closely associated with the Jerusalem temple (cf. Isaiah 6). The King's presence will dispel all anxiety (v. 15b), and Jerusalem will be called the fearless one (v. 16). No one will drop his hands and abandon his work in a gesture of despair (v. 16). The Hebrew text of the following vv. 17-18 is beset with difficulties. Part of v. 17b is best rendered with: "he will renew (you) in his love" (not: "he will be silent in love"). The full v. 17 conjures up the picture of Yahweh the warrior who shows his love in victory. V. 18b may read: "I will sweep from you the disgrace, and lift from you the reproach." The nature of the shame to be removed is specified in v. 19. The dispersion of Israel will come to an end. Those who are lame and outcast, i.e., deported, are the exiles of the Diaspora (v. 19b; cf. v 3:10). The name of Israel, held in scorn by the nations, will be exalted the world over.

Judgment is no longer the center of gravity. History inclines toward the

Day of Victory, when Yahweh the King will rally all displaced compatriots at his chosen place of Jerusalem.

Second Lesson: 1 Cor. 9:16-23. In the first part of chap. 9 (vv. 1-15) Paul speaks in defense of his apostolic freedom (cf. vv. 1a, b; 3). His custom of waiving some fundamental apostolic rights has caused some opponents to question his credibility as an apostle of Jesus Christ. Chief among the issues under scrutiny has been the right of apostles to receive material and financial aid from communities in and for which they worked. Without disputing the legality of this privilege, Paul asserts his personal freedom to abstain from it. With this decision the apostle is—according to his own words—in defiance of a command by the Lord (v. 14). The justification for his extraordinary practice of apostolic freedom is given in vv. 16-23.

He begins his plea for freedom by mentioning a "necessity" which has been imposed upon him (v. 16b). This "necessity" points to his Damascus conversion (cf. Phil. 3:12), and ultimately to his election prior to birth (cf. Gal. 1:15-16). His life as an apostle is not the result of his own free choice. Appointed in the manner of prophets (Jer. 1:5; Isa. 49:1), Paul is under a divine constraint which he cannot escape. In this sense he is a wholly unfree person. Only if he were a free man and acting on his own, could he claim earthly remunerations (v. 17a). But since he has been commissioned by God against his own will, he is like a slave deprived of all privileges. As a servant of God he has no right to ask for material rewards (v. 17b). His only personal reward is the gratifying experience of his selfless service (v. 18).

Paul's choice to forgo the right of material rewards is therefore an expression of his servitude to God. In assenting to this divine necessity, however, he gains a new freedom in his service to the people. Truly independent of any man, he can "become all things to all men" (v. 22b). He can live as a Jew with the Jews (v. 20), and act as a man freed from the law in the company of Gentiles (v. 21). Any possible misunderstandings are dispelled. His is neither a case of lapsing into legalism, nor of indulging in lawlessness. He operates from a norm which both binds and frees him.

Constrained by "the law of Christ" (v. 21) Paul strives for personal self-reliance. The freedom gained thereby allows him to serve with unreserved love. He can truly "win" the people if he speaks their language, experiences their sins, and enjoys their pleasures.

Gospel: Mark 1:29-39. Jesus' first public activity, the exorcism at Capernaum (1:21-28), is followed by an act of healing (vv. 29-31). That exorcisms and healings are a crucial aspect of Jesus' ministry is confirmed by vv. 32-34a, a Markan summary. Both activities are instrumental in implementing Jesus' major objective, the kingdom of God on earth (1:14-15).

The presence of the four disciples (v. 29) signals the importance of the healing. These same disciples will be privileged to receive Jesus' farewell speech (13:3 ff.). Peter, James, and John witness the raising of Jairus' daughter (5:21-24a, 35-43), Jesus in his transfiguration glory (9:2-8), as well as the Gethsemane agony (14:32-42). It is noteworthy that Jesus performs his first exorcism on a man and his first healing on a woman. The kingdom embraces both male and female. The significance of the healing cannot have been lost on Simon (Peter). By healing one of Simon's family, Jesus reveals his divine authority in a special way to the disciples' leader. Throughout, Simon will be both privileged by Jesus and entrusted with special responsibilities.

V. 34b is the first instance of the theology of the messianic secret. Jesus prohibits the demons to publicize his fame, not because they have the wrong conception, but because they have the right one. Silence is imposed upon them, *because* they know who Jesus is (cf. 3:11-12). Scholars are not agreed on the scope and function of the messianic secret in Mark. One obvious effect is that a veil of secrecy covers Jesus' ministry. His full identity remains hidden to men, including his disciples. It is only at the moment of his death that it dawns on the man in charge of the execution who Jesus had been (15:39).

Vv. 35-38 mark the beginning of a conflict between Jesus and his disciples. Simon and the other three "pursue" (v. 36: *katedioxen*) Jesus who had withdrawn to a place outside of Capernaum. They wish to call him back to the city of his first triumphs (v. 37). But Jesus stresses the necessity to move elsewhere so as to disseminate the message (v. 38). His mission is to cover all of Galilee (v. 39).

One might entitle our passage (1:29-39) "Jesus and Peter" (J. Schniewind). Notwithstanding Jesus' healing revelation, Simon fails to grasp Jesus' purpose. Simon seems inclined to divert Jesus from a course which is to lead beyond the city of Capernaum. While Jesus has a dynamic vision of his ministry, Simon has a more limited goal in mind.

HOMILETICAL INTERPRETATION

The passage from Zephaniah must be used by the preacher with caution. As our exegete has pointed out, the substance of the prophecy is one of judgment, a day of doom, and this is an epilogue which, if preached out of context, could be a cheap twist into a prophecy of "smooth things." Sentimentality is long range cruelty and is a besetting sin of the ecclesiastical institution. People need to be prepared for the inevitable shocks, disappointments, and tragedies concomitant with all life. Easter without Good Friday, the day of deliverance without the day of doom, deprives the worshiper of hooking his own hurt, despair, and doom to the elevating leverage of deliverance and resurrection.

The idolatry of nationalism obscures from its victim the vision of God's judgment in the action of the nation's enemy. This enemy of Israel has been the rod of God. There is enormous popular resistance in modern times to the idea of God's punishment but it is unquestionably the prophet's message that God's love includes his wrath and judgment. When a people or individual faces misfortune without considering the possibility of the prophet's message that it could be a judgment of God, they are left with the misfortune but bereft of its meaning. The defeat of the South in the war between the states is a defeat with judgment and meaning if the "national enemy," the North, can be seen as "executioner of divine judgment" (in the appropriate phrases of the exegete). Otherwise it is simply defeat. Even though this prophetic view of history does not require the instrument of God's judgment to be worthy, righteous, or better than one's own nation, still it is easy to see how the prophet's message is often regarded as unpatriotic or treacherous. However unpopular, the end result can be grace in adversity and meaning in tragedy, rather than mere adversity and mere tragedy. With a complete reliving of doom and judgment the present is combined with a foretaste of the final deliverance that brings relief, hope, serenity, and confidence.

The alternative OT reading from Job gives an opportunity for the preacher to sanction some ventilation of despair and anger in the face of innocent suffering. In important ways this is a balance to Zephaniah's prophecy from which one could falsely infer that everything that happens is the just punishment of God. On the contrary, it is the false friends alone who insist that there is some mechanical, one to one, relationship between suffering and sin, between tragedy and justice. Instead, Job can properly be presented to anyone in agony as a model for objection, protest, and anger. Heaven knows how much disguised and smoldering resentment and anger over suffering there is in any congregation but is quite likely to be underestimated by everyone. When this anger has no ventilation it will seek devious and destructive ways of expressing itself. Controlled anger is not redeemed anger. All anger needs an object and will find one. Hence, the irrational need for scapegoats in even the most sophisticated cultures. Job expresses his anger toward God, as does the psalmist, but, sadly, too few conventional Christians believe this is possible or proper. It is urgent for any congregation to be shown the simple truth that Job and the Psalms (by which this people worshiped for more than twenty centuries) allow us the opportunity to express these honest feelings of injustice and anger to

God himself. And God can take our anger so much better than our spouses, leaders, children, parents, authorities, and selves who are the scapegoats of much unconsciously projected anger that is not allowed or given appropriate release or ventilation.

The Corinthian passage gives the preacher an excellent opportunity to correct the pervasive misunderstandings of the age in regard to freedom. The popular idea of freedom is "getting what you want" and has its roots in Voltaire, Leibnitz, and the persistent Pelagianism within the church. It is a view that ignores the necessities. Lenin's view that "freedom is the recognition of necessity" is closer to the biblical view of Paul than the common assumption that one is free when his will is implemented. The latter view begs the question of "the will" and ignores the fact that many people with obvious hang-ups and in cruel bondage are choosing and getting their will's wish. The alcoholic is choosing what, when, and how much to drink but those choices are not making him free. Robert Penn Warren in his epic poem *Brother to Dragons* has a better insight than Lenin's when he observes, "For the recognition of necessity is the beginning of freedom."

Paul's ". . . . I do it apart from my own choice, I am simply discharging a trust. Then what is my pay? The satisfaction of preaching the gospel . . ." (NEB) is a view that blends freedom, necessity, and satisfaction together. The Pelagian view of freedom sees Christianity as a religion of control instead of Paul's religion of redemption. The Christian moral life is not a mere "ability not to sin," against which St. Augustine warned us, but something better, the change of our wills by being grasped and even bound as a "prisoner of the Lord" (Eph. 4:1) to the gospel. So many have a sad picture of the moral life in which we are finally able to refrain from sin, to clench our fists and teeth in a grim persistence over temptation. Instead we have something much better than mere control. We have the hope of transformation, change, redemption. The NT portrait of our Lord is certainly not one of a "teeth gritting Jesus" who was "able not to sin" but one in which he is so compelled by love that he wishes and wills to do what he must.

In this passage Paul shows the satisfaction at being grasped by the necessity of the gospel. Ernie Banks once said that if the management only knew, he'd play baseball for nothing, he loved the game so much. His enormous salary did not compel him to endure the work to earn it, but the game itself was so enticing that the love of it tied, bound him to baseball. Certainly he is more free than a person who must make himself endure his job. Similarly the gospel so claimed Paul that it was more than his will that set him free, it was being bound to the gospel. Thus he is "a free man and owns no master" (v. 19) and is able to be a servant of all.

Perhaps no text is so often quoted to deny its original meaning as "all things to all men." It is so often quoted in criticism or derision of one's having no consistent center or integrity and adjusting one's views and values to suit any condition. Paul is radically different from this. He is free to be a servant (bondman) to all for their salvation's sake. It is not helpful to tell an alcoholic, "Joe, the trouble with you is that you drink too much." One must feel as he feels, be with him where he is in order to be of any real help. It is a paradigm for being a minister (servant) to anyone. Without empathy, identification, and understanding from the position of another person's shoes no significant grace or help is possible.

Paul's view of this ministry, this servanthood in freedom, is a key to understanding in Mark the priority for teaching and preaching the kingdom even over healing the sick. Before the exorcism in the temple and the healing of Peter's mother-in-law Jesus is preaching and teaching concerning the kingdom. After he has healed many he departs to other towns to preach "for therefore came I forth." The Greek word *therapuo* ties together all three meanings of the ministry. It is translated worship, service, and health. Paul's worship is at the same time his service and satisfaction. Our service and ministry in the kingdom of God are our worship and, at the same time, our health and wholeness. Hence, the teaching and serving of the kingdom are also the healing and redeeming of the sick. Sin is bondage, service is freedom.

The Sixth Sunday after Epiphany

Lutheran	*Roman Catholic*	*Episcopal*	*Pres./UCC/Chr.*	*Methodist/COC*
2 Kings 5:1-14	Lev. 13:1-2, 44-46	2 Kings 15:1-14	Lev. 13:1-2, 44-46	Lev. 13:1-2, 44-
1 Cor. 10:31-11:1	1 Cor. 10:31-11:1	2 Cor. 4:16b-18	1 Cor. 10:31-11:1	1 Cor. 10:31-11
Mark 1:40-45	Mark 1:40-45	Mark 1:40-45	Mark 1:40-45	Mark 1:40-45

EXEGESIS

First Lesson: 2 Kings 5:1-14. Elisha, disciple and successor of Elijah, was prophet in the north of Israel during the second half of the ninth century B.C. Known as the leader of a prophetic guild (2 Kings 2:15-16), he greatly influenced the politics of Israel and foreign nations (2 Kings 8:7-15; 9:1-3). His primary function, however, was that of a miracle worker. The memory of the man and his deeds of power was preserved in prophetic circles, and ultimately incorporated into the Deuteronomic work of history (probably Deuteronomy through 2 Kings). The bulk of the Elisha tradition consists of 1 Kings 19:19-21; 2 Kings 2–9:3;

13:14-21. Nowhere in the OT are so many miracles reported within such a small space.

Our passage (2 Kings 5:1-14) reports Elisha's healing of Naaman's leprosy in the face of adverse circumstances. The healing story begins with a captive Israelite girl recommending Elisha, "the prophet who is in Samaria" (v. 3). Naaman, equipped with a letter and stately presents, travels to the king of Israel. The latter interprets the message as a provocation to war. Elisha interferes and challenges his king's suspicion. But there is still no healing in sight because Naaman refuses to comply with Elisha's instruction. Only at the prompting of his servants does Naaman condescend to obey the prophet's word. Naaman immerses himself seven times in the Jordan and emerges a cured man.

The miracle is primarily told for didactic purposes. No special interest is manifested in the miraculous. The healing is not done by a powerful word of prayer. Nor does it occur by the force of incantations, formulae, or gestures. Indeed, such a magical performance was exactly what Naaman the Syrian had expected (v. 11). Instead, Elisha is set apart from the miracle proper. This serves to direct attention to Yahweh, the source of all power. Elisha demonstrates through his miracle the superiority of Yahweh, the God of Israel (cf. v. 15).

On another plane the miracle tells the story of Naaman. The healing occurs to benefit a man who is both a foreigner and a leper. Yahweh proves his incomparability by extending help to a foreigner who would normally be considered unclean (cf. Lev. 13–14). This provocatively humanitarian aspect will be brought out in the Christian tradition. In his inaugural sermon at Nazareth Jesus mentions Naaman's healing as an example of God's movement toward the Gentiles (Luke 4:27). Elisha's miracle serves as a demonstration of Jesus' mission: it is to the Gentiles of the world.

Second Lesson: 1 Cor. 10:31–11:1. In chaps. 8-10 of 1 Corinthians Paul develops the principles of freedom and love, using the test case of meat sacrificed to idols. Our four verses summarize this discussion.

As a matter of principle, the eating of sacrificial food is permissible (v. 31; cf. 8:8; 10:25), because things are not in themselves unclean (Rom. 14:14). For the members of Christ the goods of the earth have lost their cultic and magic quality, because "the earth is the Lord's, and everything in it" (10:26; Ps. 24:1). A thoroughgoing application of the doctrine of creation (cf. also 8:6) expunges all enclaves of holiness or unholiness from the face of the earth. Paul does not base this notion of clean and unclean on a word of the Lord. This is all the more remarkable since his view comes close to that expressed in sayings and stories embraced by the

Synoptic tradition. It seems that access to such material was not available to him. In any case, Pauline ethics is not built on a *material* separation between clean and unclean.

The emancipation from the power of idols gives no pretext for rampant abuse of freedom, because the space of freedom is controlled by the application of love (v. 32). Love is guided by concern for the other person. If one eats in the company of Gentiles for whom this meal constitutes a *status confessionis* (10:27-29a), or if a weaker brother still believes in the efficacy of the meat (8:7-13), abstention ought to be practiced for the sake of the brother. What determines one's course of action is not things in and of themselves, nor personal preference, but the other person's conscience.

Love is also guided by concern for the common whole. Paul seeks "not his own advantage (*to emautou symphoron*), but that of the many" (v. 33b). What is "helpful" (*symphoron*) is what benefits the community. Paul would agree with Aristotle who considers a tyrant a man who "looks after his own profit" (Eth. Nic.: *to hauto sympheron skopei*). In Pauline ethics the profit of the individual is to be subordinated to the good of "the many" (Phil. 2:4). The ultimate good is "the church of God" (v. 32), which transcends national, social, and sexual boundaries.

Christians are entitled to "freedom from all human conventions and norms of value" (R. Bultmann). But freedom is qualified by an obligation to God and a concern for the brother. This does not mean the surrender of freedom, but its exercise in love.

Gospel: Mark 1:40-45. The Galilean ministry of Jesus is saturated with healings and exorcisms. Jesus authenticates his divine authority by deeds of superhuman power; he triumphs over sickness, mental instability, and even death. This Christology of power is not representative of the whole gospel. Jesus is also subjected to suffering and death. But the passion narrative is not to be understood in the sense that it cancels out the deeds of power (thus many interpreters, past and present). Jesus' control over the perils of human life is not invalidated by his humiliation on the cross.

There exists a close affinity between the miracle of the healing of the leper (1:40-45) and the exorcisms in Mark. The healing is described in terms of a cleansing. The leper begs Jesus to make him clean (v. 40: *katharisai*), and Jesus responds by performing a cleansing (v. 41b: *katharistheti*; v. 42: *ekatharisthe*). It seems as though the leper is a demoniac plagued by an unclean spirit (*pneuma akatharton*, cf. 1:23, 26-27; 3:11, etc.). Jesus' state of agitation also fits the nature of an exorcism. In v. 41a many commentators prefer the *lectio difficilior*: "Jesus was angered" (*orgistheis*), rather than "he was moved by pity" (*splangchnistheis*). Jesus is moved by anger because he recognizes the leprosy to be a manifestation of evil; the sick man brings him face to face with the powers of evil. V. 43 (dropped by Matthew and Luke!) fits the milieu of an exorcism. Even though the man is healed, Jesus still holds strong feelings toward him, and orders his departure similar to the way in which he casts out demons (*exebalen auton*; cf. 1:34, 39). The dramatic depiction of the story indicates a power struggle between Jesus and an evil spirit.

On a different plane the healing brings Jesus closer to a confrontation with the religious establishment. The unclean man is disqualified by society and considered a sinner before God. By letting this leper come near and touch him Jesus violates the protective laws of his religion (Lev. 13-14). The successful healing carries an indictment against the priestly establishment, if the establishment recognizes the healing, while refusing to acknowledge the person and power of the healer. (The last clause of v. 44 reads: "as testimony *against* them," cf. 6:11; 13:9.)

The manifestation of Jesus' miraculous powers is directed against the forces of evil, and puts a heavy burden on the religious authorities. Despite Jesus' effort to keep the healing hidden (v. 44b), the man cannot but make it public (v. 45).

HOMILETICAL INTERPRETATION

The story of Naaman's cure provides the preacher with an opportunity of continuing the theme of the mission imperative in Epiphany. God is not merely the God of the Israelites but it was by Naaman that "the Lord had given deliverance to Syria." Jesus uses the example of Naaman, pointing out that there were many lepers in Israel during Elisha's time but only Naaman, a Gentile, was cleansed. This example evoked wrath and attempts to kill Jesus on the part of his hearers. The anger evoked by the wider claim of God's rule versus the idolatrous attempts by fallen man to limit God's sway is an abiding tension in all times. It is no wonder that Luther could remark, "The heart of man is an idol factory." The tendency to draw one's horizons ever closer is the direction of death for individuals as well as institutions. The breaking down of walls frees those who are the victims of their own incarceration.

A theological student once spent a summer working in a parish serving native British West Indians in the Caribbean. On his return to the States he expressed doubts concerning any contribution he may have made but enormous gratitude for having his horizons widened. Citing Thomas Wolfe's *You Can't Go Home Again* he exclaimed how his home could never again be the limits and measure of his life's view. He now had a view of the world from which to see home rather than his home as a way to view the world. It is very close to the statement in the early church's

Epistle to Diognetus about a Christian's view of the world: "Every fatherland is a foreign land and every foreign land is a fatherland." The surprising grace about the Christian mission is that the giver and sender is the inadvertant recipient of a freedom from his own incarcerating idolatries.

Mission and ministry are inseparably connected, and the story of Naaman provides a congregation with an occasion to recall the essential character of ministry, servanthood. As the mission imperative erases narrow horizons, the ministry of servanthood breaks the armor of pride, *hubris*. Naaman's knowledge of Elisha's power is dependent on a servant girl. When he gets the prophet's directions he refuses to follow them because Elisha did not seem to treat him with the dignity he deserved. His arrogant condescension toward Israel's river prevents him from bathing in the Jordan. It is again through servants that this "mighty man of valour" is humbled and healed.

The relationship between humility and healing is the crucial and decisive one. There is a bit of Naaman in each of us. In all sick marriages and broken friendships our pride is an inevitable barrier, and it must come down in humility for healing to take place. Humility, however, is not claiming that you are unable to play the piano when you can. Usually false humility is but subtle pride that seeks to shield us from exposure. Nothing we can try to do produces humility. It is the by-product of true servanthood. When we have become committed to the service of the kingdom all effort and accomplishment are less than the subject deserves.

When we take seriously St. Paul's injunction in the lesson from Corinthians that whatever we do we "do all for the glory of God" the duties of our servanthood are under such demand that humility is the only possible result. This humility, however, is not mere humiliation but a deeper freedom. The sinful aspect of pride is the attempt to fashion such an armor of our own dignity that we are immune from attacks, from all charges of being wrong. To do all for the glory of God is to transfer our dignity to this kingdom. Hence as such a servant Paul showed his freedom from condemnation by saying, "Why am I blamed for eating food over which I have said grace?" (NEB). This freedom is extended to all that we do when we have in gratitude done it for God's glory. The function of pride is replaced by dedicated service and we no longer need the armor that more effectively separates us from love than it defends our dignity.

Mark continues the theme of cleansing the leper. It would be ill-advised for the homily to contain much digression into dermatology. The point for both OT and NT lessons is that leprosy to them was a symbol of sin, and like sin it is contagious, more to be cleansed than healed. Jesus violates the code by touching the leper but his power over unclean spirits, sickness, and death is demonstrated by the miraculous cure. Having broken the code he then follows the code by sending the man to show himself to the priests following the Mosaic requirements spelled out in Leviticus in the alternative OT lesson. This action of breaking and fulfilling the law at the same time is a symbolic act summing up the entire meaning of Jesus' ministry. Although he touches the leper, heals on the sabbath, and forgives sinners in violation of the law, he comes not to cancel but fulfill the law. Jesus placed before the priests the radical decision to break the code themselves in not accepting the leper's cleansing, or to accept it, thereby recognizing the power and authority of Jesus over the law.

The proclamation of Jesus as Lord should similarly place contemporary hearers in the predicament of the priests, calling them to transform their present commitment to a higher call, their present loyalty to a deeper faith. Jesus violates the very standards we live by when he breaks the code of race, group, denomination, and nation with a love that cannot be contained within the limits of any tradition.

The so-called messianic secret has the same function for a modern ear that it did in Mark's time. The miraculous power of Jesus over suffering and death cannot be denied without doing violence to both the biblical data and the continuing witness. However, Mark does not want Jesus followed for the wrong reason, because he is a miracle worker, but because of his victory on the cross. Jesus heals the leper for "He was moved by compassion." He is teaching and preaching about the kingdom of God but incidentally cannot refrain from healing those he encounters. This attracts crowds to him who are there not to discern who he is but what he can do. He tries to avoid the crowds because the claim of the kingdom is higher than the claim of being a walking hospital, even though healing is a derivation of the kingdom as well as the fruit of genuine compassion.

Only in Jesus' full disclosure of himself are human hearts transformed. The leper's disobedience of Jesus' injunction not to tell indicates that healing his skin has not changed his heart. He has not become a disciple. Where were all those countless persons who were healed by Jesus when he was betrayed, brought to trial, offered to the crowd to be released, and finally crucified? Because of his compassion he heals them. That is what love must do. But his love seeks a deeper goal than miracles of external change, the very heart of a person must be evoked by his life, buried in his death, and raised in his discipleship.

A dermatologist of long experience once observed that his patients urgently wanted a medicine they could put on their skin to cure their disease but characteristically resisted any prescription that would change their diet or their way of life. What is true of his patients is true of congregations. We wish to have the symptoms treated and healed but resist the deeper and more radical transformation occasioned only by the cross.

The messianic secret is that the transforming faith is not that of superhuman miracles but that which has been born not on the skin but in the heart on the cross. Some have attempted to preserve the secret by denying the miracles but that would seem to be a perverse way to make the secret functional. Instead it seems obvious that faith is a conjugation of many different levels of trust. Without the miracles it is doubtful that the disciples would have been brought to the deeper meaning and miracle of the cross. Likewise with us, trusting on the surface can begin a process by which successive encounters in life move us from faith to greater faith.

The Seventh Sunday after the Epiphany

Lutheran	*Roman Catholic*	*Episcopal*	*Pres./UCC/Chr.*	*Methodist/CO*
Isa. 43:18-25	Isa. 43:18-19, 21-22, 24b-25	Isa. 43:18-19, 22, 24b-25	Isa. 43:18-25	Isa. 43:15-25
2 Cor. 1:18-22	2 Cor. 1:18-22	2 Cor. 1:18-22	2 Cor. 1:18-22	2 Cor. 1:18-22
Mark 2:1-12	Mark 2:1-12	Mark 2:1-12	Mark 2:1-12	Mark 2:1-12

EXEGESIS

First Lesson: Isa. 43:18-25. Deutero-Isaiah, the author of Isaiah 40-55, spoke the will of Yahweh to a people in exile. Aroused by the sweeping conquests of the Persian King Cyrus, he anticipated a momentous turnabout in the life of the Babylonian exiles: Cyrus, the "Lord's anointed" (Isa. 45:1), will defeat the Babylonian empire (Babylon was taken in 539 B.C.), and the expatriates will return to the Promised Land. Our passage (Isa. 43:18-25) is divided into a word of hope (vv. 18-21), a word of accusation (vv. 22-24), and a word of forgiveness (v. 25).

Of the three fundamental confessions of Israel—exodus, David, and Zion—the exodus tradition is the most prestigious in Deutero-Isaiah. Salvation equals exodus. But the exodus which lies ahead for the Israelites will prove to be an unparalleled experience. "The former things" (v. 18), e.g., the exodus of old (cf. vv. 16-17), are past and ought not to be remembered. The rescue out of Egypt belongs to a phase which was concluded with the exile. Now "a new thing," the first stirrings of which are already in the air (v. 19a), is close at hand. The exiles will return to the homeland, all things will be restored to the state of perfection (vv. 19b-21a), and the renewal will be echoed in the people's praising of Yahweh (v. 21b). The very newness of this experience dissociates Israel from her past. Deutero-Isaiah directs attention toward the future, preparing for an eschatological view of history.

This declaration of hope is further enhanced by the statement of accusation (vv. 22-24). Israel has brought the misfortune of exile upon herself, because she did not truly give Yahweh the honor due to him. The people had not offered their lavish sacrifices to Yahweh. The "me" of v. 22 is emphatic by position: "it was not me that you invoked, O Jacob." The prophet deplores the abuse and misdirection of the sacrifices; he does not, like Amos, denounce the cult *in toto*. Vv. 22-24 pronounce a sweeping indictment against Israel's worship of Yahweh up to the exile. Instead of serving Yahweh, the people made him their servant. V. 23b ("I did not burden you to serve me") and v. 24b ("you made me serve—with your sins") use the same word for serve, *abad*. For a moment a key concept of Deutero-Isaiah, the Servant (*ebed*) of Yahweh, comes into view. Despite Israel's guilt, the "new thing" remains valid. Yahweh's forgiveness does not depend on the worthiness of the people (v. 25).

Second Lesson: 2 Cor. 1:18-22. Paul's chief purpose in writing 2 Corinthians is to vindicate his apostolic authority and personal integrity against people who had serious misgivings about him as an apostle and as a man. The fact that he was bold on paper, but unimpressive in person, that his appearance belied his literary genius, raised the specter of deception (10:10). He was considered a coward (10:1), a mentally disturbed person (5:13), as well as an embezzler of funds marked for the Jerusalem Christians (8:20-21; 12:16-17). Our passage (1:18-22) answers to the charge of inconsistency. Due to a change in travel plans Paul did not pay the Corinthians a previously promised visit (vv. 15-16). This breach of promise further confirms the opponents' suspicion that Paul is dishonest and hence not an apostle at all.

Paul opens with a solemn formula, "God is faithful" (1 Cor. 1:9; 10:13b), which underscores the gravity of the issue (v. 18). Although Paul changed his mind on the visit, the substance of his gospel should not be affected. ("Our word to you" refers to the message of the gospel.) The sincerity of his word rests on God, the author of the word. In v. 19 the apostle further distracts from the specific charge by focusing upon Jesus, the Son of God. The full title Son of God is virtually absent in Pauline theology (Gal. 2:20; cf. also Rom. 1:4). Its use in v. 19 may be precipitated by Paul's concern to trace the gospel through Jesus back to God. As Son of God Jesus was unwavering in his obedience to the will of God. The three witnesses to the gospel may have been introduced as an additional guarantee of authenticity. V. 20a describes Jesus' affirmative role in his people's history. This history does not end in vacuity, for the questions that had remained unanswered have found their answer in Jesus (Rom. 15:8b). Beginning with v. 20b Paul's language reflects the sphere of worship. The "Amen" refers to the Christians' acceptance of God's will in public worship (1 Cor. 14:16). The congregation responds with a confessional affirmation of Jesus, the Yes of God. The anointing (v. 21: "God who anointed us," not "commissioned us"), sealing, and giving of the Spirit as a foretaste of future glory represent baptismal terminology. The relationship between Paul and the Corinthians is indestructible, because through baptism they were joined into one Body. Paul challenges the charge of inconsistency by pointing to God's affirmation in Jesus. This is the embracing consistency which unites them all.

Gospel: Mark 2:1-12. Form-critically, the story of the healing of the paralytic exhibits an unorthodox structure. It contains a conventional type of healing miracle (vv. 1-5, 11-12) and inserted into it a controversy dialogue (vv. 6-10) focusing on Jesus' authority to forgive sins. By and large redaction critics identify the insertion as Markan. This insert was not, however, meant to cause an entire shift from the miraculous to the forgiveness of sins. To claim that the forgiveness debate dominates the physical healing so that the word overshadows the deed would distort the wholeness of the story. Mark combines miracle and controversy without taking the edge off either one. On the one hand, he reports the miracle in considerable detail; on the other, he adds the aspect of controversy. Accordingly, Jesus forgives in response to people's faith (v. 5) and heals as a demonstration of his power to forgive sins (vv. 10-11). Since sickness manifests the destructive effect of sin, healing and forgiveness are inseparable.

The introduction of the title Son of man in v. 10 marks a crucial stage in the history of Jewish-Christian thought. The conjunction of Son of man with earthly authority to forgive sins is unprecedented in the Jewish tradition as well as in the Christian tradition prior to Mark. In Jewish apocalyptic the sovereignty of the Son of man belongs to the heavenly world; forgiveness of sins is not one of his attributes. While Q knows of the Son of man's earthly ministry (Matt. 11:19/Luke 7:34), Mark is the one who for the first time uses earthly "authority" (*exousia*) in connection with Jesus the Son of man (N. Perrin). The title is fundamental to Mark's christological purpose. It holds together Jesus' identity from life (2:10) through death (8:31) to glory (14:62). The Jesus who demonstrates earthly power through healing and forgiveness is the same who will suffer and return in heavenly glory.

On his authority as Son of man Jesus challenges the scribal authorities who regard forgiveness of sins as the prerogative of God. These scribes are the spokesmen of the Jerusalem establishment (3:22). Their charge against Jesus is blasphemy (v. 7), the very charge which in the end brings the death sentence (14:64). At an early point Jesus' manifestation of power is pitted against the Jerusalem power structure. His very display of authority as Son of man provokes the forces which will bring about his destruction.

HOMILETICAL INTERPRETATION

The prophet's declaration is threefold as our exegete points out. "The new thing" calls to mind Gal. 6:15: "Circumcision is nothing; uncircumcision is nothing; the only thing that counts is a new creation" (NEB). Circumcision was a sign of the covenant but it could not enable men to keep the covenant. Second Isaiah brings to a close the old exodus and discloses "a new thing." We are neither to remember nor consider former things. In spite of the accusation there is the promise not to remember Israel's sins. God gave the inheritance to Abraham by promise (Gal. 3:18). The Second Lesson adds: "He is the Yes pronounced upon God's promises, every one of them" (NEB). That Yes to all the promises is revealed in the Gospel lesson as one who performs miracles and forgives sins. The interrelated themes are: the new creation, the promise, the power, and the forgiveness of sins.

What makes Mark's account so difficult to grasp today is that little in contemporary times corresponds to the scribes' view that only God can forgive sins. Forgiveness of sins seems so easily available, for the price of a newspaper and the time to read an advice column. There is little sense that the law is God's and only he can forgive. In fact it was blasphemy to the scribes for Jesus to forgive sins and, as the exegete points out, it was this charge on which he was put to death. It is observed that there is "no such thing as a free lunch"; someone has to pay for it even if the recipient doesn't. For the recipient of forgiveness, like the recipient of the lunch it is not cheap but free. The cost is elsewhere, on a cross. The power of this confrontation with the scribes is lost unless the force of their high esteem for the law is appreciated.

W. B. Yeats, although not seeing himself as a Christian appreciated more the cost of saving man than many theologians.

> Odour of blood when Christ was slain
> Made all Platonic tolerance vain
> And vain all Doric discipline. [1]

If we can take "Platonic tolerance" to stand for all "sensible" restraint, acceptance, and permissiveness; and "Doric discipline" for all law and order, civilized demands, and moral imperatives; then Yeats is telling us what Paul had proclaimed in Galatians, namely, "that neither circumcision

1. *The Collected Poems of W. B. Yeats* (New York: MacMillan, 1956), p. 211.

nor uncircumcision availeth." The problem of being human is so great that, as Auden put it, "Nothing that is possible can save us." So much modern theology is unable to smell the "odour of blood when Christ was slain."

Most modern Christians have been squeezed between the pressure of liberal theology that tends not to appreciate sufficiently the absolute demands of the law and conservative reactions that tend to moralism without forgiveness. In terms of our lesson, when the strength of the scribes' position is unappreciated the transforming power of Jesus' "new thing" is lost. Thomas Wilson (whose writings Charles Simeon was reading when he was converted) once observed, "The greatest of all disorders is to think we are whole, and need no help." Jesus pointed out that "they that are whole have no need of the physician, but they that are sick . . ." (Mark 2:17)

The law, then, has the function in its awesome majesty to deprive us of our self-righteousness, our false sense of well being. The scribes, not knowing who Jesus was, were properly concerned that no mere man could wipe out the demands of God. Jesus, seeing the helpless man and the faith of his friends, forgives him his sins. He is the promise of Isaiah that God will blot out transgressions. The decisively important phrase "for my own sake" should not be overlooked for it fits logically with "when Jesus saw their faith." It is not the worth of Israel nor of man nor of the effort of the friends, but the trust in the power and righteousness of God. The greater miracle is the inner healing, although the scribes and the crowd are now more impressed by the physical miracle.

Kierkegaard knew that redemption was even more a miracle than creation. "God creates out of *nothing*. Wonderful you say. Yes, to be sure, but He does what is still more wonderful: He makes saints out of sinners." [2] The unfaithfulness of Israel does not disannul the faithfulness of Yahweh. So many people can accept something of the fact that God forgives them but they can not forgive themselves. "If our heart condemn us, God is greater than our heart" (1 John 3:20).

Paul is telling the Corinthians that Christ is the Yes pronounced on all God's promises, "every one of them." If the preacher is to do justice to God's demands in the law he must not by any means fail to do equal justice to his forgiveness. Clinical personnel will rightly insist that it is virtually impossible to overestimate people's disesteem. This is no new perception but one noticed by Bishop Thomas Wilson in the early eighteenth century. "There is no man but knows more evil of himself than of any other." If this is true then anyone's flock is saturated with many more feelings of unworthiness than can be judged by conventional conversation.

2. Soren Kierkegaard, quoted in J. Baillie, *A Diary of Readings* (London: Oxford University Press, 1955), p. 341.

There is a poignant and urgent need then to declare as a "dying man to dying men" (Richard Baxter) that "Christ is the Yes pronounced on God's promises, every one of them." John Donne said it quite well.

> One of the most convenient hieroglyphics of God is a circle; and a circle is endless. Whom God loves He loves to the end; and not only to their own end, to their death, but to His end, and His end is that He might love them still. [3]

An important minor point is the phrase "reasoning in their hearts." (The NEB's use of "mind" to translate *kardia* is unjustified.) The biblical view of man was three dimensional with his mind in his head, his feelings in his abdomen, and his reasoning center in his heart. The seventeenth century marked a movement upward with reason in the head, emotions in the heart, and the deeper instinctual feelings were orphaned. Pascal's famous quote is an example of this transition and a protest against it. "The heart has its reasons that reason doesn't know." What makes this matter of importance is that so much religious insight is dependent on a whole and total perception. Moderns are often victims of thinking themselves relegated to merely animal means of knowledge. With what organ did Jesus perceive their faith? With what organ did he see the thoughts of the scribes? It is by so many unseen human attributes that things of the spirit are known. Many realities are accessible only to caring, courage, compassion, recalling, and commitment. A congregation could be helped to see this through the example of Helen Keller who was blind and deaf from infancy yet was able to "hear" and "see" more reality than most people with their animal faculties unimpaired. With the peculiarly human faculty of a "reasoning heart" we are able to perceive and to know God in Christ, the Word in scripture, and the Body in the bread.

3. Quoted from John Baillie, *A Diary of Readings* (London: Oxford University Press, 1955) p. 284.

The Eighth Sunday after the Epiphany

Lutheran	*Roman Catholic*	*Episcopal*	*Pres./UCC/Chr.*	*Methodist/COC*
Hos. 2:14-16 (17-18), 19-20	Hos. 2:14b, 15b, 19-20	Hos. 2:14-23	Hos. 2:14-20	Hos. 2:14-23
2 Cor. 3:1b-6	2 Cor. 3:1b-6	2 Cor. 3:17-4:2	2 Cor. 3:17-4:2	2 Cor. 3:1b-6
Mark 2:18-22	Mark 2:18-22	Mark 2:18-22	Mark 2:18-22	Mark 2:18-22

EXEGESIS

First Lesson: Hos. 2:14-16 (17-18), 19-20. Hosea is the only one of our writing prophets who was active in the Northern Kingdom. His ministry may be dated between 750 and 725 B.C. Witnessing the decline of Israel, he may not have lived to see the Assyrian conquest of Samaria in 721 B.C. He is a prophet of both judgment and hope. In this sense his theology conveys an insight basic to the OT and NT: as sin persists, so does the possibility for salvation.

The bulk of Hosea's criticism is directed against the Canaanite cult of Baal. The north was known for its syncretism. Under King Ahab and his wife Jezebel Baal worship had received strong royal backing. By Hosea's time this cult had virtually become the religion of the masses. Its appeal lay in a sensuous approach to life. Cultic prostitution and vegetation rites celebrated the victory of life and fertility over death and sterility. Hosea, although utterly opposed to the cult, nevertheless uses images of love and metaphors of nature which betray his indebtedness to the prevailing Baal milieu of his day.

As a lover woos his girl, so does Yahweh lure his people into the desert for deliverance (v. 14). Even though there once was "trouble" in the desert, now it is the place of hope. (In the Valley of Achor, i.e., Valley of "Trouble," Achan was stoned for stealing forbidden spoils; his guilt brought "trouble" upon Israel; cf. Josh. 7:22-26.) Despite the incident in the Valley of "Trouble," the wilderness stay is considered Israel's ideal time. Then and there the relationship between Yahweh and his people had been uncorrupted by false lovers. This ideal time will now be restored. The salvation to come is a return to the past (v. 15a). Out of the wilderness a new creation will arise. Yahweh's bride, i.e., Israel, will once again be to her bridegroom what she had been "in the days of her youth" (v. 15b). The adulterous relationship with the Baals is to be replaced by the kind of love a wife shows toward her husband (vv. 16-17). The marriage will be sealed in a covenant of peace (v. 18). All hostilities between man and beast, and man and man will be terminated (cf. Isa. 11:6-9; 2:4). Nature and history are to be reconciled. Yahweh offers his bridal gifts of righteousness, justice, love, and mercy (v. 19). Israel in turn will "know" Yahweh with the intimacy that exists between a woman and a man (cf. Gen. 4:1).

Second Lesson: 2 Cor. 3:1b-6. In a widely acclaimed study on Paul's opponents in 2 Corinthians, D. Georgi succeeded in illuminating certain aspects of Pauline theology. In 2 Corinthians Paul contended against Jewish-Christian missionaries who were primarily engaged in prophetic interpretation of Scripture, pneumatic ecstasy, and the performance of miracles. These missionaries considered themselves endowed with divine energy, and they saw their main function in the display of signs and wonders. When Paul characterizes these opponents as "super apostles" (11:5; 12:11), he refers to their manifestations of power. In broad historical perspective, these "super apostles" were representatives of a prevalent religious mode of expression, the Hellenistic Divine-Man (*theios aner*) ideology.

The Divine-Man missionaries had arrived at Corinth equipped with letters of recommendation, written no doubt by influential Christians of other communities. These documents in all probability were epistolary summaries detailing the missionaries' apostolic virtues and spiritual accomplishments. Paul criticizes his opponents (v. 1b) for adopting the conventional practice of using such reference letters. (Paul himself, however, wrote a letter of recommendation—to Philemon on behalf of Onesimus.) His own letter of recommendation is the people of the Corinthian church (v. 2; cf. 1 Cor. 9:2b). The very existence of this church is indelibly written on the heart of Paul; at the same time the church's existence is for all the world to see (v. 2). While the opponents, despite their spiritual exhibitionism, rely on the force of ink and paper, Paul's "letter from Christ" is written with the abiding quality of the living Spirit (v. 3). Paul's living letter is superior even to the Mosaic tablets at Sinai (v. 3). The people themselves form the basis of Paul's apostolic confidence, a confidence "through Christ toward God" (v. 4). No further credentials are needed. The opponents are likely to have mistaken their personal appearance in power for the source of all power. Paul reminds the Divine-Man apostles that there is no such thing as religious self-sufficiency (cf. 2:16b); his and their power are from God (v. 5).

Paul argues that the very ones who preach and practice the supremacy of the Spirit are crucially dependent on certificates of paper. It is implied that the opponents still serve under the Old Covenant (v. 6). This is Pauline polemic which should not be understood in the historical sense that the missionaries were Judaizing representatives of the Jerusalem church (Tübingen thesis!). Paul's point is that the opponents still live spiritually under the Mosaic code, because they have failed to grasp the Spirit of the New Covenant.

Gospel: Mark 2:18-22. This fasting pericope reflects a complex process of transmission and interpretation. It is immediately obvious that the final version resulted in a reversal of the story's earlier, and possibly original intention. Initially, the disciples' nonobservance of fasting is set in contrast with the fasting practice of John's disciples and the Pharisees (v. 18). In direct response to this situation Jesus sanctions his disciples' total noncompliance with the fasting regulations (v. 19a). Vv. 19b-20, however, assume a time when fasting had become a fact of Christian life. Now the Christian observance of fasting is justified.

The difference between the two versions on fasting is due to Jesus' presence and absence respectively. During the lifetime of Jesus his movement in part claimed independence by violating the practice of fasting which had been sacred to both John and the Pharisees. Many scholars regard v. 19a as an authentic Jesus saying (cf. J. Jeremias, N. Perrin). The presence of Jesus proved to be incompatible with the traditional days of fasting. The eschatological novelty of his mission forced the break with Judaism and the movement of John. Vv. 19b-20, however, appear in the form of an amendment which is designed to deal with changing conditions. It is safe to assume that this latest version makes contact with the Markan situation. The death of Jesus brought about a reconsideration of earlier practices. Now complete freedom from fasting has lost its appeal for Mark, and one day is officially assigned for fasting. "On that day" (emphatic by position) specifies the preceding reference to the days of Jesus' violent removal, and points to Good Friday. In its present form, the pericope serves to endorse Friday as the day of weekly fasting.

The Christians' resumption of fasting after the death of Jesus does not, however, denote a return to Judaism. The day of crucifixion has provided the stimulus for a reconsideration of time. If during Jesus' lifetime the disciples were at variance with Judaism by their nonobservance of fasting, after Jesus' death the Christians' fasting on Friday contrasts with the Jewish fasting on Monday and Thursday.

The amended version of the fasting pericope continues the eschatological thrust of Jesus' ministry. This is expressly stated in the sayings collection (vv. 21-22) concerning new patches on old garments, and new wine in old wineskins. No compromise is allowed between the new and the old. The new life of the kingdom is gained at the price of breaking loose from the traditional order of life.

HOMILETICAL INTERPRETATION

Hosea's situation in the eighth century B.C. is much closer to ours than one would first expect. Baal worship was essentially an attempt to resolve the problem of being human by means of the powers of nature, particularly fertility power. Within the history of Christianity there has been a tendency to combat the seduction of nature worship and the danger to community latent in sex by going to otherworldly extremes. K. S. Latourette points out that most of the world-denying heresies condemned by the early church found their way back into Christianity via monasticism; as a result traditional ascetic practices have molded to a great extent the mind of modern men concerning the content of the Christian faith. Hence, the prevailing assumption today concerning flesh versus spirit is a far cry from its OT and NT significance.

At the same time our culture has become religiously preoccupied with sex. The lesson from Hosea offers the preacher an opportunity to disclose this deeper religious dimension to what is often regarded as merely a moral problem. As one does not need be a Fascist to be against Communism, or vice versa, so the preacher must be careful not so to oppose one error as to appear to condone its opposite. Hosea provides a golden opportunity for a modern person to see the exceedingly dangerous tug of nature worship in unhooking us from our fidelity and commitment to the righteous God of history.

Such people as Norman O. Brown urge modern man in a direction comparable to Baalism in the OT. In his ending of *Love's Body* he proclaims a new garden, a new Eden, where there "will be no one to answer to." If there is no God and Father to call to account the sons of Adam, Brown argues, then there is no guilt and we are freed from all the neurotic results of guilt (which Christianity has called sin), while at the same time there is enough at the breast of Mother Nature for everybody. It is a utopian vision that accounts for sin and evil, not in man and a fallen nature (often not so much a mother as a stepmother) but in man's being held accountable by a God of history. Norman O. Brown seems to offer an elimination of sin and evil by eliminating accountability. There is an accelerating growth in modern groups reflecting in varying degrees just such spiritually seductive aspects reminiscent of Baal worship.

At the same time Hosea's example helps us avoid the opposite error in any flight away from history or any identification of nature and sex with evil. On the contrary, what is wrong with such things as prostitution is not that they are dirty but that they are unfaithful. Hosea does not hesitate to use the language of romance and sex as illustrations of our relationship with Yahweh. There is a strange blend of Victorianism and Freudianism that giggles or gives sly grins at the sexual analogies of God's relationship with his people. C. S. Lewis' chapter on "Eros" in *The Four Loves* is an excellent source for treating this subject with the proper appreciation of the goodness but demonic inadequacy of *eros*. The eighteenth century poet, Christopher Smart, expresses this aspect of Christianity:

> God all-bounteous, all creative,
> Whom no ills from good dissuade,
> Is incarnate, and a native
> Of the very world he made.[1]

This incarnational theme is carried on in the Corinthian lesson. Paul contrasts the external credentials of his critics' letters of recommendation with those of his converts whose changed lives are his credential letters, written not with ink but on the "fleshy tables of the heart." His being beset by detractors, claiming the authority of the Spirit, is especially relevant to our times. There are a growing number of similarly conflicting claims in many churches and this rule of thumb could equally apply today: "By their fruits ye shall know them" and the true Spirit writes on the "fleshy tables of the human heart." The charismatic movement today is a combination of great grace mixed with sin and manipulation (most frequently unconscious). Paul's way of dealing with conflicting authorities is to put them to the incarnational test: which authority redeems, transforms, loves, and brings more life and light?

An even wider application is the contrast Paul makes between fleshy tablets (community of people) and stone tablets (Mosaic code), between the spirit of the law and the letter of the law. In the academic and professional world institutions are threatened by an exclusive reliance on external credentials—Ph.D.'s, professional diplomas, and accrediting standards—and need always to be drawn back to the reason for their existence: the student, the patient, the client, and the parishioner. Are their credentials written on the transformed hearts of their charges, or are they merely etched on paper behind glass hanging on a wall?

The issue of fasting treated by Mark has had something of a similar history to that of sex. Because fertility cults abused religion in their affirmation of sex, so in reaction the church has tended to undervalue sex. Similarly, because fasting has been abused in the church in negative and legalistic ways, the reaction has been to undervalue fasting altogether. As our exegete points out, the church's resumption of fasting must not entail a return to Judaism. To fast on Friday rather than on Monday and Thursday could be to fall back to an old legalism and lose the new dimension of freedom given to Christians.

1. *The Hymnal* (New York: Oxford University Press, 1940), no. 320.

Traditional functions for fasting have been to keep the body in subjection, to express repentance, to influence the action of God, and help relive portions of Christ's life. Jesus himself fasted but he explicitly dissociated his mission from the fasting traditions of John and Judaism. The Christian dimension to fasting similarly must offer fasting to a congregation on a level of freedom inaccessible to legalistic traditions and the world.

Christ's victory over sin and death enables a Christian to fast as a celebration, a celebration of independence. "Man does not live by bread alone" and Christians need to be reminded of the victory that has set them free from the powers of this world. A body needs food to survive but fasting is not starvation. Fasting declares the Christian's sure and certain hope that the end of this body is not the end of man. Our citizenship is in heaven against which the gates of hell shall not prevail. As we set aside a time to recall our independence as a country, we set aside a time to fast to celebrate our independence, to declare our freedom in Christ.

The Transfiguration of Our Lord
The Last Sunday after Epiphany

theran	*Roman Catholic*	*Episcopal*	*Pres./UCC/Chr.*	*Methodist/COCU*
ings 2:1-12a	Dan. 7:9-10, 13-14	1 Kings 19:4-12	Dan. 7:13-14	2 Kings 2:1-12a
or. 3:12-4:2	1 Peter 1:16-19	2 Cor. 4:3-6	Rev. 1:4-8	2 Cor. 4:3-6
rk 9:2-9	Mark 9:1-9	Mark 9:2-9	John 18:33-37	Mark 9:2-9

EXEGESIS

First Lesson: 2 Kings 2:1-12a. Our passage is a prophetic succession story which sanctions the transfer of power from Elijah to Elisha. It is as much a story of Elijah and his mysterious departure, as it is of Elisha and his singleness of purpose.

The setting of the story is Elijah's last journey, which is a journey, not unto death, but to the ascension (cf. v. 1 with Luke 9:51). Accompanied by his disciple Elisha, Elijah travels from Gilgal to Bethel and from there to Jericho and across the Jordan. Three times along the way Elijah asks his companion to let him proceed alone (vv. 2a, 4a, 6a), but each time Elisha declares with a solemn oath that he will not leave his master (vv. 2b, 4b, 6b). At Bethel and Jericho guilds of prophets remind Elisha of the journey's end and purpose (vv. 3, 5). The possible implication of their reminder is to talk Elisha out of following Elijah, because Elijah's departure was to be a mystery, not witnessed by anyone. But Elisha asks the prophets to remain silent, and continues his journey with Elijah. As they reach the Jordan, Elijah reproduces Moses' miracle of the cleaving of waters (v. 8; cf. Exod. 14:16, 21-22), whereupon the two cross through the river on dry ground. This feat is witnessed by fifty prophets from the distance (v. 7). On the other side of the Jordan Elijah permits his persistent companion one last request, and Elisha asks for a "double share" of Elijah's spirit (v. 9). This request is based on the law concerning the first-born (Deut. 21:17), and it reveals Elisha's determination to become the principal successor to Elijah. In his response Elijah leaves the gratification of his disciple's desire to the divine will; Elisha must be found worthy of the sight of Elijah's mysterious ascension (v. 10). Instantaneously Elisha witnesses his master's triumphal procession in a fiery storm (v. 11). As eyewitness to the translation, Elisha is finally qualified to bear the mantle of Elijah.

Elisha is rewarded with the crucial sight of Elijah's glorification because he has traveled his master's road to the end. The journey has served him as preparation for his succession to Elijah. Elijah's mysterious translation in the wilderness east of the Jordan has inspired the concept of his return in Jewish and Christian tradition alike. Under the impact of apocalypticism Elijah is assigned the role of eschatological precursor (cf. Mal. 4:5). The Synoptic tradition identifies him with John the Baptist who may have ministered in the general area of the ascension scene (cf. John 1:28)!

Second Lesson: 2 Cor. 3:12–4:2. Our passage is a Midrash on Exod. 34:29-35, directed against the opponents of Paul. Recent investigations into the nature of the opposition theology in 2 Corinthians (S. Schulz, D. Georgi) allow us to follow Paul's argument more accurately than was hitherto possible.

Paul's opponents in 2 Corinthians are Jewish–Christian missionaries who hold the Torah and Moses in high esteem. According to their understanding of Exod. 34:29-35, Moses had put a veil over his face because the people would not have been able to bear the sight of it. "The skin of Moses' face shone" because he had gained direct insight into the Sinai mystery. The missionaries consider themselves, and only themselves, to be in possession of the Spirit. This permits them, like Moses, to perceive the glory of Sinai so that their bodies and faces reflect the presence of God.

Against these missionaries Paul argues that Moses had used the veil to prevent the Israelites from realizing that the glory reflected on his face was fading. The Mosaic veil illustrates the deficient nature of the glory. It had not been a protective device, but a means of deception, used to cover up the incompleteness of the old covenant (vv. 12-13). With this argument Paul disavows his opponents' primary source of revelation, i.e., Moses and the Sinai tradition. The veil which had concealed the face of Moses still lies upon the hearts of the people (vv. 14-15). The reference to "heart" (v. 15: "a veil lies upon their heart," not "minds") polemicizes against the opponents' claim to physical manifestations of power. Even if they glory outwardly, inwardly they have remained imperceptive and unredeemed (cf. 5:12). Only in Christ is the veil of incomprehension removed and the truth in Scripture perceived (v. 16). The difficult v. 17 is an argument against the missionaries' definition of their spirit alone as the Spirit of God. Paul breaks their exclusive claim to the Spirit by identifying it with the Lord, i.e., Jesus. As a result of the freedom won in Christ all people (v. 18: "and all of us"), not just the few, reflect as in a mirror the glory of the Lord. One does not, however, possess the presence of Christ as an ontological substance, rather one grows into it in a process of transformation (v. 18).

Paul dismisses his opponents' commitment to Moses and the Old Covenant, because this position betrays a superficial and exclusive understanding of Christ.

Gospel: Mark 9:2-9. The transfiguration scene is located on a mountain; of the mountains mentioned in the Gospel (3:13; 6:46; 13:3), it is the only "high mountain" (v. 2). Towering above all other peaks of revelation, the "high mountain" ascended by Jesus and his three confidants designates the transfiguration as the epiphany of all epiphanies. The transformed status of Jesus is described by the whiteness of his garments (v. 3). White, the color of the end time (cf. Rev. 6:2; 7:9; 14:14), imparts an eschatological quality to the transfigured Jesus. The Jesus the disciples are privileged to witness is Christ in his final, future glory. Both Moses and Elijah figured prominently in Jewish and Christian expectations of the end time. Their joint appearance on the "high mountain" further underscores the eschatological character of the transfiguration epiphany (v. 4). The cloud is the traditional manifestation of the presence of God (cf. Exod. 24:16), and the voice coming out of the cloud is none other than the voice of God (v. 7a). This heavenly voice marks the only direct intervention of God in the ministry of Jesus—outside of baptism. At Jesus' beginning God had in a similar way and with nearly identical words taken the initiative (cf. 1:11 with 9:7). At baptism Jesus, the Son of God, was installed into the office of the eschatological king. But the installation ceremony was shrouded in secrecy; nobody witnessed the eschatological irruption of the Spirit, not even the Baptist himself. With the transfiguration the disciples are informed of Jesus' future installation as the Son of God. The transfiguration, closely modeled after baptism, anticipates Jesus' coming in apocalyptic fullness, i.e., his parousia.

Unlike all other epiphanies in the gospel, the transfiguration is provided with the date of its final disclosure (v. 9). It is to remain under cover until the resurrection of the Son of man. The resurrected Jesus is thus not identical with the Jesus of the transfiguration. Rather, the resurrection marks the *terminus post quem* of the realization of Jesus' transfiguration glory. The transfiguration points outside itself into the post-resurrectional life of Christ—to his parousia in glory.

Throughout the Gospel of Mark the disciples fail to understand Jesus. The transfiguration is no exception. In a state of fear and confusion Peter suggests the building of three booths (vv. 5-6). His idea is motivated by the compulsion to seize upon what was only meant to be a prolepsis of the future. Peter mistakes the future for the present.

HOMILETICAL INTERPRETATION

The transfiguration offers the preacher several themes on which to concentrate. It is certainly the eschatological way to view the present and it gives to the present its transforming hope (cf. 2 Corinthians 12: "Seeing then we have such hope"). In Mark's account the disciples could not understand this event until after the passion and resurrection. For us, this side of Easter, the transfiguration is a renewed opportunity to look at our present situation in the light of its future and purpose and thereby to redeem it. W. P. DuBose in his *Soteriology of the New Testament* insisted that no definition is complete without including its purpose (or its final cause). It is not enough to say what a thing *is*. One must go on to say what it *is for*, what it was to be, its intention and destiny. This is true of everything from a monkey wrench to a person. One would not think of explaining to a child what a pipe wrench *is* without saying what it is *for*. But unfortunately we often assume the identity of a person merely on the basis of his *is* without including also his purpose and end, what he is *for*.

One quite moving illustration of the transforming power of the transfiguration way of discerning the present is in the figure of Don Quixote in *Man of La Mancha*. This comic figure tenaciously refuses to let the "is" take final precedence over "what will be." He insists on calling, naming, wording, regarding Aldonza the Whore as "My Lady Dulcinea." This wording from the eschatological perspective of her destiny, end, and purpose begins to transform Aldonza. Near the end of the play Don Quixote is dead and his comrade Sancho Panza speaks to Aldonza. She replies to him in a quiet but powerful serenity, "My name is Dulcinea."

It was from the mountain top of the transfiguration that Martin Luther King, Jr. found his inspiration and vision for that great speech in Washington, D.C. "I've been to the mountain top . . ." His vision was not the vision of what had been, nor what is now, but of what is to be. This vision of the end and destiny of things applies not only to people and situations, redeeming them, but also to suffering.

Scholars of Mark's Gospel have argued that the purpose of the secret here is to lay emphasis not merely upon the power of the Son manifested in miracles but upon the suffering of the Son manifested in his passion. The mystery of suffering is an ambitious subject for any sermon but the transformation by the transfiguration should be an important part of any approach. For many years the most requested copy of all sermons preached on "The Protestant Hour" was one on suffering by the Rev. John Redhead. There can be no question of the widespread need for attention to this subject. In whatever way God is, or is not, involved in the cause of suffering, all can agree in all cases that he is Lord over all suffering. In Rom. 8:18 Paul connects the glory of the transfiguration with the way we are enabled to regard any suffering now. "For I reckon that the sufferings of this present time are not worthy to be compared with the glory which shall be revealed in us" (Rom. 8:18).

This glory is common to the three lessons. For Paul the ministration of Moses was glorious but not to be compared with the glory of Christ's new covenant. The veil that was over Moses' face hides the limitations of the law's glory. Even now, the veil over the hearts of his adversaries hides from them the new more glorious service. Paul's contention against the Judaizers in Galatians and against the more subtle distorters in Corinth, continues down through the history of the church into our own times. John Wesley, after his conversion, wrote a blistering letter to William Law complaining that the latter had never told him of this new and more glorious ministration. One has but to read some traditional devotional writings, looking in vain for any declaration of acquittal, forgiveness, and justification, to realize that there yet persists those whose hearts are veiled with the old law and are strangers to the freedom of this righteousness. (cf. 2 Cor. 3:17)

V. 12 of the Second Lesson begins with an important assumption, "Having therefore such hope . . .," that must not be overlooked. It comes as a great surprise to many church people that the opposite of "condemnation" is "righteousness!" "For if the service of condemnation be glory, much more doth the service of righteousness exceed in glory" (v. 9). The word "righteousness" here is the same as justification, and the doctrine of justification has been interpreted in recent times as mere "acceptance" or as a permissiveness inconsistent with this biblical term "righteousness." On the other hand, in each age and in each congregation, there remain hearts veiled from the knowledge of this righteousness which is the opposite of condemnation.

We then are moving from the condemnation of the old service to the righteousness and freedom of the new service. The key word for Paul seems to be "glory" as it appears in v. 18. It is the glory that comes to us from beholding the glory of the Lord, and our identity moves "from glory to glory" by the Spirit of the Lord. There is a lie taught by the world that our glory comes from within ourselves. It was the advice of Polonius to Laertes in *Hamlet*, "to thine own self be true," and is correctly diagnosed as the pull of death in the contemporary musical comedy *Pippin*, "But I've got to be me." Both themes beg the question of who Laertes and Pippin really are. Paul is telling us that neither they nor we know who we are except in the service of him who is the expressed image of both God and our eschatological identity, our true intention, destiny and purpose. Hence the word "service" (*diakanos*) should not be obscured by the King James "ministration" nor by the NEB "dispensation" (v. 9).

When Elijah replies to Elisha that he will be granted what he asks if Elisha sees the departure, the transfer of power is left to the divine will. It is a foretaste of the request by the disciples of Jesus to sit on the right and left side and of Jesus' reply that this was not his to give but was related to their willingness to drink of the cup that he drank of (Mark 10:38). Elisha's persistence, as a follower of Elijah's ministry, is the occasion of his receiving the latter's power. Similarly, the disciples' persistence in following the way of Jesus was the occasion of their empowering. Likewise today, our doing God's service is the occasion of our glory (as his grace and word are its cause).

Peter, missing the true meaning of the transfigured Christ, wishes to make tabernacles to memorialize the event rather than see it as a way to view all events. Like Peter the ecclesiastical institution is always tempted to freeze and memorialize the vision rather than transform events by the power of its hope.

PROCLAMATION:

Aids for Interpreting the Lessons of the Church Year

LENT

William Hordern
and
John Otwell

PROCLAMATION:

Aids for Interpreting the
Lessons of the Church Year

LENT

SERIES B

William Hordern
and
John Otwell

FORTRESS PRESS Philadelphia, Pennsylvania

Library of Congress Catalog Card Number 74-24901

ISBN 0-8006-4073-X

4697B75 Printed in U.S.A. 1-4073

General Preface

Proclamation: Aids for Interpreting the Lessons of the Church Year is a series of twenty-six books designed to help clergymen carry out their preaching ministry. It offers exegetical interpretations of the lessons for each Sunday and many of the festivals of the church year, plus homiletical ideas and insights.

The basic thrust of the series is ecumenical. In recent years the Episcopal church, the Roman Catholic church, the United Church of Christ, the Christian Church (Disciples of Christ), the United Methodist Church, the Lutheran and Presbyterian churches, and also the Consultation on Church Union have adopted lectionaries that are based on a common three-year system of lessons for the Sundays and festivals of the church year. *Proclamation* grows out of this development, and authors have been chosen from all of these traditions. Some of the contributors are parish pastors; others are teachers, both of biblical interpretation and of homiletics. Ecumenical interchange has been encouraged by putting two persons from different traditions to work on a single volume, one with the primary responsibility for exegesis and the other for homiletical interpretation.

Despite the high percentage of agreement between the traditions, both in the festivals that are celebrated and the lessons that are appointed to be read on a given day, there are still areas of divergence. Frequently the authors of individual volumes have tried to take into account the various textual traditions, but in some cases this has proved to be impossible; in such cases we have felt constrained to limit the material to the Lutheran readings.

The preacher who is looking for "canned sermons" in these books will be disappointed. These books are one step removed from the pulpit: they explain what the lessons are saying and suggest ways of relating this biblical message to the contemporary situation. As such they are springboards for creative thought as well as for faithful proclamation of the word.

The authors of this volume of *Proclamation* are William Hordern and John H. Otwell. Dr. Hordern, the editor-homiletician, is President of the Lutheran Theological Seminary, Saskatoon, Sask., Canada. He studied at the University of Saskatchewan (B.A.) and St. Andrew's College (B.D.)

and then did graduate work in theology at Union Theological Seminary, New York (Th.D.). Prior to becoming president of the Lutheran Theological Seminary in Saskatoon in 1966 he held teaching positions at Swarthmore College and Garrett Theological Seminary. He is the author of several books, the most recent being *New Directions in Theology Today* (Philadelphia: Westminster, 1966). Dr. Hordern is a member of the Evangelical Lutheran Church of Canada. Dr. Otwell, the exegete, is Professor of Old Testament at the Pacific School of Religion, Berkeley, California. He studied at Kenyon College, DePauw University (A.D.), and Garrett Biblical Institute before he moved out west to the Pacific School of Religion from which he received both the B.D. and the Th.D. degrees. Dr. Otwell has been on the faculty of the Pacific School of Religion since 1947. His most recent book is *I Will Be Your God: A Layman's Guide to Old Testament Study* (Nashville: Abingdon, 1967). Dr. Otwell is an ordained Methodist minister and an active member of The First Congregational Church of Berkeley.

Introduction

Traditionally Lent has been a period of intensive activity in our churches. In many cases it is the only period of the year during which mid-week worship services can draw a significant number of worshipers. Special giving projects often make it a crucial period for the economic well-being of the congregation. Christians have seen it as a period for self-discipline and denial, for heart-searching and repentance. But in recent years we have had a number of second thoughts about the traditional observance of Lent.

The traditional Lent was a solemn and joyless period which emphasized a sackcloth and ashes mood. Special celebrations, such as the famous Mardi Gras, were held just prior to and following the season because there was no opportunity for joy or fun during the bleak days of Lent. But in recent years we have come to appreciate the place of joy and celebration in the Christian faith. It goes against this understanding to make Lent into an orgy of gloom.

The self-sacrifices with which Lent was once observed often seem hypocritical and legalistic today. Christians solemnly decided to give up some pleasure of life for the six weeks of Lent. Often the self-denial was, in fact, good for the health or general welfare of the person and hence in no sense a real sacrifice. But in our world of hunger and starvation, it is difficult to feel righteous because, for a few weeks in the year, we cut back on the enjoyment of our affluence. The basic trouble with traditional Lenten "sacrifices" was that all too often they were aimed at enhancing the spirituality of the person making the sacrifice. But a Christian sacrifice is one that is inspired by love and is made for the sake of the persons who can be helped by the sacrifice. The self-denials of Lent all too often inspired people to look more at themselves rather than to look to their neighbors.

As Christians are wrestling with how to observe Lent today, these readings are highly significant. They do not direct our thoughts to our inner life and spiritual condition but rather they concentrate upon what God has done and is doing. In one way or another, most of these readings direct our thoughts to the covenant which God has made with his people. The word "testament" means "covenant" and it is no accident that our Bible is divided into the Old and the New Covenants. The biblical God was not content to sit in heaven and wait for human beings to turn to him. On the contrary, God took the initiative to seek all people. He entered into a covenant with Abraham and his descendants in order that through them there might be blessing for all the people of the world (Gen. 12:1-3).

A covenant implies a binding of two parties together in mutual agreement. The most widely observed covenant in human relations is the marriage covenant and so we find that again and again the Bible compares God's relationship with his people to the relationship of wives and husbands. The story of God's covenant with his people is the story of God's faithfulness to the covenant and the people's unfaithfulness. Repeatedly God renews his covenant by forgiving his people and starting anew. Most decisively this occurred in the coming of God's Son to inaugurate the new covenant that had been promised.

Because our readings for Lent are centered around the covenant, they direct our attention to God and his action. In so doing they remind us that Lent is properly observed not by intense self-examination but by lifting up our eyes to God. By concentrating upon God we are pulled out of ourselves and filled with the desire to serve God who has faithfully kept his covenant with us.

It is human nature to assume that we must repent, reform our lives, and do good works in order that God may forgive us, love us, and accept us. The net result is that whatever we do, we have one eye upon our own self-interest in the doing of it. When Lent is observed in that spirit we perform various acts of piety and self-denial in order that we may enhance our status before God. But when our attention is turned to God's covenant we find that before we have repented or performed good deeds, God has forgiven us, loved us, and accepted us. As a result we do not repent and serve God in order to win his favors but rather to express our love and gratitude to God because we have already received his favors. Lent observed in the light of the message of the covenant, therefore, pulls us out of ourselves and directs our attention to God's acts and, through them, to our neighbors whom God also loves.

Table of Contents

Ash Wednesday

theran	*Roman Catholic*	*Episcopal*	*Pres./UCC/Chr.*	*Methodist/COCU*
el 2:12-19	Joel 2:12-18	Joel 2:12-19	Isa. 58:3-12	Joel 2:12-19
Cor. 5:20b-6:2	2 Cor. 5:20-6:2	2 Cor. 5:20b-6:10	James 1:12-18	James 1:12-18
att. 6:1-6, 16-18	Matt. 6:1-6, 16-18	Matt. 6:1-6, 16-21	Mark 2:15-20	Mark 2:15-20

EXEGESIS

First Lesson: Joel 2:12-19. The word of the Lord came to Joel during a plague of locusts (1:4; 2:25) and a drought (1:17, 19 f.). These scourges have appeared often in the Near East, and references to them do not help us to date a writing. Joel 2:2 describes a rite to be performed in the temple precincts. The temple, therefore, was standing when Joel prophesied. But was it the pre-exilic structure destroyed in 586 B.C. (2 Kings 25:9) or the building erected during the Persian period? Joel 3:1 presupposes the exile following 586 B.C., yet this verse is in the part of the book containing eschatological visions held by many scholars to be of a different authorship than 1:1-2:29. In 1:1-2:29, however, Joel likened the locusts to a ravening army (2:4-9) and the drought to cosmic fire (1:19) and believed them to be manifestations of the Day of the Lord (2:10-12). The tradition of the Day of the Lord is itself eschatological, even when used by Amos (5:18-20). Thus it can be concluded that Joel 2:30 ff. is merely a spelling out of a belief already present in 1:1-2:17. This conclusion then enables us to use 3:1 to help date the prophet's ministry to the Persian period. He thus comes to us as a prophet preaching after the great age of prophecy.

The message of the book is clear. The prophet interprets the plague and drought as an hour of total judgment, the Day of the Lord. The people are called to repent (2:12-17). A second oracle announces that God has heard and will respond (2:18-27, interrupted with a summons to praise the Lord in vv. 21-23). The redemption from plague and drought are then seen to be the beginning of an outpouring of divine favor (2:28 ff.).

Joel was a cult prophet. The first word of the Lord which he proclaimed commanded a series of cultic acts: fasting, weeping, mourning, the sounding of the shophar (the ram's horn blown during the New Year's festival), the calling of a cultic assembly, and the ritual weeping of the priests before the altar. The solemnity of the summons is seen in the unusual range of those ordered to attend, everyone from nursing infants to the recently married (who normally were exempted from some public duties: Deut. 24:5). There is no indication in the surviving oracles of Joel of any understanding of the source of divine displeasure, as there so often was in the prophets of the eighth to sixth centuries B.C. Correspondingly, there is no statement of abuses to be corrected. This may reflect the limited autonomy of Jews under Persian rule. It may also be the result of the understanding of the will of the Lord that separated the cult prophet from an Amos or an Isaiah.

Nonetheless, the people are exhorted to "return to me with all your heart" and "to rend your hearts and not your garments." In biblical Hebrew, "heart" (*lebh*) refers to the physical organ, to the whole self, or to the mind or the will. The context determines the precise meaning intended. When Jeremiah proclaimed it as the will of God that the people should circumcise the foreskins of their hearts (Jer. 4:4), and Joel proclaimed that they should "rend their hearts and not their garments," a ritual act was internalized. What was done to flesh or cloth in a rite was commanded to be done to man's heart. In both instances, man's "will" would seem to be a valid translation. The rending of garments often was a part of the rite of mourning (2 Sam. 1:11; 3:31). At other times, it was either an expression of agitation as intense as mourning (2 Sam. 13:19) or a form of self-abasement (1 Kings 21:27; 2 Kings 5:7 f.). Here, the phrase "rend your hearts" is an exhortation to subdue the will.

Fasting, weeping, mourning, and the rending of the heart are elaborations of the twice-repeated command "to return." In the first appearance of the exhortation, the people are urged to return "with all your heart," i.e., decisively and without qualifications. In the second, they are asked to return to "the Lord your God." The deity to whom they are to turn is thus identified precisely and in a title with strong convenantal associations.

Each renewal of the exhortation to return (vv. 12, 13ab, 15-17) is balanced by a divine response. Joel first encouraged the hope that God might respond to the people's turning to him by turning toward them (*shubh*, "to turn," commanded of the people in 12b and 13c is applied to God in 14a). In vv. 18 f., the hope voiced in vv. 13 f. becomes the proclamation that the Lord will act. The restoration promised is the revival of the productivity of the land.

Second Lesson: 2 Cor. 5:20b–6:2. During the course of his turbulent relations with the church at Corinth, Paul found his authority as an apostle and the standing of his fellow workers challenged by persons from Jerusalem who claimed a higher authority for themselves (cf. 2 Cor. 11:5, 13; 12:11; 13:2 f.). These verses are part of his defense of his mission. In 5:20a, Paul applies the term *presbeuomen* to himself and his co-workers, rather than *apostolos*. *Presbeuomen* was the title borne by representatives of the Roman Senate charged with making peace with a defeated enemy or by the representative of the emperor in an imperial province. Since Paul and his co-workers were pleading for reconciliation between God and man, the peace-making role of the senatorial representatives may have been uppermost in his mind.

The means by which the relationship between God and man is to be restored is described tersely in v. 21. God adjudged Christ to be sinful so that we, who are sinful, could achieve mystical union with Christ ("be in Christ"). But there is no estrangement between God and Christ since Christ "knew no sin." As we come to be "in Christ," we become "a new creation" (v. 17) because we share Christ's true nature and are accepted into the unbroken relationship between God and Christ.

As a co-worker with Christ, Paul pleads in 6:1 that the Corinthians should avoid accepting the salvation which God has offered in such a way as to invalidate it. Rather, they should receive it now, on the day that it is offered them (quoting Isa. 49:2).

Gospel: Matthew 6:1-6, 16-18. These sayings are found only in the Gospel of Matthew and thus may have come either from oral tradition or from a written source used only by this evangelist. They are a part of the Sermon on the Mount, a collection of teachings reported in this Gospel to have been given by Jesus to his disciples after he and they had withdrawn from the crowds to a mountain top. Since parallels to many of the sayings in the Sermon on the Mount appear in different contexts in Luke, it is likely that the Sermon on the Mount is a collection of utterances by Jesus removed from their original settings. The intention of the Matthean collection may have been to portray Jesus as a new Moses founding a new Israel and giving it laws.

Three rites are discussed: almsgiving (6:2-4), prayer (6:5-6), and fasting (6:16-18). All were well established in Judaism, and the validity of each is assumed here. All, however, are described as invalid when performed for human approval (6:1).

Vv. 2, 5, and 16 contain a formula: the disciples are urged not to be like the *hypokritēs* who "have received their reward." Our word hypocrite is a transliteration of the Greek *hypokritēs*, but *hypokritēs* could mean interpreter, orator, or actor, as well as one claiming moral or spiritual excellence falsely. The phrase "they have received their reward" seems virtually to have been a technical term for a legally valid receipt.

The significance of the sounding of the trumpet before giving alms is unclear. It may have been intended merely to indicate ostentation, but such exaggeration would be out of character with the naturalism of the parables. It has been suggested that it is a reference to the blowing of trumpets during a Jewish ritual. We know nothing of a ritual for almsgiving, however. Trumpet blasts were sounded in the temple during the payment of the temple tax, and the limits put upon the number of blasts permitted suggests that ostentation had become a problem (Mishnah: Arakhin 3, 5). The payment of the temple tax was not almsgiving, however. Apuleius, writing shortly after A.D. 150, described the sounding of a trumpet between dances and the play which followed (*The Golden Ass*, Bk X).

V. 16 is not wholly clear. It is widely held that the disfiguring of the faces of the *hypokritēs* during fasting was done either by facial expression or the use of ashes. The Greek verb means to cover, or to conceal, and again there seems to be an exaggeration: to use so much dirt that the face was hidden. It should be noted that actors in classical antiquity wore masks on stage.

There seems to have been no Jewish drama until well into the Christian Era. The theater was so prominent in Graeco-Roman culture, however, that many of its features would probably have been known to Jews who would have rejected it both because of its immorality and its Hellenistic associations. The remains of Roman theaters can still be seen in such sites as Gadara and Scythopolis in Galilee. All three of the sayings before us contain material consistent with the hypothesis that their intended context was the Hellenistic stage: the trumpet blasts before the actor begins, the translation of *hypokritēs* as actor, the emphasis on a human audience, and the concealment of the face of the *hypokritēs*. Two of these features create difficulties (one insoluble) if the context is held to be first century Palestinian Jewish life.

If these three sayings are interpreted as suggested here, the condemnation of acts of piety performed to gain status in man's eyes gains intensity. The almsgiving, prayer, and fasting not only are directed toward the wrong recipient, the only comparison appropriate to describe them is the degenerate theater of the Roman empire. The applause of the human spectators is the full and sole payment.

In contrast to practices which have a high visibility for men, Jesus commended forms of these rites which concealed their practice from others, the better to insure their performance solely for God. His teaching that alms should be given so surreptitiously that one hand did not know what the other had done is even more inward than the Jewish practice mentioned in Mishnah, Shekalim 5, 6, of leaving alms in a special chamber in the temple where the worthy needy could go privately to help themselves. The commandment on prayer has the effect of making it a private rite. The preparation for fasting (v. 17) would effectively conceal its presence since anointing one's head and washing one's face would be proper preparation for a wedding rather than for fasting.

In each case, the motivation for the radical change in the form of the rite is the same: the relationship between man and God is intensely private even though the consequences of it are not so restricted.

HOMILETICAL INTERPRETATION

As we noted in the Introduction, Lent is the time in the Church Year that has been particularly associated with repentance and renewal of spiritual life. It is a time when Christians have examined their lives, confessed their sins, performed acts of penitence, undertaken rigorous acts of piety such as fasting, and given more generously. It is fitting, therefore, that the scriptural passages assigned for the first day in Lent should direct our thoughts to these themes. Our readings remind us that the performance of such actions is not necessarily a sign of spiritual health. In fact, such apparently good deeds may separate us from God. These readings for Ash Wednesday force us to look past the mere performance of certain actions and ask about their motivation.

Repentance is taken for granted as a good and necessary thing in religious circles. A person who repents loudly often gains far more prestige in religious communities than the person who has no lurid past to narrate. Christians often play games with each other in which they try to establish that "I am more repentant than thou." In a similar way other acts of piety, such as giving alms, praying or fasting, can be used to gain public approval and prestige. Politicians who carefully end their political speeches with reference to the Deity are by no means alone in using piety for personal advantage.

Both the OT Lesson and the Gospel for Ash Wednesday speak out against the use of repentance or piety for ulterior motives. Joel calls upon the people to "rend your hearts and not your garments." True repentance, the prophet is saying, is not a matter of dramatic public acts but a matter of the whole will and self of the person. (See exegesis.) In the same vein,

Jesus calls his followers to be so secretive in their piety that not even their left hands will know what the right hands are doing.

Jesus says that those who engage in dramatic acts aimed to win public approval "have their reward." That is, they get what they are seeking—they win the approval of the uncritical public. They establish their names as people of great piety. Over against this, Jesus calls us to come to God in secret. Such piety or repentance will win no public approval or prestige. But Jesus says that God, who sees the secret action, will reward us. God's reward is not of the kind that the hypocrites receive; it does not raise us higher on the social ladder or shower us with material wealth and reward. God's reward consists of the relationship with himself. To the people who live for the things of the world, this will not seem like a reward at all. But the person of faith will ask, what higher reward could there be than the wondrous glory of being in fellowship with God?

In Lent, as we search our lives, we find that all too much of our piety is not directed towards God himself but has an eye upon a host of extraneous rewards. When we repent it is not that we are really sorry that we have sinned, it is just that we fear that we shall have to pay the consequences of our sin. Like a boy who has been caught stealing candy, we are very sorry, sorry that we have been caught, but not sorry that we have committed the sin. Similarly, whether we are praying, fasting, or giving to the poor, we have one eye upon a host of ways in which we hope to reap benefits for ourselves. When the chips are down, in religion as in the rest of our life, we ask, "What is in it for me?" What can we do to move ourselves out of this self-seeking piety so that we find our "reward" solely in the joy of the relationship between God and ourselves? It is easy to rend our garments and make a great show of repentance, but how do we manage to rend our hearts? How do we find sufficient reward in knowing that we are related to God in the secrecy of our room? The answer is obvious: there is nothing that we can do to change the basic orientation of our lives. We are self-centered individuals and so even in our religion we are seeking to promote our own advantage.

This is why the Protestant Reformers emphasized that we cannot save ourselves by our works. By an effort of our wills we can bring ourselves to do a number of things. We can rend our garments, we can give to the hungry, and we can pray and fast. But the Reformers recognized that true righteousness does not consist of going through motions, even if the motions consist of such good things as these. Luther reminds his readers again and again that true righteousness is never a matter of doing certain good deeds, but of deeds that are performed with a willing, joyful, and glad heart. We cannot save ourselves by our works, for although we can make ourselves do a number of fine works, we cannot make ourselves do them for the right reasons.

Joel does not leave the appeal to "rend your hearts and not your garments" stand alone as a commandment over the people. Immediately Joel goes on to add, "Return to the Lord, your God, for he is gracious and merciful, slow to anger, and abounding in steadfast love, and repents of evil" (v. 13). These words remind Joel's hearers that God is "your God." That is, he is the Lord who has called his people into the covenant relationship with himself. He is the God who has shown himself to be loving and forgiving. No matter how the people might try to repent honestly and completely, they could not succeed in doing so by their own efforts. But when they are reminded of God's steadfast love, when they experience his amazing willingness to forgive his stiff-necked and stubborn people, their hearts are moved. They are moved by God's love to respond with love, their hearts are won so that they are pulled outside of themselves. And then they become truly sorry for what they have done and for what they are. And thus God's love moves them to rend their hearts rather than their garments.

Paul's passage in 2 Cor. 5:20b–6:2 places Joel's point in light of the New Covenant that comes in Jesus Christ. Paul calls his readers to be reconciled to God because of what God already has done to reconcile them. "For our sake he made him to be sin who knew no sin, so that in him we might become the righteousness of God" (v. 21). We cannot change our inner lack of motivation by an effort of will. But what we cannot do for ourselves has been done for us in God's sacrificial approach to his people through Jesus Christ.

These readings for Ash Wednesday speak to us about how we may properly keep Lent. Traditionally we have been led to think that in Lent we should spend a great deal of time in taking a critical look at ourselves. This is not necessarily a bad thing to do, but it is dangerous. It can very easily lead us into an outward form of repentance or of piety. It leads to a rending of garments rather than hearts. True repentance and true piety are much more likely to come if we do not begin with looking at ourselves. In Lent we ought to begin by recalling the steadfast love whereby God originally called his people and the forgiveness that he extended continually to them when they fell away from him. We ought to recall how God has acted to reconcile us through Jesus Christ. When the meaning of God's love begins to come home to us, and only then, we shall begin to rend our heart, not our garments. We shall serve God in secret because the only reward that we seek is the parent-child relationship into which he has called us.

There was a time in the ministry of Jesus when his disciples began to see the impossibility of saving themselves and they asked him, "Who then can be saved?" Jesus responded, "With men this is impossible, but with God all things are possible." (Matt. 19:25-26.) Our readings for Ash Wednesday drive home this point to us. If in Lent we spend our time simply in looking at ourselves we can do no more than rend our garments. Only if we concentrate upon God and what he has done and is doing for us will we be pulled out of our self-centeredness and into the relationship with him in which we shall truly repent and truly serve him.

The First Sunday in Lent

Lutheran	*Roman Catholic*	*Episcopal*	*Pres./UCC/Chr.*	*Methodist/COCU*
Gen. 22:1-14	Gen. 9:8-15	Gen. 22:1-14	Gen. 9:8-15	Gen. 9:8-15
Rom. 8:31-39	1 Pet. 3:18-22	Rom. 4:2-3, 20-25	1 Pet. 3:18-22	1 Pet. 3:18-22
Mark 1:12-15	Mark 1:12-15	Mark 1:9-13	Mark 1:12-15	Mark 1:12-15

EXEGESIS

First Lesson: Gen. 22:1-14. This story, often described as the noblest of the patriarchal narratives, is from the Elohist (E) Pentateuchal source. The use of Yahweh in vv. 11, 14 is the work of the editor who merged this material into the Yahwist (J) source.

Gen. 22:1-14 is a saga, a narrative in which all of the skills of the storyteller were used to make a point. There are only five actors, two of whom (God and Abraham) wholly dominate. Dramatic tension is built up through the brief conversations, the pacing of the events, the lack of realism in crucial details, the vocabulary, and the incongruity of the role of God. Thus each of the terms used by God to describe Abraham's son magnifies the enormity of the command that Isaac be sacrificed, and the terse description of events early in the story contrasts with the fuller reporting as Abraham prepared to sacrifice Isaac. The impossibility of the child carrying enough wood to burn his body (v. 6) would have been obvious to the audience, and it must have been a calculated exaggeration. And were sacrificial animals killed after being bound and placed on the altar (v. 9; cf. Lev. 1:3-9)? All of these traits indicate that we have before us a skillfully told story.

Many of the details are significant. "God" in v. 1 is given the definite article and is at the beginning of the clause where the verb normally stands. Thus "God" is given such emphasis that we are warned that the primary concern throughout will be with him. His intent is "to test" Abraham's faith (the "tempt" of AV is a now archaic usage meaning "to test"). The description of the child (v. 2), "your son, your only son Isaac, whom you love," both conveys the magnitude of the test and implies the anguish of the father. The location of "the land of Moriah" is unknown. It cannot be Jerusalem (cf. 2 Chron. 3:1) because it is a land, not a mountain. The locality may have been fictitious, a further indication that this is a saga, not history.

We are struck by the pathos of the conversation in vv. 7 f. between the father, who knows the purpose of the journey, and the son, who was to be the victim. Abraham's reply to Isaac contains the first appearance of *r'h*, translated in the RSV in v. 8 as "provide," in v. 12 as "fear," and in v. 13 as "looked." *r'h* then appears twice in v. 14, once in the place name and once in the concluding proverb where it is in the passive mode (both are translated in the RSV as "provide"). Since the basic meaning of the Hebrew root *r'h* is "to see," the original force of the saga would be better preserved with translations which have been proposed by commentators for decades: in v. 8, "God will see for himself the lamb," in v. 12, "I know that you see God," in v. 13, "looked," in v. 14a, "the name of that place, 'The Lord sees,' " and in v. 14b (with emended text), "on this mount the Lord is seen."

Gen. 12:1-14 seems to preserve a tradition with the following history. In its earlier form, it was a tradition about a shrine where God sees and is seen, perhaps through human sacrifice. The Elohist transformed the shrine tradition. He first intensified the magnitude of the divine command. Abraham is asked not only for the sacrifice of a son, but of the son through whom the divine promise of progeny would have had to have come. Abraham's obedience, carried to the point where he had raised his arm to strike, became the occasion for a theophany. The supreme sacrifice of man, to which God responds by appearing, is changed from human sacrifice to the sacrifice of total obedience.

Second Lesson: Rom. 8:31-39. In these verses, Paul concludes his argument for justification through faith in Christ rather than by the doing of the law. He does not recapitulate his earlier argument. Instead, he states what is to him the significance of what has been presented, and he does it with such intensity of conviction that his words take on a hymnic tone.

The question in v. 31b, "If God be for us, who can be against us," seems at first to be incomprehensible. The persecutions Paul and his fellow Christians had already experienced surely were adequate proof to them that there were those who were against them!

The interrogative pronoun "who" (*tis*) reappears at the beginning of vv. 33, 34, 35. It designates someone, or something over against the God "who is for us" and remains unidentified until the end of the passage (vv. 35-39). There, Paul provides an inclusive catalogue of seven kinds of suffering (v. 35b, expanded by a quotation from Ps. 44:22 in v. 36), seven superhuman entities (vv. 38 f.), as well as "death or life" and "anything else in all creation." It is this baneful host which "is against us" (v. 31b), seeks to "bring . . . (a) charge against" us (v. 33), "condemns us" (v. 34), and attempts to "separate us from the love of Christ" (v. 35). Thus Paul groups together both adversities and adversaries. These are the antagonists who seek to alienate Christians from God and from the love of Christ.

The proclamation of divine love, implied in the first clause of v. 31b, is described in three different ways before the final affirmation of it at the end of the passage.

The first is the evocation of Gen. 22:1-14 in v. 31. This is a study in contrasts. Abraham acted in response to divine command; God acted on his own initiative. Abraham did not complete his act; God sacrificed his son. Abraham demonstrated his faithfulness to God; God demonstrated his love for mankind. The second is the image of the trial in vv. 33, 34a in which God is the judge who has already decided against those who accuse. It should be remembered that the judge in antiquity presided over a trial; he (or they, in ancient Israel) evaluated testimony, pronounced, and executed sentence. The third is the description of Christ as the advocate (v. 34). Paul's knowledge of the Scriptures would make him familiar with the dual role of God in trial scenes in which he was both the accused and the judge (e.g., Jer. 2:5-13), or accuser and judge (e.g., Isa. 41:21-29). Here, however, God is judge only. Christ, risen from the dead and seated in a place of honor in the heavenly court, is the Christian's advocate. A check with the various versions will demonstrate that the Greek text here can be translated either as a declaration or a question. The choice ultimately is exegetical, and the exposition given here calls for a declaratory rendering (with AV, RSV margin, NEB).

Gospel: Mark 1:12-15. Mark 1:12-15 contains two of the three stages of the Markan prologue to the ministry of our Lord: the baptism (1:1-11), the temptation (1:12 f.), and the introduction to Jesus' Galilean ministry (1:14 f.). The second stage is set off from the first by a change in word order and tense. In the verses with which we are concerned, the Markan temptation story is so much shorter than the accounts in Matt. 4:1-11 and Luke 4:1-13 that it may be simpler to posit a separate tradition rather than a Markan editing of a single temptation tradition. The beginning of the Galilean ministry is reported in all four Gospels, with Mark and Matthew giving a summary of the content of Jesus' message. This is given in fuller form in Mark than in Matthew.

A sense of urgency infuses the Gospel of Mark, and it appears first in the story of the temptation. The spirit came upon Jesus with such force that he was driven at once into the wilderness. The verb used here is employed elsewhere in the Gospel for the expulsion of demons and conveys a sense of irresistible power. The dynamism of the spirit recalls its role in such OT passages as 1 Kings 18:12 and Ezek. 3:14 f.

In the scriptural tradition to which the author of Mark was heir, the attitude toward the wilderness was ambivalent. It could be remembered as the place in which Israel had had (or would again have) a special relationship to God (Exodus 19; Hos. 2:14; Jer. 2:2 f., etc.). It was a place where Israel repeatedly had rebelled against God (Ezek. 20:13-22; Psalm 78). It also was a hostile place to be feared (Jer. 2:6) in which wild animals and demonic powers lived (Isa. 34:8-14).

A forty day interval is reported in Moses' stay on Sinai (Exod. 34:28) and Elijah's flight from Jezebel (1 Kings 19:8). It should be noted that Moses and Elijah emerged from their solitude with their missions clarified and matured.

The verb "to tempt" (*peirazo*) in v. 13 is used in the Septuagint to translate the *nissah* ("to tempt") in Gen. 22:1. Satan appears in Job 1:6-8 and Zech. 3:1 f. as an angel of testing or of accusing man on God's behalf. Only later (in such intertestamental writings as The Assumption of Moses 10:1, Lives of Adam and Eve 9:1, and 2 Enoch 29:4 f., where it is Satanail) is Satan the antagonist to God he has become in the Gospels. Since wild animals were sometimes described as a part of the kingdom of evil (Ps. 22:13, 21) over which the righteous will triumph (Ps. 91:13), it is likely that the presence of wild beasts with Jesus in the wilderness is a further description of the kingdom of evil by which he was beset. The angels serve him throughout his trial (not merely at its end, as in Matt. 4:11).

Mark 1:14 f. is the introduction to Jesus' Galilean ministry. There is no report of John the Baptist's ministry (as in Matt. 3:7-12 and Luke 3:7-18), merely the notation that Jesus' ministry began after John's had ended. Although it is possible to interpret v. 14 as suggesting that Jesus had been with John earlier (as intimated in John 1:29-42), the context more naturally suggests that Jesus came to Galilee immediately after the temptation in the wilderness.

V. 15 represents a summary of the early church's understanding of the essence of Jesus' proclamation. The phrase "gospel of God" appears in 1 Thess. 2:2, 8 f.; 2 Cor. 11:7; Rom. 1:1; 15:16, and the summons to repent occurs both in Petrine and Pauline speeches in Acts (5:31; 11:18; 20:21). "Kingdom" (*basileia*) is better understood as rule or reign (so Moffat and Goodspeed). The word translated as "time" (*kairos*) is used in the Septuagint for the Hebrew *eth*. An *eth* is a unit of time bearing a distinctive character (as in Eccl. 3:2-9 where a sequence of such "times" is given).

Thus the proclamation asserts that the time in which God's will will be done is close at hand. Confronted by the immanence of the breaking-in of divine sovereignty, man is summoned to repent.

HOMILETICAL INTERPRETATION

It is natural that human beings search to find a religion of "glory." That is, they seek a religion that will obviously shower them with blessings of health, wealth, and happiness. They do not want a "peace that passes understanding" (Phil. 4:7), they want a peace which everyone can understand as peace. Naturally when we try to win converts to our faith, it is most tempting to hold out promises that acceptance of our faith will bring the converts success beyond their dreams. We appeal to the natural urges of the prospective convert by trying to show that it pays to be religious.

In the season of Lent we are reminded that Christianity is not a religion of glory, it is a religion of the cross. All three of the Scripture selections for this Sunday help us to understand what this means. In three different ways they raise the problem that Christians must always face: again and again our experience in life seems to contradict our faith. In the face of so much suffering, evil, and adversity, how can we believe in God's goodness? How dare we affirm that he is a God of love?

Abraham had been called from out of his native land and given the promise that through his descendants God would bring a blessing to all the peoples of the earth (Gen. 12:1-3). Abraham was to be the father of the people chosen by God to be his covenant people. But Abraham had no children and as the years passed and his wife, Sarah, moved past the child-bearing age, it began to appear that the promise would not be kept. Just as it seemed that God had forgotten his promise, a son was born to Abraham and Sarah miraculously in their old age. Isaac, the son, was thus the link between Abraham and the promised people, he was the living sign that God would keep his promise.

It is against this background that we must see the twenty-second chapter of Genesis. God tests Abraham by asking him to sacrifice his son. To any parent this would be a painful test of faith. Down through the centuries parents have been asked to sacrifice their sons for the sake of their countries. When the grim word has come, "killed in action," most parents have wondered deep in their hearts how God could allow such things to happen. They have asked how they could continue to believe that God is good and loving. But in Abraham's case the problem went even deeper. Not only was he, a parent, asked to sacrifice his son, but this was the son of the promise. If Isaac were dead there would no longer be any reason to believe that God would keep his promise to make a covenant with Abraham and his descendants. How can Abraham keep his faith in such a situation? How can he trust a God who cannot seem to make up his mind?

Paul, in the conclusion to Romans 8 faces all of those things in life that seem to deny God and his goodness. Paul does not promise his readers that Christians will be spared from any of the tragedies that fall upon other people. He assumes that Christians, like others, will know tribulations, distress, persecution, famine, nakedness, peril, and death. If all of these adversities fall alike upon the just and the unjust, the good and the evil, then to the wisdom of the world it would not appear that it pays to be good.

Mark, in his succinct way, sums up the beginning of Jesus' ministry. When Jesus was baptized by John he received, like Abraham before him, God's word of promise. And like Abraham, he was tested. Immediately he was driven by the Spirit into the wilderness to be tempted by Satan. At the baptism Jesus had been told that he was God's beloved Son in whom God was pleased (Mark 1:11), and yet here he was being tempted like any other human being. Surely there must have been times during the forty days in the wilderness when Jesus asked whether, in light of what was happening to him, he could take seriously God's words about his sonship. And the problem did not end when Jesus came out of the wilderness because he was met with the news that John had been cast into prison. Could Jesus hear of this without knowing in his heart that it was a foreshadowing of what fate would hold in store for him too?

All three of these passages squarely face the fact that Christianity is not a religion of glory. In our sinful hearts we all desire a God who will be on our side, a God who will use his omnipotent power to protect us from the ills that beset those around us. Jesus, however, again and again warned those who would follow him that they had to take up their crosses, and these three Scripture passages help us to see the meaning of the cross that lies at the center of Christian discipleship. Christian faith is not a form of magic that will preserve the true believers from the slings and arrows of an outrageous fortune. On the contrary, it would seem that the believers may be in for more than their share of the trials and tribulations of life.

But our three selections for this Sunday have more to say than that our faith will not protect us from the woes of life. Each of them also affirms that it is precisely in the moments of trial and testing that the triumph of faith appears. Abraham goes out to sacrifice his son, hoping against hope.

And at the last dramatic moment, God provides the ram as the alternative sacrifice. Paul lists the problems that the Christian will face in order to affirm that none of these is able to separate us from God's love. The love of God that is manifested in Jesus Christ is a love that carries us victoriously through all of life's tribulations. Jesus emerges from his temptations and, despite John's arrest, he proclaims that "The time is fulfilled, and the kingdom of God is at hand, repent and believe in the good news." It was precisely in and through the temptations that Jesus saw most clearly the reality of God and his kingdom.

The Christian can continue to believe in God's love despite all that seems to deny it because the Christian knows that God himself has suffered and continues to suffer with us. As the exegesis points out, in Rom. 8:31-32 Paul is obviously evoking the story of Abraham and Isaac as a background for his affirmation that nothing can separate us from God's love. The Christian cannot read about Abraham's testing without remembering that God gave his own Son and there was no ram offered as a substitute. During World War Two a story was told about a Sunday School class that was studying the crucifixion of Jesus. When finally the teacher had finished telling how Jesus died one little boy leaped up in anger and cried out, "But where were the marines?" And that is the point of Christian faith. Jesus died without the marines coming in for the last minute rescue. No legion of angels intervened to rescue God's Son from the cross. Had an intervention saved Jesus, Christianity would have been a religion of glory rather than a religion of the cross. We would seek the evidence of God in our triumphs and successes. But because God did not spare his own Son we dare to find God's love in our sufferings and defeats.

The religion of glory always wants to have Easter without Good Friday. The Greek philosophers denied that God could suffer. To them it seemed obvious that an omnipotent God could not share the finite and human weakness of suffering. But Christianity is a religion of the cross because it is the Good News of a God who did not stay in the remote protection of heaven, far from the struggle of earth. On the contrary, God came into our life through his Son and here he drank to the full the cup of suffering, temptation and sorrow. Jesus could call his followers to take up their crosses because first he bore his own cross. Similarly, God's love can come to us in our sufferings precisely because God himself has first suffered in, with, and for us.

Suffering, particularly the suffering of the relatively innocent, remains the greatest barrier to believing in God. Down through the centuries human wisdom has argued that if God is all good and all powerful, there would be no suffering. Since there is suffering either God is not all powerful or he is not all good. Most modern forms of atheism put a great deal of emphasis upon the facts of suffering in the world.

Paul found the answer to suffering in God's love from which none of the adversities of life and death can separate us. It is important, however, to see what kind of an answer this is. It is not a philosophical answer which enables us to understand the whys and wherefores of suffering. Rather it is an answer that comes from out of the experience of life itself. A few years ago I visited a woman who was dying a painful death from cancer. I marvelled to see that in the midst of her suffering she had a radiant and triumphant faith in God's love. The next day I sat in a religion seminar on a college campus where the students were arguing that it was impossible to believe in God because of the suffering in the world. I could not help but compare the two events. The dying woman, in the very midst of her suffering, knew the love of God and gratefully expressed her thanks to God for his goodness. The students, most of whom had no firsthand knowledge of any real suffering, could not believe in God because of the suffering in the world. What was the difference? The students were wrestling with a philosophical question upon the intellectual level alone. On that level, we have few answers. But the woman was speaking from out of her experience of life, suffering and approaching death. In her experience she had found the answer that philosophy still seeks. She knew in her life the love of God in Christ and because she knew it, she had an answer to suffering. It was not an answer to a philosophical question, it was an answer to a problem of life. It did not give her any glib solutions to intellectual puzzles but it enabled her to live and die victoriously. That is the nature of a religion of the cross.

The Second Sunday in Lent

utheran	*Roman Catholic*	*Episcopal*	*Pres./UCC/Chr.*	*Methodist/COCU*
en. 28:10-17	Gen. 22:1-2, 9a, 10-13, 15-18	Gen.28:11-17	Gen. 22:1-2, 9-13	Gen. 28:10-17
om. 5:1-11	Rom. 8:31b-34	Rom. 10:8-13	Rom. 8:31-39	Rom. 8:31-39
ark 8:31-38	Mark 9:1-9	John 2:13-22	Mark 9:1-9	Mark 10:32-45

EXEGESIS

First Lesson: Gen. 28:10-17. Gen. 28:10-17 is a passage in which J and E, the two major narrative strands of the Pentateuch, have been fused. The identification of the once separate sources is based upon the changes in the name of deity, the twice-reported response of Jacob to his encounter with God (vv. 16 and 17), and the different content of each strand.

Vv. 10-12, 17 are assigned to E. Fleeing from Esau, Jacob, while en route from Beer-sheba to Haran, stopped for the night at an unnamed but specific place. It is mentioned twice in v. 11 ("a certain place," "the place" RSV), as is also the time of day ("that night," "to sleep"). A stone made an odd pillow, and Jacob's sleep was enlivened by the dream of a ramp or stairway extending from earth to heaven on which angels ascended and descended. The Hebrew term is derived from the root *sll* which means "to heap up," "to raise." The angels—not winged beings in the OT—used the ramp to come and go from heaven to earth. The word translated here as angel designates a messenger or agent. Jacob's response, according to E (v. 17), was fear. He recognized the place to be "the house of God" (*Beth-el*), "the gateway to heaven."

Some are tempted to see in this story only a survival of an ancient belief that one could receive a vision of a god dwelling in a stone while sleeping in the shrine at Bethel, but we must grant our narrator more subtlety than this. The evocations of an incubation (sleeping in a shrine) are too many to ignore. Bethel, the name given the place in v. 19, had been a Canaanite shrine long before Israel entered the land. The ramp between earth and heaven is reminiscent of the ramp, or stairway up a Babylonian ziggurat, the tower shrine of the god standing beside the earthly temple in which men worshiped. "The gateway to heaven" recalls the gateway into a royal palace, and the angels coming and going evoke the messengers and emissaries of an earthly king. In light of the complex features of the E narrative, we seem to hear the author asserting that the divine king of all the earth revealed his activity to Jacob, an Israelite patriarch, when Jacob, fleeing for his life, faced an uncertain future.

E reports Jacob as having a vision, as seeing divine activity. J reports an audition (vv. 13-16). The scene has changed. The Lord is standing beside (rather than "above" as in RSV) Jacob, who is lying on the ground, presumably sleeping. Jacob is given the same promise of land and posterity earlier given Abraham (Gen. 13:14-17; 22:17) and Isaac (Gen. 26:4, 14). Even though he now is a fugitive, Jacob is assured that God's promise is so certain that he will protect Jacob while he is in an alien land and return him safely to the land he is to possess (v. 15). Jacob, awakening, acknowledges that the deity he had known in Beer-Sheba was God in this strange place also (v. 16).

The themes of J in vv. 13-16 are those which dominate all of this author's patriarchal narratives: the promises of land and progeny, and the transmission of those promises through all hazards. When vv. 13-16 are read in the context of the E story given them by the J editor, however, the resuit is a statement of the magnitude of the God making and guaranteeing the promises. It is the heavenly king, served by myriads of angels, who has covenanted with Israel.

Second Lesson: Rom. 5:1-11. In Rom. 5:1, the strongest ancient witnesses to the text read "let us have" (present subjunctive). Correctors of Sinaiticus and Vaticanus changed this to "we have" (present indicative). Translators of AV, AS, RSV, and a majority of commentators, have chosen the present indicative, apparently on theological grounds. The subjunctive is the more strongly attested reading and is followed here (with Moffatt, Goodspeed, NEB, and some commentators).

Rom. 5:1-11 is part of Paul's transition from his discussion of election by faith (1:16—4:25) to a consideration of the life of faith (6:1—8:39). Vv. 1-11 reflect the logical disorder sometimes found in lyrical outbursts. This exposition will attempt to deal with the thought of the passage rather more systematically than did the apostle, unfortunately at the price of a loss of power and beauty.

The concept upon which the whole rests is that we are judged righteous by God when we accept with faith the act of God in Christ. This act is described as Christ's voluntary death for sinners (vv. 6-8), an act contrasted by Paul with our reluctance to die even for a good man (the contrast between our unwillingness to die for a righteous man and our grudging willingness to die for a good man seems to be more a false start by Paul than a contrast of substance). We are not told here what "faith" means, whether it is mystical union with Christ, trust, or intellectual assent.

The effects of being justified through faith are three: we may now accept the peace of God, we may be allowed to share in his glory, and we know joy.

Paul appears to assert that we are given the choice to accept or to reject the peace of God (v. 1). The volitional element here echoes a like note in 2 Cor. 6:1 (the Second Lesson for Ash Wednesday). The phrase "the peace of God" is to be read in the light of Paul's Hellenistic-Jewish vocabulary. The Hebrew *shalom*, wholeness rather than the absence of strife, is likely to have been the meaning of "peace" for Paul. Since his Jewish heritage also was wholly theocentric, the phrase "the peace of God" would seem to have meant for Paul that wholeness, or completeness of life possible only when one stood in good relationship to God, the source of all life.

The second consequence of justification is the hope that we may "share in the glory of God" (v. 2). Paul's use of *doxa* (glory) was complex. We are told in v. 9 that we will be saved from "the wrath of God." Since we are also told that we already have experienced God's love (v. 5), the phrase "wrath of God" in v. 9 appears to be a reference to the final judgment. Those who escape the final judgment enter the eschatological kingdom, according to first century Jewish apocalyptic hope, in which the splendor of God's reign is complete. This could be described as his glory (cf. Isa. 40:5), and the saved who lived in that kingdom would share in his glory (cf. Isa. 43:7; 60:1-3).

The third consequence of justification is joy. This is the fruit of the knowledge of God's love given us by the Holy Spirit. Our knowledge enables us to endure adversity with equanimity and confidence since we are experiencing in the present the love of God which makes us confident of the future (vv. 3-5, 11).

Gospel: Mark 8:31-38. This passage falls into two parts: vv. 31-33 (Jesus teaching the disciples only) and vv. 34-38 (Jesus teaching both the disciples and a multitude).

Vv. 31-35 record one of the turning points in the dramatic structure of the Gospel of Mark. In response to Jesus' question about the popular reception of his ministry, Peter declared Jesus to be the Messiah (v. 29). From this point on, Jesus began to instruct his companions on the nature of his messianic vocation.

All of the evangelists consistently attribute the use of the term "Son of man" to Jesus and to him alone (14 times in Mark; 33 times in Matthew of which 14 are shared with Mark; 24 times in Luke of which 8 are shared with Mark and Matthew and 8 with Matthew only; 12 times in John). The title is used only once elsewhere in the NT (Acts 7:56). Although it is not clear in the Synoptic Gospels whether Jesus meant it to be applied as a messianic title to himself or to another than himself, it is clear that the early church remembered Jesus' frequent use of it. Thus we have reason to believe that these verses contain a reliable memory of Jesus' ministry even though v. 31 is in indirect discourse.

A suffering Messiah was not unknown in Judaism (cf. Isa. 52:13—53:12), and the final outcome of the consistent animus of Jewish leaders to Jesus' ministry (Mark 2:6 f., 16; 3:6, 22, etc.) may already have become clear to him. The prominence of the figure of the triumphant, even regal, Messiah in first century Jewish hopes, however, may still have dominated Peter's expectations for Jesus. Whatever the reason, he took Jesus aside to protest his predictions of his death (v. 32).

Jesus rejected Peter's protest before the whole company (v. 33). The reproof seems strangely harsh. Peter is addressed as Satan in a command echoing Matt. 4:10, and the inference is that Peter's protest was a temptation to Jesus as strong as those offered by Satan in the wilderness. Peter had advocated something other than God's will as Jesus had come to know it. Nevertheless, Peter was a close follower, one already able to recognize Jesus to be the Messiah. Was Peter's being "on man's side," having let his affection for Jesus blind him to God's will? If this be correct, this is a difficult teaching!

Vv. 34-38 preserve three sayings. Each is reported twice in Matthew and Luke (Mark 8:34 = Matt. 16:24; 10:38; Luke 9:23; 14:27; Mark 8:35-37 = Matt. 16:25 f.; 10:39; Luke 9:24 f.; 17:33; Mark 8:38 = Matt. 16:27 10:33; Luke 9:26; 12:9). This attests to the strength of the tradition that these were Jesus' sayings, but it also suggests that the circumstance in which they originally had been spoken had been lost. A comparison of each saying with its parellels further indicates that the precise wording of each was uncertain. Thus we would be well advised to concentrate on the primary thrust of each rather than on its details.

In v. 34, we are commanded to serve Christ and his gospel with such devotion that we will risk death for him. Crucifixion was a well-known form of execution, and the condemned often was forced to carry his own cross. Bearing a cross in this passage, therefore, is accepting the risk of death for the sake of Christ, not bearing the misfortunes of life with fortitude (even though that is admirable in itself).

Vv. 35-37 describe the primacy of the decision to be for or against

Christ. NT writers consistently affirm Jesus to be "the way, the truth, and the life" (John 14:6). He who denied being a follower of Christ when interrogated during persecution might survive physically, yet he would lose the life given through Christ. We should remember, when reading this, Papias' report that the Gospel of Mark was written in Rome by a companion of Peter after his martyrdom.

The title "Son of man" appears again in v. 38 in a way which underscores the problem of the identity of this figure. Is Jesus distinguishing here between himself and the Son of man, is he speaking of himself as the Son of man at that future time when he was to come again, or is the early church here affirming its belief that Jesus either was, or would become the Son of man? We cannot now decide with complete confidence which (if any) of these is correct. V. 38 is an apocalyptic statement of the theme of vv. 35-37. Those who repudiate Jesus now will be repudiated by the Son of man when he comes in the full panoply of his power at the end of this age. Only here and in Jesus' prayer in the Garden of Gethsemane (Mark 14:36) does this evangelist use "father" as a term for God.

HOMILETICAL INTERPRETATION

At the center of the biblical message is the good news that God is a God of gracious love. The gods of philosophy are supreme beings who remain clothed in awesome secrecy. Some truth about them may be discovered by a few great thinkers who probe the secrets of the heavens but to the rest of humanity they are unknown entities. The biblical God is not one who waits for human beings to discover him. On the contrary, he takes the initiative and seeks his people. He chooses the Jewish people that through them he might approach all peoples. Before ever we thought of seeking God he was seeking us. Jesus said to his disciples, "You did not choose me, but I chose you . . ." (John 15:16). Those words can be used to sum up the relationship between God and his people throughout the Bible.

God's gracious love means that God seeks us, but it also means that God receives and forgives sinful human beings. The popular view of religion always pictures God as the great judge in the sky. His heavenly computer is keeping a daily record of everyone's good and bad deeds. When the time of judgment comes those whose score of good deeds outweighs their score of evil deeds will be accepted and rewarded by God. But those whose evil deeds weigh more heavily will be cast into punishment. The biblical God, however, breaks radically from this popular picture. He accepts not only the good people but he seeks the sinful and the outcast. He is a God who desires to save rather than to destroy or punish.

The gracious love of God comes out clearly in both the First and Second Lessons for this Sunday. Jacob is fleeing from the justifiable wrath of his brother. To this point in his life Jacob has proven himself to be a scheming cheat who has misled his aged father and stolen his brother's birthright and blessing. As time passes he will add still further sharp practices to his record. It seems unlikely that God would choose such an unsavory character as Jacob for his purposes. But the whole point of this passage is that God comes to the renegade Jacob and renews with him the covenant made with Abraham, his grandfather. Jacob is promised that he is to be the one through whom the covenant will be transmitted to the coming generations. "For I will not leave you until I have done that of which I have spoken to you" (v. 15). Jacob has not proven himself to be particularly trustworthy, but God pledges to Jacob his trustworthiness.

The Second Lesson is a beautiful rendition of the same theme. As God came with promise to the scheming Jacob, so Paul tells us Jesus came to die for sinful humanity. "But God shows his love for us in that while we were yet sinners Christ died for us" (v. 8). This is startling news! As Paul sees, most of us would be reluctant to give our lives for a righteous person. How can we comprehend one who so willingly gave his life for all of the unrighteous ones? But this is the nature of God's love. He does not love us insofar as we have acted to deserve it. On the contrary, he loves us in our sin and seeks to deliver us from our sinful state. And so, as Jacob received God's promise and blessings despite his sinful state, Paul assures us that in Christ we are blessed. We have been reconciled to God so that we may accept the peace of God, share in God's glory, and know joy. (See exegesis.)

At first sight the Gospel reading does not seem to fit in with the theme of the First and Second Lessons. As the exegesis points out, it seems unduly harsh when Jesus calls Peter "Satan." We must read this passage in light of its context within Mark's Gospel. Peter has just made his epochal confession "You are the Christ" (Mark 8:29). No doubt, in the minds of the disciples there had been the hope or even the belief that Jesus was God's promised Christ. But none had dared to speak the hidden hope until Peter blurted it out. According to Matthew's version of the same story, Jesus told Peter that his words had been a revelation from God and hence Peter would be the rock upon which the church would be built (Matt. 16:13-20). All of this meant, of course, that the disciples would see Jesus as the one in whom God's covenant with his people would be fulfilled.

The passage for this Sunday follows immediately after Peter's confession. Jesus began to teach his followers that the Son of man must suffer, be rejected by the religious and political authorities, and be put to death. This teaching is similar to Paul's words in today's Second Lesson. Christ has come to give his life for a sinful humanity. But the words must have sounded strange and dismaying to the disciples. Obviously they were not prepared to find that God's Christ would come as a suffering servant. Probably, like most people in their time, they were hoping for a conquering-hero type of Messiah, one who would bring victory over the foes of his people. And so it was Peter who again spoke out the thoughts that were in the minds of all the disciples. He rebuked Jesus' view that the Christ should suffer and die. This rebuke brought upon him Jesus' stern words "Get behind me, Satan! For you are not on the side of God, but of men" (v. 33).

Jesus probably calls Peter "Satan" for two reasons. In the first place, Peter has failed to see God's basic purpose. Peter is speaking "for men" in that he is expressing the presuppositions of the world that God and his Christ will come on behalf of the good people. To the good, Christ will give his rewards. Peter could not yet understand the gracious love that would die for sinful people. But perhaps even more important, Jesus calls Peter Satan because Jesus hears the temptation of Satan coming through Peter's words. In Gethsemane Jesus was to pray in agony as he sought to have the cup of suffering taken from him. Our temptations are always most difficult when they come to us from our friends. It is not too difficult to resist the temptation that comes from one that we despise. Upon such a one's lips the temptation appears in all of its loathsomeness. But when the friend expresses the same thing, it suddenly appears harmless, nay, it even seems good because it becomes part of our relationship with our friend.

Jesus' words to Peter may be harsh. They rebuked the ideas that Peter was expressing. But it is important to see that they were not a rejection of Peter himself. On the contrary, in the next chapter Mark reports that Jesus took Peter along with James and John to witness his transfiguration. Jesus, who gave his life for sinners, would not cast away from him a disciple even when he became a voice of Satan.

The concluding verses in the Gospel reading can be seen as Jesus' advice on how we ought to respond to God's gracious love. God has given himself totally for us in his grace and so Jesus calls us to give ourselves totally to God. Because Christ has taken up his cross for us, we are called to take up our cross for him. God's grace comes to us freely. We do not earn it, deserve it, or in any way receive it as our right. But it is not, in Bonhoeffer's phrase, a "cheap grace." When God's love lays hold upon us we find that we are changed. Because we have been loved by God we love God in turn and thus we love those whom God loves, our neighbors. When we love someone, we are prepared to give ourselves in costly service to them.

In v. 35 Jesus speaks paradoxically by saying that those who seek to save their lives will lose them while those who are ready to lose their lives for Jesus' cause will find them. The paradox brings out the nature of responding to God's grace. In our natural state we are all self-centered and thus we naturally seek salvation for ourselves. Because we think that God is like we are, we assume that to get God on our side and to win salvation we must do things which will please and flatter him. And so we use God for our own ends. This self-centered determination to advance and save ourselves, says Jesus, ends up in alienating ourselves from both God and ourselves. Our dedication to save our lives destroys them. But when God's gracious love takes hold of us we are literally pulled outside of ourselves. Whenever we love we do tend to forget ourselves and seek to please the loved one. When we experience God's gracious love we are won to love in return and in the love for God we quit worrying about ourselves, our salvation, our interests. We are prepared to give our lives to God and the strange wonder is that it is in such a giving up of the self that we begin for the first time to experience true selfhood.

Taken together, our three readings for this Sunday describe the essence of justification by grace through faith. In the Old Testament reading we see the forgiving love of God that pursues even the shifty sinner, Jacob. In the Second Lesson we learn of how God's son died for the enemies of God that they might be reconciled to the God against whom they had rebelled. In the Gospel we are invited to respond to God's gracious love with a responding love whereby we give ourselves to the God who has first given himself to us.

The Third Sunday in Lent

Lutheran	*Roman Catholic*	*Episcopal*	*Pres./UCC/Chr.*	*Methodist/COCU*
Exod. 20:1-17	Exod. 20:1-17	Exod. 3:1-8b, 10-15	Exod. 20:1-3, 7-8, 12-17	Exod. 20:1-17
Rom. 10:5-13	1 Cor. 1:22-25	Eph. 5:8-14	1 Cor. 1:22-25	1 Cor. 1:22-25
John 2:13-22	John 2:13-25	John 3:14-21	John 4:19-26	John 2:13-22

EXEGESIS

First Lesson: Exod. 20:1-17. The Ten Commandments in Exod. 20:1-17 (found also, with a few important variations, in Deut. 5:6-21) are unconditional demands or prohibitions. They are called apodictic (i.e., absolute) laws. They had a long history before reaching their present form. The brevity of vv. 3, 13-16 contrasts sharply with the explanatory or hortatory expansions in vv. 4-12, 17. This, and the differences between Exod. 20:1-17 and Deut. 5:6-21 suggest that all of the laws originally were brief. The expansions may have arisen as the circumstances of life changed or in response to major shifts in worship (e.g., from emphasis on God acting in the exodus [Deut. 5:15] to God acting in creation [Exod. 20:11]). No date or origin can be given the commandments in their original form. All of the evidence used in discussions of these questions is taken from the later expansions of the original, brief commandments.

The laws are identified in v. 1 as "the words of God." In Deut. 4:13, they are called "the Ten Words" (whence our decalogue). V. 2 gives the basis of the Lord's right to make demands of Israel. The declaration "I am Yahweh your God" is a covenantal title, and it recalls the self-designation used by Hittite emperors in treaties with vassals. In those treaties, the emperor's right to the vassal's obedience had been won in battle, and the victory was always reported in the treaty. The similar element here is the reference to the Lord's display of compassionate might in delivering Israel from slavery. Just as the Hittite treaty included a list of the forms of obedience demanded of the vassal, so here also the will of God for Israel is described in the commandments which follow (vv. 3-17).

V. 3 prohibits bringing other gods into the presence of the Lord, although it does not deny their existence. Vv. 4-6 prohibit the worship ("you shall not bow down") of a representation of any god. The deity in the waters under the earth (the abyss) may be the god of chaos in the Semitic creation myth: Rahab, Leviathan, or The Serpent (cf. Isa. 27:1;

51:9; Ps. 89:10; Job 26:12 f., etc.). Because the Lord was jealous of his right to Israel's allegiance, he would hold an entire household (which might include four generations) guilty for apostasy. His love, however, was greater than his anger and would flow out to a large number of those related to the faithful. Since the name was believed to contain a person's essence, v. 7 prohibits violating the Lord's sovereignty by using his name for any false reason (i.e., for a reason desired by man—including witchcraft and false witness—rather than those commanded by God). Vv. 8-11 prescribe Sabbath observance. In biblical Hebrew, "to remember" includes acting upon a recollection. That which was holy was set apart from the common. Therefore a holy day was lived differently than other days. On the Sabbath, all of the household was to stop work because God rested after creation (cf. Gen. 2:1-3; P. Deut. 5:12-15 bases Sabbath observance on the exodus).

The Ten Words conclude with six commandments governing human relationships. Honoring authority of parents (who ruled the family until they were quite old) is commanded (v. 12). Unauthorized killing (excluding judicial execution and killing in war, acts for which different verbs were used), adultery, theft, and the corruption of the judicial process by giving false testimony are banned. The list ends with a prohibition of desiring strongly to possess all that belongs to another (v. 17). "House" here seems to mean "household" since what follows constitutes the household (with the wife given the place of honor).

Second Lesson: Rom. 10:5-13. In Rom. 10:5-13, Paul uses free quotations from Lev. 18:5 (v. 5), Deut. 30:11-14 (vv. 6-8), Isa. 28:16 (v. 11), and Joel 2:32 (v. 32) as part of his argument that all those, whether Jew or Gentile, who accept Christ will be counted righteous by God. Since Paul's ways of expounding Scripture differ so sharply from the methods of modern critical exegesis, the force of his argument here can be described only when the context in which he wrote is understood.

The OT Lesson for today makes it clear that ancient Israel viewed the law as a statement of the will of the God who had established his sovereignty by an act of compassion. Thus the basis for obedience was responding to the divine act in love. The God acting in the exodus was Yahweh, translated in the Septuagint used by Paul as *kurios*. Early Christians called Christ *kurios* (lord, master), and God was affirmed as acting to save men in the ministry, death, and resurrection of Christ. Thus Paul had both a linguistic and a functional basis for equating what Yahweh had done for Israel and what Christ had done (and was doing) for Christians. As a result,

Paul applied Joel 2:32, originally said about Yahweh, to Christ as *kurios* and to all who can affirm Christ to be *kurios*.

When these aspects of Paul's thought are kept in mind, it becomes clear that his use of Deut. 30:11-14—even though it is a commentary, or midrash, formed by explanatory interpolations—does justice to the basic viewpoint of Deuteronomy. Paul is contrasting righteousness achieved by the performance of all of the law—said to be possible (v. 5) on the basis of Lev. 18:5—with the righteousness of faith in Christ by which the Christian lives. To defend the latter, he quoted phrases excerpted from the Greek text of Deut. 30:11-14, interspersing explanations of what he believed the phrases being quoted to mean for Christians. It is not an exegetical method in good standing today, yet Paul did express by means of it the basic Deuteronomic insistence that God saved Israel because of his grace and not Israel's merit (Deut. 7:6-8; 8:17; 9:4).

Paul's interpretations, when read in the light of the material quoted from Deuteronomy, are significant. Men could not hasten the coming of the Messiah by their devotion to the law (they cannot "ascend into heaven" to bring the Messiah down)—some Jews held that the Messiah or the new age would come when the law had been perfectly obeyed (2 Baruch 15:7; 44:7-14; Jubilees 23:16 f.)—because he had already come. Nor did they need to seek the Messiah in Sheol (descending into the abyss to raise Christ from the dead) because he is already raised from the dead. As a living, present reality, he is as close to them as the lips with which they confess him to be Lord.

Paul's Jewish heritage encouraged him to understand that there was an integral relationship between the inner person and what the person says. Both had to affirm the act of God in Christ (vv. 9 f.). All who do this, whether Jew or Gentile, will be saved (vv. 11-13). Since Paul here again speaks of a future salvation in addition to the present knowledge of the love of God (Rom. 5:5), the salvation of v. 13 is probably eschatological.

Gospel: John 2:13-22. John 2:13-22 contains the Johannine report of traditions recorded in different contexts and words in the Synoptic Gospels. The story of the cleansing of the temple in Mark 11:15-17 (Matt. 21:12 f.; Luke 19:45 f.) is placed early in Passion Week. Here, it comes early in Jesus' ministry. In Mark 11:17, Jesus protests the dishonesty of the merchants in the temple (echoing Jer. 7:11). In John 2:16, Jesus protests any commerce there (possibly recalling Zech. 14:21). The Markan account ends with the Jewish authorities reacting to the cleansing by plotting Jesus' death (v. 18). John concludes with the Jewish leaders' challenge of the basis of Jesus' authority and with a discussion of the destruction and rebuilding of the temple. A similar challenge is reported in Mark 11:27-33 as happening on a different day and for a different reason, and a prediction of the destruction of the temple is recorded in Mark 14:58 as part of the false witness against Jesus during his trial.

In all of this, we seem to be faced with different uses of early Christian traditions. The Synoptic Gospels appear to be somewhat the more historical. It is unlikely that the rulers in Jerusalem would let a direct challenge to essential services in the temple to go unheeded for two years. This conclusion does not deny Johannine use of early traditions. It does encourage us to find the theological content being conveyed by the fourth evangelist in his arrangements and reporting of his sources.

Writing for Greek Christians aware of themselves as non-Jewish, the evangelist may also be distinguishing between a Jewish and a Christian passover ("the passover of the Jews," v. 13; cf. 1 Cor. 5:7). The sale of animals for sacrifice and the exchange of coins unlawful for use in paying the temple tax because they displayed a human likeness were a convenience to worshipers coming from a distance (v. 14). These businesses were carried on in the temple court (*hieron*). Jesus expelled the tradesmen because any commerce there was improper (vv. 15 f.). This may have been an attack on the whole of the temple cult since both sacrifices and the support of the temple through payment of the tax were made more difficult. The phrase "my Father's house" rather than "our Father's house" implies a special relationship between Jesus and God, and it may have been a messianic claim.

The Jewish response was to ask for proof of Jesus' authority (v. 18; cp. 2 Kings 19:29; Isa. 7:10-16). Jesus replied, in effect, "If you want a sign strongly enough to destroy the temple (*naos* here rather than *hieron*), I will give it to you by rebuilding the temple in three days."

The evangelist has expanded his sources in vv. 17, 20-23. In v. 17, Ps. 69:9 is quoted from the Septuagint in a retrospect gaining its force by changing the past tense in the psalm to a future tense. The disciples are thus reported as realizing that Jesus' zeal for a proper use of the temple caused his death. In this, v. 17 echoes Mark 11:18. V. 20 is a literary device used in Hellenistic literature (and often in the Fourth Gospel) to set the stage for a clarification of meaning—here the explanation that the temple to be raised up is Jesus' body (v. 21). The forty-seven years' building time for the temple reported in v. 20 has created more problems than it has solved. According to Josephus (Antiquities XV, xi. 1), Herod the Great began the building in 20/19 B.C. It was not completed until A.D.

63. The obscurity is deepened by the comment in John 8:57 that Jesus was not yet fifty. It may be that the evangelist had no interest in, or knowledge of, the precise chronology of the building of the temple. V. 22 records how the disciples remembered Jesus' statement about rebuilding the temple after the resurrection, recognizing at the same time the messianic significance of Ps. 69:9 (cited in v. 17), and "believed" both.

If it be concluded that the fourth evangelist recast received traditions to convey a message in his narrative, his meaning should be sought in the narrative as it now stands. In John 2:13-22, the message seems to be the presentation of Jesus as the Messiah. Devotion to him would replace the Jewish temple cult. It was this threat that aroused the implacable opposition of those responsible for that cult, and it was the acceptance of such a messiahship that constituted the disciples' post-resurrection belief.

HOMILETICAL INTERPRETATION

The Ten Commandments are often referred to as the basic ethical code for all human life. As such the Ten Commandments are seen as the Judaeo-Christian version of the ethical principles that are universally accepted by the human race. This is partly true. The last six of the commandments (vv. 12-17) are most certainly not unique to Jews and Christians. All peoples extol the honoring of parents. Some, such as the Chinese, have put even greater emphasis upon this than Jews and Christians do. All societies prohibit murder, adultery, stealing, and false witness against neighbors. Coveting of the neighbor's possessions is discouraged in all societies. Certainly this group of commandments is known to people quite apart from biblical revelation. It would be difficult to find a society anywhere that did not extol or enforce these ethical ideals.

When we turn, however, to vv. 1-8 we find a framework for all of the commandments that gives a uniqueness to the Judaeo-Christian statement. We are told that God spoke and identified himself as "the Lord your God, who brought you out of the land of Egypt, out of the house of bondage." The ethical commandments are thus put into the framework of the relationship of the people with their God who, having made his covenant with them, delivered them from bondage in Egypt. The commandments are not orders sent down from on high by the ruler of the universe, they are part of the covenant relationship between God and the people whom he has chosen and loved.

And because the Lord who brought them out of Egypt is speaking, his first commandment is: "You shall have no other gods before me" (v. 3).

The second commandment (v. 4) is really just an expansion of the first. If the people are to have no gods before their Lord, then they should not make graven images. At first sight these two commandments do not seem particularly difficult for modern man. We are a monotheistic culture and we agree that the one God is the God of Judaism and Christianity. In the ancient world a person had a choice between a vast number of gods. But in North America it would appear that we have only a choice between atheism and the one God. Even when other religions are brought to our continent, the gods of such religions are usually identified with our God. Furthermore, it would not seem that we are tempted today to make graven images because that is not the way any religion operates in our culture. A typical joke tells of a man who listens to a fiery sermon on the Ten Commandments. As he leaves the church he says to his wife, "Well, at least I have not made any graven images." The point of the joke lies in the assumption that graven images are irrelevant in our culture.

But a second look quickly shows that the first two commandments are far from irrelevant. Paul Tillich described faith as "being ultimately concerned." In life we are concerned with many things and some concerns are obviously more important to us than others. We are concerned to save money but that concern is not as important to most of us as caring adequately for our families. The concern for the family thus proves more ultimate than the concern to increase our savings. Life consists, therefore, of continually weighing our priorities and deciding which concerns should take precedence. Tillich's point is that a religious faith is an ultimate concern, a concern that takes priority over all other concerns. It is Tillich's philosophical translation of Jesus' words about loving God with all our heart and soul and mind (Matt. 22:37). In light of this, the first two commandments are asking us whether God is our ultimate concern. A graven image is not something that we carve out with our hands, a graven image is a concern which we allow to take priority over God. Idolatry, said Tillich, consists of giving our ultimate allegiance and concern to that which is not ultimate. By that standard we are not as innocent of disobeying the first two commandments as we would like to think. We have been created to have God at the center of our lives but we have allowed a host of concerns to push God to the periphery of life. That is having other gods before him. It is the modern way of making graven images.

The third commandment (v. 7) prohibits taking God's name in vain. This follows from all that has been said. Because God has entered into covenant with his people, because he has kept his promise and delivered them from bondage, the relationship between God and his people is a serious one. Therefore, they should not take the name of God lightly or thoughtlessly. Such a use of God would be a denial of their relationship to him. The problem here is that all too often we assume that this is simply a prohibition of what we call cursing or swearing. Actually the third commandment probably has little to do with most forms of cursing and swearing in today's world. The man who lightly tosses off "god-damns" or uses Jesus' name as an expletive is not really taking the *Lord's* name in vain. He has not stopped to think what his words mean, they are but a part of the thoughtless vocabulary that he has inherited.

Much more serious than the mindless swearing or cursing of the modern age is the tendency of believers to use God's name to bless their many personal causes and concerns. The truly blasphemous taking of God's name in vain is that which uses God and the Bible to justify racial discrimination, aggressive war, and a host of other things that are contrary to God's revelation in Christ.

The fourth commandment (v. 8) calls the people to "remember the sabbath day." As God rested, so his people are to have rest. Because God has entered into the covenant relationship with his people it is important to have set aside a time and place where the relationship is remembered and where it is renewed. In the service of worship, as the community hears God's word and speaks their words to God, the covenant relationship is renewed.

The Ten Commandments are a vivid reminder that the covenant between God and his people is a two-way agreement. God took the initiative to form the covenant, he pledged himself to his people and bestowed upon them his many blessings. And then he called them to respond to his initiative by living as the people of the covenant. The story of the OT, however, is the story of the people's failure to keep their covenant. When we turn to the Second Lesson for the day we find that it is written from the perspective of the new covenant that has been made by God in Christ. Paul is contrasting the righteousness of faith with the righteousness based on law. God gave his law to the people whom he had chosen and delivered in order that the relationship between himself and his people might be continued. But the people used the law to exalt themselves rather than to glorify God. When that happens people dream that they might "ascend into heaven." (See exegesis.) And so it is that people continually think that if they can just live the good life they will solve all problems. If we can just get a bit more of the right technology, if we can just get the right economic system working, if we can just have less governmental action or if we can just have more governmental action, then we shall have solved the problems that beset us. But no matter how fine the methods we assemble or how proficient we become in using them, so long as people are self-centered the good methods are used again to try and "ascend into heaven." We are more concerned to exalt ourselves than to serve God.

In describing the righteousness of faith, Paul says, "if you confess with your lips that Jesus is Lord and believe in your heart that God raised him from the dead, you will be saved" (v. 9). It is interesting that he links confessing with the lips to believing with the heart. The righteousness of faith is not just a matter of saying the right things when stimulated in the correct way. A person may affirm a host of orthodox doctrines and not really have faith at all. Nonetheless, Paul seems to be saying that verbal confession is an important part of faith. Where there is faith it has the desire to make itself known and to share the good news it has heard through confession with the lips. Such confession will be an effective witness, however, only if the speaker also believes in his or her heart. To believe in the heart is to have the ultimate concern that we discussed in connection with the OT Lesson.

At first sight it is not clear just how the Gospel should be related to the First and Second Lessons for the day. The exegesis concludes, however, that John has used this story in order to present Jesus as the Messiah. His coming has meant the replacement of the temple cult which represented the old covenant. So interpreted, we can see the three readings for the day blending together.

The OT Lesson consists of the center of the law that God gave to his people. Laws, such as the Ten Commandments, can be seen in two ways. They can be seen as a response of the covenant people to their God. Because God has delivered his people, the people desire to know what they can do to please God who has done so much for them. But such laws can also be seen, as the Second Lesson makes clear, as a way whereby people exalt themselves and storm heaven. The laws are no longer seen as a way of continuing what God has started and as an expression of love to God who first loved us. Instead, they are seen as a means whereby we can exalt ourselves, win favor with God, and earn our place in the universe. Given the first view, the laws are an expression of the people's unity with God. Given the second view the laws are an expression of the division between the people and God. In the first view the laws are a means of communication with God, in the second they are barriers to be hurdled if the people are to come to God.

Where the laws are seen as a barrier to be overcome, it is inevitable that worship itself will be commercialized. The keeping of the sabbath, worship, and obedience to God, are no longer precious opportunities to express fellowship with God, they become tasks to perform in order to earn God's pleasure. The father's house becomes "a house of trade" (John 2:16). Since it is the place where we try to buy our way to God, it does not seem out of place to do other business there. And so we have the temple in Jesus' day with livestock and birds being sold and coins being exchanged. In cleansing the temple, John is saying to us, Jesus was doing more than chastising the villains on the spot. He was introducing a new order. In his messianic claim he was bringing to an end the whole idea of buying our way to God with good deeds. So understood, the Gospel for the day calls us to see how Jesus, in his life, death, and resurrection has freed us to be in the true covenant relationship with God.

The Fourth Sunday in Lent

Lutheran	*Roman Catholic*	*Episcopal*	*Pres./UCC/Chr.*	*Methodist/COCU*
Num. 21:4-9	2 Chron. 36:14-16, 19-23	Exod. 16:2-8, 13-15	2 Chron. 36:14-21	2 Chron. 36:14-2
Eph. 2:4-10	Eph. 2:4-10	Gal. 4:26-5:1	Eph. 2:1-10	Eph. 2:1-10
John 3:14-21	John 3:14-21	Mark 8:12-21	John 3:14-21	John 3:14-21

EXEGESIS

First Lesson: Num. 21:4-9. This is one of several passages in the OT which describes Israel as complaining during the wilderness wanderings (cf. Exod. 14:10-12; 16:1-31; Num. 11:1-34; 20:2-13; Psalm 78; Ezek. 20:5-26, etc.). The narrative is introduced by a note which describes tersely the Israelites as retracing their steps from Mount Hor (where they had stopped according to Num. 20:22-29: P) southward to the Sea of Reeds (*Yam Suph*; cf. Exod. 13:18) in order to detour around Edom. The Edomites had prohibited the Israelites from passing through their land (Num. 20:14-21).

As the Israelites moved back into the desert, they became testy (lit: short of *nephesh*: v. 4), and their complaints swiftly became a reproach against God and Moses for leading them out of the security of Egypt into the perils of the wilderness. The exodus is the divine act in the OT upon which the Lord's sovereignty over Israel is primarily based. Speaking against the guidance of God in the exodus was a serious denial of his sovereignty. The Lord's response was to send fiery serpents among the people which caused widespread death (v. 6).

The serpents are called *nehashim seraphim* in v. 6, *nahash* (serpent) alone in v. 7, and *seraph* (fiery) alone in v. 8. *Nahash* is used throughout v. 9. The fiery serpents, or the fiery ones of vv. 6 and 8 call to mind the *seraphim* of Isa. 6:2, 6 where one of them is the agency through which Isaiah is cleansed of his sin. The bronze serpent mentioned twice in v. 9 recalls Nehushtan, the bronze serpent worshiped in the temple in Jerusalem as late as the reign of Hezekiah (2 Kings 18:4).

The danger created by the serpents caused the people to recognize their grumbling to be rebellion against God and against Moses, his representative. They repented (v. 7), and Moses prayed to God on their behalf. Their request that the serpents be removed was not granted. Instead, Moses was commanded to make a likeness of the fiery ones to put in a prominent place. Those who looked at it when bitten would survive.

This narrative had a tangled history, little of which we can reconstruct now with confidence. Ps. 78:67-72 and Ezek. 20:5-26 suggest that the motif of revolt against God's guidance in the wilderness was a Jerusalem, or Zion tradition (Ezekiel had been a priest in Jerusalem before becoming a prophet in the exile). It may be more than coincidence that a figure of a "fiery one" was an agent for God in the call of Isaiah, a Jerusalemite (Isa. 6:2, 6), just as an image of a "fiery one" was the agent of God's salvation in Num. 21:9. A naturalistic interpretation would reject the pattern of cultic traditions just outlined. It would identify the *seraphim* as poisonous reptiles whose bites caused inflammation. The story could then be judged to be the report of a memory of a crisis in the wilderness during which snake bites were treated either by the kind of sympathetic magic described in 1 Sam. 6:1-16 or by recourse to one of the healing cults associated with snakes which were so common in Semitic antiquity. The primary point of the story as it now stands is clear. God provided the means for the healing of his people from the ravages caused by their sin after they had repented.

Second Lesson: Eph. 2:4-10. Paul is identified as the author of Ephesians in 1:1 (and 3:1). The earliest confirmation of this appears in Marcion's "canon" (A.D. 140-160). There are strong reasons to question Pauline authorship, however: the frequent parallels to phrases found elsewhere in the Pauline corpus suggest quotations from Paul by another writer; the elevation of the "holy apostles" as the founders of the church (2:20) contrasts with Paul's occasionally jaundiced view of them (2 Cor. 11:5; 12:11); views stated here contrast with those found in Paul (cf. vv. 5 f., 10 here below); and there is a vocabulary of about 100 words unique to this letter. The view is held here that the letter reflects a response to Paul's epistles. The author's identity is unknown, as also is the audience to which he was writing since the phrase "who are at Ephesus" is lacking from 1:1 in Codex Sinaiticus and Codex Vaticanus (and thus from modern translations).

Our passage opens with the affirmation that God has restored us to life because of the immensity of his love for us, even though we had died because of our sins (2:1-3) by making us to share in Christ's life (vv. 4 f.). V. 5 concludes with a terse recapitulation of this theme. Paul had written often of life "in Christ" (cf. Gal. 2:20; Phil. 3:10 f.; Rom. 6:1-11, etc.), always affirming that such life included being crucified with Christ. That is lacking here.

V. 6 describes the Christian as united with the risen Christ seated on his heavenly throne (cf. 1:20). The verbs here (and in v. 5), compounded with *syn* (with), "alive together," "raised up with," and "sit with," are all aorists. God has already done these things. The Christian is enthroned now beside Christ (a statement not found in other letters usually judged to have been written by Paul). The phrase "in the heavenly places" is applied to the risen Christ (1:20), to people living in this life (2:6), and to supernatural powers (3:10), suggesting that it describes a state of existence before God rather than life in either a future or supramundane realm. V. 7 extends God's display of love toward us into the future. The phrase "the coming ages," which normally in the NT refers to the age after the return of Christ, seems here simply to designate an indefinite future.

Vv. 8 f. return to the theme of the divine initiative in our salvation. When "faith" is defined as belief, we can will ourselves to believe and thus achieve for ourselves the faith by means of which God saves us. V. 8 rejects this possibility. "Faith" itself is given by God. "Trust" (with NEB) thus is a good translation for *pistis* here. All good works enable us to magnify ourselves (v. 9) and thereby diminish the love of God which redeems us precisely when we do not merit it.

V. 10 is striking. The redeemed have been created by God in order to do the good deeds he has prepared. Thus, even though trust in God's love is not divorced from conduct, conduct is as much foreordained by God as is salvation. This contrasts markedly with the responsibility Paul imposes upon the saved (as in Gal. 6:10; Col. 1:10, and, implicitly, in his instructions about conduct throughout his letters).

Gospel: John 3:14-21. The problem of the authorship of sayings attributed to Jesus in the Fourth Gospel is acute in John 3:14-21. These verses seem to be part of Jesus' reply to Nicodemus, yet the shift from the first person singular to first person plural in v. 11, the consistent use of the third person when speaking of the Son of man or the Son (clearly identified as Jesus in this Gospel) in vv. 13-21, and the impression of a post-resurrection perspective throughout encourage the conclusion that this passage is a statement by the evangelist. It will be so treated here.

V. 14 draws a parallel between the elevation of the bronze serpent by Moses (Num. 21:8 f.) and the elevation (*hypsoun*) of Jesus, both of which had salvific results. *Hypsoun* refers to being lifted up upon the cross in John 8:28, but it is used to describe the ascension in Acts 2:33 and 5:31. The Johannine usage of the verb, especially in the light of John 12:32, may include both the resurrection and the ascension. The parallel to Num. 21:8 f. is in the act of being elevated. The serpent is not a "type" for Christ or for his work (as in Barnabas 12:5-7 or in Tertullian, *Against*

Marcion iii 18, where the pole on which the serpent was fastened is a type for the cross). The "eternal life" of vv. 15 f. that is given those who believe in the Son is a quality of existence available now. It is the Johannine equivalent to the term "kingdom of God" in the Synoptic Gospels. It is life lived fully in accordance with God's will and thus as he had created it to be lived. Death was held to be an intrusion into life as intended by God (Paul's statements in 1 Cor. 15:21 f. and Rom. 5:12 are so terse and categorical that they seem to be quotations of widely known Christian aphorisms). Life without end would thus be a part of "eternal life," but only one aspect of it.

V. 16, probably the best known and loved verse in Scripture, opens an exposition of vv. 14 f. in which the themes of the love of God and judgment are intertwined. The verb *agapao* (to love) is used in the Fourth Gospel to describe God's relationship to man (cf. 14:23; 17:23). It is not so used in the Synoptics. The object of the love of God in 3:16 is "the world" which had been created by God through the *logos* (John 1:10). Elsewhere in this Gospel, God is said to love only those who love his Son (John 14:21, 23; 17:23) or, of course, the Son (John 10:17, etc.). The words used in v. 16 to describe God's relationship with his Son recall the story of the sacrifice of Isaac (Gen. 22:2; Tertullian, *Against Marcion* iii 18 declared that Isaac bearing the wood for his own sacrifice was a type of Christ bearing his cross). In both passages, the magnitude of the sacrifice is described by portraying the closeness of the relationship between the father and the son to be killed. Abraham was not divine, but human analogy is used often in Scripture to describe the ineffable God.

God acted because of his love. Therefore his purpose was to save, not to judge (v. 17). The outpouring of divine love was on such a scale, however, that the decision to accept or to reject it is an ultimate decision. Thus God's act of love becomes the occasion for judgment. Those who believe in the gift given in the Son escape condemnation and receive eternal life. Those who reject the Son condemn themselves.

To "believe in him" (vv. 15 f.) seems to be both to share the experience of the presence of the risen Christ and to assent to propositions about him. Those who experience the risen Christ have already entered into the eternal life where the elevated Christ now is.

The description of judgment in vv. 18b-20 is consistent with statements elsewhere in the Gospel. God has turned over the role of judge to his Son (5:22, 27), and the Son's judgments are just (5:30; 8:16). Yet men judge themselves by their response to the Son (12:47 f.). "To judge," especially in Semitic antiquity, included establishing the facts, determining standing before the law, pronouncing sentence, and executing it (cf. Jer. 26:7-19, 24). The Son embodies man's true life before God. Belief in him enables Christians to enter into it. Who, then, has judged those who reject the Son and close off eternal life for themselves?

The polarities of light versus darkness, and doing good versus doing wickedness (vv. 19 f.)—found also in the Dead Sea Scrolls (Manual of Discipline ii, iv)—clarify further the nature of the choice to accept or to reject the Son of man. Those who do wickedness love wickedness. They shun the light that created the world as the *logos* which has returned as the Son (John 1:1-5, 10). Those who "do the truth" (v. 21) come to the light, the source of the truth (cf. 1:4, 9), that their deeds of truth may be seen.

HOMILETICAL INTERPRETATION

In the Gospel for the day we read, "For God sent the Son into the world, not to condemn the world, but that the world might be saved through him" (v. 17). This verse could well serve as the text to sum up the basic themes that run through the three readings for the day. The text assumes that there is reason why God might justly have condemned the world and each of the passages brings out the fact that "men loved darkness rather than light" (v. 19). But even more the readings emphasize that God was not content to let the world drift from him and destroy itself in its darkness. God has continually acted that the world might be saved.

As pointed out in the exegesis, the exodus was the primary divine act in the OT. God acted as the covenant God of the people when he delivered them from out of the degrading slavery into which they had fallen in Egypt. One might hope that the people would be eternally thankful for God's act in delivering them. But alas, that would not have been in keeping with human nature. We forget so quickly the gracious acts of God and his goodness towards us. How quickly, when troubles strike, we complain, "Why did this happen to me?" All of us have our own ideas about how God should govern his universe. And so it is not surprising to find that once delivered from slavery, the people of God began rather quickly to complain about the hardships that they met in freedom. It was not long before some of them wanted to be back with the "fleshpots" of Egypt (Exod. 16:3). In the reading for this day we find that the people were impatient and complained against both God and Moses, their leader.

The writer of Ephesians describes the wondrous gift of salvation that God, in his mercy, has given in Jesus Christ. If the Jews had been delivered from their slavery to the Egyptians, Christians have been delivered from their slavery to sin. One might hope that the Christians would be eternally grateful. When the passage concludes with the words, "For we are his workmanship, created in Christ Jesus for good works, which God prepared beforehand, that we should walk in them," (v. 10) we can only say "Amen!" We who have known the wondrous grace of God in Christ surely ought to give our lives to walking in Christ's spirit and way.

But even as the Jews looked back longingly to the fleshpots of Egypt and complained about God, Christians consistently have failed to walk in the good works for which God has prepared them in Christ. In the NT itself we know that the church was torn with acrimonious debate, back-biting, and unseemly disunity (e.g., see 1 Cor. 1:11-13; Gal. 1:6-7). Gross immorality appeared in the church and was tolerated (1 Cor. 5:1-2). Even among Christians themselves there was a lack of love (e.g., 1 Cor. 6:1-5), and the Lord's Supper became an occasion for a selfish expression of disregard for each other (1 Cor. 11:18-22). Down through history the church has failed miserably to walk in the way prepared for it in Christ. Christians have stained their name with bloody crusades that were fought for no good purpose and included wanton murder, rapine, and theft. They have sided with the exploiters against the exploited. They have supported racial and sexual exploitation. They have persecuted and cast out fellow Christians for difference in doctrine or practice. Truly, as the day's Gospel says, we have loved darkness rather than light.

In all three of our readings, therefore, we are reminded that the behavior of the world has been such that God would have been fully justified if he had simply acted in judgment upon it. But the basic theme of all three readings is that God has never been content to act simply in judgment. God has never desired the destruction of sinful persons, he has always sought their reform and renewal.

In the OT Lesson, the complaints of the people against God result in a plague of poisonous snakes. Surely the ingratitude of the people was such that they deserved what they were getting. But God was not content to let the situation continue. Moses was directed to make a bronze snake that would enable the people to survive the poisonous bites of the living snakes. The marvel of the story is that the only thing required of the people was that they should look at the bronze snake and they would be preserved. Surely, if you or I had been setting the requirements, we would not have let the thankless people off so easily. Most of us would have said, "If you do penance for your ingratitude, if you quit complaining, if you show some thanks, then the bronze serpent will save you." But God did not set up such requirements, the people were delivered simply by looking at the snake.

In the reading from John's Gospel we find a direct comparison drawn between Moses lifting up the bronze snake and the "lifting up" of Christ himself (v. 14). As looking upon the bronze snake saved the Jews from death, so belief in Christ delivers the believer. As the Second Lesson for the day sums it up, "For by grace you have been saved through faith; and this is not your own doing, it is the gift of God. . ." (v. 8). The three readings bear the same message and yet it is a most difficult one for us to accept. How can God let the guilty Jews off by simply looking at the bronze serpent? Why does he not demand first a change in attitudes? How can God's grace bring salvation through faith? Should God not require that people set their lives straight and reform their behavior before they can be saved?

We begin to see God's point when we meditate upon the fact that "God sent the Son into the world, not to condemn the world, but that the world might be saved." God is not primarily interested in punishing or destroying sinners. His primary concern is that sinners be saved. But salvation does not simply mean a rescue from destruction or punishment, it means a new life of fellowship with God. It means entering into the parent-child relationship that God seeks to have with his children. It means that we become so motivated by our love for God who first loved us that we do his will gladly and freely. But if this is God's goal, could any other method achieve it than the one God has chosen?

Let us look again at the situation of the Jews in the wilderness. The threat of death by snake bite would have a powerful motivation upon the people. In fact, it did move them to see a relationship between their sin and the plague of snakes. God had an opportunity to put great pressure upon the people. He could have offered them a bargain whereby those who repented, cleaned up their lives and generally behaved themselves, would be preserved from death by snakebite. But in that case the change in behavior would have been motivated by fear and self-interest alone. The people would not be truly changed, they would not be motivated by love for God. Despite the fact that their behavior might be changed by their fear, they would still be curved in upon themselves. Fear and the desire to escape punishment can do wonders to change outward behavior but it cannot change the inner motivation of the heart. And therefore it cannot bring about the kind of salvation that God desires.

So God makes no bargain with his people. He offers them the bronze serpent, that anyone who looks at it will live. The bronze serpent becomes a concrete symbol of God's forgiving love and concern for his people. No doubt many will accept God's grace with relief to know that they have nothing further to fear from the snakes and so they will continue to grumble against God. The later history of the people makes it clear that sin did not disappear from their midst because of God's grace. But some did truly repent and believe because of God's gracious act. The way of God's grace bringing salvation through faith is not one that will be universally successful. Paul found that people in his time used God's grace as an excuse to sin so that grace might abound (Rom. 6:1). It might even seem that God is taking a rather dangerous gamble in acting with grace rather than punishment and judgment. But the point is that although grace through faith may not always succeed, no other way can ever succeed.

The success that God seeks is never a matter of outward behavior. In our readings for Ash Wednesday we saw that God calls his people to rend their hearts and not their garments. That is, the outward forms of repentance are meaningless if they are not performed for the right reasons. The change of the "heart," that is the inner self of a person, only comes when people are drawn out of themselves by a love that comes from beyond them. In the wilderness the bronze serpent was a symbol of such a love. But the full meaning of love only comes home to us when we realize that "God so loved the world that he gave his only Son, that whoever believes in him should not perish but have eternal life" (John 3:16).

The Fifth Sunday in Lent

Lutheran	*Roman Catholic*	*Episcopal*	*Pres./UCC/Chr.*	*Methodist/COC*
Jer. 31:31-34	Jer. 31:31-34	Jer. 31:31-34	Jer. 31:31-34	Jer. 31:31-34
Heb. 5:7-9	Heb. 5:7-9	Heb. 5:7-9	Heb. 5:7-10	Heb. 5:7-10
John 12:20-33	John 12:20-33	John 12:20-33	John 12:20-33	John 12:20-33

EXEGESIS

First Lesson: Jer. 31:31-34. Jer. 31:31-34, once often judged to be late (and inferior), is now widely held to report faithfully an oracle by Jeremiah even though the words may be those of Baruch, the prophet's secretary and companion.

The phrase "behold, the days are coming" is characteristic of predictions of an indefinite (often eschatological) future. The ejaculation "utterance of Yahweh" repeated in each verse, indicates the prophet's certainty that he is proclaiming God's word and not his own opinion (cf. Jer. 2:2-29; 31:10-20, etc., and cp. 28:5-9). Jeremiah is the herald proclaiming God's "new covenant" with the nation. A covenant was an agreement between two parties which could be entered into by mutual consent (if the parties were equal) or by the imposition by the stronger of his will on the weaker. Often in the OT, God, the stronger, proffers man, the weaker, a covenant in such a way that man is free to accept it or to reject it. Not so here, as will be seen.

The former covenant, based upon the exodus, is described as a marriage contract (v. 32) which had been made null and void by Israel's faithlessness. (Cf. also Jer. 2:2; 3:6-13 where the Lord is pictured as a husband. The AT in v. 32, "so that I had to reject them," translates an emendation based on the Greek and Old Latin. The Hebrew text is intelligible without emendation.)

There is no suggestion in Jer. 31:31-34 that the laws of the old covenant were wrong. The new covenant differs from the old only in that it will be written on the nation's heart, i.e., in the will (cf. the discussion of the heart in the exegesis of Joel 2:12 f. for Ash Wednesday). The new covenant will not have to be taught. No one will have to urge another to obey it.

Jeremiah used the Hebrew root *ydh* (to know) to describe the relationship with God in the new covenant. This root, often used in Hosea (2:20; 4:1, 6; 5:4; 6:6, etc.) and Jeremiah (2:8; 4:22; 9:3, 6; 22:15 f., etc.) also described sexual relationships in marriage (as in Gen. 4:1, 17, 25). It conveyed a sense of intimate, intense, mutual involvement. The Israelites' wills will be so changed by the inauguration of the new covenant given by God that they all will know him without instruction, urging, or punishment. Because they will live in intimate fellowship with him, he will forgive the sins that no longer will alienate them from him.

Jer. 31:31-34 is quoted in Heb. 8:8-12 in a description of the new covenant within which Christ officiates as the heavenly high priest. The term "the new covenant" (Jer. 31:31) appears in the sentences pronounced during the Last Supper as reported by Paul (1 Cor. 11:25).

Second Lesson: Heb. 5:7-9. Even though Christ, the heavenly high priest, is the Son of God (1:2–2:9), he also must be human in order to mediate between God and man (2:11-18; 4:15 f.; 5:1-4). Heb. 5:7-9 is the exposition of the humanity of Christ.

V. 7 refers to the prayer of Christ in the Garden of Gethsemane (Mark 14:34-36 = Matt. 26:39 = Luke 22:42). The phrase "with loud cries and tears" is lacking in the Gospels but may either have been taken from an independent tradition or have been a natural expansion of Jesus' words as reported in Mark 14:34. V. 7 ends with an elliptical clause. The Greek reads, "being heard from (*apo*) his reverence (*eulaleia*)." If the preposition *apo* be given a causative force, the various modern translations result. Since it is the human Christ that is being discussed, the implication of the phrase is that all who pray in reverence (or godly fear) will be heard.

The report of the prayer in Gethsemane in Mark implies that Christ sought to escape his crucifixion. This petition was denied (so v. 8 implies), even though it was a Son of God who prayed. Thus the divine-human Christ learned the obedience required of men and women. There is no suggestion that the human Christ was sinful (cf. 4:15). He participated in our humanity by sharing with us temptation and our need to be obedient to the will of God. The divine-human Christ sharing humanity's finitude contrasts with the impassivity of deity in Greek philosophy, but it would not have been alien to participants in the Hellenistic mystery religions with which Christianity was in competition. As a result of his obedience, Christ is made the agency for man's salvation.

Gospel: John 12:20-33. John 12:20-33 is a decisive turning-point in this Gospel. Prior to v. 23, the time for Jesus' passion had not yet come (John 2:4; 7:30; 8:20). Now it has. The earthly ministry carried on among the Jews is to become the ministry of the risen Christ to all peoples. The passage contains three closely related parts: the report of the interest of Greeks in Jesus (vv. 20-22); sayings about the nature of discipleship to the risen Lord (vv. 23-26); and a description of the means by which Jesus' ministry will become available to all people (vv. 27-32).

The "Greeks" coming to worship in Jerusalem during the Passover (v. 20) may have been "God fearers," non-Jews attracted to the ethical monotheism of Judaism who did not accept fully the demands of the law. Their appearance and their desire to see Jesus indicates that interest in his ministry has broken out of the confines of Judaism. Philip and Andrew are reported as being the intermediaries, possibly because of their Greek names (and Philip's home as reported here), or possibly because both disciples may have been related to a church in Asia Minor in which this Gospel may have been written (i.e., Ephesus. A letter by Polycrates, bishop of Ephesus from 189-198 reports Philip's death in a community near Ephesus, and Andrew is linked with the churches in Asia Minor by Eusebius, *Ecclesiastical History* III i.1).

The Greeks are not mentioned again, and the answer to their request is given only indirectly. Vv. 23-26 describe the circumstances in which Gentiles might "see" Jesus. The Son of man must first die in order to be glorified (v. 24). Then those who wish to see Jesus must surrender themselves to him as fully as he had surrendered himself to the will of God that he be crucified (vv. 25, 26a). Such persons will then become servants of Christ and be where he is (v. 26b). Thus it is the risen Christ whom the Gentiles may see.

"Glory" often has the meaning of reputation or status in the OT (cf. Exod. 33:18 f.; Job 19:9; 1 Chron. 16:29. Cp. Exod. 24:16 where a different meaning is required). A person's reputation is a record of his or her acts. Habitual action discloses one's nature. Thus the glory of the Lord to be revealed in the restoration of the exiles (Isa. 40:5) is his nature as a God of redemptive power because this restoration is like earlier divine acts on behalf of Israel. So here also. Christ's nature (his "glory") cannot be disclosed until he is released by the resurrection to do his work fully. His death must precede his glorification, and Jesus can move toward this now that Greeks have become interested in him. In this Gospel, Jesus cannot have been crucified without his consent (John 10:18).

The aphorism in v. 24 may have been intended to refer both to Jesus and to his followers. It has no parallel in the Synoptics (but cf. 1 Cor. 15:36). The saying in v. 25 has parallels in Mark 8:35 = Matt. 10:39; 16:25 = Luke 9:24; 17:33, although the settings and the words used differ. The point being made is the same in all, however. Complete surrender to Jesus and to the way of his cross is opposed to the cultivation of one's own life in this world. The outcome of devotion to Christ is "eternal life." "Life (*psyche*, here equivalent to the Hebrew *nephesh*) in this world" is placed over against "eternal life" (*zoen aionion*), just as "loving" contrasts with "hating," and "losing" with "keeping." V. 26b lacks any parallel in the Synoptics, but note Eph. 2:6 (cf. the exegesis of the Second Lesson for Lent 4).

V. 27 opens with an echo of the scene in Gethsemane reported in the Synoptics. Here, the hint of the struggle of the earthly Jesus against his approaching death becomes the occasion for a statement of Jesus' complete acceptance of his role. He prays for God to act rather than to escape from the crucifixion. One's name epitomized one's essence. For God to glorify his name is for him to act wholly in character, i.e., to do that upon which the redemption of mankind depends. The divine answer is the assurance that God has so acted (in Jesus' ministry) and will again so act (in Jesus' passion, resurrection, and ascension).

Vv. 29 f. record a typical Johannine device. Responding to the reactions of the onlookers becomes the means by which a clarification of meaning is given. Thunder was regarded as the voice of God in Jewish tradition (cf. Exod. 19:19!). If the comment attributed to the people present be read in the light of this tradition, Jesus' reply (v. 30) becomes the means by which his standing before God is doubly affirmed. Jesus did not need a divine attestation to himself, but the people did need to be persuaded of his standing before God.

John 12:20-31 reaches its climax in the two declarations in vv. 31 f. V. 31 is the mirror image of v. 32. The hour has come (v. 23). The iterative emphasis of "now is . . . now is . . ." in English translations of v. 31 is a faithful rendition of the Greek. The judgment (*krisis*: decision or judgment) is in contrapuntal actions by God: the expulsion of the Evil One who rules this age (a divine being over against God; cf. John 8:44; 13:27; 14:30; 2 Cor. 4:4, etc.), and the elevation of Christ (*hypsoun*; cf. the exegesis of John 3:14 in the Gospel for Lent 5). The repudiation of life in this world and the choice of eternal life (vv. 25 f.) is the human response to those divine acts. In v. 33, the evangelist makes it clear that he has been speaking about the crucifixion. Other methods of execution, such as stoning, would not have been described as being lifted up.

HOMILETICAL INTERPRETATION

We are moving through Lent and are coming closer to Palm Sunday, Holy Week, Good Friday, and Easter. It is fitting, therefore, that the readings for this day direct our thoughts to the new covenant that is ushered in by the life, death, and resurrection of Jesus. The word "testament" means "covenant," so the division of the Bible into Old and New Testament is a witness to the importance of the concept of the covenant relationship between God and his people. As the exegesis points out, the concept of a new covenant probably originated with this passage from Jeremiah.

The new covenant is not completely different from the old and certainly it does not contradict it. Jesus said that he had come to fulfill and not destroy the law (Matt. 5:17). In a similar way the new covenant is the fulfillment of the old. The covenant began when God called Abraham to be the father of a people through whom all nations would be blessed (Gen. 12:1-3). It was confirmed and renewed when God delivered his people from slavery in Egypt, gave them his commandments, brought them to the promised land and rescued them from the exile. Jeremiah likens the covenant relationship between God and his people to the covenant relationship of a man and wife (v. 32). But, Jeremiah notes, Israel has been an unfaithful spouse in its marriage relationship to God.

When a marriage has been broken by the unfaithfulness of one of the parties there may be a renewal of the marriage. If the injured party is willing to forgive and the guilty party is willing to accept forgiveness a new relationship may come about. In one sense it is the same marriage as before, but because of the lessons that have been learned, because costly forgiveness has been extended and received, the marriage relationship has been put upon a new level. Jeremiah has such an analogy in mind as he speaks of the new covenant that God will make with his people. God, the injured party, is prepared to forgive so that the covenant relationship can be renewed.

The full nature of the new covenant, of course, cannot be found in Jeremiah. Although Jeremiah heard God's promise that there would be a new covenant, the full implications of it could not be seen until after the life, death, and resurrection of Christ. Nonetheless, Jeremiah has some important clues that we can see fulfilled in Christ.

First, Jeremiah says that God will write the laws upon the hearts of the people. This, of course, is contrasted with the old covenant in which the laws were written on tablets of stone. Under the old covenant God's laws were given by God's gracious love as the way in which the people could respond to God in the covenant relationship. But when the people became unfaithful to God they came to see the law as something over against them, a demand that had to be fulfilled. As we saw in the discussion of the readings for the Third Sunday in Lent, the laws came to be seen as a barrier between God and his people rather than a means of communication.

By the time of Jesus it was all too apparent that the law had become a burden that divided the people from both God and each other. Many of the people seem to have given up hope of ever keeping the law. They were the sinners and outcasts of Jesus' society with whom he mixed so freely. Others, however, were doing a pretty good job of keeping the law in comparison with the "sinners." As a result, they were filled with pride and thanked God that they were not like their sinful neighbors (Luke 18:9-14). To such a situation the promise of the new covenant is a promise that the law will not be seen as an external command to be fulfilled in order to make oneself righteous. Instead, the people will be filled with a desire to do God's will. This happens when Jesus is lifted up on the cross and draws people to himself (John 12:32). The love of God revealed in the death of Christ moves the hearts of people to an answering love. In this relationship there is a true desire to do that which will please God. The law is written on their hearts. Jeremiah foresaw that this desire to keep the law would arise out of a relationship in which "I will be their God, and they shall be my people" (v. 33). We see this relationship established through Christ and his work.

The second clue that Jeremiah gives is that in the new covenant "no longer shall each man teach his neighbor. . ." (v. 34). There would seem to be two implications in this. First, it implies that in the new covenant there shall be no elite group who are experts in the faith and have the duty of passing it on to others. It is not for the clergy, the theologians, or the elect to go out and "save souls." It is God himself who shall make himself known. As Luther put it in his Small Catechism, "I believe that by my own reason or strength I cannot believe in Jesus Christ, my Lord, or come to him. But the Holy Spirit has called me through the Gospel, enlightened me with his gifts, and sanctified and perserved me in true faith, just as he calls, gathers, enlightens and sanctifies the whole Christian church on earth and preserves it in union with Jesus Christ in the one true faith." This comes about because, as we read in the Hebrews' passage, Christ has become our "high priest" (v. 10). The priest is one who mediates between God and the people and so Christ has become the mediator between God and his people.

In the second place, the absence of one person teaching another has implications about the relationship to the will of God. Where the law is seen as a barrier to be overcome to get to God, it results in judgment of others. Because we have kept the law to some degree we thank God that we are not like those who have not done so well in keeping the law. When we take it upon ourselves to teach the law to another there is an implicit implication of judgment. We are the ones who have and keep the law and those we teach are lesser breeds without the law. Luther says that everyone who is apart from Christ ends up passing judgment upon others. Perhaps so, because if we feel that we have to earn our way to God by being righteous, we need some evidence that we are passing the test. Since none of us can claim perfection, the best evidence that we can usually get for our own righteousness is to find someone who is less righteous than ourselves. We look around with a critical eye at our neighbors so that we can assure ourselves that we are not too bad. On the other hand, when we know that we stand before God because of his goodness and not because of our own, we dare to see that we are fellow sinners with our neighbors. We are not in the position to cast the first stone.

This leads us to the third clue that Jeremiah gives us about the new covenant. The law shall be in people's hearts and one shall not have to teach his neighbor because God promises "I will forgive their iniquity, and I will remember their sin no more" (v. 34). This is a wondrous promise. In human relationships we do sometimes forgive those who have injured us. But all too often we do not forget what has been forgiven and we do not let the forgiven party forget it either. As a result, the misdeed hangs like the skeleton in the closet, it remains a barrier between us. Worst of all, we remember the forgiven act so that we can use it as a lever at some future date when we shall work upon the gratitude of the forgiven ones so that we can bend them to our will. God's forgiveness is not of that kind. When we are forgiven the sin is forgotten, it is past and obliterated.

In the new covenant we are shown that forgiving and forgetting is a costly process. The short passage from Hebrews brings to mind in a few words the agony that Jesus experienced in Gethsemane. To be the high priest that mediates between God and his people, Jesus had to learn obedience through what he suffered (v. 8). In the Gospel we see the same thing, as Jesus indicates that his soul is troubled (v. 27). He does not even know how to pray. Shall he ask to be delivered from this hour? No, it is for this hour that he has been sent. And so he anticipates his being raised upon the cross. Salvation may be free, but it is not cheap.

Throughout Lent our assigned readings have reminded us of God's covenant relationship with his people. Because God loved us he sought for us. He entered into the covenant relationship which we have broken time and time again. But God did not give up on us. As Karl Barth says, we may give up on God and become atheist but God never gives up on us and becomes ahumanist. And so it is that to those who have failed to keep the old covenant there comes the promise of a new covenant. We stand today in the new covenant, remembering that it was instituted by the sacrifices of God in Christ. The church exists today, the people of God, as a fulfillment of Christ's promise: "and I, when I am lifted up from earth, will draw all men to myself" (v. 32).

PROCLAMATION:

Aids for Interpreting the Lessons of the Church Year

HOLY WEEK

William C. McFadden
and
Reginald H. Fuller

PROCLAMATION:

Aids for Interpreting the
Lessons of the Church Year

HOLY WEEK

SERIES B

William C. McFadden
and
Reginald H. Fuller

FORTRESS PRESS Philadelphia, Pennsylvania

Library of Congress Catalog Card Number 74-24932

ISBN 0-8006-4074-8

4698C75 Printed in U.S.A. 1-4074

General Preface

Proclamation: Aids for Interpreting the Lessons of the Church Year is a series of twenty-six books designed to help clergymen carry out their preaching ministry. It offers exegetical interpretations of the lessons for each Sunday and many of the festivals of the church year, plus homiletical ideas and insights.

The basic thrust of the series is ecumenical. In recent years the Episcopal church, the Roman Catholic church, the United Church of Christ, the Christian Church (Disciples of Christ), the United Methodist Church, the Lutheran and Presbyterian churches, and also the Consultation on Church Union have adopted lectionaries that are based on a common three-year system of lessons for the Sundays and festivals of the church year. *Proclamation* grows out of this development, and authors have been chosen from all of these traditions. Some of the contributors are parish pastors; others are teachers, both of biblical interpretation and of homiletics. Ecumenical interchange has been encouraged by putting two persons from different traditions to work on a single volume, one with the primary responsibility for exegesis and the other for homiletical interpretation.

Despite the high percentage of agreement between the traditions, both in the festivals that are celebrated and the lessons that are appointed to be read on a given day, there are still areas of divergence. Frequently the authors of individual volumes have tried to take into account the various textual traditions, but in some cases this has proved to be impossible; in such cases we have felt constrained to limit the material to the Lutheran readings.

The preacher who is looking for "canned sermons" in these books will be disappointed. These books are one step removed from the pulpit: they explain what the lessons are saying and suggest ways of relating this biblical message to the contemporary situation. As such they are springboards for creative thought as well as for faithful proclamation of the word.

The authors of this *Holy Week - Series B* volume of *Proclamation* are William C. McFadden and Reginald H. Fuller. Dr. McFadden, the editor-homiletician, is a member of the Society of Jesus and Associate Professor in the Department of Theology, Georgetown University, Washington, D.C. He is a graduate of Woodstock College, Woodstock, Md. (B.A.), Bellarmine College, Plattsburgh, N.Y. (Ph.L), and Fordham University, New York (M.A.). He studied theology at College St.-Albert-de-Louvain, Belgium (S.T.L.), in Muenster, Germany, and at the Gregorian University in Rome (S.T.D.). Dr. McFadden has served as chairman of the Department of Theology at Georgetown University since 1966. Much of his preaching experience comes from his association with Holy Trinity parish in Washington. Dr. Fuller, the exegete, is Professor of New Testament, Virginia Theological Seminary, Alexandria, Va. He is a native of England and a graduate of Cambridge University (B.A., M.A.). He served parishes in England and taught in colleges in England and Wales prior to coming to the United States in 1955. From 1955-66 he was Professor of New Testament Literature and Languages, Seabury-Western Theological Seminary, Evanston, Ill., and from 1966-72 he was Baldwin Professor of Sacred Literature, Union Theological Seminary, New York. Dr. Fuller is a prolific author and translator. His most recent work, which is directly related to this present volume, is entitled *Preaching the New Lectionary* (Collegeville, Minn.: The Liturgical Press).

Table of Contents

The Sunday of the Passion, Palm Sunday

utheran	*Roman Catholic*	*Episcopal*	*Pres./UCC/Chr.*	*Methodist/COCU*
ech. 9:9-12	Isa. 50:4-7	Zech. 9:9-12	Zech. 9:9-12	Zech. 9:9-12
hil. 2:5-11	Phil. 2:6-11	Phil. 2:5-11	Heb. 12:1-6	Phil. 2:5-11
ark 15:1-39	Mark 15:1-39	Mark 14:32—15:39	Mark 11:1-11	Matt. 26:14—27:66

EXEGESIS

First Lesson: Zech. 9:9-12. Chapters 9-14 of Zechariah consist of a collection of messianic prophecies quite distinct from the prophecies of the first part of the book. These latter chapters formed an important quarry for the primitive church in its search for material for its passion apologetic, an apologetic which sought to answer the questions: Why should Jesus have suffered? How, if he suffered, could he be the Messiah?

Today's reading combines two quite distinct messianic prophecies. The first (vv. 9-10) pictures the messianic king as a man of peace, whereas in vv. 11-17 he is depicted as a warrior. By stopping at v. 12 our selection plays down this contrast and allows us to read vv. 4-11 in the light of Jesus' entry to Jerusalem on Palm Sunday and vv. 11-12 in the light of his redemptive death ("my blood-of-the-covenant," Mark 14:24) on Good Friday. It thus covers both the minor (except for the Pres./UCC/Chr. Ch. lectionary, where it is the sole theme) and major theme of this day. In v. 11b the captives were for the original author the exiles in Babylon after 586 B.C. In the Christian interpretation they stand for all men under the bondage of sin. The stronghold (v. 12a) in the original text meant the earthly Jerusalem. In the Christian interpretation it becomes the heavenly Jerusalem, the kingdom of God.

The Roman Catholic selection (Isa. 50:4-7) is the second of the four servant songs, which recurs in sequence in Wednesday in Holy Week and is commented upon there.

Second Lesson: Phil. 2:5-11. This passage occurs every year and so was commented upon in *Proclamation* last year. For many reasons vv. 6-11 are regarded by most contemporary exegetes as an early Christian hymn which the apostle has utilized and commented upon. The immediate context is an exhortation to humility (v. 5). Among the reasons for supposing that the hymn is pre-Pauline we may note its rhythmic character, its concern with basic kerygmatic affirmations, the large number of un-Pauline words (this disposes of the common British view that it was a hymn composed earlier by the apostle himself) like "form," "equality," "a thing to be grasped," (or, as we should translate it, "a thing to be clung to"), "in human form," "highly exalted." Note, too, that the apostle continues to quote from the hymn after it has ceased to be relevant to his immediate purpose: he passes beyond the humiliation of the Christ to his exaltation.

Despite the general agreement that it is in verse form, the division of the hymn into lines and stanzas is much controverted and affects the interpretation. Some divide it into two stanzas and interpret the first stanza to refer exclusively to the earthly life of Jesus, the second to his exaltation. We prefer a four-stanza division which would yield the pattern pre-existence and incarnation—incarnate life—exaltation—final triumph:

I

(Christ Jesus) who though he was in the form of God
did not regard equality with him a thing to be clung to,
but emptied himself
and took a bond-slave's form.

II

So he was born like any other man
and in his human mode of existence
he humbled himself
and became obedient to death (yes, a death on a cross).

III

Consequently God exalted him higher (than all the powers)
and gave him the name
which is above every name,

IV

that in the name of Jesus
every knee should bow
and every tongue confess
"Jesus is Messiah and Lord."

In this four-fold division stanza I covers the pre-existent life of the Redeemer as the divine Wisdom, enjoying a mode of existence like that of God himself. Wisdom, however, did not cling to this status, but divested itself of it and became incarnate in Jesus, being subject like all men to the onslaughts of the powers of evil. Stanza II: in this human mode of existence, however, the incarnate wisdom reversed the human situation by refusing to succumb to the powers (unlike Adam) and lived a life of complete obedience maintained to the point of death (Paul adds as a gloss, that this death was a death on a cross; for the cross is not merely the exit of wisdom from this world and its return to eternity, but the culmination of the incarnate One's obedience). Stanza III: the exaltation and enthronement of Christ affirm the efficacy of the incarnate One's obedience and death on a cross; they do not cancel them out or relegate them to the past. Stanza IV: the final goal of his enthronement is that the exalted One should be acknowledged by all the cosmic powers as Messiah and Kyrios, universally recognized for what he has become as a result of his obedience unto the death of the cross.

Heb. 12:1-6 (Pres./UCC/Chr. Ch.) contains in summary form the same christological pattern of humiliation/exaltation, but develops the parenesis in a different direction. Instead of an exhortation to humility, it leads into an exhortation to perseverance and endurance. Hebrews envisages a community or a group within a community which has become bored and tired with the Christian life.

Gospel: Mark 15:1-39. Since the form of the passion story is that of a continuous narrative rather than a series of isolated units strung together, it does some violence to its literary form when only a section of it is read. Note that the Episcopal reading runs from the arrest to the death; that is the earliest form. Later the narrative was extended backward to start from the plot of the Sanhedrin (Mark 15:1). The episodes covered in today's selection are: the trial before Pilate, the release of Barabbas, the mockery, the *via dolorosa*, the crucifixion and accompanying incidents, the death of Jesus, and the centurion's confession. The passion narrative, though it allows the outline of the story to be reconstructed, was designed primarily to express the following kerygmatic truths: (1) that Jesus died as Messiah; (2) that he died for our sins; (3) that he died in accordance with the scriptures (1 Cor. 15:3-4). Of these points (1) is expressed in the trial scene and in the *titulus*; (2) does not figure in the body of the narrative but is confined to the cup word at the supper (a restraint that increases our confidence in the historicity of the main outline); (3) is expressed in a number of details in the passion story (the wine mingled with myrrh, the dividing of the garments, the cry from the cross, etc.) It is always a moot point whether the OT prophecies have created the particular incident or whether the incident has led to search for the prophecy. But these considerations affect the peripheral details, hardly the central core of events. This basic outline may be summarized as follows: Jesus was sentenced to crucifixion by the Roman authorities, to whom the Jewish authorities had handed him over as a messianic pretender. He carried his cross to the scene of his execution (Simon of Cyrene is probably adduced as an eyewitness, his two sons being known very likely to the community where Mark wrote). There Jesus was executed with two criminals (perhaps Zealot guerrillas), and died a premature death. Thus far we have noted the original history and its development in the tradition. Finally there is the evangelist's redaction. This can be seen in the wording of the centurion's comment on Jesus' death: "Truly, this was the Son of God." The christological title, Son of God, plays an important role in the structure of Mark. It occurs (probably, though the text is uncertain) at Mark 1:1, at the baptism, and at the transfiguration. In the first part of the Gospel it remains a secret known only to Jesus himself and the demons. It is disclosed to the inner group of disciples at the transfiguration but they are silenced until after the passion. Then it is finally revealed to the Gentile centurion at the foot of the cross. Mark is telling his readers that Jesus can be confessed as Son of God only as the crucified One. To call him Son of God does not mean that (as people were saying in Mark's church) he was merely a miracle worker or "divine man," i.e., an epiphany of the divine. The title refers not to Jesus' "divinity" considered as an abstraction, but concretely to the saving act which God has wrought in him.

HOMILETICAL INTERPRETATION

In the gospel narrative of the passion, first the story of Jesus is told, then the teller of the story gives his comment. It is suggested in today's exegetical notes that Mark's comment on Jesus' death is contained in the cry wrung from the lips of the centurion: "Truly, this was the Son of God."

The homilist may profitably dwell on this process since it is the same sort of process which is taking place between him and his hearers. Like the evangelist he is telling the story of Jesus and adding to it his own comment. It is of paramount importance that he not overlook this aspect of his role in the liturgy. He is not simply to bear the Book in solemn procession and read from it to his congregation. He is not simply to explain some difficult passages. He must make his own personal comment on the sacred text. He must take a position with respect to it. He must also point out to his hearers that they are under the same obligation of adding their personal comment to the biblical word (and to the word of the homilist!). Only in this way are they truly hearers of the word.

There is, of course, another possible order. When the readings are very lengthy, or when for any other reason less time is available for the homily, it can be a very effective move for the homilist if he makes some remarks *prior* to the reading of the sacred text. This serves to orient the mind of the listener to certain key ideas and helps him to hold together a long reading.

In fact, even on ordinary days this method may open up the word of God so that it speaks directly and with added power to a congregation which has in this fashion been prepared ahead of time to hear it. Too often congregations are forced to sit patiently through readings which they cannot easily follow. This puts the homilist in the position of having to explain the texts before proceeding to the homily itself.

The selection from Philippians is a good example of a homilist taking the story of Jesus and applying it to the lives of his people. Paul is writing to a church he dearly loved. He wanted them to do all in their power to remain united with a common purpose and a common mind. That, he tells them, is the one thing that would make him completely happy. He wanted them to avoid self-glorification and conceit. They were to think always of the good of others first. That is how Paul pictured life in the ideal Christian community.

How was he to motivate them to this self-forgetful way of living? His answer is to take the story of Christ and focus on the first part of it, the downward movement that begins with the exalted state of the pre-existent Christ, proceeds through various stages of humiliation, and finally climaxes in his pitiable death on the cross. This whole downward movement was not thrust on him. He chose it. Though enjoying equality with God, he emptied himself out completely and utterly. This self-emptying disposition is characteristic of the mind of Christ Jesus and the Philippians are exhorted to put on this same mind and let it re-fashion the way they live with one another.

Today's reading from Zechariah weaves together two messianic themes, the greatness of the royal descendant of David and the lowliness of the One through whom Yahweh brings about salvation and universal peace. The result is a strong paradox which is only intensified by employing these verses on Passion Sunday. At the beginning of the solemn commemoration of Jesus' final days on earth, we are invited to rejoice and shout with gladness. A king arrives in Jerusalem. He is triumphant and victorious. And yet he does not ride in on a warlike steed, but on a simple donkey, and his victory in war is a victory over war. By passing through war he establishes peace.

The acceptance of Jesus on Sunday with waving palm branches and hosannas is contrasted sharply with the rejection he received a few days later. It is worth noting that it is not simply a case of Jesus having to undergo suffering. You can suffer as a hero, receiving great admiration and support. The rejection robs his passion of any halo of earthly glory. It is suffering without honor. The cross means death as a despised reject. Those like Peter who refused the whole notion of his being destined to suffer grievously (Mark 8:33), ended up fleeing into the night, leaving him alone. This is not the kind of Lord they wanted.

This is suggestive of the various paradoxes of the passion: Jesus walks through sorrow to attain the joy of heaven, experiences rejection to enter into glory, endures suffering to come to eternal rest, undergoes death to pass over to life.

These paradoxes have become too familiar to our ears. We need someone to help us feel again the sense of shock at the reversal of human standards they embody. Only in a flow of words does someone glibly pass "through death to life." If a homilist can properly evoke the reality of death, its darkness, its helplessness, its apparent finality, he may re-awaken in us the sense of this mystery of faith: how strange and unlikely that this should lead to that, that the path to death is the path to life!

In evoking a sense of the reality of death, the homilist may find some help in Tom Stoppard's play *Rosencrantz and Guildenstern Are Dead*. In it the leader of an acting troupe remarks that the only kind of death audiences believe in is melodramatic stage death. One time an actor in his troupe was condemned to hang for stealing a sheep so the leader got permission to have him hanged during the play. It was a disaster. The man just was not convincing. He did nothing but cry all the time. The audience jeered at him and threw peanuts, but he just stood there and cried.

Rosencrantz observes that there must have been a moment when it first became clear to each of us that we were not going to live forever. It must have been a shattering moment, one that is stamped indelibly in one's memory—and yet he cannot recall it. Maybe we are born knowing we are going to die, or maybe we cannot allow ourselves to realize that fact.

The exegetical notes recall the problem of the early Christian apologetic: If Jesus suffered, how could he be the Messiah? We are not dealing here with a simple paradox, but with a grave scandal. How can this be the Messiah?

The scandal continues to our day. We are too used to the idea of a suffering Messiah to feel the original scandal. Perhaps another scandal strikes closer to home for us: If Jesus is the Messiah, if he is the one foretold by Zechariah, then what of the promise that "the bow of war will be banished"? If he is the one to proclaim peace for the nations, why do wars still rage and grow in virulence? Why do we live under the present possibility that one mad day of war could obliterate mankind from the face of the earth?

The homilist should face this scandal squarely, or better locate the proper source of the scandal. It is not so scandalous that God's anointed one should suffer and thus enter into his glory. It is not so shocking, to use the imagery in today's second reading, that one who was in the form of God should give up that exalted rank and take the form of a slave, or even that he would humble himself, obediently accepting death on a cross. The real scandal is that we have been so monumentally slow to heed the admonition Paul attaches to these words: "Your attitude must be Christ's." The truly shocking thing is that we are so persistent in refusing to act like people who have been redeemed, whose lives have been purchased at such a great price.

The second reading in the Pres./UCC/Chr. Ch. lectionary is the solemn climax in a litany of heroes of faith. The author of the Epistle to the Hebrews is trying to exhort his readers to perseverance in the face of difficulties. His strategy is to go through the list of biblical ancestors who in one way or another make his point: "Only faith can guarantee the blessings that we hope for, or prove the existence of the realities that at present remain unseen" (Heb. 11:1). He invokes the memory of Abraham and Jacob and Moses and so many others. "These were men who through faith conquered kingdoms, did what is right and earned the promises. They were weak people who were given strength to be brave in war and drive back foreign invaders" (Heb. 11:33-34).

Jesus is the final example, the one who is our leader in faith and who brings faith to perfection. There is a very significant phrase used here, which gains added force by reading this passage on Passion Sunday, as we stand at the beginning of Holy Week. The author does not simply exalt the quality of Jesus' faith, or praise his courage in putting up with the opposition of his enemies. We read that Jesus endured the cross "for the sake of the joy which was still in the future" (Heb. 12:2).

This recalls the parable of the man who found a treasure hidden in a field and who with great joy goes off and sells everything he owns in order to possess it (Matt. 13:44). The joy he looks forward to is so great he thinks nothing of giving up all he owns to possess it.

The homilist may choose to use this theme of joy to set a tone for the whole of the passion. All the heroes of faith were persons who drew strength and courage from a joy they hoped for. The victory they reached for was still unseen but they were firm in their conviction that it would be theirs.

So Jesus, as he enters the time of his passion, is fortified by faith to remain firm. But his faith gives him strength and courage because it is an unshakable conviction of the joy that is in his future according to the promise of the faithful God.

Monday in Holy Week

.utheran	Roman Catholic	Episcopal	Pres./UCC/Chr.	Methodist/COCU
sa. 42:1-9	Isa. 42:1-7	Isa. 42:1-7	Isa. 50:4-10	Isa. 42:1-9
Ieb. 9:11-15		Heb. 11:39—12:3	Heb. 9:11-15	Heb. 9:11-15
ohn 12:1-11	John 12:1-11	John 12:1-11 or Mark 14:3-9	Luke 19:41-48	John 12:1-11

EXEGESIS

First Lesson: Isa. 42:1-9. The first four verses of today's reading form the first servant song (the other songs, all read this week, are 49:1-6; 50:4-9; and 52:13–53:12).

The servant songs raise two main problems: (1) Their origin. Were they by Deutero-Isaiah himself, were they earlier compositions, or were they subsequent additions to the text? They stand out clearly from their surrounding context. It is most likely that Deutero-Isaiah took them over as preformed materials since he offers his own comments on them, and these comments are consistent with his theology as a whole. (2) Who is the figure of the servant? Many suggestions have been made. Those who think that he is an individual figure identify him variously with the prophet himself, with some other prophet, with a historical Hebrew king of the past, or with a future messianic king. Others regard the servant as a corporate symbol standing either for Israel as a whole, or for an ideal remnant. The trouble is that the servant songs seem to differ among themselves as to the individual or corporate character of the servant. Whatever the servant's original identity, for Christian faith the figure of the servant comes ultimately to rest in Jesus of Nazareth. There is still one remaining problem. Did Jesus in his lifetime identify himself with the servant? Did he take it as the inspiration or blueprint for his mission? Such was the prevailing opinion until quite recently. Now the identification is seen to be rather the result of the christological development of the post-Easter church—very early, but still not the earliest Christology. Read consecutively (and for this reason it is regrettable that the Pres./UCC/Chr. Ch. lectionary has departed from the consecutive order) the four servant songs cover the career of Jesus from his baptism to his death and subsequent vindication.

The first servant song (Isa.42:1-4) speaks of the servant's call and his endowment with the Spirit for his role in salvation history (v. 1). It then proceeds to characterize his activity (vv. 2-4a) and the goal of his career (v. 4b). The pre-Marcan tradition already saw v. 1 as a model for narrating Jesus' baptism and Matthew later saw in vv. 2-4a a prophecy of his ministry (Matt. 12:18-21) as characterized by the messianic secret. It is the whole preceding ministry of Jesus, from his baptism to his arrest, his proclamation of the inbreaking of God's eschatological reign, his call of the disciples to follow him, his eating with the outcasts, his exorcisms and healings, that provide a structure and meaning for the cross. There were hundreds of crosses in first century Palestine. This cross is different. It has saving significance only because of Jesus' prior self-understanding and his activity which expressed his self-understanding and intentionality. That is why this first of the servant songs comes fittingly on the first weekday of Holy Week.

The Pres./UCC/Chr. Ch. reads the third servant song today. For comment see Wednesday in Holy Week.

Second Lesson: Heb. 9:11-15. This is the core of the central argument of Hebrews, which runs from 7:1—10:25. Point by point the author builds up his case for the use of "high priest" as a title for Christ and as a framework in which to describe his redemptive work. In doing so he has provided a point by point comparison of the two priesthoods, Christ's and the Levitical. Now he sums up his conclusions in a succinct declaration. Christ as high priest entered once into the holy place, i.e., into heaven, taking with him his own blood, his life surrendered unto death. The effect of his work is to secure for mankind an eternal redemption, further defined as purging our conscience from dead works (=sins), to serve (the Greek word for "serve" is a cultic word, meaning worship) the living God.

The importance of this passage is that it indicates that the redemptive work of Christ upon the cross, his sacrifice, is a work which is of abiding efficacy. It is a work, as the writer so strongly emphasizes, which was accomplished "once for all" in a decisive moment of the past. Christ still applies his atoning for us and our salvation. Charles Wesley based one of his great eucharistic hymns on this passage:

O thou before the world began
Ordained a sacrifice for man,
And by the eternal Spirit made
An offering in the sinner's stead;
Our everlasting Priest art thou,
Pleading thy death for sinners now.

Thy offering still continues now
Before the righteous Father's view;
Thyself the lamb forever slain,
Thy priesthood doth unchanged remain;
Thy years, O God, can never fail,
Nor thy blest work within thy veil.

The Episcopal selection is less weighty doctrinally (Heb. 9:11-15 occurs on Wednesday). It consists of the conclusion of the great passage on the OT heroes of the faith and the exhortation to look to Jesus (see Pres./UCC/Chr. Ch. Second Lesson for Passion Sunday).

Gospel: John 12:1-11. On the Johannine dating the anointing takes place the Saturday before Holy Week. In Mark-Matthew it takes place early in Holy Week, hence its use today. This story presents a tangled series of problems in synoptic relationships and in the history of tradition. It exists in no less than three different forms in the Gospels (Mark-Matt., Luke, John). Here we can only say that in our view the Johannine version is independent of the other two but that there has been an intertwining of traditions of two basically different stories. John's version, like Luke's, represents a combination of the story of a penitent woman who wetted the feet of Jesus with her tears and wiped them with her hair, and a quite different story of a woman who anointed Jesus.[1] Several different interpretations of these actions have been given in the various traditions. In John the following interpretative motives are apparent: (1) The great extravagance of Mary's action. This extravagance is indicated by the statement that the fragrance of the ointment filled the whole house. The suggestion that this is an allegorical expression of the universality of the gospel (Hoskyns) is not convincing. (2) The theme of the poor is accentu-

1. See R. E. Brown, *The Gospel according to John*, Vol. 1 (New York: Doubleday, 1964), *ad loc.*

ated by the intervention of Judas. (3) The nuancing of the theme of Jesus burial by the curious statement that the woman is to keep "it" (the ointment?). If so, how could she perform this extravagant act?

The real problem is, what did the evangelist intend by including the story of the anointing at this point? The only place where his hand can be clearly traced is in the cross-reference to Lazarus in vv. 1-2 and in the identification of Mary with Lazarus' sister. Clearly for him the anointing has some connection with that episode. Is it just that the same people and the same locale are involved, or is it some theological connection between the raising of Lazarus and the anointing? Probably the latter. The evangelist is telling us that the Jesus who raised Lazarus from the dead was in that very act proclaimed to be the resurrection and the life precisely because he was also the one whose day of burial was at hand, the one whom they would not have with them always as they would have the poor. Therefore Jesus is the resurrection and the life only because he himself died and was buried, and so glorified.

The Episcopal alternative Gospel reading (Mark 14:3-9) is the Marcan version of the anointing. Note that this version is uncontaminated by the other story of the penitent woman who wetted the feet of Jesus with her tears and wiped them with her hair. The two motifs of the poor and the anointing for the burial appear here and are again traditional. The Marcan redaction is to be seen in v. 9 (there is a growing consensus that the word "gospel" in Mark is always redactional). Mark is saying that the woman's action, pointing as it does (according to the tradition) to the burial of Jesus, calls attention to an essential aspect of the gospel. Jesus is not just a divine man or wonderworker. He is the crucified one whose crucifixion is constantly re-presented in the kerygma, and along with it the woman's action as a witness to his burial.

The Pres./UCC/Chr. Ch. Gospel reading (Luke 19:41-48) is the continuation of the Lucan version of the Palm Sunday entry (chosen for today despite the fact that the *Marcan* version was the Pres./UCC/Chr. Ch. reading yesterday). It consists of two episodes, Jesus' weeping over Jerusalem and the cleansing of the temple. Both emphasize that Jesus comes to Jerusalem to fling down the gauntlet of his final challenge to his people at the center of the national and religious life. This—rather than any theological purpose (e.g., to die as an atoning sacrifice)—was the historical intention of Jesus in his last journey to Jerusalem.

HOMILETICAL INTERPRETATION

Today's texts reflect various attempts to find language to express the mystery of the passing over of Jesus to his Father.

The passage from John's Gospel focuses on the body of Jesus, which the evangelist has earlier described as the sanctuary of the new temple (2:21). The anointing of Jesus' feet is a foreshadowing of the preparation of his body for burial, the last sorrowful gestures with which his loved ones will consign him to the grave. There is sadness in Jesus' words, sadness not because of foreseen suffering, but because of the coming separation from those he loved. Those who watched him in action and heard his words knew of his deep affection for the poor. But this is not the time to think of their needs. These are his last days with them: "You will not always have me" (12:8).

In such a critical time Mary knew the right thing to do. This is the same Mary who on another occasion was praised by Jesus for having chosen the better part when she sat down at his feet and listened to him, and let her sister Martha bustle about in the kitchen doing less important things (cf. Luke 10:38-42).

The Episcopal alternate reading is Mark's account of the anointing of Jesus at Bethany. The woman is not identified as Mary and she pours the precious ointment over Jesus' head (not on his feet, as in John). Jesus' speech is somewhat longer, and emphasizes the extraordinary sensitivity of the woman to the significance of the moment. Though others became indignant over the waste (in Mark Judas is not the culprit) and were upsetting her with their grumbling, the woman had followed her heart. She took ointment worth nearly a year's salary and poured it all out in a gesture of unrestrained generosity. Jesus sides with her against the others. Her open-handed giving was closer to his heart than the prudent calculation of the other possible uses of the ointment. He is moved to declare solemnly that her story will be remembered wherever the gospel is proclaimed.

The homilist may wish to explore this point further. Why will her story be remembered wherever the gospel is proclaimed? How is it that in an account of the mighty works of God worked through his Son Jesus this small incident is raised to such prominence?

One possible answer is that this woman recognized what the others had failed to perceive: Jesus' presence was not a permanent possession which they could deal with in their own way and in their own good time. It was a gift offered to her then and there for an immediate response.

If this is the case, then she is remembered as an ideal of discipleship. Consequently, the question about giving the money instead to the poor should be seen in a different light. No special importance should be attached to Christ's words about the poor being always with us. The care of the poor is really not at issue here. It rather takes its place as one of many reasons men come up with to refuse or postpone the giving of themselves completely to Christ.

One man wishes to go and bury his father first (Matt. 8:21). Another man wishes to say goodbye to his people at home (Luke 9:61). In the parable of the great banquet Jesus describes the same pattern. The invitation goes out from the great king and the excuses come back: "I have bought a piece of land and must go see it. . . I have bought five oxen and am on my way to try them out. . . . I have just got married and so am unable to come" (Luke 14:18-20).

The glory of this woman is that she seized the moment and responded to it fully. Putting aside the normal considerations of prudence, ignoring the disapproval of others, she celebrated the gift of Christ's presence, holding back nothing. We need her story. For this her story will be remembered wherever the gospel is proclaimed.

The identification of Jesus as the suffering servant in the Book of Isaiah was a particularly effective way in which the early church gave expression to the mystery of Christ. Today's passage helps to illuminate further the significance of Jesus' death. We are led to consider Good Friday not as a single great act of sacrifice but as the culmination of Jesus' life, growing out of the logic of all that had gone before.

Just as the servant is chosen by God and endowed with his Spirit, so Jesus begins his ministry by being baptized and receiving the Spirit from heaven (Mark 1:10). Jesus' entire ministry is conducted under the influence of the Spirit.

The mission of the servant is described as one of deliverance: the eyes of the blind are to be opened. So, too, are the doors of prisons and dungeons. John will describe the mission of Jesus in similar terms: he is the light of the world (8:12) and opens the eyes of a man born blind (9:1 ff.). Those who believe in him will know the truth and the truth will set them free (8:32). There is an echo here also of Luke's description of the day when Jesus read at a synagogue service in Nazareth those powerful lines from Isaiah:

> "The Spirit of the Lord has been given to me,
> for he has anointed me.
> He has sent me to bring the good news to the poor,
> to proclaim liberty to captives
> and to the blind new sight,
> to set the downtrodden free,
> to proclaim the Lord's year of favor" (61:1-2)

Here the homilist may choose to explore the implications of Christian baptism with its anointing of the new Christian to strengthen him in undertaking the same mission of bringing liberation to those who are unfree.

The author of Hebrews explores another image to bring out the mystery of Christ, the image of Jesus as the high priest of a new covenant. He has a special purpose in mind, however, and it is one which makes his words particularly appropriate for us. He is addressing a group of Christians whose situation is like ours today. They are trapped in a mood of discouragement and of disillusionment. Their earlier hopes have lost their vitality. Their certain expectation of deliverance by the coming of the Lord has become smothered under a mountain of doubts. They have lost their zest for a life lived in the service of God. Their actions seem to them "dead."

The form of Hebrews is that of a homily, but the homilist is faced with a group of people who are indifferent to the word of God. They radiate to him an attitude which says, "Preacher, it's all been said before many, many times for many, many years, and we still find ourselves in a very difficult situation, prey to fears and doubts, wondering if there is any point in coming to church anymore" (cf. 10:25).

The biblical author's strategy is to try to re-awaken hope in their hearts by showing that in Christ, the new high priest, we have access to God. The same Christ who offered himself in sacrifice to God has been established by God as the mediator between God and his people.

Christ lives before the Father, always interceding for us (7:25), so that we may be confident in approaching the throne of grace (4:16), and we may have hope through the prayer of Christ to have our spirits renewed. This very day he can "purify our inner self from dead actions" (9:14), and restore to our lives the sense that we are living them in the service of the living God.

The homilist may wish to undertake the formidable task of doing for his congregation what the author of Hebrews attempted to do: meet the challenge of indifference in the congregation to the Christian message. The categories of high priest, sacrifice, mediator, etc., may not be sufficiently forceful for his purposes. The basic need, however, of both groups may really be the same: to have a living experience again of the *presence* of God in their lives, of his fatherly interest in them, and thus a renewed sense that what they are doing really does matter.

In the Pres./UCC/Chr. Ch. lectionary the first reading today is the third servant song from Deutero-Isaiah, which is commented on in the notes for Wednesday of Holy Week. The Gospel reading is taken from Luke and the homilist should situate this text for his listeners as it fits into the theological program of Luke.

Jerusalem is the center of Jewish religious life and Luke begins his narrative with events which center around the temple, including the presentation of Jesus at the temple (2:22 ff.) and the visit of Jesus to the temple when he was twelve years old (2:41).

From that time on Luke never records any visit of Jesus to Jerusalem, but describes his ministry in such a way that it represents a gradual movement toward the holy city which brings together the growing interest of the people in Jesus and the rise of hostility towards him. The exegetical notes say that Jesus comes to Jerusalem finally in Luke to fling down the gauntlet of his final challenge. But, as he does so, Luke presents us with the touching picture of Jesus weeping over the city, lamenting over the fate of the city which he knew would not recognize the message of peace he was bringing.

It is good to have this image in mind as we continue through the events of the passion. In its own way it gives us an insight into the heart of Jesus as his ministry comes to its climactic phase, the confrontation in Jerusalem. It is a poignant picture of a gentle prophet who loved his Father and his people and foresaw the failure of his attempts to bring them together and the consequent ruin that would befall this beloved city.

Tuesday in Holy Week

Lutheran	Roman Catholic	Episcopal	Pres./UCC/Chr.	Methodist/COCU
Isa. 49:1-6	Isa. 49:1-6	Isa. 49:1-9a	Isa. 42:1-9	Isa. 49:1-9a
1 Cor. 1:18-25		1 Cor. 1:18-31	1 Tim. 6:11-16	1 Cor. 1:18-31
John 12:20-36	John 13:21-30, 36-38	John 12:37-38 42-50	John 12:37-50	John 12:37-50

EXEGESIS

First Lesson: Isa. 49:1-6. This is the second of the servant songs. The additional verses, 7-9a, included in the Episcopal and Pres./UCC/Chr. Ch. readings, are not part of the song, but the beginning of another prophecy in which the nation's plight in exile is contrasted with the glorious times which will follow upon its restoration.

A unique feature of the second servant song is its explicit identification of the servant with the people of Israel (v. 3). This identification, however, by no means clears up the problem of identity in the other songs. For "Israel" could mean one who as an individual embodies and represents either the whole people (e.g., the king or the messianic king, or perhaps even a prophet), or the true remnant of the people. In any case, Christians can read this song, like the others, in terms of Jesus and his mission. In the NT it is used only once christologically (in the song of Simeon, Luke 2:32) and twice of the apostolic ministry (Gal. 1:15; Acts 13:47). The song itself contains no direct reference to suffering, and the addition of vv. 7-9a from the other prophecy supplies this lack in a reading for Holy Week. The song's main theme is the universality of the servant's mission (vv. 5-6), a mission for which the servant has been destined from his mother's womb (v. 1b). This is why Isaiah 49 is more usually associated with the epiphany season in Christian usage rather than with Holy Week. However, the accompanying Gospel Lesson from John 12 ties up the theme of universality of the servant's mission explicitly with the cross, a link lacking in the Roman Catholic gospel reading.

Second Lesson: 1 Cor. 1:18-25. This section is the opening part of Paul's reply to the Corinthian problem described in v. 12, the tension between the various groups in the community. This reply extends from

1:18 through 3:23. (The Episcopal selection runs through the second paragraph, in which Paul gives a concrete illustration of the general principle he has laid down in vv. 21-25 in the first paragraph.) The Corinthian parties (not just one of them; all the parties are equally under attack) are priding themselves on their wisdom. They were probably influenced by an early form of gnosis (we follow the practice of distinguishing between first century gnosis and second century gnosticism, reserving the latter for the developed gnostic systems of the later period). They thought that man's basic need was not a redemption of the whole man but the knowledge of his true self. For Paul, man's fallenness is total and his need of redemption much more radical. He requires not information but transformation. Hence Christ came not to bring gnosis, not information about man's true being, but complete transformation. Hence too the necessity of the cross. The cross is "folly" to those who are unaware of their radical fallenness. If all man needed was information, the cross would have been unnecessary and meaningless, a stumbling block for the Jews and folly to the Greeks. Paul contrasts two programs for man's salvation, the gospel ("word," v. 18, and "kerygma," v. 21) on the one hand, and "wisdom of this world," (v. 20), on the other. In defining the gospel here exclusively in terms of the cross, Paul is not excluding other aspects of the saving event. The cross epitomizes the whole saving act of God in Christ which includes the sending of the Son (Gal. 4:4), his whole observable history, his whole career (what elsewhere Paul calls *sarx*, flesh) and his resurrection-exaltation (see the summary of the kerygma in 1 Corinthians 15 and the hymn in Phil. 2:6-11). The cross would not be a saving act if God had not first sent his Son, and its efficacy would not continue into the present as the saving act of God if it were not for the resurrection-exaltation, which alone makes the cross a present word of salvation. The wisdom of this world which Paul condemns is not the enterprise of philosophy as such. Christian theology has always been dependent upon philosophy for its terminology and conceptuality and often for the issues to which it has responded. Philosophy has always been the handmaid of theology. What Paul condemns is the existential attitude that registers itself in particular philosophies, the illusion that man can discover the ultimate truth about himself and so save himself, not needing an act of God to save him. The cross, however, is perceptible as the saving act of God only to the eye of faith ("who believe," v. 21), only to those who are being saved (v. 18), who are called (v. 24). This involves predestination. Insight into the saving significance of the cross as the power and wisdom of God (v. 24) is the gift of God. Yet, those who are perishing, those who do not see in the cross the saving act of God, blind themselves by their own choice.

Gospel: John 12:20-36. This passage is a collection of materials derived from different sources and representing different forms of tradition. It falls into three main sections: (1) vv. 20-22; (2) vv. 23-33; (3) vv. 34-36.

(1) Vv. 20-22. These verses must at one time have served as an introduction to an earlier pericope, probably as the setting for a pronouncement story. But the original pronouncement has been lopped off, and in its place a Johannine one substituted. The Greeks never see Jesus and drop out of the picture. The evangelist intends the real answer to the request to be found in the discourse.

(2) Vv. 23-33. Here are several items. V. 23 is a Son of man saying evolved in the Johannine tradition out of the primitive parousia sayings (note the word "glorify," derived ultimately from Dan. 7:14).

V. 24 is a parabolic saying, with good claim to be authentic.[1]

V. 25 is a saying about losing one's life to save it, a Johannine variant of the similar synoptic saying. It was evidently combined with the parabolic saying prior to the composition of the Fourth Gospel in order to interpret the parabolic saying. The principle of dying in order to produce fruit is the principle of the Christian life.

V. 26 is a variant of the synoptic saying about discipleship. It further interprets the parabolic saying, relating the life of discipleship to Jesus' passion.

Vv. 27-30 are a variant of the Gethsemane story. It is characteristic of the evangelist's procedure to place episodes from the passion story at an earlier point in his Gospel. Placed here, it elaborates further the passion theme already broached in the preceding verse.

V. 31 is a saying rooted in the apocalyptic tradition of the primitive church. But it has been modified by Johannine language ("of this world") and the future eschatology of the primitive church has been transposed into the present. "Now" is the judgment, "now" is the ruler of this world to be cast out. Note, however, that the "now" is not the now of Jesus'

1. See Dodd, *Historical Tradition in the Fourth Gospel* (Cambridge: University Press, 1963), pp. 266-67).

revelatory discourses in the earlier part of the Gospel, but the now of his passion. All that Jesus was revealed to be in the discourses he became concretely in the hour of his passion.

V. 32 is also a saying rooted in earlier tradition, namely, in the primitive Christian proclamation of Jesus' exaltation and in the proclamation of the universal efficacy of his atoning death (Mark 10:45; 14:24). But the saying has been developed in the Johannine school: the verb "draw" is characteristically Johannine and may be due to gnostic influence (Oepke). V. 33 is a typical Johannine redactional note both in form and in content. It explains that exaltation refers to Jesus' lifting up on the cross.

Here we have the response to the Greeks' question. They cannot see Jesus until he has been lifted up on the cross. Only then can the Gentiles gain access to his saving presence. Thus the theme of the whole pericope is the universality of God's redemption in the cross of Christ. It is the fulfillment of the universal mission of the servant of Yahweh (First Lesson).

(3) Vv. 34-36. It would have made the commentators', the preachers', and probably the hearers' task easier had the pericope ended with the great pronouncement in v. 32 and the appended comment of the evangelist. For the ensuing sayings develop a rather different line of thought. Indeed, Bultmann, who resorted to wholesale rearrangement of the text, attached these verses to John 8:29. V. 34 takes up the theme of the lifting up of the Son of man, but in terms derived more from 8:28 than from 12:32. Jesus' answer to the crowd's question looks a bit of a *non sequitur*, and forces upon his hearers the urgency of decision in view of the challenge of his revelation. The dualism light/darkness has some connection with the hour of the cross, but its main reference is to the dualism of decision which permeates the Johannine discourse material.

There is considerable variation between the lectionaries of the four traditions at this point. The Roman Catholic selection (John 13:21-30, 36-38) comprises the unmasking of Judas and the prediction of Peter's denial. The Episcopal reading (John 12:37-38, 42-50) and the Pres./UCC/Chr. Ch. (John 12:37-50) form the conclusion of the first half of John's Gospel, the signs and discourses. It consists of a testimonium from Isaiah 6, bringing to a climax the challenge to decision presented in the discourses and summarizing the teaching of the revelation discourses. This material seems less directly related to the theme of the passion than the Roman Catholic and Lutheran readings.

HOMILETICAL INTERPRETATION

Today's readings suggest a sort of drama being enacted by God and those he has chosen. There is the divine call and man's response, a divine mission and man's labor. Then man falls into discouragement and God's response, strangely enough, is to extend his mission further. This does not discourage man but rather makes him aware that his thoughts are not God's thoughts and his ways are not God's ways. Man is moved therefore to put aside his fears and to trust completely in God.

The suffering servant of Isa. 49:1-6 is confident of his call and had been looking to become the one in whom God would be glorified. But his mission seems to him a failure and he asks himself, "Where is the glory of God that I hoped to see?"

Then God speaks to him in his grief and despair. The word is scarcely what the servant expects to hear. The servant is thinking, "I have toiled in vain, I have exhausted myself for nothing," and God says to him, "I have even greater plans for you. For I plan through you to bring all mankind to salvation."

The despair lifts and the servant comes to realize he has been judging by too human standards. There was no need for discouragement. "All the while my cause was with Yahweh, my reward with my God. I was honored in the eyes of Yahweh, my God was my strength" (vv. 3-4).

The story of Paul manifests striking similarities to that of the servant. The Lord makes his claim on the young Saul on the road to Damascus and after suitable preparation sends him on the mission of preaching the gospel. Paul is zealous in undertaking this apostolate, but regularly encounters opposition, persecution, or indifference. He finds himself unequal to the task, only to hear the Lord tell him, "My grace is enough for you; my power is at its best in weakness" (2 Cor. 12:9). So Paul makes it his special boast that he is weak, for then he is strong with the power of Christ. In the same way in today's second reading Paul boasts of the foolishness of the message he is preaching. For him that is a sign that God is at work.

Paul seems to have perceived a pattern in God's dealings with men. God regularly chooses the weak to overthrow the strong, the foolish to confound the wise. He calls Abraham out of his homeland and sends him to an unknown land without posterity and with no hope of having any, with the extraordinary promise that he will raise up from him a great nation. The infant Moses is marked for death, but is saved to become the leader who will free Israel from captivity in Egypt. Gideon is chosen to drive the Midianites out of the promised land, though he is the lowest member in his father's house and in the weakest clan in all Israel. When he raises a force of 32,000 men the Lord directs him to reduce the force until only 300 remain (Judg. 7:1 ff.). In this way it will be evident that it is the power of the Lord which is delivering Israel. Likewise, the young David went out against a heavily armed Goliath, taking with him only a slingshot and five smooth stones (1 Sam. 17:40).

Paul has perceived how regularly God challenges human wisdom and overturns human expectations. In this way God is calling us to listen for *his* word. Mostly we tell him what he may say to us. Like the Greeks we are looking for a wisdom which is like the wisdom we already have. Like the Jews we are looking for signs, but we want signs which confirm us in our present way of acting. Who of us is prepared to find the wisdom of God and the power of God in the broken, dying body of a man hanging on a cross?

The selection from the Fourth Gospel continues in its own way the same theme as the first two readings. Since Jesus is presented in this Gospel as already possessing, even in his life on earth, some share of his heavenly glory, we do not meet here a scene such as the agony in the garden, which would most closely approximate the picture given of the suffering servant as the suffering man of faith. The equivalent scene in John is in 12:27, where Jesus acknowledges that his soul is troubled.

Today's theme is present in the Gospel selection through the word that some Greeks wish to see Jesus, which is John's way of introducing the universality of the mission of Jesus. The whole world will only come to see Jesus, however, when he is glorified. Glorification comes in a way men could never dream possible: if Jesus is lifted up from the earth on a cross, he will draw all men to himself. John tries to soften the shock to our sensibilities by giving an analogy from nature. Why should we find it so strange that more abundant life comes out of death? After all, look at what happens in nature. If a grain of wheat falls on the ground and dies, it yields a rich harvest. Otherwise it remains alone.

In the concluding verses to this section of the Gospel, vv. 37-50, we read of the unbelief of so many Jews who acted out of fear. In their case it is fear of the Pharisees, or fear of being expelled from the synagogue. We have similar fears that keep us from coming to full belief. But perhaps the best formula for summing up our various fears is the one contained in 12:25. The man who clings to his life loses it. Let this stand for all of the fears that would close us off from the grace of God. Let it stand for the fears of the good men: of the suffering servant who thought all his labors were in vain and who doubted he would see the glory of God, of Paul who feared that his weakness would bring about the failure of his mission, and of Jesus himself whose soul was troubled as the hour of his passion came upon him.

And let it stand for the fears of other men, of people we know so well, who cling to their lives with both hands, afraid to let go. When Christ is lifted up, we are told, he will draw all men to himself—but not those men who fear death in all its forms, not only the death of the body but each day's little deaths of sacrifice, of loss of money or pleasure or comfort, and especially the difficult death of dying to oneself.

The man who clings to his life has all he can do to protect himself from the erosion of time and the encroachments of others. He must be careful, too, to keep under control the claims and demands of love. Such a man cannot afford to hear a divine call or undertake a divine mission. He cannot place all his trust in God or his faith in the love of another. He cannot "see" Jesus, even if Jesus is lifted up on the cross, or rather, especially since Jesus is lifted up on the cross. He cannot feel himself drawn by the example of such a life of unreserved giving. And so he loses his life.

The Pres./UCC/Chr. Ch. lectionary includes an exhortation made by Paul to Timothy. This selection may lead the homilist to develop some of the richness contained in the theme of light.

In 1 Tim. 6:16 God is said to dwell in inaccessible light, i.e., light symbolizes in this way the transcendence of God, "whom no man has seen and no man is able to see." Cf. also 1 John 1:5: "God is light; there is no darkness in him at all."

More commonly, light serves as a symbol of revelation or of the one who brings the truth. So John's Gospel speaks of the Word of God as "the true light that enlightens all men" (John 1:9).

In the story of the passion, though, it becomes especially clear that John does not picture darkness as an absence of light patiently waiting for illumination. Darkness is a power which is locked in a struggle with the light. When Jesus says in today's Gospel selection, "I, the light, have come into the world" (John 12:46), the context does not imply a serene manifestation of truth. As the exegetical notes today indicate, the main reference of the light/darkness dualism is to the dualism of decision. Thus Jesus continues by saying that his presence brings the conflict to the point of life or death. Whoever believes in Jesus escapes from the power of darkness. If a man rejects Jesus, he remains the captive of darkness. But a man cannot ignore him. He must choose.

Faith, then, is a struggling against the darkness, and Paul picks up this same theme with his exhortation to Timothy to "fight the good fight of the faith" (1 Tim. 6:12). At the time of his baptism Timothy made a profession of faith and spoke up for the truth in front of many witnesses. Paul here seems to suggest that this baptismal testimony is best understood in terms of the great profession of faith made by Jesus. Paul may be thinking specifically of Jesus' testimony before Pilate, when he proclaimed he had come into the world to bear witness to the truth (John 18:37), or more generally of the testimony Jesus gave throughout his entire passion. It matters little since these both are parts of a single testimony which came forth in a time of great struggle when Jesus resolutely decided to undergo the baptism wherewith he had to be baptized (cf. Mark 10:38). This suggests that Christian baptism is to be understood not so much as a permanent acquisition of truth as a taking sides in a continual struggle against a hostile power.

The Roman Catholic Gospel selection concerns the Lord's foretelling of his betrayal by Judas and of Peter's denial. Homiletical reflections on these two topics may be found in Wednesday's section.

Wednesday in Holy Week

utheran	*Roman Catholic*	*Episcopal*	*Pres./UCC/Chr.*	*Methodist/COCU*
sa. 50:4-9a	Isa. 50:4-9a	Isa. 50:4-9a	Isa. 52:13-53:12	Isa. 50:4-9
om. 5:6-11		Heb. 9:11-15, 24-28	Rom. 5:6-11	Rom. 5:6-11
Iatt. 26:14-25	Matt. 26:14-25	John 13:21-35 or Matt. 26:1-5, 14-25	Luke 22:1-16	Matt. 26:14-25

EXEGESIS

First Lesson: Isa. 50:4-9a. This is the third servant song. Here we may speak for the first time of the suffering servant. Here, too, the servant is much more clearly an individual figure than was the case with the second song. Three things are said about the servant, all of which find their fulfillment in the history of Jesus. First, the servant receives day by day a message from Yahweh to pass on to his hearers. He has first to hear the word himself before he can speak it to others. This picture of the servant's inner life corresponds remarkably to the portrait of Jesus in the Fourth Gospel. In the Johannine discourses Christ says "I have given them the words which thou gavest me" (John 17:8). He says, too, that after he has been glorified the Jews will learn the secret of his authority: "then you will know that I am he, and that I do nothing on my own authority but speak thus as the Father taught me" (John 8:28). Second, the fact that he declares to the world the word he has received from Yahweh involves the servant in rejection and suffering (v. 6). This reminds us that in the Gospels the death of Christ is not an absurd, irrelevant end to a life which had quite a different meaning, as Bultmann portrayed it in his book *Jesus*, but is absolutely integral to it, the climax of his ministry as the servant of God.

The Pres./UCC/Chr. Ch. reading (Isa. 52:13–53:12) will receive comment under Good Friday.

Second Lesson: Rom. 5:6-11. Paul's plan in chaps. 5-8 of Romans was apparently to outline the kind of life made possible for those who have been justified by the grace of God alone through faith, a case which he had argued in 3:21–4:25. He starts off in 5:1-5 to describe his life but his restless mind causes him to return again and again to the saving event which made this new life possible. This pericope is just such a reversion. Having spoken in v. 5 of the love of God, he expounds precisely what is meant by love. (1) Vv. 5-8 stress its completely unmerited character. (2) In v. 9 he reverts directly to the subject of the previous chapters, but this time under the same rubric of love. God's love in Christ is his act of justification. This is very important. Too often, we take the love of God as an abstract quality which must be reconciled with the harsh realities of life: How could a God of love allow this or that to happen? In the NT, however, the love of God is his act of justifying us in Christ. It is often forgotten that Charles Wesley's hymn, "Jesus, lover of my soul" is all about justification. (3) The saving event is described under the image of reconciliation (v. 10) which—and here Paul returns to the Christian life—is an occasion for rejoicing.

For the Episcopal reading (Heb. 9:11-15, 24-28) see above, Monday in Holy Week.

Gospel: Matt. 26:14-25. Once again, on formal grounds it is not entirely satisfactory to isolate part of the passion narrative in this way, since with one or two exceptions, like the institution of the Lord's Supper, the passion narrative is continuous. However, today's Gospel reading covers part of the prelude to the narrative proper. It consists of three paragraphs: (1) Judas' plot to betray Jesus; (2) the preparation for the passover; (3) the unmasking of Judas. Clearly the role of Judas (paragraphs one and three) occupies the center of our attention today. The preparation for the passover serves here to provide the setting for the unmasking of Judas. We are not concerned at this time with the Last Supper as such. Our modern curiosity is very anxious to know what motivated Judas to betray Jesus. The NT has no such interest. Any answers we give to that question are inevitably speculative. Perhaps the most plausible conjecture is that Judas was somehow infected with Zealotism and because Jesus did not fit in with his program he sought to get rid of him. But we shall never know. For the early Christian community the problem of Judas lay elsewhere: How could God allow such a thing? The early Christians were convinced that everything that happened in Jesus' passion happened by the foreknowledge and predetermined counsel of

God. They sought to alleviate the scandal of Judas by searching the (OT) scriptures. Hence we find the assertion that "the Son of man goes as it is written of him" (v. 24). Surprisingly, Matthew does not seek to elucidate his Marcan *Vorlage* as he so often does, and we are left wondering what scriptures the text has in mind. It is fairly certain that the passage in mind was Ps. 41:9 (cf. RSV margin): "Even my bosom friend in whom I trusted, who ate of my bread, has lifted his heel against me." Note, however, that the reference to God's will as declared in scripture does not relieve Judas of responsibility: "woe to that man . . ." Here we touch once more (see Second Lesson) upon the mystery of God's foreknowledge and man's free will. Both have to be held together in tension and paradox. God has foreknowledge and we have free will. God uses man's sin to overrule the consequences of his deeds for his own good purpose. *O felix culpa!*

The first alternative in the Episcopal selection (John 13:21-35) covers much of the same material as the Roman Catholic selection for Tuesday. Most of it is the Johannine version of the unmasking of Judas. But in John the theodicy question is ignored. Here is the bold assertion that Judas acted as the agent of Satan.

The Pres./UCC/Chr. Ch. reading (Luke 22:1-16) begins with the parallel Lucan account of the compact of Judas. But it diverts attention from Judas by running on into the first part of the actual supper narrative, a questionable procedure since vv. 15-20 form a single block of pre-Lucan tradition.

HOMILETICAL INTERPRETATION

The readings for Wednesday may be viewed as unfolding in climactic fashion the special quality of Jesus' death.

The first reading is the third of the servant songs. The pattern is one that is familiar. The servant hears the word that the Lord addresses to him. When he preaches that word, he creates opposition. Like the prophets before him, he is subjected to persecution. He does not fight back but trusts in the Lord, who finally does come to his aid. His enemies will all fall to pieces like a moth-eaten piece of cloth.

Paul in the second reading fastens on a remarkable aspect of Jesus' death. We are no longer in the pattern of the third servant song. Despite certain similarities the whole thrust of the action is radically different. Christ died, we are told, not simply in fidelity to his mission of preaching. Christ died *for* men—helpless, sinners, enemies of God, men in no sense deserved such an extraordinary demonstration of love. Paul goes a step further. The fact that Christ died for us while we were still sinners is not only a sign of Christ's love for us. It is proof that God loves us.

Paul gives a picture of the redemption which is utterly removed from that of an angry God who demands retribution and who is moved to pity by the sufferings of Christ. On the contrary, it is out of his love and compassion for sinful men, who have set themselves up against him, that the Father sends his own Son to save mankind. The Son willingly accepts this mission despite the suffering and rejection it entails. God further pours out the Holy Spirit on men's hearts to bring them back into union with him. Given this reaching-out on the part of God to save mankind, the redemption would only be frustrated if God's enemies were destroyed.

The Gospel selection for today focuses our attention on the figure of Judas Iscariot. Perhaps in so doing it heightens dramatically a very special dimension of the love Jesus showed in his passion. For Judas is not simply a sinner, one among many whom Christ came to save. Nor is Judas simply one of those who rose up in opposition to Jesus and his mission. Judas is the one who is referred to as "the traitor." (Matt. 10:4; Mark 3:19; Luke 6:16).

There is a special shrug reserved for dismissing the traitor, the man whose malice consists in profiting from violating a trust. An opponent can be respected, but the man who betrays a trust can never be trusted again.

Judas is one of the intimates who shares with Jesus his final meal. They both dipped bread into the same bowl. He was entrusted with the common purse and, John tells us, he was a thief and used to help himself to the money that had been given to Jesus (John 12:6). When he decided on his act of treason, we find again the desire to turn this act to his own profit: "What are you prepared to give me if I hand him over to you?" (Matt. 26:15).

The betrayal finds its culmination in Judas' choice of a way to identify Jesus in the darkness of Gethsemane: "The one I kiss, he is the man. Take him in charge" (Matt. 26:48).

It is worthwhile to dwell a moment on this scene. Jesus has just been through the long and difficult agony in the garden. Now he must face one of his chosen twelve, who comes up to him and singles him out for arrest with greetings and a kiss.

In Mark's Gospel Jesus does not respond to Judas. But Luke and Matthew wish to give some expression to Jesus' response to Judas. In Luke Jesus says, "Judas, are you betraying the Son of man with a kiss?" (Luke 22:48) Matthew records the words, "Friend, do what you are here for" (Matt. 26:50).

It is tempting to see in the expression "friend" a demonstration of Jesus' abiding affection for one of his close followers, even in the act of betrayal. This is surely what comes across in respect to Peter's denial.

Perhaps the word, though, does not bear that meaning. It only occurs three times in the NT, and all three are in the concluding pages of Matthew's Gospel (20:13; 22:12; 26:50). The first instance is in the parable of the vineyard laborers. Those who had been working all day grumbled at the landowner for paying the latecomers as much as them. His answer is, "Friend, I am not being unjust to you," etc. The second instance is in the parable of the wedding feast where the king notices one of the guests is not wearing a wedding-garment and questions him, "Friend, how did you get in here without a wedding-garment?"

In both these instances the speaker has been subjected to some provocation and, while he continues to speak courteously, he is pointing out his dissatisfaction with the other man's conduct. This suggests that Matthew does not wish to make the point that Jesus continued to show affection to his betrayer. Perhaps there is some irony in the use of the word "friend," and surely a great deal of sadness at being so used by one he had trusted.

But the meaning of Jesus' reply is best found in the words which follow: "do what you are here for." Matthew is underlining the fact that Jesus has come through his agony in the garden. He has resolved what his course of action must be. He is being betrayed by one of his close friends. No matter. No more than it matters that "all his disciples deserted him and ran away" (v. 56).

The Jesus we see here is not a weak and submissive man, someone being carried away, helpless before larger forces. We see instead a man so strong and fixed in his resolve to drink the chalice of suffering according to his Father's will that he has no time to concern himself with the betrayal of Judas or the desertion of all of his disciples. The end is coming and he goes forth to meet it alone.

If the homilist is interested in pursuing the story of Judas, the picture unfortunately becomes very unclear. Still, it may be profitable to explore it.

The Acts of the Apostles contains a tradition that Judas purchased a field with the thirty pieces of silver and that he fell, apparently by accident, and died there (Acts 1:18-19). Matthew, on the other hand, relates a different tradition. On learning that Jesus had been condemned, Judas repented of his deed. He took the pieces of silver back to the chief priests and confessed, "I have sinned. I have betrayed innocent blood." Then, flinging the coins into the sanctuary, he went out and hanged himself (Matt. 27:3-6).

A comparison with Peter is unavoidable. Just a few verses earlier in his Gospel Matthew described Peter's triple denial of Jesus, which culminated in Peter's calling down curses on himself and swearing, "I do not know the man." The cock crowed at that moment and Peter remembered that Jesus had foretold his denial. Peter then went outside and wept bitterly (Matt. 26:69-75).

Why do these men react so differently to their sin? There may be a salutary lesson here. Judas, we read, repented of his deed. He confessed his sin. He rid himself of his ill-gotten money. What did he lack? Why was he unable to turn back to Jesus? One is tempted to speculate that it is because he is turned in on himself. His repentance is not productive of forgiveness because it does not even lead him to ask for forgiveness. "*I* have sinned. *I* have betrayed innocent blood." Is there an accent here that comes from deeply wounded self-esteem? When a person cannot tolerate the fact that *he* has sinned, he often uses the expression, "I cannot forgive myself for what I did." If someone is locked up this way inside himself, it is impossible for him to turn and ask forgiveness of another.

Peter, however, follows a different course. He wept bitterly, but his sorrow does not prevent him from coming to receive forgiveness. One indication that Peter was not caught in a paralyzing self-recrimination is that the story is preserved for everyone to know. Far from suppressing all trace of his denial as incompatible with his growing importance in the early church, the record of his weakness forms a permanent part of the preaching of the good news and enters into the composition of the NT. It is as if Peter does not wish to forget it, and wants us to benefit as well from its being remembered. It is an unforgettable testimony to the weakness of man and the mercy of God.

Perhaps the best comment on these two men can be found in some words of Paul. In a previous letter to the Corinthians Paul had caused them some distress, but their sorrow led finally to repentance, and this is the kind of sorrow God approves of. While not thinking of Peter and Judas, Paul's words are most appropriate: "The wound which is borne in God's way brings a change of heart too salutary to regret; but the hurt which is borne in the world's way brings death" (2 Cor. 7:10 NEB).

Maundy Thursday

Lutheran	*Roman Catholic*	*Episcopal*	*Pres./UCC/Chr.*	*Methodist/COC*
Exod. 24:3-11	Exod. 12:1-8, 11-14	Exod. 12:1-14a	Deut. 16:1-8	Deut. 16:1-8
1 Cor. 10:16-17 (18-21)	1 Cor. 11:23-26	1 Cor. 11:23-26	Rev. 1:4-8	1 Cor. 10:16-2
Mark 14:12-26	John 13:1-15	John 13:1-15 or Luke 22:14-30	Matt. 26:17-30	Mark 14:12-26

EXEGESIS

First Lesson: Exod. 24:3-11. Today we break the sequence of the servant songs (the fourth will be read tomorrow in all lectionaries except the Pres./UCC/Chr. Ch.). This reading comprises the inauguration of the Mosaic covenant. The narrative is composite: vv. 3-8 are from E, 9-11 from J. Moses enters into a book the words of Yahweh revealed to him on the mount (chap. 20), inaugurates the covenant by a blood sacrifice (vv. 4-5), throwing half of it on the altar and sprinkling the rest on the people (v. 8). By this rite the people are involved in the covenant. Vv. 9-11 are unconnected with this rite, and consist of a quite separate report of a theophany. The vision of God is consummated in "eating and drinking" (v. 11, a sort of communion rite). It is doubtless for this reason that the second paragraph is included in today's reading. We have here a double typology of the Lord's Supper: the inauguration of the covenant with blood and a participation of the people of God in that covenant by means of a communion meal. This typology has a biblical sanction, for Exod. 24:8b, "Behold the blood of the covenant," has shaped the cup word in the institution narrative at Mark 14:24.

The Roman Catholic and Episcopal reading from Exodus 12 is the institution of the passover. Since the Lord's Supper has a paschal background in the Marcan passion narrative (though not in the institution narrative itself) and in the Lucan Supper narrative throughout (including the institution narrative) this reading is quite appropriate for today. However, in Judaism it was used precisely at the passover rite itself, and this usage passed in early Christianity into the paschal liturgy (see, e.g., the passover homily of Melito of Sardis), so it would seem to belong more properly to the vigil services on Easter Eve. The Pres./UCC/Chr. Ch. readng (Deut. 16:1-8) is the Deuteronomic version of the institution of the passover. Unlike the exodus parallel, which comes from JE, the D account combines the two rites of the unleavened bread and the passover lamb. Both aspects of the meal play a role in Christian typology (1 Cor. 5:7-8), but in connection with the Christian passover celebration, not directly with the Lord's Supper.

Second Lesson: 1 Cor. 10:16-17. This is one of Paul's two *loci classici* on the Last Supper. The context of the present passage is as follows. Certain groups in the Corinthian community, probably influenced by early gnosis, thought they had already attained salvation. They therefore felt free to participate in pagan sacrificial meals with impunity. Paul, however, regards such practices as dangerous. Celebration of the Lord's Supper involved a *koinonia* (i.e., a communion participation, a term which implies a thoroughgoing sacramental realism, according to Conzelmann) in the body and blood of Christ. Participation in Christ is exclusive because it places one under obedience to the *Kyrios.* It can tolerate no participation in other cult deities.

To make this point Paul draws upon some traditional liturgical formulations. The "cup of blessing" is a Jewish phrase, meaning the cup over which the name of Yahweh is blessed (Jews did not bless things, but rather blessed Yahweh in thanksgiving for his gifts). Similarly, the phrase, "the bread which we break," did not symbolize the breaking of the Lord's body on the cross, an idea not found until later textual tradition in 1 Cor. 11:24 (see RSV margin). It was a purely utilitarian procedure necessary in order to have the common loaf distributed among all present so that they would be involved in the blessing said over it. Similarly with the blessing said over the cup. Paul would have regarded both individual wafers and individual communion cups as an unfortunate obscuring of the eucharistic symbolism! To these traditional phrases Paul adds his own questions, "Is it not a participation in the blood/body of Christ?" It is a striking fact that Paul here reverses the usual order of bread/cup, and some have thought that this represents an actual liturgical custom. This is not so. Paul is not citing a complete liturgical formula here, but only excerpts from such a formula, and he reverses the order because he wishes to comment at further length upon the bread part (v. 17). Elsewhere Paul follows the normal order of bread/cup (see 1 Cor. 10:3-4, and especially 1 Cor. 11:23-25, where he is actually citing the liturgical agenda of his communities). One further point before we leave v. 16. Body and blood are not things, stuff, but the one central event of salvation—the sacrificial death of Christ. The bread and wine are the body and blood of Christ in the sense of sacramental identification (Conzelmann) of one event (partaking of the bread/cup) with another (the saving event). The one event is brought out of the past and made contemporaneous with the other.

In v. 17 Paul makes further comment on the bread word. Partaking of the one loaf unites the participants into one body. The Lord's Supper has thus a horizontal as well as a vertical dimension. It involves *koinonia* with each other as well as with the Lord. But the horizontal dimension is created by the vertical.[1] The eucharist is not just a celebration of ordinary human togetherness.

The *koinonia* aspect of the communion was not in itself an original contribution of Paul to eucharistic thought. It was merely his comment on what the tradition already implied. Here he draws out what is implied by the *esti* ("is") in the bread and cup words of the traditional institution narrative and by the anamnesis formula (Do this for the recalling of me, as the passover was the recalling of the exodus salvation event). The further comment about the bread in v. 17 is, however, an original contribution. It was Paul who first gave a double meaning to the *Corpus Christi.* It is for Paul both sacramental and ecclesial, and the ecclesial depends upon the sacramental.

The Roman Catholic and Episcopal reading consists of the other *locus classicus* in 1 Corinthians (11:23-26), the institution narrative. Much of what we have said in our comments above relates also to this passage.

The Pres./UCC/Chr. Ch. reading (Rev. 1:4-8) consists of the initial vision of the exalted Christ in the Apocalypse. Presumably it is chosen today because of vv. 5-6 which speak of the saving event in the blood of Christ and the establishment thereby of the royal priesthood of the whole church.

Gospel: Mark 14:12-26. This pericope consists of part of the continuous passion narrative (vv. 12-21, 26), into which has been inserted at some stage of the pre-Marcan tradition the institution narrative (vv. 22-25). The

1. See Luther's profound remarks on *koinonia* given in J. Pelikan, *Luther the Expositor* (St. Louis: Concordia, 1959), pp. 191-204.

surrounding framework consists of: (1) the preparation for the passover (vv. 12-16), (2) the narrative of the supper in which Judas is unmasked (vv. 17-21), and (3) the exit to the Mount of Olives (v. 26). We regard the institution narrative as an originally separate tradition for the following reasons: (a) in 1 Cor. 11:23-25 Paul cites it as a separate pericope; (b) the Johannine passion supper narrative contains no institution; (c) the surrounding narrative presents the Last Supper as a passover meal while the institution itself ignores this point; (d) a particularly telltale piece of evidence is the repetition in v. 22 of the phrase "and as they were eating" from v. 18 as a peg on which to hang the institution. Therefore we conclude that the function of the institution is that of a separate aetiological cult narrative (i.e., it is concerned not to relate what happened at the Last Supper, but how the Marcan community was celebrating the Lord's Supper). Our commentary will concentrate on this narrative (14:23-25). It consists of three parts: (1) the actions and words over the bread (v. 23); (2) the actions and words over the cup (v. 24); (3) the eschatological saying (v. 25).

(1) The actions and words over the bread. The bread is *artos* (leavened), not *azuma* (unleavened). Mark's account presumes the ordinary weekly eucharist, not the annual Christian passover. Four actions with the bread are prescribed: taking, blessing, breaking, and giving, and a fifth implied (see the command "take" and cf. the statement that they drank of the cup). "Take" means lifting up the bread "a hand's breadth." It has nothing to do with the "offertory," as is often thought. That is only a preliminary to the taking. "Blessed" is a more primitive term than "gave thanks," which appears later with reference to the cup. For its meaning see the commentary on the Second Lesson above. The words over the bread are very brief: simply words of sacramental identification. An interpretative addition is not added as in 1 Cor. 11:24, "which is for you." In this respect Mark is more primitive than 1 Corinthians. Less primitive, however, is the dropping of the reference to the intervening meal (contrast "after supper" in 1 Cor. 11:25). In Mark's church both the bread and cup followed the meal.

(2) The actions over the cup correspond to those over the bread, except, of course, there is no breaking. The bringing together of the bread and cup rite through the removal of the meal between has resulted in assimilation of the bread and cup words: this is my body/this is my blood,

instead of: this is my body/this is the new covenant (1 Cor. 11:24-25). Here again Mark is less primitive, but it is still clear that blood means not the stuff but the saving event. In Mark, too, the cup word has to bear the whole weight of the covenant/atonement theology. The Pauline tradition identified the covenant with the new covenant of Jer. 31:31 ff. But in Mark the covenant saying is based on the typology of the Mosaic covenant in Exodus 24 (see above, First Lesson). It is now *my* blood-of-the-covenant, as opposed to the Mosaic blood-of-the-covenant. "Poured out for many" is tacked on awkwardly to the preceding phrase. The passive participle is a reverential periphrasis indicating that it is God who pours out the blood of his Messiah. The messianic sacrifice is the redemptive act of God (Jeremias). "For many," in accordance with contemporary rabbinic usage, does not mean "some but not all" but precisely "all"—all of the nations. The language is derived from Isa. 53:12. So the atoning, covenant theology has a double background, Exodus 24 and Isaiah 53.

(3) The eschatological saying has the highest claim to authenticity (Bornkamm, Schweizer), since the tendency in the history of the tradition is for the eschatological saying to become atrophied. Already in 1 Cor. 11:26 it is reduced to "until he comes" and finally in the later liturgies it disappears altogether. It contains implicitly all that is asserted in the bread and cup words about the Lord's Supper. "I will no longer drink" implies that Jesus will not, but they will. He is going to die, they will be left behind. The next time Jesus drinks wine, it will be in the consummated kingdom of God. This implies that the death of Jesus is the decisive event which lies between the Last Supper and the realization of the kingdom. Unfortunately, Mark does not add "with you" (Matt. 26:29), but it is apparently implied. Since the church continued to celebrate the eschatological meal in the joy of Christ's risen presence, it understood its rite as the fulfillment of Jesus' prediction at the Last Supper.

Mark contains no command to repeat (1 Cor. 11:24, 25 and Luke 22:19). But the very fact that form-critically Mark 24:23-25 is a cult aetiology (i.e., it gives the reason for the church's practice) is enough to indicate that the command to repeat is implied. And that it was done for the recalling of the Lord is indicated by the words of sacramental identification over the bread and cup.

The Roman Catholic and Episcopal Gospel reading (John 13:1-15) comprises the other main incident in the supper tradition, the foot washing (these lectionaries consider the institution of the eucharist sufficiently covered by the Second Lesson). This story has two levels of meaning. First, in the pre-Johannine tradition, it was an example of humility and service (cf. Luke 22:24-27). Second, in the Johannine redaction it became a piece of dramatic symbolism, expressing the total way of Christ: as he lays aside his garments, washes the disciples' feet, and resumes his garments, so he lays aside his eternal glory to become incarnate, stoops to redeem men throughout his humble incarnate life culminating on the cross, and then in the resurrection and exaltation resumes his heavenly glory.

The alternative Episcopal reading (Luke 22:14-30) is the Lucan account of the Last Supper. It should be read with the full text including vv. 19b-20 (RSV margin, Common Bible text). There has been a remarkable shift of text-critical opinion in recent years in favor of the long text and the RSV was undoubtedly wrong in relegating it to the margin. The long text is again aetiological: it represents the Christian passover as celebrated in Luke's church, with an initial cup breaking the pre-paschal fast, no lamb, and the Christian eucharist. The shorter text was produced by the puzzlement over the two cups at a time when the Christian passover was no longer celebrated in this way, and the church was familiar only with the weekly eucharist with bread and one cup.

The Pres./UCC/Chr. Ch. Gospel reading (Matt. 26:17-30) is the Matthean narrative of the Last Supper. It follows closely the Marcan version, but its institution narrative is more rubrical (Matthew was a churchman), placing the cupword during the drinking, not after as in Mark, and adding a further theological explanation to the word, "for the remission of sins" (v. 28; RSV: forgiveness).

HOMILETICAL INTERPRETATION

There is a great deal of variety in the readings selected by the different churches for today.

The principal focus is to be found in the Gospel narration of the institution of the eucharist (Lutheran, Episcopal alternate reading, Pres./UCC/Chr. Ch.). The first and second readings mostly pick up the theme of blood, an enormously rich theme in terms of the Bible, but one which is hardly apt to prove rewarding to a congregation today. Perhaps the best the homilist can do is evoke something of its symbolic meaning to our ancestors in the faith.

The blood of the Mosaic Covenant, poured around the altar and sprinkled on the people, sealed a bond of union between them and God. The blood of the lamb, sprinkled on the doorposts of the Israelites, marked them as chosen people, as belonging to the Lord, and delivered them from the angel of death. So Jesus shed his blood as a way of bringing about union. His desire was to break down the barriers between God and his fellow-men, and to bring all men into a living harmony, delivering them from the power of death.

The Gospel reading in the Roman Catholic and Episcopal lectionaries deals with a distinct event at the Last Supper, viz., the washing of the feet of the disciples.

The homilist may choose to join both of these accounts by means of the notion of "prophetic action." Those who are preaching on the eucharist will find that the foot washing helps to interpret it, and those who are preaching on the foot-washing will find that this scene is illuminated in terms of the subsequent institution of the eucharist. For each of these two in its own way is a prophetic action which aims at revealing the meaning of Jesus' death on the cross. It finally comes down to this: What can it mean to me that this man was put to death outside of Jerusalem so many centuries ago?

We have, unfortunately, seen far too much of killings, executions, and assassinations. We find ourselves asking what these deaths mean. What significance should be attached to the killings of Martin Luther King, John and Robert Kennedy? What of the deaths of so many other nameless ones, whose passing was as unnoticed by our world as Jesus' death was in his?

A man's death may come suddenly, accidentally, and the meaning of it may be for us only this: the life of a man is a fragile thing. Or a man may be executed and the meaning of his death may simply be that superior force carried him away against his will and snuffed out his life.

But Jesus' death was not like that. In a variety of ways we hear Jesus saying, "I see this coming. I accept it—for your sake."

Let us look at some of the ways he tried to help us to see the meaning of his death. He did not use the method beloved of teachers. He did not give a lecture on the subject. He performed instead a couple of prophetic actions. We recall that at times the prophets engaged in symbolic actions that in their own way gave notice of what was to come and its meaning, e.g., by taking an earthenware jar and smashing it on the ground (Jer. 19:10-11) or by taking a cloak and cutting it into twelve pieces (1 Kings 11:30-31). What were these prophetic actions which Jesus performed to instruct us in the meaning of his coming death?

For one thing, he gave a dinner and invited his closest friends. It is difficult for us to place ourselves imaginatively in that scene but we should try. We are too accustomed to eucharistic services which may serve well as memorials of the Lord's death but bear no resemblance whatever to the Last Supper.

A college group once tried to recapture something of the atmosphere of the Last Supper by celebrating the traditional Jewish seder service during Holy Week. They invited a rabbi to be present but conducted the service themselves. The group was properly reverent. They said all of the prayers with a great solemnity. Finally the rabbi could not keep silent any longer. "You're much too stiff and formal," he said. "When we do it, we say a prayer, then talk or laugh a bit, then we have a glass of wine, and after some more conversation we say another prayer. It's a big family thing. If you people keep going the way you're going, you'll be done in twenty minutes."

So they did as he suggested and gradually began to enjoy themselves very much. The result was that the service lasted over three hours. If we wish to imagine for ourselves this dinner, we need to remember that these were friends gathered together to celebrate the passover.

Of course, this was not simply a passover meal between friends. Jesus did not act simply as a good host who provides food and drink to his guests. There is something special here and we must give it our closest attention, but we must keep in mind the setting Jesus chose in which to explain to his friends and to us the meaning of his coming death.

What is special is that at one point in this meal he took some bread and broke it and gave it to each one, and he took a single cup of wine and passed it to each one in turn. What is special is that the same food and the same cup are *shared*. He gave it to them.

How do I understand the meaning of the cross? How do I interpret the brute fact of his being put to death like so many hundreds of thousands of others in the course of history? I return to this picture of Jesus saying that this bread is his body and then breaking it and sharing it with his friends.

And I see him taking a cup and saying that it holds his blood which will be poured out as a sign of his love for his fellow-man. And I get the message that communion with him is sharing his way of dying.

All of us who eat of the one bread are called to live out the promise of unity with each other symbolized by the single loaf of bread we share. And all of us who drink from the cup of the new covenant should be moved by the example of our ancestors at Sinai who, when they had listened to the commandments of the covenant, cried out, "We will observe all that the Lord has decreed; we will obey" (Exod. 24:7). Sharing in the blood of the new covenant would be an empty memorial if we did not likewise pledge ourselves to observe all that the Lord has decreed and obey the new commandment that he gave us: "love one another; just as I have loved you, you also must love one another" (John 13:34).

There is a second prophetic action, the one described in the Roman Catholic and Episcopal reading from the Gospel of John, the washing of the feet. There are really two levels of meaning here. The first and basic one is that Jesus tells us that his death on the cross means that he submits himself to his death like a slave, like a servant who comes in to wash the feet of guests reclining at table, a man hardly noticed whose service is scarcely recognized. This humble obedience was very pleasing to his father.

The second meaning is in terms of the example he gives to the disciples. We could take this, as Peter seems to do at first, as the institution of a new ritual, a new rite of purification that the disciples were to repeat in his memory. It is interesting how little the church has made of the washing of the feet as a ritual. Perhaps this is because it was too clear from the beginning that it was not a ritual that Jesus had in mind. In a ritual the roles are already assigned, and carrying them out, even the role of a servant, can be an honorable thing.

No, Jesus did not have a new ritual in mind, and neither did he mean by his example that just as he has died for us, or washed our feet, so we should wash his feet or be ready to die for him. Think of the character in Camus' novel *The Fall*, whose friend is imprisoned and who therefore sleeps on the floor so that he may not have comforts which are denied to his friend. Jesus is not saying, "I have slept on the floor for you so you should sleep on the floor for me." His example is that he, being lord and master, has washed our feet and *therefore* we should wash each other's feet. There would have been something consoling about washing the feet of the Lord, but this is not the example he gave us.

And so this second prophetic action helps us to understand what happened on Calvary because it helps us to understand the spirit that moved Jesus to embrace his death. It helps us also to come to the conviction that, if we would have some share with him, we must live and go to our deaths not for him but, as he did, for our fellow man.

The Episcopal lectionary gives as an alternate reading Luke 22:14-30. The special material that is of interest here is that, immediately after the narration of the institution of the eucharist, Jesus in this account announces that one of those eating at that table was betraying him.

The disciples at once begin to ask one another who the traitor might be. In this context then we are startled to learn that a dispute arose between them about which of them was the greatest!

Jesus replies with what seems to us incredible patience. It is the same lesson he has been trying to communicate to them for a long time now. It is the lesson of his life and of his death. It is the same lesson that is contained in the prophetic action of the washing of the disciples' feet. Therefore, whichever lectionary he is following, the homilist may wish to introduce this material as well. It certainly does catch our attention and it is something we all have firsthand experience of: the desire to be reckoned as the greatest!

But it is this very desire which sets us against one another, which provokes disputes and dissension, and which, therefore, is diametrically opposed to the spirit of Jesus, the nature of his kingdom and the meaning of the eucharistic meal.

Jesus tells them that his kingdom is not modeled after those of pagan rulers. To be great is to act toward others with deference, and to be a ruler is to act as one who serves.

This is a very difficult lesson for men to learn. We have yet to do so. That may be why we find it difficult to grasp the spirit of Christ himself. It is so much easier to worship Christ and sing praises to his name. But how deal with the fact that he came among us as one who serves, and that he will not let us take him out of that role? Rather, as he serves us, he steadfastly insists that we learn the spirit that moves him, the spirit of the servant.

This is the lesson of his life and the lesson of his death. This is the teaching that is sacramentally present in the eucharist he gave us. As we learn it, we will come to know him, and will more joyfully assemble to celebrate the eucharist, and will become ourselves sacraments of Christ's presence in the world.

Good Friday

utheran	*Roman Catholic*	*Episcopal*	*Pres./UCC/Chr.*	*Methodist/COCU*
a. 52:13-53:12	Isa. 52:13-53:12	Isa. 52:13-53:12	Lam. 1:7-12	Lam. 1:7-12
eb. 4:14-5:10	Heb. 4:14-16; 5:7-9	Heb. 10:1-25	Heb. 10:4-18	Heb. 10:14-18
hn 18:1-19:42 ohn 19:17-30)	John 18:1-19:42	John 18:1-19:37 or John 19:1-37	Luke 23:33-46	Luke 23:33-46

EXEGESIS

First Lesson: Isa. 52:13–53:12. Today we read the last and greatest of the four servant poems. It contains many problems of text, translation, and interpretation, but the general sense is clear. Whatever the precise identity of the servant (cf. first reading for Monday), he plays a crucial role in salvation history. Through him Yahweh brings the world to salvation through the knowledge of himself. In the process, the servant is rejected and humiliated, but God vindicates him, and those who had rejected and humiliated him come to recognize that he had suffered as an innocent victim and that by his sufferings their sins have been taken away.

The song falls into five parts (see RSV paragraphing). 52:13-15 forms an introduction, assuring us in advance that the servant will finally triumph despite his humiliation. 53:1-3 summarizes the sufferings of the servant. In vv. 4-9 the servant's tormentors acknowledge in the light of his vindication that his sufferings were vicariously undergone for their own sake, though they themselves inflicted them. Vv. 10-12 speak of the servant's vindication.

It is amazing how closely the fate of the servant corresponds to that of Jesus. The traditional view was that the prophet was predicting consciously and under divine inspiration the fate of Jesus. When this mechanical conception of prophecy was abandoned through the application of historico-critical methods to the OT, the view was substituted that Jesus himself consciously and deliberately modeled his own career on that of the suffering servant. Now that view in turn has broken down through the advance of tradition-criticism. The interpretation of Jesus in terms of the suffering servant (e.g., Mark 10:45; 14:25) is now seen as the result of early Christian attempts to understand the meaning of the Lord's death. From the earliest days after the first Easter his death was seen as having taken place in accordance with the Scriptures. At first Christians turned to Psalm 118 which gave them the interpretation of the Lord's death as the Jews' NO and the resurrection as God's YES. Later they hit upon Isaiah 53 and found there that the Lord's death was a vicarious atonement. Is the fourth servant song, then, nothing more than a quarry for early Christian theology? In what sense is it the word of God himself? We may understand it thus: the composer of the songs has a profound insight into the ways of God with man, and out of it he painted a picture which came to rest finally in the fate of Jesus of Nazareth. Hence Christian faith may in a very real sense read this fourth servant song as a song about Jesus of Nazareth, although that was not its original meaning. Texts do not have a static meaning through history. They acquire new meaning in the light of new events and experiences.

The Pres./UCC/Chr. Ch. substitute (Lam. 1:7-12) was apparently necessitated by the preemption of the fourth servant song for the Wednesday in Holy Week. Lamentations, traditionally ascribed to Jeremiah, consists of a series of poems bewailing the destruction of Jerusalem and the exile of the southern kingdom of Judah in 586. In Christian tradition the lamentations have been interpreted in terms of Jesus' passion, and readings from this book have been traditional in the office lectionaries in Holy Week from early times. Lam. 1:12 has a particular pathos for Good Friday, but it is not so theologically profound or as important for the *theologia crucis* as the fourth servant song.

Second Lesson: Heb. 4:14—5:10. The procedure of Hebrews is to follow a theological exposition by an exhortation. As we have seen, its major theological theme is the high priesthood of Christ. For this theme the author builds up his case gradually, enunciating it several times before developing it fully in the central section. Having first stated the theme at 3:1, the author now introduces it again, and this time expands on it by showing that Jesus had some of the necessary qualifications to be a high priest. His primary qualification was the sharing of our common humanity. He thus knew what temptation was and therefore is able to sympathize with our weaknesses (4:15) and to deal gently with the ignorant and wayward (5:2). The second qualification for a high priest is divine appointment; he must not put himself forward for the job. That this is true of Christ is proved from Pss. 2:7 and 110:1. Both Psalms 2 and 110 were used in the primitive church as testimonies for the resurrection. The author attaches particular importance to Melchizedek. He is concerned to show that there is another, eschatological high priesthood, distinct from the Aaronic priesthood. Unless there were another order of high priesthood it would not have been possible to claim high priesthood for Christ. The true Christ is like the Aaronic priest in some respects. He is human, was called by God, and appointed from among men. He was tempted as we are, is able to sympathize, offers a sacrifice. But in other ways he differs significantly. He is without sin (which has a positive rather than a negative meaning: Jesus committed himself totally to obey the will of his Father, Heb. 10:5-10). He was "made perfect," i.e., he achieved the goal for which he was appointed, and became the author of salvation. Yet, being truly and fully human, he had to learn obedience by overcoming temptation (v. 8).

V. 7 has been thought to refer to Gethsemane. In what way was this prayer of Jesus heard? Not by the removal of the cup of suffering, but rather through his exaltation (cf., the fourth servant song) in which he was designated as High Priest.

The Episcopal and Pres./UCC/Chr. Ch. readings (Hebrews 10) contain the crucial passage (vv. 5-10) to which we have already alluded as the quintessential definition of what is meant when we speak of Jesus' death as a sacrifice, viz., a life of total commitment in obedience to the will of God, culminating in death. The Episcopal reading, which runs through v. 25, goes beyond the doctrinal exposition to the exhortation (vv. 19-25), urging the baptized worshipers (v. 22b) to "draw near" (a cultic word), to love and do good works, and not to neglect assembling together for liturgical purposes.

Gospel: John 18:1—19:42 (John 19:17-30). The passion narrative of the Fourth Gospel begins at 18:1. Here the Johannine style exhibited in discourses couched in typically Johannine language is abandoned for a straightforward narrative. Only in a few places (e.g., in the trial before Pilate with its dialogue about truth, John 18:36-38), is there an echo of distinctive Johannine themes. It is probable that John's passion narrative represents a distinct and independent tradition from those of the synoptists. We will note here some of its distinctive features. It is remarkably well oriented on the topography of Jerusalem (Kidron, the praetorium, Gabbatha), and history (Annas as the power behind the high priestly throne). More primitive, too, is the absence of Jesus' prayer in Gethsemane, the self-identification of Jesus with the coming Son of man at the investigation before the high priest (18:19). Also its chronology is more plausible (the dating of the crucifixion on the eve of the Passover, rather than on the day itself, 19:14). On the other hand, later apologetic is at work in the participation of the temple police in the arrest. There are legendary features, such as the naming of Malchus and Peter (18:10), the episode between the mother of Jesus and the beloved disciple, which perhaps has allegorical significance, as does the omission of the breaking of the legs (identifying Jesus with the passover lamb) and the story of the lance and the outflow of water and blood, symbolizing perhaps the gospel sacraments. The overall effect of the Johannine passion narrative is to stress the glory of Jesus in the midst of his passion. Note how at every point Jesus remains master of the situation. See, for instance, the arrest (18:5-10), Jesus' behavior before the high priest (18:23), and finally Jesus' making his own will and deciding himself on the moment of his death (v. 30). He dies with the triumphant cry, *consummatum est* (19:30). The weakness of the RSV (KJV), "it is finished," is unpardonable.

The Pres./UCC/Chr. Ch. lectionary again goes its own way, following the Lucan passion (Luke 23:33-46). It thus opts for the least theological, though most affecting, of the passion stories, the one which has transposed the passion from the key of tragedy to the key of pathos (Dibelius). This transposition is shown in the three Lucan words from the cross. First, there is Jesus' prayer, "Father, forgive them" (the omission of these words, noted in the RSV margin, is apparently due to later antisemitism). Second, the episode of the penitent and impenitent thieves, which looks like a homiletic elaboration of the earlier tradition that both the thieves railed on Jesus. Third, the last word, from Ps. 31:5, the Jewish bedtime prayer, instead of Ps. 22:1. Then there is the substitution of "this man was an innocent man," for the more theologically motivated confession of the Marcan centurion, "Truly this was the Son of God." But perhaps Luke was closer to history in attributing the darkness to an eclipse. In Mark it is supernatural and a piece of eschatological symbolism. The overall tone of the Lucan passion narrative is the culmination of the life of the gracious savior who goes out in love to others.

HOMILETICAL INTERPRETATION

Today's readings, except for the Pres./UCC/Chr. Ch., appear at first glance to put the homilist in something of a bind. If he follows the indications in the first two readings, then he may develop the theme of Jesus as the man of sorrows, as one who shared our humanity in every way, who was tempted and experienced weakness, especially the great weakness of man, the fear of death; and yet in the midst of his dying he showed that fear of death may be overcome by one who is firmly rooted in hope.

If, on the other hand, he chooses to follow the indications of the Gospel according to John, then he will be singing the victory of Jesus over all the forces that opposed him. In John's account Jesus is always the master of every situation.

This picture seems at variance with the first, or at least seems to put the homilist in the position of having to establish two quite distinct moods. Perhaps approaching John's Gospel from a certain viewpoint will bring the readings into harmony.

First of all, the homilist has at his disposal one of the most powerfully moving passages ever composed. In fact, the language of the fourth servant song is so extraordinary and so easily grasped by the listener, the homilist would do well to make his comments prior to the reading of this selection. In that way he can prepare his hearers to receive its impact directly.

He should ask them to recognize that the church saw in the figure of the servant a prophetic description of Jesus: by his sufferings our sins have been taken away. The point of this is not for us to feel guilty or to try and work up some sense of shame. The servant is a hero who has won a great victory for us. We should rejoice and be grateful.

In the original meaning of the fourth servant song the Gentiles are the ones who despise the people of Israel and hold them of no account. And yet out of the sufferings of this people came salvation for the Gentiles: Who could believe it? It was to this lowly people that the power of Yahweh was revealed (cf. 53:1).

It is true that over the centuries we have continued to act as the Gentiles did, to look down on certain races and classes of people, to lay heavy burdens of suffering on them and then attribute their unhappy condition to a punishment inflicted on them by God.

Yes, we have a great deal to learn about the ways of God with man, but let us not fail to hear the glorious words of salvation which the fidelity of the servant has called forth: "on him lies a punishment that brings us peace, and through his wounds we are healed" (53:5).

The first reading in the Pres./UCC/Chr. Ch. lectionary must have special treatment. It directly pertains to a tragedy that befell Jerusalem and attributes this to her having sinned grievously. She laments the fact that her enemy has triumphed over her. This can be applied to the passion only with the greatest care. The final verse is very touching if placed on the lips of Jesus: "All you who pass this way, look and see: is any sorrow like the sorrow that afflicts me," but the remainder of the sentence makes it very inappropriate as attributed to Jesus: "[the sorrow] with which Yahweh has struck me on the day of his burning anger?" (Lam. 1:12).

To attribute these verses to the proper subject, Jerusalem, runs the risk of summoning up images of a wrathful God wreaking vengeance on Jerusalem for having crucified his Son Jesus. This is wholly alien to the spirit which moved Jesus during his passion, and it is from him that we learn the attitude of his Father; out of love he sent his Son into the world so that through his sacrifice all men might be saved.

The second readings continue the theme of Jesus as the man of sorrows. He has now come into his glory but the author of Hebrews is at pains to establish the permanent importance for us of how he got there. In Heb. 4:14–5:10 we are told that Jesus deserves to be *our* high priest because he fully shares our humanity. To put it more precisely, he was so subject to the condition of being human that he was tempted in every way that we are. The author is not thinking of the three temptations by Satan in the desert at the beginning of his public life. Jesus was subjected to the test throughout his ministry, but especially at the end of his life.

We are not presented with the masterful Jesus of the Fourth Gospel here. No, we see rather a Jesus struggling against his weakness, especially before the prospect of his being handed over to be put to death. He is a Jesus who cries aloud and who sheds silent tears, praying to the one who had the power to save him out of death.

Having learned obedience in the school of suffering, he is acclaimed by God with the title of high priest, but he remains *our* high priest. In his glory he has the power to bring us to salvation, but he reached that state by struggling with his weakness. He remembers what it is to be tested. He is a high priest who can sympathize with our weakness. In our need we can turn to him in perfect confidence that he will reach out to us with compassion.

In Heb. 10:1-25 the power of our high priest to save us is described. In contrast to the old sacrifices that needed to be repeated again and again, we learn that the perfect obedience of Jesus has given all of us access to the Father. Because he hoped in God, we too may have hope.

A most dramatic example of Jesus' hope is in the Gospel selection from the Pres./UCC/Chr. Ch. lectionary. Jesus is being mocked and jeered at as he hangs nailed to the cross. If he has any power, now is the time to use it—on his own behalf. The leaders of the people, the Roman soldiers, even one of the criminals hanging beside him, all urge him in mocking tones to save himself.

Something in us urges him also to pop the nails from his hands and feet, and by his show of strength to confound his enemies and give comfort to his grieving followers. But he has no power to come down from the cross. Unless his Father acts, and acts quickly, he will pass into the darkness of death with the mocking cries still being hurled at him, the derisive epilogue that sums up the failure of his mission.

Abandoned, powerless, alone, on the point of death, Jesus still clung fast to his hope in God. Luke writes: "when Jesus had cried out in a loud voice, he said, 'Father, into your hands I commit my spirit' " (Luke 23:46, citing Ps. 31:5).

When we turn to the Gospel according to John the atmosphere is in many respects quite different. In the garden of Gethsemane there is no mention of an agony scene. Instead Jesus is presented as "knowing everything that was going to happen to him" (18:4). The soldiers who come to arrest him fall to the ground at the mention of his name (v. 6). Jesus directs them to arrest him and let the disciples go (v. 8). In the dialogues with Caiaphas and with Pilate Jesus is clearly in command. In fact, it is established that he is a king (v. 37). He speaks three times from the cross: once it is to commit his mother to the care of the beloved disciple; the second time he says, "I am thirsty," and John notes the reason is to fulfill the scripture perfectly (v. 28); finally Jesus proclaims the victory, "It is accomplished" and gives up his spirit (v. 30).

John, of course, is aware of Jesus' sufferings, but is pointing out that the same events viewed with the eyes of faith may be transformed from a seeming defeat into a glorious exaltation. It may indeed be the supreme revelation of God to man in Jesus. John uses a number of images to describe the climactic moments of Jesus' life. The passion is conceived as Jesus' return to the Father, a gracious way to describe the suffering and death Jesus was to undergo. John begins his account of the Last Supper with the solemn words that "Jesus knew that the hour had come for him to pass from this world to the Father" (John 13:1). Again he notes that Jesus knew that "he had come from God and was returning to God" (John 13:3).

A second image which John uses to refer to the crucifixion/resurrection/ascension is that of being "lifted up." The first step in his return to the Father is his being lifted up on the cross. Just as Moses lifted up a bronze serpent in the desert, so, Jesus said, the Son of man must be lifted up in order that each one who believes in him may possess eternal life (cf. John 3:13-15). Jesus will be recognized then as having divine rank: "when you have lifted up the Son of man, then you will know that I am he" (John 8:28). The effect of his being lifted up on the cross will be so powerful and so magnificent as to make men forget its original grim appearance: "And when I am lifted up from the earth, I shall draw all men to myself" (John 12:32).

A third image is taken from the language of royalty, but John employs it in his own special way. The Jesus who is proclaimed "King of the Jews" by Pilate and by the Roman soldiers is indeed a king. His crown, though, is a crown of thorns and he is dressed in a rough purple robe. He is slapped and whipped and finally nailed to a cross and, strangely enough, this is what reveals him to be a king: "Yes," he says to Pilate, "I am a king. For this was I was born and for this I came into the world: to bear witness to the truth" (John 18:37). So it was that when Pilate handed Jesus over to be crucified he had a notice fixed to the cross. The notice was written in Hebrew, Latin, and Greek so that all men would be able to identify this man, "Jesus of Nazareth, King of the Jews."

These lines on the kingship of Jesus are heavy with irony. A pagan governor confers the title on him. The chief priests and the people reject it. None of them understands what kind of king Jesus really was.

Today a homilist may be tempted to avoid the title altogether. Royalty has fallen to a very low estate in our day. The external trappings remain but a monarch no longer rules alone. Even if a homilist should re-create for his congregation the former glory of the king, he then must face the problem that Jesus was not that kind of king. And yet there is something about that title. Even today it speaks to something deep in us, a longing that no earthly king could ever respond to. We may at times thrill to the sight of a magnificent king who rules with power from a mighty palace. But our heart yearns for another kind of leader, one who is close to us and shares our life and who calls forth from us, not awe, but love.

Luke seems to have caught this aspect of the kingdom of Christ perfectly in his description of the good thief, contained in the Pres./UCC/Chr. Ch. lectionary for today. As Jesus is hanging on the cross, he is mocked by those about him. If he is the man he says he is, then he ought to save himself. This challenge is hurled at him by the leaders of the people (Luke 23:35), by the Roman soldiers (v. 37) and finally by one of the criminals crucified with him (v. 39). But the other thief surprisingly takes Jesus' part, then turns to Jesus and says, "Jesus, remember me when you come into your kingdom" (v. 42). Older translations had him saying, "*Lord*, remember me," but that misses the whole point. He does not see a "Lord." He sees only Jesus, and yet somehow he knows that Jesus cannot save himself. The thief understands that Jesus is a very special kind of king and asks to be with him in that kingdom.

A fourth image used to express this mysterious revelation of God in Jesus is found in John's use of the term "glory." The first events of the passion itself are referred to as the beginning of Jesus' glorification: "Father, the hour has come. Glorify your Son in order that the Son may glorify you" (John 17:1).

It is not simply the case that John is too sensitive a spirit and so is unable to face the harsh reality of Jesus' passion. He is sensitive but in a different sense of the word. He is not simply anticipating the splendor of the resurrection in order to brighten up the gloom of the crucifixion. John is saying that the glory of God shines magnificently through all the events of the passion for those with eyes to see.

This same glory of God accompanies his manifestations throughout the OT. When God gave Israel the Ten Commandments, the glory of Yahweh settled on Mount Sinai and "to the eyes of the sons of Israel the glory of Yahweh seemed like a devouring fire on the mountain top" (Exod. 24:17). This glory is the radiance, the epiphany to men, of God's majesty, his power and his holiness.

All these mighty attributes are also revealed in the passion of Jesus but in a strikingly different way. John does not view the cross simply as a stage that Jesus must pass through so that the glory of God may then appear, i.e., what we would recognize as glory. John is saying that in the very suffering of Jesus the glory of God appears, or better, in his passion Jesus is revealing to us God himself.

From this point of view John's account does not seem so much at variance in spirit with the first two readings. God's glory is manifested in the weakness of Jesus and in his strength, in his humiliation and in his exaltation, in his fear of dying and in his unshakable conviction that it was into God's hands that he was handing over his spirit.

PROCLAMATION:

Aids for Interpreting the Lessons of the Church Year

PENTECOST 2

SERIES B

Eduard Riegert
and
Richard H. Hiers

ORTRESS PRESS Philadelphia, Pennsylvania

Table of Contents

Library of Congress Catalog Card Number 74-24960

ISBN 0-8006-4077-2

4752F75 Printed in U.S.A 1-4077

General Preface

Proclamation: Aids for Interpreting the Lessons of the Church Year is a series of twenty-six books designed to help clergymen carry out their preaching ministry. It offers exegetical interpretations of the lessons for each Sunday and many of the festivals of the church year, plus homiletical ideas and insights.

The basic thrust of the series is ecumenical. In recent years the Episcopal church, the Roman Catholic church, the United Church of Christ, the Christian Church (Disciples of Christ), the United Methodist Church, the Lutheran and Presbyterian churches, and also the Consultation on Church Union have adopted lectionaries that are based on a common three-year system of lessons for the Sundays and festivals of the church year. *Proclamation* grows out of this development, and authors have been chosen from all of these traditions. Some of the contributors are parish pastors; others are teachers, both of biblical interpretation and of homiletics. Ecumenical interchange has been encouraged by putting two persons from different traditions to work on a single volume, one with the primary responsibility for exegesis and the other for homiletical interpretation.

Despite the high percentage of agreement among the traditions, both in the festivals that are celebrated and the lessons that are appointed to be read on a given day, there are still areas of divergence. Frequently the authors of individual volumes have tried to take into account the various textual traditions, but in some cases this has proved to be impossible; in such cases we have felt constrained to limit the material to the Lutheran readings.

The preacher who is looking for "canned sermons" in these books will be disappointed. These books are one step removed from the pulpit: they explain what the lessons are saying and suggest ways of relating this biblical message to the contemporary situation. As such they are springboards for creative thought as well as for faithful proclamation of the word.

The authors of this volume of *Proclamation* are Eduard R. Riegert and Richard H. Hiers. Dr. Riegert, the editor-homiletician, is a graduate of the University of Saskatchewan (B.A.), the Lutheran College and Seminary in Saskatoon (B.D.), the Lutheran Theoolgical Seminary in Philadelphia (S.T.M.), and Princeton Theological Seminary (Ph.D.). He has been teaching at Waterloo Lutheran Seminary, Waterloo, Ontario, since 1965 and is currently Associate Professor of Homiletics and Liturgics and Dean of the Chapel. In addition, he is also Lecturer in Archaeology,

Wilfrid Laurier University, Waterloo, Ontario. Dr. Riegert is an ordained Lutheran minister and a member of the Lutheran Church in America. Dr. Hiers, the exegete, is a graduate of Yale Divinity School (B.D.), with a major in New Testament, and Yale University (Ph.D.), with a major in biblical theology. He is Professor of Religion, University of Florida, Gainesville. He is a member of the Protestant Episcopal Church and an ordained minister in the Presbyterian Church, U.S.

Introduction

One of the intimidating and yet liberating lessons the preacher must learn is that he becomes an interpreter of Scripture. Nowhere is this lesson better learned than in close dialogue with a biblical scholar. This volume, like others in this series, invites the reader to join the dialogue a preacher and a biblical scholar have had.

We have offered exegesis (thought not exposition) of all the denominationally appointed texts, and wish to record our impression that remarkable insight has gone into the selection of these combinations of lessons by the several traditions, especially with respect to the related and ultimate issues they coherently embrace. We have not, however, attempted to smooth out all differences in interpretation between us. Both the Scriptures and human life are too rich for a "party line" approach. Occasionally one or the other of us does take a fairly definite theological and/or ethical position or follow a different perspective or interest; but we think we ought to do so, for the preacher must do so, too.

It is only fair, furthermore, to acknowledge that we assume, necessarily, a series of critical and historical positions which, given the limits of our assignment, we cannot explicate or even define adequately; nevertheless, we have endeavored to avoid premature cloture with respect to traditional interpretations as well as to the latest conclusions in biblical research (e.g., the authorship of Ephesians; the historical value of the Markan tradition). Our assumption is that the reader will have access to major commentaries, monographs, and journals. For this reason, too, as well as because of limitations of space, we have not provided footnotes to scholarly literature.

The homiletical expositions were born out of independent study of and meditation upon the texts, and subsequently shaped by direct confrontation with the exegetical studies. Their intent is not so much to provide clusters of sermon ideas as to move imaginatively into the realm of human life as this is suggested, challenged, and illuminated by the text. A basic principle underlying the expositions is that kerygmatically and experientially the story of the text is our story. Historically Joshua and Jeremiah and even Jesus are far removed from us, but their struggles with faith and life are not. Any good story grips us and takes us into it, so that we identify with the characters and the situations; thus it articulates at least some of our experiences and problems. The Bible does this too. Thus, the shift from Jeremiah, for example, to ourselves occurs in a split second: we *are* Jeremiah complaining to the Lord. And through this imaginative process we gain meaning for ourselves, and through faithful exegesis we find also correction.

While it may be obvious, it is nevertheless well to set forth the reminder that the exegetical studies themselves are prime material for sermons. The wide range of biblical references given (to mention only one facet) forms a reservoir of material for "expository" sermons which teach the Scriptures, and for "doctrinal" sermons which treat theological themes. It goes without saying that neither the exegesis nor the exposition will make sense to the reader unless he has before him and carefully attends to the biblical text.

We wish to acknowledge the use of the Revised Standard Version in most direct quotations, as well as Kittel's and Nestle's texts.

E.R.R.
R.H.H.

The Tenth Sunday after Pentecost

Lutheran	*Roman Catholic*	*Episcopal*	*Pres./UCC/Chr.*	*Methodist/COCU*
Exod. 24:3–11	2 Kings 4:42–44	2 Kings 4:42–44	2 Kings 4:42–44	2 Kings 4:42–44
Eph. 4:1–7, 11–16	Eph. 4:1–6	Eph. 4:1–6	Eph. 4:1–6, 11–16	Eph. 4:1–6, 11–16
John 6:1–15	John 6:1–15	Mark 6:35–44	John 6:1–15	John 6:1–15

EXEGESIS

First Lesson: Exod. 24:3-11 (and 2 Kings 4:42-44). Exodus 20-23 reports the various "words" and ordinances which, according to the tradition, God spoke to Moses on Mt. Sinai as the law for Israel. Because of the holiness of God, the people had to keep their distance from God, but Moses had drawn near to him (20:21). Our lesson describes what follows, when Moses comes down and tells the people what God has said. Immediately and unanimously they declare their intention to keep the law (24:3). [In later times, the elders of Israel enacted a more elaborate ceremony of ratification or renewal of the covenant. See Deuteronomy 27–30.] Afterwards, Moses "wrote all the words of the Lord," thereby producing "the book of the Covenant" (24:7) which, presumably, contained both the Ten Commandments (20:1–17) and the numerous other laws recorded in 20:23–23:33. Moses then built an altar at the foot of Mt. Sinai, erected twelve pillars, representing the tribes of Israel, and ordered sacrificial offerings. The blood of the animals was drained off, in accordance with the ancient belief that it was their life (Gen. 9:4–5). Having thrown half the blood against the altar, Moses then read the "book of the Covenant" to the people, who again vowed fidelity to it (v. 7). Then he threw the rest of the blood upon the people, symbolizing, perhaps, the sacred bond of unity or community between God and people. Nadab and Abihu were sons of Aaron, according to later priestly belief (Exod. 6:23; Num. 3:2 ff.). They, together with Moses, Aaron, and seventy (other) elders then went back up Mt. Sinai and "saw the God of Israel"—an unusual episode, since God was only rarely *seen* (Isa. 6:1 ff.; Ezek. 1:26–28; cf. Exod. 3:3–6). God is not described, but only that on which he stood: "as it were, a pavement of sapphire stone," through which translucent surface, perhaps, he was visible. God did not come into direct contact with the men, but they were allowed to see him and to eat and drink in his presence (v. 11). Possibly it was thought that Moses and the others were given a share of the sacrificial offerings, though what they ate and drank is not stated. The meal, like the sprinkling with blood, indicated communion with God. Later Jewish traditions looked forward to eating and drinking in the presence of God or his messiah in the kingdom of God (Isa. 25:6; 2 *Baruch* 29; cf. Gen. 49:10–12).

2 Kings 4:42–44. A man brings Elisha a supply of "bread of the first fruits" (see Exod. 23:16), namely, twenty barley loaves and a sack of grain. This may have been a typical offering to the priests or prophets who presided at the cultic altars in those days. Elisha orders his servant to set this before "the men," i.e., the group of cultic prophets mentioned in 2 Kings 4:38. The servant protests that this will not be enough for a hundred men. Elisha insists. The servant then did as directed, the men ate, and there was some left. The story was told, with others in 2 Kings 2–7, to commemorate Elisha's not always beneficent miraculous powers (see 2:23 f.), and to show that God could take care of those in special need (4:1–41). It is noteworthy that few such miracle stories are reported in the OT, and that most of them are associated with Elisha.

Second Lesson: Eph. 4:1–7, 11–16. We come now to a series of five lessons (Pentecost 10–14) from chaps. 4 and 5 of the Epistle to the Ephesians. The words "who are at Ephesus" (1:1) are absent in the earliest manuscripts, suggesting either that this was a general or "catholic" letter for reading by several churches, or that it was intended for some church whose identity was undesignated or lost. There is little in the letter to suggest that the author was personally acquainted with its intended recipients (cf. Acts 19), and several hints that he had not been with them before, e.g., 1:15; 3:1–4. Of course, the letter might have been written before Paul first came to Ephesus. But there are other reasons to question whether Paul was its author. References to the apostles in 2:20 and 3:5 imply composition in the post-apostolic age. Numerous words are used here that are not found elsewhere in Paul's letters, and there are other stylistic differences. The letter parallels or reproduces a great deal of the distinctive content of Colossians, whose authorship also is disputed. Nevertheless, much of the faith-understanding in the letter is basically Pauline. Edgar Goodspeed and John Knox have proposed that it was written around A.D. 90 as a compend of Paul's thought and an introduction to a collection of Paul's letters then being assembled for copying and wider circulation among the churches. The main concerns of the letter are to appeal to readers to maintain the unity of the church, faithfulness to Christ, and renewed moral life befitting those who have been saved, brought near, called, or forgiven.

Here as elsewhere in Paul's letters, the author refers to himself as a "prisoner" (e.g., Phil. 1:7, 13; Philem. 23). Paul had been imprisoned on several occasions, including the final years of his career (Acts 21–28). The understanding of the Christian life in 4:1–3 is typical of the Pauline "indicative/imperative" (Bultmann). In effect: Strive to be what already, through the grace (gift) of God in Christ, you have become. There are a number of echoes of Paul's exhortations in 1 Corinthians 12–14 here: The summons to lowliness, meekness, patience, forbearance, and love (1 Cor. 13:4–7); to unity in the one Spirit (1 Cor. 12:4–13); and to peace and honoring all members of the community as members of the one body of Christ (1 Cor. 12:14–31). In Eph. 4:11 the different offices of the church are described as "gifts"; cf. 1 Cor. 12:4 ff., 27 ff. But in both, the final mark of the Christian life is love, doing that which contributes to building up the church (1 Cor. 13:13; 14:12; Eph. 4:12, 16). A special feature in Ephesians is the idea of growing or maturing into the stature or person of Christ: 4:13, 15–16. The emphasis in Ephesians is less on the future coming of Christ than on the transformation or confirmation of Christians by Christ to the measure of his perfection (see also 1:22; 2:16–19, and esp. 4:13). Paul's "Christ-mysticism" was similar in some respects, though Paul looked for final perfection, transformation or fulfillment only at the resurrection of the dead and the coming of Christ (1 Cor. 13:8–12; 15:42–55; Phil. 3:8–21).

Gospel: John 6:1–15; Mark 6:35–44. The Fourth Gospel generally presents a quite different account of Jesus, his message and activity, from that given in the first three (synoptic) Gospels. To what extent John contains historically reliable tradition beyond what we find in the synoptic Gospels is still debated. In any case, this Gospel represents the faith-understanding or theology of an important segment of the late first century Christian community. In our lesson today, we have John's version of Jesus' feeding of the five thousand. It is not very different from that given in Mark 6:32–44. John locates the meal "in the hills" (cf. Mark 6:46); omits reference to Jesus' compassion on the crowd and teaching (Mark 6:34); places the event near or at Passover (6:4); reports that Jesus knew what he would do and deliberately tested Philip by asking him how they would buy bread (cf. Mark 6:37); and that a lad, rather than the disciples, supplied barley loaves (cf. 2 Kings 4:42) and fish. In other respects, the stories are quite similar, including such details as two hundred denarii, five loaves, two fish, five thousand participants sitting on the grass, and twelve baskets of fragments left over.

In both versions, Jesus' procedure parallels or anticipates his actions at the last supper and the church's later reenactment of that event: the people are seated, Jesus takes bread, blesses or gives thanks, distributes to the crowd, likewise the fish (cf. cup). In Mark 6, Jesus also breaks the bread and distributes it through the disciples. If the procedure is already eucharistic in Mark, it is still more so in John. Such key terms as *anapesein, anakeimenois* (sit down), *elaben* (take), *eucharistēsas* (give thanks), and *edoken* (give), lacking in Mark but used by John, parallel and probably derive from the synoptic and Paul's accounts of the last supper

(Matthew 26, Mark 14, Luke 22, 1 Corinthians 11). In John, the story of the feeding of the five thousand seems to function as the "institution" of the eucharist, since John does not describe any such procedures at the last supper (chap. 13). As we shall see in the next three lessons, in the later verses of chap. 6 Jesus discourses about the bread which gives eternal life, identified with himself or his flesh, in what are, evidently, a series of eucharistic sayings (6:26–58). John may have intended the reader to understand that the bread about which Jesus spoke here was related to the ceremony involving bread and fish reported in the earlier verses of chap. 6.

Only John's Gospel describes any of Jesus' actions as "signs"; in this Gospel, signs are reported for the benefit of the reader: "that you may believe that Jesus is the Christ, the Son of God, and that believing you may have life in his name" (20:30–31). Thus the signs themselves have a kind of sacramental or saving value. But the people mentioned in 6:14–15 misread the sign: they identified Jesus as "the prophet who is to come" (a "prophet like Moses," Elijah, or Elisha?). And they desired to "snatch" or "seize" (*harpazein*: cf. Matt. 11:12; 12:29; 13:19; John 10:12) him and make him king. But this was not the kingship Jesus sought: My kingdom (or kingship) is not of (or from) this world (John 18:36; cf. Matt. 4:8–9).

HOMILETICAL INTERPRETATION

First Lesson: Exod. 24:3–11. Exotic narratives: on the one hand a "primitive" (barbaric? savage?) scene of covenant-making and covenant-ratification; on the other hand a sublime theophany and a feasting with God!

But the covenant has to do with life (the blood is the life), and life is messy . . . and sublime! The covenant is made here in the midst of life—in the midst of slavery-freedom, sin-grace, the blood of violence and the blood of brotherhood. We are all in that together even as all Israel was sprinkled with blood, and we are all "washed in the blood of the Lamb" and receive "the blood of Christ shed for you" (note the movement in John 6, covered progressively over the next several Sundays). We cannot escape this solidarity of mankind—nor should we want to; we are all inextricably bound to one another (note "one body, one Spirit . . ." in the Second Lesson, Ephesians 4); to be bound to one another is life; to be separated is death (quite dramatically so in our "spaceship earth" and our "global village").

If life is messy, it is also sublime. The covenant is from God and with God—already here in our messy and frequently dehumanizing life-together we catch glimpses of his presence. There is enormous commitment on the part of God; already he "humbles himself" to become part of our oft barbaric human existence, showing us in the midst of it the magnificent dimensions of life: the mountain of splendor, the vision of clarity, the feast of united celebration. All biblical feasts have that ultimate dimension: they are "foretastes" (see exegesis, v. 11).

Second Lesson: Eph. 4:1–7, 11–16. There is much here that is instructive for the peculiarly Christian community. The churches (as do other institutions and groups) too often exaggerate their *differences* in order to justify their existence; Paul admonishes us to exercise watchful care over the *unity* which is already given through our calling. It is the unity of one body activated by one Spirit and motivated by one hope; it is made possible by one Lord with whom we are all united by one baptism which demonstrates and expresses one faith; it is a unity under one Father-God who permeates all (4:4–6). This unity is fragile; to care for it requires worthy living (4:1–3), which in turn produces worthy results: a mutual nurture leading to full maturity as measured in Christ (4:7, 11–16).

This unity held in the bond of peace recalls the ancient covenant with God (First Lesson). That covenant is here neither negated nor superseded, but expanded to its fullness: Gentiles are included in it (cf. Eph. 2:11 ff.)! This is a magnificent vision, an expansion of the ancient covenant which the writer calls a "mystery" (Eph. 3:3–6, 9–10). Over the centuries that ancient covenant became narrow and exclusivistic—that is a danger the people of the "new covenant" in later times, unfortunately, have not escaped! The writer to the Ephesians wrote from an *inclusive* perspective; the church's perspective on Jews and other non-Christians has been largely *exclusivistic*. Fragmentariness is a mark of our lives and of the world. Paul's vision of one body with distinct yet integrated members is not only a model for congregations but also for the community of nations.

Gospel: John 6:1–15. The whole of John 6, with a few omissions, is read over the next five Sundays, Pentecost 10 through 14. We need therefore to grasp the movement of the entire chapter. One may see the thought moving on three levels: (1) the purely materialistic level in which hungry folk receive bread; (2) the still materialistic but advanced level in which bread signifies Jesus' flesh; (3) the illuminating level of the Spirit. Again, one may see a progression in a series of questions and answers, initiated by Jesus and concluded by Jesus:

6:5—How feed the people?	6:9—We can't. Can you?
6:25—When did you come here?	6:26 f.—Labor for the food of eternal life.
6:28—How do the work of God?	6:29—Believe in the one he sent.
6:30 f.—What sign do you do?	6:32 f.—God gives the bread of life.
6:34—Give us this bread.	6:35 ff.—I am the bread.
6:41 f.—How can he say he came down from Heaven?	6:43–51—I am the living bread=my flesh.

6:52—How can he give us his flesh to eat?	6:53–58—Mutual abiding.
6:60—Who can listen to this hard saying?	6:61–65—The spirit gives life.
6:66 f.—Will you also go away?	6:68 f.—You are the Holy One of Israel.

In today's Gospel Jesus initiates the discussion by feeding the 5,000. It is a "sign," says the evangelist, and this should alert us that interesting and even profitable themes like Jesus' compassion which triumphs over his weariness, Andrew still bringing people to Jesus, the boy and his lunch, the "facts and figures" Philip, and the abundant leftovers are definitely secondary themes. As a "sign" the miracle reaches *back*: back to Elisha's feeding miracle (2 Kings 4:42–44; Elisha is the carrier of Elijah's mantle, and Elijah was very important in Jewish messianic expectations); back to the feast with God of Moses and the 70 elders (First Lesson); to the Passover (6:4) and its themes of exodus and wilderness wanderings; and to Deut. 18:15, the "prophet who is to come" (6:14). As a "sign" the miracle also points *forward* to the advent of a New Age when God intervenes to save his people; to the cross and resurrection; to the eucharist; and to the eschatological banquet.

The "sign," discernible only to the eyes of faith, sets Jesus at the center of history as the one who makes clear God's constant and saving presence. The same God who led Israel out of Egypt, who fed them in the desert, who sustained them through centuries of convoluted history, is savingly present—incarnate—in this Jesus whose life is the life of the world, and remains savingly present in the eucharist, and indeed, into the ultimate future.

The Eleventh Sunday after Pentecost

Lutheran	*Roman Catholic*	*Episcopal*	*Pres./UCC/Chr.*	*Methodist/COCU*
Exod. 16:2–15	Exod. 16:2–4, 12–15	Exod. 16:2–4, 12–15	Exod. 16:2–4, 12–15	Exod. 16:2–15
Eph. 4:17–24	Eph. 4:17, 20–24	Eph. 4:17–24	Eph. 4:17–24	Eph. 4:17–25
John 6:24–35	John 6:24–35	John 6:24–35	John 6:24–35	John 6:24–35

EXEGESIS

First Lesson: Exod. 16:2–15. The story picks up here immediately after the escape from Pharaoh's armies by the Red Sea (Sea of Reeds) celebrated in the songs of Miriam and Moses, chap. 15. Moses had purified the "bitter" water of Marah, and the people, having encamped at the oasis of Elim (15:27), now come into the Wilderness of Sin (= Zin, Sinai?). It is still only a few weeks after their deliverance by the sea (16:1), but already the people complain against Moses and Aaron, that it would have been better if they had never left Egypt with its ample supply of meat ("fleshpots") and bread. In their anxiety and discomfort, they profoundly mistrust Moses' intentions or ability: "You have brought us out into this wilderness to kill this whole assembly with hunger" (v. 3). Moses correctly perceives that their "murmurings" are not so much against himself and Aaron, as against the Lord (vv. 7–8).

The "murmuring" or complaining of the people of Israel in the wilderness is a characteristic feature of the biblical reports concerning this period. (Thus also, e.g., Numbers 11, 14 and Exodus 32, which give mainly J and E traditions.) Probably we have here a P (Priestly) account: Note the prominence of Aaron, provision for obviating the necessity of gathering (doing labor) on the Sabbath (v. 5), and the typically P description of God's visible presence in terms of his "glory" *(kabōd)*, vv. 7, 10. Only a few days after the exodus events, the people are again (cf. 14:11–12) doubting whether the Lord cares or is able to sustain them. They do not pray, but only complain. Nevertheless, the Lord hears their "murmurings" and undertakes to provide for them. So quails "came up and covered the camp," supplying flesh or meat *(basar)*, and in the morning "there was on the face of the wilderness" a peculiar substance, identified, perhaps, as manna *(man)*, and as bread *(lechem)*. Thus God provided the flesh and bread for want of which they had complained (v. 3). What the "manna" may have been was a mystery then (v. 15), and has remained so since, though interpreters have offered many more or less naturalistic explanations. It is described as a "fine, flake-like thing, fine as hoarfrost on the ground," and also "like coriander seed" (vv. 14, 31). The term *lechem* may mean simply "food" as well as "bread"; we should not visualize loaves of bread, though this is suggested in later times, e.g., John 6:31. In any case, here, as in the great exodus event, God showed himself willing and able to care for his people. Later in the chapter, it is said that the people continued to eat manna all their years in the wilderness until they came to the land of Canaan (v. 35).

It is remarkable that these reports of Israel's complaining and mistrust are found in their Scriptures. Yet it is typical of the faith and historical traditions of Israel that the faults of the people are openly reported. Jacob, David, Solomon, and even Abraham and Moses, are shown in their moments of disbelief, disobedience, and—in the case of Solomon—apostasy. There are heroes, but no saints in the OT. The basic distinction between God and people central to Israel's faith permitted the story of Israel to be told realistically, with surprisingly little self-glorification (cf. Ezra 9:2). The sermons in the early chapters of Deuteronomy continually emphasize that it was not because of Israel's importance or virtue that God made covenant with them and blessed them, but because of his promise to the fathers and his love for them (e.g., Deut. 7:6–8; 9:4–6). We see here already the understanding that God's favor and blessings flow from his love or grace, not because of man's—even Israel's—righteousness (cf. Rom. 3:20–26; 1 Cor. 1:26–31).

Second Lesson: Eph. 4:17–24. Paul (or the Pauline author) exhorts the readers to live the kind of life befitting the new humanity which has been made possible for them. Vv. 17–19 contrast the life that Christians must live with that of the Gentiles; vv. 20–21 refer to the standard of Christ which they should have learned; and vv. 22–24 call upon the readers to put off their old nature (literally, "old man") with its corrupt ways of life, and put on the new one of true righteousness and holiness.

Paul does not usually speak disparagingly of the Gentiles: they were, in fact, the subjects of his special theological concern and missionary activity (Gal. 1–3). Eph. 4:17–19 echoes Paul's description in Rom. 1:18–32 of those, presumably Gentiles, who failed to perceive the "power and deity" of God in the world, who "became futile in their thinking and their senseless minds were darkened," and consequently were given up to "dishonorable passions" and all kinds of improper conduct. Increasingly the churches of the latter part of the first century were composed of Gentile-Christians, who had not been brought up in accordance with the law and customs of Jewish morality. If Ephesians was written to such a church (or churches), its summons to live differently from the ways of the Gentile neighbors and from the readers' own former Gentile patterns of behavior, would be very much to the point. Thus, probably, Eph. 4:22; cf. 1 Cor. 6:9–11.

The expressions "learning Christ," "hearing about him," and being "taught in him" (vv. 20–21) are unusual. Paul only infrequently refers to traditions about Jesus or his teaching. Here, however, the sense may be more the mystical participation of the believer in Christ, an immediate perception of his being and will, as in Phil. 2:5: "Have this mind among yourselves, which you have in Christ Jesus . . ." Here the author calls on his readers to be renewed in the spirit of their minds (Eph. 4:23).

Paul's insistence that those in Christ are already a "new creation" (*kainē ktisis:* see 2 Cor. 5:17; Gal. 6:15) is presupposed in the summons to put off the old man and put on the new (*ton kainon anthrōpon*), "created [*ktisthenta*] after the likeness of God" (4:22–24). A quite similar saying is to be found at Col. 3:9–10, again contrasting the "old man" with the "new," but with the slight difference that the latter is indicative rather than hortatory, and it is a matter of "*being renewed in knowledge* after the image of its creator." Cf. 1 Cor. 15:49: "Just as we have borne the image of the man of dust, we shall [or "let us"] bear the image of the man of heaven." Paul normally thinks of the believer's being conformed or transformed to the image of Christ, rather than to the likeness of God. On being like God in righteousness and holiness, see, e.g., Lev. 19:2 ff.; Matt. 5:48. The idea that the Christian already is, or should be transformed is basic both to Paul and—if not the same person—the author of Ephesians (see also Rom. 12:1–2).

Gospel: John 6:24–35. After feeding the five thousand, Jesus and also his disciples crossed the Sea of Galilee to Capernaum. Jesus walked the first part of the way on water, rather than traveling by boat with his disciples, to the temporary mystification of the people who had not seen him leave by boat and so looked for him the next morning in the vicinity of the meal of bread and fish (6:16–24). Afterwards they find him at Capernaum. Despite what seem to be several non sequiturs in the dialogue that follows between Jesus and "the people" (later identified as "the Jews," vv. 41, 52), there are a number of related contrasts and associations of terms and concepts.

The people address Jesus as "rabbi" or teacher (v. 25), but he refers to himself as "Son of man" (v. 27), a title with divine connotation in John. They ask him when he came there (v. 25). But Jesus ignores this, and tells them that they do not seek him because they saw signs (presumably this refers to the feeding of the five thousand the day before, John 6:14), but they seek him, he says, because they ate their fill of loaves (v. 26), as if they were simply interested in another free or filling meal. (The expression, "you ate your fill" is reminiscent of the feeding of Israel in the wilderness from the First Lesson: Exod. 16:8, 12, 16. This is referred to explicitly in John 6:31–33 where the expressions "bread from heaven" and "bread which comes down from heaven" probably allude to Exod. 16:4. See also Ps. 78:23–24.) Jesus admonishes them not to seek such food, but to seek the food or true bread from heaven which endures to and gives eternal life (vv. 27, 33, 35). As in the eucharistic-soteriological sayings that follow (esp. vv. 48–58), the Johannine Jesus identifies this food or bread with himself. It is he who has "come down from heaven" (6:38, 50–51).

Strangely, they reply, "What must we do, to be doing the work (*ergon*) of God?" (v. 28). Perhaps the connection is by verbal association with Jesus' statement in v. 27, "Do not labor" (or "work," *ergazesthe*). Or it may be that the evangelist intended to contrast Jewish emphasis on doing the works of the law with believing in Jesus. At any rate, the work of God they should do, Jesus tells them, is to believe in him (v. 29). Then they do ask for a "sign" or demonstration as basis for believing him (v. 30), but not, significantly, for believing *in (eis)* him (cf. vv. 29, 35).

It is not certain whether these sayings really refer to the eucharistic bread. In this lesson, Jesus does not call on the people to eat (or drink), but to *believe in* him. This is the "work of God" that they must do (v. 29). He who comes to Jesus and believes in him will not hunger or thirst (v. 35). Jesus is bread, then, in the spiritual or symbolic sense that those who believe in him receive the "food" or "bread" of life, eternal life (vv. 27, 33, 35, 40).

HOMILETICAL INTERPRETATION

First Lesson: Exod. 16:2–15. Moses is angry! It is no small thing to be accused of leading a people into the wilderness to perish—and that they might do so may well have crossed his own mind more than once. Besides, "murmuring" is at once irritating and infectious. To be reminded of "how things used to be"—before all these precipitous changes occurred—makes one's teeth grate, especially if one is the initiator of change and has no more than a future hope to set forth as justification. Yet how can the people of Abraham (and of Jesus!) keep forgetting the promise, and keep mislaying their commitment to the covenant (see Pentecost 10, First Lesson)? It is hard to shake a slavish mentality, to put off the old and put on the new (Second Lesson), to venture from the known—no matter how dreary it is—into the unknown. Yet that is our human journey.

While Moses is angry, God, against whom the murmuring is ultimately directed, is magnificently lenient: "I will rain bread from heaven . . ."! But not vapidly lenient: "that I may prove them, whether they will walk in my law or not." God's grace is also a judgment! He sets before us "exodus" opportunities, and our immediate reaction is one of shrinking back. Yet it is precisely *in* the opportunity that his sustaining grace can be discovered. The wilderness is a sore place that calls for "dying," and for those with the courage (or the desperation!) to die, it leads to the promised land of a new beginning and a new status. Miraculously, unexpected resources do appear.

Second Lesson: Eph. 4:17–24. Any convert, whether to or from a religion, an ideology, even an opinion, can grasp the dynamic of transformation detailed in this pericope. A conversion is a terrible invigoration! It is terrible because it means forsaking the familiar "old" for the strange "new," and that is a wrenching experience, full of pain, loss, sorrow, anguish. It is also invigorating, for it is fresh air, elbow room, excitement, adventure. It is like that moment when, having let go of one trapeze bar while reaching for the other, you hang suspended in sheer terror and sheer ecstasy. The people of the ancient exodus from Egypt knew it (see the First Lesson); so did Paul on the Damascus Road, Marx in the British Museum, and indeed, if we reflect on our progress in thought and life, we will find a variety of "conversions" we have experienced and/or backed away from.

We ought then to beware of reducing the transformation described in this pericope to a series of moralistic changes. Although ethics are definitely involved (v. 19), the writer is talking about a shift from one "manner of life" to another, from one stance or posture to another, from one "nature" to another, from being "in sin" to being "in grace." Unlike the shift made by the trapeze artist, this transformation does not occur in the twinkling of an eye (though the decision to change may so occur), but is a process that needs helping along—even with pointed reminders, 4:20–21. (Notice the progress toward understanding in John 6.) If we take our theological and experiential understanding of ourselves seriously *(simul justus et peccator)* we will glimpse something of the depth and length of this transformation, and its increasing radicalness: "after the likeness of God."

Gospel: John 6:24–35. It is amazingly difficult to rise above a sheerly physical and materialistic level of life (see under Pentecost 10, John 6:1–15). We are overwhelmingly preoccupied with survival ("the food which perishes"), yet vaguely hungering. As we struggle hard for the food which perishes, so we think we must also struggle hard for "the food which endures to eternal life"—unless there is a short-cut: "give us this bread always"!

Somewhere at the root of it is our self-understanding and our subsequent God-understanding. We are "nature's man," and like every other creature strive to survive today and tomorrow, and any windfall extends survival to the day after tomorrow. We are "manipulative man" who, if he does the right thing (pushes the right button, knows the right people, obeys the right rules, "operates" adroitly) will get an instant reward (like Moses in the wilderness). We are "absurd man," valiantly or resignedly going the weary round, pathetically hoping for a delivering miracle, yet suspicious of any promise ("What sign will you do?").

Is there something more? That's the sometimes sluggish, sometimes poignant question. Is there deliverance: a diamond ring in a box of antique junk? a winning lottery ticket? perhaps a wonder-working God?

Open your eyes and see! Deliverance is *here* (even as Jesus stands there before them, saying, "Believe in me"). We don't see it because we ask the wrong questions—penultimate questions related to our survival and to the immediate problematic situation. Are we (can we stretch that far?) "God's man"? If so, then "nature's man" is also a decision-maker; "manipulative man" is also a creator; "absurd man" is also transcendent. Man, like bread, can be only a chemical mixture, pummelled and subjected to enormous stress . . . or, like bread, he can be a medium of life, a sacrament, a means of grace.

How? That's the wrong question. Can I, like the grain of wheat in the earth and the loaf on the plate, die and thus bring life? Can I subsume my history into a greater history so that my history becomes part of God's history?

The Twelfth Sunday after Pentecost

Lutheran	*Roman Catholic*	*Episcopal*	*Pres./UCC/Chr.*	*Methodist/COCU*
1 Kings 19:4–8	1 Kings 19:4–8	1 Kings 19:4–8	1 Kings 19:4–8	1 Kings 19:4–8
Eph. 4:30–5:2	Eph. 4:30–5:2	Eph. 4:30–5:2	Eph. 4:30–5:2	Eph. 4:30–5:2
John 6:41–51	John 6:41–52	John 6:41–51	John 6:41–51	John 6:41–52

EXEGESIS

First Lesson: 1 Kings 19:4–8. Elijah, the great ninth century prophet in Israel, has just been vindicated in his contest with the prophets of Baal and Asherah on Mt. Carmel—that scene dramatized so memorably in Mendelssohn's "Elijah." Baal did not answer the cries of his prophets, but the Lord brought fire upon the offering Elijah had prepared. Then, at Elijah's command, the prophets of Baal were killed and, strangely obedient to Elijah's direction, the mighty but malevolent King Ahab meekly returned to his palace at Jezreel and his Phoenician wife, Jezebel (chap. 18). She was no believer in the Lord, and vowed vengeance upon Elijah by her pagan gods (19:1–2). He had humiliated, then (presumably) killed the four hundred prophets of Asherah who once sat at her table (18:19). Asherah probably was a female Canaanite deity. Jezebel regarded her own royal power as absolute; she was not one to stop at anything (see 1 Kings 21). Not surprisingly, Elijah was frightened by her threat (19:3).

He went a day's journey south into the wilderness, sat down, and asked that he might die (19:4; cf. Jonah 3:4; 4:3, 9). "*I am no better than my fathers,*" i.e., as good as dead (see 19:10, 14). This is quite a letdown after his tremendous victory, and it might be thought that God's astounding intervention at Mt. Carmel would have given Elijah confidence that God could now spare him from the machinations of Jezebel. But just as Israel, after the great deliverance by the sea, lapsed into complaining and mistrust, so here, Elijah gives way to anxiety and self-pity. It is not said that he was hungry—though after his phenomenal run to Jezreel (18:46) and day's journey into the wilderness, he might well have been. As with Israel in the wilderness, so here, God provides food for Elijah: not manna, but a "cake baked on hot stones and a jar of water," brought by an angel (cf. Bel and the Dragon 34–36). "*And he ate, and drank, and lay down again.*" There is no reason to think that the food was supernatural. A later apocalyptic and messianic text possibly alludes to the situation of Elijah, but is transformed into hope for the resurrection of the dead and, perhaps, a messianic meal: "And with that Son of man shall they eat and lie down and rise up for ever and ever" (Enoch 62:14).

After he rested, the angel again came, perhaps with more food and drink, and urged him to partake in preparation for the long journey ahead. "In the strength of that food," without eating anything else, it seems, Elijah then went forty days and forty nights, as later, Jesus did, in Matthew's story of his "temptation in the wilderness" (Matt. 4:1–2). Elijah's destination was Mt. Horeb, the mountain of God where Moses received the law, as it is named in E and Deuteronomic tradition (Exod. 3:1; Deut. 5:2). Here Moses also had spent forty days and forty nights (Exod. 24:18; 34:28). In this setting, later in the chapter, the "still small voice" of the Lord calls Elijah from his self-pity and dejection, to go forth and anoint Hazael to be king over Syria (!), Jehu to be king over Israel, and Elisha to be his own successor as prophet.

Second Lesson: Eph. 4:30–5:2. These verses are part of the section on Christian living or ethics that runs from 4:1 through 6:9 The pericope begins with "And" (4:30), while 5:3 begins with "But" *(de)*, indicating, as does content analysis, continuity with the preceding and following exhortations.

"Do not grieve the Holy Spirit" (4:30a): The Spirit is associated with the unity of the church (4:3–4). Evil talk (4:29) together with other forms of dissension (4:31) contrary to unity or community in the church would thus grieve the Holy Spirit. "In whom you were sealed for the day of redemption" (4:30b): This phrase recapitulates the declarations made in 1:13-14. Those who "believed in him [Christ] were sealed with the promised Holy Spirit." The understanding is that those who read the letter had received the "seal" of the Holy Spirit when (or shortly after) they first believed, possibly at the time of baptism (4:5). The Holy Spirit, moreover, is understood as "the guarantee of our inheritance until we acquire possession of it" (1:14). "Inheritance" *(klēronomia/nachalah)* is used in the OT for promised land, and in the NT for the "eternal inheritance," i.e., "salvation," e.g., Eph. 5:5. This is probably the sense of "the day of redemption" at 4:30b. These references (1:14; 4:30; and 5:5) are the principal suggestions in the letter as to future eschatological fulfillment. As in Gal. 5:21, so in Eph. 5:5 the author warns that those who practice immorality will not "inherit" the kingdom of God.

V. 31 picks up the thought of v. 26: Anger may be inevitable, but it is to be put away, along with kindred feelings and expressions of bitterness, wrath, clamor, slander, and malice. The readers are called to be "kind" or "gracious" *(chrēstoi)* to one another, goodhearted, and "freely giving" or "forgiving" *(charizomenoi)*, just as God in Christ "gave freely" (to) or "forgave" them (4:32). This *didachē* closely parallels Col. 3:12–13. It is also similar to Paul's admonitions to the Galatians in Gal. 5:16–23, where he calls on them to renounce the works of the flesh (including enmity, strife, jealousy, anger, dissension), and to manifest the fruit of the Spirit: "love, joy, peace, patience, kindness, goodness, faithfulness, gentleness, self-control." Paul does not generally speak of God's forgiveness, but rather of justification or reconciliation (e.g., Rom. 5:8–11). But the teaching of 4:31–32 is characteristic of the Pauline "indicative/imperative."

So is the exhortation to "walk in love, as Christ loved us and gave himself for us" (5:2). In Gal. 5:16, Paul called on his readers to "walk by the Spirit." The idiom, "to walk" is Hebraic, referring to the manner of conduct. As in Eph. 4:24, so in 5:1 f., he summons the readers to imitate God in mutual self-giving love (cf. Rom. 5:8; Phil. 2:1–8). The expression "beloved children," and the call to love as Christ loved us are reminiscent also of Johannine exhortation or paranesis: John 13:33–35; 1 John 4:9–11. The phrase "a fragrant offering and sacrifice to God" is used by Paul in Phil. 4:18, referring to the money the Philippian church has sent for the Jerusalem church. Paul does not describe Jesus' death in such terms elsewhere.

Gospel: John 6:41–51. In view of the earlier allusions in John 6 to Israel in the wilderness, it may be that the author referred to the "murmuring" of "the Jews" against Jesus (6:41) with the earlier "murmuring" of Israel (Exodus 16) in mind. John's Gospel dates from a period when Christians had drawn apart from Judaism; the author commonly sets "the Jews" over against Jesus, as if Jesus' own first followers—and he himself—had not also been Jews. (See, for example, 6:49: "*Your* fathers . . .") They protest that they know Jesus' parents: how then can he have "come down from heaven"? (John 6:42; see also 7:27). Reference here, and at Luke 4:22, to Jesus' father indicates that he may still have been alive at the time.

Instead of answering their rhetorical question, Jesus warns them not to murmur, and makes a series of statements about himself, God, and eternal life (6:43–51). Only those can come to Jesus who are drawn or led by God (v. 44). This is not strictly predestinarian, but God's grace or initiative is primary (see also 6:65). Such persons, Jesus says, "I will raise up at the last day." That Jesus himself, rather than God, will raise men from the dead at the resurrection is intimated only in this Gospel (see also 12:32). Some commentators, following Bultmann, propose that such references to "the last days" were not part of the original Gospel of John, where emphasis centers on the fact that the Son has already come, so that judgment, resurrection, and eternal life are already present possibilities. Others see the tension between actualized and futuristic eschatology as a basic feature of the original gospel. V. 45, picking up from v. 44a, also emphasizes the priority of God's initiative, but inclusively, rather than restrictively: "Everyone who has heard and learned from the Father comes to me." But no one has *seen* the Father, "except him who is from God" (v. 46), i.e., Jesus himself (cf. 1:1–5, 18).

Again (as in vv. 29, 35, 40), the stress is upon *believing in* Jesus: "He who believes has eternal life" (v. 47). The fathers ate bread in the wilderness, but they died (v. 49). Jesus as "the bread of life" (v. 48) or "living bread" (v. 51), gives eternal life. The conception of the eucharist as "medicine of immortality," formulated soon afterwards by Ignatius of Antioch, may be anticipated in these verses: "If anyone eats of this bread, he will live for ever" (v. 51; see also vv. 50, 54). Yet is should be noted that the Fourth Evangelist often writes in "figures" and attributes such also to Jesus (e.g., 10:6). In John 4:32–34, "food" represents Jesus' doing the will of God. In chap. 6, it may be that "eating bread," identified with Jesus, is a metaphor for believing in him, which itself, without sacramental partaking, leads to eternal life (6:40, 47). As the manna came down from heaven, so did Jesus (3:13; 6:38, 51).

HOMILETICAL INTERPRETATION

First Lesson: 1 Kings 19:4–8. It seems that an enraged and humiliated Jezebel is more terrifying to Elijah than forty-five prophets of Baal; be that as it may, Elijah is seized by despair, futility, weariness—and panic. He is both "beating a retreat" (fleeing) and "making a retreat" (going into solitude to seek renewal). While concerned to put distance between himself and the threatening queen, he does not, however, flee to strange lands like Jonah, but flees deliberately—and no doubt with subconscious promptings—to the place of Israel's origins. In that sacred place of "beginning" he will either die or be renewed.

Whenever some great task or crisis faces us, our immediate reaction is to say, "I am not able." Our energies retreat, draw back to the fountainhead, back to our subconscious. It is a symbolic return to the beginning . . . and that is at once the point of danger and the point of potential renewal. We can get stuck "back there" in the "beginning": the world of babyhood and infancy, the world of dependency and security, for it is a nostalgic and romantic world full of the earliest and therefore the most potent memories; or, going back, we can be reborn, rediscover ourselves, find again the adventurous motives of life and purpose.

This whole process is played out in Elijah's symbolic (note the "forty days and forty nights") return to Horeb, the place of Israel's beginnings. Utterly weary, the threat of Jezebel is the "last straw." Can one never do enough? Must one crisis follow on the heels of another? Why does it happen to me? Why does God allow a spectacular victory to be turned into humiliating defeat? It is too much: "O Lord, take away my life." Self-deprecation sets in: "I am no better than my fathers" (which perhaps is really an excuse, "Don't expect me to be better than . . ."), and that exactly marks the danger of this return: for if I am no better I may as well stay with my fathers and make no new ventures.

Yet one *must* go back all the way . . . and that nostalgic pull enables us to do so.

Unfortunately, the pericope ends back there "at the beginning." While we know that Elijah eventually rediscovered his sources, all we can do on the basis of this pericope is to show the possibility of his doing so.

Back there, where Israel began, he can also begin again. So we can go back to our own sources, to the fountainhead of our faith, our tradition —not to remain there, parroting old formulae, but to begin again with the tasks at hand in our time.

Second Lesson: Eph. 4:30–5:2. Elijah (First Lesson) makes his return to the place of beginnings; here, the writer calls the Ephesians to make a similar return to their beginnings. The process of change (transformation, see Pentecost 11, Eph. 4:17–24) necessitates again and again at least a look backwards in order to check or reestablish bearings. It is always from that "place of beginnings" that one works forward to deal with the tasks at hand.

It is in precisely this fashion that the writer frames and expresses his admonitions. He doesn't, in parental or authoritarian fashion, simply issue commands. He says, "Do not grieve the Holy Spirit *because* you are authentically certified to be God's heritage." To get the full effect, we need to turn that around: "*Because* you are . . . therefore do not grieve . . ."; "*Because* God in Christ forgave you, therefore be tender . . ."; "*Because* you are beloved children, therefore imitate God"; "*Because* Christ loved us, therefore walk in love." The "indicative" is the basis of the "imperative." Someone has called this the "grammar of the Gospel" in distinction to the "grammar of the Law" which proceeds conditionally: "If . . . then . . .," "If you want to be forgiven, then forgive others."

It is in this way that the writer recalls the Ephesians to their "place of beginnings": "You *are,* now become what you are." You are marked as God's possession; you are forgiven; you are beloved children; you are loved . . . now let that show!

Our world and our society constantly "put us down." Like Elijah we grow weary, and our self-image erodes. "You are only the son of Joseph, the carpenter, from Nazareth. How can you offer anything?" (Gospel, John 6:41–51). Small wonder we are ready to give up, and to give vent (v. 29) to "bitterness and wrath and anger and clamor and slander" (v. 31). Of course this reveals our impotence—like the raging child who is reduced to name-calling; but the sensitive ear will hear in all that clamor the plea for recognition. And hearing that plea, the fruitful response is that of affirmation: "You are . . . Remember your place of beginnings: return there and begin again."

Gospel: John 6:41–51. Wrestling with this passage can make "murmurers" of us, too! Who can make sense of it? But that should be a warning: by trying so hard to make sense of it we may block profounder understanding. It was not the "Flat Earth Society" members who discovered the new world, but those who dared to imagine new dimensions.

We are rather prone to be "Flat God Society" members for whom God is a one-dimensional book or code or metaphysical formula. The Incarnation is still as great an offense as ever it was. Oh, it's easy enough to say Jesus was God incarnate—but can we get beyond the one-dimensionality of such a statement? Can we perceive God in the last, the least, and the lost (cf. Matt. 25:31 ff.)? Can we truly acknowledge the human (a son of Joseph!) as the vehicle for the divine? Can we dare to hear a human word as divine Word when it confronts us with judgment and/or heals us with grace?

We listen but do not genuinely hear. We do not hear because we do not believe—do not trust God as the Father who teaches directly and not by codified transmissions. Those transmissions are there, true (like the "prophets"), but they suggest, provoke, stimulate, point beyond themselves to the always incarnated word. To stop with the letter of the transmissions is to expect the Messiah to leap off the pinnacle of the temple, is to want to store up manna for the next day. That way lies disillusionment, for "signs" only whet the appetite for more signs, and stored manna becomes wormy.

After Moses and the prophets, how is it that more witnesses are demanded? After the Incarnation, how many more witnesses to God's saving presence in the world do we need? Having heard these witnesses, how is it that we cannot hear God in the human voice of the world? The offense of Incarnation!

Manna is a good case in point. "The Jews" saw it only as a "sign," an interesting marvel Moses did (6:30 ff.); they failed to see God in, with, under, and beyond it. It never became "transfigured" for their one-dimensional eyes, never became a vehicle for the saving life of God which he was sharing with his people. It is like that with Jesus. While "the Jews" saw him only as son of Joseph, we see him equally statically as Son of God. Can they and we see the life of God manifested and shared through humanity? Jesus says, "I *am* the living bread because I *give* it." When we in our life-together give each other "bread," can we celebrate that as God's saving presence among us? That is the offense of Incarnation!

The Thirteenth Sunday after Pentecost

Lutheran	*Roman Catholic*	*Episcopal*	*Pres./UCC/Chr.*	*Methodist/COCU*
Prov. 9:1–6	Prov. 9:1–6	Prov. 9:1–6	Prov. 9:1–6	Prov. 9:1–6
Eph. 5:15–20	Eph. 5:15–20	Eph. 5:15–20	Eph. 5:15–20	Eph. 5:15–20
John 6:51–58	John 6:51–59	John 6:53–58	John 6:51–59	John 6:51–59

EXEGESIS

First Lesson: Prov. 9:1–6. Wisdom, thought of as a feminine person, is described in Proverbs 8 as the first being created by God, who was with him, helping design and construct the universe (8:22–31). Prov. 9:1 possibly refers to this role: Wisdom, the master workman or, more precisely, "like a master workman" (8:30), has "built her house" and "set up her seven pillars." "House" may refer to the world, the pillars to those columns on which the sky is suspended (see Job 26:11). Or, it may refer, metaphorically, to her royal palace on earth, whence she speaks to those who will hear, and to which she calls those who will come.

"She has slaughtered her beasts . . ." (vv. 2–6): Wisdom has prepared a banquet, and sent her maidservants to summon all in town to eat of her bread, and drink her wine. We have here an allegory or parable rather like the Parable of the Great Supper (Luke 14:15–24) to which all are invited. There, the house and the banquet represent salvation in the kingdom of God. But not everyone will "eat bread in the kingdom of God" (Luke 14:15); only those who respond to the invitation, or when they fail to do so, those who are compelled to come in. In Proverbs, it is also a question of salvation, but thought of in a different way.

V. 4 exactly duplicates v. 16, later in the chapter. The latter is the invitation of the foolish, shameless, wanton woman (a harlot), who calls "from the highest places of the town" (9:14–15; cf. 9:3), trying to seduce male passersby to their unwitting destruction. In contrast, Wisdom invites those who are "simple" and "without sense" to eat of her bread, and drink of her wine (cf. v. 17), which means, to "leave simpleness," "walk in the way of insight" which leads to life (v. 6). This parable illustrates the basic understanding of the wisdom theology, which is that the righteous (those who heed wisdom) shall have their reward in prosperity and long life, while the foolish, who give way to wickedness, shall suffer adversity and an early death. (Thus, e.g., Prov. 12:7, 21; 14:11; Psalm 37). As in the Book of Deuteronomy and the earlier prophets, so in the wisdom writings, the individual is summoned to insight, wisdom, knowledge, and righteousness, all of which have their beginning in "the fear of the Lord" (9:10).

Second Lesson: Eph. 5:15–20. We have more here from the extended section of exhortations on Christian living in Eph. 4:1–6:9. As in 5:2 and 5:8, the term "to walk" refers to conduct. The contrast between "wise" and "foolish" resembles the terminology of the wisdom writings (esp. Proverbs and Ecclesiasticus where wise = righteous, and foolish = wicked.

"Making the most of the time": This expression may derive from Col. 4:5. It probably refers to the expectation which is not, however, particularly emphasized in Ephesians, that the end of this age and the beginning of the age to come is near (cf. 1:13–14, 21b). "*Because the days are evil*" (v. 16b): As in the synoptic Gospels and 1 John, Satan's power, if not dominion, on earth is taken seriously. The "prince of the power of the air," an evil spirit, probably *the* evil spirit, the devil (6:11), "is now at work in the sons of disobedience" (Eph. 2:2). The devil and his "principalities and powers" are the rulers of the world in its present darkness (6:12; cf. 1 John 5:19 and Gal. 1:4). But the evil one and his horde can be resisted by "putting on the whole armor of God": truth, righteousness, the gospel of peace, "above all" the "shield of faith," salvation, and the spirit (6:10–17). Because time is short, and the days evil, it is all the more important not to be foolish, but to "understand what the will of the Lord is" (5:17). The will of "the Lord" may refer to God or Christ; textual variants support both readings. In any event, it is probably understood to refer to the whole range of matters reviewed in chaps. 4–6, if not the letter as a whole and Paul's other writings and the Gospels.

The readers are cautioned to renounce the way of false joy or enthusiasm: getting drunk with wine, for that is "debauchery" (RSV) or, more precisely, "wastefulness" *(asōtia).* Paul elsewhere had cautioned that those who engage in "drunkenness" and "carousing" would not inherit the kingdom of God (Gal. 5:21). Instead (of being filled with wine), Christians are to be filled with the Spirit. Their joy and celebration are to be experienced and expressed in psalms, hymns, and spiritual songs (Eph. 5:19). Thus they are to address one another, we infer, in coherent and edifying expressions of the Spirit (cf. 1 Cor. 14). And they are to address, or sing to and praise the Lord joyfully, "in [or "with"] their heart."

Vv. 19 and 20 closely parallel Col. 3:16–17, as do the admonitions to wives, husbands, children, slaves, and masters that follow in each letter (Eph. 5:21–6:9; Col. 3:18–4:1), indicating probable literary dependence. The instruction to give thanks "always" and "for everything" is certainly characteristic of Paul, who based it on his assurance that death, sin, and the law have been overcome by Christ (1 Cor. 15:51–58), and that the coming of the Lord is near (Phil. 4:4–6).

Gospel: John 6:51–59. The first two-thirds of v. 51 accords with the apparently metaphorical description of Jesus as the bread of life which came down from heaven, to which one may come and eat (= believe), and so have eternal life (e.g., John 6:35–40, 47–50). But in vv. 51c–57, a more literally sacramental or eucharistic meaning seems to be asserted (see esp. v. 55). Six references to Jesus' "flesh" *(sarx)* are featured here, four associated with the verb "to eat," the other two with "food" or "bread." With these references to Jesus' (or the Son of man's) flesh are four suggestions or invitations to drink his blood. Those who eat Jesus' flesh and drink his blood (cf. v. 57, "he who eats me") have eternal life. All this would seem to refer to the eucharistic eating and drinking of bread and wine, understood as Jesus' body and blood, after the fashion of Ignatius' conception of the eucharist as the "medicine of immortality," if not also the idea of transubstantiation. Consequently, on critical if not also dogmatic grounds, Bultmann considers the passage a secondary interpolation intended to add emphasis to the eucharist which is otherwise lacking in the Gospel.

Elsewhere in John, the basic understanding is that *believing in* Jesus (or Christ) is the way to eternal life (e.g., 3:16, 17; 6:29, 35, 40, 47). In John 6:40, Jesus states that it is God's will that everyone who believes in him "should have eternal life, and I will raise him up at the last day"; but at 6:54, that *"he who eats my flesh and drinks my blood* has eternal life, and I will raise him up at the last day." The prospect of eternal life and resurrection is constant in both cases, but the "means of grace" seem different. The expression, "abides in me, and I in him" (v. 56) is characteristically Johannine; but in other contexts it is not used in a eucharistic sense, but rather in reference to Jesus' and God's love and commandments (John 15:4–10; 1 John 2:6; 3:24; 4:12–16). It is a question, then, whether the language about eating Jesus' flesh and drinking his blood was intended literally, i.e., sacramentally, or as a still more concrete or vivid version of the metaphor: eating the bread of life, which is Jesus = "seeing" or "coming to" him and believing in him. It does seem that v. 58 picks up again the more symbolic understanding expressed in 6:27–51b. Jesus, like the "bread" or manna in the wilderness, "came down from heaven"; the fathers ate that bread but died; but "he who eats *this* bread (= believes in Jesus) will live forever" (cf. esp. v. 51a–b).

HOMILETICAL INTERPRETATION

First Lesson: Prov. 9:1–6. We have here an appeal to partake of Wisdom's feast, i.e., to benefit from the experience of man's past and our own past, rather than continue being stupid and acting stupidly (contrast Folly's feast, 9:13–18). Heaven knows, we need to be wise today; our greedy exploitation of the earth and its natural resources, our insane economic policies of constant growth and constant consumption, our inhuman abuse of peoples are all very stupid—and deep down we know it. We sup at Folly's table, while Wisdom's feast goes unattended; we are fools, not wise persons (cf. Second Lesson).

Thankfully, we are beginning to realize the urgent need to be wise; and yet it is there we touch the heart of an ancient dilemma: knowing does not guarantee doing. Perhaps that is why Israel's wise men eventually connected wisdom with God himself, even personifying it to stress this connection, and thereby making the point that wisdom is attainable *only* from God.

We are, I think, again at that stage. Our technology raises the serious question whether our vaunted wisdom is really wise. For if it were, it wouldn't constantly backfire on us. The results of our "wisdom" leave us with ever new and more devastating threats to life; our well-intentioned efforts produce monstrous Frankensteins. To begin now to ponder afresh what it means that wisdom is a gift from God will be a hard process. It may demand a confession of our bankruptcy, and thus an uncomfortable humility and tentativeness about our "way of life" and our personal and corporate "rights." It will require a renewed struggle with the problem of how to live and work in the world while yet acknowledging the overarching priorities of God (cf. Paul's discussion of "wisdom" and "foolishness" in 1 Cor. 1:18–25); of how to keep our feet on the ground while yet trusting in his guidance of the world (cf. Jesus' admonition to be "wise as serpents and innocent as doves," Matt. 10:16).

Central to this struggle will be our conception of God. This text assumes that God blesses the wise person's righteousness, and punishes the fool's wickedness. Popular theology—even as it is played out in national and international councils—assumes the same (e.g., "the poor are poor because they are lazy, stupid, etc."). In the end that makes God an enemy of man. But the God of Jesus Christ is *not* our enemy, he is not a competitor. God, to use a strange phrase, has built himself into our human life, he has not just added himself on to it. That is what the personified Wisdom of the text is getting at, and that is what the Incarnation demonstrates and expresses.

Second Lesson: Eph. 5:15–20. This lesson, like the First Lesson, urges us to be wise, and goes on to show us how the gift of wisdom is received from God: cast out your foolishness, it says, and "be filled with the Spirit."

The foolish person does not know what time it is, nor who he is, and thus does not know what to do (what the will of the Lord is). A consistent mark of the authentic prophet was his ability to discern the time: the right time to speak, the opportune moment to act. He knew, in short, when the *kairos* arrived. Foolishness manifests itself most vividly in its misjudgment of or insensitivity to the right time. Even a right word at a wrong time misses its mark. "The days are evil," true; the wise person knows when the opportunity arrives to counteract that evil. The foolish person, secondly, does not know who he is, and thus is not only "out of character" but worse, characterless. The wise person knows he is "sealed," forgiven, a beloved child (Pentecost 12, Eph. 4:30–5:2), "light in the Lord" (5:8). Finally, the foolish person does not know "what the will of the Lord is." Of course not, because the will of the Lord emerges out of the matrix wherein we, knowing who we are, engage the *kairos*. This engagement will certainly demand risk; at the same time it will reveal any pretensions and arrogance we have—but that is part of discovering what is the will of the Lord.

"Empty out this foolishness and be filled with the Spirit." That sounds charismatic, ecstatic, even glossollalic; these dimensions surely may be involved. It certainly sounds "pious" in the negative sense the word has acquired: Who wants to go around singing hymns? While it might be interesting to try, few of us are prepared to do so. At any rate, the emptying out of foolishness and the filling up of the Spirit are of one piece with Eph. 4:17–24 (Pentecost 11) and 4:30–5:2 (Pentecost 12): a change from one lifestyle to another, and that at very practical levels. What comes out of a man, Jesus remarked, is what is already in him, and language is surely an immediate indicator of the content of the heart. Thus the language of the Spirit-filled person, of the new lifestyle, will be characterized by joy and celebration, a language that cherishes, respects, reverences, affirms, heals. Secondly, this new language will demonstrate a new attitude, that of thankfulness. An aged Amerindian woman said, "Wherever the white man touches the world, he leaves it sore." Would thankfulness halt our trails of environmental and human soreness?

Gospel: John 6:51–58. There are many ways in which we humans can and do explain the meaning and purpose of our existence and express our hopes for some kind of salvation. For example, we can take a naturalistic stance and tell a story of a seed germinating, flowering, bearing fruit, and dying, and say that that is the story of human existence. Or, we can take the stance of faith and tell a story of "God and his relationships with man." The Scriptures clearly tell such a "faith story," and, for the Fourth Gospel, as for all the NT writers, this story is essentially embodied in Jesus of Nazareth. The realistic (cannibalistic!) language of the evangelist preserves the insistent claim of the church that the historical Jesus is the mediator of God's eternal life, accomplished through his death on the cross. A specific life was given, in history, for the life of the world. At the same time, the life that was given transcends history, or, better, incorporates history: quite specifically that means that the meaning and purpose of my life and my hopes for redemption and salvation are to be found in the story of Jesus of Nazareth.

That is, of course, an affront to me. After all, I come from a good family (Abraham . . . Peter . . . Luther . . . Calvin!); I have a proud history (Red Sea . . . baptism!); I have had profound experiences (Manna . . . the "bread" of the Torah . . . the eucharist!). I have life, I know the ultimate meaning of life, I know what the will of the Lord is. My own life is measure enough; it is sufficient standard and norm. All I want is a little "extra" to corroborate my story: a "sign" or two to show me I'm on the right track; a baptismal certificate to hang on the wall; a fragment of bread and a sip of wine . . .

The evangelist says, "No! Unless you eat the flesh of the Son of man and drink his blood you have no life in you." My story, no matter how noble, is not sufficient to incorporate the height and depth and length and breadth of life under God, nor is it sufficient to offer redemption to the world. Even the story of a people (Israel, church) is not sufficient. So the evangelist points us beyond these stories to the greater story of Jesus in whom all our lesser stories find fulfillment and correction. Our eucharists and baptisms and Bibles push us into that larger story. His images flow one into the other: flesh and blood are the same as door, vine, bread, water, light—all of which represent Jesus in his ultimate significance. To eat and drink are the same as "abiding in," "coming to," "believing in," "having life," "seeing," that is, full participation in the story of Jesus, realizing it (i.e., making it real) in our lives, realizing it (i.e., discovering its reality) in our own existence.

The Fourteenth Sunday after Pentecost

Lutheran	*Roman Catholic*	*Episcopal*	*Pres./UCC/Chr.*	*Methodist/COCU*
Josh. 24:1–2a, 14–18	Josh. 24:1–2a, 15–17, 18b	Josh. 24:1–2a, 14–18	Josh. 24:14–18	Josh. 24:1–2a, 14–18
Eph. 5:21–31	Eph. 5:21–32	Eph. 5:21–32	Eph. 5:21–33	Eph. 5:21–33
John 6:60–69	John 6:61–70	John 6:60–69	John 6:60–69	John 6:60–69

EXEGESIS

First Lesson: Josh. 24:1–2, 14–18. As the story is told in the Book of Joshua, the Israelites defeated the indigenous population of the land of Canaan (chaps. 1–12), after which Joshua allotted each tribe its own territory (chaps. 13–22). Chaps. 23–24 report Joshua's "farewell address" to the tribes of Israel considerably later (23:1), and shortly before his death (24:29). Chap. 23 is generally attributed to the Deuteronomistic Historian (RD or DH); chap. 24 to the old Northern or Elohist (E) tradition.

Historians have found evidence suggesting an annual ceremony of covenant renewal in ancient Israel during the days of the Judges (ca. 1200-1000 BC), when the leaders or elders of the tribes would gather, if possible at Shechem, to hear the reading of the Covenant (Law), and exhortations to keep it faithfully (Deuteronomy 6–11), after which, seated on Mts. Ebal and Gerizim, they would shout blessings and curses upon themselves—the latter as sanction lest they fail to keep the ordinances and statutes (see Deut. 11:26–29; chaps. 27–30; Josh. 8:30–35). Part of this ceremony, Gerhard von Rad has proposed, consisted of a recitation of the "cultic credo," reviewing the great acts of God on behalf of his people in the past in fulfillment of his promises to the patriarchs. This "credo" or recitation of God's acts has been preserved in three versions, according to von Rad: at Deut. 26:5–9, Deut. 6:20–23, and a more detailed or expanded statement, at Josh. 24:2–13.

Whether read as the last words of Joshua to the tribes of Israel on this particular occasion, or as a confession of faith deriving from the ancient renewal ceremony at Shechem (mentioned in Josh. 24:1, 25), the statement in vv. 2–13 testifies to Israel's belief that it was the Lord (Yahweh) who called them into being and sustained them, beginning beyond "the flood" (Euphrates) with Abraham (24:2), through Egypt and exodus, wilderness and enemy peoples, into possession of the land.

Following the conclusion of the "credo" (v. 13,), Joshua exhorts the people assembled to fear the Lord, serve him and him alone, sincerely and faithfully. "Choose this day whom you will serve" (v. 15): Here is a great summons to faithfulness and obedience to God, epitomizing the central theme of the prophetic (e.g., Elijah, Hosea) and Deuteronomistic paranesis. "But as for me and my house, we will serve the Lord." Joshua (or the leader of the congregation) declares his own choice: devotion to the Lord. The people respond—possibly in the words of the renewal ceremony's liturgy—with a shortened form of the "cultic credo" (vv. 17–18a), and their own pledge, renouncing service to other gods, and dedicating themselves to serve Yahweh, "for he is our God" (vv. 16, 18b).

Second Lesson: Eph. 5:21–33. The basic concerns of the author of Ephesians are the unity of the church, and the faithful moral life of its members. The author now turns to the subject of the right attitude and conduct of husbands and wives toward one another (cf. Col. 3:18–19), and compares this with the relation between Christ and church.

"Be subject to one another in (reverent) fear *(phobos)* of Christ" (v. 21): The principle here is mutual submissiveness, in recognition of the lordship of Christ over all. But then the writer calls on wives to be subject to their husbands, "just as" *(hōs)* to Christ (vv. 22–24). There is no doubt that Paul regarded wives as second in authority to husbands: woman was made from man and *for* man (1 Cor. 11:8–9). However, the analogy, husband is head of wife as Christ is head of church, is not found in the incontrovertibly Pauline letters. Instead, we find the principle—if not consistently applied—of full equality in Christ: Gal. 3:28 cf. Col. 3:11.

But it is not only a matter of *subjection*. Husbands are to *love* their wives as Christ loved the church (v. 25). The theological affirmations about Christ's self-giving love for and cleansing of the church (vv. 25b–27) are unusual. In Paul's letters, reference usually is to Christ's (or God's) love or self-giving "for us" (Rom. 5:8; 1 Cor. 15:3, 57; Gal. 3:13; 4:3–5), for "the world" (2 Cor. 5:19; cf. John 3:16), for "many" (Rom. 5:15), or for "all" (Rom. 5:18; 11:32; 2 Cor. 5:14–15), but not "for the church." "Having cleansed her by the washing of water with the word . . ." (v. 26): Perhaps "water" here represents baptism, though elsewhere Paul speaks of baptism in association with the "one Spirit" (1 Cor. 12:13) or "into Christ" (Gal. 3:27). Here the association is with "the word" *(hrēma),* which may suggest that the cleansing of the church is through Christ's and, perhaps, the apostles' instruction or teaching. The conception of the church as the bride of Christ also appears in 2 Cor. 11:2, though as a simile, and with reference to the Corinthian church in particular; cf. the eschatological holy city, Jerusalem, "coming down . . . prepared *as* a bride adorned for her husband" (Rev. 21:2).

V. 28 returns to husbands and wives, with the argument that since man and woman are "one flesh" (Gen. 2:24), "he who loves his wife loves himself." Moreover, both are members of Christ's body (v. 29). Vv. 29b–32 again take up the love of Christ for his church, interpreting Gen. 2:24 allegorically, "to mean Christ and the church." But "even if" *(plēn)* this is its intended meaning, the writer says, each one should love his wife "as himself"; (cf. Lev. 19:18), and the wife should "respect" *(phōbetai:* reverently "fear") the husband.

Gospel: John 6:60–70. Perhaps some of the disciples had been absent during Jesus' discourse with "the Jews" about the bread of life (6:25–59), and only later (v. 60) heard about it. Many of them now complain, "This is a hard saying" (v. 60). It is not clear whether "this" refers to the saying at 6:57, the whole series of sayings in 6:51c–57, or the more symbolic saying at v. 58. Jesus' reply corresponds more to the symbolic or allegorical sayings in 6:27–51b, 58, than to the apparently eucharist sayings in vv. 51c–57. If the disciples "take offense" (lit., "are scandalized") at "this," how would they react to his (the Son of man's) "*ascending* where he was before" (vv. 61–62)? "This," in vv. 60 and 61 would seem, then, to refer to Jesus' claim that he *came down* from heaven (6:33, 38, 50, 51a, 58a), the claim that had also occasioned the "murmuring" of "the Jews" (6:41–42).

V. 63 apparently repudiates the kind of materialistic and eucharistic understanding represented in 6:51c–57. The "*flesh* is of no avail," it is "the spirit that gives life." The *words* Jesus has *spoken* to them "are spirit and life" (cf. v. 68). On the basis of these words, the disciples should have believed, "but there are some of you who do not believe" (v. 64). Here, as in numerous other verses in 6:27–51, the way of life is to believe in Jesus; in that sense he is "bread of life" to those who "eat," i.e., believe in him. (So also John 3:16.) It is almost as if vv. 63–64 had been written to counter or correct the apparent literalism and sacramentalism of John 6:51c–57, where *believing* is not mentioned. V. 65 continues the thought of v. 64a: here as elsewhere in chap. 6, "coming to" Jesus is equivalent to "believing in" him (cf. vv. 44a, 47). As generally in this Gospel, Jesus knows in advance what is to happen: here, who will not believe, and who will betray him (vv. 64b, 70–71).

"After this many of his disciples drew back . . ." (v. 66): The more "spiritual" interpretation of vv. 51-57 given in vv. 61-65 evidently does not satisfy them. These disciples, not specifically identified with "the Jews" (v. 52), represent a larger circle of followers than the twelve. After "many" of them left, Jesus asks the twelve if they, too, will go away. Peter responds for them with a confession of faith which some interpreters regard as John's equivalent to Peter's "confession" at Caesarea Philippi (Mark 8:27–30): "You have the words of eternal life; and we have believed, and come to know, that you are the Holy One of God" (vv. 68–69). Jesus' words are the basis for belief. They, not eucharistic food, give eternal life. Not only have the disciples *believed*, they have come to *know* who Jesus is (cf. 1:10b).

HOMILETICAL INTERPRETATION

First Lesson: Josh. 24:1–2a, 14–18. It is highly significant that when the chronicler proceeds to record the "last will and testament" of Joshua, he has Joshua tell a story (24:1–13). It is the familiar story which begins with Abraham and moves on through the captivity in Egypt to the exodus and the conquest of Canaan.

Every community of people articulates its own history, and this history is essentially a story which is first told orally and eventually is recorded in writing. Such a story is always a profound interpretation of human existence: by depicting a people's origins and the crucial events which they have experienced it answers the basic religious questions of "Who am I? Who are we? Why are we?" That is, their story affords a people a common rootage, a common self-understanding, and a common destiny. This story shapes a people, it gives them identity, makes them distinctive, sets them apart; and it serves as a standard by which to understand and interpret subsequent events, and by which to assess other stories, other interpretations of existence. It is ultimately a statement of faith, which both preserves faith and creates faith.

Such a story is never static—though always in danger of becoming static, frozen in formula, closed. Periodically momentous events necessitate a reinterpretation of the story. In the Judaic-Christian story, the Babylonian Captivity, Jesus of Nazareth, the Reformation were such times, and certainly our present chaotic era is again such a time.

We, like Joshua's Israel assembled in their newly acquired land, are poised in a "threshold" situation. We know where we have come from, but we have only hints of what the world we have entered will be like.

It is then that we have doubts about the validity, the truthfulness, the relevance of our story, of our interpretation of human existence. Is our story adequate in this new world? Is the story of Yahweh covenanting with his people adequate to an agrarian Canaan? Is the story of Jesus and the church (note how the Gospels and the creed essentially tell a story!) adequate to a technological and pluralistic world? Can this story still shape us and hold us together? Can it still make meaning of our new existence? Above all, can it still save us and others from meaninglessness and fear and guilt?

Joshua believed Israel's story could, though he feared that his people might fall easy prey to the stories of Canaan. Jesus put the question to his followers (Gospel Lesson), and Peter's answer is affirmed to the Ephesian readers (Second Lesson).

Joshua's question is ever again our question: How will we tell our story? How we will interpret our existence? Which God will we choose to serve?

Second Lesson: Eph. 5:21–31. Suppose you are living in a society in which (1) marriage is held in light esteem and as a consequence degradation and de-humanization are corrosive forces; and (2) women are not even "second-class citizens." What analogy or model would you advance in order to expose and hopefully correct the situation?

It is not difficult to "suppose" such a society—it is very much our own. Nor is it difficult to select any number of explanations or rationalizations of marriage from the many being recommended and practiced today. A biological model suggests that marriage is only for the purpose of bearing children; prior to and apart from that task and after its completion marriage is unnecessary. A psychological model suggests that marriage is a mutually supportive structure, valid only so long as it indeed mutually supports. A sociological model suggests that marriage and the family are the bedrock units of a society. Further models grow out of romantic, sacramental, economic, and sometimes very exotic, soils. Are any of these, or even combinations of these, capable of doing the twofold task of exposing and correcting a bad marital situation in society?

The writer to the Ephesians laid hold of an extraordinary and singularly impressive model: the relationship between Christ and his body, the church. While we are hypersensitive to his seeming male chauvinism, we ought not allow this to blind us to the revolutionary power of his model. While he speaks of the husband as head of the wife even as Christ is head of the church, he takes pains to show that this does not mean *control.* He goes out of his way to stress that Christ saves, cleanses, sanctifies, nourishes, cherishes, and glorifies the church. If this is "power over" or "control over" it is indeed a very peculiar power and control!

If we can then discard the idea of control-obedience, we still find offensive that the husband should do this *for* the wife as Christ does it for the church. We must admit that at this point the analogy breaks down. The Pauline writer is conscious of the limitations of his analogy: at the end he admits, "This is a great mystery!" Nevertheless, his point is powerful: marriage is a new and profound relationship, analogous to Christ and the church. When the Spirit enters (cf. Pentecost 13, Eph. 5:15–20), marriage too is transformed.

As an important event in life, marriage also poses the question, "How will we interpret and tell our story?" (First Lesson). Shall it fall outside our story (be simply biological or psychological, etc.), or become an integral part of it? If part of it, then it must be incorporated into the paradigmatic story, that of Christ and the church.

Gospel: John 6:60–69. The evangelist reviews the scope of his dialogue in swift fashion before posing the ultimate question. Again the murmuring—but now there is a note of hard-nosed intolerance in it. Jesus cuts through the murmuring and the earlier one-dimensionality: "When I die and ascend, there will be no flesh and blood to see, much less to eat and to drink. Then there will be only my spirit left, and my words. *These* give life."

Joshua pleaded with his people (First Lesson) to remain faithful to the "Yahwistic" story, to the traditional interpretation of the origin and meaning of their existence. To depart from that story would mean departing from their understanding of themselves as Yahweh's people, and would result in disintegration. The evangelist has, in this chapter, set forth a reinterpretation and a fulfillment of that same story: the story of Israel is played out afresh, and to its fullest dimensions, in Jesus of Nazareth: Passover (6:1–14, 51); Exodus crossing of Red Sea (6:16–21); Covenant (6:56); wilderness wandering (6:25 ff.); Moses (6:14, 31–32, 49); the Promised Land (eternal life). It is still the *same story,* only now the full dimensions of God's presence in it and his purposes are revealed. If we murmur at eating his flesh and drinking his blood, this is the counterpart to the murmurings done at the original Passover, exodus, wilderness wanderings, for it is a murmuring against a God who is too near. We don't want a God who is too near: It seems unworthy of God to be so closely identified with our world and our existence; furthermore, a God so intensely near is threatening! Yet he *is* near. Even when Jesus is removed he will still be near. For Jesus, like manna in the desert or the eucharist on the altar or the speaking of the prophets, has demonstrated how near and involved God is. The removal of Jesus' physical presence, the close of the eucharistic service, the end of the sermon, or the close of a deeply communicative conversation, do not mean the close of an intimate involvement with God. The event of Jesus Christ has shown once and for all that God won't go away—he is present in all the interchanges and interactions of life.

Faith is therefore required—not only in those special moments (like sacraments and sermon) but in all moments. Is the Joshua-Jesus story our story, or is it not? Is our personal story illumined, explained, directed, and transformed by that story, or is it not? In short, will we be God's people or some other kind of people? What is our credo, our story?

The question is asked in an always dramatic setting: On the one hand the growing disaffection of Judas (apostasy in the First Lesson); on the other the tragedy of defection. The former plumbs the depths of evil consequences; the latter reveals the terrible blindness of not recognizing the true "sign" of God's presence to save.

The Fifteenth Sunday after Pentecost

Lutheran	*Roman Catholic*	*Episcopal*	*Pres./UCC/Chr.*	*Methodist/COCU*
Deut. 4:1–2, 6–8	Deut. 4:1–2, 6–8	Deut. 4:1–2, 6b–8	Deut. 4:1–8	Deut. 4:1–8
James 1:17–22 (23–25), 26–27	James 1:17–18, 21b–22, 27	James 1:17–18, 21b–22, 27	James 1:19–25	James 1:17–22, 26–27
Mark 7:1–8, 14–15, 21–23	Mark 7:1–8a, 14–15, 21–23	Mark 7:1–8, 14–15, 21–23	Mark 7:1–8, 14–15, 21–23	Mark 7:1–8, 14–15, 21–23

EXEGESIS

First Lesson: Deut. 4:1–2, (3–5), 6–8. The first four chapters of Deuteronomy consist of relatively late material, and probably were composed as a preface or introduction not only to the Decalogue (5:6–21) and the other laws in Deuteronomy, but to the entire "Deuteronomic History Book": Deuteronomy, Joshua, Judges, 1 and 2 Samuel, and 1 and 2 Kings. These writings were collected, revised, and arranged by an editor or editors influenced by the religious viewpoint of the Deuteronomic code (chaps. 12–26) and reform (ca. 622 BC), perhaps during the exile. These first four chapters present a narrative, as told by Moses to all Israel (Deut. 1:1, 5), reviewing what happened after the law was given at Mt. Horeb, as Israel moved on in the wilderness and into the land east of the Jordan River toward Jericho, and calling on Israel to obey this law.

It is not stated at 4:1, 2, 5, 6 or 8 *what* statutes, ordinances and commandments Israel is to keep, but as the book now stands, we can assume that the laws in question are those that follow in chap. 5, and particularly, chaps. 12–26, where the terms "commandments, ordinances, and statutes" are used in the preliminary and concluding exhortations (12:1; 26:16–19). A second collection of introductory exhortations or sermons follows in chaps. 6–11. Possibly some of these "sermons" date back to the ancient assemblies at Shechem in the days of the Judges (see above, Pentecost 14, First Lesson).

"That you may live, and go in and take possession of the land . . ." (4:1b): This is typical of the prophetic theology of history and also of the paranesis of Deuteronomy 6–11: the people can lose God's blessing if they fail to keep the covenant or laws which he has given them, particularly if they worship other gods. The laws are not to be added to or diminished (4:2a). Later rabbis understood that the law of Moses included 613 commandments. Jesus warned that the law was to remain in full force, without relaxation of even the least commandment (Matt. 5:18–19; cf. Luke 16:17). See also Rev. 22:18–19. The law is to be preserved as given so that the people will keep it as commanded (4:2, 5, 6a), and that it may go well with them in the land (4:40).

The incident at Baal-Peor is invoked as further sanction for keeping the covenant: God had destroyed those who worshiped Baal (Canaanite fertility god) there (Num. 25:1–9). The implication is that God will destroy those who worship other gods; cf. also, e.g., Deut. 4:26; 6:14–15; 7:3–4. Moreover, by keeping "all these statutes," Israel will commend itself in the eyes of other peoples, who will be impressed with their wisdom and understanding and the greatness of their nation which has such righteous statutes and ordinances (vv. 6–8).

Second Lesson: James 1:17–27. James is one of the "catholic" or general letters, addressed to all the churches, described metaphorically as "the twelve tribes of the dispersion" (1:1). The author does not claim to be James, the brother of Jesus, or even an apostle, but simply "a servant of God and of the Lord Jesus Christ" (1:1). He writes to encourage Christians to live in accordance with the "royal law" of love (2:8), patiently and helpfully in relation to others in the days of one's life (4:13–17), and in the time that remains until the coming of the Lord, which is near (5:7–9). God's grace is emphasized in 1:17–18. Every good and perfect gift is from God. The new life or creation which Christians enjoy is given by God who "of his own will . . . brought us forth by the word of truth."

"Let every man be quick to hear, slow to speak, slow to anger"(1:19b): In form, this balanced, triadic admonition is reminiscent of some of Jesus' sayings. James has more to say about speaking in 1:26 and 3:3–12. Here, he cautions particularly against anger: it does not "work the righteousness of God" (v. 20, cf. Gal. 5:20). All kinds of filthiness and evil (or "trouble," *kakia*), which may have been meant in relation either to speaking (cf. Mark 7:15–23; or to anger (cf. Matt. 5:22; Eph. 4:26, 31), are to be "put off" (cf. Eph. 4:22, 25).

"And receive with meekness the implanted word . . ." (1:21b): "Meekness" is in contrast to anger. The "implanted word" is the "word of truth" (v. 18), but whether this refers to Christ (John 1:14), the gospel

(Rom. 1:16), or Jesus' teaching (cf. Mark 4:14) is not certain. It is, in any case, the word that enables salvation. V. 22 suggests that it means the will of God: "Be doers of the word, and not hearers only" (cf. Matt. 7:21–27 = Luke 6:46–49; cf. Rom. 2:13). This is further suggested by the terms "perfect law," "law of liberty," and "royal law," which are equivalent, it seems, to the scriptural statement of the will of God, "You shall love your neighbor as yourself" (1:25, 2:8). Those who hear the word but do not do it, accomplish nothing and forget the word (vv. 23–25). The doer of the word does not forget, but acts; and "he shall be blessed in his doing" (cf. Matt. 5:3–10; 25:1–40).

Religion is not a matter of the tongue (1:26), whether thought of as mere talk, "filth" or gossip. Pure religion "before God" (v. 27) means both responsive action for one's neighbor—"to visit orphans and widows in their affliction"—and withdrawal from the contaminating influence of "the world" *(kosmos;* cf. 1 John 2:15–17).

Gospel: Mark 7:1–8, 14–15, 21–23. For about a hundred years, most scholars have regarded Mark as the earliest Gospel, dating its composition between A.D. 60 and 70. One of the great issues in NT criticism for nearly that long has been the question whether Mark's Gospel presents authentic reports of Jesus' words and actions, and to what extent it reflects the viewpoint of the church where it was composed and/or peculiar interests of its author-editor.

The controversy in 7:1–13 concerns the validity of the "tradition" or oral law of the Pharisees. Wishing to keep the written law, pious Jews as early, perhaps, as the first century B.C., had begun asking scribes to interpret its implications for certain situations not expressly defined therein. A body of such interpretations came to be passed on by word of mouth, initially, perhaps, to avoid confusion with the written law. This became known as "the tradition" or oral law, first written down, after A.D. 200, eventuating in the two Talmuds. In our Gospel Lesson, the scribes and Pharisees (traditionalists) ask Jesus why he does not require his disciples to wash their hands in accordance with the "tradition of the elders." Jesus' reply, quoting from Isa. 29:13 (LXX), distinguishes between the precepts or tradition *of men,* and the commandment of God. To illustrate, Jesus goes on, in vv. 9–13, to show that observance of "religious" practices may not be used as an excuse for refusing to assist one's parents in their need. Jesus elsewhere berates scribes and Pharisees for tending to minor, but neglecting the major parts of the law, for "straining out a gnat but swallowing a camel" (Matt. 23:23–24).

Jesus' attitude toward the law, and probably the oral tradition, is also suggested in the "antitheses" of Matt. 5:21–48. In these places, Jesus does not say that the law no longer applies; quite the opposite; Matt. 5:17–20; Luke 16:17; Matt. 23:23 = Luke 11:42. In Matthew, he even endorses the oral law of the scribes, though not their practice (23:3). But in Mark

7:1–8, if Jesus does not oppose the tradition regarding hand-washing, he certainly does not require his disciples to follow it.

In vv. 14–23, it is no longer a question about keeping the tradition. Rather, Jesus tells "the people" a "parable" (v. 17), namely, the saying given at v. 15. As with many of the parables in Mark, the disciples fail to understand, so Jesus has to explain the meaning to them: vv. 17–19, cf. 4:10–20, 33–34. Critics usually hold that these explanations are mainly Mark's own. This is clearly the case in 7:19b. The "parable" or riddle contrasts two kinds of defilement: ritual (from contact with "unclean" things), and that which arises "from within, out of the heart of man" (v. 21). See also the admonitions to this same effect in Matt. 7:17–20; 12:33–37; Luke 6:43–44; James 3:8–12; and Paul's list of the "works of the flesh" in Gal. 5:19–21.

HOMILETICAL INTERPRETATION

First Lesson: Deut. 4:1–2, (3–5), 6–8. How is faithfulness engendered and encouraged? In last Sunday's First Lesson Israel's story in creedal form is rehearsed, and the challenge to faithfulness is articulated as a consequence or follow-up (Pentecost 14, Joshua 24); in the Gospels from John 6 Jesus is set forth as the embodiment and fulfillment of that same story, and the challenge to faith is articulated (Pentecost 14, John 6: 60–69). The same procedure is at work here in Deuteronomy 4, but with one distinctive difference: in Joshua and John we meet a very "lively" God; in Deuteronomy we meet "statutes," "ordinances," and "commandments." (Note how in today's Gospel, Mark 7:1 ff., we also meet "the tradition of the elders.")

Faithfulness is engendered by teaching, and in order to teach ("hand on") a tradition of faith it must be codified in some way. The danger is that the focus will inadvertently shift from the God to whom the tradition witnesses to the codification, and obedience will follow this subtle shift. It is not surprising then to hear people say, "I live rightly; why did this happen to me?"

We need therefore to ask continuously: Faithfulness to what? To codes, formulaic creeds, statutes, and ordinances—or to the God out of whose involvements with us these codifications have arisen and to which they witness? Perhaps the two words, "faithfulness" and "obedience," will point the way toward making the distinction. "Obedience" will become anxious and exceedingly meticulous about "You shall not add to the word which I command you, nor take from it" (note again today's Gospel); while "faithfulness" will attune itself to the holiness and mercy of God, and the vitality of relationship with him.

Thus in vv. 9 ff. the text makes the important injunction: "Do not forget . . . but remember . . . how you stood before the Lord at Horeb . . ." Remember the story! The "statutes and ordinances" are *reminders,* and this is singularly significant. They remind, recall, re-present the shaping events of God's encounters with his people, and of the consequences and implications of those encounters, all the way from Abraham to Pentecost and beyond!

Second Lesson: James 1:17–27. The Epistle of James, from which the Second Lessons for this and the following three Sundays are drawn, has, since Luther's day, been suspect in Protestant circles for its seeming confusion on the faith-works issue. However that may be, James is an "activist," for whom religion can never be divorced from daily conduct. In a day when such slogans as "It doesn't matter what you believe so long as you are sincere" get translated into "It doesn't matter what you do so long as it is your thing," we need very much to hear James who sees as disastrous any divorce between faith and works, religion and life, words and actions.

James is very conscious of the grace of God: God gives every gift, and his giving is good; he brings new life to birth not out of coercion but "of his own will," freely, voluntarily; he is unchangeable and invariable in his being and giving; he grants us to be a first fruits of a vast harvest; he has implanted a saving word. But how credible are such affirmations today? Can we believe them? If James' readers could be reassured that the stars were controlled by the "Father of lights," does that control extend to man-made satellites? If what he calls "gifts" have become fought-over human *rights,* is God as "giver" still credible? If the world is over-populated, is "first fruits" a bad joke? And if words spill out in cacophanous din, however are we to hear, much less do, *the* word? How can we make James' celebration of grace credible again to ourselves and others?

James points to fundamentals. "Be quick to hear, slow to speak, slow to anger" so as not to obstruct the righteousness of God. We usually respond to anger with anger; instead we need to be "quick to hear" what is behind the anger, for it is often the shout that says, "You're not hearing me!" By speaking too soon, the cry for understanding is silenced and justice–rightness–is circumvented. Injustice can continue, squelching any hesitant shoots of reconciliation and new life.

"Be doers of the word and not hearers only." One person against the kind of world we have described is overwhelmed. But if the whole community of faith stands together, "doing the word," then revolutions may happen. A whole community reflecting the perfect law of liberty is a force to be reckoned with. It can be the mirror held up to society which exposes evil and wickedness in high and low places; it can be a loud word of truth uttered in the face of distorted and emasculated words; it can be the sign of a new humanity over against inhumanity. There is a challenge to the church!

Gospel: Mark 7:1–8, 14–15, 21–23. Legalism is what we call an obsessive and rigid attention paid to observance of law. Its potential roots lie in worthy concerns, namely, to be fair (no exemptions from the requirements of law), and to be respectful of law. It comes to full flower when, in the name of respect for law, the principles of fairness which have been established take precedence over the persons involved. Israel's law was an eminently "fair" expression of God's relationship with his people; it was "people oriented"; it was right (righteous), appropriate. But somehow we always manage to shift the focus. Perhaps it is because "God" or "justice" or "righteousness" are so intangible that we focus on the concrete thing: the law, the codes, the body of legislation. We become "code oriented," and before we know it we are legalists. The results would be comical were they not so tragic. The very effort to "protect" the law—to give it proper respect and honor—results in the establishment of numerous "bylaws" (the "tradition of the elders") which in the end not only nullify the law but bury people under "red tape," thus defeating the purpose of being fair. The laudable attempt fully to obey the law deteriorates into manipulation of the law (do we not search for loopholes in tax laws, for example?) in order to gain control of it and so escape it! There is nothing quite so revealing of our sinfulness as our encounters with law!

In the final analysis, legalism—whether practiced with the ten commandments, ritual, the Bible, theology, societal values, or universal principles, etc.—is an attempt to control God and the neighbor. The legalist, of course, is not aware of this, and it is always a great shock to realize that his zeal for fairness and for respect of law has in fact thwarted the just intent of law, and enabled him to escape responsive love to the neighbor. For it is not a question of whether or not to have law—we need it!—but of how we use the law we have. To paraphrase a saying of Jesus: "Law is made for man, not man for the law."

The saying of v. 15 is one of the most revolutionary statements in the NT. Jews in Maccabean and other times had suffered and died to uphold their dietary laws; Christians in many ages have suffered and died to uphold specific doctrinal interpretations and theories about the Bible. They all will have their reward; yet Jesus breathtakingly sweeps away everything that impedes the direct relationship to God. The only absolute is God. We ought not invest with divinity that which points to, represents, witnesses to God.

The Sixteenth Sunday after Pentecost

Lutheran	*Roman Catholic*	*Episcopal*	*Pres./UCC/Chr.*	*Methodist/COCU*
Isa. 35:4–7a	Isa. 35:4–7a	Isa. 35:4–7a	Isa. 35:4–7a	Isa. 35:4–7a
James 2:1–5	James 2:1–5	James 2:1–5	James 2:1–5	James 2:1–5
Mark 7:31–37	Mark 7:31–37	Mark 7:31–37	Mark 7:31–37	Mark 7:31–37

EXEGESIS

First Lesson: Isa. 35:4–7a. Interpreters usually place Isaiah 35 either in the late exilic period, in connection with Isaiah 40–55 ("Second Isaiah"), or in the early post-exilic years, along with chaps. 33–34. Thematically, chap. 35 relates closely to Isaiah 40. Both look forward to the joyful return of the exiles through a supernaturally transformed wilderness to Zion (cf. also Isa. 55:12–13).

The chapter begins with a proclamation that the wilderness through which the exiles are to pass itself will "rejoice and blossom," manifesting the glory and majesty of the verdant mountains, Lebanon, Carmel, and Sharon, indeed, the glory and majesty of God himself (vv. 1–2). There will be a safe highway through this wilderness, over which "the ransomed of the Lord shall return" (vv. 8–10; cf. 40:3–5). "Say to those who are of a fearful heart, 'Be strong, fear not!' " (v. 4). "Fear not!" is one of the great, recurring Isaianic assurances: God is in control of history and will bring about the promised redemption of his people. The assurances to this effect here correspond to a related Isaianic theme: "A remnant shall return." This declares both God's judgment—only a remnant shall return—and his steadfast love for his people, and thus the basis of their hope for the future: a remnant *shall* return. Here the prophet goes on, God will come with vengeance and recompense (cf. 34:8; 40:10). "Vengeance" may refer to the fate in store for those nations that have oppressed the Jewish people, as in the various prophetic oracles against foreign nations (e.g., Isaiah 34). Or, it may refer to the punishment which God's people must complete before they are redeemed, God's action seen as both "smiting and healing" (Isa. 19:22; cf. Hosea 1–2; Isaiah 10–12). In Isa. 40:1–2, the prophet announces that the people have now completed their punishment.

"He will come and save you." This is the gospel of the OT: God will not only deliver his people from their present oppression, but also bring about a new, transformed and everlasting era of peace for the whole creation (cf. Isa. 2, 9, 11). The verb "to save" *(yasha)* is probably represented in such significant biblical names as Hosea, Isaiah, and Joshua (Greek: Jesus), and is familiar in the transliterated cry for deliverance, "Hosanna!" Salvation means not only the ultimate condition of "everlasting joy" (v. 10), but restoration of the blind, deaf, lame, and dumb to the full use and enjoyment of their faculties while still in the wilderness, both as a foretaste and anticipatory celebration of the ultimate salvation to come, and to ease the difficulties of their remaining journey through the wilderness (cf. 40:29–31; Luke 4:18). For this latter purpose also, in an unusual fourfold poetic statement, the exiles are promised that waters/streams/pools/springs will break forth or come to be in the wilderness/desert/burning sand/thirsty ground (vv. 6b–7a).

Second Lesson: James 2:1–5. James often addresses his readers as "my brethren." In this lesson he urges, in effect, that in Christ there is neither "rich nor poor." Thus, he argues against partiality and discrimination within the assembly (lit., synagogue) in favor of the rich or against the poor. Possibly the christological title, "Lord of Glory" (v. 1), contains an implicit reproach against the pretensions to glory of the rich. In any event, the members of the assembly are not to show deference to the rich (politely seating the man "in splendid clothes") or humiliate the poor (ordering him to stand or sit in an inferior place, lit., "under the footstool"). Such discrimination has no place in the churches. Those who so discriminate against each other become judges with evil, inward questionings (v. 4). We might see here a call for unity in the faith (v. 1) and in the churches, as in 1 Corinthians and Ephesians. Paul had admonished the Corinthians not to humiliate those who had nothing (1 Cor. 11:22).

Something else, however, seems to be said in v. 5: that it is the "poor of the world" whom God has chosen to be "rich in faith" and heirs of the kingdom. This is also the apparent meaning of James 2:6–7 and 5:1–6: Because of their unrighteousness, the rich are to be condemned. Several of Jesus' sayings in the Gospels are to the same effect, e.g., Mark 10:17–31; Luke 6:24–25; 16:19–31 [see below, Pentecost 19, Second Lesson]. But in James 2:1–5 the author is not arguing against the rich, but against invidious treatment of the poor. What he has to say in v. 5 is a further reason for paying proper respect to the poor man who comes into the church. Such persons are rich in faith (cf. Mark 10:29–30). Moreover, they are heirs to the kingdom of God. Such also was the reported understanding of Jesus himself: Luke 6:20–21 (cf. Matt. 5:3–10); 12:33; 16:9; 20–22, 25. Other sayings of Jesus and statements of Paul indicate that it is the righteous, those who do the will of God, who will inherit the kingdom of God (e.g., Matt. 7:21; 13:43; 25:34–39; 1 Cor. 6:9). Perhaps it was generally understood that those who chose to seek the kingdom and serve God in love of neighbor would give up their possessions (Matt. 6:24 = Luke 16:13; Mark 10:21–25; cf. Luke 16:19–31).

James himself argues that discrimination against the poor man is in violation of the "royal law" of love, since it fails to meet the test, "You shall love your neighbor as yourself" (2:8–9). This suggests, incidentally, that James understood that the churches to which he wrote, if not wealthy, were for the most part composed of persons more affluent than the "poor man in shabby clothing." But each person is of equal worth: to humiliate or dishonor the poor man (2:6a) is against the law of love.

Gospel: Mark 7:31–37. In Mark 7:24–30, Jesus had extended his travels into Gentile territory, and there exorcised the demon who was troubling the Syro-phoenician woman's daughter. Now he returns, circuitously, "through the region of the Decapolis" (an extensive area in northern Palestine and east of the Jordan comprising ten Greek cities), to Galilee. As is common in Mark, the conjunction "and" *(kai)* stands at the beginning of every verse in the passage, tying the action together, and suggesting urgency or speed.

A man who was both deaf and had a speech impediment *(mogilalos)* is brought to Jesus to be healed. Healing is mediated by Jesus' touching the man's ears and tongue. Jesus looks to heaven, prays (cf. 6:41; Matt. 6:9), sighs (in compassion or as part of the treatment), and says, "Ephphatha," meaning (in Aramaic), "Be opened." The man's ears were "opened," "the bond of his tongue" was loosed, "and he spoke plainly" or "correctly" *(orthōs,* v. 35).

The story very probably was understood by Mark to fulfill the prophecy given in Isa. 35:5–6:

> Then the eyes of the blind shall be opened,
> and the ears of the deaf unstopped;
> then shall the lame man leap like a hart,
> and the tongue of the dumb *(mogilalos,* LXX) sing for joy.

Elsewhere Mark reports Jesus' healing the blind (8:22–26; 10:46–52) and a paralytic (2:3–12). Probably Mark saw these episodes as evidence for the long-awaited time of salvation, whether preliminary and preparatory to the coming of the kingdom of God, or somehow marking its presence. In any case, these actions bring salvation (wholeness) to those who are freed from their afflicting demons or healed.

Neither Mark nor any of the other synoptic evangelists designates such cures as "signs" or "miracles." Though there are no Jewish traditions to the effect that the Messiah would heal, it is shortly after Jesus' healing of the blind man of Bethsaida that Peter makes the startling announcement that Jesus is "the Christ" (8:22–29).

V. 36 introduces the highly problematic question of the "messianic secret." Jesus tells those who witness this healing "to tell no one"—that he is the Messiah (cf. 8:29–30), or about the healing (cf. 1:44)? The actual cure was performed privately (7:33). But, as elsewhere, the warning is to no avail: "The more he charged them, the more zealously they proclaimed it" (7:36b; cf. 1:28, 45). However, though the witnesses to the healing are impressed (v. 37; cf. 1:27; 2:12b), they apparently do not infer that Jesus is the Messiah or that the prophesied era of salvation has begun or come near.

HOMILETICAL INTERPRETATION

First Lesson: Isa. 35:4–7a. The background against which the prophet speaks is exile (specifically, the Babylonian Exile, cf. exegesis). The twentieth century has, in all probability, known more exiles and refugees than any other period of history. Countless people in congregations across our continent have grim memories of exile; many more across the face of the earth are in the midst of the harsh experience. But twentieth century man, wherever he is, feels he is a refugee. Our world—even if not upset by war—has become an alien place, from which the God of our ancestors has seemingly withdrawn, or in which he has grown dim and increasingly impotent. The call, "Fear not!" seems unforgivably naive; the invitation to hope, "He will come and save you!" sounds incredible. Yet we *want* to hope . . . and we *must* hope or go to ruin.

The experience of exile—a mix of loss, suffering, pain, doubt, anger, despair, depression, unfaith, guilt, fear, defiance, hope, grief—shatters everything the person holds dear, shatters the meanings with which he has invested his life, shatters the "story" he has thus far told. Thus the exile shattered Israel's faith, her theology, her concept of God, her self-understanding, her destiny. Could her faith-story be resurrected? The prophet, significantly, uses her old story to interpret this disastrous exile experience: He announces a "new" Passover ("He will come and save you"), a "new" covenant ("*Your* God will come"), a "new" wilderness trek (vv. 6–7), a "new" wholeness (vv. 5–6). What God did he will do. In short, the God of judgment and mercy works judgment in order to show his mercy; his judgment *is* merciful because his purpose is to save.

The way of God's working in the world comes clear in Jesus: life is attained through death because God is present in the dying to give life. So we exiles shall look for signs of life not from some ethereal realm remote from us, but precisely in the realm where we are: waters in the *wilderness,* streams in the *desert,* pools in the *burning sand,* springs in the *thirsty ground;* or, to change the figure: rays of light when we wander blindly, the redeeming word penetrating deafness, invigoration of feebleness, songs of joy where mute despair reigned.

Salvation is perceivable in these unexpected places—precisely there where all hope seems absent and irretrievable. It is the message Jesus announced: The kingdom of God is breaking in; blessed are those who, with eyes of faith, look to see it.

Second Lesson: James 2:1–5. The temptation to prefer and defer to the rich is an almost irresistible temptation. There are many reasons for it: fear, desire for gain, status, protection, power, influence. Cinderella winning the prince, and thus triumphing over not only her wretched circumstances but also her own oppressive family, is a powerful motif in any society. On the other hand, however, we equally rejoice when the "apple-polisher" is exposed and humiliated—as when Haman was hanged on the very gallows he had had made for Mordecai (the Book of Esther). There is thus an ambivalence in us over against the rich person: we feel impelled to honor him, and yet realize that in so doing we dishonor ourselves and lose our integrity and freedom. There is no feeling quite so devastating as the feeling of having "sold out" to financial interests; perhaps that is why the rich person in the world's stories is so often portrayed as a Scrooge. We *know* we can be bought, and we hate ourselves and the buyer the more!

The church in ancient times was the first to break social and class distinctions; it was revolutionary for a master to receive communion from the hand of his slave. Little wonder James speaks so passionately against showing partiality. He knew, as we are inclined to forget, that partiality is above all destructive. It destroys the "faith of our Lord Jesus Christ" in that it engenders and expresses a divided allegiance to God and Mammon. It destroys human relations because it permits a double standard. It destroys people themselves in that it nullifies the "law of love" by diametrically opposing God's purposes of compassion and salvation.

There is a wealth of sardonic irony in James' plea. The rich oppress the poor—how strange then to give the oppressor special honor! It seems singularly masochistic. But more: Stranger still that those who follow the Lord Jesus—he who had no place to lay his head—should bow down to gold rings and fine clothing. As that shaft of irony begins to penetrate our affluent mentality, we may well begin to feel uncomfortable in our comfortable pews. Where is the prophetic word and the prophetic action coming from today? Has the church willingly entered another "Babylonian captivity"?

For behold: God chose the poor in the eyes of the world to be rich in faith and heirs of the promised kingdom. No, poverty *per se* is not a ticket to the kingdom. Rather, the kingdom is at least this: *Justice;* and if God is to be fair (impartial!) to *every* person, then "the least of these my brothers" becomes the norm: the shabby man, the man who has nowhere to lay his head. In the days of the early church he had no one to champion him except the church; who is his champion today?

Gospel: Mark 7:31–37. It is a commonplace to reach to past events (or experiences or formulations) in order to interpret a present event. In such a process of reflection the past and present events illuminate and fulfill ("fill full") each other. After having caught a glimpse of a person's past we frequently exclaim, "Aha! Now I know why he did (or said) what he did." Similarly, the NT church, as it strove to fathom and communicate the meaning and effect of Jesus, constantly reached back into the OT. In that process they not only discovered the meaning of Jesus, but came to understand the depth of meaning of the OT reference. Two such "reachings back" may be noted in this pericope.

The one is the reference to Isaiah 35 (see the First Lesson) with its glowing visions of God visiting and redeeming his people; the other is the reference to the creation story where an unresponsive and mute chaos is tamed and opened to light and creativity by the power of God's utterance ("He has done all things well," cf. Gen. 1:31). Jesus, therefore, is God present to save, loosing the bonds of oppression *(desmos,* bond, fetter, v. 35; cf. Luke 13:16); his effect is re-creation. Conversely, where there is deliverance and the creation of life, there we shall be "open" to God's presence and ready to sing his praise.

Most of the time our faith works only in retrospect. It is only when we look back that we are "opened," becoming aware of a providential guidance, or of the re-creative power of a harrowing experience, or of the shaping force of an influential word. It is not too late then to speak the word of praise and recognition—but we do feel remorse at being so slow of heart that we had not done so earlier.

But perhaps it is just this slow and agonizing process that must be lived through for opening and loosing to happen: To be "taken aside from the multitude, privately," and thus experience the full bewilderment of our deafness and muteness and the horrifying reality of our isolation. It is there, when we "hit bottom," that we may finally *hear,* and finally find fumbling words: "I was on the road to dissolution, but now I may begin again. Praise God!" There faith is created again.

Can this faith also be directed forward? One of Jesus' arguments with the leaders of the people is, in effect, "If you knew what Moses and the prophets were all about, you would know what I am all about." So Mark is saying in his pericope, "If you know what Isaiah (35) was saying, you will know what is going on here." The past interprets the present and points us toward the future. Our faith can do that too as it is nourished by the past traditions of faith and boldly sings praises into the present oppressions and future darknesses.

The Seventeenth Sunday after Pentecost

Lutheran	*Roman Catholic*	*Episcopal*	*Pres./UCC/Chr.*	*Methodist/COCU*
Isa. 50:4–10	Isa. 50:5–9a	Isa: 50:5–9a	Isa. 50:4–9	Isa. 50:4–10
James 2:14–18	James 2:14–18	James 2:14–18	James 2:14–18	James 2:14–18
Mark 8:27–35	Mark 8:27–35	Mark 8:27–38	Mark 8:27–35	Mark 8:27–38

EXEGESIS

First Lesson: Isa. 50:4–10. Isaiah 40–55, and sometimes 34–35, are commonly attributed to an anonymous prophet, Second Isaiah, who lived, perhaps among the Babylonian exiles, shortly before the end of the exile, ca. 540 BC. Isaiah of Jerusalem (c. 760-690 BC) was the first and greatest of a series of Southern or Judahite prophets. Second Isaiah may have been a fourth or fifth generation follower in this school.

Vv. 4–11 are sometimes designated "the third servant song," the others being Isa. 42:1–4; 49:1–6; and 52:13–53:12. Each refers to "the servant" of the Lord, and in the last two, interest is focused upon the past suffering or persecution of this servant and his hoped-for vindication. Who is the servant? In 42:1–4, the servant seems to be the Persian emperor, Cyrus (cf. 45:1). Elsewhere in Isaiah 40–48, however, the servant probably represents Jacob (= Israel) or the exiles. But in 49–55, the servant appears more as a single individual, perhaps the prophet himself. In 50:4–9, the writer evidently speaks of his own experience. Like other prophets, he attributes to God's inspiration the message given him to proclaim: God "wakens" his ear "morning by morning" (50:4; cf. Jer. 1:9). His task is to "sustain with a word him that is weary": presumably the tired and discouraged exiles. In vv. 5b–7, he reports the abuse to which he has been subjected because of his prophetic proclamation, and his persistence, through God's help, despite it (cf. Jer. 1:18; 15:20). Other prophets before him also had been persecuted by those who preferred to hear them prophesy "peace," "smooth things," and illusions. When the prophets would not oblige, such people regarded them as conspirators or enemies and treated them accordingly. See, e.g., Amos 7:10–12; Matt. 23:37.

Since Second Isaiah proclaims mainly the good news of coming deliverance, it is surprising that people would have taken offense. Possibly some of the exiles resented his message of coming salvation for the Gentiles (42:6; 49:5–6; cf. Jonah 4:2). Or perhaps they preferred to pity themselves (Psalm 137). Or, as some of the ancient Israelites preferred the comforts of Egypt to the hazards of the wilderness, perhaps some of the exiles did not care for Isaiah's summons to go forth (48:20).

Like Jeremiah, this Isaianic prophet looks to God for vindication and the condemnation of his oppressors (50:7–9, 11; Jer. 11:20; 17:18; 18:19–23). Like the psalmists, Second Isaiah expresses profound confidence in God's righteousness and power to make things right for those who trust in him. Vv. 10–11 probably are sardonic: The prophet is "unenlightened"—in the eyes of those who do not fear the Lord. They do not obey the voice of his servant, the prophet, but walk by their own lights. In turn, they will have to endure torment, "from my [God's own] hand" (cf. v. 9b).

Second Lesson: James 2:14–18. Luther's contemptuous characterization of James as "that straw epistle" derived mainly from his reaction to the discussion of faith and works in 2:14–26. Luther's attitude, very likely, was colored by his rejection of Catholic excesses, notably the sale of indulgences (later repudiated at Trent), and by his confusing works of the Jewish law with works of love in response to God and neighbor.

James was arguing against a kind of piety which claimed that faith or belief *(pistis)* was all that mattered. Proponents of such piety dispensed cheap spiritual blessings—"Go in peace, be warmed and filled"—as an excuse for failing to respond with needed help that might cost them something. James rightly rejects such faith as "dead" (2:17). John, Paul and Jesus would not have disagreed. "But if any one has the world's goods and sees his brother in need, yet closes his heart against him, how does God's love abide in him? Little children, let us not love in word or speech, but in deed *(en ergō)* and in truth" (1 John 3:17–18). For Paul, grace and faith were fundamental. Yet he could write, "If I have all faith, so as to remove mountains, but have not love, I am nothing" (1 Cor. 13:2b). Love is the greatest spiritual gift. Genuine faith "works" *(energoumenē)* through love (Gal. 5:6). It is not enough to say "Lord, Lord," or recite the Apostles' Creed, as Karl Barth put it, commenting on Jesus' saying at Matt. 7:21, Luke 6:46.

"If a brother or sister is naked *(gumnoi)* . . ." (v. 15): The translation "ill-clad" is possible, but weakens the point. It is not a question of fashion, but of being cold (v. 16). The same term is used in the great judgment scene in Matthew 25, translated simply as "naked." In both James 2 and Matthew 25 it is a question of responding to those in need, or failing to do so. In Matt. 25:44 those who have ignored their hungry, thirsty, lonely, naked, sick, and imprisoned neighbors address the Judge devoutly as "Lord" (cf. Matt. 7:21). But such piety will not save them.

"Go in peace, be warmed and filled . . ." (v. 16): The hypothetical Christian who pronounces this "blessing" is eager for the needy persons to *go;* "in peace" hints that they had best do so before the authorities are sent for. In any case, it is left to God, someone else, or the cold and hungry themselves to provide for their needs. "What does it profit?", literally, "What help *(ophelos)* is it?" None, to those who need help. Or the meaning may be as in 2:14: What is the advantage to the man who claims to have such faith? Clearly, conduct matters: cf. Mark 8:36; Luke 6:33–35; Rom. 2:13; 1 Cor. 3:14; Gal. 6:7–9.

A hypothetical respondent argues, in effect: There is a variety of gifts; some have faith, others have works (v. 18). James refutes this disjunction as invalid: Faith, if it is real, is expressed in what the believer does. It is to be professed with our lips *and* shown forth in our lives.

Gospel: Mark 8:27–38. We have here three major units of tradition: Peter's "confession" that Jesus is the Messiah (vv. 27–30), Jesus' first "passion pronouncement" and Peter's response (vv. 31–33), and a group of sayings about self-denial and following Jesus.

On the way to Caesarea Philippi, Jesus asks his disciples who people say he is. To the reader, familiar with the NT witness to Jesus as the

Christ, it may seem an odd question. But Jesus had not proclaimed himself Messiah or Christ. The disciples did not yet realize who he was; cf. Mark 4:41. Peter announces a new discovery! Some people thought he was John the Baptist (8:28). Others said Elijah, the great preacher of repentance who was expected to come "first" (Mark 9:11–12). Others said he was one of the (other) prophets; they, like Jesus, had proclaimed coming judgment and salvation. Jesus does not acknowledge Peter's confession, but charges the disciples to say nothing "about him," in effect, to keep his identity as Messiah a secret. Some interpreters propose that this is what Jesus himself intended (Schweitzer). Others attribute the "messianic secret" to the editorial hand of Mark (Wrede).

Jesus then teaches the disciples that the Son of man must suffer, be killed, and rise from the dead (v. 31). "And he said this plainly" (8:32a), lest there be any doubt. Peter, however, rebukes Jesus, apparently finding the prospect of his suffering and death intolerable. But then Jesus rebukes Peter, and actually identifies him with Satan! What God has ordained, and what Jesus has taught, is what must happen.

Jesus then calls the multitude, and summons any who would "come after" him, to deny himself, take up his cross and follow (8:34). Elsewhere, Jesus called on those who sought the kingdom to renounce all and follow him (e.g., Mark 10:21; Matt. 8:19–22; Luke 9:57–62; 12:33–34; 14:16–33). "Take up his cross" may be a later Christian revision if cross *(stauros)* has come to replace "staff" *(hrabdos,* Mark 6:8). Whoever would try to preserve his life in this world by keeping his own goods for himself or otherwise "playing it safe" will lose it; those who give up all else for the sake of life in the kingdom of God will save it. What does it profit *(ōphelei)* if a man gains the world, but loses eternal life, the greatest of all treasures (vv. 36-37, cf. Matt. 13:44–46)? Emphasis here is less on responding to others (cf. James 2:14–16) than upon self-denial. But unless one is willing to deny self, one will not be able to respond to others. Jesus and his words are the messenger and message to "this generation." Soon the Son of man (= Jesus, himself?) will come to judge each one according to the measure of his response to Jesus and his words (v. 38.)

HOMILETICAL INTERPRETATION

First Lesson: Isa. 50:4–10. The exegesis raises the fascinating question of why good news should cause offense. It obviously still does. In any "exilic" situation, which is filled with individual and national disillusionment, good news is received with suspicion and incredulity, and the bearers of good news are looked upon either as interesting lunatics or as dangerous radicals.

Whatever theories we may have about the identity of the "Servant" in Deutero-Isaiah, eventually we must say that the Servant represents the faithful in all times and places, whether these happen to be one or many.

God does not at any time leave himself without a witness, or, to turn that around, a witness is always embodied somewhere—even, let us remember, in a Cyrus! We must say, then, that the church is also this Servant . . . and then we must ask about her faithfulness, and how she is being regarded by the world.

What is the nature of the Servant-church's task? On the one hand it is to be a servant like Moses, that is, to stand in the gap between the people and Yahweh, bringing them "home." On the other hand it is to be like the ultimate Servant, Jesus, who is the incarnation of God's own redeeming servanthood (note that Isa. 50:4–9 is also the First Lesson for the Sunday of the Passion in Series A). While Isa. 42:1–7 gives a summary of the task in cogent breadth, and Isa. 52:13 ff. plumbs its redemptive depths, this "song" describes the task as being "the servant of the word."

Like the Isaianic Servant, the faithful community is entrusted with the word. This is no frozen, timeless word; it is not a word calcified in scroll or book. It is given "morning by morning" to the receptive ear. It is never a possession, but always a gift to those who are teachable. And the word is God's justice and mercy (cf. Isa. 42:1–7), it is God's way of working in the world. The Servant-church listens for that word, and embodies it, for the word can have reality and visibility only in a *people.*

Small wonder this word offends! Being heard afresh morning by morning it is always timely and thus disconcerting; being just it hurts, yet in the hurt is its healing. Small wonder the church's adversaries insult and shame and accuse—for the faithful community is always writing a different history than the world writes.

But beware the martyr-complex as well as the elemental pride or pretension to embodying *all* truth and virtue! The very determined and at times defiant faith that "the Lord God helps me; who will declare me guilty?" can calcify the word of the living God, and then he must seek embodiment elsewhere. Better this humility: "Anyone who fears the Lord, obeying the word of his servant, who (nevertheless) gropes in darkness and has no glimmer of light, let him trust in the name of the Lord" (v. 10, North).

Second Lesson: James 2:14–18. James is indeed a passionate preacher; his illustration is devastatingly to the point! He must have seen something like this happen, and the memory of it will not leave him. It is in an actual life-situation that we must see James' argument.

In any controversy, especially in passionate controversy, the positions tend to become polarized. That seems to be the situation out of which James writes: "I have faith" vs. "I have works" (v. 18). In the abstract, such polarizing seems inevitable and from the point of view of faithful theology, quite essential: James and Paul do seem to be "poles apart." In a real-life situation, however, such polarization becomes absurd and unproductive ("What does it profit . . .?" v. 14). It is immensely sobering for the "I have faith" side to realize that the naked neighbor would be much better off with the "I have works" side; it is equally sobering for the "I have works" side to realize that the naked neighbor has become nothing more than a peg on which to hang one more good work (cf. v. 18). Polarities profit neither the needy neighbor (v. 14) nor the Christian (v. 16).

James, who likely knew the way of "works righteousness" very well, perhaps was also particularly sensitive to a subtle and yet devastating perversion taking place, namely, fideism. He points out that the demons too "believe," in surface fashion, but they at least have the decency to shudder (v. 19). The proponents of "faith alone" are always in danger of falling back into the very morass from which Christ has rescued them; inadvertently they make faith into a justifying work. It is easily done. For the Christian whom Christ has freed from the tyranny of works righteousness, "faith alone" is a doxological reception of salvation as an undeserved and unearned gift from God. But when that "faith alone" becomes an admonitory "Only believe!", then faith has been subverted into a justifying work. Thereupon the trusting reliance upon God (Matt. 6:25 ff., "do not be anxious . . .") becomes a passing of the buck to God ("You do it, God"), and the exhortation to faith becomes a patronizing condescension to the needy neighbor ("God will supply all your needs. Only believe"). The miserable naked neighbor is left unassisted.

And it is, in the end, that needy neighbor whom we dare not remove from our sight. Faith and works both find reality—and corrective—in him. He is *needy*: no volume of words and well-wishes, however sincere or fervent or faith-full, will relieve his condition; action is required. And he is *neighbor*: he is not an opportunity to be used for well-doing (a good way to assuage a guilty conscience, by the way!), but a human being, a person with whom relationships are to be established; faith is required.

Gospel: Mark 8:27–35. In Mark's narrative the process of opening the disciples' eyes to the identity of Jesus is long and slow, and is depicted by him in a series of healing miracles which climax in the healing of the deaf-mute (Pentecost 16, Mark 7:31–37), and of the blind man of Bethsaida (8:22–25). It is perhaps not unimportant to note that Bethsaida was Peter's home town, and it is Peter who, with eyes finally opened, also finds his tongue released to speak plainly, "You are the Christ."

It is an exciting moment when a scientist, after much searching and experimentation, discovers the key formula which unlocks the mystery that has eluded him. It is a truly moving moment when a person, after much greater soul-searching and heartache and weary journeyings, discovers the key to the meaning of life. Too few of us press on to the ultimate meaning of life; it is always easier to make do in Egypt or Babylon; it is less fretful to settle for whatever meanings are handed us by current pundits and gurus and politicians. Better to pull down the horizons and be content with our little world and our cozy little meanings.

And yet there is always an Everest looming on the horizon, no matter how narrowly we limit it, inviting and terrifying. There is always the shattering blow, or the scent of something in the air, or an expression in the eye, that speaks of mystery: the mystery of life and death and complex humanity and spirit and the beyond.

We unashamedly (see v. 38) present Christ as the key to the mystery, as the bridge that links the here and the beyond, as the profound reality of God intertwined in our human existence and transcending it.

But how quickly we recoil! We want the mystery to be unravelled in keeping with our cozy little meanings—with our vision of what God should be and do, with our yearnings of how things should be set right, and our opinions as to how we should be vindicated. But no! The key to the mystery won't fit the locks of our treasure chests. It is a strange key, shaped cross-like. It opens the way to suffering and death—beyond which lies life. And that seems so contrary! But there it stands: "The Son of man must suffer . . . and be killed . . . and after three days rise again." Not "Messiah," the "anointed one" as kings and priests and prophets were anointed, but "Son of man" which includes these and, indeed, every mother's child past, present, and future; not only includes but represents them, in fact *is* them in all their glory and shame, power and weakness, honor and dishonor, grandeur and misery, suffering and death . . . and hope.

"And lead us not into temptation . . ." There is no royal road to life and its ultimate meaning. There is only the integrity of life itself, of its ambiguities. Suffering and death are not unfortunate misadventures we should seek to avoid, but are part and parcel of what it is to be human, to be sons of man and sons of God. By accepting this hard mystery of life—this is how we follow.

The Eighteenth Sunday after Pentecost

Lutheran	*Roman Catholic*	*Episcopal*	*Pres./UCC/Chr.*	*Methodist/COCU*
Jer. 11:18–20	Wisd. 2:17–20	Wisd. 2:1, 12–20	Jer. 11:18–20	Jer. 11:18–20
James 3:13–18	James 3:16–4:3	James 3:16–4:3	James 3:13–4:3	James 3:13–4:3
Mark 9:30–37	Mark 9:29–36	Mark 9:30–37	Mark 9:30–37	Mark 9:29–36

EXEGESIS

First Lesson: Jer. 11:18–20; Wisd. of Sol. 2:1, 12–20. Jeremiah reports more of his own personal experiences and feelings than any of the other prophets. Some earlier prophets also had their trials: Elijah fled in terror before the threats of Jezebel (see Pentecost 12, First Lesson), and Amos was ordered out of "the king's temple" (Amos 7:10–13). Here we have one of Jeremiah's several "confessions" or complaints. We learn from 11:21 that certain men of Anathoth, offended by Jeremiah's prophesying, told him to desist or they would kill him. We infer that Jeremiah has persisted and that his persecutors do seek his life. But the prophet has been warned by the Lord (v. 18), and declares as the word of the Lord that these would-be persecutors, and their sons and daughters, will themselves perish (vv. 22–23; cf. Amos 7:16–17). In fact, Jeremiah was frequently attacked for his unpopular prophecy of God's impending judgment. He was beaten (chap. 20), threatened with lynching (chap. 26), imprisoned (chap. 32), and thrown into a cistern (chap. 38). Anathoth had been his home (1:1), and 12:6 implies that even his own family was involved in the plotting against him (cf. Mark 6:4). Jeremiah survived their evil schemes, and lived to see the Babylonian conquest and at least the early months of the exilic period (chaps. 39–45). The prophets, along with the righteous of all ages, were an offense to those who perceived them as a challenge to the cruelties of their self-serving ways. (See Wisd. of Sol. 2:12, 14–20; Matt. 23:34–35 = Luke 11:49–51).

Like most of the other writings of the OT Apocrypha, the Wisdom of Solomon is retained in Roman Catholic and Greek Orthodox scripture to the present day. Chaps. 1:16–2:24 describe the philosophy and ethics of "ungodly men." Their philosophy is quite materialistic and "modern": Life is short, afterwards there is nothing, God is unreal. Their ethics follows logically: Enjoy life while it lasts, anything goes. "Let us crown ourselves with rosebuds before they wither"; "Everywhere let us leave signs of enjoyment"; "Let our might be our law of right" (vv. 8, 9b, 11a). To such folk, the righteous man is "inconvenient" (v. 12), for he reproaches those who live by oppression. "The very sight of him is a burden to us" (v. 15a). Such was Jeremiah to the men of Anathoth. The obvious solution is to lynch him and see if the God he trusts will deliver him (vv. 17–20; cf. Ps. 22:7-8; Matt. 27:39–43). "But the souls of the righteous are in the hand of God," while "the ungodly will be punished as their reasoning deserves" (Wisd. of Sol. 3:1, 10). If not in this life, then in the next, God will vindicate the righteous (3:2–9) and bring the wicked to their just condemnation (1:12–16; 3:10–19).

Second Lesson: James 3:13–4:3. Like the wisdom writings in the OT, James contains an extended series of exhortations to right living. One admonition follows upon another, but it is not always clear where one section ends and the next begins. Our lesson could be seen either in connection with the discourse on the perils of wrongful speaking (3:3–12), or with the warnings against passions, covetousness, worldliness, pride, double-mindedness, and judging one's neighbor in 4:1–12. As frequently in the letter, James begins here with a rhetorical question.

Those who claim to be wise are advised to manifest their "works" (cf. 2:14–18) by good conduct "in the meekness *(prautēs)* of wisdom" (3:13). James distinguishes two kinds of wisdom. The one "from above" is "pure, peaceable, gentle, open to reason, full of mercy and good fruits, without doubting or insincerity *(anupokritos,* unhypocritical)" (v. 17). Those who conduct themselves thus hold to what they know, but without boasting or putting others down. Jesus had commended the meek as fit heirs to the kingdom (Matt. 5:5); and gentleness or meekness *(prautēs)* was commonly listed by Paul and later NT writers among the proper characteristics of the Christian life: e.g., Gal. 5:23; 6:1; Eph. 4:2 = Col. 3:12; 1 Pet. 3:15.)

The other kind of wisdom is not "from above" but "earthly, physical (or "natural," *psuchikos),* and demonic" (3:15). This use of *psuchikos* is found also in 1 Cor. 2:14 and Jude 19. Claimants to such wisdom, like the "spiritualists" in Paul's Corinthian church, are jealous and boastful. Ambition, rivalry, or selfishness *(eritheia)* prompts their behavior (3:14, 16; cf. Rom. 2:8; 2 Cor. 12:20; Gal. 5:20; Phil. 1:15–17; 2:3). The consequence of such wisdom is "disorder" or "confusion" *(akatastasia:* cf. 1 Cor. 14:33; 2 Cor. 12:20) and "every vile practice" (3:16). But those who make peace (cf. Matt. 5:9) sow [their wisdom] in peace, and bring forth the fruit of righteousness (3:18; cf. Phil. 1:11; Heb. 12:11). As in 1 Corinthians, where Paul urged the Corinthian spiritualists to test their gifts—including wisdom and knowledge—by love, which is helpful, edifies, and builds up the church, so here James calls on Christians who think themselves wise to act so as to promote peace, mercy, and gentleness and thus be true to the truth.

Self-centeredness is the main problem in 4:1–3 also. Wars, fightings, and killing derive from capitulation to one's passions (or pleasures, *hēdonai)* and coveting. There may be echoes of Rom. 7:23 in v. 1b, and of Matt. 7:7–11 in vv. 2b–3. To ask rightly is to ask for "good gifts," not those that feed one's pleasures.

Gospel: Mark 9:30–37. Mark here reports Jesus' second "passion pronouncement" (vv. 30–32), and follows it with an account of his response to the disciples' discussion as to who was "the greatest" (vv. 34–37).

"They went on from there and passed through Galilee" (v. 30a): Jesus' general direction is now toward Jerusalem, via trans-Jordan (10:1, 32, 46). "And he did not wish anyone to know" (v. 30b): This suggests that Jesus preferred to remain out of view, lest he be detained on his way to Jerusalem, where his death and resurrection were to be accomplished (cf. 10:33–34). "After three days he will rise" (v. 31): Textual variants read "on the third day," following, perhaps, Matt. 17:23. "But they did not understand . . . and were afraid to ask" (v. 32). Mark often points to the disciples' lack of understanding. Here they do not grasp the mystery of Jesus' coming passion (cf. 8:32). They acted later as if they were unprepared for what had happened. If Jesus anticipated his death, he might plausibly have looked also for his resurrection at the beginning of the new age (thus Schweitzer and Pannenberg).

Capernaum had been Jesus' home (Mark 2:1). He asks his disciples what they had been discussing "on the way." Their silence indicates that they are ashamed. Probably they had been speculating as to which of them would be greatest in the coming kingdom. Something of the sort is suggested at Mark 10:35 ff.: James and John merely wish to be given the seats of greatest glory next to Jesus when he is enthroned! In both places, Jesus replies, "If anyone would be first [in the coming kingdom], he must [now] be last of all and servant of all" (9:35; 10:43b–44; cf. 10:31).

"And he took a child . . ." (vv. 36–37): Perhaps Jesus intended to illustrate what it means to be a servant of *all* by taking and receiving *even* a child. Far from being idealized in those days, children, along with women, tax-collectors and "sinners," were considered at best second-class persons. Yet, Jesus says, who receives such a one, receives "me," indeed, God himself (v. 37), even, or particularly, in the case of those neighbors commonly regarded as inconsequential or strangers (see Matt. 25:31–46; Luke 10:25–37). But there are many sayings about children in the Gospels, and it may be that vv. 36–37 should be read in relation to these. Mark 9:41–42 refers, apparently, to new disciples; Matt. 18:2–4 to *becoming like* children in respect to humility as requisite for entering the kingdom (cf. John 3:3); Matt. 20:26–27 = Mark 10:43–44 = Luke 22:24–27; Matt. 23:11–12 refers to becoming a *servant;* and Mark 10:13–16 to receiving the kingdom as a child receives [it?], *or,* to receiving the kingdom as one receives a child *(hōs paidion).*

HOMILETICAL INTERPRETATION

First Lesson: Jer. 11:18–20. It is on the basis of Jeremiah's "confessions," one of which we have before us in the present pericope, that some scholars have advanced the theory that Deutero-Isaiah's "Servant" was Jeremiah himself. Certainly last Sunday's First Lesson, Isa. 50:4–10, has much in common with this "confession" of Jeremiah, and both carry the profound nuances of today's Gospel, Mark 9:30–37, the second pronouncement of the Passion in Mark.

As Peter recoiled from the first pronouncement of the Passion (last Sunday's Gospel), so too Jeremiah recoils with shock and anger that his *faithfulness* should precipitate the heinous conspiracy mounted against him by his own household. Both have run into the hard mystery of life under God.

Jeremiah reacts with shock, incredulous innocence, and anger—a constellation of emotions which we would today describe as part of the "grief process." And it would be no help at all, at this stage, to say to

Jeremiah, "Hush up, you blasphemer. You are saying things you don't mean. You are doing bad theology by crying for revenge." No. *We* would be doing bad theology by shutting his mouth like that (cf. Psalms 3, 10, 17, 28, 35, etc.). For Jeremiah, in crying for vengeance, is being faithful to the covenant which he has been bidden to proclaim (11:1–17); and if God himself is faithful to his own covenant, he will surely not permit this assault upon his covenantal messenger. Or will he? That is a staggering question which Jeremiah can only resolve by positing a new covenant (chap. 31); at this moment he is still short of that revelation, and so he must proceed with the shock and anger. For at this stage a word of comfort, "There, there, Jeremiah, everything's going to be all right," would be premature and unrealistic. It is always a temptation to protect ourselves and others from the ambiguities and harsh realities of life. We offer comfort too readily, and thereby deny the only reality the afflicted one knows at that moment, namely that he *hurts;* by denying his hurt we deny him. And unless that hurt is given and permitted its own integrity, healing and insight and revelation and new life cannot occur.

As Jeremiah must face the betrayal perpetrated upon him, so we too must face those circumstances which seem to contradict a God of love and justice. It is not enough to protest innocence: "But I was like a gentle lamb led to the slaughter. I did not know it was against me they devised schemes . . ." (v. 19). The covenanting God did not initiate the covenant under any illusions; he entered it "for better and for worse," with eyes wide open (cf. the "passion pronouncements," Mark 8:31; 9:31). His servants need to learn that too, else their commitment to God will be but a half commitment. For God *is* committed to his people—but that can be learned only to the degree that one suffers the sin of one's own people.

Second Lesson: James 3:13–18. Thematically we may connect this pericope with what James has to say about teachers and teaching (3:1 f.), or the unruliness of the tongue (3:3 ff.), or the various warnings in chap. 4, or, of course, treat it as a self-contained unit.

James' comparison of the two kinds of wisdom is clearly of a piece with ancient Wisdom literature, as is evidenced by the similarity of this lesson to Prov. 9:1–6, 13–18 (cf. Pentecost 13, above). Like the Hebrew Wisdom literature, James understands true wisdom to be a gift from God—it is "from above" (v. 17). He does not speculate about this, however; he keeps his eye firmly upon what happens when people interact with people.

Quite possibly James was not only aware of but also very sensitive to the dynamics of Jewish-Christian relations, and the unavoidable polarizations that were taking place not only between Jews and Gentiles but also within individual Jewish Christians themselves (himself included?). How does one deal with such and similar polarizations? Each side claims to have the right understanding and thus to be wise; competition begins and jealousies develop, fed by personal ambitions; positions are overstated and then need to be defended—and thus the "very devil" is raised. In the end truth is not served, because personal victories take the place of truth, and are won at the expense of truth.

Truth, like wisdom, comes "from above." It is no person's and no party's possession. No one "has" truth; all have glimpses of it. As two parties dialogue they may, hopefully, develop a larger glimpse of it, discovering in the process that they have made peace and are harvesting a new respect (righteousness) for one another, a profounder respect for truth, as well as a humility derived from the acknowledgement (with Paul) that we now see only dimly and know only in part (1 Cor. 13:12). And all that, put together, is surely wisdom!

We should note that James says, ". . . the wisdom from above is pure, peaceable, . . . without uncertainty . . ." A close study of these characteristics will reward us with criteria to test the glimpses of truth we have and gain—as well as of our methods of communal discourse! Secondly, like James we need to keep a close watch on the dynamics of our interactions and conversations; surely if they create "disorder and vile practices" neither righteousness nor peace will be sown or harvested. And that, in the end, is contrary to God's very nature and to his desires for the community of man. It is likewise contrary to him who said, "If any one would be first, he must be last of all and servant of all" (Mark 9:35, Gospel).

Gospel: Mark 9:30–37. A new element in this second pronouncement of the Passion is that "the Son of man will be delivered into the hands of men, and they will kill him" (v. 31). It is a chilling statement.

A child coming upon a picture of the crucifixion for the first time is deeply perplexed. Why was it done? And why was it done to *him?* We meet here the stubborn and terrifying reality of sin. There lies in the hands of men the power to *kill* (cf. Cain and Abel). When the newborn baby is delivered into the hands of parents and family, the baptized infant into the hands of a congregation, the child into the hands of teachers, the employee into the hands of a company, each "delivery" is always fraught with comfort and terror, hope and fear, growth and destruction, life and death. So much good and so much harm can be experienced and perpetrated, so much life can be created and so much killing can be done. The ultimate risk of being human—for the Son of man and for every son of man—is to be killed by the hands of men (cf. First Lesson).

The child (v. 36), whether that be a literal child or any vulnerable person (cf. exegesis), is the perfect example of "being delivered into the hands of men." Will he be "received" or not? The evangelist wrote poignantly of Jesus, "He came to his own home, and his own people received him not" (John 1:11). Therefore, "Whoever receives one such child in my name receives me; and whoever receives me, receives not me but him who sent me" (v. 37). For "receiving" is the opposite of "killing"; it is giving life instead of taking it.

But "receiving" requires the servant posture, else it is not genuine "receiving," only condescension and patronage. For this reason the aspiration to be "the greatest" (v. 34) is always potentially participation in destruction, if only in the fact that to be greatest necessitates someone else to be less and someone to be least.

But now the strange paradox: To be "servant of all and last of all" is to be vulnerable; and vulnerability, given the reality of evil, is an invitation to the destructive hands of man; "they will kill him." Yet Jesus, the ultimate servant (see Mark 10:45), expresses a confident hope: "After three days he will rise." The church, like its Head, is called to be servant (see above, Pentecost 17, First Lesson), and to suffer the vulnerability of servanthood in hope of the promise of resurrection. But she should not entertain illusions of grandeur (v. 34); rather, by "receiving" the children of men, witness to the world that "delivery into the hands of men" is also participation in salvation.

The Nineteenth Sunday after Pentecost

Lutheran	*Roman Catholic*	*Episcopal*	*Pres./UCC/Chr.*	*Methodist/COCU*
Num. 11:24–30	Num. 11:25–29	Num. 11:25–29	Num. 11:24–30	Num. 11:24–30
James 5:1–11	James 5:1–6	James 5:1–6	James 5:1–6	James 5:1–6
Mark 9:38–50	Mark 9:37–42, 44, 46–47	Mark 9:38–43, 45, 47–48	Mark 9:38–48	Mark 9:38–50

EXEGESIS

First Lesson: Num. 11:24–30. Here is a marvelous fragment of early tradition describing those ancient days when Moses and the people of Israel were still in the wilderness. The law had been given, but the people were not yet in the Promised Land. The episode is framed by accounts of the Israelites' complaining that they had no meat such as they had enjoyed in the good old days in Egypt, and of the Lord's punishing them with a surfeit of meat and a terrible plague.

In Num. 11:16–17 the Lord had instructed Moses to gather seventy of the elders to whom he would then give some of the spirit that earlier had been put upon Moses alone. Thus Moses would not have to "bear the burden of the people" by himself (11:17). Moses gathered the seventy and placed them in a circle around the tent, which was outside the

Israelites' camp. The Lord then put some of the spirit upon the seventy elders, whereupon—on that occasion only—they prophesied (vv. 24–25).

Eldad and Medad, also apparently elders, perhaps among the seventy Moses had chosen, remained in the camp, but nevertheless received the spirit and prophesied there. Joshua—who later led Israel into the land of Canaan—was indignant at this irregularity, and urged Moses to forbid their prophesying in the camp. Moses' response shows that he was not thinking of his own prerogatives, but of the wonderful gift of the spirit and prophecy: "Would that all the Lord's people were prophets, that the Lord would put his spirit upon them!" Moses' reply to Joshua foreshadows Jesus' answer to John regarding the "strange exorcist": "Do not forbid him; for he that is not against you is for you" (Luke 9:49–50; cf. Mark 9:38–40).

The location of the tent of meeting outside the camp (cf. Exod. 33:7–11 and the later Priestly concept in Num. 2:2) probably expressed God's holiness or "separateness," and the corresponding importance of the people's keeping their distance from him (cf. Exod. 19:10–24). The spirit of God was associated with prophecy from quite early times, possibly going back to ecstatic Canaanite prophetism, e.g., 1 Sam. 10:6, 10. All Israel, if not all mankind, would receive the spirit and prophesy in the "latter days," according to Joel 2:28–29. The early Christians in Jerusalem had such an experience on the day of Pentecost (Acts 2:1–21).

The account in Num. 11:24–30 is similar to the story in Exod. 18:13–27 in which Moses accepts his father-in-law's advice, and appoints judges who "will bear the burden" (18:22) of judging the innumerable disputes among the Israelites in the wilderness. In Numbers, however, it is not clear how the seventy were to assist Moses, and we hear no more of them afterwards.

Second Lesson: James 5:1–11. Our lesson has two parts: Vv. 1–6 call on the rich to bemoan the judgment in store for them. Vv. 7–11 call upon the "brethren" to be patient and steadfast, for the *parousia* of the Lord has come near *(ēngiken)*.

Elsewhere James has inveighed against the rich, and declared that the poor would inherit the kingdom (2:2–7). Numerous traditions, especially in Luke, report that this had been Jesus' understanding also, e.g., Luke 6:20, 24; 12:16–21. In the Parable of the Rich Man and Lazarus (Luke 16:19–31), Lazarus was not said to have been righteous, just poor; nor the rich man wicked—other than by living in luxury while Lazarus starved at his gate—just rich. Perhaps Jesus' saying at Matt. 6:24 sums it up: "You cannot serve God and possessions" (=Luke 16:13). See also Mark 10:17–25, where Jesus called on the rich "young" man to sell all and give to the poor if he wished to have treasure in heaven. "All things are possible with God" (Mark 10:27) has been seized upon by latter-day Christians who hoped to have it both ways. But as J. Weiss observed, it would be more pious to honor Jesus' command than to hope for a miraculous dispensation (see also Luke 12:33). The early church in Jerusalem evidently did sell all, gave to the poor, themselves became poor, and awaited the fulfillment of the promise (Acts 2:43–47).

That those excluded from the kingdom of God would weep and howl (or "gnash their teeth") is often stated, especially in Matthew (also Luke 13:28). On the decay and rust of earthly treasures, see Matt. 6:19–21. Holding back the wages of laborers was one of the offenses proscribed by the ancient law (Deut. 24:14–15), while living in luxury, heedless of God's law and impending judgment had been condemned by the prophets (Amos 6:4–7; Isa. 5:8–23). It is not clear who "the righteous man" condemned and killed by the rich may have been (v. 6). Perhaps he represents all the righteous who have perished through neglect and oppression (see Wisd. of Sol. 1:16–2:20; Luke 11:49–51).

James urges the church (or churches) of his day to keep the faith, for the time of judgment and redemption is near. The image of the farmer awaiting the fruit of the earth draws upon messianic symbolism and assures the readers that this time is coming, though they still may have to wait (cf. Mark 4:26–29). James' admonition against grumbling recalls the tendency of Israel in the wilderness to complain as if doubting God's ability to bring them into the Promised Land or care for them in the meantime (Exod. 16; Num. 11). It also echoes Jesus' saying against judging (Matt. 7:1–2; cf. Rom. 2:1–3; 14:10). So near is the judgment that the Judge is already standing at the doors! (cf. Mark 13:29). But those who have kept the faith in patience and steadfastness need not be anxious, for "the Lord is compassionate and merciful."

Gospel: Mark 9:38–50. Here we have at least five different sayings collected by Mark (or an earlier "redactor") and arranged on the basis of catchwords or verbal association. Beginning in v. 37, three sayings are given, all involving reference to Jesus' "name." The first declares that one who, mindful of Jesus' name, receives a child, receives Jesus himself (cf. Matt. 25:31 ff.). The exorcist of v. 38 who uses Jesus' name is not to be stopped simply because he is not a disciple. Like Moses (Numbers 11), Jesus recognizes that God may act through other persons than those authorized by men. Strangers who do the will of God may be thought of as fellow-workers. (But cf. Matt. 12:30; Acts 19:13 f.) A third saying referring to Jesus' name follows in v. 41: Those who do even a minor service to Jesus' followers will have their recompense. This saying may reflect the later question of hospitality to Christian missionaries: cf. 3 John 5–8; Luke 10:7–8.

The "little ones" who believe in Jesus (v. 42) seem to be Jesus' followers, perhaps new converts, rather than believers who are children (cf. Matt. 10:42). Paul expresses similar concern lest supposedly more mature Christians cause new converts to "stumble" (1 Cor. 8:7–13).

The longer saying, vv. 43–48, is linked to the foregoing by the verb *skandalizein,* translated (RSV), "to sin," at vv. 42 and 43, and by other associations. The idea elaborated in the threefold saying about hand, foot, and eye is that eternal life is worth any sacrifice, for the alternative is eternal torment in gehenna. The saying may be offensive to many (cf. Matt. 19:12). It is the most vivid statement by Jesus in the Gospels as to the prospective fate of the condemned, even with vv. 44 and 46 omitted. But it is consistent with his other summons to repent, to choose between saving one's life in this world, or abandoning all for the hope of life in the kingdom of God. The idea of eternal torment in gehenna (v. 48) is omitted in Matthew's and Luke's versions. V. 49 may have been a separate saying (cf. Luke 12:49 f.) added to v. 48 on the basis of the catchword, "fire."

Two other sayings about salt then follow. The first, v. 50a, seems to parallel Matt. 5:13 = Luke 14:34 f., and, like numerous other sayings (e.g., at Matt. 5:14–16; 6:19–24), calls for radical obedience or choice between the life of discipleship, and the comfortable way of accomodation to the world. The final "salt" saying, in v. 50b, may correspond to the exhortation to gracious speech in Col. 4:6. It calls for mutual accord or peace, a fitting ending to the group of sayings that began with the disciples' dispute about which of them was the greatest (9:33–35).

HOMILETICAL INTERPRETATION

First Lesson: Num. 11:24–30. In Exod. 18:13 ff. we have a straightforward accounting of how Moses, acting upon his father-in-law's recommendations, appoints trustworthy "rulers" to settle day-to-day disputes. In this First Lesson, however, that narrative has become an "ordination" service, complete with a theophany and impartation of "the spirit that was upon Moses." Judging by what happens again and again in liturgical history, we may have here an example of how institutions, appointments, traditions, etc., which were born of practical concerns, in time are sacralized and divinely rationalized. Joshua's negative reaction to the two "unordained" prophesiers is therefore all the more interesting. For once an appointment or tradition has been divinely sanctioned, enormous energy is invested in maintaining "good order," "proper procedures," and "legitimate certification." Moses' wistful prayer, "Would that all the Lord's people were prophets," is a wish breathed whenever the church becomes rigid and unresponsive, or when leaders become jealous of their own power when a wider distribution of authority is proposed.

Moses' prayer is also the hint of major developments in the conception and experience of the spirit of God. Moses has the spirit; here it is shared —at least for a short time. In later eras the prophets especially are "seized by the spirit," and as the exegesis points out, Joel envisaged a general outpouring of the spirit, which the church has subsequently celebrated on Pentecost. The movement is from the few to the many; and certainly in the church today there is a new recognition and appropriation of the gift of the spirit by all God's people, independent of denominational lines. While God "is not a God of confusion but of peace" and therefore "all things should be done decently and in order" (1 Cor. 14:33, 40), this is not to be interpreted statically. The Spirit "blows where it wills" (John 3:8), and blessed is he who, like Moses, recognizes his manifestations in unexpected places and rejoices (see also the Gospel). God always breaks out of the strictures we place upon him; our anxiety about "irregular" religious beliefs and practice has left its sad trail of heresy and witch-hunts.

Coupled with this freedom of the spirit is the interesting location of the tent of meeting *outside* the camp. While this is an expression of God's holy separateness, the author of Hebrews sees as highly significant the fact that Jesus, like the ancient sin offerings which were burned outside the camp, "also suflered outside the gate" (Heb. 13:11 f.) "Therefore," he writes, "let us go forth to him outside the camp, bearing abuse for him" (Heb. 13:14). God, who is always also outside the camp, keeps beckoning us on; he is "for us" and "with us," but can also always take a stand "against us" (cf. the Second Lesson: "Behold, the Judge is standing at the doors").

Second Lesson: James 5:1–11. When the hardships, oppressions, and injustices of life strike hard, what sort of hopes do we nourish? Surely they involve at the very least some vague anticipation of better days to come. James details two ways in which the faithful community has tried to handle the evil and wickedness of life.

Vv. 1–6 of this Second Lesson reflect vividly the Jewish and early Christian apocalyptic expectations of late OT and early NT times. The "Day of the Lord" would signal God's cataclysmic intervention on behalf of his people, inaugurating the New or Messianic Age in which Israel would be vindicated and enthroned over all her enemies. Here we observe how oppression and injustice can gall to the point of violence. The anger in these verses comes from centuries of Jewish subjugation by foreigners in which faith in the eventual triumph of righteousness has well-nigh evaporated. It is the anger our age has been experiencing from minority groups, and as Martin Luther King invoked the ancient exodus images, so here James invokes the ancient "Yahweh of hosts," Yahweh the *warrior* God of Israel (cf. also Revelation). That the "rich" become the symbol of oppressive wickedness is not surprising, for the oppressed minority has little choice but to assume that the oppressors have all the wealth, since they themselves have none. A theological student working in a black ghetto had in his apartment a picture of his parents' home. Though it was a "modest bungalow," to the teen-agers it was a mansion, and they automatically expected he had bushels of money to share with them!

Their voiced and unvoiced expectations were for a great upheaval that would put "whitey" in his place.

Vv. 7–11 reflect the Christian community's eschatological hopes: The Lord will come, is indeed at the door; therefore be watchful and prepared to meet him and enter his promised kingdom. Here the emphasis is on patient suffering, buoyed up by the shortness of time left and by examples of outstanding steadfastness (the prophets and Job). God here is not the warrior "God of hosts," but rather the Judge who dispenses justice, motivated by compassion and mercy for his faithful suffering ones.

The church has largely adopted this latter attitude, and has consequently been accused of quiet, other-worldly withdrawal, depending upon the Last Judgment to condemn the unrighteous. But a growing realization of the oppression and exploitation of minority groups and native peoples is forcing the church to adopt a more aggressive stance in keeping with James' castigation of the "rich." That is a painful message to a church established in an affluent society, and therefore the church must herself first hear James' strong words before she can with credibility and power attack wider patterns of oppression.

Gospel: Mark 9:38–50. This Gospel is a veritable "catch-word quilt." Here is an opportunity, however, to share some of the history of the formation of the Gospels (see exegesis and parallel passages). As well, here is an opportunity to trace the development of "hell" from the Valley of Hinnom (Hebrew, gê hinnōm), the infamous ravine where Ahaz instituted the sacrifice of children through fire to Molech (2 Chron. 28:3; 33:6; Jer. 7:31; 19:5 f.; 32:35). Josiah ended these rites (2 Kings 23:10), and the valley eventually became the perpetually smouldering dump for Jerusalem's garbage. The burning, smokey, wormy (vs. 48), unclean vale produced the imagery for the place of divine punishment (cf. Enoch 27:2; 90:26 f.; 4 Ezra 7:36).

The strange exorcist narrative recalls the First Lesson. The power of the name is an intriguing conception. The ancient notion that a demon could be exorcised by means of the name of a more powerful spirit is not so strange when we realize we still "exorcise" law-breakers "in the name of the Law," and threaten policemen "in the name of" the Chief of Police who "is our friend"! The power of a name—and not least the name of Jesus—has been used to achieve innumerable good and bad ends, and our religious divisions have been maintained "in the name of" both worthy and perverse reasons. Whatever may be said against the disciple John, he deserves praise for being jealous of the name of Jesus. He will not have that name used for nefarious enterprises. Would that we had a like concern for that name, and the names of our fellows.

The statement, "he who is not against us is for us," is a marvelous expression of tolerance; yet it seemingly contradicts another saying of

Jesus, "He who is not with me is against me" (Matt. 12:30). While the contexts of the two sayings are different, it is just that difference that can lead us into consideration of the vexing question, "When does tolerance become wishy-washiness?"

The "cup of cold water" saying raises the issue of reward. The NT speaks of rewards in the context of a merciful and caring Father who sees even the sparrow fall, and thus recognizes such small services as expressions of his own will. In light of this, causing others (v. 42) and oneself (vv. 43–48) to stumble is all the more heinous.

The "salt" sayings are difficult to understand. Salt for the ancients was a valuable preservative as well as a seasoning; in addition, salt made OT sacrifices acceptable (Lev. 2:13), thus perhaps symbolizing purity or covenantal faithfulness. Fire usually symbolized purgation, judgment, persecution. These verses thus stress the radicalness of the call to discipleship and the imminence of judgment. For God—*because* he is a caring God—is not a loosely permissive God.

PROCLAMATION:

Aids for Interpreting the
Lessons of the Church Year

PENTECOST 1

SERIES B

David Randolph
and
Jack Kingsbury

FORTRESS PRESS Philadelphia, Pennsylvania

Library of Congress Catalog Card Number 74-24959

ISBN 0-8006-4076-4

4695I75 Printed in U.S.A. 1-4076

General Preface

Proclamation: Aids for Interpreting the Lessons of the Church Year is a series of twenty-six books designed to help clergymen carry out their preaching ministry. It offers exegetical interpretations of the lessons for each Sunday and many of the festivals of the church year, plus homiletical ideas and insights.

The basic thrust of the series is ecumenical. In recent years the Episcopal church, the Roman Catholic church, the United Church of Christ, the Christian Church (Disciples of Christ), the United Methodist Church, the Lutheran and Presbyterian churches, and also the Consultation on Church Union have adopted lectionaries that are based on a common three-year system of lessons for the Sundays and festivals of the church year. *Proclamation* grows out of this development, and authors have been chosen from all of these traditions. Some of the contributors are parish pastors; others are teachers, both of biblical interpretation and of homiletics. Ecumenical interchange has been encouraged by putting two persons from different traditions to work on a single volume, one with the primary responsibility for exegesis and the other for homiletical interpretation.

Despite the high percentage of agreement between the traditions, both in the festivals that are celebrated and the lessons that are appointed to be read on a given day, there are still areas of divergence. Frequently the authors of individual volumes have tried to take into account the various textual traditions, but in some cases this has proved to be impossible; in such cases we have felt constrained to limit the material to the Lutheran readings.

The preacher who is looking for "canned sermons" in these books will be disappointed. These books are one step removed from the pulpit: they explain what the lessons are saying and suggest ways of relating this biblical message to the contemporary situation. As such they are springboards for creative thought as well as for faithful proclamation of the word.

The authors of this volume of *Proclamation* are David James Randolph and Jack Dean Kingsbury. Dr. Randolph, the editor-homiletician, is Senior Minister of Christ Church United Methodist in New York City. He was President of the American Academy of Homiletics in 1968-69. Dr. Randolph has taught homiletics at Drew University, Princeton Theological

Seminary, and The Divinity School of Vanderbilt University. He has also served as a denominational executive in the field of worship. Dr. Randolph is the author of *The Renewal of Preaching* (Fortress Press, 1968) and *God's Party* (Abingdon Press, 1975). He is also the editor of the *Ventures in Worship* series (Abingdon Press). Dr. Kingsbury, the exegete, is Associate Professor of New Testament at Luther Theological Seminary in St Paul, Minn. He is a graduate of Concordia Seminary, St. Louis, Mo. (B.A., B.D.) and the University of Basel (Dr. Theol.). In addition to numerous articles in scholarly journals, Dr. Kingsbury has written two books: *The Parables of Jesus in Matthew 13* (S.P.C.K. and John Knox Press, 1969) and *Matthew: Structure, Christology, Kingdom* (Fortress Press, 1975).

Introduction

The purpose of this volume is to support the preaching ministry by offering exegetical and homiletical interpretations of the lessons for Pentecost Sunday and the nine subsequent Sundays of Series B in the three-year series of lessons of the church year.

The pattern in this volume will be to present the exegetical study in a way which deals both with the uniqueness of each lesson and its relatedness to the other lessons of the day with special attention to the unifying theme, or intentionality, of the texts. This intentionality becomes the *concern* of the sermon, the major meaning to be communicated. This *concern* will then be related to *confirmations* (material which corroborates, ingrains, illustrates) and *concretions* (material which deals with the concrete responsibilities, decisions, actions). Attention will then be paid to possibilities of *construction* by which the message of the text may come to expression in the situation of the hearers.

This pattern is designed for the person who understands preaching to be a creative process. The authors have sought to make important materials available so that from the preacher's own unique angle of vision he may allow the creative spirit to make the truth real to the particular congregation which is to be addressed. Interpretation is one task with many acts. It is the preacher himself who unites the diverse acts into one task of meaningful interpretation. The exegetical movement is basic. Here the spokesman seeks to understand by the best scholarly means available the original intention of the text, i.e., what the text *said*. The homiletical movement extends the exegetical into the present situation of the hearers, i.e., what the text *says*. The preaching event—the actual presentation of the sermon—occurs when the meaning of the biblical text is interpreted into the concrete situation of the hearers in a transforming way.

Jack Dean Kingsbury, the exegete of these lessons, has written of them: "The new three-year lectionary system is so devised that it focuses attention each year on one of the Synoptic Gospels. The Fourth Gospel is used to supply the readings for special feasts and festivals. In recognition of this principle, the discussion of the Scripture readings appointed for each Sunday begins in this book with the Gospel for the day. The strength of this approach is not only that the Gospel reading receives the position of stress, but also that it is followed in each case by a treatment of the OT reading, which as a rule has been chosen precisely because it can be correlated with the Gospel reading. Once the internal affinities between these two texts have been observed, one can move the more easily to a study of the second lesson, which may or may not be related thematically to the other two readings. On the matter of text selection in general, it soon becomes apparent to anyone working with the readings appointed for Pentecost 1 that remarkably good judgment has determined their choice."

Exegetically, the stress falls on the Gospel lesson for theological as well as practical reasons. Homiletically, however, the stress may fall on the second lesson or the OT lesson because that text offers the more compelling vehicle for communication in a specific situation. Whatever lesson may become the preaching text, the sermon should be responsible to the underlying intentionality of OT, Gospel, and Epistle.

Moreover, it must not be assumed that we can simply jump from exegesis to sermon, from what the text said originally to what the text says. We are historical beings. The texts also have a history of interpretation which must be taken into account. Moreover, we are interpreters of the Christian faith and not merely commentators on scattered texts. The question of dogmatics or systematic theology must be dealt with. Through all this we are communicators, sensitive to the people whom we are addressing. Therefore, we look for the material which will confirm the meaning of the text and the concrete ways in which this meaning will come to expression in the lives of the hearers.

These are exceedingly complex matters. Yet, the preacher consciously or unconsciously must deal with them for every sermon. This heightens the challenge of a book like this, for it is not presented as a complete road map to a territory already charted. Rather it is an invitation to an adventure in search of the Word that saves.

To Mrs. Jacqueline Danyo who typed the homiletical portions of this manuscript, the editor expresses thanks.

David James Randolph

Table of Contents

The Day of Pentecost

Lutheran	*Roman Catholic*	*Episcopal*	*Pres./UCC/Chr.*	*Methodist/COCU*
Ezek. 37:1–14	Acts 2:1–11	Joel 2:28–32	Joel 2:28–32	Joel 2:28–32
Acts 2:1–21	1 Cor. 12:3b–7, 12–13	Rom. 8:14–17, 22–27	Acts 2:1–13	Acts 2:1–21
John 7:37–39a	John 20:19–23	Luke 11:9–13	John 16:5–15	John 16:5–15

EXEGESIS

On the festival of Pentecost, the church celebrates its "founding" by commemorating the outpouring of the Holy Spirit upon the disciples. According to John, Jesus imparted the Holy Spirit to his disciples on the same day on which he arose (20:19–23). According to Luke, the Holy Spirit descended on the disciples on the Jewish feast of Pentecost (Acts 2:1), which was fifty days after Jesus' resurrection. As far as the church calendar is concerned, it is of course the Lucan scheme that has determined the date for the Christian celebration of Pentecost. Nevertheless, the Scripture readings for the day invite us to take a synoptic look at theological emphases drawn from both John and Luke, and Ezekiel as well. In combination, these emphases suggest the unifying thought for the day: Jesus, the author of salvation, is the dispenser of the Spirit (Gospel), who renews God's people (First Lesson) and empowers them to proclaim the word of salvation to persons everywhere (Second Lesson). As dictated by this thought, the mood of Pentecost is one of joyful anticipation: Christian worshipers await once again the descent of the Spirit, who will enable them to respond to God's grace in Christ with a life of witness and service.

Gospel: John 7:37–39a. Chap. 7 is a well-defined unit in John's Gospel. It reaches its culmination in the words of the text, which is embedded in a context of controversy. Jesus' opponents are out to kill him (v. 1). In teaching in the temple (v. 14), Jesus claims for his words and deeds the authority of God (vv. 16–18, 21). Some people hear him and believe (v. 31), but the Pharisees send officers to arrest him (v. 32). With great solemnity Jesus pronounces the words of the text, which create division among the crowd and confound the arresting officers (vv. 43–44).

V. 37 opens with a reference to the "last, great day of the feast." This

Jewish feast, however, is not that of Pentecost (Lev. 23:15–21) but of Tabernacles (7:2; Lev. 23:39–43). To avoid confusing the hearers, therefore, the preacher should perhaps forego explanation of the historical background of these feasts and concentrate instead on the words of Jesus.

These words in vv. 37b–38 admit of two quite different ways of punctuation. The first has traditionally been favored by the eastern church and is found in the RSV: "If any one thirst, let him come to me and drink. He who believes in me, as the Scripture has said, 'Out of his heart shall flow rivers of living waters.' " Should the text be read in this manner, then it is the "believer," and not Jesus, from whom the "rivers of living water" flow. The difficulty with this, however, is that elsewhere in his Gospel John does not speak of the believer in specifically these terms.

The second way in which vv. 37b–38 can be punctuated has been advocated historically by the western church and is found in the NEB: "If anyone is thirsty let him come to me; whoever believes in me, let him drink. As Scripture says, 'Streams of living water shall flow out from within him.' " So punctuated, these words now point to Jesus himself as the one from whom the "streams of living water" flow. The reason for preferring this reading is that it enjoys the support of other passages in which John portrays Jesus as the dispenser of "living water" (cf. 4:10, 14; also 19:34). Then, too, we know from v. 39 that the image of "living water" applies to the Spirit; but in John's Gospel, it is exclusively Jesus or the Father who gives the Spirit (20:22; 15:26; 16:7–15).

V. 39 is a parenthetical remark John makes in order to put the entire passage into proper theological perspective. "Water" was well known to the Jews as a symbol for spirit and pointed to the coming age of salvation (cf. Isa. 12:3). In that John depicts Jesus as the one from whom the waters of salvation, or the Holy Spirit, flow, so he is affirming that in the person of Jesus salvation is a present reality. In the Fourth Gospel, the work of the Spirit is to "bear witness" to Jesus (14:26; 15:26; 16:12–15). By so doing, the Spirit mediates salvation, or "life," to those who "believe" in Jesus, that is to say, to those who confess him to be the "Christ, the Son of God" (20:31). The new life which is in Jesus and is mediated by the Spirit to the church—this is the message this Gospel text proclaims on the occasion of Pentecost.

First Lesson: Ezek. 37:1–14. Ezekiel discharged his prophetic ministry over a period of more than twenty years (593–571 B.C.) as an exile in Babylon (1:1, 3; 33:21; 40:1). The destruction of Jerusalem and of the temple in 586 B.C. caused him and his fellow Israelites no little consternation. Whereas in the forepart of his book Ezekiel inveighs against the sins of his people (chaps. 2–24) and pronounces oracles of doom against the surrounding nations (chaps. 25–32), in the latter part of his book he foretells the future restoration of both Israel and the temple (chaps. 33–48). Our text is situated in the latter section.

In the vision of the valley of dry bones, made famous by the celebrated Negro spiritual, Ezekiel describes himself as caught up by God and transported to a wide plain that was strewn with the bones of countless men long dead (vv. 1–2). Asked by God whether these bones would ever live again, Ezekiel has no answer (v. 4). But God commands him to prophesy breath and life for these bones (vv. 4–6). Ezekiel obeys, and to his astonishment the bones order themselves once again as bodies (vv. 7–8). By means of a second prophecy these bodies receive breath, or life, and the "exceedingly great host" then takes to its feet (vv. 9–10).

In vv. 11–14, Ezekiel explains his vision. The dry bones represent the house of Israel (v. 11). Cut off from the temple and without hope, these exiles are as dead and buried (vv. 11–12). In the power of his Spirit, however, God opens their graves and restores them to life. What Ezekiel predicts, therefore, is that God will give proof of his Lordship by returning Israel to her land and reconstituting her as a nation (vv. 13–14).

The theme of this text is not that of resurrection per se. Rather, it proclaims faith (v. 3) in the power, or Spirit, of God to imbue a people, despite utterly hopeless circumstances, with that life that only God can give (vv. 13–14). For Christians, the new people of God, such life is theirs by virtue of God's grace in Jesus and is the gift of the Holy Spirit in word and sacrament.

Second Lesson: Acts 2:1–21. The setting for the extraordinary events surrounding the day of Pentecost is Jerusalem (Acts 1:4). For Luke, Jerusalem is not merely a geographical location but is also of theological significance: it is the place of temptation (Luke 4:9–13) and of death (Luke 9:31; 13:33; 18:31–32). Thus, the way of Jesus is towards Jerusalem, where he suffers, dies, and rises (Luke 9:51; 18:31–32). By contrast, the way of the church is from Jerusalem towards Rome (Acts 1:8), occasioned to no small degree by the same manner of rejection Jesus encountered (Acts 4–9).

The text divides itself into three parts: it tells of the outpouring of the Holy Spirit upon the disciples (vv. 1–4), of the reaction to their preaching by the great crowd of Jews and proselytes (vv. 5–13), and of the first half of Peter's speech to the crowd (vv. 14–21).

Gathered together in a house, the disciples are filled with the Holy Spirit (vv. 1–4). The sudden sound from heaven of the rush of a mighty wind (v. 2) portends the approach of the Spirit (v. 4). The "tongues as of fire" (v. 3) point at once to the gift the disciples receive to "speak in other tongues" (v. 4) and the fact that the word they will proclaim will effect division, or judgment, among people (cf. Luke 12:49–53). The phenomenon itself of "speaking in tongues" seems to refer here to the ability to discourse in other recognizable languages (vv. 6, 8, 11).

At the speaking of the disciples in other languages, a huge crowd of Jews and proselytes from many nations gathers and asks as to the significance of this (vv. 5–12). The names of the lands and regions cited can be correlated with the signs of the zodiac, the inference being that Luke's geographical catalogue constitutes a representative list of all the nations of the world. Consequently, one purpose of the text is to show that the word of the "mighty works of God" (v. 11), which the disciples proclaim in many languages on Pentecost, is able to dispel the confusion of tongues that long ago resulted from humankind's presumptuous effort to find its unity in its own strength, in the construction of the tower of Babel (Gen. 11:1–9).

In response to the taunt that the disciples are perhaps drunk (v. 13), Peter addresses the crowd and interprets what is taking place as the outpouring of the Holy Spirit in fulfillment of the prophecy of Joel (vv. 14–21). According to Peter's speech, a new time has dawned (vv. 17, 20), for Jesus, crucified, raised, and exalted to the right hand of God, has now poured out the Holy Spirit upon his disciples (vv. 22–33). Empowered by the Spirit, the disciples bear witness in these last days to God's mighty acts in Jesus (Acts 1:8), and the word they proclaim is one of salvation: it summons all people, Jew and Gentile, to call upon the name of the Lord and be saved (v. 21).

Accordingly, the major thought of the text is that empowered and therefore guided by the Holy Spirit, the disciples of Jesus attest to God's mighty acts in him and so proclaim the word of salvation which is meant for all people.

HOMILETICAL INTERPRETATION

1. Concern

Jesus imparts the Spirit who renews God's people and empowers them to proclaim the word of salvation with joyful anticipation to persons everywhere.

2. Confirmations and Concretions

The valley full of bones is one of the most contemporary of ancient images. It represents life outracing its limits, the abandonment of hope, ultimate desolation.

Ezekiel's vision is our reality. As real as My Lai, Dachau, Hiroshima. As real as burned out buildings in Dresden and the South Bronx. As real as the weariness which leads us to say at times, "I am bone tired."

The Mexican artist, Jose Guadalupe Posada, developed a large corpus of work showing persons engaged in a wide range of activities but depicted as skeletons. In one drawing he depicted a soldier riding through a valley of bones full of skulls.[1] Picasso's work "Guernica" expresses in one master painting the skeletal consequences of war. Terrible as that state is, however, it is overcome early in Ezekiel's vision: the prophet speaks and the bones come together. Sinews cover the bones; next skin covers the flesh.

Then comes the most terrifying aspect: bodies to all appearances human but without the breath of life. This is the essence of tragedy—not that we die but that we do not live. The flesh without spirit, not the dry bones, is the most haunting aspect of the vision. It is the zombie, the living dead, who is even a more frightening representation of our time than the skeleton.

These are the bodies T. S. Eliot described in "The Waste Land." Movement I, "The Burial of the Dead," refers to interment not in the cemetery but in the modern city. We see a crowd of people flowing across the London Bridge, sighing, each with his eyes fixed before his feet. The poet had not thought that "death had undone so many."[2]

The Day of the Locust by Nathanael West shifts the scene to Hollywood.[3] There a commercial artist, Tod Hackett, works on a master painting to be called "The Burning of Los Angeles." Before the painting can be completed, however, Hackett is crushed in a mob which riots while awaiting the arrival of movie stars at a premiere. The novel ends with Hackett's scream blending with the sound of the police siren, even as his fantasy blends with the reality of his painting.

This novel, and the film of it directed by John Schlesinger, is about the people who slave at dull jobs until they save enough to go to California—the land of dreams. Once there they discover that sunshine and oranges

1. See Justino Fernandes, *A Guide to Mexican Art* (Chicago and London: University of Chicago Press, 1969), especially p. 154.

2. T. S. Eliot, *Collected Poems 1909–1962* (New York: Harcourt, Brace & World: 1930–1963). "The Waste Land," with notes, is found on pp. 51–76. "The Hollow Men," pp. 79–82, carries on the theme. "Ash Wednesday," pp. 83–95, employs the "dry bones" imagery from Ezekiel in Movement II.

3. Nathanael West, *The Day of the Locust,* with an introduction by Richard B. Gehman (New York: Bantam Book, 1959).

are not enough. One wave of the Pacific looks just like the one which came before. The American continent and the Dream end at the Pacific. These people haven't the personal resources to improve their situation and long for excitement and violence to pull their senses tight. They feel cheated and betrayed.

The novel is not about the big stars and producers of the film world, but the *pretenders* who seek the meaning of their lives by assuming the poses of celebrities. West's vision cuts to the bone of our modern malaise: our capacity to imitate has outrun our capacity to create. We have traded the humble but holy reality of our lives for the spectacular illusion.

The valley of dry bones cuts through the Hollywood Hills across the continent, and throughout the world. It is an inescapable region in the landscape of our time.

The word of the Lord which brought flesh to the bones in Ezekiel's vision was summoned again and this time brought the Spirit which gives life to the flesh. Jesus Christ was that word incarnate. Jesus is to spiritual dryness what a spring of water is to thirst. The Christian faith knows of no other source from which "the streams of living water flow." There is no way out of the valley full of bones except by way of the mountain full of life, Calvary. Only the Day of the Lord is more potent than the Day of the Locust.

Nathanael West also had a glimpse of this possibility which he shared in *Miss Lonely Hearts,* the story of a writer of an advice-to-the-lovelorn column. "Miss Lonely Hearts," actually a man, reads through the correspondence which floods him with the lamentations of persons suffering from kidney pain, from unwanted pregnancy, from being born without a nose, from those assaulted by others and by their own endless fears. He stops reading. He knows that Christ is the answer to these cries, but feels that he had better stay away from "the Christ business."

"Miss Lonely Hearts" becomes sick and his view of religion is part of this sickness. Yet, as a boy in his father's church, he had discovered that when he shouted the name of Christ something powerful stirred within him. Then West offers what may be the explanation of the sickness of "Miss Lonely Hearts": "He had played with this (Christ) thing but had never allowed it to come alive."[4]

We stay in the valley full of bones as long as we "play" with Christ without really letting him come alive.

The Day of Pentecost marks the advent of hope as the valley of bones marks the advent of despair. It might be said that until that day the

4. Nathanael West, *Miss Lonely Hearts,* with an introduction by Stanley Edgar Hyman (New York: Avon Books, 1955–1964), p. 42.

early church had been "playing" with Christ. Playing, not altogether frivolously, but in the sense that they had not allowed the fullness of his power to occupy them. Then on the Day of Pentecost, Christ really came alive. The something for which they had longed, happened.

The imagery of the event is incandescent. It glows with tongues of fire and the bewilderment of other languages. People stagger like drunken men. But when Peter speaks and the air clears that which is testified to is nothing other than the mighty works of God.

That mighty work goes on in the church wherever the dreams of the old and the visions of the young refuse to "play" with Christ but allow the risen Christ to come alive. For this mighty work is the work of salvation: "Whoever calls on the name of the Lord shall be saved."

Now what concrete response can be given to such a mighty event? Here we are at the very heart of man's response to the gospel. Man's predicament without God is so desperate and man's possibilities with God are so enormous that any response seems incidental. Does one fall to his knees in prayer? Does one rise to his feet in service? Does one do both? In what sequence?

Such questions are secondary. They come at a distance from the event and may be a form of "playing" with Christ. Anyone who places himself within the event of Pentecost knows the answer of faith: Repent and be baptized, receive the Holy Spirit.

Repentance is the radical turning of the whole self from itself to orientation to God. To be baptized is to enter into the life of the church. To receive the Holy Spirit is to allow the Spirit to shape our lives in obedient witness and service. It may mean selling what we don't need, distributing our goods to the needy, sharing a common life with others, worshiping daily and breaking bread in homes—as it did to the early Christian community described in Acts 2:37–47.

In our time it will certainly mean the distribution of the waters of grace into the valley of dry bones where life is dehumanized and destroyed. This will take many concrete acts of witness and service in a lifetime of commitment. But unless these acts are to evaporate and lead back to the valley of dry bones, they must proceed from that repentance which is the total turning of self to God.

3. Construction

The concern of these texts unfolds logically and poetically from OT Lesson, to Gospel, to Second Lesson. If the essay form is used, each text may supply a point. For example:

1. Life without faith is desperate.

2. Life with Christ overcomes despair.
3. Life with Christ finds empowerment through the Spirit in the church for mission in the world.

A more poetic development would cluster symbols around three master images. For example:

1. The Day of the Locust.
2. The Day of the Lord.
3. The Day of Pentecost.

In either case the sermon, theologically and structurely, finds its center in the Gospel.

The Holy Trinity, The First Sunday after Pentecost

Lutheran	*Roman Catholic*	*Episcopal*	*Pres./UCC/Chr.*	*Methodist/COCU*
Deut. 6:4–9	Deut. 4:32–34, 39–40	Exod. 3:1–6	Isa. 6:1–8	Deut. 4:32–34, 39–40
2 Cor. 13:11–14	Rom. 8:14–17	Acts 2:32–39	Rom. 8:12–17	Rom. 8:12–17
John 3:1–17	Matt. 28:16–20	John 3:1–16	John 3:1–8	Matt. 28:16–20

EXEGESIS

Gospel: John 3:1–17. As the Gospel reading for Trinity Sunday, this text has been appointed because it makes direct reference to God the Father, to his Son Jesus, and to the Holy Spirit. Indeed, one way of outlining the text serves to highlight each of the three: vv. 3–8 pertain above all to the Spirit, vv. 11–15 to the Son of man, and vv. 16–17 to God.

Vv. 1–8 focus on the theme of "begetting from above." John reports that Nicodemus, who is a Pharisee, a member of the Sanhedrin, and a teacher, comes to Jesus by night to converse with him (vv. 1–2, 10). He is the spokesman, as it were, of those Jews who had seen the signs Jesus did during the feast of the Passover and had consequently begun to believe in him (v. 2; 2:23). Nicodemus initiates the dialogue by telling Jesus that he considers him to be a teacher approved by God (v. 2). To this Jesus solemnly replies that unless a person is begotten from above he is unable to experience the gracious rule of God (v. 3).

Nicodemus misconstrues Jesus' words. He understands "begotten from above" as "being born again," and therefore asks Jesus how it is possible for a man to enter his mother's womb a second time and be born once more (v. 4).

Jesus does not give specific answer to this query, but instead speaks of the working of the "Spirit." Nicodemus, however, still does not understand him, for he takes the word "Spirit" to mean "wind." More particularly, Jesus tells Nicodemus that a person, simply as he is by nature, that is to say, simply as one born into the world by reason of his father's begetting him, is unable to enter into the sphere of God's rule; to enter this sphere, what is necessary is that one be begotten "from above," that is to say, regenerated by the power of God's Spirit (vv. 5–7). Moreover, such regeneration by the Spirit is something that is beyond human comprehension and accomplishment; it can only be effected by the Spirit himself: even as the "wind blows where it wills, and you hear the sound of it, but you do not know whence it comes or whither it goes," so the "Spirit breathes where he wills, and you hear his voice, but you do not know whence he comes or whither he goes" (v. 8).

In response to Jesus' words, Nicodemus puts one more question to him, thereby giving evidence of his continued ignorance as to what Jesus is talking about (v. 9). In reply, Jesus chides Nicodemus (vv. 10–11), but does tell him how regeneration by the Spirit takes place. It takes place, says Jesus, through faith in the Son of Man, whom God has decreed should be "lifted up" on the cross. Regenerated by the Spirit through faith in the Son of man, a person receives the gift of "eternal life" (vv. 14–15).

In conclusion of his dialogue with Nicodemus, Jesus broadens the scope of the discussion by pointing to God as the ultimate source of salvation (v. 16). His great love for humankind is what has impelled him to send his Son into the world and to the cross (v. 16). Through faith in the Son, people need not perish but can receive the gift of eternal life mediated by the Spirit, and so be saved (vv. 16–17).

In sum, the main point of this text is that one receives salvation, or eternal life, as the gift of the Spirit through faith in the Son, whose coming into the world and death on the cross are God's absolute demonstration of his great love for humankind.

First Lesson: Deut. 6:4–9. In chap. 5, the Deuteronomist depicts Moses as reminding Israel of the covenant God has made with her and of its statutes and ordinances. Chap. 6, in which we find the text, has to do with the meaning of the so-called First Commandment (v. 1).

The text is known in Jewish tradition as the "Shema," after the Hebrew word with which v. 4 begins and which means "hear." The Shema captures in a word the faith of Israel, and is Judaism's highest confession. On the basis of the words of v. 7, ". . . when you lie down, and when you rise," rabbinic law early stipulated that the faithful Jew should recite the Shema both morning and evening.

Vv. 4–5 are essentially a restatement in positive form of the First Commandment of the Decalogue (cf. 5:7–10). This is termed "*the* commandment" in v. 1, and was known as such also by Jesus (Mark 12:28–30; Matt. 22:36–38). The point of v. 4 is that there are not many gods or forces in the universe but one Lord, who is unique and sovereign (cf. 4:39). The point of v. 5 is that one is to love the one, sovereign God utterly and completely.

By postexilic times, if not earlier, v. 8 was taken literally and thus gave rise to the custom of wearing phylacteries. Phylacteries are small leather receptacles in cubical form which every male Jew above thirteen years of age was required to tie on himself, one on the left arm and one on the forehead, during morning prayer. Whereas the phylactery for the arm had one compartment, that for the forehead had four. Each compartment contained a piece of parchment on which was written one (or, in the case of the arm phylactery, all four) of the OT passages that were regarded as giving sanction to the practice (Exod. 13:1–10, 11–16; Deut. 6:4–9; 11:13–21).

On Trinity Sunday, the reading of the Shema is most appropriate. It reminds Christians that though they worship three persons, God is nevertheless in essence one.

Second Lesson: 2 Cor. 13:11–14. The text culminates in v. 14 with what has become a familiar Christian benediction. The great creeds of the church are, from one standpoint, later theological elaborations of passages such as this (cf. Matt. 28:19).

V. 11 reflects the fact that the Corinthian congregation had been wracked by factionalism and dissension. False Jewish-Christians from Palestine with Gnostic-pneumatic tendencies had invaded the congregation with a theology of glory, deprecating Paul's theology of the cross. Combined with this was a fierce attack on the very person and apostleship of Paul, against which the latter vigorously defended himself (2:14–7:4). In v. 11, then, Paul bids the congregation farewell and urges the members to pull themselves together, to encourage one another, and to let harmony and peace prevail. If they do so, Paul assures them that God will himself bless them by showering his own love and peace upon them.

In v. 12, mention is made of "greeting one another with a holy kiss." It appears that at the very least this was a liturgical gesture that had its place in the celebration of the Lord's Supper and gave demonstration of the fellowship that united all Christians as members of God's end-time people in Christ (cf. Rom. 16:16; 1 Cor. 16:20; 1 Thess. 5:26).

The meaning of the benediction in v. 14 is that the grace which Jesus Christ, who is now Lord of the church, has manifested towards humankind in the cross (2 Cor. 8:9) flows from the love of God, which love also enables Christians to participate in the life of the Spirit (cf. Gal. 6:18; Phil. 4:23). This thought tallies well with the Gospel for Trinity Sunday.

HOMILETICAL INTERPRETATION

1. Concern

The one God reveals himself in love as Father, Son, and Holy Spirit.

2. Confirmations and Concretions

The homiletical emphasis for this Trinity Sunday clearly falls with the Gospel lesson dealing, as it does, with the Trinity. The Trinity is approached existentially, that is, through the concrete situations of the existence of Nicodemus. The sermon has rich resources, for Nicodemus is one of the most intriguing persons recorded in the Scriptures.

Nicodemus was a ruler of the Jews. He was a teacher of Israel. He was a big man in Jerusalem. Nicodemus is a very "modern" type of man. Picture him as he would, and probably does, appear in your city or town.

Nicodemus has it made. And yet he is not quite sure why he wakes in the night. Nor is he sure why he wakes in the morning. The point of his life has grown dull. Perhaps he has lost it altogether. We can imagine him on a restless night going to Jesus, the visiting preacher, with the hope that perhaps this new figure on the religious horizon will be able to offer what he is looking for, even though he is not sure what that is.

When Nicodemus finds Jesus he begins with a complimentary approach. Jesus must have looked not so much at Nicodemus as through him. In effect he says, "Oh Nicodemus, come off it. Why are you giving me this Madison Avenue stuff? Are you wanting to fit me into a comfortable niche in your comfortable life? Are you hoping somehow that religion is going to be just another trophy you can put on your shelf? Nicodemus, face it. I am involved in a kingdom of the Spirit. You are not going to be able to fit this kingdom into your life, your life is going to have to fit into this kingdom. You must be born again."

Today we don't find Jesus' words any more comfortable than Nicodemus did. We, too, would like the world of the Spirit to be another thing in our well-ordered lives. We would like the kingdom of God to be one of the many places we could visit on some future itinerary.

But there is something in the nature of spiritual reality which will not let us rest with that. No matter how materialistic we may be, no matter how absorbed we may be in our quest for success, we sense somehow another possibility. We may sense it with the sophistication of an Edward Arlington Robinson who saw a dark night all around him in his poem entitled "Credo." Yet even Robinson felt "the coming glory of the Light." Less sophisticated were the dance-hall girls pictured in the Broadway show and film, "Sweet Charity." Night after night they danced with any man who had the money to buy their time. Always there was the hope that someone would come in and dance them into a new life. They sang, "There's got to be something better than this."

No matter how much we get caught up in the material realm there is a wind that blows through our lives. We can't keep it out. This is the wind of the Spirit. The Spirit does not occupy some other world far away. The Spirit occupies a plane which cuts right through all that we do and all that we are. The Spirit isn't located somewhere else but right in the midst of the world where we live and work. To be born of the Spirit is to share that plane and to give it primacy.

Nicodemus' response to Jesus was to attempt to put him down. "Born again . . . Am I to enter a second time into my mother's womb?" Jesus unmasked that evasiveness by insisting that Nicodemus deal with the concrete reality of that very moment. What it came down to was whether or not Nicodemus would accept Jesus as the door by which he was to enter the world of the Spirit.

This is what the NT frankly admits is the scandal of Christianity. For what Christianity is about is not some fairytale in a never, never land. Christianity has to do with the concrete reality of our everyday life. It has to do with whether we are going to find in this man, Jesus, our Lord and Savior. The Christian sees in this Jesus of Nazareth the Son of man and the Son of God. It is a staggering claim which Jesus makes about himself. No wonder that the character in Nathanael West's novel wants to "play" with Christ rather than to deal with him.

We today find it no less scandalous than Nicodemus. Jesus says to us, as he said to him, that we have to choose. We did not choose to be born, but we must choose to be re-born, as Hermann Hesse reminded us. We must choose the name by which we are to be born into the Spirit. And for the Christian that name is Jesus Christ.

We owe an enormous debt to the religions of the world. Personally, I find myself in awe of the truths which come from Judaism, Buddhism, Hinduism, and Islam. I have learned much from them. The world of the

Spirit is infinite and its winds blow from many directions. Christians are those who enter the world of the Spirit through the door of Jesus Christ.

Jesus continues with Nicodemus by pointing out that once the name is named, once we open the door to Jesus Christ in the concrete situations of our life, then it is as if a whole universe of energy rushes through that door. Jesus' reference is to a life which is eternal, to a world that is cosmic in its dimensions.

God is the cosmic reality, present in and through Jesus of Nazareth. It is incredible to our normal way of experiencing things. But in the moment when we are able to sense God in this man Jesus, then the whole universe rises up in support. "For God so loved the world that he gave his only begotten Son, that whosoever believeth in him should not perish, but have everlasting life."

We do not know how the encounter between Jesus and Nicodemus ended that night but there are two other references to Nicodemus in the NT: John 7:50 depicts him in his role as a leader of the Jews pleading that a fair chance be given to Jesus; and John 19:39 depicts Nicodemus caring for the body of Jesus which places him very near the crucifixion. We do not know the details of where and when, but at some point this ruler, this man, came to know that "God so loved . . . Nicodemus."

This entire discussion has been about the Trinity. The God of the Christian revelation is the God who meets us as Spirit, as Son, and as Father. This understanding, drawn from the Gospel lesson, is enriched by reference to the OT lesson which emphasizes the oneness of God and the Epistle which stresses his love.

J. S. Whale in his book *Christian Doctrine* sums up the discussion of the Trinity in a way which also sums up these three lessons for the day: "The transcendent God of Israel, who had revealed himself in Christ as the God of infinite grace, was now and always the life-giving Spirit of his Church. . . . The Bible speaks of one God, and of one God only. It speaks of him in three distinct ways which are normative for Christian thinking."[1]

We have been considering the Trinity in its existential meaning rather than in its philosophical presuppositions. In this existential, practical meaning the doctrine of the Trinity teaches us that the God who met Nicodemus in Jesus Christ is the God who meets us here and now.

In relation to the lesson and sermon of last Sunday, this sermon should stress that the Spirit of Pentecost must be "tested" against the Spirit of the God of the Trinity. And in relationship to our lives, this doctrine assures

1. J. S. Whale, *Christian Doctrine* (New York: MacMillan and Cambridge, England: At the University Press, 1941), p. 114.

us that the rebirth which is so desperately needed in our day is no harder for us than it was for Nicodemus. Nor is it easier. Many know that rebirth must come. The Christian knows that it can come through Jesus Christ.

3. CONSTRUCTION

The structure which emerges from the Gospel lesson builds on three distinct supports:

1. God as Spirit.
2. God as Son.
3. God as Father.

The contemporaneity of the passage can be shown by use of the narrative/application method. That is, identifying the major element in each passage of the text then showing its application to contemporary life. The OT lesson and the Epistle relate most directly to the third point. The summary should include both a statement on the Trinity in its existential expression and exposition of how that relates to our life of today, building on confirmations such as those suggested above.

The Second Sunday after Pentecost

Lutheran	*Roman Catholic*	*Episcopal*	*Pres./UCC/Chr.*	*Methodist/COCU*
Deut. 5:12–15	Deut. 5:12–15	Deut. 5:6–21	Deut. 5:12–15	Deut. 5:12–15
2 Cor. 4:5–11	2 Cor. 4:6–11	2 Cor. 4:7–11	2 Cor. 4:6–11	2 Cor. 4:7–11
Mark 2:23–28	Mark 2:23–28	Mark 2:23–28	Mark 2:23–3:6	Mark 2:23–3:6

EXEGESIS

Gospel: Mark 2:23–28. From the second through the ninth Sunday after Pentecost, the Gospel for the day is taken from the first half of Mark.

The story of plucking grain on the sabbath is situated in the first major section of the Gospel (1:14–3:6), which treats the opening phase of Jesus' public ministry in Galilee (1:14–15). The emphasis in this section is on, respectively, the call of the disciples (1:14–20), the miracles Jesus performs (cf. 2:1–12), and his debates with the leaders of the Jews (cf. 2:1–3:6). The section closes on the ominous note that the Pharisees and Herodians go out and hold counsel on how to destroy him (3:6).

The text clearly has the form of a debate: the setting is established (v. 23); the Pharisees lodge a charge against the disciples (v. 24); and

Jesus refutes the charge with his authoritative word (vv. 25–28). Since the reply of Jesus falls into two parts (cf. "And he said to them," v. 27), it is in the latter part, which occupies the position of stress, that we can expect to find the climax of the narrative.

Mark writes that the Pharisees, in a question to Jesus, accuse the disciples of breaking the law because they pluck grain on the sabbath (vv. 23–24). Technically, since the act of gleaning itself is not, according to Deut. 23:24–25, a violation of the law, it would seem that we are to think of Exod. 34:21, a statute that prohibits reaping on the sabbath, as furnishing the grounds for the accusation. However this may be, Jesus responds to the Pharisees with a (double) counter-question, a literary device that is characteristic of rabbinical arguments (cf. Mark 12:10, 26).

To trace the logic of vv. 25–28, the Markan Jesus refutes the charge against the disciples in three steps. The thing to observe is that each step is of greater weight than the preceding one, so that it is in the final one that the answer of Jesus culminates. In vv. 25–26, the purpose for which Jesus recalls the OT story that tells how David and his men, hungry and in need, entered the house of God and ate the holy bread of the Presence (cf. 1 Sam. 21:1–6) is to remind the Pharisees that it has always been permissible, under exceptional circumstances of human need, to set aside the statutes that regulate the sabbath. This illustration alone is tantamount to a rebuttal of the Pharisees' charge against the disciples.

But Mark appends to this two further assertions of Jesus. The first (v. 27) bases the legitimacy of setting aside the sabbath law on the principle of "creational priority": in the order of creation, even as God's making man (Gen. 1:26–31) preceded his institution of the sabbath rest (Gen. 2:1–3), so "the sabbath was made for man, not man for the sabbath." The second assertion (v. 28), which is climactic, bases the legitimacy of the disciples' behavior on the authority of Jesus himself: if v. 27 is true, then Jesus Son of man, who wields the very authority of God, is in the last analysis the one who determines what is permissible on the sabbath.

In sum, the central thought of this text is that it is the will of Jesus, the authoritative Son of man, that compassion and love, not the blind observance of regulations, are to be the hallmark of the Christian life.

First Lesson: Deut. 5:12–15. More than anything else, Deuteronomy concerns itself with the revelation of God's will and with all that this implies. Consequently, the section 4:44–6:3, which depicts Moses as presenting to Israel the Decalogue (5:6–21; cf. Exod. 20:2–17), is central to it. Depending upon how one counts, we may regard the text as the Third Commandment.

The Decalogue begins with a fixed formula by means of which God is portrayed as introducing himself to Israel (5:6). The idea is that with these words the divine "I" is thought to approach Israel and to address her as his own possession. Theologically, this is of great importance for understanding the Decalogue, for it means that God speaks to Israel as one who, in bringing her out of bondage, has already demonstrated his saving will towards her. Accordingly, in that Israel adheres to the Decalogue, she is not saving herself by works, but is responding to the grace God has shown her.

The OT gives two reasons why God should enjoin observance of the sabbath. In Exod. 20:8–11, such observance is explained in terms of creation: God rested on the seventh day from his work and therefore so should humans. By contrast, in Deuteronomy we learn that the purpose of the sabbath is both to provide rest for man and beast (vv. 13–14) and to establish an occasion on which Israel might ponder her deliverance from Egypt (v. 15).

The Gospel text, we saw, places love above casuistry. But Christians are not antinomian per se (cf. Matt. 5:17–20). The text, then, complements the Gospel reading well, for it reminds the church that in response to God's grace in Christ, the Christian, too, does the will of God as expressed in the Decalogue.

Second Lesson: 2 Cor. 4:5–11. The text is a part of the larger section 2:14–7:4 in which Paul speaks of the ministry that has been entrusted to him and explains its purpose. In the text itself, Paul sketches in one sentence the content of his ministry and of his gospel, and then tells of the impact it has upon his life. Although he writes in the first person plural ("we"), Paul's statements are primarily reflective of his own situation.

In v. 5 Paul succinctly describes his ministry and summarizes his gospel. Unlike his Jewish-Christian, Gnostic-pneumatic opponents at Corinth, Paul asserts that he does not preach, or exercise his ministry, so as to secure status for himself (cf. 3:1; 5:12), but so as to proclaim Christ Jesus as Lord and to serve (i.e., to assume pastoral responsibility for) the Corinthian Christians. As a capsule-summary of his gospel, the meaning of the words "Christ Jesus as Lord" is that Jesus of Nazareth, the Messiah who was crucified, has been exalted by God through resurrection to the right hand of power, as a result of which he is presently Lord of all (cf. Rom. 10:9; 1 Cor. 1:18; 2:2; 12:3; 15:3–4). The relationship for Paul between gospel and ministry is that to accept the gospel, that is, to acknowledge Christ Jesus as Lord, is both to be saved (Rom. 10:9) and to become his slave (Rom. 1:1; Phil. 1:1). But to become the slave of Christ is likewise to become the slave ("pastor") of those who are his (e.g., the Corinthians).

Paul traces the origin of his ministry to God himself (v. 6). The very God who in the beginning created light (Gen. 1:3) is the one who has enlightened him. In the encounter with Christ on the road to Damascus, God made the glory of his saving ways known to Paul. Through his ministry, Paul now shares this knowledge with others.

Thus, it is "earthenware vessels," frail human beings such as Paul, to whom the "treasure" of the gospel has been entrusted (v. 7a). In this way, the source of the extraordinary power of the gospel for salvation will always reveal itself to be God and not Paul (v. 7b). Indeed, no matter what the experience that threatens to crush Paul, God's power sustains him (vv. 8–9). And although his life is such that he is gradually being killed for the sake of Christ, through him the resurrected Christ makes manifest the new life that is his (vv. 10–11).

Whereas the First Lesson and the Gospel point out, respectively, that obedience towards God and love towards others are hallmarks of the Christian life, this text brings the two thoughts together: to know Christ Jesus as Lord is to serve him by serving one's fellows.

HOMILETICAL INTERPRETATION

1. Concern

God has faced us in Jesus Christ and therefore we can face him and our world with confidence and joy.

2. Confirmations and Concretions

Nobody likes to be left in the dark. At the physical level it is frightening and we try to avoid it with costly lighting systems.

Nobody likes to be left in the dark figuratively. We want to be in the know, not in the dark. To be in a situation where we don't know what is going on is threatening. And yet the truth of the matter is that for a great deal of our lives, we *are* in the dark.

Who of us, for example, thinking about his or her past feels completely in the know about their own life? Can we speak with certainty about who we are? About the forces that have made us? About how we got here? When we look back on our own lives in many ways we are in the dark.

Who of us in thinking about his or her future can speak with assurance? Who can predict accurately our economy? Our relations to our friends? Our employment? When we think about our future much of it is in the dark.

The great power of the Christian faith is that while we may be in the dark about many things in terms of the ultimate issues of human existence, there is light. The God who created heaven and earth and who commanded the light to shine out of darkness, has not left us in the dark. "We have seen the light of the glory of God in the face of Jesus Christ." We may never be able to get quite straight all the details of our past nor our future, but there is no doubt that God's love is eternal and that this love shines from the face of Jesus Christ. No matter how dark our situation may be, the splendor and the radiance of God shines forth in the face of Jesus Christ.

God could have made all kinds of spectacular displays for his glory. Yet he chose to make his ultimate revelation in a human face—a face like yours and like mine. The ordinariness of the human face is in itself a mark of the uniqueness of the Christian revelation. So when we ask who and where is God? the answer is the face of Jesus Christ, a face like yours, a face like mine.

Most of us at some point in our life have seen glory in a face. A mother, a father, a teacher, a preacher, a truck driver, a shop keeper has given us a glimpse of the glory of God. I imagine that few of us would be Christians if there were not a face like that in our lives. But in someone, somewhere, we saw a face in which there was such peace, joy, and togetherness rooted in Christ that had we not been a Christian we would have wanted to become one because of the glory in that face.

Because of that we turn toward God with confidence. Because Jesus has shown us his face we do not cringe before some overpowering cosmic bully, we do not bow in obeisance before the raw forces of nature. Rather ultimate reality has turned toward us and shown us a face to which we can relate with trust and love.

Because God has turned his face toward us, we can turn our face toward the world. We can face life with its problems and perplexities. We can face the problems of the world creatively and redemptively. The OT lesson today draws our attention to the importance of moral law. We are to observe the sabbath day. The Gospel lesson, however, describes a situation in which Jesus found himself in conflict with the law as the Pharisees understood it. The Pharisees held that Jesus was breaking the law when he plucked grain and ate it on the sabbath.

Yet, we may argue that Jesus was keeping the law in its central meaning when he placed dealing with hunger above keeping the letter of the law. In our time hunger has reached global proportions. It is common knowledge that the United States with a relatively small portion of the world's population possesses and uses a disproportionate amount of the world's energy and resources. C. P. Snow's vision seems to become more realistic day by day—he foresaw the possibility of one-half of the world watching on color television while the other half starved to death.

What does this mean? What are we to do? The Jesus who placed the priority with the feeding of the hungry rather than with the preservation of an abstract law, leaves us little room to doubt what our priority should be. If we wish to feed the hungry, we must work for changes that affect the economic structure which allows such a disproportionate consumption. There are vast changes which must be made in the structure of our world economy. Our systems must be changed as numerous studies point out.[1]

In addition, however, each of us must get hold of hunger where we can and do what is best to ease it. We must exercise our own priorities. For example, if Americans substituted chicken for one-third of their beef consumption we could release enough grain to feed 100 million people every year.

Or, for example, if a pound of fertilizer from the 3 million tons which we use in America for non-food purposes (lawns and golf courses, etc.) could be transferred to Indian soil it would produce at least twice the additional yield as a pound of fertilizer on American soil.

Every church-going Christian in America has, through church channels, a means of concrete response to the world's hunger. The Christian can not only face this problem, he can help solve it.

3. Construction

The construction which emerges most naturally from this concern builds on the Epistle.

1. God has faced us in Jesus Christ.
2. Therefore, we can face God . . .
3. And face the world.

The OT and Gospel lessons come to bear especially on the third point.

1. See James A. Scherer, *Global Living Here and Now* (New York: Friendship Press, 1974).

The Third Sunday after Pentecost

Lutheran	*Roman Catholic*	*Episcopal*	*Pres./UCC/Chr.*	*Methodist/COCU*
Gen. 3:9–15	Gen. 3:9–15	Gen. 3:9–15	Gen. 3:9–15	Gen. 3:9–15
2 Cor. 4:13–5:1	2 Cor. 4:13–5:1	2 Cor. 4:13–5:1	2 Cor. 4:13–5:1	2 Cor. 4:13–5:1
Mark 3:20–35	Mark 3:20–35	Mark 3:20–35	Mark 3:20–35	Mark 3:20–35

EXEGESIS

Gospel: Mark 3:20–35. The text finds its place in the second main part of the Gospel (3:7–6:29). The immediate context encompasses the following units: the massive summary-passage describing Jesus' ministry in Galilee (3:7–12); the story of the choosing of the twelve (3:13–19); the text itself, which highlights sayings of Jesus concerning his alleged collusion with Satan (3:22–30) and his true family (3:20–21, 31–35); and Jesus' discourse in parables (4:1–34). Though a distinct unit, one purpose of the text is to prepare the reader for the parabolic speech to follow (cf. 3:23 to 4:2; 3:34 to 4:11).

The pericope on Jesus' true kindred (vv. 20–21, 31–35) forms a bracket around the pericope entitled "On Collusion with Satan" (vv. 22–30). This is a literary device of which Mark is fond (cf., e.g., 5:21–43; 11:12–25; 14:54–72) and indicates that the two pericopes are in some sense related. In this case, the unifying factor is the theme of "madness": the family of Jesus believes that he is mad mentally (v. 21), whereas the scribes believe that he is mad theologically (v. 22).

Mark records that Jesus goes home (v. 20a). A crowd gathers, with the result that he and his disciples are not able to eat (v. 20b–c). Meanwhile, news of Jesus' public activity has reached his family (v. 21; cf. 3:7–12). They think he is mad, so they leave home to seize him (v. 21). At this juncture the story breaks off.

The intervening scene describes Jesus in conflict with scribes from Jerusalem (vv. 22–30). The mere fact that these scribes are identified with Jerusalem is sufficient already to characterize them as being inimical to Jesus, for Jerusalem is the place where he will suffer and die (10:32–34). The scribes level a double charge against him: he is possessed of an unclean spirit and guilty of casting out demons by means of the prince of demons (vv. 22, 30). In reaction to the double charge, which reveals the scribes to be perverse and blind, Jesus addresses them in parables, that is, in speech they do not comprehend, in this way confirming their blindness (v. 23; 4:11–12). He asserts that it is absurd to accuse him of being in league with Satan, for Satan would then be at war with himself (vv. 24–26). On the contrary, he is "mightier" than the "strong man" Satan (v. 27; 1:7). God has endowed him with the Spirit so that the power of the kingdom is at work in him (1:10, 15). In driving out demons, he is releasing people from the bondage of Satan's rule, thus "plundering Satan's house," or kingdom (v. 27). In principle, God stands ready to forgive humans all their sins (v. 28). The one exception, however, is that one willfully and knowingly declare the Spirit's activity in him, the Son of God, to be "satanic" (vv. 29–30; 1:10–11). The scribes, therefore, had better beware.

With this, Mark returns to his story concerning the family of Jesus (vv. 31–35). They arrive at the house where Jesus is staying and send word, summoning him outside (v. 31). Upon hearing that his family stands without, Jesus looks searchingly at his followers seated around him (vv. 32–34a). Then, in solemn tones he announces that it is not his blood relatives as such who are his real mother and brother and sister, but those who do the will of God, that is to say, those who become his disciples (vv. 33b–35).

To conclude, the essential point of this text is that only the disciples of Jesus, those who follow him, can penetrate the mystery of his person, viz., that in him God is at work in the Spirit to rescue humans from Satan and all evil and to bring them into the gracious sphere of his rule. "Outsiders," on the other hand, contemplate the person and activity of Jesus and think him mad.

First Lesson: Gen.3:9–15. The whole of chap. 3 is of the nature of an aetiological legend explaining the origin of sin and the consequences of the fall. It is with the latter that the text has to do.

The fall of the man and of the woman into sin is described in 3:6: the woman plucks fruit from the tree of the knowledge of good and evil and eats, and the man takes from her. What motivates them is the thought that by eating this fruit they will suddenly possess the capacity to know everything. Their intention, therefore, is to expand the horizons of their existence beyond the limits set for them by God, which is rebellion against him.

Instead of increasing in wisdom, however, the man and the woman experience the results of sin described in the text. Thus, when the man hears God in the garden calling to him, he flees for fear because, he says, he is naked (vv. 9–10). In Israel, to appear naked before God was an abomination, expressly forbidden in connection with the cult (Exod.

20:26). In the text, nakedness connotes the shame the man feels towards both God and another human being (3:21). In addition, the man is afraid, and so flees from God (v. 10). Consequently, it is fear and shame, according to the text, that are the elemental symptoms of guilt.

Interrogated by God as to what he has done, the man blames the woman (vv. 11–12) and the woman blames the serpent (v. 13). Harmonious relationships have been destroyed. The text closes with the curse that God pronounces upon the serpent (vv. 14–15). This curse offers at once an ancient explanation of the physical make-up and of the behavior of the serpent (v. 14) and characterizes the species as emblematic of the evil with which the man must forever struggle without hope of victory (v. 15).

Theologically, the story of the fall prepares the worshiper for the word concerning forgiveness which is sounded in the Gospel for the day (Mark 3:28).

Second Lesson: 2 Cor. 4:13–5:1. As was the case with the Second Lesson appointed for Pentecost 2, Paul, in writing in the first person plural ("we"), is reflecting above all on his own situation. The immediate context is 4:7–5:10, and the principal subject under discussion is Paul's ministry.

In 4:7–12, Paul has argued that he, frail "earthenware vessel" that he is, has been entrusted with the "treasure" that is the gospel. Developing this theme, Paul declares in the text that the reason he proclaims, or "speaks," the gospel is that the same spirit who engendered faith in the Psalmist of old and so impelled him to speak has engendered faith in him (v. 13). Indeed, he proclaims the gospel in the manner he does because he is firmly convinced that God, who raised Jesus from the dead, will likewise raise up both him and the Corinthian Christians, so that together they will, with Jesus, triumphantly stand in the presence of God (v. 14). In point of fact, all the things Paul has been discussing, viz., his suffering (vv. 8–13), his faith, and his preaching, have but one purpose to serve: the benefit of the Corinthians (v. 15a). And what results as the grace of God supplies their every need is that it causes thanksgiving to abound to the glory of God (v. 15b).

Therefore, says Paul, he does not become tired and consequently neglect his duty (v. 16a). Because although the natural man is wasting away, day by day the spiritual man is being renewed (v. 16b–c). Present affliction is, after all, "light," and produces to an extraordinary degree an eternal "weight" of glory (v. 17). For this reason, he keeps his eyes fixed, not on the things seen but on the things unseen (v. 18). In the last analysis, his ultimate hope is rooted in the sure knowledge that should his earthly body be destroyed by either death or the second coming of Christ, he will receive from God a new, imperishable body (cf. 1 Cor. 15:51–57).

The Scripture readings for Pentecost 3 combine to set forth the following thought: in Christ, God forgives man his sin, enables him to do his will, and gives him a sure hope that will sustain him no matter what he encounters in life.

HOMILETICAL INTERPRETATION

1. Concern

In Christ, God forgives us our sin, enables us to do his will and gives us a sure hope.

2. Confirmations and Concretions

"Sin" seems to be an ugly little word that moderns want to hide away. The reality of it, however, is not so easily disposed of. The psychiatrist, Karl Menninger, asks boldly, "Whatever became of sin?"[1] The psychiatrist discovers that we violate moral boundaries even while trying to ignore them at terrible costs to ourselves.

"Whatever became of Adam?" might also be asked. The notion of an objective individual whose sin is genetically transmitted to the human race would get little support today, but the reality of the human condition symbolized in Adam's fall is inescapable. Sin is not just the acts we commit but the persons we are. Sin has to do with the communities in which we have our personal existence. Sin is a function of our social inheritance as well as of our choices. The modern man who looks for Adam need not search for the location of a garden in the ancient Near East. He should look instead at Washington, Los Angeles, New York, or, preferably, in his own mirror. The story of Adam and Eve continues to have power because it is the story of our lives. We transgress the moral boundaries and find ourselves expelled from paradise.

When the Lehman Wing of the Metropolitan Museum of Modern Art in New York City opened recently, thousands of persons saw a classic expression of this theme in Giovanni di Paolo's "Expulsion from Paradise," one of the fifteenth century treasures in that collection. Adam and Eve are seen hastening from the garden obviously very embarrassed. God hovers over them, unmistakably pointing the way out. That gesture may be said to sum up the OT lesson today.

1. Karl Menninger, *Whatever Became of Sin?* (New York: Hawthorn Books, 1973, 1974).

The NT lesson, however, might be summed up by the gesture of Jesus beckoning everyone to come unto him for forgiveness. The Gospel lesson assures us that all sins will be forgiven except the sin against the Holy Spirit. That sin, presumably, would be the denial of the power of God's Spirit to forgive sin.

The thanks which Jesus got for offering forgiveness, as recorded in the Gospel for today, was to be called "crazy." It is "mad" to believe that this Jesus can forgive us our sins and yet it is the "madness of God."[2] The forgiveness of our sins opens the way to do God's will and to hope for glory. The theme of the Epistle lesson is beautifully developed in a sermon by C. S. Lewis entitled "The Weight of Glory".[3]

Another useful resource in this area is the book *Images of Hope* by William S. Lynch.[4] Father Lynch has written a poetic and practical book which effectively links imagination and reality. The book was written out of conversations with psychiatrists and patients under psychiatric care. The author relates hope not only to our ultimate future, but to "The City of Man." He writes:

> "We can decide to build a human city, a city of man, in which all men have citizenship, Greek, Jew, and Gentile, the black and the white, the maimed, the blind, the mentally well and the mentally ill. This will always require an active imagination which will extend the idea of the human and which will imagine nothing in man it cannot contain."[5]

Hope is one of the most practical assets anyone can have.

3. Construction

The construction of this sermon follows the development of the concern in the sequence of the lessons.

1. Fall (OT lesson).
2. Forgiveness (Gospel lesson).
3. Fulfillment (Second Lesson).

2. Cf. Elie Wiesel, *Zalman or the Madness of God* (New York: Random House, 1974) for a study of this theme in a Jewish context. Wiesel has offered a powerful story which argues that it is mad today to believe in God and in man. He urges us, however, to be mad.

3. See Roger Lancelyn Green and Walter Hooper, *C. S. Lewis: A Biography* (London: Collins, 1974) pp. 203–204.

4. William Lynch, S. J., "*Images of Hope: Imagination as Healer of the Hopeless*" (New York and Toronto: The New American Library, 1965).

5. Ibid., p. 21.

The Fourth Sunday after Pentecost

Lutheran	*Roman Catholic*	*Episcopal*	*Pres./UCC/Chr.*	*Methodist/COCU*
Ezek. 17:22–24	Ezek. 17:22–24	Ezek. 17:22–24	Ezek. 17:22–24	Ezek. 17:22–24
2 Cor. 5:6–10	2 Cor. 5:6–10	2 Cor. 5:6–10	2 Cor. 5:6–10	2 Cor. 5:6–10
Mark 4:26–34	Mark 4:26–34	Mark 4:26–34	Mark 4:26–34	Mark 4:26–34

EXEGESIS

Gospel: Mark 4:26–34. The text comprises the latter part of Jesus' discourse in parables (4:1–34). Both the seed growing secretly (vv. 26–29) and the mustard seed (vv. 30–32) are parables of the kingdom and therefore, to the eyes of faith, provide insight into the mystery of God's rule (v. 11).

The seed growing secretly and the mustard seed are what are known as companion, or double, parables. This means that though the message of each may differ, the two are similar in structure and content. Common to these parables are the features of contrast and growth.

In the parable of the seed growing secretly, reference is made to both seedtime (v. 26) and harvest (v. 29). This suggests contrast. The emphasis, however, does not lie here but on the element of growth (vv. 27–28): once the seed has been planted, the process of maturation begins, and "of itself" moves inexorably to completion. So it is, claims Mark, with the kingdom of God. In the person of Jesus of Nazareth, God has brought his rule to mankind (1:15); presently, in the time following Easter, he is unremittingly at work in the resurrected Jesus (cf. 14:28; 16:6–7) ordering the course of events (cf. 13:10) to the end that, at Jesus' parousia, he will establish his rule over all the world in majesty and splendor (8:38; 9:1; 13:24–27). As for the Christians of Mark's church, the message of this parable strengthens them in their belief that God, in the crucified and resurrected Jesus, is indeed in control of things, guiding them unswervingly towards the establishment in splendor of his end-time kingdom.

To turn to the parable of the mustard seed, the importance of the elements of contrast and of growth is the opposite of what we found in the parable of the seed growing secretly. While the element of growth is indeed present (vv. 31b–32a–c), the stress is on the element of contrast (vv. 31a, 32d). To make this clear, Mark has enclosed the key words "which is the smallest of all the seeds" (v. 31) in verbal brackets by having the same clause, but in reverse word-order, both precede and follow them: "whenever it is sown on the earth . . . on the earth, and whenever it is sown . . ." (vv. 31–32a). Thus, the thought of the parable is that the mustard seed, which was proverbial among the Jews as the smallest of quantities, grows up and miraculously becomes a tree in which the birds of the air can nest. Again, so it is, says Mark, with the kingdom of God. From such insignificant beginnings as the ministry of Jesus of Nazareth there will one day issue that splendid kingdom which will embrace all the nations of the world (cf. Dan. 4:1–12; Ezek. 17:23; 31:6). Accordingly, this parable, too, contains a message of confidence for the Christians of Mark's church.

The point of vv. 33–34 is that whereas the parables of Jesus strike "them," that is, the "outsiders" such as the Jewish crowds (cf. v. 2), as riddles, the "insiders," those who follow Jesus (cf. 4:11), are told their meaning. Applied to today, these verses set forth the basic Christian truth that genuine insight into the mystery of the kingdom is possible only by God-given faith in Jesus Christ.

First Lesson: Ezek. 17:22–24. Chap. 17 contains the allegories of the eagles (vv. 1–21) and of the cedar (vv. 22–24).

In the allegory of the eagles, Ezekiel reviews and evaluates events surrounding 588 B.C. Thus, Nebuchadnezzar, king of Babylon ("a great eagle," v. 3), had marched on Jerusalem ("Lebanon," v. 3) a decade earlier and had taken Jehoiachin ("the topmost of its young twigs," v. 4) captive, deporting him to Babylon ("land of trade," v. 4). In his place he had left Zedekiah ("seed of the land," v. 5) as a vassal king. Now, however, Zedekiah has decided to join forces with Pharaoh ("another great eagle," v. 7) in order to gain freedom from Babylon (v. 7), thus breaking his treaty with Nebuchadnezzar. Using the allegorical mode to speak out against Zedekiah, Ezekiel contends that Zedekiah's breach of treaty is tantamount to rebellion against God (v. 19). What will finally come of it, he predicts, is deportation to Babylon for Zedekiah and death for his army (vv. 20–21).

In contrast to this message of doom, the allegory of the cedar (vv. 22–24) is a word of promise. In place of the king of Babylon, Ezekiel describes God himself as choosing one from the house of David ("a tender shoot," v. 22; cf. Isa. 11:1; 53:2) and establishing him upon Mt. Zion ("a high and lofty mountain," v. 22). This son of David will become a mighty ruler ("a noble cedar," v. 23), and to him all who need help will look for protection ("birds of every kind," v. 23). Then, too, as they gaze upon him, all the kings of the world ("all the trees of the field," v. 24) will know that it is none other than God who humbles the mighty and exalts the lowly (v. 24; cf. Isa. 2:2–4; Luke 1:52).

While the OT writer did not, of course, have Jesus in mind when he told the allegory of the cedar, from a Christian standpoint it is in him that this allegory ultimately reached its fulfillment. Jesus, crucified and resurrected, is that one in the line of David whom God has made regent in the sphere of his rule.

Second Lesson: 2 Cor. 5:6–10. We recall that Paul has been speaking of the ministry and of the gospel entrusted to him (4:5, 7). He has referred to himself as an "earthenware vessel" (4:7) and depicted his sufferings (4:8–12). Starting with 4:16, however, he has begun to look to the future and talks of his hope (4:16–5:5). In the text he describes his person in the light of this hope.

Paul states that if he were to have his way, he would prefer to remain alive until the parousia of Christ, that is, until that time when his body will be changed and his mortal nature will put on immortality (5:4; cf. 1 Cor. 15:51–56). As the first step in the realization of this hope of future life, God has bestowed on him the gift of the Spirit (5:5).

Accordingly, Paul continues in the text, he is supremely confident (v. 6a), regardless of whether he should live or die. So long as he lives, he is separated, as it were, from Christ, who is at the right hand of God (v. 6b). Separated from the exalted Christ, he must walk by faith, without the capacity to see him (v. 7). But should he die, he would be at home with the Lord (v. 8). Still, either way his one goal is to be obedient to Christ, for the disciple is utterly responsible to him and must one day give him account for his life on earth (vv. 9–10).

HOMILETICAL INTERPRETATION

1. Concern

The Christian walks by faith in the confidence that history finds its fulfillment in Jesus Christ.

2. Confirmations and Concretions

Faith in a simple or "animal" sense is basic to human life. Without faith we would have to examine the floor every morning before getting out of bed, have our car checked before driving it, and do an interrogation of every individual before talking with him.

To say that we walk by faith is to describe a simple condition of human life. However, when the author of the Epistle to the Corinthians wrote, "We walk by faith, not by sight" he was referring to faith in Jesus Christ—faith far more radical and demanding than mere "animal" faith.

This is the faith in Jesus Christ which issues in the confidence that however much our life on earth may seem an exile, we do have an ultimate destination.

This faith issues in courage. The word the author of the Epistle uses is a form of *Tharrēo.* The RSV translates this as "courage" in place of the King James' "confidence," and courage seems the more accurate word for the original carries the meaning of boldness and daring. Faith in Christ gives us such daring.

John F. Kennedy, while a Senator, wrote a book entitled *Profiles in Courage.* The book is about moral courage on the part of parliamentary leaders who because of principle confront the opposition of colleagues, constituents, and a majority of the general public. The book contains many examples worth study including James W. Grimes who cast one of the deciding votes of "not guilty" in regard to the impeachment of President Andrew Johnson. Because of his stand, Grimes was burned in effigy, accused by the press of "idiocy and impotency," and repudiated by his state and friends. His political career never recovered but before he died, he declared to a friend:

> "I shall ever thank God that in that troubled hour of trial, when many privately confessed that they had sacrificed their judgment and their conscience at the behest of party newspapers and party-hate, I had the courage to be true to my oath and my conscience . . ."[1]

Such courage does not always mean that the possessor of it is in the right. Yet, our parliamentary system could not exist at all if it were not for persons of courage who were able to put what they believed to be right above the pressures of the immediate. And courage, wherever we find it, is in the long run one of the most compelling of human virtues.

Courage is also one of the most essential qualities. Paul Tillich has emphasized the courage to be as the act by which a person affirms himself in the face of all the uncertainties and anxieties of life.[2]

Christian faith affirms that God is at work even where it is not obvious, just as we have confidence that a seed is growing even when it is hidden in the ground.

We are called to labor wherever we can; to participate in the kingdom of God. There may be little recognition and less applause for our acts to allay wounds and heal the hurts in our complex society. We may often

1. John F. Kennedy, *Profiles in Courage* (New York: Pocketbooks, 1957), p. 128.
2. See Paul Tillich, *The Courage to Be* (New Haven: Yale University Press, 1952).

work alone or seem to, but our faith in God gives us confidence to take the next step. That one step by faith may lead us nearer our ultimate destination than the many circuitous steps which lead us away from our immediate responsibilities in our daily lives.

3. CONSTRUCTION

These passages suggest a doctrinal sermon on faith:

1. The introduction would deal with the definition of faith as distinguished from "animal" faith and would draw heavily on the Second Lesson.
2. A major portion of the sermon should be the development of faith as courage.
3. Another major portion of the sermon should deal with faith as confidence, the assurance that God is at work even when we may not be aware of it.

The Fifth Sunday after Pentecost

Lutheran	*Roman Catholic*	*Episcopal*	*Pres./UCC/Chr.*	*Methodist/COCU*
Job 38:1–11	Job 38:1, 8–11	Job 38:1–11, 16–18	Job 38:1–11	Job 38:1–11, 16–18
2 Cor. 5:14–17	2 Cor. 5:14–17	2 Cor. 5:14–17	2 Cor. 5:16–21	2 Cor. 5:14–17
Mark 4:35–41	Mark 4:35–40	Mark 4:35–41	Mark 4:35–41	Mark 4:35–41

EXEGESIS

Gospel: Mark 4:35–41. The text begins a section of the Gospel in which Jesus and the disciples are depicted as undertaking six voyages back and forth across the Sea of Galilee (4:35–8:21; cf. 4:35; 5:1, 21; 6:45; 8:13). In this way Jesus is pictured as discharging his ministry among both Jews and Gentiles.

Mark writes that towards evening on the day on which Jesus has delivered his parabolic discourse to the crowd (4:1–34), he summons his disciples to go with him to the other side of the lake (v. 35). The disciples dismiss the crowd and, in the company of other vessels, embark with Jesus on the voyage (v. 36; cf. 4:1). Out on the lake, a fierce squall suddenly arises, and the boat of Jesus and the disciples is in danger of being swamped by the waves (v. 37). Jesus, at peace, is asleep in the stern of the boat, but the disciples, afraid, arouse him with the reproach: "Teacher, do you not care if we perish?" (v. 38). Awakened, Jesus rebukes the wind and the sea with the words, "Be silent, be muzzled," and at his command the wind abates, giving way to a great calm (v. 39). Then Jesus turns on the disciples and asks them why they are so cowardly and lacking in faith (v. 40). The disciples, who receive Jesus' question with fear and hence incomprehension, can only look at one another and ask who he might be, that even wind and sea obey him (v. 41).

Several features of this miracle-story are of weighty theological significance. Thus, Jesus commands the wind and the sea with the same word ("be muzzled") with which he casts out demons (1:25). This and the great calm that ensues are reminiscent of God's power over the waters of chaos at the creation (Pss. 74:13–14; 104:5–9; Job 38:8–11; Jer. 5:22). Mark, then, portrays Jesus in this story as the one whom God has invested with divine authority and who consequently has control over the demonic forces of nature. Therefore it is in the question the disciples pose in v. 41 that the narrative reaches its climax: Who, exactly, is Jesus? In the succeeding paragraph, Mark provides the answer: He is the almighty Son of God (5:7; cf. 1:23–27; 3:11).

The disciples in the story are said to be cowardly, without faith, and fearful (vv. 40–41). Instead of being like Jesus, who, at peace in the care of his Father, sleeps in the midst of the storm, they are without the courage of faith and so awaken Jesus in order to reproach him for not being concerned about their welfare (v. 38). Furthermore, the fact that they react with fear to Jesus' admonition of their cowardice and lack of faith (v. 41) discloses that they have failed to grasp the significance of the miracle and therefore of the person of Jesus. Hence, this story, too, reflects the familiar Markan theme of persistent ignorance on the part of the disciples about the mystery of Jesus' person and work (cf. 6:52; 8:17, 21; 9:6, 32).

As he directs this pericope at the Christians of his church, one thing Mark does is to use the negative example of the disciples to proclaim faith in the all powerful Son of God. In him these Christians are to find courage to withstand the vicissitudes of life.

First Lesson: Job 38:1–11. The Book of Job is not unlike a Greek tragedy. In it, the protagonist is made to ask a question that is innate to life itself: Why must a human being endure suffering? The fact that Job is characterized at the outset as a "blameless and upright man" (chaps. 1–2) only makes the question more acute.

At the conclusion of his dialogues with Eliphaz, Bildad, and Zophar (chaps. 3–31), Job boldly reviews his past behavior in order to assert his moral innocence before God and his fellows (chap. 31). Indeed, at this point Job challenges God to meet with him and to argue with him his case (31:35–37). In two discourses at the end of the book, God meets Job's challenge (38:1–40:5; 40:6–42:6).

Taken together, these discourses of God, of which the text is a portion, comprise the dramatic and theological high point of the book. Dramatically, following the inconclusive counsel of Job's friends, the scene is set for God to deliver the final word. And theologically, in speaking with Job, God gives answer to his question.

The text states that God addresses Job from a "whirlwind" (v. 1), which is a common setting in the OT for divine appearances, or theophanies (cf. Ps. 50:3; Ezek. 1:4; Nah. 1:3; Zech. 9:14). But although Job believes that his innocence entitles him to call God to account, God immediately makes it clear that he has come to call Job to account (vv. 2–3).

In essence, God's answer to Job's question about suffering is the revelation that he, who is the author of all creation, cannot be comprehended in his ways by human beings. Hence, the final resolution of the problem of righteous suffering must be seen to lie hidden in the mystery of his divine person.

To convey this message to Job, God overawes him in the text with a description of two acts of creation. Referring to his creation of the world, God pictures the earth as a building so gigantic that he alone can know its make-up and dimensions (vv. 4–7). And referring to his creation of the seas, God gives illustration of his limitless power: calling forth the "cosmic birth" of the waters of the world, he has clothed them with clouds and darkness and has prescribed for them their boundaries (vv. 8–11). Appropriately, Job responds to God's words to him by taking cognizance of his smallness and by stilling his tongue (40:3–5).

The text complements the Gospel especially with regard to the second illustration: the power of God to create and control the waters of the world manifests itself in the Son of God, whom both sea and wind obey.

Second Lesson: 2 Cor. 5:14–17. The text's wider context is 2:14–7:4, and its immediate context is 5:11–21. The broad objective of Paul in the former is to treat of his ministry and its purpose, and he accomplishes this in the latter by discussing the message of reconciliation. The focus of the text itself is on the "new creation" that arises out of the death and resurrection of Christ.

Using the editorial "we," Paul declares in the text that his person and his actions are governed by one thing only, viz., the love that Christ has shown him in the cross (v. 14a). The reason Christ's love controls him is that his death on the cross is of benefit for all mankind (cf. 1 Cor. 15:3): when he died, all people died (v. 14b–d). How is this to be understood? In Christ's death all people died in the sense that, when appropriated by faith, this death releases people from the necessity to lead a life that is centered on the self and frees them to lead a life that finds its center in him, the One crucified and resurrected (v. 15; cf. Rom. 6:1–14).

Of course, continues Paul, a death of this sort is of enormous consequence for daily life. Thus, negatively speaking, the shape of one's existence is no longer determined by purely human values and standards (v. 16a). In this respect, consider even Christ. Once he was seen solely as a human being (v. 16b). But he is not now so to be regarded, for he is the resurrected and exalted Lord (v. 16c).

From a positive standpoint, the result of dying with Christ is that one thereafter is "in Christ" and therefore a "new creation," viz., one lives in this age as one who, by faith in Christ, has already passed through death and resurrection and so is a member of the glorious age to come (v. 17a–b; Gal. 2:20). For such a one, the old, self-centered way of relating to the world is gone; it has been replaced by the new, Christ-centered way (v. 17c–d).

In relation to the Gospel for the day, Paul's description of the new being in Christ is the gospel-counterpart to the negative example the disciples set in Mark. On this score, this text is the necessary balance to that one.

HOMILETICAL INTERPRETATION

1. Concern

The power of God to create and control the waters of the world manifests itself in the Son of God, whom both sea and wind obey, and in the creation of the new being.

2. Confirmations and Concretions

The Board of Trustees of a college once appointed a committee to install a heating unit in the administration building. The new heater was installed but the heating problem was not solved. For it was then discovered that the pipes were inadequate to handle the heat produced by the new unit. The entire system had to be replaced.

Something like this occurs when Christ comes alive for us. We may wish that that new center of energy might fit easily into the apparatus of our old conveniences and desires. We soon discover, however, that a whole new system is demanded. "If anyone is in Christ he is a new creation: The old is passed away, behold, the new has come."

Writers know the importance of the point of view. Every story has to be written from a certain P.O.V., as it is sometimes called. That determines everything else in the story. The writer of 2 Corinthians knows that basic to the new being is a new point of view. We don't look at anyone from a human point of view any longer but from the point of view which comes with Christ.

Indeed we do not look *at* Christ any longer. That is, Christ is not an object totally outside us, a figure for historical investigation. We are, rather, *in* Christ. We actually participate in the new being he brought. This is the complete antithesis of the "playing" with Christ which we have spoken of earlier. We do not "play" with Christ, we *participate in* Christ.

This new being is a gift, a gift from God through Christ. "God was in Christ reconciling the world to himself, not counting their trespasses against them, and entrusting to us the message of reconciliation"—surely this is one of the greatest lines of Scripture.[1]

The new being in Christ does not mean that we are not troubled. Indeed our sensitivities are heightened and we may be more anguished than before. The message of Job, therefore, is not to be dismissed.[2]

The Gospel lesson is also relevant here because even the disciple of Christ will find himself in rough waters and that is a threatening experience. Rembrandt gave it a classic expression in his painting of "The Calming of the Sea" which may be found in The Isabella Stewart Gardner Museum in Boston. The different reactions of the disciples are depicted with painful detail: We see one clutching the mast, another leaning over the side of the boat. Christ, however, remains secure and asleep. There is a radiance about his calm which suggests the power with which he will soon calm the sea.

3. Construction

These texts suggest a sermon on the new being with three major sections each dealing with one of the lessons for the day.

1. Being New (Second Lesson).
2. Being Troubled (the OT lesson).
3. Being Calm (the Gospel).

1. See especially Donald Baillie, *God was in Christ* (New York: Scriptures, 1948).

2. See especially Archibald MacLeish, *J. B.: A Play in Verse* (Boston: Houghton Mifflin, 1958), and Robert Frost, *A Masque of Reason* (New York: Holt, 1945).

The Sixth Sunday after Pentecost

Lutheran	*Roman Catholic*	*Episcopal*	*Pres./UCC/Chr.*	*Methodist/COCU*
Lam. 3:22–33	Wisd. 1:13–15; 2:23–35	Wisd. 1:13–15; 2:23–24	Gen. 4:3–10	Lam. 3:22–23
2 Cor. 8:1–9, 13–14	2 Cor. 8:7, 9, 13–15	2 Cor. 8:1–9, 13–15	2 Cor. 8:7–15	2 Cor. 8:1–9, 13–15
Mark 5:21–24a, 35–43 *or* Mark 5:24b–34	Mark 5:21–43 *or* Mark 5:21–24, 35b–43	Mark 5:21–24, 35b–43	Mark 5:21–43	Mark 5:21–43

EXEGESIS

Gospel: Mark 5:21–24a, 35–43. The text, the story of the raising of Jairus' daughter, is one of four miracles Mark associates with Jesus' first voyage to the eastern, or Gentile, side of the Sea of Galilee (4:35–5:20) and his return to the western, or Jewish, side (5:21–43). Literarily, it surrounds the story of the healing of a woman with a hemorrhage (5:25–34). Earlier we encountered this same compositional device (cf. 3:20–25: vv. 20–21, 22–30, 31–35), and noted that it indicates that the units so combined are closely related to each other. In this case, the relatedness is in terms of structure, since both units are miracle stories, and of content, since there is in both an emphasis on the dual themes of restoration (cf. vv. 29, 34 to v. 42) and of faith (cf. v. 34 to v. 36).

Mark writes that when Jesus returns to the western shore of the Sea of Galilee, a great crowd gathers around him (v. 21). There beside the sea, Jairus, who is either the president of the local synagogue or one of its seven leaders, approaches him, falls down in homage before him, and fervently pleads with him that he should come and place his hands on his sick daughter so that she might be healed and live (vv. 22–23). Jesus goes with him (v. 24a).

Because Jesus is delayed on the way to Jairus' house by a woman who has suffered from hemorrhages and whom he heals (vv. 24b–34), news reaches Jairus that his daughter no longer lives (v. 35). Though the situation now appears hopeless, Jesus ignores the report and exhorts Jairus to cast aside fear and doubt and to believe (v. 36). Later, taking with him Peter, James, and John, Jesus enters the house of Jairus, only to encounter mass confusion, with people (perhaps professional mourners) weeping and wailing loudly (vv. 37–38). Seeing this, Jesus asks the mourners why they are so distressed and weeping, and tells them that the girl is not dead but merely sleeping (v. 39). The mourners reply with ridicule, for to them the girl is beyond help (v. 40a). Jesus, however, expels them from the house, and then ushers his three disciples and the parents into the room where the girl is lying (v. 40b–c). Taking her by the hand, Jesus bids the girl in Aramaic to arise, and she responds at once, getting up and walking (vv. 41–42a). When the disciples and the parents witness this, absolute astonishment grips them, a sign that the "impossible" has in fact happened (v. 42). In addition, Jesus' command to silence likewise underlines the unique thing that has taken place, and the fact that the girl can eat is proof that she has indeed returned to life (v. 43).

For the Christians of Mark's church, this story bore the following message: the disciple of Jesus is to be like Jairus and in faith look to the resurrected Son of God for life and salvation; he it is who commands the very power of God which can break the bonds of death itself.

First Lesson: Lam. 3:22–33. Chap. 3 is a tripartite acrostic poem composed in such a way that in Hebrew each three verses begin with the same letter of the alphabet. The first main part is a psalm of personal distress ending on a note of praise (vv. 1–24); the second is paraenetic in content and counsels submission under affliction and penitence (vv. 25–51); and the third is a psalm that calls upon God for vindication and the requiting of the enemy (vv. 52–66). If vv. 34–36 and 43–48 can be pressed historically, the poem was written for Israelites for whom the invasion of their land and the destruction of Jerusalem (587 B.C.) were still a vivid memory. It may be that it had its place in the cult and was read at prescribed times to the gathered community.

The text overlaps parts one and two of the poem. The individual speaking is "the man" of v. 1, who regards himself as authorized to address the lamenting community because he, too, knows what it is to experience the judgment and wrath of God (vv. 1–3). Some commentators identify "the man" with Jeremiah, but this is unlikely.

Vv. 22–24 constitute a confessional hymn of thanksgiving that articulates the basis for renewed hope. Vv. 22–23 recall Exod. 34:6 and remind the suffering assembly that throughout the history of the covenant God has fundamentally revealed himself to be a God of love and mercy. The statement in v. 24, "The Lord is my portion," expresses the notion that God, just like the land from which and upon which one lives, is the true sustenance of every Israelite.

The second three verses of the text enjoin the community to patience in the present time of affliction. The key word in them is "good." Because God is "kind," or good (v. 25), so it is "good" for humans to submit to his will and quietly await his salvation (vv. 26–27).

The third section counsels the community not to resign itself to suffering, but willingly to accept it (vv. 28–30). For, declares the speaker in the final three verses of the text, God, because he is loving by nature and not wrathful, will not "cast off" his own forever but will look upon their "grief" and visit them with his compassion (vv. 31–33).

In line with the Gospel reading, the text calls Christians to patience and hope in times of affliction. Such an attitude springs from trust in the God who in his Son has destroyed the power of death.

Second Lesson: 2 Cor. 8:1–9, 13–14. While Paul makes mention in no fewer than four of his letters of the collection he was gathering among the Gentile churches for the Jewish Christians in Jerusalem, nowhere does he discuss this more extensively than in 2 Cor. 8–9 (cf. Rom. 15:25–29; 1 Cor. 16:1–4; Gal. 2:10). Sketching the background of this collection will shed light on the text.

The church that grew up in Jerusalem following Pentecost was impoverished from the outset (cf. Acts 6:1). Jewish hostility and persecution only contributed to its financial plight (Acts 4:1–3; 5:17–18; 6:12–14; 8:1–3; 9:1–2; 12:1–3). At the same time, theologically this church was suspicious of any mission to the Gentiles, believing that the Jews had priority in God's plan of salvation (cf. Acts 10; 11:2–3).

In A.D. 40 or 41, a Jewish-Christian prophet from Jerusalem named Agabus visited the church at Antioch and prophesied that famine was about to engulf the world (Acts 11:27–28). Realizing the precarious situation of the Christians in Jerusalem, the church in Antioch set about gathering aid for them (Acts 11:29).

Between A.D. 40 and 48, a severe shortage of food did in fact develop in Judea. In these same years, Paul also began concerted missionary work among the Gentiles. By A.D. 48, the shape of events made it necessary to convoke the so-called Apostolic Council. It convened in Jerusalem in order to deal with the question of fellowship between Christians of Jewish and of Gentile background (Acts 15:1–35; Gal. 2:1–10). But it also provided the occasion for Paul and Barnabas to bring to Jerusalem the relief that the church at Antioch had finally gathered (Acts 11:30).

The outcome of the Apostolic Council was the emergence of two wings within the early church: the Gentile wing, under Paul; and the Jewish wing, under Peter, James, and John (Gal. 2:7–9). The latter, however, urged Paul not to forget the poor in Jerusalem (Gal. 2:10).

Paul's collection among Gentile Christians originated with this plea. He saw it as a means to maintain "fellowship" between the two branches of the church (2 Cor. 8:4; 9:13) and to facilitate "equality" in the sense that "those who have" might share their abundance with "those who have not" (2 Cor. 8:13–15). And the Gentile Christians, reasoned Paul, will be all the more pleased to contribute to their Jewish-Christian brothers because they are in debt to them for the gift of the gospel (Rom. 15:27).

In the text, Paul holds the Macedonians up as an example for the Corinthians to emulate in meeting their obligations for the collection (vv. 1–5). The thing to note, however, is that Paul motivates the collection theologically. In v. 5, he speaks of first giving oneself to the Lord, and in v. 9 he refers to God's grace in Christ. Paul's point is that it is response to God's love in Christ which produces true liberality towards the neighbor.

In conjunction, the three Scripture readings for the day suggest the following related thoughts: God, who reveals himself in Jesus Christ, is the Christian's hope in times of affliction; as the recipient of God's love, the Christian deals liberally with his neighbor.

HOMILETICAL INTERPRETATION

1. Concern

The disciple of Jesus Christ looks to the resurrected Son of God for life and salvation, trusting God in times of affliction and serving others.

2. Confirmations and Concretions

"There may yet be hope." This line from the OT lesson (Lam. 3:29) comes out of a desperate situation. It was written by one who may well have been an eyewitness to the fall of Jerusalem and to the destruction of the temple. A profound sense of grief is expressed throughout Lamentations as well as a sense of horror worthy of Ezekiel. The author is familiar with people who brood in silence. He has seen good people with their faces in the dust. But he believes "there may yet be hope," for the faithfulness of the Lord is "new every morning" (Lam. 3:22).

An important novel of recent years was entitled *Nectar in a Sieve*. It was the story of a woman in India whose life bore the double burden of poverty and sexual discrimination. Yet the theme of the book, from Samuel Taylor Coleridge, is that life without hope is like nectar in a sieve; for we cannot live without hope.

The author of Lamentations knew that. But even more he knew the authentic hope which finds the Lord as its source.

Such hope is put to a severe test in the face of death. Jesus' raising of the daughter of Jairus is a miracle or "wonder" which carries the message that the resurrected Christ brings hope even in hopeless situations. Death will appear to be an end. Anyone who has looked literally into the face of death would be forgiven that conclusion. Yet the testimony of faith, again and again, is that death is not an epilogue at the end of life, but an episode in endless life.

A good friend of mine suffered with his wife through a terrible illness. Yet they faced that suffering with faith. Later he said to me, "I have come to a new and deep understanding of the lines of the hymn, 'Those angel faces smile, which we have loved long since and lost awhile.'" His name was Edward. It could have been Jairus.

The author of the Epistle to the Corinthians did not hesitate to link his hopes with the stewardship of the hopeful. The Second lesson for today is a powerful plea for cheerful giving. The author assumes that the love of the Corinthians is real and asks that they express it in more than words. It is as if we are being reminded that Christians are to be not only the recipients of hope but the givers of hope. We are so to contribute our material resources that we may give hope to others–hope for the suffering, hope for the hungry, hope for the needy, hope for the desperate. The source of that giving is plainly God himself. He was rich but he became poor for us. Therefore, we are "to give and give and give again as God has given us."

3. Construction

There are two major ways of developing this concern. One is to prepare a doctrinal sermon on hope. Such a sermon might take the following outline:

1. "There may yet be hope" (the OT lesson).
2. Even in the face of death (the Gospel).
3. When we share our resources we may get hope to others (Second Lesson).

Another possibility is to preach an expository sermon based on the Second lesson dealing with stewardship and making reference to the other lessons. Yet another possibility is to take the direction suggested by Lamentations and preach a sermon on "New Every Morning" which deals with the perpetual freshness of God's providence and which proceeds through treatment of the other lessons.

The Seventh Sunday after Pentecost

Lutheran	*Roman Catholic*	*Episcopal*	*Pres./UCC/Chr.*	*Methodist/COCU*
Ezek. 2:2–5	Ezek. 2:2–5	Ezek. 2:2–5	Ezek. 2:1–5	Ezek. 2:1–5
2 Cor. 12:7–10	2 Cor. 12:7–10	2 Cor. 12:7–10	2 Cor. 12:7–10	2 Cor. 12:7–10
Mark 6:1–6	Mark 6:1–6	Mark 6:1–6	Mark 6:1–6	Mark 6:1–6

EXEGESIS

Gospel: Mark 6:1–6. The story of the rejection of Jesus at Nazareth recalls the Gospel reading for Pentecost 3, which tells of Jesus' true family (Mark 3:21, 31–35). There the family of Jesus, reacting to his public activity (3:7–12), is portrayed as thinking him mad (3:21), with the result that they leave home to get him (3:21, 31–32). Instead of submitting to his family, however, Jesus looks around him at his followers and declares that his real mother and brother and sister are those who do the will of God (3:33–35). In other words, Jesus turns from his family and towards his followers.

If the Gospel for Pentecost 3 depicts Jesus' break with his family, the text depicts his break with the townspeople of Nazareth (vv. 1, 4), especially with his relatives (v. 4). In this case, too, the disciples are made to contrast sharply with those who oppose Jesus. Whereas the disciples are said to "follow" him (v. 1; cf. 1:16–20; 2:14–15; 8:34), the townspeople and relatives become "astonished" at his teaching (v. 2a–b) and "offended" by his wisdom and mighty works (vv. 2c–e, 3d). They know him to be a carpenter and are acquainted with his mother and brothers and sisters (v. 3a–c). Therefore in their view he is not to be attributed the divine dignity and authority to which his teaching and healing allude. As the conclusion to this pericope, v. 6a is most fitting, for the word "unbelief" shows clearly that the "astonishment" of the people and the "offense" they take at Jesus do indeed indicate a rejection on their part of his divine sonship as implied by his miracles or message of the kingdom (cf. 1:11, 14–15, 23–28, 32–34; 3:7–12).

V. 4 seems to imply that the title "prophet" is appropriate to Jesus. The saying, however, has the character of a proverb and possesses many parallels in Greek, Hellenistic, and Roman literature. It should not be pressed as a title of majesty for Jesus, because the Christology Mark develops in his Gospel is that of Son of God and Son of man. "Prophet" for Mark signifies no more than the way in which the populace regard both John the Baptist and Jesus (cf. 6:15; 8:27–28).

The strange comment in v. 5a, "And he could do no mighty work there . . . ," should not be taken to mean, as v. 5b plainly reveals, that Jesus was unable as such to perform a miracle. Instead, it is intended to call attention to the enormity of the unbelief of the townspeople of Nazareth and of the relatives of Jesus (v. 6).

One thing this text illustrates well is the challenge of faith with which Jesus confronts all who encounter him: Will one confess him to be the Son of God and follow him, or will one take offense at him and deny his claim to fealty?

First Lesson: Ezek. 2:2–5. In chap. 1, Ezekiel describes his vision of the glory of the Lord (c. 594 B.C.). In it God discloses to him that, Israel's deportation to Babylon notwithstanding (1:1), he is still the ruler of the universe (1:26–28). As such, he has determined, Ezekiel writes in the text, to declare his will to the exiles (2:4). For this purpose he calls (1:28b) and commissions (2:3–4) Ezekiel to be his prophetic mouthpiece to them (2:5).

God addresses Ezekiel in the text as "son of man" (v. 1). This designation is not to be confused with the use Jesus makes of it in the Gospels, for here it underlines the creatureliness and finitude of Ezekiel over against God (cf. Job 25:6; Ps. 8:4). In point of fact, for Ezekiel even to be able to stand upright and to converse with God it is necessary that God empower him with his Spirit (v. 2; cf. Job 34:14–15; Ps. 104: 29–30).

Ezekiel receives his commission in vv. 3–4. Following the demise of the northern kingdom, Judah had proudly arrogated to itself the title "house of Israel." But this people, God announces to Ezekiel, has become a "house of rebellion" (v. 5). Accordingly, he is to go to them and fearlessly to proclaim in their midst the word of the Lord (vv. 3–4). Whether he succeeds or fails in his mission is to be of no concern to him (vv. 6–7). Regardless of how the people receive him, the decisive thing is that God's word will have sounded forth and "they will know that there has been a prophet among them" (vv. 4–5).

It should be recognized in passing that the true link between this text and the Gospel for the day is not to be found in the word "prophet" (cf. v. 5 to Mark 6:4) but in the theme of rejection and rebellion. Both Ezekiel and Jesus are sent to a "rebellious house."

Second Lesson: 2 Cor. 12:7–10. The congregation at Corinth had been invaded by Jewish Christians from Palestine of Gnostic-pneumatic stripe whom Paul terms in his letter "superlative apostles" (11:5; 12:11). These individuals have, on the one hand, cast aspersions upon the person (4:2; 5:11–12; 7:2; 10:2; 12:16), gospel (4:3; 13:3), ministry (6:3), and apostleship (3:1; 10:13–14; 12:12) of Paul, and, on the other, have boasted of their own credentials (3:1; 10:12, 18), position (5:12), mission (11:12, 18), apostleship (11:5; 12:11), and revelatory experiences (5:13; 12:1, 7). In chaps. 11–12, Paul suddenly turns the tables on them and bids the Corinthians to bear with him in a "little foolishness" (11:1). Specifically, he, too, will boast (11:16, 21; 12:1), but only of his weaknesses (11:21, 30; 12:5, 9). The text comprises four verses of Paul's exercise in "boastfulness."

If the "superlative apostles" are bent on boasting of their ecstasies, then Paul asserts in the text that he, no less than they, has also had an "abundance of revelations" (v. 7a; cf. 12:1–4). But because God did not want him to get a "swelled head" over them, he gave him a "thorn in the flesh," that is to say, a messenger of Satan, to beat him (v. 7). In prayer, Paul has earnestly and repeatedly pleaded with God to remove this from him (v. 8). But God's final answer is that the love he has shown him in Christ (8:9) is sufficient to sustain him, for it is in weakness that his divine power comes to its full strength (v. 9a–c; 4:7). In order, therefore, that the power of Christ may dwell within him, Paul is only too happy to boast of his weaknesses (v. 9d–e). For him it is a spiritual law: when he is weak, then he is strong (v. 10).

Paul's reference to a "thorn in the flesh" (v. 7) has elicited a welter of speculation. Some have reasoned that it was a physical or emotional malady, such as epilepsy (2 Cor. 12:7), hysteria, periodic depressions, headaches, eye-trouble (cf. Gal. 4:15), malaria, leprosy, or a speech impediment (cf. 2 Cor. 10:1, 9–10; 11:6). Others have argued that it was a spiritual affliction, such as temptation brought about by opponents or pangs of conscience. In the last analysis, the evidence is simply too meager to permit anything but the most calculated guess. Furthermore, one must remember that Paul's health was not so fragile that he could not endure the many hardships he lists in the text (v. 10) and elsewhere in his letters.

HOMILETICAL INTERPRETATION

1. Concern

The secret of the Christian's strength is that God's power is made perfect in his weakness. This "weakness" offends the unbeliever but sets the believer on his feet.

2. Confirmations and Concretions

Some people are "survivors." No matter how rough life gets they come through. Other people seem to wilt or be destroyed by relatively lighter demands. What is the secret strength of the survivor?

For the Christian the secret of strength is to know one's weakness. "When I am weak, then I am strong" (2 Cor. 12:7–10). This is a paradox, but like all paradoxes in the end its truth proves out. To pretend that we are strong all the time is an invitation to disaster. To act as if we can be "on top" of every situation, "the master of all we survey," is to prepare ourselves for defeat.

Emily Dickinson once wrote about such people:

> How awful to be somebody,
> How public like a frog,
> To tell your name the livelong day
> To an admiring bog.

Such activity may be good public relations for a frog, but for a human it reveals insecurity, not strength.

Real strength comes from knowing that we do not have to be masters of every situation precisely because we know the One who is. Confident about God's strength, we can be humble about our own. That is the secret of survival.

Faith in God's power is an ingredient of strength. We know that his grace is sufficient for us. Helen Kim was the moving spirit behind the founding of the great Ewha University in Korea. The odds against her were enormous, but she created one of our great Christian institutions. When she told the story of her life she took as her title, *Grace Sufficient.*[1]

The prophet Ezekiel faced an overwhelming situation. An inventory of his own resources would have left him in despair, but he allowed the Spirit to enter into him and the Spirit set him on his feet. Ezekiel in his weakness let the mighty God speak through him. Therein lay the power of the prophet for Ezekiel and for ourselves.

Jesus himself appeared "weak" to many of his contemporaries. They were expecting a kind of Superman. They anticipated spectacular signs and unmistakable evidences of his divinity. They saw only a carpenter's son, a local boy, a prophet without honor. Yet all the power of God came to expression in that "weakness." The "weakness" of God proved mightier than the strength of men.

1. See *Grace Sufficient: The Story of Helen Kim by Herself,* edited by J. Manning Potts (Nashville: The Upper Room, 1964). Dr. Kim's Ph.D. dissertation is entitled "Rural Education for the Regeneration of Korea" (Columbia University, 1931).

How can we survive in difficult times? Through the paradox of strength —God's strength made perfect in our weakness.

3. CONSTRUCTION

The Epistle Lesson is a key stating the paradox of strength. The sermon could build from this, with an introduction exploring the paradox. The development of the meaning could be related to:

1. Ezekiel.
2. Jesus.
3. Ourselves.

The Eighth Sunday after Pentecost

Lutheran	*Roman Catholic*	*Episcopal*	*Pres./UCC/Chr.*	*Methodist/COCU*
Amos 7:10–15	Amos 7:12–15	Amos 7:10–15	Amos 7:12–17	Amos 7:10–15
Eph. 1:3–14	Eph. 1:3–14	Eph. 1:13–14	Eph. 1:3–10	Eph. 1:3–14
Mark 6:7–13	Mark 6:7–13	Mark 6:7–13	Mark 6:7–13	Mark 6:7–13

EXEGESIS

Gospel: Mark 6:7–13. The story of the commissioning of the twelve is one of a series of narratives (6:1–33) which Mark has inserted between two cycles of miracle-stories (4:35–5:43; 6:32–56). The first narrative of this series is Jesus' rejection in Nazareth (6:1–6), which is the Gospel reading for Pentecost 7. Next comes the text, which finds its logical conclusion in Mark's report of the return of the disciples and hence forms a bracket around the pericope on the death of John the Baptist (6:7–13, 14–29, 30–31).

Mark states that Jesus, following his rejection in Nazareth, goes around among the villages teaching (v. 6b). Then he summons the twelve and sends them out, giving them instructions about their mission (vv. 7–11). A terse description of this mission concludes the pericope (vv. 12–13).

The twin facts that Jesus is portrayed as teaching in the villages around Nazareth (v. 6b) and that mention is made of the twelve (v. 7a) indicate that the missionary journey of the disciples is to Israel. The Greek verb translated "to send out" (v. 7a) emphasizes the circumstance that the disciples carry out their mission as the special representatives of Jesus (cf. the cognate noun "apostles" in 6:30). The notion of going out "two by two" is thoroughly Jewish (cf. Luke 10:1; Acts 8:14; 13:2; 15:40), and the "authority" on which the disciples act is derived directly from Jesus (v. 7c).

Jesus commands the disciples to take along what is essential ("staff," "tunic," "sandals"; vv. 8a, 9) but nothing more (not "bread," "knapsack," "pin-money," or extra "tunic"; vv. 8–9). The point is that they are not about to become professional itinerant preachers but have before them the eschatologically urgent task of extending Jesus' ministry to Israel. Moreover, when they enter a village, they are to stay in one house only and not move about seeking more comfortable quarters (v. 10). Should a locality not welcome them or accept their message, they are to "shake off the dust that is on their [your] feet for a testimony against them" (v. 11), that is to say, they are to give the people of that place a sign of warning to the effect that they have become as the "heathen" and stand under the judgment of God (cf. Matt. 10:14–15; Acts 13:51; 18:6).

As for the missionary journey itself, Mark writes that the disciples go out and proclaim repentance, exorcise demons, and heal the sick (vv. 12–13). This description of their mission parallels exactly the mission of Jesus (cf. 1:14–15, 32–39; 3:7–12).

Applied to the church of Mark, this text reminded these Christians that they, too, have been entrusted by Jesus with a mission. Their mission, too, is an extension of his mission.

First Lesson: Amos 7:10–15. Amos, a layman from the Judean village of Tekoa (1:1; 7:14), was sent by God around 750 B.C. to the northern kingdom of Israel to denounce its errant sense of security (cf. 6:1–3, 13), its tolerance of social injustice (cf. 3:9–10; 4:1; 5:7, 10–15), its immorality (cf. 4:1; 6:1, 4–6, 12), and its false piety (cf. 4:4–6; 5:5–6). It was towards the close of the long and prosperous reign of Jeroboam II (786–746 B.C.) that Amos undertook his ministry. He appeared publicly first in Samaria, the capital of the northern kingdom (chaps. 3–6), and then at Bethel, the site of the royal sanctuary. The setting for the text is Bethel, and it depicts Amos' clash with Amaziah, the supervising priest at the temple.

The text opens with the news that Amaziah has sent a message to King Jeroboam to the effect that Amos should be charged with treason for having conspired against the palace (v. 10). Indeed, he has so filled the land with his message of judgment that it can no longer endure another word from him (v. 10). In essence, he is predicting the violent death of the king and the deportation of the nation into exile (v. 11).

Before Jeroboam can receive the message and react, Amaziah takes it upon himself to counsel Amos. He respectfully addresses him as "seer," as a "charismatic" prophet, and advises him to return home to Judea and there prophesy for a living (v. 12). Bethel, however, is henceforth "off limits" to him, for it is a national sanctuary (v. 13).

In his reply to Amaziah, Amos punctuates his words with three references to himself ("I," v. 14) followed by three references to the "Lord" (vv. 15–16). He contends that he is neither a professional prophet (cf. 1 Sam. 9:6–10; Mic. 3:5–8, 11) nor a member of a prophetic guild (cf. 1 Kings 22:6; 2 Kings 2:3; 1 Sam. 10:5). On the contrary, he is a shepherd by profession and a dresser of sycamore trees (v. 14). The reason he prophesies as he does has nothing to do with earning a living. It is because God has interrupted his life, himself choosing him and compelling him to go and to prophesy to the people of Israel (v. 15).

Amos is the first Hebrew prophet whose words have been preserved in a book. He is also the first to proclaim the "day of the Lord" as bringing judgment upon Israel and not salvation (cf. 5:18–20; chaps. 8–9). The text admirably conveys the powerful sense of mission that one can have when one knows oneself to have been called into service by God.

Second Lesson: Eph. 1:3–14. If Paul was the author of the Letter to the Ephesians, he most likely wrote it in the early 60s while a prisoner at Rome. If he was not the author, the Epistle was most likely written in Asia Minor sometime between A.D. 80 and 100. Be that as it may, the addressees were Gentile Christians and the writer's principal topic is the church. An important facet of this topic is the oneness within the church of Jew and Gentile who, "united in Christ through his reconciling death, have access by one Spirit to the Father" (H. Chadwick, "Ephesians," *Peake's Commentary on the Bible* [London: Nelson, 1962] 980).

The text presents a variation of this thought and, in the original Greek, captures in a single sentence the fundamental contents of the letter. Formally, it is what may be termed a hymnic benediction (cf. the word "blessed" in 1:3).

By a wide margin, the single most prevalent expression in the text is "in Christ" or its equivalent ("in him," "in whom," "in the Beloved," "in the Messiah"; cf. also "through Jesus Christ"). Since the entire benediction is a paean of praise to God the Father (1:3), the repeated use of this expression shows that, for the author, the locus of God's activity towards humankind and of his revelation of himself is solely Jesus Christ.

With this in mind, we can trace the flow of the text as follows, even though the basic themes intertwine. Our praise, says the author, is to God the Father, who in Jesus Christ has poured out upon us from heaven his blessing (v. 3). In Christ, God has elected us before creation to be free from sin and resplendent before him (v. 4). In Christ, God has graciously adopted us to be his sons (vv. 5–6). In Christ, God has graciously redeemed us, granting us the forgiveness of our trespasses (vv. 7–8). And in Christ, God has revealed his will and purpose to us, namely, that in the fulness of time all things in heaven and on earth might be united under Christ's governance (vv. 9–10). And with respect to this governance, both "we" Jews and "you" Gentiles have the Spirit as a guarantee of the life to come (as a first installment which assures future payment).

Compared with the First Lesson and the Gospel for the day, this text has none of the particularity about it of the call of Amos and of the commissioning of the disciples. It is thoroughly cosmic in sweep as it treats of God's eternal purposes as worked out in the Son and sealed by the Spirit in baptism.

HOMILETICAL INTERPRETATION

1. Concern

The mission of the church is cosmic in its support and concrete in its demands.

2. Confirmations and Concretions

Henrik Ibsen's drama *Brand* depicts a man struggling through a tempestuous blizzard in the icy wastes of Norway. "Go back," an observer cries. "I can't," says Brand, "I am on a mission for someone great whose name is God."[1]

Everyone who has ever been called of God understands Brand's response. He is also likely to understand the call of the observer. That would certainly have been true of the twelve who were first sent out. They had nothing for their journey except a staff, no bread, no bag, no money. They wore sandals and had only one tunic. There were people who refused to hear them and they ran into many demons, not all of which they could cast out. But they could not go back—they were on a mission for someone great.

Nor can we! The mission to which the church is called is cosmic in its support. This is the great burden of the Epistle. The writer sees the fellowship of Christ flowing from the eternal mystery of God which unites

1. See Henrik Ibsen, *Brand* (London: Rupert Hart-Davis, 1960).

all things in heaven and earth. The language is poetic, admittedly sublime. Yet unless the church understands its resources to be cosmic in their sweep, it is soon likely to run out of energy.

God is the eternal source of blessing. He never fails to love. A grand claim was once made for a commercial product: "Ice Never Fails." These words were spread on a huge sign in a city on the Eastern seaboard before refrigeration became widespread. With what confidence it spelled out its message, "You can count on ice. Ice will never fail to preserve your food, to cool your drinks."

That sign is laughably dated, yet strangely contemporary. The public is still looking for something that will not fail. And others are forever offering us some product to meet that need. Their names make their boast. *Sure* a product is called, clearly advising us that if we use it we will be not only more fragrant but more confident. For some time there has been a line of sports products named *Everlast*. Such abiding security they seemed to offer. It is always a little amusing to someone outside the boxing ring to see some fighter keeling over from a knockout blow with the word *Everlast* emblazoned on his trunks.

What a search for support we carry out! And again and again we discover in spite of all our billboards, ice *does* fail. We can not always be sure. The things we call everlasting seem forever to be knocked out by the temporary. Everything that is except God, who isn't a "thing" at all but the eternal source of love who chose us in Christ even before the foundations of the world were set in place. He is everlasting! You can be sure of him. *God* never fails.

God never fails to care for us. The eternity of God is best expressed not in some kind of advertising slogan but through biblical faith in which we see his constancy revealed. God has a constant care for us and an abiding concern for his Creation.

We have been thrilled to see the success of the Apollo-Soyuz space experiment. We are glad that we have come to a time when Americans and Russians can work together for mutual benefit. The handshake of friendship takes the place of handsfull of weapons. I remember a cartoon from the earlier years of space shots. It showed a father who had taken his little boy out under a starry sky when one of the first satellites was visible on the horizon. As they looked intently up at the sky the boy pointed his finger. But the father said, "No, Son, that one has been up there all along." The father was saying that in a time when the sky seems filled with satellites and other kinds of hardware that go up and come down there are still stars in the sky that have been up there all along.

The Christian faith gives us an assurance like this. We see space shots go up, we see space shots come down. We see the triumphs of technology and we are faced with the horrendous questions of priorities they raise. But God's love is like a star. We reach out toward it many times even though we cannot touch it, with the knowledge that God's love has been there all along.

This image can only suggest that aspect of God's love which becomes flesh, which walks among us. For the constancy of God is best imagined not as an object in space but as a person in history. That constancy is most real in the person of Jesus Christ who is with us to suffer when we suffer, to rejoice when we rejoice.

God never fails to do justice. The mission of the church is cosmic in its support but concrete in its demands. Amos understood that, as this Old Testament lesson makes clear, and the legacy of Amos must always be inherited by every generation in the church.

The God of biblical revelation is a just God. He measures the walls we build between people with his moral plumbline. He is the God who holds his will against the wills of men and measures our achievements by his law. Amos is called to serve *this* God. Amos is not comfortable about it. The "proper" priest says, in effect, "Amos, these are sacred precincts. We don't want that message in here." But Amos can not help trying to get that message through. He, like Ibsen's Brand, cannot turn back. He is not an official prophet nor an accredited priest. He is no part of the Establishment. But he is part of God's design. So are we.

We are never comfortable with the justice of God. But no less than Amos you and I must seek to participate in that justice. To try to voice it, but even more to embody justice. Every church, every minister, every lay person—Amos was a layman!—must be constantly involved in discovering and ministering to the concerns of persons around them.[1] This means dealing with justice in the concrete even if it means standing against the King—or a President. It means confronting the forces that make for war. It means dealing with criminal law, and with criminals in prison (with persons as well as with principles). It means coming to grips with exiles and refugees. It means plunging into the world of history.

The justice of God demands that we do all that we can to see that every person gets what is due them. There is always room for work and

1. One way of getting at these from a theological base may be found in *Faith Alive!:* A Study Book for Doing Theology, edited by David James Randolph (Nashville: Tidings, 1969). Compare Wallace E. Fisher, *From Tradition to Mission* (Nashville and New York: Abingdon Press, 1965) and Robert K. Hudnut, *Arousing the Sleeping Giant* (New York, Evanston, etc.: Harper and Row, 1973).

never room for self-righteousness. For the justice of God will be done, if not through us then upon us. We who would be prophets stand under that justice no less than anyone else.

The Christian mission to which you and I are called is cosmic in its support and concrete in its demands. Our love falters. Our justice is often fragmentary. Ice melts and all our sureties are at last unsure. But God never fails to care for us. God never fails to do justice. We can count on God. Trust him. Seek to walk in his way and you step on foundations laid before the world began.

3. CONSTRUCTION

These passages suggest a sermon on the church which deals with:

1. Mission (the Gospel).
2. Cosmic support (the Epistle).
3. Concrete demands (OT lesson).

The Ninth Sunday after Pentecost

Lutheran	*Roman Catholic*	*Episcopal*	*Pres./UCC/Chr.*	*Methodist/COCU*
Jer. 23:1–6	Jer. 23:1–6	Jer. 23:1–6	Jer. 23:1–6	Jer. 23:1–6
Eph. 2:13–22	Eph. 2:13–18	Eph. 2:11–18	Eph. 2:11–18	Eph. 2:13–22
Mark 6:30–34	Mark 6:30–34	Mark 6:30–34	Mark 6:30–34	Mark 6:30–44

EXEGESIS

Gospel: Mark 6:30–34. The text spans two units: 6:30–31 and 6:32–34. Vv. 30–31 form the conclusion to the pericope on the commissioning of the twelve (6:6b–13), and vv. 32–34 introduce the miracle of the feeding of the five thousand. Taken together, however, vv. 30–34 do cohere.

Mark designates the returning disciples as "the apostles" (v. 30). Although this expression is not the technical term in the Second Gospel that it is, for example, in Paul's writings, it does have recognizable content. Thus, it is applied to the twelve and refers to the fact that Jesus "sends them out" both to preach and to exorcise demons (3:14–15; 6:7, 12–13). For Mark, therefore, the word "apostles" describes the twelve as those who, on the authority of Jesus, function as an extension of his ministry.

The text reports that the apostles return to Jesus and tell him of all they have done and taught (v. 30), that is, of their preaching and healing activity (6:12–13). Jesus summons them to come away to a lonely place where they can rest for awhile and find relief from the hubbub around them (v. 31; cf. 3:20). Accordingly, they leave in a boat and head for a deserted spot (v. 32). But there are many who see them embarking and recognize them, the upshot being that people from all the surrounding towns run to the place towards which Jesus and the disciples are sailing (v. 33). Getting out of the boat, Jesus sees the great crowd of people, has compassion upon them, and teaches them at length, for they are as leaderless and aimless as sheep who have no shepherd (v. 34).

In consideration of the sheep-and-shepherd imagery in the OT (cf. Num. 27:17; 1 Kings 22:17; Jer. 23:1–6; Ezek. 34), the implication of the text is that Jesus is the messianic Shepherd who in love "gathers" and through his authoritative teaching "feeds" the eschatological flock of Israel (cf. Matt. 9:35–38).

First Lesson: Jer. 23:1–6. Jeremiah began his prophetic ministry in 627 B.C. when Josiah was king of Judah (640–609 B.C.). He was active through the subsequent reigns of Jehoiakim (609–598 B.C.), Jehoiachin (598–597 B.C.), and Zedekiah (597–587 B.C.), remaining in the land even after the destruction of Jerusalem (587 B.C.). But about 582 B.C., upon the assassination of Gedaliah, the newly appointed governor of Judah, a band of Israelites, fearing reprisals from the Babylonians, fled to Egypt, taking Jeremiah with them. What became of Jeremiah in Egypt is not known.

The Book of Jeremiah falls into four main sections. The first (1:1–25:14) contains his prophecies of doom against Jerusalem and Judah, and the second (25:15–38; chaps. 46–51) his oracles against the nations. By contrast, the third section (chaps. 26–36) is devoted to his prophecies of salvation for Israel and Judah, and the final one (chaps. 37–45) is the so-called passion story of Jeremiah.

The text is located in the first main section. It comprises sayings of the Lord which have the form of threat (vv. 1–2) and promise (vv. 3–6). God's wrath, says Jeremiah, is against the shepherds, or rulers of Judah, who destroy, scatter, drive away, and neglect the flock of Israel (vv. 1–2). In their place, God himself will gather the remnant of the flock from all the countries of the world, and he will set shepherds over the sheep who will truly care for them (vv. 3–4). In point of fact, in the future God will raise up from the line of David one who will rule in accordance with his will ("a righteous Branch"), one who will be his instrument of salvation ("justice and righteousness") towards his people (v. 5). Under the governance of this ruler, Judah and Israel will be restored as one nation, so that unlike king Zedekiah, who is indebted for his throne to Nebuchadnezzar and is a mockery to his name ("the Lord is my righteousness"), this new son of David will act in full concert with his name ("the Lord is our righteousness [salvation]") (v. 6).

The text is well suited to the Gospel for the day because, for Christians, Jesus is the one in the line of David who is the true Shepherd of God's people.

Second Lesson: Eph. 2:13–22. It is said that the entire Epistle reaches its culmination in vv. 11–22. The text itself may be divided as follows: v. 13 introduces the hymn of vv. 14–18, which extols the peace Christ has established between Jew and Gentile and between God and mankind, and vv. 19–22 set forth the consequences of this peace.

The reference to the "far" and the "near" in v. 13 alludes to Isa. 57:19. But there the contrast is between Israelites in exile and Israelites in Palestine. Here the contrast is between Gentile and Jew. The thrust of v. 13 is that through the blood of Christ the Gentiles have become part of the people of God.

Intoning the great hymn of peace (vv. 14–18), the author writes that, in the person of Christ, oneness now reigns between Jew and Gentile; former hostility has given way to peace (v. 14). Through the death of Christ, the law, which served to separate Jew from Gentile, has been abolished, so that in place of these two men Christ has created one new man, the church (v. 15). What is more, in the church these two have also been reconciled by Christ to God, so that hostility between God and mankind has also been brought to an end (v. 16).

But Christ is not simply the ground and source of peace. He it is (and his ambassadors) who has likewise come and proclaimed the fact of this peace to both Jew and Gentile. Moreover, like a high priest he furthermore gives access to Jew and Gentile in the one Spirit to God the Father (v. 18).

The effective result of the peace Christ has established is that Gentiles are no more to be regarded as aliens or resident aliens as far as the household of God is concerned; in Christ they are members of this household with full citizenship-rights (v. 19). Then, too, the whole structure, with Christ as the cornerstone (cf. Isa. 28:16; Matt. 21:42), tends upwards towards God and is his dwelling place (vv. 20–22).

If the Gospel and the First Lesson emphasize the truth that Jesus is the prophesied Shepherd of the eschatological flock of Israel, this text emphasizes the truth that in Christ Gentiles, too, have their place in this flock, which is in fact the church.

HOMILETICAL INTERPRETATION

1. CONCERN

Jesus is the shepherd of his flock, the church in which Jews and Gentiles are welcome.

2. CONFIRMATIONS AND CONCRETIONS

In the Candid Camera series on television some boys were once chosen to receive what they were told was a big prize. They were paraded before their classmates and the master of ceremonies went through an elaborate buildup about their selection for the award. At the climax came the words: "You have been chosen . . . shepherds of the month!"

The looks of disappointment on the boys' faces filled the screen. Being a shepherd of the month is not very exciting to the contemporary imagination. However, if we think of the shepherd as the person who cares for a bunch of noisy, straggling creatures, then we realize how essential that task is. John Updike has a story called "Lifeguard" in which he describes the attentions which the man on the beach gives to those struggling in the waters. That image of the lifeguard may be more appropriate for our time. Try reading Psalm Twenty-three with that image in mind, "The Lord is my lifeguard."

Whether "shepherd" or some other image may be sought for the one who cares, the image of the strangers drawn from Ephesians is very real to us. Vance Packard has written a study of contemporary America entitled *A Nation of Strangers.*[1] The Christian community offers an alternative. We can be members of a community where we are strangers no more. That community is what the Letter to the Ephesians is about.

The Christian community, however, is not only a group which is concerned about internal relations. The Christian community moves out into the world to bring together all persons in a new understanding of humanity. Jesus Christ has broken down the walls between persons.

The church is potentially God's family. Several expressions of this truth are worth exploring. One is that the church should build family relationships at a time when many forces are working against this. Secondly, the church should develop family-like groups where persons may come together face to face to be truly human with one another. Thirdly,

1. Vance Packard, *A Nation of Strangers* (New York: David McKay, 1972). See also Morton Thompson, *Not As A Stranger* (New York: Scribners, 1955).

the church can actually become the "family" for many persons, especially in our modern cities, who otherwise would live alone.

The eschatological dimension of these passages is inescapable. The privileges and demands of life in the kingdom now are enormous. At the same time we look beyond the limits of all that we know to that Jesus who transcends all our languages and our images in his eternal caring.

3. CONSTRUCTION

The concern of this sermon could be developed in the following steps:

1. The need for belonging (the OT lesson).
2. The Caring Christ (the Gospel).
3. The Church as God's family (Second Lesson).

Last Things: A Summing Up

A Theology in Outline: these lessons have offered us no less. We began with the God who addresses the valley full of bones to bring life and who calls the church into being on Pentecost. We saw how this God reveals himself as Father, Son and Holy Spirit in the lessons for Trinity Sunday. Successive lessons have provided the basis for an elemental if unsystematic study of the church in its mission to the world. The interpreter makes no claim that in this limited space all the terrain has been explored. He simply observes that it has come into view and that it is beautiful.

Faith in every specific expression reaches toward wholeness. Christian theology after all is not an arrangement of words, a collection of texts, an arbitrary categorization of data. Theology is rather a way of seeing faith in its wholeness and living life in its fullness.

Thus the preacher who understands his task knows himself not to be serving snacks from his own little kitchen but breaking the Bread of Life to the hungry. This truth will shame him, for he knows how often he has handed out crumbs. But it will also redeem him, for is not he who breaks the Bread also nourished by it?

In any case, it is appropriate that these lessons end on eschatological themes, even as doctrine dealing with the Holy Spirit has from ancient times.

"Last Things" is the language often associated with eschatology and the title of a novel by C. P. Snow. In it we read a kind of summary of a series of books dealing with a scholar who comes to walk "the corridors of power" in Great Britain. In the novel, the central character tells his son that he has refused a job in the government. The son observes that this must be the end of one line for him. The father agrees. The son asks, "It never was a very central line, though, was it?"[1]

Soon or late we all come to the end of one line, the line of our earthly life. Christian faith does not alter that. Christian faith simply guarantees that the life lived in loving God, neighbor, and self is the central line. You can know that you have not been sidetracked in selfishness.

The central line of God's purpose is a great line to be on. I heard once of a minor employee in a small British rail station who was meticulously going about his work. A skeptical tourist asked why he was doing such a thorough job in such an obscure place, visited by so few people. In amazement the workman replied that though his was a small station it was part of the national system! He felt involved in a mighty transportation network. Those who do Christian work may feel that their labors are insignificant, their work unrecognized. But these lessons remind us that however remote from the heavenly our daily tasks may seem, Christian discipleship carries us on the central line.

The central line has a destiny beyond all earthly destinations. The Christian "looks to the resurrection and the life of the world to come."

F. Scott Fitzgerald knew and described the wasteland of modernity as few have. At the conclusion of his novel, *The Great Gatsby,* the narrator Nick Carraway wanders down to the beach at Gatsby's house and sits brooding. He thinks back to the time Gatsby looked across the waters of Long Island Sound and first saw the green light at the end of Daisy Buchanan's dock.

"Gatsby believed in the green light, the orgiastic future that year by year recedes before us. It eluded us then, but that's no matter. Tomorrow we will run faster, stretch our arms farther. . . . And one fine morning——

"So we beat our boats against the current, borne back ceaselessly into the past."[2]

It is often claimed that Gatsby represents the "great American dream." If so, no wonder there is a wasteland. Gatsby confuses quantity with quality. He seems to know the surface of everything and the depth of nothing. Fitzgerald, moralist as well as storyteller, knew that. But had Fitzgerald been writing of the Christian hope instead of the American dream he would have written a different story. The story would have been set in the Wasteland but it would be about a person who finds the Christ leading him to the living water. It would picture a life refreshed by the

1. C. P. Snow, *Last Things* (New York: Scribners, 1970), p. 137.

2. F. Scott Fitzgerald, *The Great Gatsby* in *Three Novels* (New York: Scribners, 1953), p. 137.

waters of grace, waters which irrigate the wasteland with the possibility of renewal. That story might conclude:

The Christian believes in the green light, the joyful future that day by day comes toward us. We never completely grasp it in any one day, but that's no problem, because tomorrow we will respond more fully, stretch out our arms farther. . . . And one bright morning——

So we sail on, boats with the current, borne ceaselessly toward God.

PROCLAMATION:

Aids for Interpreting the
Lessons of the Church Year

EASTER

SERIES B

Charles Rice
and
J. Louis Martyn

FORTRESS PRESS Philadelphia, Pennsylvania

Table of Contents

Library of Congress Card Number 74-24958

ISBN 0-8006-4075-6
Second Printing 1976

5736C76 Printed in U.S.A. 1-4075

General Preface

Proclamation: Aids for Interpreting the Lessons of the Church Year is a series of twenty-six books designed to help clergymen carry out their preaching ministry. It offers exegetical interpretations of the lessons for each Sunday and many of the festivals of the church year, plus homiletical ideas and insights.

The basic thrust of the series is ecumenical. In recent years the Episcopal church, the Roman Catholic church, the United Church of Christ, the Christian Church (Disciples of Christ), the United Methodist Church, the Lutheran and Presbyterian churches, and also the Consultation on Church Union have adopted lectionaries that are based on a common three-year system of lessons for the Sundays and festivals of the church year. *Proclamation* grows out of this development, and authors have been chosen from all of these traditions. Some of the contributors are parish pastors; others are teachers, both of biblical interpretation and of homiletics. Ecumenical interchange has been encouraged by putting two persons from different traditions to work on a single volume, one with the primary responsibility for exegesis and the other for homiletical interpretation.

Despite the high percentage of agreement between the traditions, both in the festivals that are celebrated and the lessons that are appointed to be read on a given day, there are still areas of divergence. Frequently the authors of individual volumes have tried to take into account the various textual traditions, but in some cases this has proved to be impossible; in such cases we have felt constrained to limit the material to the Lutheran readings.

The preacher who is looking for "canned sermons" in these books will be disappointed. These books are one step removed from the pulpit: they explain what the lessons are saying and suggest ways of relating this biblical message to the contemporary situation. As such they are springboards for creative thought as well as for faithful proclamation of the word.

The authors of this volume of *Proclamation* are Charles Rice and J. Louis Martyn. Charles Rice, the homiletician, is Associate Professor of Homiletics in The Theological School of Drew University. Before assuming his present post in 1970, Dr. Rice taught at Salem College in Winston-Salem, N.C., Adams United College in South Africa, and The Divinity School of Duke University. Dr. Rice is a graduate of Baylor University (B.A.), Southern Baptist Theological Seminary (B.D.), and Union Theological Seminary in New York (S.T.M.) where he studied homiletics with Edmund Steimle. He received the Ph.D. in American Religious studies from Duke University in 1967. A minister of the United Church of Christ, Professor Rice has served as interim pastor of the United Church of Chapel Hill, N.C., and of Pilgrim United Church, Durham, N.C. He is associated with a movement that emphasized contemporary narrative preaching patterned after New Testament storytelling and is the author of *Interpretation and Imagination: The Preacher and Contemporary Literature* (Philadelphia: Fortress Press, 1970). J. Louis Martyn, who has provided the exegesis for this volume, is Edward Robinson Professor of Biblical Theology at Union Theological Seminary in New York and Adjunct Professor of Religion at Columbia University. He has taught at Union since 1959. Dr. Martyn is a graduate of Texas A & M (B.S.), Andover Newton Theological School (B.D.), and Yale University (M.A., Ph.D.). He has also studied in Göttingen, Germany, on a Fulbright Scholarship. In 1963-64 he was awarded a Guggenheim Fellowship and in 1974-75 he was at the Ecumenical Institute for Advanced Theological Studies in Jerusalem. His publications include *Studies in Luke-Acts* (Nashville: Abingdon, 1966), of which he was co-editor, and *History and Theology in the Fourth Gospel* (New York: Harper & Row, 1968).

Introduction

Amos Wilder was among the first to point us toward the story as a natural speech-form for the gospel. The anecdote, the sort of simple story that people everywhere tell, belongs to the earliest speech of the church and is essential to the community's initial and continuing celebration of the Resurrection. Wilder gives us an example of such an anecdote; Jesus' cure of the blind Bartimaeus at the gate of Jericho (Mark 10:46-52):

> What would this story convey as it was told and retold orally well before there were any written gospels? For its meaning we should put it in the context of the post-Resurrection faith. The believers lived in vivid realization of the time of fulfilment. The Old Testament promises were there and then coming to pass. These were the times when, as we read in Isa. 35:5-6:
>
> Then the eyes of the blind shall be opened,
> and the ears of the deaf unstopped:
> then shall the lame man leap like a hart,
> and the tongue of the dumb sing for joy.
>
> But such salvation in the order of physical well-being was only one aspect of the general redemption. The cure of Bartimaeus was then a dramatic sign of what God was bringing to pass. Like other wonders in what we call the natural order and like certain parables of Jesus it conveyed the truth that God had bared his mighty arm and wrought salvation: being thus a small companion piece to the Resurrection-drama itself. This small anecdote was the Gospel in miniature. [1]

". . . a small companion piece to the Resurrection-drama itself." We could hardly do better in trying to say what we hope for in this booklet and in the stories we hope they will evoke from Christian communities and those who preach for them.

Some say that every Sunday is Easter, and there is no good historical or theological reason to disagree so long as the notion does not lead us to live in that flat liturgical landscape where everything is shouted, or reduced to a muffled beige, so that we hear and see less of the drama than we need. But we can agree that not only every Sunday but the other six days as well have to do with Easter, as surely as Bartimaeus' new eyes celebrate the Resurrection. Our weekday, get-up-and-go-to-work and come-home-and-get-ready-to-do-it-again lives are companion pieces to the day of trumpets and hot-house lilies. And it is there, in our story, that *the* Story finds both its hearing and its continuing, earthy celebration. And there, too, lie the affective sources of preaching. Whether we want simply to pull out the stops and shout "He is risen!" or to try to figure out how to live in the world when the shouting is an echo, we hear and tell both stories. Wilder says that even "the road to moral judgement is by way of the imagination." [2]

1. Amos N. Wilder, *Early Christian Rhetoric* (Cambridge, Mass.: Harvard University Press, 1971), p. 62.

2. *op. cit*, p. 60.

We have tried, in this booklet, to hear as clearly as possible the voices of the early church, and we have tried to hear our own communities speaking their "gospels in miniature." We hope that the end of this will, to some degree, realize the artist's aim: "Not so much to speak as to cause to speak."

The exegete expresses appreciation to a number of interpreters among whom four should be mentioned in particular: Raymond E. Brown for *The Gospel According to John (xiii-xxi)* (Garden City, N.Y., Doubleday, 1970); Ernst Haenchen for *The Acts of the Apostles* (Oxford, Blackwell, 1971); Joachim Gnilka for *Der Epheserbrief* (Freiburg, Herder, 1971); and Rudolf Schnackenburg for *Die Johannesbriefe* (Freiburg, Herder, 1970). I wish to thank Ronald Allen, formerly a student of Professor Martyn's, and now a graduate student in homiletics and New Testament studies at Drew University, who read the manuscript with a holy eros.

Charles Rice

The Resurrection of Our Lord
Easter Day

Lutheran	*Roman Catholic*	*Episcopal*	*Pres./UCC/Chr.*	*Methodist/COCU*
Isa. 25:6-9	Acts 10:34a, 37-43	Isa. 25:6-9	Isa. 25:6-9	Isa. 25:6-9
1 Cor. 15:19-28	Col. 3:1-4	Col. 3:1-4	1 Peter 1:3-9	1 Peter 1:3-9
Mark 16:1-8	John 20:1-9	Mark 16:1-8	Mark 16:1-8	Mark 16:1-8

EXEGESIS

First Lesson: Isa. 25:6-9. It is a fact of the faith and history of ancient Israel that, while God was known always to be King, it was nevertheless necessary for the people repeatedly to experience and to celebrate his kingship. The knowledge of yesterday and of today, important as it was, seemed never in itself to suffice for tomorrow. Note 24:23—"The Lord of Hosts *will* reign on Mount Zion and in Jerusalem."

The present, rather apocalyptic text is the heavenly counterpart, so to speak, of the earthly coronation in the temple of Jerusalem of the kings of Israel. As the recognition of Yahweh's coronation, it has several components: (a) The feast of extraordinarily rich food and fine wine is a symbol, of course, of fullness of life which can be had only in God's realm. (b) The universalism is quite unmistakable. All nations are incorporated in the birth of God's kingdom at Zion. (c) As so often in Hebraic thought, the nations are conceived as being under the domination of angelic powers. Hence a presupposition of the universal establishment of God's kingdom is the vanquishing of these patron angels who have previously blinded the nations (24:21).

This last element now receives a remarkable heightening: not only are the misleading angelic powers put down, but also death itself is swallowed up by Yahweh (cf. the role of Mot [death] in the Canaanite Baal myth). Vv. 7-8 form a powerful part of the poem, evidencing Hebrew parallelism in the words "covering" and "veil," both serving here as symbols of death; similarly "tears" and "reproach." The prophet sees that there is no ultimate celebration of Yahweh's coronation banquet until this last enemy—the enemy of *all* nations and of *all* peoples—has been destroyed. V. 9 is the joyous celebration, not of an annual agricultural "miracle," but rather of this victory over death itself by the one who is the cosmic Lord.

Second Lesson: 1 Cor. 15:19-28. The place of chap. 15 in the epistle is quite clear: it is the climax which has been in Paul's mind from the outset. In the period since Paul's departure from Corinth, a weighty part of the Corinthian church has made an astounding "discovery": They have come to see that the Christ event consisted of nothing other than the revelation of the Essential Man who appeared to die, but whose "resurrection" was actually an illumination of his timeless and spiritual immortality, making clear that he passed through death as easily as one passes through a door. They have also come to see that they themselves share his timeless, spiritual essence, and are thus, in their essential selves, already living in glory. There is no historical drama to human life. Everything is already in hand, at least for those who, like themselves, are truly spiritual (4:8).

Paul perceives clearly that these "spiritual" Corinthians have sacrificed the gift of life which comes "from God," and understandably he does not consider their having done so to be a matter of indifference. At point after point he takes issue throughout the first fourteen chapters. Then, in chapter fifteen, he comes to *the* issue: the death and resurrection of Jesus.

From v. 12 it is clear that reports have reached Paul informing him that some of the Corinthians deny "the resurrection of the dead." From this we can rightly conclude that they affirm *Jesus'* resurrection, but only in the sense indicated above: his "death" was a momentary passage, and his "resurrection" was a revelation of his timeless essence. That means, in turn, that the thought of a general and future resurrection has no meaning to them. Hence Paul comes, in vv. 20-28, to the crux of the matter, which he expresses to some considerable degree with the terms "first fruits" (v. 20) and "order" (v. 23). Notice also the studied use of the word "then" (vv. 23-24). The coming of Christ (cf. Gal. 4:4), his death, and his resurrection are not points at which one may get a glimpse of a timeless essence. They are in fact events in God's overarching deed of re-grasping the world under his sovereignty. *And*, the whole of that overarching deed is by no means already accomplished. Christ's resurrection is only the "first fruits," the surety of God's ultimate victory. It is not an isolatable event, which may be studied in and of itself. It is, on the contrary, the beginning and guarantee of "the resurrection of the dead" (v. 21), that is to say, of the general resurrection. As such it involves us all, whether we know it or not. Paul has no doubt that in Christ "*all* shall be made alive" (v. 22).

But, again, he does not speak of the general resurrection as something which has already been accomplished. All *shall be* made alive; each in his own *order* (v. 23). Christians, and, in fact, all of creation (cf. Rom. 8:18 ff.) are not yet at the goal. Hence the temporal use of the word "then." In short, Easter is not the end, but rather the beginning.

The beginning, precisely, of what? The beginning of God's new creation (2 Cor. 5:17), which he is bringing into being by vanquishing all hostile and enslaving powers (v. 24), the last of which is death itself (v. 26). It is sheer folly to deny the existence and potency of these enemies (4:8). Nor are they overcome by one's coming to a knowledge of his own essential self. It is Christ who overcomes them, and he is even now doing that, in order finally to deliver the regrasped world, and even himself, to God. God's new creation is, thus, not a *thing* that is completely given; it is, rather, the unfolding drama of Christ's past in the reality of death, and of Christ's presence as risen Lord, and of Christ's future as the one who continues to bring under his subjection the tyrannous powers in human life; and ultimately it is the drama which is our liberation because it ends in God's being "all in all."

Gospel: Mark 16:1-8. We begin by noting the broader context of this paragraph. To a large degree the Gospel of Mark is stretched out on the background of extraordinary dramatic tension. Already in the first chapter, the reader senses that the coming of the Spirit on Jesus impels him into tense conflict with the evil spirits which imprison human beings. Jesus himself speaks of the necessity first to bind the strong man (Satan) before he can enter his house (the orb of human sin and enslavement) and plunder his goods (free those who are possessed). Nor is the conflict simply an otherworldly one. Just as Jesus embodies the liberating power of God's new age, so many of the religious and political authorities embody the enslaving powers of the old age. Consequently it becomes clear that the struggle will find at least one of its climaxes in the real and painful, yes, horrible death of Jesus (3:6). The authorities of the old age cannot tolerate this man. The preservation of their hegemony necessitates putting him out of their world.

In the passion narrative itself there are weighty symbols pointing to the fact that Jesus' death is not an "unfortunate incident," but is rather *the* point at which the two ages collide. One pair of these symbols is provided in 15:33 and 16:2. In these two verses Mark is not giving his readers the time of day; he is bearing witness to the eschatological conflict. There can be little doubt that for Mark the darkness at the crucifixion stands for the ultimate show of strength on the part of the "powers of darkness," the demonic, religious, and political forces of the old age with whom Jesus has been doing battle through the whole of the gospel story. Similarly the perfectly "natural" dawn of a new day (16:2) is in actuality a sign of the victory of the inbreaking kingdom of God, the new age. Mark's attentive reader already perceives that God does not intend to leave Jesus in the grave. But, what form, precisely, does God's victory take?

One will not want to forget that the victory has already taken proleptic form in the course of Jesus' life: the possessed have been liberated, the sick have been healed, the hungry have been fed, the ignorant have been taught the words of life. These forms of victory remain the good news which Mark calls the good news of Jesus Christ (1:1). The passion narrative shows, however, that the drama is yet larger, the opposition yet fiercer and more desperate, and the dimensions of God's kingdom yet more comprehensive. "The last enemy to be vanquished is death."

Thus our paragraph unfolds. The women come in order tenderly to perform the anointing rite due the dead. But the body is not to be found. Instead they encounter an angel who announces to them that Jesus of Nazareth (the really crucified one) has risen! God's victory takes the form of the vanquishing of death.

But there is more. We are at one of those points at which careful literary criticism and synoptic comparisons bring out weighty dimensions of the text. One notes, first, that Mark 16:7 repeats a promise made by Jesus in 14:28. That fact in itself gives a strong hint that the verse may be Mark's redaction. Second, one notes that 16:8 follows more easily on 16:5-6 than on 16:7. Fear is a standard reaction to an angelophany.

Having seen the angel and having discovered the empty tomb, the women flee in fear.

If Mark provided 16:7, what was his intention? Comparison of Mark 16:7 with Matt. 28:7 will show how Matthew understood the verse. He takes the promise, "there (in Galilee) you will see him," to point forward to the appearance of the risen Lord to his disciples on a mountain in Galilee (Matt. 28:16 ff.). But is this necessarily Mark's intention? Pondering the question will remind us of the remarkable fact that Mark is content to close his Gospel without narrating an appearance of the Risen One. (The question of the genuineness of Mark 16:9 ff. has been recently reopened in an impressive way; yet in what is written here the secondary nature of these verses is assumed.) To what, then, does he intend to point with the promise of 16:7?

There are good grounds for seeing it as a promise of the parousia. Perhaps, however, one should not compel the text to yield a single level of meaning. The promise may refer both to a resurrection appearance and to the parousia. In that case, we see that the form of God's victory encompasses the gospel story, and Jesus' resurrection, and also what has been so suggestively called in our time "the future of Jesus Christ."

HOMILETICAL INTERPRETATION

The momentum of this weekend may leave us speechless. One event converges upon another from Thursday to Sunday, and the pace tries our powers. When were sorrow and joy, alienation and love, death and life so impacted, or when were men and women called on to find words to accompany such events? Do our musical and homiletical extravagances, services and sermons as overdressed as the congregation, betray our feeling of inadequacy?

As a matter of fact, standing speechless before the Easter event may be the best preparation for preaching today. Günther Bornkamm suggests that it may be so:

> The contrast between what men did and do and what God has done and accomplished in and through this Jesus, belongs . . . inalienably to all the New Testament testimony of the resurrection. In this the first Christians do not consider themselves in any way as confederates of God and comrades-in-arms with their Lord, as we might put it. They regard themselves as those who have been conquered, whose former lives and beliefs have come to naught. The men and women who encounter the risen Christ in the Easter stories, have come to an end of their wisdom.[1]

What is the mood of Easter morning? Why bother to get up before dawn if not to keep a vigil and, as befits mortal flesh, to keep silence for a time and to stand in fear and trembling?

That is the mood which John Killinger, too, suggests for moving toward the pulpit today. He warns us away from trying to *prove* something, as if

1. Günther Bornkamm, *Jesus of Nazareth* (New York: Harper & Bros., 1960), p. 184.

we had to roll the stone away. God has done it already, as he has created and continues to create his alleluia-singing people:

> In the church, then, as the community of the Restoration, the preacher is not called on to be an orator or public advocate. He is instead a listener, a mediator, a friend, a fellow, a catalyst. And he is all of these primarily as a man among men who is always seeking more and more wholeness for himself and is never inhibited about saying this to his congregation, that is responsible for the sense of Restoration, and, by that token, for the preaching of the church as well.[2]

When we feel that way about it, that it is God's doing, that the resurrection has made this church in the first place, and that the restoration to new life is a tangible kind of fact that people know today, then we can enter into the joy of this day.

1 Cor. 15:19-28; Isa. 25:6-9. We arrived at the church early, before eight, on that day of high celebration. Someone had been there before us. That is the way it happened on Easter Day, isn't it? Some Easter angel had done it, scooped us and said it all before we had a chance to put on our black gowns and get up in the high pulpit and announce loudly that he was risen and that everything was therefore OK. Speak of non-verbal communication and standing there upstaged in your wordiness! There it was, smack in the middle of the narthex, just sitting there in all its battered rusty brown and sunshine yellow glory, stark and beautiful as fine linen lying on a stone floor. It was a garbage can which had been run over by the truck a dozen times and flung aside empty on a hundred times that many Monday mornings. Now, at the gate of heaven it overflowed with six or seven dozen chrysanthemums. "Christmas anthems" we used to call them. Easter alleluias at least.

Easter is God's day. It is hard to find metaphors as apt as that unlikely bouquet, but that *is* what the day is about. It may be possible on other days and in other circumstances to speak less theologically, but when we come to the crucifixion of Jesus, the dispersion of his followers, and the general gloom of what appeared very likely to be a lost weekend, only to receive from these same defeated people the witness of Jesus' resurrection, like all of the lections for today we can only witness: "It is the Lord's doing, and it is marvelous in our eyes."

Paul could not be clearer: everything depends upon the resurrection of Jesus, and it is God who has raised him. Where we might be inclined to point to the success of the church or even of our own ministry as "proof" of the resurrection, Paul takes just the opposite view. If God has not raised Jesus from death, then he is not at work in him or in us and it is all a washout. Paul, however, does not tarry over such speculations: "But in fact Christ has been raised from the dead . . ."

Paul is pointing to God's adequacy for his people: God has not left his Holy One in death, and he will in the same manner deliver his people from the "last enemy." Paul almost personifies death, and he hangs a great deal

2. John Killinger, *Leave It to the Spirit* (New York: Harper & Row, 1971), p. 162.

on God's overcoming the threat which it poses. We can appreciate the meaning—and the threat of meaninglessness—attached to the death of Jesus. Here is the innocent being put to a criminal's death at the hands of the guilty. The death of Jesus is loaded with our deepest moral questions. But as to death in general, would we wish to put the matter just as Paul states it? Is death for us the last (ultimate?) enemy of mankind? In an overpopulated, underfed world, is the death of a person at home in bed among friends at the end of a long life an "enemy" at all? Where is God winning his victories in our world? Where is Jesus Christ crucified? Where is he vindicated? Where in our day do we see the salvation of the Lord? Is there being realized among us today the hope of Isaiah for plentiful food, good wine, and the Lord's glory which will dispel the cloud that covers the land? For what do we wait, even on this side of Easter?

The earliest church, even while rejoicing in the resurrection, waited for the parousia. We can be sure that Isaiah's cultic feast which celebrates God's kingship is at the same time a feast of waiting for the victory yet to come. Such a feast is always a having and a not having, a foretaste. That is certainly the mood of the central feast of our faith in which we remember, rejoice, give thanks, and yet wait for more to come. Having, yet not having, filled, yet hungry, saved from death, yet dying. Has that way of waiting changed since the first Easter? Do we not wait still for Isaiah's day of peace and plenty and the hope that Jesus' victory will indeed have its final fruition in us and all peoples? To have God's blessing is to wait for more, just as to celebrate God's greatest day, this Easter, is to wait still for the day of the Lord. "Blessed are they that hunger, for they shall be filled."

Mark 16:1-8. What a picture of surrender, of the first dawning of hope, of not daring to believe. It is like a person who has been very ill who takes a tentative walk and feels something in the air and in the forgotten pleasure that he takes in it that he is getting well, and yet he walks carefully.

Mark's story of the women coming with fragrant oils to the garden tomb evokes in us quietness, vulnerability, even passivity. Here are people who have come to the end, who have done all that they can do. Now they come to the tomb with their pitiful offering not even sure that they can get to his body to make this last gesture.

Then, to make us feel even more deeply our helplessness, Mark fixes our attention on the great stone at the entrance of the tomb. The monolith is blunt fact, certain death, the way things have always been and always will be, the undeniable power of the state, our doubts, our not daring to hope. The stone preoccupies the women.

Then the stone is no longer there. How else do you handle a stone as huge as that? It is simply rolled away. The women enter the tomb and the messenger tells them what they can plainly see: "He is not here." The stone is removed, and Jesus is not here. The assurance that he has been raised and that he is going before them into Galilee seems lost on the women, for at the end of Mark's account, they are both silent and afraid.

To what degree do the people to whom we preach today experience the Easter message in this way, or would they do so if we could get past the twittering birds and sentimental optimism of a haberdasher's Easter? Why do we have a story like Mark's at all? Does such a story complement Paul's more straightforward catalogue of witnesses to the resurrection (cf. 1 Cor. 15:3-9)? Mark is not so much interested in proving the truth of Jesus' resurrection as in evoking the sense of awe and mystery surrounding it. We might do well to balance, at least, the more blatant and trumpet-like announcement with this tradition.

In his understatement of the story—Mark does not give us a resurrection *appearance* at all!—the Gospel writer suggests, in his own way, that this is *God's* doing. Who can help but tremble and keep the holy silence? The Russian Orthodox Church, before it displays the full glory of its celebration of the resurrection, keeps the Easter vigil. It is in that mood that Mark brings us to the tomb where we feel in the emptiness of the place our absolute dependence upon God. Perhaps we are never closer to the Easter celebration than in that fearful, hopeful, vulnerable mood in which we wait for God to move the stone which is too big for us.

The major celebration of Easter among the Moravians of Winston-Salem, North Carolina, takes place in the cemetery, or "God's Acre" as they call it. There the saints have been buried for generations under simple white stones which bear testimony by their simplicity to the faith of a plain people and to the "democracy of death." Between the love feasts of Holy Week and Easter morning the people come with brushes and pails to scrub the stones, and on Holy Saturday every stone gets a bouquet of fresh flowers. And then on Easter Day, before dawn, the whole community meets at the church and to the subdued sound of brass bands, they march to the cemetery. Among the orderly rows of marble, in the very teeth of death, they celebrate the resurrection of Jesus Christ from the dead. It is as if that were the only proper place to have such a celebration, out there among the tombs where death is unavoidable, even in the dawning light of an April day among the people's flowers that have not yet begun to wilt. It is the *mood* which strikes a worshiper there. It is not brassy: even the bands sound slightly cold as they play antiphonally from hill to hill. There is hardly a sermon at all, mostly just the familiar words. It is all understated, and there is about it a quiet waiting, for the sun to come up, and for more.

Easter Evening *or* Easter Monday

Lutheran	*Roman Catholic*	*Episcopal*	*Pres./UCC/Chr.*	*Methodist/COC*
Dan. 12:1c-3	Acts. 2:14, 22-32	Acts 2:14, 22-32		
1 Cor. 5:6-8				
Luke 24:13-49	Matt. 28:8-15	Matt. 28:9-15		

EXEGESIS

First Lesson: Dan. 12:1c-3. Who are "your people"? And why are they in need of deliverance?

The Book of Daniel was written shortly before 164 B.C., in a period when external political and military might (the Seleucid ruler Antiochus Epiphanes) got linked up with the attractiveness of Hellenistic culture to threaten the preservation of the Jewish faith. The author was one of the Chasidim who initially greeted the Maccabean resistance as God-inspired, only to find that it too unfolded unidimensionally on the humanly political and military level. At the time of writing he lives in a group of faithful Jews who refuse to defile themselves "with the King's rich food" (1:18), as they search for the meaning of a brutal history which finds them not infrequently mourning the death of loved ones slain by the Seleucid army.

In order to read the author's book from the "inside," therefore, we need to imagine ourselves hiding from Seleucid soldiers by huddling together in a Judean cave with fellow Chasidim who, in the face of such brutal experiences, have come to believe without a doubt that history is doomed to remain an enigma both to persecuted and to persecutor if their eyes are fixed solely on what they perceive to be events transpiring on an earthly stage (2:10; 2:27; 5:8, etc.), as though there were a human orb from which God were absent. These Chasidim are sure the enigma is interpreted only when God grants stereoptic vision, enabling one to see both the (dependent) earthly stage and the (determinative) heavenly one. Such God-given stereoptic vision, is, in fact, the genius of "apocalyptic," and the seed bed in which the crucial hope for resurrection took root and grew. Antiochus Epiphanes proudly saw only the corpses of the defeated weak ones, and, correspondingly, he saw only his own might and glory. Moreover, he successfully invited seducible Jews to see exactly what he saw. However, to the suffering and martyred Chasidim God granted (and grants) quite a different (angle of) vision, enabling them to see "that the Most High God rules the kingdom of men" (5:21; cf. 11:32b) and that while they themselves may "fall by sword and flame, by captivity and plunder" (11:33), God and his purpose for them are *never* in fact defeated. He sends a hand to write on the wall words which spell the doom of monoptic earthly rulers who preen their own feathers while violating their fellow human beings (chap. 5). And *in his time* he will deliver the

:hasidim who are living, will raise to everlasting life their comrades who ave fallen, and will raise to judgment the persecutors and their ac- omplices. It is, thus, not surprising that Daniel sees a general (or cor- orate) resurrection, for the hope of resurrection is not at all at home in n individualistic frame of reference. It is, rather, part of God's word to he otherwise hopeless enigma of corporate human destiny in the face of vil.

Second Lesson: 1 Cor. 5:6-8. None of Paul's letters shows more clearly han 1 Corinthians the interpenetration of what we call "ethics" and what ve call "theology." In the course of the first four chapters Paul confronts he Corinthian Christians with the essential dimensions of their near postasy precisely by indicating God's present and powerful activity in reas where they thought they were themselves doing the deciding (recall he monoptic view of Daniel's persecutor, and, more important, note arefully the studied imbalance of 1 Cor. 1:18; the jolting penultimate lause of 3:23; the scorn Paul pours on the Corinthians' discriminatory owers in 4:3). The *Christian* gospel (2:1 ff.) does not describe the novement from a heteronomous to an autonomous conscience, thus nabling human beings to celebrate themselves and their potential with quanimity (4:8). *That* gospel is rather God's powerful action (1:18) in nd through the ignominiously crucified Christ, and in and through pparently weak and foolish apostles in whose daily death for others the ruly liberating life of Jesus is effectively manifested (15:31; cf. 2 Cor. 4:7 f.).

Now, in chap. 5, Paul turns to a specific instance of the Corinthian endency to celebrate naked human vitality: A member of the church has shacked up" with his stepmother, and a good many of the Corinthians re proudly boasting over his and their liberation. Paul's horror (focused onsiderably more on the boasting than on the deed) reveals again the elation of *the indicative* of God's powerful invasion to *the imperative* of thical command: "*Cleanse out* the old leaven . . . just as in fact you *are* nleavened." *The* event has now occurred. At Passover time, the time vhen Israel's hopes for deliverance were brought to fever pitch, God in act delivered us from the reign of malice and evil. The community is lready unleavened (cleansed) from the power of self-deceit by Christ's aschal death. Paul, therefore, in *exhorting* them to celebrate not them- elves, but rather the Paschal Easter Feast of the crucified one who is iod's power and God's wisdom (1:24), exhorts them only to be what in act God has already caused them to be: people who are singularly ocused not upon themselves but upon God's truth. Good Friday and aster form the locus of the transforming miracle which is "in us" only ecause God has placed us "in it."

Gospel: Luke 24:13-49. No single chapter in Luke's two-volume work more revealing of his theological commitments than this final one of the ospel. He carefully structures it from three primary literary units, the story of the empty tomb (23:56b–24:11), the Emmaus story (vv. 13-35), and the story of a Jerusalem appearance (vv. 36-43). In and around these traditional units Luke accents certain points of crucial importance to him. In each he portrays a movement from perplexity and consternation (vv. 4, 21, 37) to the granting of a new hermeneutic (vv. 5b ff., 27, 45) and climactically to the knowledge of Christ's resurrection (vv. 31, 34 f., 46, 52). God's lordship over all of history (recall the First Lesson from Daniel) is now grasped in the new hermeneutic which focuses the message of scripture in three infinitives (vv. 46 f.): The Christ is *to suffer*, and *to rise* from the dead (Luke's volume no. 1); and in his name forgiveness of sins is *to be preached* to all nations (Luke's volume no. 2). The third infinitive is no less a part of God's effecting his lordship over history than are the first two. But where is he to find those who will do the preaching?

This question leads us back to the second of the traditional units, the famous Emmaus story, which may have a new ring when read on the heels of the two lessons. Cleopas and his companion are not strangers to the kind of Chasidic hope which burned in the breast of Daniel. Moreover, for them, this hope has received a powerful impetus in Jesus' preaching and deeds, so that they have begun to suppose that God's deliverance and vindication are to appear momentarily (cf. Luke 19:11). At this point comes the Pasch and the taut eschatological stretching of the nerve of hope. And then what? The bubble bursts, the picture shatters, the hope evaporates in the merciless afternoon sun. God's prophet of imminent deliverance is himself arrested and summarily executed.

At this juncture one supposes that the disciples could have returned to Daniel *et al.* to find comfort in the hope of resurrection. "Together with other fallen martyrs," they could have said to themselves, "Jesus will be raised in the (general) resurrection." But God puts his stamp on this eschatological hope, while also transforming it. He raises Jesus from the dead *now* and sends him to the distraught disciples in order to make them into his witnesses who shall march in the power of the Spirit from Jerusalem to the ends of the earth. "To rise" is the middle of the three programmatic infinitives (vv. 46 f.), binding the other two together. It is the risen Lord and he alone who opens eyes (v. 31) and minds (v. 45), so that persons are transformed from disciples who have imperfectly learned Jesus' teachings into witnesses through whom God in fact effects his lordship over the whole of human history (Acts). The resurrection of Jesus is not an isolatable event, a freak happening which may be investigated in and of itself, or even a *private* warming of the heart to which an individual may return over and over. It is God's re-creative deed by which he inaugurates the communal transformation to life which is his will and intention for all humankind.

HOMILETICAL INTERPRETATION

These days if you had seen what Luke's two travelers had witnessed you could more easily divert yourself. There is always television, which numbs us to human suffering by showing it every day and then helps us forget about it by flip-of-the-switch distraction. How much can be put out of mind, and how much lost, sitting in overstuffed chairs stuffing ourselves with our minds completely engaged by the cool medium? It is hard to imagine anything that could be reported on the Friday evening news that we couldn't live with through a weekend of electronic diversion.

We may, nevertheless, be able to enter into the story of Cleopas and his friend as they leave Jerusalem where hopes have risen so high only to be brought so low. Where do we go when our hopes have been dashed, when a beaten up garbage can expresses us? It is bad enough when your private ship of dreams runs aground, but what do you do when the *world* you have come to believe in falls down around your head and the best people you know suffer? If we stopped to think about it we would probably count ourselves lucky to have one friend to walk along with us and talk it out. Luke offers us more even than that, and the other lections point toward finding our real identity and making sense out of what happens by seeing God at work.

Dan. 12:1c-3. Who could fault a newscaster for signing off every weekday: "And that's the way it is"? What else is a news reporter to say about the sorry scene he must survey day after day? Only occasionally, when some poetic reporter forgets the news and turns the camera on someone who has stopped watching television and lives off by himself or herself someplace close to the earth or animals or God, do we get some slight view past the way it is to the way it really is, or at least might be. And we wish we could go "on the road" more often! But, for the most part, to read the newspapers and watch the evening news is to become what Richard R. Niebuhr calls "radial man," who is constantly hooked up by the media to the sorry show of the way it is.

That is not the way it is with the writer of Daniel. The writer is in a state of mind not unlike that of a black slave singing about freedom to the rhythm of chopping cotton. What this Jew has seen in Jerusalem does not let him rest, and his imagination is stretched to its limits by the disparity between the events of the day and his faith that God is the Lord of history. Vision, more real to the prophet than the events that a newscaster would report, moves him to hope and to chaste living. He speaks of the "book," in which are written the individual names of all those who have kept themselves unsullied. Even those whose bodies have been reduced to dust will awake and will shine as the stars. These are the "wise" who know that the way things appear on the bald face of history is not the way things are in God's economy, and that to do right and to try to turn others to righteousness is not, even in such times as when the high altar is defiled, a waste of time.

Here is John of Patmos, holding out for a new heaven and a new earth on the very island from which the Caesars quarried stone for their eternal city. Here is the dogged hopefulness of Dilsey in Faulkner's *The Sound and the Fury*, as she is able to endure the world because she has seen "the first and the last." Here is the church, as human as underwear and sometimes as quaint as prunes, demonstrating in its life that the kingdom of this world is become the kingdom of our Lord and of his Christ.

1 Cor. 5:6-8. Here again we are pressed by the questions: What *is*? Who are *we*? Paul takes on a case of immorality in the church, and the passage seems a bit foreign to us. When did we last see anyone excommunicated or "churched"? It is not so much the details of the matter (which the makers of the lectionary have conveniently omitted) or Paul's high standard of church discipline which concerns us on this Easter evening as his rationale for purity of life among Christians. Paul says quite simply that our behavior is part and parcel of our celebration of this holy festival.

As a matter of fact, Paul says, you *are* free from sin, "unleavened." That's the way it is! Morris Niedenthal calls it "the grammar of the gospel." You *are* set free in Christ, forgiven and redeemed; now you *can* behave that way! We are prone to reverse that grammar, to make the imperative prior and to turn the indicative toward the conditional. When we do that, "God is good, therefore be good," becomes "Be good, and then God will be good to you." But Paul never falters in this matter. It is what God has done which is decisive. Paul spends the first eleven chapters of Romans showing how God's grace overcomes our sin, abounding all the more where our sin abounds, and it is only in chapter twelve that he moves to "Therefore, I beseech you, brethren, to present your bodies a living sacrifice . . . by the *mercies* of God . . ." As God raised Jesus from the dead, so he acts in unconditional grace toward us, overcoming by his power both sin and death. It is from that knowledge that we act, not in fear but in the confidence of people who celebrate *God's* triumph at Easter. Edmund Steimle has well said: "Behind and beneath the summons, the call to commitment, the charge to act responsibly, must be the word of the gospel addressed to the 'need of man for a basic security from within which he can be free for change.' "[1] Does not the whole ethical imperative of our faith unfold from this day? "And every man that has this hope in him purifies himself, even as he is pure" (1 John 3:3).

Luke 24:13-49. It is a long way from the opening of Luke's closing chapter to its end. The evangelist begins with Mark's story of the fearful women and ends with the disciples embarked on a mission to the world. Three distinct accounts move us along this road: the empty tomb, the travelers to Emmaus, and Jesus showing his feet and hands to his disciples in the upper room. These stories meet us in the various moods in which we come to Easter. But in the whole of the Gospels, does any story help us to celebrate more than Luke's narrative of the two friends who, even as they talk it over, are overtaken, fed, enlightened, and sent running with good news? Don't we still walk along wondering, speaking of snowed-under hopes, trying to make sense of it, at least trying to be with each other?

1. Edmund Steimle (ed.), *Renewal in the Pulpit* (Philadelphia: Fortress Press, 1966) p. xii.

And then he stands beside us, opening the scriptures and breaking the bread and warming up hearts that are cold and giving life to spirits as dry as a navy bean. This story says a lot more to us than some would say if we were in the shoes of those two heads-down travelers: "Shoulders back, head up, stomach in; one, two, three . . . ."

It stood in the front gallery at the Museum of Modern Art, so that I could go by to see it without even going into the building. Sometimes as I stood there peering through the glass a passerby would stop and try to see it. One guy looked at me sideways and then asked, "What is it, a wasp?" Like Mama Younger and her droopy geranium, there were days when I needed to see "Large Soft Fan." It seemed, as Mama said, to express me. It stood about twelve feet high, maybe ten, and it was one of those old black fans that used to turn slowly back and forth in your grandmother's parlor like someone listening to a conversation and turning from speaker to speaker, or like someone watching a slow ping pong game. "Large Soft Fan" drooped. Its black plastic blades and the guard around them seemed to need fanning, and "Large Soft Fan," despite its size and what it obviously was, seemed about to collapse at any moment. It had a great long power cord, as big around as a fire hose, and at the end a plug as big as a fireplug. But it wasn't plugged in, and there was about the whole thing a great helplessness. It was beautiful.

Cleopas and his friend were simply going home, but by that Easter evening they found themselves back in Jerusalem, and who knows where they went from there. Luke's story suggests the birth of the church, and we are aware already of the power that will be poured out at Pentecost. The meal which they share in Emmaus that evening is for us—whatever it was for Luke—a eucharist. And we have difficulty thinking that it was not so for Luke: the restraint of the account, the evening hour, and the familiar language—"He took bread and blessed and broke it, and gave it to them." Luke does not let us forget that this is God's doing. These people had lost heart and were speaking of their hopes in the past tense. Easter breaks in upon them, as Bornkamm sees:

> The men and women who encounter the risen Christ in the Easter stories have come to an end of their wisdom. They are alarmed and disturbed by his death, mourners wandering about the grave of their Lord in their helpless love, and trying like the women at the grave with pitiable means to stay the process and odour of corruption, disciples huddled fearfully together like animals in a thunderstorm. So it is, too, with the two disciples on the way to Emmaus on the evening of Easter day; their last hopes, too, are destroyed. One would have to turn all the Easter stories upside down, if one wanted to present them in the words of Faust: "They are celebrating the resurrection of the Lord, for they themselves are resurrected."[2]

They are, in fact, more like "Large Soft Fan" until they are *overtaken* with Easter's joy, fed and cheered at the Lord's hand. And when that happens, everything becomes possible.

2. Günther Bornkamm, *Jesus of Nazareth* (New York: Harper & Bros., 1960), p. 184.

The Second Sunday of Easter

Lutheran	*Roman Catholic*	*Episcopal*	*Pres./UCC/Chr.*	*Methodist/COCU*
Acts 4:32-35	Acts 4:32-35	Acts 4:32-35	Acts 4:32-35	Acts 4:32-37
1 John 5:1-6	1 John 5:1-6	1 John 5:1-6	1 John 5:1-6	1 John 5:1-6
John 20:19-31	John 20:19-31	John 20:19-31	Matt. 28:11-20	John 20:19-31

EXEGESIS

First Lesson: Acts 4:32-35. This lesson follows easily on the heels of the Gospel for Easter Evening. The community of witnesses, whom God is transforming to life and through whom he is transforming the whole world, has now encountered sharp opposition and persecution. Will such events turn it aside from "the way"? Luke is sure that left to its own power and wisdom it would indeed be turned aside (5:38 f.). But God creates the community of his witnesses in the invincible and closely linked events of his raising Jesus from the dead and of his sending his Spirit upon the church.

Regarding the former, note carefully the opening sentences of Peter's speech in Acts 3:12 ff., particularly 3:13. When was it that God "glorified his servant Jesus"? Luke probably intends a double reference (a) to God's deed of raising Jesus from the dead, (b) to the present dimension of that deed in God's making Peter a witness through whom he (God) raises to health the lame beggar. Jesus' resurrection is both back there and here now.

Regarding the latter, Luke mentions the Holy Spirit's filling the community not only at Pentecost (2:4), but also here in the midst of persecution (4:31). It is, then, *both* in the contemporary power of Jesus' resurrection *and* in the renewed coming of the Spirit that the witnesses act and speak with joy and without fear.

Some of the inner-community dimensions of this picture are now given in the paragraph which forms the lesson. In fact, the dual character of the community's source—the resurrection of Jesus of Nazareth, and the sending of the Spirit—is reflected as a literary problem in the paragraph. Commentators have long puzzled over v. 33. It seems to interrupt a well-structured report about a pattern of communal sharing brought about by the coming of the Spirit. Clearly, however, Luke did not see it as an interruption, but rather as a link. The miracles which God powerfully effects on the public scene (4:33a) by glorifying the risen Jesus *in* the testimony of his witnesses find their inner-community counterpart in a miraculous economic sharing to which the young church is led by the Spirit (4:31-32; cf. 2:44). This sharing—certainly not "an unsuccessful experiment in communism"; note the juxtaposition of 4:33b and 34a: God's grace leads to the sharing, so that it is not "man's deed"—is effected both by holding property in common (v. 32) and by some persons (note 12:12) selling property to raise money for the needy. Luke is probably consciously aware that in these deeds God fulfills his promise of Deut. 15:4, for the LXX of that verse is essentially reproduced in Acts 4:34a.

Second Lesson: 1 John 5:1-6. It may be well to read this text backwards as well as forwards. The author of 1 John had to do contest with gnostics who denied the reality of Jesus' death, an error into which we may ourselves easily slip in a post-Easter euphoria. By the words of v. 6 the author wants to make clear that the cross was not merely a door through which the heavenly redeemer passed momentarily. He really *died*. Nor does the resurrection obliterate the cross. It is the Jesus who really died who is the risen Son of God.

Moving back, we can see that while the author's gnostic opponents divorce from one another (a) questions of belief and (b) issues of everyday life in community, the author perceives an inextricable connection between Christology and community ethics. His opponents, the gnostics (2:19), deny that the earthly Jesus is the heavenly Christ, *and* they haughtily look only to their own interests (4:20). In the author's view by contrast, to affirm that the Son of God is none other than Jesus the crucified one (in 5:1 the word Jesus receives the emphasis) is to die to "the world" of self-interest and pride (2:15-17) and to live in the practical love of the brothers and sisters (5:1 ff.). If one is offended by the fact that the author speaks of love *within* the community, he may want carefully to consider the import of 5:1b. Pondering one's own experience in family life (also in re-reading John Steinbeck's *East of Eden*), one must realize that to say that every child who loves the parent loves also the siblings is in fact to speak of a miracle which is to be observed and experienced only in the *family of God* where God effects a birth that overcomes the world of self-interest and hate (5:4). The author is well aware of the inherent integrity of the God-Neighbor-Self triangle as he says of the miracle of human love: "We love, *because* he first loved us." Just as self-interest and hate spring precisely from disobedience vis a vis God ("I shall set up on my own"), so brother/sister love springs from obedience (faith) to God who grants to such active faith the victory over evil in the life of everyday love.

Gospel: John 20:19-31. It is instructive to compare the original ending of John's Gospel (chap. 21 is probably an appendix, an important one to be sure, from a later hand) with the ending of Luke commented on above (Easter Evening) and below (Easter III). For making such comparisons, use, if possible, a parallel of the four Gospels. In the section of John 20 under perview the evangelist seems to have employed (1) a piece of old tradition, that of Jesus' appearance to the disciples in Jerusalem (vv. 19-23), which is also reflected in Luke 24:36-43 (cf. Mark 16:14). He follows this piece (2) with a two-paragraph story of his own composition designed to dramatize the emergence of doubt among Christians of his own day in the late first century (vv. 24-29) and (3) with the conclusion to his Gospel (vv. 30-31).

In the traditional piece (1) Jesus utters three sayings, all of which have essential counterparts in Luke: (a) John 20:21; Luke 24:48. (b) John 20:22; Luke 24:49; Acts 2:4; (c) John 20:23; Luke 24:47 (cf. Matt. 16:19 and 18:18). Yet the fourth evangelist has heard the sayings in his own setting, as is particularly evident in the case of the first two. (a) Luke hears the risen Lord tell his disciples that they are "witnesses of these things"; John (v. 21) hears words about the disciples' being "sent" by one who in this Gospel so often refers to himself as having been sent by the Father. (b) Luke hears the risen Lord promise later to send the Spirit; John (v. 22) hears him utter words awesome beyond measure, as, in the moment, he breathes the Spirit upon them (cf. the five Paraclete sayings in chaps. 14-16 and the motif of Jesus' ascension in chap. 17). We shall return to these sayings in a moment.

Searching for the fourth evangelist's major intentions in our text, one may recall that the tradition of a Jerusalem appearance was worded, in at least one form, in order to combat the threat of docetism (see Luke 24:39b and 43). This threat seems to be of no concern to John. He can calmly portray a body of marvelous powers, able to pass through closed doors, while elsewhere he speaks explicitly of perceivable parts of a tangible body. He is interested not in the nature of the body, but rather in the identity of the risen Lord with the man of Nazareth. Yet even this is not his major concern.

That concern emerges, rather, in the remarkably bold reshaping of the traditional sayings behind vv. 21 and 22, and in the linking of those boldly reshaped sayings to the paragraphs about Thomas. It is precisely this linking which should help us answer the old question whether the utterance of v. 21 refers only to the eleven (ten?) or to all Christians. If John's concern in the Thomas story centers in the emergence in his own time of debilitating doubt within the Christian circle, he will scarcely be interested in reshaping the saying behind v. 21 in a way which refers only to the eleven. Thus, the sayings of vv. 21 and 22 are so deeply awesome precisely because in them John hears the risen Lord (a) send every Christian into the world (15:18-27) *just as* the Father sent him into the world, (b) breathe into *every* Christian the Holy Spirit, the Paraclete.

In order to sense the *full* import of these twin utterances one must turn back to the farewell discourses (13:31-17:26) which are informed by many concerns, one of which is the fact that, with his ascension to the Father, Jesus is leaving his disciples behind in a hostile and menacing world. (He explicitly does not ask the Father to take them out of the world, 17:15.) Is it any wonder that the disciples are anxious (14:1)? Consider the words of Jesus in 17:11 f.:

> And now I am no longer in the world . . . While I was with them, I kept them in thy name . . .

The question is, Who will keep them now?

And, as if to make this question completely unbearable, the Lord proceeds, not only to leave his followers in the world, but in fact to send them into the world (17:18). In the face of these developments the disciples will not only be assailed by anxiety but also plagued by doubt.

Now, return to the Lord's utterances in 20:21 f. There are two *gifts*! The sending of the disciples into the world *just as* the Father sent Jesus Christ into the world and the immediate breathing onto the disciples of *the Spirit*. Is the Christian *left alone* in alien territory? Hardly. He is actively *sent* at the authority of the Father, and he is *given the Spirit* who is Jesus' "double" (14:26; 16:13 f.). As Thomas soon learns, the immediacy of this sending and the immediacy of this Spirit leave no room for insulating factors which breed fear and doubt. He who sends the disciples also gives the Spirit who is the *praesentia Christi*. Hence the climactic, face-to-face confession: "My Lord and my God."

HOMILETICAL INTERPRETATION

The trumpet which celebrates the church's new life in the resurrection plays a triplet, three inseparable yet distinct notes: Jesus is present among his disciples; they have everything in common; fear is overcome and the Holy Spirit is present in power. The living Lord is present with God's gathered, sharing people, and the victory he has won over the powers of death is celebrated by the cripple who walks and the people who are together, first behind closed doors and then to the ends of the earth. Though the last two lines limp for putting the wrong foot first, and peter out into a mere "something," the quatrain holds:

> The ground of all celebration
> is a circle of people
> who believe in one another
> and in something together.[1]

Acts 4:32-35. Could we live together without the cash nexus around which society coheres? How do we answer Eliot's question:

> When the Stranger says: "What is the meaning of this city?
> Do you huddle close together because you love each other?"
> What will you answer? "We all dwell together
> To make money from each other"? or "This is a community"?[2]

Isn't our status in society directly related to what we own? Would we have any community *or* identity without property lines? The communes which have sprung up in recent years have, at least, roused in us feelings of ambivalence. We cannot readily see how such a community could stay together, and we wonder if we wouldn't lose our identity in an environment like Walden II. Who would we be if we put everything we have in one pot?

An American traveling in New Zealand was warned by a European New Zealander, a *pakeha*: "The Maori people are shiftless and have no ambi-

1. Ross Snyder, *Contemporary Celebration* (New York and Nashville: Abingdon, 1971), p. 36.
2. T. S. Eliot, "Choruses from 'The Rock,' " *The Complete Poems and Plays* (New York: Harcourt, Brace and Co., 1952), p. 103.

tion, and you ought not to judge our country by them." What the traveler found, after living among the Maori for a few months, was that these polynesian New Zealanders had a different set of values from the *pakehas* in both New Zealand and America. The Maori person values, above all, talking and playing and eating with family and friends. A Maori father likes nothing better than to stay home all day telling stories to his children. A Maori's status is not determined by how much property he has, but by how well he is related to family and community. The quality of life in the community determines the Maori's attitude toward money (and the work that gets it), rather than the reverse.

The early church is bound together in the joy of the risen Lord, in the power of the Spirit, and so they share everything. That is the sequence: "And all who believed were together and had all things in common . . . ." (Acts 2:44). This is the community of teaching *and* fellowship, breaking of bread *and* prayers, daily worship *and* laying it on the line for people in need. In a community like that, it doesn't even occur to someone to say, "That's mine." Isolation from the community, as Ananias and Sapphira learn, is the way of death (cf. Acts 5).

Notice how it is put: ". . . no one said that any of the things that he possessed was his own, but they had everything in common." Doesn't that offend the works righteousness by which we lay heavy demands on people without supporting them in a nourishing community? Edith Wharton, in her novel *Ethan Frome*, paints a picture of Starkfield, the wintry gray town in Puritan New England which demands hard work and duty and even self-sacrifice of Ethan but offers him no real sustenance for living up to its law. Starkfield is all demand and no grace; it is Sinclair Lewis's unsatisfying society which demands that Babbitt, at all cost to himself and the humanity of those around him, be a "success" on *its* terms. Babbitt lives in our Starkfield, does he not?

But we see in the early church a group of people who have found a new kind of status. They move beyond a mere jockeying for position or the grudging admonition to "pay your own way" and "carry your own weight." This is not the petty economy of "If you don't work you don't eat" or the dues-paying club where status is for sale. This is the utter generosity of people who have found a new set of values. The community itself is a gift, God's gracious creation in Jesus Christ, and it is received, valued, and shared as such. What's yours is mine and what's mine is yours because what we have together is more valuable than anything I could have apart from this community. With healing and joy breaking out among them, these Christians got their priorities straight.

1 John 5:1-6. We could, of course, press the idea of community to the point of equating salvation with "togetherness." Life in the church too easily becomes, as Nels Ferré once suggested, living under an umbrella of mutual congratulation, intellectual coziness, and pot luck suppers which does not so much overcome the world as fend it off. The preacher in the *New Yorker* cartoon stands in a contemporary pulpit proclaiming "I'm OK and you're OK," and his enthusiastic congregation answers, "Amen, brother, you're OK and we're OK." That is not the picture we get from the author of 1 John.

It is a real, unavoidable world in which everything is *not* OK, and the writer holds our noses to that. The world is in the power of the "evil one" (5:19), and it is the kind of world that actually put to death the very life and light of God (cf. 1:1 ff.). No more than Jesus escaped real suffering and death at the hands of the world can we expect to live like disembodied spirits in a docetic church. This church that prays daily in celebration of Jesus' victory and rejoices in the Spirit is still *in* the world.

How do we overcome the world? More characteristically the writer would answer with what Frederick Buechner calls "consonants" rather than a blatant vowel (cf. *The Alphabet of Grace*). The writer would tell us to "have fellowship," "walk in the light," "love one another," "do right." But here it is "our faith," words which seem to flash like a neon sign with a blinking arrow pointing toward *us*. In fact, however, the writer holds together the victory of faith—"Who is it that overcomes the world but he who believes that Jesus is the Son of God"—with more homely words: "We know that we have passed out of death into life, because we love the brethren." The writer does not allow any separation between "our faith" and "loving the brethren," as if one were a noun which we have and the other something we do. Even God's commandments are both gift *to* us and demand *upon* us, as Jesus Christ is both Savior and Lord, the Spirit both impetus and power, our being together—kind, tenderhearted, forgiving one another—inseparable from the gift *and* command of forgiveness.

John 20:19-31. Here are the disciples in shuttered seclusion on the evening of that day. And here is the bold confession, "My Lord and my God." In so brief a story we follow the trajectory of faith, from fear to joy, from doubt to confession, from retreat to witness, from asking a sign to bowing down.

Here is the embryonic church, huddled between hoping and not daring to hope. Mary Magdalene has brought the news: "I have seen the Lord." But who can believe it? They have not seen him, and a knock at the door would heighten their fears more than raise their hopes. But can we doubt that hope is there, that they would be gathered at all were not the first movement toward faith already afoot, the first blush of believing already on them? There is no knock at the door, but Jesus comes and stands among them, shows them his wounds, speaks peace, and tells them, in so many words, to unlock the doors: "As the Father has sent me, even so I send you." The wounded healer, the crucified king, gives them freedom and with it a mission to make freedom mean something. The stone is rolled away, the doors are open. The power they need will be theirs as they receive the Holy Spirit, and the authority promised to Peter the Rock is promised this little band: "If you forgive the sins of any, they are forgiven . . . ." (cf. Matt. 16:19). But how can they receive such peace and power on the third day after they have seen that vulnerable flesh on the cross and their hopes sealed in the tomb? Jesus stands among them, showing them his hands and side, speaking peace and power, sending them out. Is there any sight they could see, any experience they could go through, which cannot be accommodated by the suffering, death, and resurrection of the one who has been their friend and teacher and is now their Lord and Savior? Will not the story of the cross be adequate to the ends of the earth and the end of time so that the mission on which they are sent is provided for by the very message which they are sent to tell? "Take up the cross and follow me" is both final succour and ultimate demand.

Eight days later when they are gathered in the same house with the doors shut—but here there is no mention of their being afraid—Jesus stands among them speaking peace.[1] He speaks at once to faith and doubt, to the Thomas that is in them all and in us all. "Peace be with you," Jesus says, and he invites Thomas not only to see but to touch with his hands: "Do not be faithless but believing." And Thomas, who tradition says went all the way to India from that room, speaks for them all, for the whole church: "My Lord and my God." In the world they all had, as Jesus said, tribulation. But before they left the room, the world had in fact, in them and among them, been overcome.

The Third Sunday of Easter

Lutheran	*Roman Catholic*	*Episcopal*	*Pres./UCC/Chr.*	*Methodist/COC*
Acts 3:13-15, 17-19	Acts 3:13-15, 17-19	Acts 3:13-15, 17-19	Acts 3:13-15, 17-19	Acts 3:13-15, 17-19
1 John 1:1-2:2	1 John 2:1-5a	1 John 1:3-2:5a	1 John 2:1-6	1 John 2:1-6
Luke 24:36-49	Luke 24:35-48	Luke 24:35-48	Luke 24:36-49	Luke 24:35-49

EXEGESIS

First Lesson: Acts 3:13-15, 17-19. The Book of Acts—is it surprising?—contains its own supply of apostolic miracle stories. It also presents several times a brief encapsulation of what Luke understands to be the core of apostolic preaching about Jesus. And finally, Acts presents, as is well known, several rather finely developed "speeches" of some length. Our text is one of the passages in which these three literary forms are brought together.

(1) The miracle story presents the basic outline expected: I. A Hopeless Situation (3:2); II. The Miracle (3:6 f.). III. Confirmation (3:8-10). Prior to Luke's editing, the story probably concerned only Peter and the lame man ("with John" looks secondary in v. 4; Peter does all of the talking and acting; Luke is concerned to have two witnesses appear before the Sanhedrin in 4:5 ff., especially 4:20). There is also little doubt

1. See the hymn, "They Cast Their Nets in Galilee," *Pilgrim Hymnal*, p. 340.

that in its traditional form the story placed emphasis on the healing act "in the name" of Jesus Christ. For Luke, as for the traditioner from whose hand the story came to Luke, the "name" of Christ is one of the loci in which the risen Lord exercises his gracious power on earth. It is not the name of Luke's culture but rather of his Lord.

(2) The brief encapsulation of "the Jesus Kerygma" may be seen when one compares 3:13b-15 with 2:23-24, 32; 4:10; 5:30-32; and 13:29-31. It seems to have three major elements: (a) The Jewish authorities *delivered* Jesus up, (b) but God reversed that line of action by *raising* him from the dead, and (c) by bringing into existence faithful *witnesses.* Luke never presents this encapsulated kerygma by itself. He always ties it to a setting by means of at least two of its elements. The word "raised" in v. 15 points back to the word "glorified" in v. 13, which, in turn, points back to the miracle.

(3) Peter's speech (vv. 12-26) contains "the Jesus Kerygma," but also goes far beyond it. Compare Acts 2:14 ff.; 4:8 ff.; 5:29 ff.; 13:16 ff.

Luke shows both great literary skill and theological potency in the combining (and composing) of these three elements. Regarding the possibility of a double entendre in the word "glorified" (v. 13), see the second paragraph of the exegesis for Acts 4:32-35 (Easter II). Beyond that one notices that Luke extends the miracle story and the brief kerygma into a speech which indicates that it is *God's grace* and nothing else which *calls man to repentance* (v. 26). There is no presupposition which the lame man must fulfill before he can be healed. God simply chooses to glorify his servant Jesus by bringing people to health. Do you believe that God's grace precedes your faith? Believing that is what repentance is all about.

Second Lesson: 1 John 1:1–2:2 (or 2:6?). Re-read the exegesis of John 20:19-31 (Easter II), especially the comments about the farewell discourses and their importance for understanding John 20:21 f. Now, come to 1 John. We are listening to a preacher who has faced the threat of being left as an orphan (John 14:18), and who, in the face of that threat, has been allowed to hear (note the primacy of this biblical verb), to see, and even to touch the life which was from the beginning. Where and How?

Part of the answer is given by the literary probability that our author is a preacher who has lived with the fourth Gospel so closely for so long that its message has permeated his manner of speaking as well as his theology. Beyond this it is clear that the "major character" of that Gospel has himself spoken to this preacher through its pages, and in those moments the preacher has heard and seen and touched the one who says so majestically,

> I am the resurrection and the life; he who believes in me, though he die, yet shall he live, and whoever lives and believes in me shall never die. (John 11:25 f.)

Our preacher has also heard this one say:

> I am the light of the world; he who follows me will not walk in darkness, but will have the light of life. (John 8:12)

The one who is life did not remain in a distant sphere, but rather came to be manifest and to be heard, seen, touched. The preacher has heard, seen, touched. He stands, therefore, on solid ground.

But one notices also that all of these verbs of perception are plural. It is *we* who have heard and seen and touched. While one can be sure that 1 John was written by an individual (2:1, etc.), he does not understand his essential existence to be individual in character. He has heard the one who speaks in the pages of the (fourth) Gospel *as* that Gospel is read in the Christian fellowship. It is not in a lonely trance, therefore, but in the fellowship that he and his brothers and sisters perceive.

Perceive whom and perceive what? In our author's setting the second question is as necessary as the first. For he lives in the real world in contact with people who use a word dear to his heart—fellowship—while showing in their daily lives a pride and self-assurance which annuls the gift of life. They are not irreligious people. Exactly the opposite. Indeed one of their favorite sayings has an unexceptionable ring to it:

> We have fellowship with him (1 John 1:6).

There is a tip-off, however, in another of their sayings:

> We have fellowship with him and are without sin (1 John 1:6, 8).

And while they are very lively people who believe they have discovered their own essential congeniality with the eternal light, perhaps intending to refer to nothing less than John 8:12 (above) as they say

> We are in the light (2:9),

they straightway prove that they are still in the darkness by showing no love for the brother.

Our author makes no compromise with such people (2:19); yet neither is he mesmerized into a preoccupation with them. His concern is for the building up of the fellowship of Christians who are in every way forgiven sinners, and whose love for one another springs precisely from their knowledge that in their daily confession of their sins they are bound to the Lord who faithfully forgives both them and every other member of the human family (2:2).

Gospel: Luke 24:36-49. The Gospel for today consists literarily of a pre-Lucan tradition regarding Jesus' post-resurrection appearance in Jerusalem (vv. 36-43) and of a penultimate paragraph in which Luke is able to communicate in powerfully dramatic form major dimensions of the story of Jesus and his new people (vv. 44-49). For literary analysis see the exegesis on Luke 24:13-49 for Easter Evening.

It is not difficult to see that Luke has allowed the traditional piece to set the scene for the crucial pronouncement of the risen Lord which follows it. In its pre-Lucan use the traditional piece clearly had some anti-docetic dimensions (note vv. 39 and 43). In the technical sense these seem of no great concern to Luke. He is intent, rather, on the motif of *empowered continuity*. The path followed by the one who healed the sick and who taught the way of the Lord did not find its end in the cross. On the contrary, that same one now comes to his frightened, erstwhile followers and puts their feet on the extension of that path. How?

In the first instance by showing them the path in a book! In its long journey (Acts 1:8) the church will need again and again to search the scriptures for guidance (a lamp to the path); and this need makes necessary, in turn, a true hermeneutic. Hence Luke's concern with the hermeneutical question.

Notice, however, that this question is not merely a matter of scribal acuity. It involves making the scriptures an "open book" in a radically new manner. In fact Luke uses the verb "to open" in remarkably instructive ways: twice in the Emmaus story and once in the Lord's crucial pronouncement. The reader first learns that the Emmaus stranger is suddenly recognized because in the moment of his breaking the bread the *eyes* of the two disciples *were opened* (v. 31; cf. v. 16). Next, after the Lord's withdrawal, these two disciples ponder the fact that their hearts had burned within them as he talked with them along the road and as he *opened the scriptures* to them (v. 32). Finally, these two motifs are brought together, as the risen Lord *opens* the disciples' *minds* to understand the *scriptures* (v. 45).

Of what, exactly, does this "new hermeneutic" consist? In the main, of two points. (1) The scriptures bear witness to Jesus as the Christ (v. 27); the hermeneutic is Christocentric. (2) The specificity of this scriptural witness is communicated by three infinitives (in Greek) which demonstrate precisely the empowered continuity: It is written in scripture for the Christ *to suffer*, for him *to rise* from the dead, and for repentance and forgiveness of sins *to be preached* in his name to all nations, beginning from Jerusalem (vv. 46 f.). The risen Lord gives his church a radically renewed vision of scripture which will guide their feet on the path already traveled by him. This is a great gift (cf. 2 Cor. 3:16-18).

Yet there is more. The disciples will walk in "the way," not only under the guidance of scripture, but also in the power of the Spirit. It is to Pentecost that the Lord points in v. 49. The Spirit will come and will clothe the young church—the scriptural interpreters—with the power of God himself.

HOMILETICAL INTERPRETATION

Easter's victory occurs among people who are lame, guilty, afraid, sometimes joyful, often disappointed. Perhaps "victory" is too triumphal: the people we know, both in and out of the Bible, will limp and cower and feel the pangs of guilt on many a fine spring morning. The texts for today point not so much to the *fait accompli*, though there is that, as to a continuing relationship and obedience to Jesus Christ. Jesus did not speak so much of final victory as of the peace that the Spirit would constantly give. The fearful women of that first Easter, the doubting Thomas, the sequestered disciples: they will all continue to fear and doubt and hide as we do. But the word we hear today witnesses to God's continual overcoming of sin and death. Isn't that just the word we need to hear two Sundays removed from Easter Day? Is there anybody here who is lame, if not from birth, then periodically? "But if we should sin. . . ." Does that hit us? And do we still walk the road to Emmaus, wondering?

Acts 3:13-15, 17-19. ". . . the God of our fathers has glorified his servant Jesus." The language points to the days of his flesh, which led some to glorify God and some to reject Jesus. What obtuseness and willful blindness could have failed to see the glory that was there all along, so manifest in his very humanity? Is it not the same alienated dullness which keeps us from seeing our own true situation as God's children? How could it happen that people with ordinary human feelings could have preferred a murderer and given over to death the Author of Life? Peter does not hesitate to point the finger: "You delivered up . . . you denied . . . you asked for a murderer." And there is the word of compassion, or at least of realism: "And now brethren, I know that you acted in ignorance, as did also your rulers." But there is no hope in that, in making excuses. Peter's brief gives way to gospel.

"But God. . . ." It is God who is at work in all of it: your denial, Pilate's cowardice, Jesus' suffering. God is using all of this, life as you have warped and spoiled and misused it, to glorify his servant Jesus. He has turned the whole affair to his own purpose. Beyond all fixing of blame, Peter witnesses: You have in your ignorance chosen death when you put Jesus to death; you have not been true to even the most elemental human instincts of decency and worth. But God has, nevertheless, raised him, and all who follow him, to life. Peter does not invite argument. What matters is that God has used the shame to show forth the servant's glory and that we are called now to read in his suffering the marks of our own true status. In Jesus God opens our eyes to what is. He causes us to walk and he turns our walking to dancing.

Peter's message lives in its context, as if the sermon were being acted out as he preaches it. The man lame from birth is raised at the hand of Peter in the name of Jesus. Jesus is raised, and people who see the meaning of that are turned away from death to life. And it is all of God: it is the goodness of God *which is always there* that leads us to repentance (cf. Rom. 2:4). Thomas Oden has said:

> The purpose of proclamation is that of calling man to an awareness of the reality of the situation in which he already exists, the reality of God's occurring love; not to introduce God to his world, as if he were not already there, but to introduce man to himself as one who is always already claimed by God.[1]

So much is God already there claiming us as his own that even in the ignominious death of an innocent man his love can shine through. There we are illumined, our eyes are opened, and we see and dance out what has been there all along:

1. Unpublished paper, Drew University, 1973.

Hear him, ye deaf; his praise ye dumb,
Your loosened tongues employ;
Ye blind, behold your Savior come;
And leap, ye lame, for joy.

1 John 1:1–2:6. The writer describes a community of grace which we have hardly known. He confesses at the same time the human condition and God's grace, and he sees the church as the people among whom we confess: "But God shows his love for us in that while we were yet sinners Christ died for us" (Rom. 5:8). In the community of grace it is possible, beyond all pretense and clamoring for status, to face up to our condition: "If we say that we have no sin, we deceive ourselves. . . ." How is it possible for people to face themselves and to know each other and make it together? We sometimes achieve it in the family. Home is, as Frost said, "the place where when you go there they have to take you in." But even families are not always at home with each other. How can any other group hold together intimately without the lubrication of the cocktail party? How does a community of *sinners* cohere?

The author points to something that has happened: We can't forget what we have seen with our eyes and touched with our hands—the word of life. And we can't help telling you what we have seen and heard. In fact, we tell you this so that you may come with us out of darkness into the clear daylight. We can look at ourselves and each other with wide open eyes because God has opened our eyes to himself. We can have life together because God has said Yes to us, and that Yes is spoken in the face of every No that we can say to ourselves and to each other. There is no longer any need to avert our eyes from the worst that we can do or the worst that could be done to us. God has pulled the stinger.

We need not pretend, lie, or even try to be "somebody." This community is built upon something prior. Where else but in the presence of God who in Christ forgives and renews could people say out loud together:

> We confess to you, God of the oppressed and oppressors, and to you our brothers and sisters, that we ourselves are not only oppressed but oppressors as well. We are black, red, yellow, brown, white; male, female; western, eastern; Asian, African, American, European; schooled, unschooled; lower class, middle class, upper class; suburban, rural, inner city; married, unmarried, divorced; heterosexual, homosexual; Protestant, Catholic, agnostic, atheist. We confess that knowingly and unconsciously we have been accomplices to imperialism, sexism, racism, consumerism, and ageism.[2]

The holy catholic church. I believe in it. I've even seen it in the flesh once or twice. I believe in God the Father . . . Jesus Christ . . . Holy Spirit . . . the forgiveness of sins.

You sit across the kitchen table from that person who has been saying no to himself for years, perhaps for all the years he has had. You are grateful for coffee that gives you something to do, or else you might speak too quickly and say what is on your mind: "O come off it. Why can't you

2. Unpublished liturgy of the Fisherfolk Community, Camden, N.J., 1975.

admit what you are and where you've been and be yourself?" But you don't say the words. Would you be heard if you could get it out: "Why don't you slow down and let the Lord love you?" or "Why not give up trying to be a nice guy and let the Lord make something good out of you?" But it all remains unspoken. What kind of environment would make it possible to speak the truth in love and to be heard? How, and where, can you let people know that God is saying Yes all the time and that even the No which they are feeling and fixating on is part of his Yes?

The writer imagines a community where that takes place, where we admit to one another how it is with us and praise God together, where redemption and worship occur east of Eden. Such a community is possible when we remember the message of Easter, that it is *God's* doing. It is when we praise God together that we are able to be together. "Where there is no temple there shall be no homes. . . ."[3] Whether we worship in folding chairs in the round or continue to sit in pews side by side, our life together is our life facing the altar in praise of him who knows us and forgives us and binds us. It is in such a community that we experience *at the same time* the two things we need all our lives: to be held responsible and to be, finally and beyond all striving, held.

Luke 24:36-49. Where do we go from here? What does it all mean, the suffering and death of Jesus, my suffering and that of people I know? Is there anything to be salvaged from wrecked hopes? What could possibly put together the pieces of the puzzling occurrences which preoccupy the two travelers to Emmaus?

Luke frames their conversation with two stories which focus on Jesus their friend and teacher. In fact, the focus is on his body. The insistent sensuality of the Christian story borders on being embarrassing. It begins with a red baby born among the redolent earthiness of a stable and moves toward the naked body on the cross, tenderly taken down by Joseph and wrapped in linen to await the women with their spices and ointments. Small wonder that artists have painted Christianity's every scene: the body is always there.

But Luke's frame is to give both context and emphasis to his central image: two puzzled companions who are moved from seeming dismay to discipleship. What happened to send them running back from Emmaus to Jerusalem?

In Grünewald's triptych, the long finger of John the Baptist points to the vulnerable body on the cross. In his other hand John holds an open book: "Behold the lamb of God!" In Luke's story, Jesus points from the book to himself, and the experience of that Friday becomes comprehensible to Cleopas and his companion. Experience is raised to the level of meaning: Jesus crucified becomes the lamb slain from the foundation of the world and through the long history of Israel, and he becomes the lamb

3. T. S. Eliot, "Choruses from 'The Rock,' " *The Complete Poems and Plays* (New York: Harcourt, Brace and Co., 1952), p. 103.

worthy to receive blessing and honor, dominion and power. The death of Jesus is caught up in the larger story of God's redemption, and in that new understanding the past transforms the present and opens toward the future.

We limp and sin and wonder, and it can all sink down to life that is out of joint with nothing connected to anything else. But God opens our eyes, in the name of Jesus, to see who he is, and our story is caught up in God's story, and we are given a mission, courage, and joy.

> Rejoice in the Lord always; again I will say, Rejoice. O Thou, Thou who didst call us this morning out of sleep and death. I come, we all of us come, down through the litter and letters of the day. On broken legs. Sweet Christ, forgive and mend. Of thy finally unspeakable grace, grant to each in his own dark room valor and an unnatural virtue. Amen.[4]

The Fourth Sunday of Easter

theran	*Roman Catholic*	*Episcopal*	*Pres./UCC/Chr.*	*Methodist/COCU*
ts 4:8-12	Acts 4:8-12	Acts 4:5, 7-12	Acts 4:8-12	Acts 4:5-12
ohn 3:1-2	1 John 3:1-2	1 John 3:1-8	1 John 3:1-3	1 John 3:1-8
n 10:11-18	John 10:11-18	John 10:11-16	John 10:11-18	John 10:11-18

EXEGESIS

First Lesson: Acts 4:8-12. This is the third of Peter's post-Pentecost speeches and the first of two which he makes while standing before the Sanhedrin (5:29-32 is the other). We need to be clear about the setting, and then about the structure of the speech itself.

The setting is specified by the note in 4:2 that the Sadducees arrest Peter and John because the latter affirm in Jesus the resurrection of the dead. If one emphasizes Luke's expression, "the resurrection of the dead," the note seems to make good sense: The Sadducees, who vigorously deny this doctrine, arrest the apostles for proclaiming it. On second thought, one will see, however, that this syllogism makes no sense at all. Were this doctrine itself the point at issue, the Sadducees would need to arrest all Pharisees, and, indeed, hosts of the general populace as well. What causes the rub is the connection between *Jesus* and the resurrection and especially the connection in terms of *current events*, such as the healing of the ame man. Pharisees who affirm the doctrine of the general and future resurrection are quite tolerable. Ignorant men (4:13), on the other hand, who are instrumental in healing people in the "name" of a condemned criminal whose resurrection they affirm already to have been accomplished by God—such men are unbearable. They must be silenced. Hence they are called to account.

. Frederick Buechner, *The Alphabet of Grace* (New York: Seabury, 1969), p. 112.

As Luke pens such scenes it is clear that he recalls Jesus' prediction:

> [Before the cosmic terrors of the end time] they will lay their hands on you and persecute you, delivering you up to the synagogues and prisons . . . . This will be a time for you to bear testimony . . . . I will give you a mouth and wisdom, which none of your adversaries will be able to withstand or contradict. (Luke 21:12 ff.; cf. Matt. 10:17 ff.)

Thus, while the formal outlines of the situation call for a scene in which prisoners speak in their own defense, the true dimensions of the situation are reflected in the fact that they do not speak in their own defense, but rather bear witness to God's contemporary deeds. For to these deeds those who propose to sit in judgment are themselves subject, whether they realize it or not.

The setting is thus not at all what the Sadducees imagine it to be. Rather than being just another day in the history of jurisprudence, it is a stage along "the way" which leads victoriously from Jerusalem to the ends of the earth.

As to the structure of the speech itself, it is in the main similar to the others: (1) A comment about the situation itself (4:8-9; cf. 3:12 and 2:15) is followed by (2) two-thirds of the "Jesus Kerygma" (cf. Easter III): (a) You crucified Jesus of Nazareth, (b) God reversed that line of action by raising him from the dead, and by (3) a clear indication of how this kerygma is related to the situation. In the present speech the relating of kerygma and situation is accomplished by focusing attention on Jesus' *name* (cf. 3:6, 16).

The ancient orientation to the name of a person and especially of a god is in play here. A name is not a mere convenience; it is rather something which participates in the personhood of the one to whom it belongs, and it is therefore not really separable from him. If he is truly named, he is at least partially present in terms of his power. Hence a wise man does not name a god lightly.

Once again we see that the road did not end in the cross. To be sure, the Sanhedrin might logically think that to be so. It had passed its judgment (Luke 22:66 ff.), and Jesus had been crucified at Pilate's hands. Yet here are these Christians standing with a healed man and saying that God gave him his health (salvation) when they demanded in the name of Jesus that he walk. In what they say about Jesus' name, they clearly affirm that Jesus is alive and active. Exegetes ponder whether the pronoun in the last clause of v. 10 should be translated "him" (so RSV), referring to Jesus, or "it," referring to Jesus' name. Perhaps the grammatical ambiguity should be accepted as an unintended index of the presence of Jesus' power in his name.

The final verse has occasioned a large literature over the centuries. Luke's intention is quite clear. *All* lines of history are flowing together into the emerging great church, in which one therefore recognizes that Jesus Christ is *the* Lord (Note Acts 14:15-17; 17:22-31). One may find it profitable to imagine a conversation between Luke and Franz Rosenzweig (see N. N. Glatzer, *Franz Rosenzweig* [1972], pp. 341-348).

Second Lesson: 1 John 3:1-2 (3:1-3). Re-reading the comments on the texts from 1 John for Easter II and Easter III will provide needed background for the present text.

The context is set partly by the note of 3:7, the danger of church members being deceived and led astray. Who might deceive them, and how might he lead them astray?

The answers are clearly enough given in 3:8 ff. The author takes for granted not only the existence of the devil, but also his active participation in human affairs. The latter is reflected in the author's affirmation that, like God himself, the devil has children. That is to say, he does not merely exist "somewhere"; on the contrary, he is active and effective in human society through children of his own. What do they look like? They might be quite attractive and highly religious people, through whom one could be led astray, but in every case they are revealed to be his children by one clear mark of distinction: Like Cain they manifest the "original sin" of the devil—they do not love their brothers.

Over against this picture the author places that of the children of God portrayed in our text. We can be sure that he has read and pondered many times John 1:12 f., verses which retain overtones of their connection with baptism. In that event the person becomes a child of God, not through any effort of his own or through any power of his biological parents, but by God's own graceful action. The thought is very old (cf. Hos. 11:1 ff.). In Jewish thought of the Hellenistic age God's action is (a) affirmed as a future hope and (b) introduced into a dualistic framework, as in the Qumran writings and in Jubilees (1:24 f.) and in the present passage: there are sons of light and sons of darkness, children of God and children of the devil. But we must understand that this does not necessarily bring with it a deterministic motif. Our author simply observes two distinct patterns of life, and wishes his readers not to be deceived into thinking there really is no difference between the two.

What guards members of the fellowship from such deception is their knowledge that God has graciously made them his children, thus both enabling (4:19) and commanding (3:11) them to love one another. All of this—and more—is gathered up in the remarkable practice followed in the author's community of calling God "*The* Father" (twice in the synoptics; 75 times in the Johannine Gospel and 14 times in the Epistles).

Whereas the author of Jubilees (see above) expected the gift in the future age, our author affirms it for the present. Correspondingly, awesome as it is already to be children of God, there is more, a very powerful "not yet." It is not powerful as a result of the painting of colorful and detailed apocalyptic pictures. On the contrary, all is focused on the Father himself and hence on the promise that seeing him—recall both John 1:12 f. and John 1:18—will bring about a marvelous transformation in us. We *shall* become similar to God!

(There is a knotty exegetical problem in v. 2; the statement just made stands on the election of one interpretative alternative. Following the words "we know," the author has employed a passive verb whose subject is difficult to fix. Should we translate, "We know that when he is revealed . . .," or should we render it, "We know that when what we shall be is revealed"? Schnackenburg makes a strong case for the latter. The result is that 3:12 speaks about God and his children and does not mention Christ. However, the other alternative is not at all to be excluded as a possibility, and, following it, one would read the text as a reference to Christ's parousia and to the children's becoming similar to him when they see him. In either case the vision is sharply focused on the Godhead, and the promise is that our present experience of God's remarkable love in making us his children will be followed by the yet more remarkable event of our becoming similar to him. [We do not meet here the thought of man's ultimate divinization. That would be a gnostic motif foreign to the author.])

Gospel: John 10:11-18. Raymond Brown in his commentary on the Gospel according to John (pp. 388 f.) has given the structure of John 10. The first five verses present two parables: (1) vv. 1-3a: There is a proper way to approach the sheep, through the gate; (2) vv. 3b-5: There is *the* shepherd, and there are alternative shepherds. Following these parables, vv. 7-10 explain the gate parable, and vv. 11-16 (to which vv. 17-18 are attached) explain the parable of the shepherd.

The latter explanation falls into two parts: (a) vv. 11-13 explain the shepherd parable by introducing new characters and new motifs. There are wolves; their coming spells danger; in that context a hired hand saves his own neck; the model shepherd, on the other hand, lays down even his own life for the sheep. It is difficult to be sure who the hired hands are, but the relationship with John 9 will suggest that those who proved themselves blind to Jesus' presence as the Light of the World by handling so roughly the formerly blind man are here thought of as hired hands who have no genuine concern for the people entrusted to their care.

(b) Vv. 14-16 (17-18) offer a second interpretation, which follows the parable itself more closely by emphasizing the shepherd's intimate knowledge of the sheep. It is a typical and impressive Johannine note to heighten the intimacy of the relationship between Jesus and his own by placing it as a typology (". . . just as . . .") with the relationship between the Father and the Son (v. 15a)!

Two further motifs call for comment. (1) The entire passage is framed by two affirmations of Jesus about his own death (vv. 11 and 18). The second of these is polemically formulated. Perhaps there are persons in the evangelist's setting who interpret Jesus' death as an execution: the responsible judges ruled that Jesus' life was to be taken, and so it was. "Not at all," replies John. Jesus is himself the one in complete authority, who lays down his life in order to re-take it!

(2) The motif of v. 16 has played a large role (along with John 17) in the modern ecumenical movement. We cannot be certain of its import for John, but many interpreters take it to be a reference to the Gentile mission. If so, it is one more witness to the early Christian conviction that

the worldwide mission is a component of Jesus' death/resurrection itself (cf. John 12:31).

HOMILETICAL INTERPRETATION

The power of the texts for today is dialectical. New life is set alongside the old, the children of God against the "world," the good shepherd over the hired sheepsitter. The collage is light and darkness, the contrasts extreme.

We meet these NT witnesses as preachers whose message can hardly be bridled to one metaphor or held back from hyperbole. The bigger the truth, the wilder the metaphor. As we hear—or better, overhear—the early church celebrating the new life, there is no need to try to make everything "fit"; that can end in gutting one text to suit it to another. The gospel cannot be homogenized, and we would be suspicious if it all turned out to be as neat as a three-point sermon. We rejoice in these disparate witnesses who reveal their humanity as they cast about for words to say the one thing they are sure of: Whereas we were in darkness, lame, hungry, and lost, now we are made whole. Overhearing them is like hearing the children's song:

> Sometimes my voice is as small as a mouse,
> And sometimes my voice is as big as a house.
> But it's all right, it's all right,
> Because the song is always beautiful.

Acts 4:8-12. The force of a sentence is at its end: "and by him this man is standing before you well." Peter is speaking before theological skeptics and political conservatives. He might have debated with them the possibility of resurrection or he might have attacked their alliance with Rome. But he simply points to the man, past forty, crippled from birth, who stands before the assembled political and ecclesiastical powers of Jerusalem. We can only dimly picture the scene: two "uneducated, common men" and a middle-aged man whose great distinction is that he can walk, before the old high priest, his family, and associates. Where does Peter get his words? From the message he has heard? A report of resurrection? From the rapidly growing, supportive community of Christians? From John, who simply stands there with him? From the lame man? What is the connection between Peter's bold speeches and the tradition that the risen Lord appeared first to him? However we account for Peter's words, Luke says that he was "filled with the Holy Spirit." He finds his voice: "This is the stone which was rejected by the builders, but which has become the head of the corner. And there is salvation in no one else. . . ." It is a very big voice indeed! The humble poor believe and the forgotten crippled dance in the temple, and the new life they know in the crucified and glorified servant is of another sort altogether than might be won by protecting one's worldly position or kowtowing to Rome. No name, not even Caesar's, could do what the "name" of Jesus has done for these three men standing here. The redeeming story accomplishes what the how-to pragmatism of political and technological manipulation could never achieve. These are people "made whole"—it is as close as we can come in English to salvation of body and spirit—metaphors themselves of the unlikely cornerstone. Peter, who has at last become a rock, would have understood the metaphor well.

1 John 3:1-2. "Beloved, we are God's children now." Here and now, just as we are, in the flesh and too often of the flesh, we are God's little family. Pretty cozy. You could get the picture here of a clutch of people gathered around a groaning table, the draperies drawn and the warm glow of congeniality fending off the hostile world outside. Or you could imagine a beleaguered cadre locked in an upstairs room, fear bordering on paranoia, or at the very least, exclusiveness. John gives us the makings of either scenario. The passage is surrounded by "antichrists," "the children of the devil," and the "world." The godless world is shut out of the little circle because it does not know God as we do.

We could set the stage that way, and there is reason to do so. John writes in the midst of contending religious cults and threatening heresy, and he is concerned for purity. He turns inward toward the community, and his central concern is that those who follow Jesus should abide in Christ and love one another in the church. But he keeps his feet. This is no mere "I'm OK, you're OK, aren't we great!" Far from it. John begins where he ends, with the unaccountable love of God.

"See what love the Father has given us. . . ." That is the only justification for calling ourselves his children, and if we have any success in loving each other and doing right, it is his doing as he works among us. And we can't even say what will become of us, how we will turn out, as if "every day in every way" we were "getting better and better." That is not John's thrust at all. We abide in him, confident that the same love which, beyond all our doing, keeps us from sin (cf. 3:9) today will shape our life together in the future. For the present and for the future, for what we are and are becoming, it is being in Christ that matters. This is not the coziness of a self-assured group living above sin, despising the "world." It is more like being grateful that you can see and walk, or feeling deep down that sense of belonging and being known when parents' love turns sharing meals and a house into a home that frees and heals. It is that awareness of the Father, and the goodness of his creation and his grace in Jesus Christ, which leads us to hope that we may become like him. The awareness of love which leads to love, holds us together and gives us the future.

John 10:11-18. The contrasts between the new life and the old are stark. "I am the bread of life." This is the true bread, as health-giving as the manna come down from heaven and as dependent upon the Father's goodness. This bread is the opposite of that which does not satisfy (cf. Isa. 55), of that "light" bread which is white and soft but does not nourish us. Anyone who eats this bread will not be hungry; this is soul food such as you can get at the H&H Cafe down in Macon, Georgia, where the menu is written out in pencil and there *is* no decor and they've never heard of MSG and you can have six vegetables and boiled beef and cornbread. Two dollars flat! And the next time you spend twenty dollars for two you remember Isaiah: "Why do you spend your money for that which does not satisfy . . .?"

"I am the light of the world," shining in the darkness "I am the resurrection and the life," shouted into the very teeth of death. "I am the *good* shepherd." We understand that, especially in a society like ours, where so much is superficially attractive, where the very economy is built on making it so. There is so much to tantalize the palate, titillate the imagination, and appeal to the insatiable need for the new, or at least the novel. Who can really feed the people? Where is life, illumination, joy, peace? Who can fend off the wolves, win the real battles, stay with us through the night and prepare the banquet table at noon? Is there another name that we can trust? Who are the hirelings, who the good shepherd, here in our town, on our main street? (Cf. Jer. 23:1-4.)

This is one of those texts that has such a voice of its own that we find preaching it like following a big anthem, or like making a sermon of Tillich's our own. We would just as soon leave such a text to itself, or to stained glass windows or Handel. We wish that we were musicians or painters, or that we could dance it out like lambs at play in the fields of the Lord.

Some would say that the difficulty of preaching on the passage is its pastoral setting. "I am the good shepherd. I know my own and my own know me. . . ." What can it mean to me? I am not sure I want to be a sheep! I have hardly *seen* a good sized flock of sheep in my life, and they had never been near a wolf. And as for shepherds, I've seen a few pictures in *National Geographic* and some in Christmas pageants. Maybe I would do better to find another metaphor: "I am the fool-proof computer: you are instantly retrievable," or "Social Security has my number, I shall not want."

But that doesn't quite do it. The heart of the passage is inseparable from the *kind* of knowledge which the shepherd has of the sheep: "I know my own and my own know me, as the Father knows me and I know the Father." When I hear the words, "I am the good shepherd," I feel that I am known where I really live. In this city, where "sheep" mean someone easily taken in, or out on this farm where sheep are managed by fences and fleeced by machinery, I know what it means, "I am the good shepherd." I feel that I am known where I myself am the wolf and the hireling, and just because of that I am the sheep in need of the shepherd who knows me and lays down his life for me. There is a place at the heart of my life—where I am afraid and run away and bare my teeth, and where I am a lamb—to which I am always trying to invite other people. But most cannot know me there at all, and some would manipulate and handle me in that place. Even my father and mother, my spouse and children, my best friend, cannot often stay with me there when the wolves come. But "thou makest me to lie down in green pastures, thou leadest me beside still waters, thou preparest a table . . ., thou anointest my head with oil."

The ironies are many. The good shepherd, himself the lamb of God, saves the sheep but cannot save himself. His rod is both grace and judgment, his kingly sceptre a shepherd's crook. He knows and guards his own flock, but the whole world is his fold. His kingdom embraces the world but is not of the world and is finally as close to me as his own relationship to the Father, as near at hand as his words: "I am the good shepherd." And I wish I were the Hallelujah Chorus to answer, "Worthy is the lamb that was slain. . . ."

The Fifth Sunday of Easter

Lutheran	*Roman Catholic*	*Episcopal*	*Pres./UCC/Chr.*	*Methodist/COCU*
Acts 9:26-31	Acts 9:26-31	Acts 9:26-31	Acts 9:26-31	Acts 9:26-31
1 John 3:18-24	1 John 3:18-24	1 John 3:18-24	1 John 3:18-24	1 John 3:18-24
John 15:1-8	John 15:1-8	John 15:1-11	John 15:1-8	John 15:1-8

EXEGESIS

First Lesson: Acts 9:26-31. We may grasp some aspects of Luke's work as a Christian historian by comparing two paragraphs in Acts 9 with the pertinent data in Paul's own letters.

Acts 9:19b-25 // 2 Cor. 11:32 f.

In this paragraph Luke paints two pictures of Paul in Damascus immediately after the latter's conversion. He seems to fill out the first picture merely from the fact of the striking contrast between Paul's activities before and after his conversion. For the second, he clearly had a tradition about a dramatic escape from Damascus, for Paul also speaks of the event in 2 Corinthians. Comparing the two texts enables one to see that an event which was probably fundamentally political has been portrayed by Luke as exclusively religious.

From Galatians we learn that immediately after his conversion in Damascus Paul went to Nabatea (1:17). Luke does not mention this fact for a simple reason. He is writing church history; Paul did not succeed in establishing any churches in Nabatea, or perhaps did not try to; hence no tradition came to Luke about Christian activity in Nabatea. What may very well have transpired there is that Paul came afoul of the king, Aretas. In any case, Paul returned from Nabatea to Damascus (1:17).

In doing so, he did not entirely remove himself from the grasp of Aretas, since the latter maintained a governor or a charge d'affaires in Damascus. Through this minister Aretas attempted to arrest (not kill) Paul, but the Christian brethren enabled him to escape by lowering him in a basket through an opening in the city wall (2 Cor. 11:32 f.).

If we assume that Luke received a tradition similar to the report Paul himself gives—and the wordings are in some regards quite close—we may note how he shapes and changes it. Luke is not interested in Paul's "political" relations with the Nabatean king and his minister in Damascus. His canvas at this point is concentrated on the "religious" tensions between representatives of Judaism and those of "the way," and he portrays these tensions as growing rapidly. Hence he presents a picture in which Paul's adversaries are not Nabatean soldiers, but rather "the Jews," and their intention is not to arrest Paul, but rather to kill him.

Acts 9:26-30 // Gal. 1:18-24.

The comparison just made will help us here. Again it is clear that Luke had at his disposal a piece of tradition: a notice of some sort about a trip made by Paul from Damascus to Jerusalem. If it was similar to the report Paul gives in Gal. 1:18 ff., we may once more see Luke's editing.

In the Galatian letter Paul speaks of going from Damascus to Jerusalem three years after his conversion. It was a brief visit of two weeks, and his contacts were severely limited. He conversed only with Peter and James. He says nothing about having preached while there.

We cannot be sure, of course, that Luke received exactly this picture in his traditions about Paul, but if he did, his handling of it is striking. He first introduces the dramatic note that the Jerusalem Christians were afraid of Paul, not believing him to be a Christian. This is probably a note of Luke's own making, since it is quite unlikely that after three years (Gal. 1:18; cf. Luke's own "when many days had passed," Acts 9:23) news of the extraordinary genuineness of Paul's conversion would not have traveled from Damascus to Jerusalem. The note is designed to catch the reader's interest.

Next, Luke says that after Barnabas showed him to be "kosher," Paul went about in Jerusalem, so to speak, arm in arm with the church leaders, preaching and entering into disputation. We can be sure Paul would have been amazed at this picture, and perhaps much more than amazed (cf. Gal. 1:20). For Luke, however, it is a natural portrait. He certainly did not intend to distort, but rather to show what he takes to be essential: Paul's mission—to the ends of the earth—grew out of and therefore developed in continuity with that of the Jerusalem church. Luke's interest is shown quite clearly, in fact, in the summary of Acts 9:31. It is remarkably ecclesiological. Whether through Peter, Stephen, Philip, or Paul, it is God who is building up and multiplying his one church.

Second Lesson: 1 John 3:18-24. Again we see the inextricable connection which the author weaves between "theology" and "ethics." God's commandment (3:23) is that we believe in the name of his Son Jesus Christ (developed in 4:1-6) *and* that we love one another (developed in 4:7 ff.) However, the new note, as compared with texts in 1 John already commented upon, is struck in 3:19-21, verses which occasioned much attention from the church fathers and which may speak in a remarkable way in our own context.

The heart stands here, of course, for the human conscience. Two possibilities are open to it. It can condemn the ego (v. 20), or it can abstain from condemning the ego (v. 21). In the author's world, as in our own, people put much store in the power of the conscience precisely for this reason. Does the author endorse the guidance of the conscience, perhaps "Christianizing" it in the process? Not at all. He clearly considers the conscience to be anything but a reliable guide. Of course it is there, and it cannot be ignored; but neither is it to be followed.

Does he then throw his readers into the chartless labyrinth of complete relativism? Hardly. For the Christian the conscience is no reliable guide precisely because God has invaded his very being with his word of grace which is also his commandment. When the author says that God is greater than our heart-conscience, he has in mind a quite specific situation: that of the Christian who is living in loving relationships within a Christian community and who is plagued by an inner accuser. He is to say to the inner accuser, "God is greater than you are. Be gone!" Obviously this does not mean that the Christian has become autonomous. Far from it. What has happened is that the quite unreliable conscience has been replaced by the direct invasion of the gracious and demanding Father who sets the person in that community in which the Father's commandment to love the brother is in fact kept. Perfectly kept? Of course not. But in instances in which it is not kept, one does not fall again under the tyranny of the conscience. One remains in the presence of God, with the advocate whom God has provided: Jesus Christ the righteous (1:9; 2:1). It is because of the gifts of Christ and the Spirit in the community of Christian love (3:23, 24) that we can know in daily experience that God is greater than our condemning conscience.

Gospel: John 15:1-8. The structure of John 15:1-17 is similar to that of 10:1-18 analysed for Easter IV: a parable drawn from pastoral or agricultural life is provided with interpretation. In both instances we find what we might call a fine interweaving of Christology and ecclesiology.

This interweaving is handled somewhat differently in 15:1-6 and in 15:7-17, so that the present reading tastes of both. In vv. 1-6 third person language dominates the imagery, without, to be sure, obliterating the use of the second person, and the relationship between Christ and his church is represented in a timeless parable. In vv. 7-17 the second person is consistently used, and we find numerous themes proper to the Last Supper. There is a resulting movement of thought from the supra-temporal unity of vine and branches to the specificity of this unity in the gospel story itself, and this movement is crucial in keeping the rich imagery of vv. 1-6 from becoming an end in itself. More on that in the comments for Easter VI.

Having heeded the warning not to read vv. 1-6 as the whole story, we may allow them their role. They constitute what the Jews call a *mashal*, a broad parabolic form from which some small degree of allegorical overtones should not be excluded: "I am the (real) vine" (vv. 1 and 5), "My

Father is the gardener" (v. 1); "You are the branches" (v. 5). Through the entire picture runs the dualistic choice of remaining or not remaining in Jesus, and the whole of life turns on it. There is no ecclesiology without the massive Christology which stands always at the center of John's picture. Given this massive Christology, the present reading, divided as it is, may be taken as a commentary on the meaning of a community of disciples which is fruitful in the world because of its thoroughly christological nature (v. 8).

HOMILETICAL INTERPRETATION

One way of viewing today's texts is to set them in the much-traveled terrain between pietism and activism. We are uncomfortable in either camp: pietism seems incapable of validating itself, and activism is all too easily prone to self-confirmation. What is the relationship between the vision and the mission? Between contemplation and getting with it, between Blake's "braces" and "relaxes"? Is it true that the end of the religious life is to glorify God and enjoy him forever, and if so, what is the profile of the person in the act of glorifying God? The readings for today do not give us the kind of answer that we can put in our pocket like a two-dollar bill. Instead, they force us in this Eastertide to think again about the source of our confidence *and* of our activity.

Acts 9:26-31. The most obvious fact about Paul is the apostle's validation of his ministry by his experience on the Damascus Road. You don't even have to press him to get him to push his chair back and say, "Well, I am doing this and telling you this story because once upon a time when I was traveling to Damascus. . . ." That is, of course, what all of us ultimately have to do in giving account of who we are and what we are doing: "Something happened to *me* once. . . ." The emphasis which Paul wishes to give to the story which lies behind his message and mission is at least part of the reason for the differences between his own account of his conversion and ministry (cf. Galatians 1) and that of Luke. What Paul wishes to stress is that the gospel he preaches is not a second-hand "man's gospel": "For I did not receive it from man, nor was I taught it, but it came through a revelation of Jesus Christ" (Gal. 1:12). And even in Luke's account, when Barnabas brings Paul before the apostles, he emphasizes the experience on the road, how Paul had "seen the Lord, who spoke to him" as a way of accounting for his reported boldness in preaching to the people of Damascus.

The way in which the question of pietism and/or activism presents itself to us would have made little sense to the early church. The very impetus for all they did was the continuing, vivid experience of the risen Lord. All of Paul's preaching and traveling, his disputing and apologetics, rose from an experience which was his own and which was constantly renewed in both his victories and in deprivation. We can only imagine the importance to his active, sometimes whirlwind ministry of the years in "Arabia," a period of withdrawal which is foreshadowed immediately after his experience on the road as he waits, blinded and immobilized, for a brother to come. How do we, as we give account of what we are doing in the name of Christ in this town here and now, relate our doing to being in Christ? What is the role of the Spirit and of our brothers and sisters in leading us from our private experience toward useful work in the community? Doesn't Luke suggest throughout Acts an inseparable relationship between worship/fellowship on the one hand and mission to the world on the other? Whether we take Paul's account, in which he lays emphasis upon the kind of experience which we usually identify with pietism, or Luke's, who is eager to tie Paul to the community, any effort to separate what we do from what God has done for us in Christ fails.

1 John 3:18-24. To do God's will: what is that? What is expected of us? What sense can we make of the language of *abiding*? The word probably suggests to us something like passive dependence. What would our lives look like if we were really abiding in God? Does that suggest a great deal of church going, or private prayer, or elevated moods, like always being on cloud nine?

Abiding in God is certainly not a passive hanging around in holy precincts. John makes that clear: "All who keep his commandments abide in him and he in them." And keeping his commandments is not just a matter of pious talk or ecclesiastical good manners: ."Little children, let us not love in word or speech but in deed and in truth." The pastoral counsel of this letter could not be more straightforward: to be in Christ is to *do* something, to demonstrate by our style of life that we are being led by the Spirit.

At the same time, we do *abide* in him. This passage seems tailor-made for the American experience in which we are constantly oscillating from one extreme to the other. But here, doing and being are not allowed to fly apart. We are called to do the deed, but we are, for all our doing, "little children." Demand is laid on us at the same moment that grace meets us. At every moment, we abide in God, even when we fail to match deed with word. Even when we condemn ourselves—when we do not live up to the most elemental responsibilities of being God's people—we abide in his grace: "God is greater than our hearts." So marching for peace and sitting down for justice and boycotting for equality, we are justified by grace, not in the doing itself. And even when we pray, we must ask the spirit to intercede for us.

There is in Graham Greene's novel, *The Power and the Glory*, that ne'er-do-well, drunken priest who, despite himself, is able to be an instrument of grace in a disrupted society. His very ineptness points to the power of the Spirit which uses him, and there is about him an integrity of purpose which Greene sets over against the dour proper missionaries whose religion seems as external to their persons as a pair of ill-fitting shoes. The priest abides, hangs on for dear life, and is able, as a "wounded healer," to minister.

It is the sense of dependence, the knowledge that no day and no deed is well undertaken which is not begun in Christ, which is life in the Spirit. To *abide* in him is to believe and to do, to speak and to act, to pray and to preach, to keep house, push pencils, and make pies. It is the same Spirit which causes all these moments to shine with new meaning. In exalted moments and common tasks, "by this we know that he abides in us, by the Spirit which he has given us." Is this a unique relationship? Is there any other in which we know such ultimate demand—"all who keep his commandments abide in him"—and such final acceptance: "God is greater than our hearts, and he knows everything"? Even the analogies of marriage and old friendships seem not quite adequate to express that kind of being at home.

John 15:1-8. By what analogy can we see more clearly the organic connection between act and being? "Abiding" and "bearing fruit" are one and the same where horticulture is concerned, whether you take it from "The Fantastics"—"plant a turnip, get a turnip"—or from the Gospels: "By their fruits you will know them." To be a grape vine *is* to bear grapes, and we assume disease or a trick when a vine which appears to be grape does not manifest grapeness in clusters of fruit. To be in Christ, to live in the fellowship of the Counsellor, is to bear predictable fruit.

When we hear the words, "bear fruit," do we think first of measurable production, of quantifiable results, such as we tally up at the end of a month or a year? What is this fruit? Do we understand the metaphor if we picture the vinedresser counting out tangible contributions to the church, or success in enlisting new church members, or our self-consciously undertaken good works? No one interpreting the passage for practical, pragmatic Americans would want to disparage those good works. On the other hand, our inclination toward the philosophy of success—"Nothing succeeds like success"—is at once our virtue and our vice. The first fruit of the spirit is love for one another. That is what issues in good works and evangelism, the sort of tangible deeds which we often equate with Christian fruitfulness.

Paul's catalogue of the fruits of the Spirit occurs in the context of pastoral counsel on Christian *freedom*. Legalism and works-righteousness "sever" us from Christ (Gal. 5:4), and the signs of being cut off from him are abusive acts toward our own bodies and toward other people. On the other hand, "the fruit of the Spirit is love, joy, peace, patience, goodness, faithfulness, gentleness, self control. . . ." (Gal. 5:22). Being in Christ produces the very attitudes which are essential to living with other people! Can we say that abiding in Christ *is* being in community? Is it Christ who makes true community possible? Do we agree with T. S. Eliot?

> There is no life that is not in community,
> And no community not lived in praise of God.[1]

1. T. S. Eliot, "Choruses from 'The Rock,' " *The Complete Poems and Plays* (New York: Harcourt, Brace and Co., 1952), p. 101.

"I am the *true* vine." We can have confidence in the fruit which comes from that vine, even hope that God may be glorified in that fruit (cf. Matt. 5:16). How many of our own motives can we trust so confidently? How many crusades and ideologies, faddish movements and pop causes last long enough to give us *hope*? Herbert Butterfield, at the end of *Christianity and History*, tells us:

> We can do worse than remember a principle which both gives us a firm Rock and leaves us the maximum elasticity for our minds: the principle: Hold to Christ, and for the rest be totally uncommitted.[2]

The more we are involved in the immediate problems which plague our society and the world, the more we could ponder those words and what it is to abide in Christ the true vine. What can both nourish and motivate us, set us free and give us security? Apart from Christ, how many of our causes will end up at the city dump as smoldering garbage?

Walter Rauschenbusch was the foremost figure in the American social gospel movement. He labored to better the lot of working people, campaigned for political candidates, and worked for such mundane social improvements as sandboxes for New York's poor children. At the same time, he preached warm, simple, biblical sermons to his small congregation in Hell's Kitchen on New York's West Side, and his own personal religious life was as deeply devout as that of his Lutheran and Baptist forebears. He spoke of prayer as stepping aside and entering through "a little postern gate," to a place where he was renewed and guided. Few have achieved Rauschenbusch's integration of action and devotion. The Gospel for today promises us such wholeness: to be in Christ the true vine is having and sharing new life.

The Sixth Sunday of Easter

Lutheran	*Roman Catholic*	*Episcopal*	*Pres./UCC/Chr.*	*Methodist/COC*
Acts 10:34-48	Acts 10:25-26, 34-35, 44-48	Acts 11:5a, 11-18	Acts 10:34-48	Acts 11:5a, 11
1 John 4:1-11	1 John 4:7-10	1 John 4:17-21	1 John 4:1-7	1 John 4:1-11
John 15:9-17	John 15:9-17	John 15:9-17	John 15:9-17	John 15:9-17

EXEGESIS

First Lesson: Acts 10:34-48. Acts 10 is often referred to as "the first conversion of a Gentile: Cornelius." That is quite correct, but only part of the picture. It also narrates the conversion of Peter, and that is where the major accent lies. Peter and his companions in the Jerusalem church—all Jews (10:45)—assume that God's new people constitute a circle within the larger circle of Israel. They are in for a surprise. God leads them into a new world-view.

2. Herbert Butterfield, *Christianity & History* (London: Fontana, 1957), p. 189.

First, by a dream Peter learns not to call any food cleansed by God (10:14 f.) or any man created by God (10:28) common or unclean. The Kosher rules do not dictate the contours of the church. Second, there is the matter of the Spirit. Jews who are Christians may learn to have some degree of association with Gentiles (vv. 28 f.), but surely the gift of God's Spirit, which empowers the church, is limited to Israel. But no, this wall also comes tumbling down. For even as Peter speaks, God breaks the "rules," by sending the Holy Spirit on *all* who are listening (v. 44). We may now notice how crucial to the speech are the little words "all" and "every":

v. 35 . . . in *every* nation . . .
v. 36 . . . He is Lord of *all* . . .
v. 43 . . . *every* one who believes in him . . .

As is always the case in Acts, the speech and its context are thus carefully inter-related.

The speech is remarkable on several counts. It gives the fullest outline of Jesus' ministry outside the Gospels. This would seem appropriate in a speech made to Gentiles in Caesarea, and so it is. But one may also note the literary artistry of Luke, who really addresses this speech to the readers of his two volumes. For it is these readers, and not Cornelius, who by having read the first of his volumes, already know the story of Jesus (vv. 36 ff.). And it is they, whether they be Jews or Gentiles, who are now to be converted as Peter was, so that they learn that God does not turn over his lordship to any set of national or racial rules as such, but rather intends the Spirit-empowered mission for *all* people. This is not a matter of a good "liberal" feeling. It is a matter of God's choice and of his action (15:7).

Second Lesson: 1 John 4:1-11. This reading comprises two sections which are distinguishable, yet closely interrelated.

(1) *4:1-6.* One may re-read the comments on 1 John 3:1-2 for Easter IV. The dualistic framework is, of course, maintained in the present passage, and specifically vis a vis a crucial matter in early Christianity—cf. 1 Cor. 12:10—the discerning of the spirits. The author is convinced that his readers live in a world in which, even as regards the church, there are numerous "options." In the face of these options one will need criteria for discernment, and the author unashamedly finds such criteria in what we call dogmatics. The matter of confession is not something which can as well fall this way as that. It is *the* question of life.

In the author's context a major option was offered by gnostic prophets (4:1) who had the "right" slogans (see Easter III) and who—surely in an "intelligent" manner—identified the savior as the essential Christ, a figure who temporarily appeared in the guise of a man called Jesus. It is not difficult to see how such people might have developed their thought on the basis of *some* elements in the Johannine Gospel. They certainly understand themselves to be Christians.

To the author this situation makes necessary a distinction between "orthodoxy" and "heresy," and he makes it on the basis of the confession that Jesus Christ came *in the flesh*. The Christology which finds its center in Jesus of Nazareth as God's Son is here distinguishing itself from an otherworldly retreat into metaphysics alone.

(2) *4:7-11*. As is clear from earlier passages, the "heresy" inevitably reveals itself not only christologically, but also in everyday relationships (4:8, 20). Hence, once again, the emphasis on love of brother.

The modern reader may find it strange, finally, that the love of brothers is the content of God's *commandment* and hence of *exhortation* (4:7). It is a result of the development of romantic love in Western culture that we speak of "falling in love," being "struck by lightning," etc. By contrast the author thinks of love as being subject to the will, once one knows that God has loved him first.

Gospel: John 15:9-17. One sees the extraordinary care expended on the composition. As Raymond Brown has shown in his commentary on the Gospel according to John (p. 667), we find one of the numerous cases in John of a chiastic pattern enclosed by vv. 7 and 17: If . . . my *words* remain in you, *ask* for whatever you want . . .; the Father will give you whatever you *ask* . . .; this I *command* you.

Several motifs call for special comment:

First, as was remarked in the exegesis for the preceding passage (Easter V), the paragraph is strongly marked by the interweaving of Christology and ecclesiology. We may see this interweaving in a kind of diagram:

Just as the Father loved me,
also I have loved you:
  Remain in my love
  (This is the place—*topos*—for the Johannine community.)
How does the community abide in Christ's love?
  By keeping his commandments,
  just as he kept the Father's commandments, abiding in his love.
What are these commandments?
  Only one: love one another,
  just as I have loved you.
Because I have elected you, you are my friends.

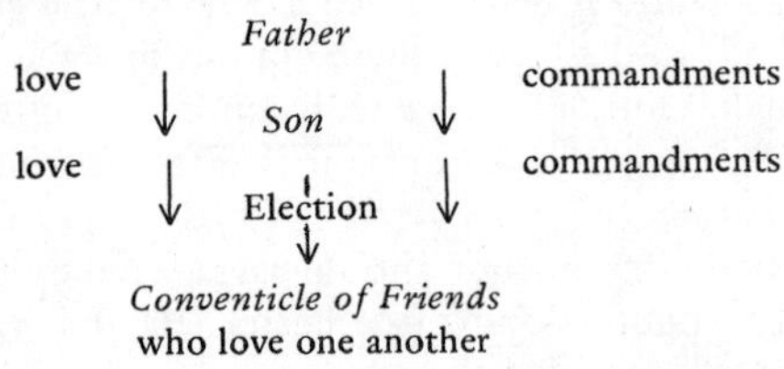

To put it boldly, the verb "remain in," which is so central to the parable of the vine and its branches, is now explicated in such a way as to suggest that the corporeality of the community with Christ is in some regards comparable to the relationship Christ has to the Father.

Second, the paragraph very nearly begins and ends with a second expression taken from the parable: "to bear fruit." What does it mean? A strong clue is given in v. 16. As is appropriate to the parable itself, bearing fruit is not something a branch decides to do of itself. In terms of v. 16, a person is a fruitful branch not because he has chosen Christ, but because Christ has elected him to the "apostolic" ministry, has laid on him the single-minded commandment to love his brothers, and has given him himself and the fellowship as the place of his abode. To bear fruit is thus not a matter of an individual's deed as such; it is rather a matter of the life of love in the community.

Only *in* the community? The question may justly be posed, not least because of the paragraph which follows (15:18 ff.). The picture of the vine and its branches is surely a portrait of what we might call conventicle piety. Outside is "the world," which hates the fellowship (15:18, 19, 23), and persecutes it (15:20), even to the point of inflicting death on some of its members (16:2). We are surely in touch here with some of the marks of the actual experiences of John's community, experiences which have reinforced its feeling of estrangement from a largely hostile environment.

Yet it is equally clear that the world is the object of God's love (3:16), and that Christ has "other sheep" (10:16). Hence the conventicle piety is no end in itself, but is rather the beachhead which God has established, and which he is enlarging for the sake of all men (12:32; 11:51 f.). It is for this reason that the conventicle-like fellowship is of such vital importance. In short, the joy of which v. 11 speaks is the joy of a community which has *both* a tightly-knit identity of mutual love *and* a world mission, just as the joy of Christ is had both in his immediate relationship with the Father and in his coming into the world.

HOMILETICAL INTERPRETATION

There is little in the NT to provide texts for the kind of navel-gazing which asks repeatedly: "Who am I?" Rather, the preoccupation of the early church is with questions of corporate identity and responsibility: "Who are *we* as the people of God?" and "What is expected of us?" The church whose internal conversation we overhear is marking itself off from the world of darkness, death, and hatred, to use John's categories. And the community is trying to get its feet for mission, to understand how it is related to its environment and how that relationship is shaped by the word which both breaks in dynamically and remains a fixed point. We can hardly miss the difference of emphasis in John and Acts: one turns in toward self-understanding, the other is moving out to the alien, even hostile "world." But in both, the church's identity *is* its mission: to be to all persons what Jesus Christ is to his people. Who we are tells us what we are to do, just as what has been done for us tells us who we are. That word "abide" crops up again, and it pushes us here beyond individualism and exclusivism toward the kind of community which is both living and sharing the new life. That was the first word we heard this Eastertide: Jesus who is raised in power among us is to be proclaimed to the ends of the earth.

Acts 10:34-48. "God has no favorites. . . ." Peter, a Jew, and now one of the favored leaders of the Jerusalem church, makes such an admission, and before non-Jews in the house of the god-fearer Cornelius. The very city of Caesarea, from which Rome ruled the province of Judah, should have put Peter on the defensive, reinforced him in provincial and conventional attitudes. But the opposite is true. Peter seems almost surprised at himself: "I need not tell you that a Jew is forbidden by his religion to visit or associate with a man of another race. . . ."

There is about the story a warm and simple humanity, an atmosphere in which ideology and doctrinaire exclusiveness, of whatever sort, do not thrive. Cornelius runs out to meet Peter and welcomes him with such respect that Peter protests: "I am a man like anyone else." The centurion has invited his family and friends to meet Peter, and they seem eager to listen to him. Luke paints a picture of the very situation which Peter describes: Peter preaches peace in a setting of peace. The Holy Spirit comes upon these people gathered at home, and they are filled with ecstatic joy.

What is it to be in peace—at peace with God's creation and all his creatures—and so to be able to preach peace? What prior, profound experience sets aside Peter's fears and his commitment to behavior which in another setting he would deem proper to his station? At that gathering in Cornelius's house, did Peter's preaching bring peace and joy, or was there already the atmosphere of being together *as human beings* which helped to open both preacher and people to the word? Peter had had his vision beforehand in Joppa, of the goodness of creation. And his sermon shows that he understood the gospel of the resurrection as breaking all boundaries of time, place, and status. He appreciates fully the history that God has been pleased to use: "He sent his word to the Israelites and gave the good news of peace through Jesus Christ. . . ." But the risen Christ is Lord of *all*. That is not a claim to special privilege for those who follow him, but genuine recognition of his lordship and of the fertile soil for his word, openness to his spirit, and readiness for his peace which are there by virtue of our common humanity.

A course is now being given in one of our seminaries on "Story, Humanity and Preaching." How often does our preaching and witnessing fail because we withdraw, exclude, and condescend? And how far is that from this family gathering and the meeting of two men which ends in the gifts of the Spirit and baptism?

1 John 4:1-11. But Christian inclusiveness is not moral anomie or a bland permissiveness. Legalism and license are not, after all, so far apart: both are essentially indifferent to the significance of human experience, to the weight of existence. The Johannine pastoral advice is direct and does not hedge in drawing sharp lines: "But do not trust any and every spirit, my friends; test the spirits to see whether they are from God . . ." John doesn't mumble when it comes to the test he would apply: those who belong to the community can be recognized by their acknowledgment that Jesus Christ has come in the flesh. It is the *man* Jesus with whom we have to do, and John wants nothing to do with people who aren't interested in the person that the apostles have heard, seen, and handled.

John goes further: he is interested in people who can be heard, seen, and handled right now. The true community is validated, finally, by the actual quality of its life in the flesh. This is God's family, inspired by God's spirit, and such a group of people can be recognized. Is that so? Where would *we* draw the lines? Are Christians healthier? Do they make more money, or use it better, or show more taste in the houses and clothes and pleasures they buy with it? Aren't we on safer ground just to stick to creedal distinctives? Christians are people who have been baptized and believe certain things. But John marks out the community of faith not only doctrinally but according to practice: "everyone who loves."

"Lifestyle" is the common coin for it today, and John describes the Christian's style with a word that is as worn as "relevance" or "my friends." "Love" has become as insubstantial as a gnostic Christ! But the writer calls us to it, and he ties the word, the hallmark of the Christian community, to what we know of Jesus Christ in the flesh, Lord of his church. Are all who live in love his? What would that look like, living in love? The answer, of course, depends upon our paradigm for the word. John makes clear who his own model is.

John 15:9-17. The gospel echoes 1 John: "Let us love one another, for love is of God." Jesus calls his disciples to be imaginative lovers, to let appear in their own daily lives the love with which the Father loves the Son and the Son his friends. The assumption here is a modern one. You can't just go out and be a lover; you need someone to imitate. A good many high-priced magazines make money on that premise. What paradigm of loving is adequate for the church? What can save us from mere sentimentality? What could bind a group of people together so that they would really want to spend more than an hour together hiding behind pews and organ music on a Sunday morning? What could make people listen to each other? Could any model of loving overcome the prejudices of economics, sex, race, and taste?

Whatever success we have in making such a community is not merely the predictable result of our autonomous planning and action, if we follow John. The branches draw their life from the true vine: new life in the community is life in Christ. The more we mature, the more we come to understand what it is to "dwell." Beyond all mere self-reliance and playing at being God, we learn what it is like to be connected, to be at home in him and with each other. Structure becomes freedom, ties become life, law becomes grace, and joy becomes full as joy was full in the obedient Jesus.

But how often is this actually realized in a human community? How often do we manage even a one-night stand of the humble, joyful loving which we see in Jesus Christ? What would it be to *dwell* in his love together? That would be the ideal community: loyal and outgoing, kind and demanding, at home and on the move. When Josiah Royce tried to imagine such a group of people, the best model he could come up with was the ideal church. But where does it exist?

The victory of the resurrection is that this new life is always breaking forth out of death. The community is constantly being created by the reality that already exists in Jesus Christ: "You did not choose me; I chose you." All that follows depends on that prevenient decision for us: "Go and bear fruit . . . love one another." God's love is there before and after all our efforts to love other people, and ourselves, and gives us the courage to stay with ourselves and other people through an afternoon and a night, or a gray morning, when we have hurt or failed or betrayed or hidden from the people who love us and whom we love. The victory of the resurrection is that this new life is always being created again in us because the separation of person from person, of persons from themselves and God, has been overcome, finally, and we only wait and try, by stops and starts, to get our eyes open to the fact and our ears and hearts open to the people around us in whom the resurrection takes flesh today. We are seeing among us today, in people being made whole as they are called from the deserts and closets and backrooms to come and be human together, the fruition of God's deed in Jesus Christ. The signs of God's victory are the unmistakable banners of love. Where are they in your church? Who has been called in, held up, supported, confronted, healed, challenged? In your family? Who has been heard, recognized, talked with, given time? Paul Tillich writes:

> Where one is grasped by a human face as human, although one has to overcome personal distaste, or racial strangeness, or national conflicts, or the differences of sex, of age, of beauty, of strength, of knowledge, and all the other innumerable causes of separation—*there* New Creation happens! . . . resurrection means the victory of the New state of things, the New Being born out of the death of the Old.[1]

Where are you celebrating the resurrection in your own life today? What is new, open, hopeful? Or if there is nothing, are you waiting, dwelling, abiding? Do you think that living with silence, failure, and loneliness could be part of abiding in Christ and showing forth his love?

1. Paul Tillich, *The New Being* (New York: Charles Scribner's Sons, 1955), pp. 23-24.

The Ascension of Our Lord

Lutheran	*Roman Catholic*	*Episcopal*	*Pres./UCC/Chr.*	*Methodist/COCU*
Acts 1:1-11	Acts 1:1-11	Acts 1:1-11	Acts 1:1-11	Acts 1:1-11
Eph. 1:16-23	Eph. 1:17-23	Eph. 1:16-23	Eph. 1:16-23	Eph. 1:16-23
Luke 24:44-53	Mark 16:15-20	Luke 24:49-53	Luke 24:44-53	Mark 16:15-20

EXEGESIS

The three Ascension texts are remarkably complementary, especially if one reads them in the order in which they were written:

Gospel: Luke 24:44-53. One may wish to review the exegetical notes on Luke 24 for Easter Evening and Easter III. The added paragraph is what calls for comment here.

As the risen Lord had broken bread with the Emmaus disciples, their eyes were opened, and he vanished out of their sight (24:31). Now, having appeared in Jerusalem, and having given the disciples a new hermeneutic and the promise of the Spirit, the Lord leads them out to Bethany and takes leave of them for the last time.

In *this* context it is an arresting note that there should be three instances of the verb "to bless" (vv. 50, 51, 53), and one mention of the word "joy" (v. 52). Taken together these are clear indices that the sorrow which wracked the hearts of the disciples as a result of the crucifixion has indeed been overcome by Jesus' resurrection; and that the anxiety which could so easily attend the risen Lord's final departure has already been vanquished by the gifts of opened eyes, a mission to carry out, and the sure promise of the Spirit to empower the mission.

Some educated readers of Luke's own day would easily think of the sorrow of Socrates' disciples upon his death. Here, by contrast, there is great joy, precisely upon the Lord's departure, for he is the victor who will shortly pour out the Spirit to guide and empower his followers. His ascension begins the mission of his church through the whole of the world.

First Lesson: Acts 1:1-11. One has to recognize, first, that the very idea of following a Gospel with a sequel, a second volume on the history of the church, was not only unheard of prior to Luke's efforts, but also almost unthinkable. From a careful reading of the other Gospels it is clear that the earliest understanding of the literary form resulted from narrating the story of Jesus in a way which included the contemporary dimensions of that story in the life and destiny of the church (see, e.g., Matthew 10). There was, in short, only one story.

Now, in Luke's hands, a new horizon appears. There is still only one story, but it unfolds in epochs which may be presented and contemplated also in their own right, and this reflects a great shift in the church's understanding of itself. We can be sure that it never occurred to any member of the highly eschatologically conscious church of the first decades to make the church an object of historical inquiry. Yet this is exactly what Luke has done. Motifs of "world-foreignness" common to the earliest communities—and continued and developed in different ways by the gnostics—are left behind in Luke's understanding of the church. Indeed, he sees the growth of the church not as a sign of the imminent end, but rather as *the key to the whole of world history*.

Several aspects of the present text make this clear. Luke is conscious of writing literature (1:1) about a movement which may be described historically and chronologically (1:8). In the first paragraph, which overlaps the penultimate paragraph of the carefully structured final chapter of his Gospel (cf. Luke 24:36-49 with Acts 1:1-8), Luke allows the disciples to speak in such a way as to place the major point in relief. They ask whether it is now the end time (1:6); and Jesus corrects them by substituting a very long—one may say linear—end time (1:8). The correction is then placed in italics by being repeated: At the ascension, the disciples gaze after their master into heaven as though that were the locale in which they themselves belonged. "No," say the two angels, "do not stand here gazing into heaven. Your task is to wait in Jerusalem for the promised Spirit, who will lead you with the gospel to the end of the *earth*."

It is not a call to mere action, of course, as constrasted with contemplation. One will not credit the angels with an exhortation to roll up one's sleeves and get to work. The correction has to do, rather, with the *scene* of *God's* action, which he will carry out, to be sure, in and through his people. Jesus' ascension means not that the sequel to his earthly life will be played out in a supraterrestrial realm, but rather precisely the opposite. He will pour out the promised Holy Spirit upon his flesh-and-blood witnesses, who will then march through the world for its healing. Luke would easily have understood John 3:16. It is the world which God is in love with, and his being in love with it is its salvation.

Second Lesson: Eph. 1:16-23. The document opens (1:1-2) in the form of a letter, yet without a clear indication of the addressees, unless, as seems unlikely, the words "in Ephesus" stood in the original text of verse one. There follows—without an exact counterpart in the letters confidently ascribed to Paul—a lengthy eulogy to God, in which the author emphasizes the comprehensive nature of God's over-arching redemptive plan, into which both he and his readers have been gracefully brought (1:3-14). For numerous reasons it appears that the document is essentially a homily written by a Jewish Christian who sees his Gentile Christian brothers to be in danger of losing vital contact with his group. The homily finds its center in the picture of the Body of Christ as encompassing believers of both Jewish and Gentile heritage. That is to say, for the author the church has itself become a large part of theology. This fact makes possible a profitable comparison of Ephesians with Acts.

Note that immediately before our passage lies a paragraph (1:11-14) which Käsemann has taught us to compare with the Cornelius story of Acts 10 (see Easter VI). One may paraphrase:

> *We Jews* who first hoped in Christ have been destined and appointed to live for the praise of the glory of him in whom also *you Gentiles* were sealed with the Holy Spirit after you had heard the word of truth . . . and had believed in him.

It is God himself who broke through the limits of the old people of God in order to include also the Gentiles (cf. 2:13 ff.). The Jewish Christian author is amazed at this; he also gives thanks for it. His thanksgiving is formally expressed in our passage, which actually consists of a brief thanksgiving (v. 16a) and a long intercessory prayer (vv. 16b-23). One senses again the Jewishness of the author when one compares this passage with the thanksgiving prayers of Qumran; just as one senses his Christian faith expressed in a kind of creed in vv. 20-23.

It is this creedal expression, of course, which makes the passage an ascension text. The author draws, no doubt, on previous formulations. Compare Phil. 2:9 ff.; 1 Pet. 3:18 ff.; and Polycarp 2:1 f. The confession has three major accents: (1) God's raising Christ from the dead, (2) his exalting him to his own right hand, and (3) his subjecting all powers under Christ's feet. The author has expanded the creed by adding a fourth element, which is designed to explain the full significance of the first three: (4) The resurrection and the ascension and the exaltation above all powers of the cosmos find their meaningful goal in the fact that God has made Christ head of the *church*, which is then specified to be both Christ's body and the fullness of Christ, who fills all in all.

The Jewish Christian author surveys what we would call the ecumenical scene, and sees that the *cosmic* lordship of Christ is effected in and through the *church*, where the dividing wall of hostility between Jews and Gentiles is broken down (2:14). It is a hermeneutical task of some proportions to try to hear the voice of this Christian brother across the years and tears of the Holocaust; and the health of the contemporary church may be to no small degree dependent on such hearing.

HOMILETICAL INTERPRETATION

With what images will *we* celebrate the elevation of Jesus to kingly power? Language strains and metaphors limp as we try to preach in the blunt way expected of us on this day at the end of Eastertide and on the verge of Pentecost. The presence of the living Lord with his people bursts the bounds of the shuttered room and reaches beyond Jerusalem to the ends of the earth and the end of the age. Time and space cannot contain what Luke and Paul have experienced in the days of Pontius Pilate and on the road to Damascus. It may be true that the cloud of glory may not be as real to us as to Luke, or even "up" so powerful an idea as it was before Mercury and Apollo became names for our technological prowess. But we, nevertheless, between Easter and Pentecost, celebrate both his absence and his presence.

Eph. 1:16-23. For the apostolic witness, the exaltation of Jesus is inseparable from the new life in Christ: "... in union with Christ Jesus ... [God] raised us up and enthroned us with him in the heavenly realms...." (2:6) We may be less able to handle language like that than images of ascension! The author describes a "high" that, to his mind, is the normal state of the church as it is raised up to a new life of forgiveness. We are, he says, delivered from "this present age" and from the "spiritual powers of the air" (2:2). The whole epistle reads like a hymnbook and the two themes play back and forth, both in the discrete pericope and in the overall composition of the book: You are raised up with Christ; in your new life you bring praise to him. "Praise be to the God and Father of our Lord Jesus Christ, who has bestowed on us in Christ every spiritual blessing in the heavenly realms ... in order that the glory of his gracious gift ... might redound to his praise." (1:3-5)

These twin themes are the background to the apostle's words: "Because of all this ... I give thanks ... I pray." Where people are forgiven and know it—only the *knowing* is problematical—Christ is exalted. All that God has done, in prophets and psalmist and lawgiver, has moved toward this: a group of men and women freed from guilt and fear, open to each other, grateful and liberated for the future. What better metaphor than "body" could we find? This visible people in its diversity, weakness, and humanity is as inseparable from Christ as body from spirit.

The apostle prays for those "inward eyes" which can see both the unbelievable freedom and power which people together in Christ actually have, and, at the same time, the enthronement of Jesus Christ above all merely earthly power. The writer searches for words to sing "Worthy is the lamb," and he comes out with what may appear to us quite a mundane picture: people at peace, living together in love and joy, are the transfigured body of Christ. Where, in the whole universe, is there greater praise to Christ than people at peace living together in love? There is that painting of Dali's showing Christ both crucified and exalted at the same time. This Christ looks down from his cross upon a scene of the greatest tranquility in which people quietly work and where even earth and sky seem to be transformed in each other's embrace. Where are the signs among *us* that the apostle's prayer has been answered?

> Grant, we beseech thee, Almighty God, that like as we do believe thy only begotten Son our Lord Jesus Christ to have ascended into the heavens; we may also in heart and mind thither ascend, and with him continually dwell, who liveth and reigneth with thee and the Holy Ghost, one God, world without end. Amen (Common Prayer, for Ascension)

Luke 24:44-53, Acts 1:1-11. It is not easy to see what is at hand, or to appreciate fully what we already possess. In fact, as Peter Rinkoping discovers in Frederick Buechner's *Entrance to Porlock*, we must sometimes have the best taken from us and returned as gift before we recognize it as precious. How often do we actually "see" members of our families and our closest friends when they are absent? Is it any wonder that the Ephesian writer prays that the church may have inward eyes to see the absolutely astounding wonder of the gospel which can take on such homely form?

Luke begins *Acts* by recalling his Gospel in which he had tried to tell all that Jesus did and taught. He recalls that Jesus had been with his followers for forty days between Easter Day and Pentecost. Then, in the very midst of that recital, we hear the plaintive disciples: "Lord, will you at this time restore the kingdom to Israel?" The kingdom was there, in their very life together and in the words and deeds of their Lord which were their inalienable possession, and they did not see it! How much distance do we need to see clearly? Jesus had promised his friends, as he prepared them in the upstairs room, that the Comforter would teach them all things concerning himself. Could that promise be kept only in his absence? The prophet is not without honor, except among people who know him *too* well. Had the kingdom been a snake, it would have bitten them many times before they saw it.

The response to their question is both understatement and the patience of a man who knows that he has done all that he can do but who knows also that God's kingdom is already coming: "It is not for you to know. . . . But you shall receive power. . . . " Jesus has made his witness to the kingdom—it is there in what he has said and done—and now they are to be witnesses. They do not bring the kingdom, as if it were indeed a governmental and geographical estate over which a king might reign from David's throne. They are *witnesses* to the kingdom as it has already appeared in Jesus. It is true that this kingdom will be ruled from Jerusalem, but not from an easily recognizable throne or by a king who would be identified by the usual marks. The "times and seasons" are in God's control.

So they are told to wait. The very idea rubs us wrong. We are people of instant breakfast and get-up-and-go, get it done and come home to supper and that satisfied feeling of something *real* accomplished. But they are told to wait, even to "tarry" until they receive power. What all of this means, that they are to carry on his ministry as his witnesses, will become clear to them. Wait. As uncongenial as the idea may be to an activistic American, it is the only way to find out what we have and what we do not have.

Paul Tillich has said that "Waiting means not having and having at the same time."[1] Tillich launches into a kind of litany in which he urges us to be willing to wait with empty hands:

> I think of the theologian who does not wait for God, because he possesses Him, enclosed in a book. I think of the churchman who does not wait for God, because he possesses Him, enclosed in an institution. I think of the believer who does not wait for God, because he possesses Him, enclosed within his own experience.[2]

But the community which watches Jesus disappear out of their sight, waits. And in the waiting they discover what they do not have *and* what

1. Paul Tillich, *The Shaking of the Foundations* (New York: Charles Scribner's Sons, 1948), p. 149.
2. Ibid., p. 150.

they do have. Jesus is no longer present with them as he once was, but in his very absence they are brought together as people who rely on each other, and they are sent out as witnesses on a vast, new scale.

But we ought not to overlook the concreteness of this story. Even as we are being dazzled by the ascending Christ and commissioned to go to the ends of the earth, the writer maintains a dogged provincialism. These witnesses are to begin at Jerusalem. Wherever they go they will tell about the events that have occurred there. They are witnesses to Jesus who set his face to go to Jerusalem and was lifted up there to draw all persons to himself. Here is the particularity and the universality of the commission: Begin at Jerusalem and go as far as feet and beast and ship can take you. Even as Jesus leaves them, the place names which Luke records tie the church to this soil and to the deeds done here: Bethany, Jerusalem, Judea, Samaria, Olivet. As W. H. Auden has it:

A poet's hope: to be,
like some valley cheese,
local, but prized elsewhere.[3]

". . . and in the act of blessing he parted from them." His going away is viewed here as part of the divine plan for the salvation of the world. Now the Spirit will come and they will understand more clearly what he meant and how they are to speak of him. The events of those last days in Jerusalem will become more and more meaningful as they experience together the reality of forgiveness and life together. So even as he leaves them, he blesses them. "And they returned to Jerusalem with great joy, and spent all their time in the temple praising God." There isn't anything about this that smacks of people standing on the platform or at the gate, to say nothing of the graveside, saying a last goodbye. His going away has made it possible for them to know just what they have, to bind them together, and to allow them no more leisure for gazing into heaven than reason for mourning his absence.

That painting, "Christ of St. John of the Cross," speaks of presence in absence. The cross is just suspended there, floating, and though Jesus is on it, there are no nails holding him there. We can see a long way and our view takes in sea and sky, sun, clouds and mountains, but everything we see is well within the view of the drooping—or is it soaring—figure on the cross. There is about even the black sky a peacefulness and the whole picture seems to hold together. Strange, though, how that can be: people working, a calm blue sea and azure sky, and the figure up there above it, not part of the scene below but not absent from it either. One thing is sure, looking at it we feel that we could easily, comfortably, cast the nets or set sail in the boat or walk along with the worker who lives under that ascending cross.

3. W. H. Auden, *Epistle to a Godson* (New York: Random House, 1969), p. 37.

The Seventh Sunday of Easter

Lutheran	*Roman Catholic*	*Episcopal*	*Pres./UCC/Chr.*	*Methodist/COCU*
Acts. 1:15-26	Acts.1:15-17, 20a, 20c-26	Acts 1:15-26	Acts 1:15-17, 21-26	Acts 1:15-26
1 John 4:13-21	1 John 4:11-16	1 John 5:9-15	1 John 4:11-16	1 John 4:11-16
John 17:11b-19	John 17:11b-19	John 17:11b-19	John 17:11-19	John 17:11-19

EXEGESIS

First Lesson: Acts 1:15-26. Several factors make clear that we have before us a speech composed by Luke, on the basis of earlier tradition to be sure, and quite appropriately placed in Peter's mouth: (1) v. 19: In the situation portrayed, Peter would scarcely need to inform the Jerusalem community of an event "known to all the inhabitants of Jerusalem," and he would certainly not interpret for such an audience an Aramaic expression, referring to Aramaic as "their language," that is to say, the language of Jerusalemites. It is Luke who, not having footnotes at his disposal, speaks to his Gentile readers, translating for them the Aramaic term. (2) v. 20: The interpretations of the Psalm texts (look them up!) presuppose the readings given in the Septuagint; they were made by persons in the Hellenistic church sometime prior to Luke's writing. Moreover, there were several traditions about Judas' death: note Matt. 27:3-10 (he hanged himself); Papias (he swelled to monstrous proportions). Luke has probably selected one from among those known to him. The statement of v. 17 is a piece of early Christian honesty and realism. There is no denying that Judas was one of the inner circle of the twelve.

This verse (17) is also one of the clues to Luke's interests and intentions. As we have seen repeatedly, Luke is keenly interested in the *linear continuity* of God's plan, as he causes it to be formed in the emergence of the great church. Hence, even a small share of "this ministry" cannot simply be dropped and forgotten. The church has a long way to go (1:18), and will need the full complement of its founding circle: Judas' place must be filled.

The requirements for the successor (vv. 21 f.) are the standards set in Acts for an apostle, and, again, these standards emphasize the need for continuity. This continuity is the product of God's acts, however, and is not the result of human "conservatism." That is made clear by the procedure followed to determine the successor's identity. There is no election, based on the principles of democracy ("the people rule"), which would have been, in fact, quite strange to the early church. God is the one who chooses, for the entire plan has been fixed by his authority (1:7). That this choice fell on a man named Matthias is known to Luke from tradition. The greatest weight falls on the continuity which links Jesus' life, Jesus' resurrection, and the "apostolic" ministry (witness) of the church (vv. 21-22). One may recall the three infinitives of Luke 24:46 f. The actions of God referred to in those infinitives, rather than any principle of organization, form the *fundamentum* of the emerging church.

Second Lesson: 1 John 4:13-21. Among the many motifs of this text, one of the most important is the statement about the mutually exclusive nature of Christian love and fear (4:18). The author lived in the Hellenistic age, one of the major marks of which was the widespread and dualistically oriented experience of anxiety. Indeed one might logically wonder whether a man who believes that "the spirit of deceit" is lurking about, seeking ways to lead folk astray into destruction (4:6), would not himself be subject to periods of fear. There is, in fact, every reason to believe that our author is personally acquainted with debilitating anxiety.

Yet he boldly affirms that love not only encompasses no fear, but also that love excludes fear from the field. How so? At least part of the answer lies in the link presupposed between fear (v. 18) and hatred (v. 20). Of whom might the author and his readers be afraid? In the first instance, perhaps, of the false teachers and of the spirit of deceit which animates the latter. But who are these teachers, precisely? They are the ones who say they love God, but hate their brothers. It seems that the author knows quite well that one hates because one is afraid. Hence the love which is perfected in the Christian fellowship is the antithesis of both hatred and fear.

Gospel: John 17:11b-19. This chapter presents the prayer of Jesus uttered virtually as though he were already in the process of ascending to the Father (vv. 11a, 12a, 13a). That will in itself remind us of the major *problem* to which the farewell discourses (chaps. 14-17) are addressed: Jesus Christ has come into the world which was created through him (1:3, 10); yet, paradoxically, the world does not, on the whole, welcome him (1:10; 12:37). To the world as such he is somehow The Stranger, and those who do believe in him become a community who are similarly strangers to the world (15:18 ff.; 17:14). Well and good, so long as he is with them. But now the time has come for the Stranger to return to the Father, and hence the problem: With his departure, his followers are left behind in foreign territory as orphans (14:18). This turn of events is bound to strike fear into their hearts (14:1).

All elements of the farewell discourses are formulated with this problem in mind. Not least 17:9-19, the sub-unit of chap. 17 of which our reading is a part. Note v. 11a: Jesus is no longer in the world, but the disciples remain in the world, and although he might consider asking the Father to remove also them out of the world (v. 15), he does not do so. What does he ask? While he was with them, he guarded them (v. 12); now he asks the Father to do that (v. 11a), and specifically to keep them from the evil one.

How is this request to be fulfilled? First, by the fact that Jesus has given to the disciples the Father's word (v. 14). The Father will now "consecrate" them in this word (v. 17), i.e., he will make them holy, as he is holy (v. 11) and will thus guard them. Second, by the paradoxical fact that the disciples are now sent into the world in a way quite analogous to the way the Father sent the Son into the world. We see here, once again, that the expression "world" is used to refer both to the largely hostile environment experienced by the Johannine community (e.g., 16:1 f.) and to the object of God's love and redemptive intentions. Note carefully 17:20 f. The Johannine community is not a collection of the last believers! There will certainly be others, and these others will believe because the apparent "orphans" are not left desolate, but are rather kept in God's word, and in fact are empowered by the coming of the Paraclete to utter that word to others.

HOMILETICAL INTERPRETATION

On this Sunday after the Ascension, close to Pentecost, we see the church in its germinal and seminal stages. What is private becomes provincial and then, in the confident power of the ascended Lord and the coming Spirit, becomes universal. In the Gospel for today, Jesus prays for his own little band. Luke tells of the community that has grown to the size of a modest parish church, and the Johannine epistle stakes out even larger territory. What has occurred in the environs of Jerusalem leaves the world different as these witnesses spread in all directions like ripples from one stone.

John 17:11b-19. Can we make too much of the power of a discrete human event? Is it true that what is most personal is most universal? We may be impressed by big scale and shiny ideology, but what is it that empowers these early Christians and keeps them going, uncowed by the power of Rome and the unbelieving hostility which they will face?

John shows us Jesus in retreat with the twelve, getting them ready to move out of the upstairs room and into the streets. He is washing their feet! It is a preparation for the sabbath. A group of friends are together for a meal of fellowship. At Jesus' hands the simple food and the washing become the sanctifying of a new sabbath, preparation for their role in God's new time which will be measured from the day of resurrection. As Jesus teaches his disciples, prays for them, and consecrates himself, he is equipping a cadre.

What great movement has not begun in privacy? And does not the church, into whatever streets it moves, find its origins and continuing identity by reference to the events of that room and immediately surrounding it? Behind the church at the barricades and rushing to the place where the action is, there is the church in retreat with the one who breaks bread and takes a towel. The Fourth Gospel gives ample room, indeed makes essential, what Marriane Moore calls "our particular possession, the sense of privacy." Elton Trueblood, too, calls the activist church, the public person, the leader, to the essential preparation of private experience. Jesus' last gift to those whom he will send into the world even as the Father has sent him, is to get them *away* from the world by a gift of intimacy.

What will, after all, hold them together? How is it possible that these men who have already shown themselves contentious, ambitious, and shallow could stay together, to say nothing of their carrying on Jesus' ministry? He prays for them: "Holy Father, keep them in thy name which thou hast given me, that they may be one, even as we are one." What we might expect here is a pep-talk or some good advice on sales technique or surefire evangelism. Instead, Jesus gives them gifts which they will not forget, the same gifts which they are to give. In the single act of washing their feet he both consecrates himself and sanctifies them. From such a seminal moment everything issues, and it is a moment which we easily recognize from our own experience. It didn't seem particularly important at the time, but it was that day when your mother came into your room for a talk, or your father kept a promise, or you received the letter. And the ripples are still going. And from time to time you remember that moment, and you place yourself by it as if it were one of those colored arrows on a map telling you "You are here."

What makes the church possible? What makes a family possible or, for that matter, enables one human life to hold together? What enables people to say "yes" to each other and to themselves and over the long haul to accept and affirm and stick with each other? The word "consecrate" is a sacrificial word. Jesus consecrates himself, gives himself up, and takes upon himself all that there is in human life which separates and says no and tears apart. And it is right there, in that washing of their feet. He consecrates himself, and the world is overcome, and the community of grace is born. As Jesus bends to them with the basin, there is a microcosm of all he meant and of all that his followers would become. Jesus' offering of himself becomes vine and door, true life and way. The friends who gather on that evening to sanctify the sabbath are themselves sanctified for the kingdom, sanctified not by virtue of their own perfectibility or competence but by the Lord whose self-sacrifice they know for themselves.

We can't make too much of the discrete event, of the particular story which we know, of what has happened to us. If we could ask any one of those men, later on, in who knows what circumstances: "Why do you speak as you do? How can you go on? Are you sure of what you are doing?", what would he say? Is Frederick Buechner right, that finally all of us have to push back our chairs and take off our spectacles and tell a story about something that happened to *us* once? Jesus has washed their feet and then sent them out without an extra pair of shoes to witness to the whole world. If we were to fish around for something like that experience today we would probably come up with a teacher or an artist "blowing our minds" and sending us out with only a pair of blue jeans and something to tell. Is that what it is like to overcome the world and to have his joy fulfilled in us?

Acts 1:15-26. Frost has it right, so far as Christianity is concerned. Swinging high on birches is fine, he says, within limits:

May no fate willfully misunderstand me
And half grant what I wish and snatch me away
Not to return. Earth's the right place for love:
I don't know where it's likely to go better.[1]

How many student ministers have lived, so to speak, way up in the birches on a seminary campus, only to find themselves on a weekend brought down to earth by people in a little country church with no indoor plumbing and a morning service that sometimes smelled more of people just in from doing the chores than of incense? Coming as we are now to the end of Eastertide, we are being brought down to earth. That is as it should be. The pattern in the NT is familiar: tarrying on the mountaintop is tolerated no more than gnostic tendencies to spiritualize the gospel.

From Olivet the disciples return to the room upstairs. The ascension of Jesus had been punctuated by an admonition: "Men of Galilee, why stand there looking up into the sky?" That we have seen God's glory shining forth in Jesus leads us down from the mountain and into the world of strategies. We remember the high moment, and we may even feel a pang when we take down the Christmas wreath in the middle of January, but finally we are brought back to our familiar places and mundane responsibilities. One of our best preachers, whose strength is his earthiness, says that we should always try to keep in mind that the church is just around the corner from St. John of the Gas Station. The room upstairs provides us a good symbol of both the mountain and the mundane. It is the place of the towel and the basin and dusty feet, of simple food and friends eating together. At the same time, it is much more, a transfiguration. But finally it is still bread and wine and human feet, common things which carry this meaning.

And so we see these early Christians, in the lees of the Ascension, turning to the election of a successor to Judas. There is about it something of the demeanor of the woman who goes to work the day after she wins the million dollar lottery or the man who cleans the gutters to celebrate a promotion. They name Matthias to succeed Judas, and we know that we have here to do with the *church*.

1 John 4:13-21. So here is the church which Jesus sanctified? Already they are fighting and threatened. The pastor is obviously appealing for community rather than contention, for the people to be together despite their differences and to live together in peace despite all that works against peace. Can it be? Can the lordship of the ascended Christ and the image of the footwasher bind these people? That is the only reassurance the writer offers: being together is a gift of God through Christ.

The images of family and home might work, as we try to get inside the

1. Robert Frost, "Birches," *Poems of Robert Frost* (New York: Modern Library, 1946), p. 128.

writer's understanding of Christian discipleship and community. Children growing up in a house learn quite early that the complex interconnections that make up "home" are held together by gifts. Oh, it's true that a house works better if everyone has duties and if certain limits are established. But finally "home" is unconditional free gift. This gift comes as many gifts, but the most significant are from the parents: the decision to have the child in the first place, the provision of food and toys and heat and light, and the tacit recognition by everyone in the house that these gifts may in fact be taken for granted. And that they are taken for granted is grounded in one fact, the love of human beings for each other. Home holds together in a house because people are *in* love. It is all the gift of love.

John paints such a picture of the Christian community. "God is love, and he who abides in love abides in God, and God abides in him." If we give the most universal interpretation to that verse, then we have reached the outermost boundary of the meaning of the ascension. John's intention is much more limited: the love we know, we know in Jesus Christ, and it is because of the love which we have seen in him that we are able to be together. John's pastoral advice could easily have for its text the story of Jesus washing his friends' feet, for the best gifts we have to give are those given to us.

My friend and I took a walk one spring morning, the kind of day when promises are easily made. He was feeling down, and the flowering magnolia tree we had left our chores to see must have been to him both joy and pain. "I will send you something," I said, as we walked back to our duties. "It is an essay by Oscar Wilde." "Fine," he said. He went home to Pennsylvania, time passed, and the promise and presence of mind and the book seemed never to get together, and there was that vague feeling of guilt not quite strong enough to move the laggard feet to the library. Then one day, I got down my friend's own book to prepare for class, and there it was as the book fell open, the very paragraph from Wilde's *De Profundis*. And I wrote to tell him: "My gift to you is your gift to me."

Set on the road, called to wash each other's feet, to forgive and bear with each other and be honest and stay at it, we have had our feet washed. And so we are able to love because he first loves us.

PROCLAMATION:

Aids for Interpreting the Lessons of the Church Year

PENTECOST 3

SERIES B

Fred Craddock
and
Leander Keck

FORTRESS PRESS Philadelphia, Pennsylvania

Library of Congress Catalog Card Number 74-25171

ISBN 0-8006-4078-0

4753I75 Printed in U.S.A. 1-4078

General Preface

Proclamation: Aids for Interpreting the Lessons of the Church Year is a series of twenty-six books designed to help clergymen carry out their preaching ministry. If offers exegetical interpretations of the lessons for each Sunday and many of the festivals of the church year, plus homiletical ideas and insights.

The basic thrust of the series is ecumenical. In recent years the Episcopal church, the Roman Catholic church, the United Church of Christ, the Christian Church (Disciples of Christ), the United Methodist Church, the Lutheran and Presbyterian churches, and also the Consultation on Church Union have adopted lectionaries that are based on a common three-year system of lessons for the Sundays and festivals of the church year. *Proclamation* grows out of this development, and authors have been chosen from all of these traditions. Some of the contributors are parish pastors; others are teachers, both of biblical interpretation and of homiletics. Ecumenical interchange has been encouraged by putting two persons from different traditions to work on a single volume, one with the primary responsibility for exegesis and the other for homiletical interpretation.

Despite the high percentage of agreement between the traditions, both in the festivals that are celebrated and the lessons that are appointed to be read on a given day, there are still areas of divergence. Frequently the authors of individual volumes have tried to take into account the various textual traditions, but in some cases this has proved to be impossible; in such cases we have felt constrained to limit the material to the Lutheran readings.

The preacher who is looking for "canned sermons" in these books will be disappointed. These books are one step removed from the pulpit: they explain what the lessons are saying and suggest ways of relating this biblical message to the contemporary situation. As such they are springboards for creative thought as well as for faithful proclamation of the word.

This final volume in the *Proclamation* series has been written by Fred B. Craddock and Leander E. Keck. Dr. Craddock, the editor-homiletician, is Professor of Preaching and New Testament in the Graduate Seminary, Phillips University, Enid, Okla. He is a graduate of Johnson Bible College, Knoxville, Tenn. (B.A.), Phillips University (B.D.), and Vanderbilt University (Ph.D.). Dr. Craddock has written two books, *The Pre-Existence of Christ* (1968) and *As One without Authority* (1971; rev. ed., 1974), and contributed numerous articles to various journals. He serves as a member of the General Board of the Christian Church and also on the

Administrative Committee of the Christian Church (Disciples of Christ). Dr. Keck, the exegete, is Professor of New Testament, Candler School of Theology, and Chairman of the Division of Religion, Graduate School of Arts and Sciences, Emory University, Atlanta, Ga. He is a graduate of Linfield College (B.A.), Andover Newton Theological School (B.D.), and Yale University (Ph.D.). Dr. Keck is the author of three books: *Taking the Bible Seriously* (1962; paperback ed., 1969); *Mandate to Witness* (1964); and *A Future for the Historical Jesus* (1971). He has also served as co-editor with J. Louis Martyn of *Studies in Luke-Acts*, a Festschrift for Paul Schubert (1966), editor of the Society of Biblical Literature's Monograph Series, and editor for the "Lives of Jesus" series published by Fortress Press. In this latter series he is translating, editing, and providing an introduction for David Friedrich Strauss's *The Christ of Faith and the Jesus of History*.

Introduction

Perhaps it would be helpful at the outset to make a few suggestions about the use and non-use of the book.

First, prior to any use of this book or any other book, read and re-read the Scripture selections. Sometimes a reader can be deceived by the structure of a book. Biblical references in small print at the top of the page may be easily passed over for the exegetical and homiletical discussions that follow. To do so would be to minimize the value of this book which presupposes careful reading of the texts and to jeopardize the quality of one's preaching. The preacher facilitates a conversation not between this book and the congregation but between the Scriptures and the congregation. There is not to be found in print an adequate substitute for this direct interaction.

Second, permit yourself, even indulge yourself, in immediate and spontaneous reactions to the biblical texts. Register on a note pad every surprise, question, doubt, recollection, feeling, idea that comes to the surface. This pre-commentary exercise will remove the inhibitions that subtly take over when approaching Holy Scripture. Reverence sometimes hinders the full use of our faculties for feeling, inquiring, thinking, imagining. In addition this exercise helps the preacher identify with his listeners who will, after all, be hearing the text without exegetical aids.

Third, resist the temptation to impose a thematic unity upon the three readings for the day. In some cases unity will be there but this will need to be discovered in the course of examining each text separately. You will notice that both exegetical and homiletical notes seek to follow this principle.

Fourth, *overhear* each text before trying to hear it. In other words, listen in on the conversation between the author and his readers before asking the author to speak relevantly to you or your congregation. To enable this overhearing is the purpose of the exegesis. Only in this way can the integrity of the past and the intention of the author be discovered and respected. Otherwise, the all-too-common error is repeated: private words become public words by disregarding their intent.

Finally, you will discover that this overhearing will soon draw you into the text. As in a theatre where the actors never speak to you directly and yet by analogy and identification you feel addressed, so it is before the carefully studied text. The result is a new hearing of the Word which at the same time provides a new way of seeing the congregation. This is what it means for the Bible to be the church's "Scripture." The homiletical sections of this book seek to help one move from overhearing to hearing, but admittedly the trip is only partial. It can be completed only by the minister who, even in the privacy of the study, is surrounded by a congregation constantly whispering, "Remember me when you come into your pulpit."

Fred B. Craddock

Table of Contents

The Twentieth Sunday after Pentecost

Lutheran	*Roman Catholic*	*Episcopal*	*Pres./UCC/Chr.*	*Methodist/COCU*
Gen. 2:18-24	Gen. 2:18-24	Gen. 2:18-24	Gen. 2:18-24	Gen. 2:18-24
Heb. 2:9-11	Heb. 2:9-11	Heb. 2:9-18	Heb. 2:9-13	Heb. 2:9-13
Mark 10:2-16	Mark 10:2-16	Mark 10:2-9	Mark 10:2-16	Mark 10:2-16

EXEGESIS

First Lesson: Gen. 2:18-24. This passage is part of the Yahwist's creation story which begins in the middle of Gen. 2:4, "In the day that the Lord God (Yahweh Elohim) made. . . ." The priestly creation story, written several centuries later, is found in Gen. 1:1—2:4a.

In the Yahwist's version, God created the man from the earth and then imparted his own life-breath to him (Gen. 2:7); in the priestly account, the emphasis is on the "image and likeness" (Gen. 1:26 f.). More important for our lesson, in the priestly account male and female humans appear to have been created simultaneously, whereas in the Yahwist account woman is created subsequently. In fact, in the priestly account, the creation of the human pair is the climax of creation, but in the Yahwist version the man is created first, then vegetation, then living creatures lest the man be alone in the world.

The Yahwist version neither teaches, nor implies, the subordination of the woman to the man, but the opposite. None of the creatures is a "fit" companion for the man, even though they too are formed from the ground as he was. Nor does the story teach or imply that woman is merely man's helper; rather, it implicitly denies this because it says that the animals were created to help man and that this quest for a "helpmeet" was unsuccessful. The woman was created as an alternative to the quest for a helper; when the man saw her, he says nothing at all about having found a helper at last. Rather, she is "bone of my bone, flesh of my flesh." That is, she shares his dignity as an equal. She is neither a work-animal nor any other kind of "lower creature."

Even though the passage (Gen. 2:18-24) is much older than the story in Genesis 1 (ca. 6th cent. B.C.), it incorporates different levels of tradition; (a) the creation of woman (Gen. 2:18-22), (b) the man's response, v. 23; (c) the reference to marriage, v. 24, (d) the mention of their nakedness—which anticipates the next phase in the overall account (Gen. 3:1-21). The translation of the second half of the couplet (v. 23) brings out the inner connection between the Hebrew words: *'ish* (man) and *'ishshah* (woman) are inherently related. The reference to marriage implicitly scores three points: The bond of marriage is stronger than that of lineal descent; the couple form a single living entity ("one flesh"); finally, marriage is not an economic necessity which results from the "fall" (as is arduous labor, Gen. 3:19), but is part of the created order. V. 24 expresses the ancient assumption that marriage is the norm, and is not a deliberate response to considered reflection on whether everyone ought to be married.

Second Lesson: Heb. 2:9-13. The longer Episcopal lection is pertinent also to the shorter ones; indeed, the entire chapter forms a coherent whole, so that Heb. 2:1-8 must be considered if we are to grasp the argument.

The anonymous Epistle to the Hebrews provides a Second Lesson for Pentecost 20-27. Consequently both the preacher and the congregation have an opportunity for a substained encounter with this subtly argued, elegantly written, and frequently neglected book. In the NT, only Romans is comparable in articulating an integrated theological argument. Therefore the exegete must always be alert to the way a given passage fits into the overall development of the argument.

A hallmark of Hebrews is the way its theological themes are related to the actual situation of the readers. There is no clear reason to think that they are in danger of returning to Judaism, nor that the readers are Qumranites (or other Jews) whom the author is trying to evangelize. The readers are clearly Christians who have lost their initial enthusiasm. The writer sees them in danger of "drifting away" from the faith (Heb. 2:1; 3:12-19; 6:4-8), of being stunted in their understanding of the faith (Heb. 5:11—6:3), of being negligent in attending worship (Heb. 10:23-25). Despite a good record (Heb. 10:32-34), their devotion is waning (Heb. 12:12). It is not clear why their faith appears to be drooping. Perhaps it was the backlash of the fact that the Lord had not come as soon as had been expected; or the earlier enthusiasm of Christian worship could not be sustained. Both possibilities have been advanced. In any case, to bolster this community, the author presents a theological argument!

The central theme of his theology is the definitive meaning of Christ, whose significance surpasses both angels (who, according to a tradition taken for granted, mediated the law, Heb. 2:2) and the whole OT cultus. Evidently the readers were impressed by the role of angels as divine mediators; the writer insists repeatedly that Christ is superior to angels, for he is the radiation (*apaugasmo*, 1:3, like "radiation" can mean both the process and the substance) of God, God's agent of creation (1:2), and now is God's regent (1:3-13). Moreover, the revelation of God mediated by angels has been supported by the gospel (inaugurated by the Son) attested by the apostles and supported by God-given wonders, including the gift of the Spirit (Heb. 2:1-4).

Today's lection carries forward the theme of the decisiveness of the event of Christ. To do so, the writer relies on a "three stage" Christology: pre-existence, existence, post-existence, though he concentrates on the second and third stages—the incarnation and exaltation of Christ. A second element in the theme is the author's use of OT passages, which he correlates to each of the three stages; a third is the soteriological meaning of the incarnation—viz., that by it the pre-existent Son established the solidarity with humanity so that it might be saved. The author anticipates a theme developed by Irenaeus (ca. A.D. 180)—that Christ became what we are so that we may become what he is.

But Christ is in glory, yet we are on earth, very much in history. Does not this disparity undermine the validity of the gospel? Not at all, argues our author. Hebrews 2 is designed to substantiate this conviction. First, he uses Psalm 8 to assert that all things have indeed been subjected to the Son; the writer understands "son of man" to refer to heavenly Son of man, not as an equivalent of "man" as in the original Hebrew. Since he has in mind the three-stage Christology as he reads the LXX, he takes *brachu* to mean "for a little time" rather than "a little less" (*brachu* can mean either), and so sees in Psalm 8 an allusion to the brief incarnation of the Son who then was made God's regent over creation. Second, he notes that now we do not see everything subject to Christ; v. 8 must not be construed to mean that now we see only some things subject to Christ and that we shall see this grow. The point, rather, is that Christ is lord and we do not see at all that everything is subject to him. Third—and here today's lection begins—what we do see is Jesus, the one who briefly had been a human among humans. For the author, the three stages are a single indivisible event; therefore the stage two which we can see—Jesus the human who suffered—guarantees the reality of stages one and three which we cannot now see. The author can reason this way because for him faith is "the conviction of things not seen" (Heb. 11:1). Those whose faith is sagging can be reassured of the truth of the gospel even though the sovereignty of Christ is not a visible phenomenon.

Fourth, to undergird his argument the author reflects further on the meaning of the incarnation for human salvation. The theological principle is stated in v. 11—there must be solidarity between the savior and the saved (see also v. 17). Precisely this solidarity was established by the incarnation (hence everything angels may have done for mankind is now superseded). Again, the writer appeals to the OT, correlating three quotations to each of the three stages of the Christ-event. (A) Ps. 22:22 is understood to be spoken by the pre-existent one to God and so is interpreted as the Son's pledge to be a heavenly messenger to mankind (only Hebrews calls Jesus the "apostle" 3:10). (B) Isa. 8:17-18 is interpreted to mean that the incarnate Son will trust God while in history (and therefore become the pioneer of faith, 12:2). (C) Isa. 41:8-9 is then interpreted as the words of the post-existent Son who presents the saved to God.

By juxtaposing lessons from Genesis 2 and Hebrews 2, the lectionary brings together the themes of creation and redemption.

Gospel: Mark 10:2-16. The third passage picks up another theme of the First Lesson—marriage and family, for in Mark 10:6-8 Jesus quotes Gen. 2:24.

Since Mark 10 appears in Pentecost 20-23, it is useful to see at the outset the chapter as a whole. Mark structured the second half of his Gospel around the three predictions of the passion (Mark 8:31-33; 9:30-32; 10:32-34); although the third prediction falls within chap. 10, it does not appear in this cycle of lessons. Nonetheless, attending to Mark's understanding of what he writes requires us to bear in mind the overall setting in which he placed these materials—namely, that each of the passion predictions is intimately associated with Jesus' teaching about discipleship and its costs. Throughout this block (Mark 8:31—10:45) Mark exposes the disciples' misunderstanding of what Jesus' call to follow—with one's own cross—really means. Because Mark has compiled and ordered these traditions, the present context of a given saying therefore comes from the Evangelist (and his tradition) and may not record accurately the context in which Jesus said these things.

Today's lesson juxtaposes two related themes: (a) divorce and marriage (Mark 10:2-12); (b) Jesus' receptivity to children (Mark 10:13-16); the first has no parallel in Luke (except for Luke 16:18), whereas the second is paralleled in Luke 18:15-17.

Jesus' views of divorce and remarriage are not easy to ascertain, for already the oldest text in 1 Cor. 7:10-11 (written 15-20 years before Mark) forbids either the wife or the husband to divorce the spouse, but applies the regulation only to cases where both are Christians. Likewise, Mark 10 and Luke 16:18 apply the regulation equally to husband and wife. This parity accords with the legal rights of women in the Greco-Roman world. In Matthew, however, matters are somewhat different. For one thing, he has Jesus deal with the subject twice, once in Matt. 5:31-32 and once in Matt. 19:2-9 (a revision of our passage); besides, he restricts the possibility to the husband's initiative in accordance with Jewish law, and provides a loophole: if the wife is faithless, the husband may divorce her. When one analyzes and ponders all of the NT teachings about divorce, three things emerge: one, each expresses an attempt to be faithful to Jesus; two, to do so in different circumstances, each must make some adaptation; three, it is likely that in his own situation, Jesus himself simply forbade divorce.

In our passage, Jesus transforms the question of what is legal into a statement of what is right. Jesus did not contest the legality of divorce which was allowed by the law (represented by "Moses"), but pointed out that the divorce legislation (Deut. 24:1-4) must be seen as a concession made necessary by the realities of the human condition—"hard-heartedness" was his word. God's original intent, however, was togetherness of man and woman, marriage not divorce. In support of this, Jesus cites *both* creation stories (Gen 1:27 and 2:24), and draws the conclusion that God himself has united man and woman in marriage. Therefore God's act should not be nullified by man's action, even if it is legal. As in the Sermon on the Mount (Matt. 5:21-48) the coming of the kingdom means that now human relationships are to be governed by what is right according to the Creator's intent, rather than according to the possibilities open to them in law made necessary by human sin.

Mark 10:10-12 expresses the church's attempt to square the unconditional demand of God with the realities and contingencies of the human situation. Public teaching and private explanation are customary Markan devices (e.g., Mark 4:10; 7:17). In this way, Mark can specify what Jesus' word *then* means *now*. To do so, he uses another piece of Jesus tradition (similar to that in Luke 16:18) on the subject, one which not only reckons with the possibility of the wife taking legal action, but which introduces a new factor—adultery. In Matt. 5:32 and 19:9 the wife's adultery (*porneia*) is an acceptable cause for a man divorcing the guilty woman; but in Mark 10:11-12 committing adultery (*moichatai*) is not the cause but the result when there is remarriage. It is not altogether clear to whom "commits adultery against her" (v. 11) refers—the divorcee or the new wife. This text seems to assume that whoever divorces a spouse will remarry, and that this involves adultery because, in the present context of the saying, divorce is contrary to God's will since one cannot be "one flesh" with two spouses simultaneously.

Today's interpreter should bear in mind three things: (a) eschatological horizons of Jesus' own view of marriage and divorce; (b) the early church's freedom to modify Jesus' view in light of the new situations it faced (Paul, for instance, had to deal with the question of "mixed marriages" [1 Cor. 7:12-16], something Jesus never contemplated); (c) both marriage and divorce have somewhat different functions in our society. A juridical application of these sayings is therefore in danger of forfeiting the intent of Jesus.

Mark evidently added 10:13-16 because it dealt with children. V. 15 interrupts the story; that at an earlier time this saying had circulated independently of its present Markan context is shown by the fact that Matthew puts a variant form of it into a quite different setting (Matt. 18:3). It is also an "amen" saying (translated "truly"). One of the distinguishing features of Jesus' sayings is his use of "amen" to begin a saying. Since this usage is taken from liturgy, where it means "so be it," the effect of using it to introduce a saying is somewhat like the colloquial "I'm here to tell you. . . ." One should guard against reading too much into the saying, as well as romanticizing childlikeness. The saying accents the importance of receptivity, openness and willingness to take a gift, and to respond joyously to the giver.

HOMILETICAL INTERPRETATION

First Lesson: Gen. 2:18-24. We have learned to refer to this passage as the second creation account, differing from the first in sequence, vocabulary, divine names, and theological perspective. Actually this second account of creation is the beginning of the story of man, focusing on the basic questions of the human condition and how it came to be. Gen. 2:18-24 is preparing the reader for the story of "the Fall."

And why is there violence and hostility in the world? Why, even in primary relationships, is there hostility and alienation? The author begins by saying, the story you are about to read (chap. 3, the Fall) does not find its cause in man's basic nature. He is different from the animals, as is dramatically discussed in God's search for a companion for man among the animals. Violence and hostility do not find their cause in man's origin. He is created by the one God who is Creator of all things. There is no intrinsic hostility and violence between man and the world in which he lives. Nor can the presence of evil be attributed to some myth that woman is of a different nature from man. Emphatically the text says "bone of my bone, flesh of my flesh," "one flesh". Neither is the reader to accept pagan views of man as originally androgynous but who, by reason of some cosmic fall, fell into two parts, each incomplete, male and female. God created them male and female. Each has value and integrity, but the unity of man and woman is also a gift of creation. This union is not a legal completion of two inadequates; not the huddling of the fearful, sinful, and dependent. Furthermore, the sexuality of the two is not the result of some fall into sin. Sexuality precedes the Fall. In summary, says the writer, you are about to read of disobedience, alienation, hostility, and frustration but the roots of it are not in the very *nature* of man and woman. Man and woman are social beings; it is not good to be alone. For this reason man and woman constantly call to and seek each other. Such is their nature by virtue of the act of creation which itself is to be understood as an act of grace, a gift of life from God.

Second Lesson: Heb. 2:9-11. The reading from Genesis 2 opened with the expression, "It is not good for man to be alone." Immediately that statement returns to mind in this passage. If man is by nature a social being, finding fulfillment and joy in another, as is beautifully imaged in the creation of woman; if being alone through death of the spouse is described in the OT with such heavy words as "desolate" and "abandoned"; if the immediate result of sin was separation, then most welcome are the sounds of reconciliation and harmony flowing through this text from Hebrews. Let the phrases sink in: "tasted of death for everyone"; "sanctifier and sanctified all have one origin"; "not ashamed to call them brethren." This is salvation by identification. While there is no doubt in the writer's mind that Christ was the agent of creation, the one for whom and by whom all things existed, neither is there any doubt that "for a little while" Christ was radically human. He who shared in man's creation now shares in his redemption by means of full identification with man's plight. That plight is summed up in the two words "suffering" and "death." Christ's reconciling work was made perfect (complete, finished) by means of that identification.

One needs no Scripture texts to know the healing, recovering, restoring, reconciling power of identification with another. It is not good for man to be alone. Experience shouts the truth of it. Prolonged distance from others is unbearable. The church has no more severe punishment than excommunication; the world has no more severe punishment than solitary confinement. And what could be more painful, confess it or not, than the experience of distance from the God with whom we had walked in the cool of the day? Now experience again Heb. 2:9-11: But he comes to us and shares in our suffering and death.

However, identification alone, regardless of how sweet the taste of sympathy and shared woe, has a limited potency. If I am in a hole and you jump in beside me, it helps, but not enough. Sympathy can be a pool of helpless pity. Therefore it ought to be borne in mind that the Hebrew writer is careful to repeat often that he who identifies with us was with God in the beginning, was lower than the angels "for a little while," and is now crowned with glory and honor. He is like us and therefore *will* help; he is unlike us and therefore *can* help.

It is important to notice that Heb. 2:1-11 is based on a Messianic interpretation of Ps. 8:4-6. Psalm 8 is a creation song, focusing upon man as God's supreme creature. The gospel does not call us to a strange and different life but rather recalls us to that which we vaguely remember from Eden. Hebrews 2 sings of the recovery of the union and harmony and completeness of life presented in Genesis 2.

Gospel: Mark 10:2-16. This passage comes within the larger unit of Mark 8:27–10:52 in which the cross of Jesus is introduced for the first time. With the cross as the symbol of discipleship, the writer spells out the meaning of being a disciple under various circumstances: in marriage (10:1-12), in relation to children (10:13-17), and in relation to possessions (10:17-31). This section may at one time have been part of a catechism.

The reader notices immediately Jesus' use of Gen. 2:24 which is our first reading for today. But notice the difference in the sequence of events, here and in Genesis 2. Genesis 2 describes the concord in which man and woman lived with each other and with God. Then follows the alienation, excuse making, and blaming of Genesis 3. Here the order is reversed. We meet first the effects of the Fall in Genesis 3: excuses, fault finding, and blaming. Without interruption since Genesis the causes and results of separation and hostility take their toll. Even the intervening law of Moses could not halt the deadly effects. To those who lack trust laws do not alter behavior but only provide occasions for being more clever and deceptive. The law *permits* us, twice the opponents said to Jesus who twice responded with the *command* of God. Unlike those who would use the law to bless the continuation of the "fallen" behavior of Genesis 3, ("The woman you gave me for a companion, she gave to me and I ate"), Jesus calls for a return to the design and purpose of God's creation presented in Genesis 2: one flesh.

But returning to the harmony and unity of God's creation does not come by a new law, "Follow Genesis 2 rather than Genesis 3." Nor does it come by firm resolve and screwing one's courage to the sticking point. Returning to the design and purpose of creation means returning to the very ground and meaning of creation: the gift of life as an act of a gracious God. And what better model than that of a child? The child comes with nothing in his hand, no claim to make, no bargain to strike. A child can "receive" the kingdom. How sharply in Mark's Gospel does Jesus rebuke his disciples on such occasions in which it is clear that they too have missed the point. By their own blindness of unbelief, by their own lack of trust, even well-intentioned disciples contribute to continued alienation and separation. And if it strikes at the very basic and primary relationships, marriage and family, who shall prevent its infecting the church, the whole family of God? If creation and re-creation are acts of God's grace, who can know this apart from trust?

The Twenty-first Sunday after Pentecost

Lutheran	*Roman Catholic*	*Episcopal*	*Pres./UCC/Chr.*	*Methodist/COCU*
Prov. 3:13-20	Wisd. 7:7-11	Wisd. 7:7-11	Prov. 3:13-18	Prov. 3:13-20
Heb. 4:12-13	Heb. 4:12-13	Heb. 3:1-6	Heb. 4:12-16	Heb. 3:1-6
Mark 10:17-27 (28-30)	Mark 10:17-30	Mark 10:17-27	Mark 10:17-27	Mark 10:17-30

EXEGESIS

First Lesson: Prov. 3:13-20; Wisd. 7:7-11. These two passages extol wisdom's virtues which she bestows upon those who find her. (Wisdom can be personified as a woman because in both Hebrew and Greek, wisdom is a feminine noun.) In the development of wisdom theology, there are three distinguishable meanings: (A) Wisdom is human insight, commonly expressed in proverbs, pithy sayings and riddles (e.g., Prov. 15:1). (B) When wisdom is personified (as in Lady Luck or Miss Liberty), it means a way of life which accords with the will of the Creator. Post-biblical Judaism began to equate this meaning of wisdom with the Torah (see Book of Sirach). (C) Finally, wisdom is thought of as a divine being in her own right; the technical term for this is *hypostasis* (substance). This is expressed clearly in Wisd. 7:22-28, espec. 25-27. What is said here of wisdom is said of the pre-existent Son of God in Heb. 1:1; similar thinking lies behind the prologue of John.

Prov. 3:13-18 congratulates the person for finding wisdom as divinely sanctioned prudence and insight. The passage is composed by juxtaposing a series of parallel lines, the simplest and commonest element of Hebrew poetry. Here each verse expresses a self-contained idea; the second line paraphrases the first. In various ways, then, the wise man is congratulated for finding a good and rewarding way of life.

Two things should be noted. First, neither this text, nor the wisdom tradition before Sirach, associates this wisdom with the Torah. One should not, therefore, read the later association back into our passage, as if it said, "He who keeps the law of God (e.g., the Ten Commandments or the Sermon on the Mount) is the wise man whose life will be blessed." Second, the limits of this view of life must not be overlooked, as the Book of Job, or the theology of Paul make clear. There is nothing in the wisdom theology comparable to Rom. 5:1-5.

Because wisdom accords with God's will, Prov. 3:19-20 can say that God created the world "by wisdom." But this is not yet the same theological point which is made in Wisd. 7:25-27, where wisdom is a pre-existent being who is God's agent in creating. Prov. 3:19-20 means rather that wisdom is in accord with creation. The simple principle that both goodness and wickedness bring their rewards is grounded in the nature of things.

In Wisd. 7:7-11, the speaker is the wise man, though it is not the historical Solomon who is soliloquizing here. This passage goes beyond that of Prov. 3:13-20 in that here God gives wisdom to the person who asks for it. Here wisdom is not the result of a successful quest, but the gift of God.

Second Lesson: Heb. 4:12-16. Having argued that Christ is superior to angels (Hebrews 1–2), the author begins a theme prominent throughout—Christ's superiority over Moses (Heb. 3:1-6). Heb. 4:12-16 deals with a quite different theme—the revealing capacity of God's word.

In Heb. 3:1-6 the christological argument stands in the service of the exhortation (developed in 3:12-19, and especially chap. 4). Assuming that clearer understanding of the person and work of Christ will yield greater fidelity, the author asks readers to reflect upon Jesus, "the apostle and high priest of our confession"—doubtless the baptismal confession. For this theologian, the highpriesthood of Christ is a central motif (see, e.g., 4:14–5:10).

Behind Heb. 3:1-6 stands Num. 12:7-8 (the RSV renders the Hebrew "entrusted with all my house"; the LXX used by Hebrews, however, has "faithful" or trustworthy). There Moses is contrasted with prophets with whom God communicates by visions; with Moses, however, God speaks directly. Our passage wrestles with the question: How, then, can the Christ-revelation supersede the Moses-revelation?

First, although both were faithful to God, Christ was a faithful son whereas Moses was a faithful servant. The second basis of superiority is somewhat ingenious. The author takes literally the LXX which speaks of

Moses' fidelity "*in* his house"; Christ, however, is *over* the house–evidently because of the post-resurrection exaltation (Heb. 1:3-4). A third contrast is only implied–that Moses testified to what was to be said later–that is, the OT points toward later revelation (see also Heb. 1:1-2).

The author's argument relies partly on the ambiguity of the word "house." In vv. 3-4, it refers to a building (so in v. 2, it can refer to the tabernacle in the wilderness); but in v. 6, it means community. The passage ends by returning to the pastoral concern–the church is God's people if it is faithful in the boldness of its hope (see also 10:19-25).

Hope is fundamental for Hebrews, as chap. 11 makes clear. The church is therefore comparable with Israel in the wilderness (Heb. 3:12-19, alluding to Numbers 14 as well as Ps. 95:7-11). Appropriately, since the church in history endures hardship and suffering (Heb. 10:32-34), the goal can be spoken of as "rest" (chap. 4). "Rest," of course, is a metaphor for salvation which is future.

Heb. 4:12-13 underscores the seriousness of the exhortation to strive to achieve that "rest." At the same time, it rounds out the first main section. Here "the word of God" is not the Bible, nor the Logos-Christ of John's prologue, but God's disclosing and judging activity. Here, it should be noted, the revelatory role of the word is focused solely on the human situation; nothing is immune to exposure by this word. God's word does not guarantee the church's security in this passage, but its insecurity. This is not the whole of the matter, even for Hebrews; yet without this component, Christian appeal to the word of God which it has heard easily becomes the basis for a self-justifying ideology.

Gospel: Mark 10:17-30. Whereas last Sunday's reading from Mark 10 dealt with the way discipleship impinges on the family, today's lection compiles sayings concerning wealth. Mark 10:17-22 (23?) is the self-contained story of a rich man, nicknamed "the rich young ruler" by Christian usage–though only Matt. 19:20 says he was young and only Luke 18:18 says he was a "ruler." Mark 10:24-27 appears to be built up from single sayings, whose introductory statements intensify the Markan theme of the disciples' misunderstanding of Jesus. It is probably impossible to recover accurately the stages by which the text as a whole came into its present form. Clearly, however, 10:28-30(31) was originally independent, for it asserts that the disciples have already made the hard sacrifice in order to follow Jesus. A compiler put vv. 28-30(31) here, partly because it also deals with forsaking wealth, and partly because it reports that the disciples have met this requirement. Because Mark himself emphasizes repeatedly the disciples' misunderstanding, this compiler probably worked before Mark.

The identity of this rich man is unknown; nor do we know of any previous meeting with, or hearing of, Jesus which would have prompted him to kneel before Jesus and address him with the unparalleled "Good Teacher!" His question, however, is typically Jewish. "Eternal life" is not a matter of quantity nor to be confused with deathlessness (immortality); it is rather a quality of life which, while it may include immortality, is akin to God's. Because this existence is derived from God, the man speaks of "inheriting" it—not as his due but as a bequest, a gift.

Jesus responds by observing that only God is good. Thereby he does not deny his own morality, let alone reflect on his sinlessness. He rather rebuffs the effort to find eternal life by learning it from a good man. Jesus refuses to be his guru. A certain kind of wisdom can be learned from a wise man, but eternal life comes directly from God. Jesus then points him to the Ten Commandments, some of which he quotes, though not in the usual order. For some reason, a new one appears: "Do not defraud," which Matthew and Luke delete. (Because love of neighbor is important to Matthew, he adds it also here.) The commandments which Jesus cites all have to do with human relationships, and omit the one which a Marxist reading of Jesus expects to find first—Do not covet. In reminding the man of the law, Jesus expresses the fundamental biblical and Jewish conviction that obedience to the law is rewarded by God with life (e.g., Deut. 30:15 f.; Ezek. 33:15). Jesus' reply is not a strategy for getting at something else; he apparently believes that whoever does what God has commanded will attain a life which is eternal. Jesus also assumes that this man can do what these commandments require; whether he thought anyone who tried could fulfill the law generally is another matter. In any case, Jesus clearly did not undertake to liberate this man from Judaism.

Whether Jesus was surprised by the man's response, "But I have done all this ever since my Bar Mitzvah," is not said. Jesus did not call this into question, but now saw that the man who "had everything going for him" neglected one thing—but he did not say what it was. Had Jesus spelled it out for this achiever, he would surely have undertaken the task of attaining it. Instead, Jesus implied it in a three-stage presentation: sell everything, give it to the poor, and become a disciple. This self-impoverished man would be rich before God ("in heaven" is a circumlocution for God; it does not mean that after death he would be recompensed richly). What the man lacked was the sort of trust in God and his kingdom by which he would rely solely on God's goodness. Jesus did not make poverty a requirement, although the man would indeed be poor. What Jesus required was radical dependence on God; had the man done as Jesus asked, he would have received the kingdom as a child (10:15; see previous Sunday).

Mark 10:23-27 comments on the story: it is impossible for the wealthy to enter the kingdom. Yet some do, because for God also this miracle is possible. Jesus has no animus against the wealthy (v. 21, to the contrary, says he loved this man); Jesus does not speak as does James 2:6-7; 5:1-6. Luke 6:24, together with v. 20 expresses the coming eschatological reversal of the perverted present. Nor does Jesus romanticize either the moral goodness of the poor or the state of poverty. Because wealth buys power and security in this world, it obscures the truth about the human situation and easily interferes with unreserved trust in God.

HOMILETICAL INTERPRETATION

First Lesson: Prov. 3:13-20; Wisd. 7:7-11. This text for today introduces to us the Wise Man, the Sage. Of the three figures representing religious leadership in Israel—the priest, the prophet, and the sage—it is the sage who is least familiar, has made least obvious impact and has least continuity with the Christian community. Not that the wise man is an obscure figure; he is found in many cultures and religions. Nor is his role unimportant. In Israel, as among other peoples, he counselled the kings and called the people to a life of peace, prosperity, longevity, and happiness. There may be several reasons, however, for the lack of attention upon wisdom and upon the wise in our time. The term sage still carries the image of a strange, isolated, eccentric person of unusual life style; a guru to be visited in crises but not to be found among us or in our social structures. In addition, the image is of one very old, and this is the time of the young. Beyond that, the sage is no reformer, no agent of change, no radical voice shaking institutions. Rather the wise man speaks in universal and timeless maxims, fables, and proverbs. "An ounce of prevention is worth a pound of cure." "Better a little in peace than plenty in turmoil." "Fools rush in where angels fear to tread." "When in doubt, take the old path." There is nothing here of how things ought to be, no prophetic reading of the signs of the times. The wise man studies the workings of God's creation, the way things are with clouds and rain, birds and trees, mice and men. Did not God create the earth by wisdom, the heavens by understanding, and the netherworld by knowledge? Careful observation and reflection will therefore yield secrets for living in harmony with life and in quiet peace.

Is there any reason the Christian community should listen to the sage and seek the way of wisdom? At this point in our history several come to mind. First, the sage, by drawing many lessons from observing creation, may have a lesson for man who has violated his environment in stupid and suicidal ways. "Go to the ant, you sluggard, and learn wisdom," was the counsel of the ancient sage of Israel. Perhaps now his word is appropriate: "Go to the earth, it was made by God's wisdom; go to the heavens, for they were made by God's understanding; go to the netherworld for it was made by God's knowledge, and there you will learn to live." Second, wisdom is available to all. It is not the special possession of a few experts nor of those with rare religious experience. All who listen, observe, reflect may be wise. Third, wisdom is a gift. Wisdom here is not an intellectual game nor a matter of being more clever. It does not distort the community of faith into an afternoon discussion group. "Reverence of God is the beginning of wisdom"; "If anyone lacks wisdom let him ask of God." It is a gift in that it comes to those open to God and to his creation. Finally, wisdom is inextricably related to lifestyle and conduct. Unlike many of her neighbors, Israel linked wisdom and righteousness. The proper working of God's wisdom among us is in character formation. All in the service of the one God, the priest calls to beauty of holiness, the prophet to righteousness, and the sage to wisdom.

Second Lesson: Heb. 4:12-13. The key term in our first reading for today was Sophia, Wisdom; here it is Logos, Word. "Word of God" is a phrase designed to express God's actively revealing himself. In the text before us God is revealing himself in discerning judgment, bringing to clear light the motives, character, and actions of his people. This is a strong statement of the moral and ethical earnestness of our faith. Of course, the word of God does not always come in judgment; his word supports, consoles, disciplines, and prompts to joy.

But still the vagueness lingers; What is "word of God"? Karl Barth has written of the threefold nature of God's word: the Scriptures, the preaching of the Gospel, and Jesus Christ the incarnate Word (John 1:14). But why "word" of God? Just as biblical descriptions of the Lord's Supper presuppose a society in which eating together is sacred; just as biblical descriptions of the church as the bride of Christ presuppose a society in which marriage is deeply reverenced, so the phrase "word of God" presupposes respect for the value and efficacy of a spoken word. In a culture in which speaking was an act of releasing a force into the world to build or destroy, heal or hurt, bless or curse, it was especially meaningful to refer to God's active presence as his "word". Pagan gods are captured in visual objects, images, static and dead. With our God it is not so. "No one has seen God at any time." We have only heard him; that is, as a word is the movement of air across the ear, fragile and brief, and yet life changing, so God is moving, dynamic, bringing his creation to its fulfillment.

It might be wise, then, for the preacher to enlighten this text by helping the congregation recover respect for a word as an event in the world of sound. Especially is this recovery important in a society prone to discount words as "talk, talk, talk." "It's not what you say but what you do that counts." "Anyone can talk, but . . . " "Sticks and stones may break my bones, but words will never harm me." In the face of such pejorative references to words, reflect upon occasions when a word created an entirely new situation, or when a word brought clarity to hours of confused struggling with an idea. Think on the performative power of words such as "I will" or "This is my body." Use significant synonyms for speaking such as "to give you my word" or "to break the silence." Recall the difficulty of speaking with husband or wife, parent or child, or with the minister when the issue was very important. How many husbands find it easier to buy flowers or candy than to say the words, "I love you"?

The minister who helps the congregation appreciate a word will have opened a door to word of God. After all, our word and God's word are related. Heb. 4:12-13 begins with "the word of God" and closes (even though it is obscured by the translation "before him with whom we have to do") with "our word." Literally the phrase is, "before him unto whom is our word." Our words stand under the clear discernment of his word.

Gospel: Mark 10:17-27. The reading from Hebrews for today gave us a strong clear statement on the penetrating and discerning power of the word of God. One could hardly find a better illustration than this text from Mark. Mark tells this story so as to make two matters clear beyond equivocation:

(1) The word spoken by Jesus is the word of God. A man (and that is all we need to know at this point; to decorate him with "rich" and "young" at the beginning of the story is to put him a special category removed from the rest of us) asks a question the answer to which must come from God. Jesus, in his opening statement, turns the man's attention from Jesus to God. The authority of Jesus lay in his ability to place his hearers immediately and directly before God. Those who experienced Jesus experienced God. Then Jesus reminded the man of God's demand already known in his tradition. The man had already known the disappointment of keeping the rules and still being unsatisfied. Like saints of old and of every age, beyond and through all the forms and means, the soul thirsts for God. The man now heard what he wanted, and did not want, to hear: When we come to the point of asking the ultimate question we must be ready for ultimate answers. The answer may seem too much but the man knew, as we do, that any less would have been too little, and insulting. To be willing to give up everything for God is not a call to poverty and privation. How simple a transaction that could be, and still not be for God. But complete trust in God, to stand stripped before him, is the path both Scripture and experience call "life full and free." Such trust discovers as a result that, rather than privation and poverty, life has now and hereafter will have a hundredfold of all the property and family that were released (Mark 10:29-30). The man is permitted to say No because, without room for No, there can be no authentic Yes.

(2) The word spoken by Jesus is the word of God *to us.* Mark makes sure that we do not regard this story as an interesting but isolated incident safely lodged back there in Jesus' ministry. The next paragraph begins, "And Jesus looked around and said to his disciples." It is a common pattern in Mark to portray Jesus giving a teaching to a person or persons and then elaborating upon it in private to his astonished disciples. Was that meant for us? Yes. What *was* true *is* true. Not only does the account through v. 30 make it clear that the demands of discipleship and the conditions of wholeness of life are there for all who would follow, but there is an unmistakable clue in the Markan style that confirms it. In responding to the man who came, Mark says Jesus looked intently straight at him and replied (v. 21). When the disciples asked if the answer were for them, Mark says Jesus looked intently straight at them and replied (v. 27). In other words, no exceptions.

The Twenty-second Sunday after Pentecost

Lutheran	*Roman Catholic*	*Episcopal*	*Pres./UCC/Chr.*	*Methodist/COCU*
Isa. 53:10-12	Isa. 53:10-11	Isa. 53:10-11	Isa. 53:10-12	Isa. 53:10-12
Heb. 5:1-10	Heb. 4:14-16	Heb. 4:12-16	Heb. 5:1-10	Heb. 4:12-16
Mark 10:35-45	Mark. 10:35-45	Mark 10:35-45	Mark 10:35-45	Mark 10:35-45

EXEGESIS

First Lesson: Isa. 53:10-12. Understanding Jesus' death through the lens of Isaiah 53 has been part of Christian faith from the start; indeed some hold that Jesus himself interpreted his death in light of this passage. In his own time, however, the anonymous prophet of the exile described and interpreted the suffering and death of God's servant, whether Israel, or a composite prophetic or "messianic" figure.

Today's reading comes from the conclusion of the fourth "Servant Song" (52:13–53:12). The others are 42:1-4 (+5-9); 49:1-6 (+7-13); 50:4-9. The change of speakers is the key to the structure. The song begins (52:13-15) and ends (53:11b-12) with God proclaiming the vindication of the servant; in between (53:1-11b) the career of the servant is reported. Although formally vv. 4-6 appear to interrupt the description, they actually interpret the career of the suffering one, and do so from the standpoint of those whose waywardness caused it and for whose redemption it occurred. Vv. 10-11a conclude the description by reporting that this suffering was not a sign of God's rejection, but rather its opposite. At 53:11b God again speaks, and restates the theme of 52:13-15. Thus today's lesson combines two clear structural elements. The difficulties inherent in the passage are revealed in the divergent translations.

The vindication of the suffering servant in 53:10-11a asserts three things: (A) God was at work in this career (whether we follow the RSV—"it was the will of the Lord"—or Westermann—"Yahweh took pleasure in him"). (B) The servant's life (death) was a sacrifice which atoned for sin (confessed in 53:4-6). (C) The servant is restored to a prosperous life.

God's own proclamation of the servant's vindication (53:11b-12) announces that (a) the righteous servant will "make many to be accounted righteous"—that is, he will cause their acquittal in court, or their "justification," because (b) he bore their sins. (c) His vindication will be manifest in the booty which he obtains. "Booty" may be a metaphor for the nations, or for their homage. (d) The suffering was not only undeserved, but vicarious. (e) The intercession mentioned in the last line need not refer to offering prayers on behalf of sinners; the preceding parallel line suggests rather that his death intervened on their behalf—i.e., he suffered in their place, as v. 5 also asserts.

Second Lesson: Heb. 4:12 (14)-16; 5:1-10. (For Heb. 4:12-13, see previous Sunday.) Heb. 4:14—5:10 begins the development of the central theme, Christ's priesthood, which had been mentioned earlier (2:17; 3:10); 4:15 reaffirms the solidarity between the savior and the saved, which had been argued in chap. 2 (see exegesis for Pentecost 20). Again, the practical consequence of Christology is emphasized: the believers who are "weak" and vulnerable to temptation need not be incapacitated by their situation vis-a-vis the holy One (see 12:29) for they are represented by Christ the high priest who knows from experience what it means to be human.

Having argued that Christ is superior to angels (see Pentecost 20) and to Moses (see Pentecost 21), the author now announces that Christ is superior to the high priest. Precisely how Christ is a Melchizedek-priest will be shown in chap. 7, where the author reflects on Gen. 14:17-20. In our pericope, however, the assertion is a quotation of Ps. 110:4, which is linked with Ps. 2:7. Nowhere in Hebrews is it said that the earthly Jesus exercised a priestly office; rather, on earth Jesus was the incarnate Son who by obedience and suffering qualified to be the heavenly priest in the heavenly sanctuary (see chap. 8). Thus Ps. 2:7 refers to the incarnation, Ps. 110:4 to the exaltation; the period in between is introduced at v. 7 with the phrase, "in the days of his flesh." Both his origin and destiny make him superior to any earthly high priest.

To argue the superiority of Christ's highpriesthood, the author must first make clear that Christ meets the qualifications. (A) Like every high priest, Christ was appointed by God rather than exalting himself (5:1, 4, 5). (B) The high priest can act on behalf of human sin and weakness because he is himself a human (5:2-3); the previous argument has already shown that the eternal Son, through whom God created the world (1:2), was incarnate as Jesus in order to establish this necessary solidarity with mankind; likewise the author has asserted that Jesus was vulnerable to sin, yet did not succumb (2:17-18; 4:15); therefore 7:27 can say that Christ's sacrifice was not for his own sins.

In 5:7-10 the human vulnerability of the incarnate one is described, and in a remarkable way. Unfortunately, the precise meaning of the details in the passage is elusive. Nor is the relation of the parts to the whole clear, for strictly speaking, vv. 5-10 are all one sentence. Many see a reference to the Gethsemane story (Mark 14:32-39, par.), though nothing is said there of Jesus praying "with loud cries and tears," nor is anything said here of Jesus' accepting his God-given fate. Rather, "he was heard for his godly fear" seems to suggest rescue from the necessity of death. Even if we take the phrase to mean rescue from the dead (NEB: "deliver him from the grave") rather than rescue from the necessity of death, there is no clear allusion to Gethsemane or to any other gospel tradition; nowhere else is it said that God rescued Jesus from the dead because of Jesus' piety (*eulabeia* is rendered "godly fear" by the RSV; "humble submission" by NEB; "submitted so humbly" by the Jerusalem Bible). Actually, "in the days of his flesh" suggests that no particular incident, such as Gethsemane, need be in view; on this basis, v. 7 emphasizes one dimension of Jesus' life as a whole, and regards the resurrection as God's response to his persistent faith (recall that 2:13 used Ps. 8:17-18 to characterize Jesus' life: "I will put my trust in him"). V. 8 asserts the paradox: even though he was Son (of God) he learned obedience from suffering—again, a point which appears to refer to the career of Jesus as a whole more than to the passion only. The precise sense in which "he was perfected" (v. 9) is to be taken is obscure, though the context suggests moral perfection by obedience in suffering.

The passage as a whole, then, presents a remarkable Christology. The Creator-Son, having become incarnate in Jesus, so fully identified with the human situation (marked by fear of death, 2:14-15!) that he himself had to learn what it is to trust God; therefore he can truly represent us before God, now that he has become the heavenly high priest.

Gospel: Mark 10:35-45. This pericope follows immediately upon the third, and final, passion prediction in Mark (10:32-34); it brings to a head the clash of perspectives between Jesus and the disciples.

Close comparison with Luke (Matt. 20:20-28 generally follows Mark) shows that Mark has skillfully combined several pieces of tradition in order to create a powerful scene. (A) Jesus' saying that he has a baptism to undergo is found in a quite different context in Luke, where it is also formulated differently (Luke 12:50). (B) In Luke the saying about the way gentile rulers acts is put at the Lord's Supper (Luke 22:24-26), and Luke feels free either to rewrite Mark 10:45 completely or substitute another form of the tradition (Luke 22:27). (C) The story is omitted altogether by Luke, perhaps because a report of the disciples' misunderstanding undercuts his view that the validity of the gospel is guaranteed by the disciples who had been with Jesus (e.g., Acts 1:21). Matthew achieves much the same result by blaming the mother's ambitions (Matt. 20:20). In short, there are three discrete pieces of tradition in the Markan account: the story, the saying about the gentile ruler, and the climactic "ransom saying" in v. 45.

The story begins with the request for the places of honor. Since Mark put this material directly after the most detailed of the three passion predictions, the brothers, in effect, hear only the last word—the promised resurrection, which they rightly construe as entry into glory. Jesus' reply is twofold. First, he rebukes them for separating what is really inseparable: the way to glory is through suffering. So he asks whether they are able to share his suffering as well. He uses two OT metaphors for suffering, baptism and cup of wrath (Ps. 95:8; Isa. 51:17, 22; Lam. 4:21). The expression "to be baptized with a baptism" alludes to flood waters which threaten to overwhelm the victim, as in Ps. 42:7; 69:1-2; Isa. 37:27-28; 43:2—though Jesus' expression itself is not used here. The LXX of Isa. 21:4, however, reads "unrighteousness submerges (baptizes) me." The point is that Jesus expects to experience the outpouring of God's wrath. Probably this expectation is grounded more in the conviction that the "Messianic woes" (sometimes called the labor pains of the Messianic age) are imminent and that he must endure them, than it is in Jesus' insight into the political realities of the situation. Even though the syntax does not make it clear, Jesus does not expect a positive answer to his counter-question. The brothers, however, have no doubts. Jesus' response is sheer disappointment: they will indeed share his suffering; even so, that will not guarantee them the places of honor. Those will go to those whom God determines shall have them (the passive "are prepared" is a circumlocution for divine action). In other words, suffering will be rewarded but glory cannot be guaranteed.

The saying in 10:41-44 has in view a different, though thematically related, problem—the quest for position within the church. The transition in vv. 41-42a appropriately speaks of intramural tension against the brothers who had sought positions of power. Jesus, however, revolutionizes the criteria for being first—and thereby distinguishes power from greatness. The identification of power and greatness is a mark of gentile rulers. Jesus is clearly not awed by the moral pretensions of power.

V. 45 grounds this perspective in the inherent character of the mission of the Son of man. This is one of the most important verses in Mark, not only because of what is said but where it is placed—at the climax of the whole narrative between the Caesarea-Philippi scene and the entry to Jerusalem (assuming that 10:46-52 is a "hinge" pericope); see next Sunday's Gospel. It formulates the point of the whole section. Many students regard the verse as the church's formulation rather than as the very words of Jesus. If correct, this view does not diminish the truth of the saying, even if it does not tell us Jesus' own thinking.

Several things must be noted. First, Jesus speaks as the heavenly Son of man whose career on earth has not asserted his regal prerogatives but instead has been one of service. The incongruity of it all is deliberate, as in Mark 14:41. The latter half of the saying carries this forward—service to the point of giving his life for humanity. Second, "ransom" is a metaphor for a death which frees captives, slaves, or hostages. A clear "doctrine of the atonement" can be read into this text but not out of it, for the necessary details are absent. The saying is commonly regarded as distilling the point of Isaiah 53, though it is not actually quoted. Third, "many" must not be pressed to mean some but not all; if our text spoke of "the many," as do certain of the Dead Sea Scrolls, it would refer to the elect community, and Jesus' death would ransom the elect. Actually, here "many" points to an unlimited number.

HOMILETICAL INTERPRETATION

First Lesson: Isa. 53:10-12. Karl Barth has said that all theology begins and ends in awe and wonder. There is more in theology to be considered than we can wrap our brains around. Such could be said about any efforts to deal with this magnificent passage. Perhaps the preacher should begin with the recognition that on this Sunday, given whatever brilliance or eloquence he may possess, the highlight of the sermon will be the reading of the text.

In this passage the prophet describes the person and work of the suffering servant of God. The portrait captures the best of the whole service and ministry of the people of God. One recognizes in the servant something of the king who, in behalf of his wayward and evil nation, publicly repents, tears his clothes, and dramatically endures mistreatment, pain, and abuse in behalf of his people whom he would restore and renew before God. Here also is the prophet, submitting himself in complete obedience to the word of the Lord. And here, too, is the priest, offering a sacrifice, in this case himself, for the sin of the people.

Who, then, is the suffering servant? Of course, the church thinks of Jesus. We no longer ask as did the Ethiopian, "About whom, pray, does the prophet say this, about himself or about someone else?" (Acts 8:34). Directly and indirectly this image has influenced heavily NT portraits of Christ. Both the Epistle and Gospel for today have been touched by it. It is a question how widely, if at all, the suffering servant passages were regarded in Israel as Messianic. Perhaps Jesus himself so adopted the ministry of the servant as his own apart from any common association of suffering servant and Messiah.

Whatever the christological implications, a remarkable feature of this passage is that the prophet and those who shared his faith had come to such a rare and profound understanding of life and the ways of God among us. The prophet belonged to a community that had long since tried to negotiate life with a simple question: the good prosper, the evil suffer. Texts abound pressing for the truth of that, but experience provides an abundance of footnotes on exceptions. Sometimes the good suffer and the evil prosper, as the Psalmist (Psalms 37, 73) and Habakkuk protest. All of us can testify that learning to live with the fact that there is often no direct correlation between one's quality of life and one's fortune calls for no little faith in God's love and care. But here in this text, the prophet has moved beyond all our calculations to the very way of God himself: sometimes the innocent submit to suffering in behalf of the guilty. Call it what you will: atonement, expiation, substitution, intercession. The point is, here end any private self-seeking negotiations with the universe because God is offering himself.

Second Lesson: Heb. 5:1-10. Isaiah 53 echoes clearly in this reading. Here there is no question about whom the writer is speaking. Neither is there any question as to the major task before the author of Hebrews. He is faced, of course, with the burden of establishing that Jesus of Nazareth, though not of the priestly lineage of Levi, was definitely a priest and that he so functions for those who believe. But the writer's larger problem is to demonstrate the Messianic role of Jesus of Nazareth who was apparently so non-Messianic. The facts of Jesus' life are honestly stated: "In the days of his flesh, Jesus offered up prayers and supplications, with loud cries and tears, to him who was able to save him from death, and he was heard for his godly fear. Although he was a Son, he learned obedience through what he suffered." What kind of Messiah is that?

Most of the NT reflects the church's sensitivity to the observer's argument that Jesus bore no traits of a Messiah. By contrast the popularity of John the Baptist is understandable. John preached that a Messiah *will come*. Promises of a coming Messiah are always welcome. There is always enough misery and suffering in the world to make the message of a future Messiah believable. Tattered faith and faint hope turn to tenacity, clutch the message, and begin framing job descriptions for the coming Messiah. Jesus comes. He participates in human misery, is a victim of it, and calls his followers into it with him. If there is always enough misery in the world to make believable a message that a Messiah is coming, there is also enough misery in the world to make *unbelievable* a message that he *has* come. It is therefore no mystery at all that a strong accent on the second coming of Christ often veils a disappointment to the point of unbelief in his first coming.

To accept Jesus as the Messiah demands a complete reversal of an ancient formula repeated enough to make it almost true: where God is, there is no suffering. Jesus demonstrated that where suffering is, God is. Therefore it remains the central miracle of the NT and of the church that men and women would confess, "The Messiah has come, and it is Jesus of Nazareth."

Gospel: Mark 10:35-45. There is hardly a better illustration of the difficulty of seeing in the work and words of Jesus the image of Messiah than that provided by this text. It confirms the truth of Matt. 16:17 in which Jesus responds to Peter's confession that Jesus is Messiah with the words, "Flesh and blood has not revealed this to you." It does not come by observation.

There is no question about it: James and John appear in bad light here. Their request contradicts all that Jesus has said and done. But this incident fits the overall pattern of Mark's portrayal of the twelve as afraid, confused, misunderstanding, and cowardly. Focus on the three predictions of the passion in Mark to feel the force of this sketch of them. After the first prediction (8:31 ff.) Peter rebukes Jesus. After the second (9:30 ff.), the disciples engage in an argument about who is the greatest. After the third prediction of his death (10:32 ff.) James and John ask for chief seats. How are we to understand this? Does Mark represent a circle of Christianity which prompts him to depict the twelve thus? Is Mark simply telling us in brutal honesty how blind and deaf they were? Maybe Mark has a suffering servant Christology and the twelve never accepted that view of the Messiah.

Some help comes by asking the question this way: Did Mark intend for his readers to identify against these disciples who missed the point or to identify with them? Do I join in criticism of those who miss the nature of Jesus' Messiahship, or do I identify with that portion of the church which has continued to miss the path of suffering, the way of the cross, the cost of discipleship? This is a good time for the preacher to pause and be reminded how important it is to be aware of where one stands in a text, where one identifies. Unless conscious effort is made, the one preaching can easily fall into the comfortable place of preaching as though he were Mark and the congregation were James and John. In a text in which Jesus speaks to Pharisees, how easy to be Jesus and let the listeners be the Pharisees. Or in the Pauline letters, the preacher can, without realizing it, assume the role of Paul and speak to his people as Corinthians, or Galatians, or Romans.

As preacher for today, am I Mark, or am I Jesus, or am I James and John? Where I stand determines what sermon will be heard. If I am in the place of the disciples, it is humbling to realize that after all this exposure to Jesus I still have missed the word of the cross. But it is also gratifying to know that he has always had room in his kingdom for those who only gradually get the point.

The Twenty-third Sunday after Pentecost

Lutheran	*Roman Catholic*	*Episcopal*	*Pres./UCC/Chr.*	*Methodist/COCU*
Jer. 31:7-9	Jer. 31:7-9	Jer. 31:7-9	Jer. 31:7-9	Jer. 31:7-9
Heb. 4:2-10	Heb. 5:1-6	Heb. 5:1-9	Heb. 5:1-6	Heb. 4:2-10
Mark 10:46-52	Mark 10:46-52	Mark 10:46-52	Mark 10:46-52	Mark 10:46-52

EXEGESIS

First Lesson: Jer. 31:7-9. This passage is part of a collection of oracles of salvation found in chaps. 30-31, for which a prose introduction sets the theme (30:1-3). Scholars are divided over the extent to which these oracles come from Jeremiah himself. Jer. 31:7-9 is among those whose genuineness is doubted, because it is so similar to Deutero-Isaiah. This might well be the result of Deutero-Isaiah's adapting an originally genuine oracle to address the exiles in Babylon.

The theme is the reconstitution of God's people, called "the chief of the nations"—a phrase reminiscent of Amos 6:1. Even though only a remnant is involved, the compiler regards it as the occasion for great joy because it will embody "all the families of Israel" (31:10); it will show that Yahweh has redeemed his people from decimation and dispersion. Although the returnees will include those for whom travel is difficult (the blind, lame, and pregnant are mentioned), God will aid them. The glorious return is portrayed in language which is akin to Isaiah 35; 40:3-5, 11; 41:17-20; 42:14-16; 43:1-7; 44:3; 48:20-21; 49:8-13. The father-son metaphor (v. 9) recalls Hos. 11:1-4, yet goes beyond it in calling Israel the first-born—the one with primary rights and responsibilities. Despite the ordeal of national destruction God has not disinherited Israel. The return is a sign of God's covenant-fidelity. God's faithfulness is as reliable as the order of creation (31:35-37). For the compiler of these oracles, the restoration is not a return to status quo ante, for he includes in the collection the promise of a new covenant in which knowledge of God shall be internalized (31:31-34).

Second Lesson: Heb. 4:2-10; 5:1-6(-9). Comments on Heb. 5:1-9 are included in the Exegesis for the previous Sunday (Pentecost 22). Heb. 4:2-10 uses the precedent of Israel in the wilderness to develop the pastoral exhortation to be faithful in history lest the church forfeit its promised salvation—a theme announced earlier in 3:6-19.

The author does not allegorize the experience of Israel but treats it typologically. Strictly speaking, allegory uses an account to identify basically timeless or ever-recurring realities. Typology, on the other hand, discerns parallels between two events, yet does not simply hold that "history repeats itself." For our author, the movement of Israel from Egypt through the wilderness into Canaan prefigures the movement of the eschatological people of God to its destiny, salvation. For Hebrews the church does not yet enjoy salvation, except by faith, precisely because it is still in history where it must suffer hardship and develop endurance (Heb. 10:32-39); it is a pilgrim people on the way, as was Israel in the wilderness.

Within this structural similarity between Israel-church, however, the author makes it clear that he does not believe that the church is fated simply to repeat Israel's experience and the consequence—those who left Egypt did not arrive in Canaan. Heb. 3:15-19 is clearly interpreting Ps. 95:7-11, which in turn is reflecting on Num. 14:1-35. Earlier, Paul too had treated Israel's wilderness experience in this way (1 Cor. 10:1-13). In other words, typologically Israel prefigures the church, but concretely the church must not be like Israel.

Our lesson begins by pointing out the seriousness of the parallel: both Israel and the church heard the good news (the promise of future salvation), but in the former case the word did not evoke faith, here understood as faithfulness. The author develops his argument by combining and interpreting texts which speak of "rest" and of the sabbath, evidently relying on Jewish exegetical traditions which used both, as well as entry to the promised land, as eschatological metaphors.

Whereas Israel's unbelief prevented their attaining the goal (the author's hortatory concern leads him to ignore the fact that some did enter

Canaan), v. 3 asserts that the believing church does enter it. This claim is supported by the rest of the paragraph. First, he returns to Ps. 95:7-11 (previously quoted in 3:7-11) in order to show that unbelieving Israel did not attain the "rest." Second, this failure must not be taken to mean that there is no goal, for it was created along with everything else and therefore exists, waiting to be reached. (The author assumes the Jewish belief that eschatological realities, such as repentance or the name of the Messiah, pre-exist before they become manifest.) This is supported by Gen. 2:2. Third, the author concludes that Ps. 95:11 means that Israel will not attain the goal. Fourth, since the goal cannot exist in vain, it will be reached by someone; moreover, since Israel failed to achieve it then, and will never achieve it, God has set another time (implicitly for another group). The author infers this from the fact that long afterward Ps. 95:7 says, "Today, do not do as they did in the wilderness."

This exhortation, he reasons, makes sense only if the "rest" is still not attained, as v. 8 observes. Therefore a Sabbath rest—a symbol of eschatological salvation ahead—is still outstanding. This is why the author could claim in v. 3 that "we who have believed enter that rest." Believers therefore are to strive to enter it and not repeat Israel's infidelity (v. 11).

It is difficult for us to appreciate the author's subtle reasoning and his exegesis. His compressed style also makes it hard for us to see the point, as does the fact that his metaphors for future salvation are foreign to us. Nonetheless, he is grappling with a real pastoral problem—how to provide scriptural warrants for persistent faith among Christians who appear to be dismayed and let down because full salvation is not yet theirs. (See Exegesis of Second Lesson for Pentecost 20.)

Gospel: Mark 10:46-52. Apart from certain details, the story itself is fairly straightforward, while Mark's use of it is much more subtle.

Why this beggar hailed Jesus "Son of David" is not clear, since the title has clear Messianic meanings; it was not customary for Jewish thought to expect the Davidic Messiah to heal. After the crowd failed to silence him, Jesus sent for him and asked him to specify what he had in mind with "have mercy on me." Curiously, the man now calls Jesus "Rabbi" (*rabbouni*, my master), evidently as a term of respect rather than in a technical sense. Jesus' reference to the man's "faith" probably means both confidence in Jesus' ability and persistence in getting his attention. Although Jesus asked him to go, he joined the throng on the road to Jerusalem.

In the structure of Mark's Gospel, this is the last healing story. More important, the story is a "hinge" between the wandering ministry of Jesus and the Jerusalem ministry, inaugurated by the entry which follows. Furthermore, the extended section which precedes our story (beginning with the Caesarea-Philippi story, 8:27 and ending with 10:45 [see previous Sunday], the "ransom saying") is permeated by the disparity between Jesus' understanding of his destiny and the disciples' misunderstanding.

The "hinge" between this section and what precedes it is also a story about healing blindness (Mark 8:22-26). Thereby Mark frames this section by suggesting that blindness must be healed if one is to understand and follow Jesus on his way. In this light, the concluding comment in our story suggests that if one's blindness is healed, he will follow Jesus. Since Mark appears to be critical of "Son of David" as a way of understanding Jesus (Mark 12:35-37), he may also suggest that only a "blind" man would call Jesus Son of David. He is really Son of God.

HOMILETICAL INTERPRETATION

First Lesson: Jer. 31:7-9. An adequate handling of this text puts upon the preacher the burden of re-creating its mood as well as its words. And that mood can be re-created by enabling the hearer to experience the contrast between this text and the chapters that precede it. After thirty chapters of doom and destruction, this passage is a diamond tossed on black velvet. A lament has turned to dancing. "Tears may linger at nightfall, but joy comes in the morning" (Ps. 30:5 NEB). The faithful remnant now returns home to Zion. Faces adorned with tears, the pilgrims come; the lame, the blind, the woman heavy in pregnancy move with joy along a smooth path and beside the fresh water God has provided.

True to the word he heard and even against his own desire and nature, Jeremiah had announced judgment. He went so far as to say what Isaiah never said: the temple will be destroyed. The prophet was no iconoclast but he understood how the temple, rather than drawing Israel closer to the source of her life, had become a talisman, a national rabbit's foot providing illusionary security. "It will not happen here. Did we not have a reformation under King Josiah? Is not King Zedekiah a God-fearing man?" But Jeremiah was right.

Then come chaps. 30-33, the little Book of Consolation. In a way, this section offers testimony to the sheer tenacity of hope. Hope sees a cloud the size of a man's hand and runs for shelter from rain. Hope sees a sprout growing out of an old stump and envisions the hills covered with cedars of Lebanon. Hope drops a seed in the ground and sees corn as high as an elephant's eye. Hope is a little girl dressed up in mother's discarded clothes. Hope is a little boy standing beside the breakfast table measuring himself against the tallest man in his world. Hope is an old man holding a child, praying "Now let thy servant depart in peace, for my eyes have seen the deliverance of Israel."

But beyond any witness to the tenacious power of hope, this passage re-affirms the faithfulness of God. This, not favorable political alliances nor the tears of the penitent, is the sure ground for hope. Is not this what Jeremiah was saying when he bought a piece of property just before the exile (Jeremiah 32)? "Even though I speak against Ephraim, he is still my child." Is not this the central affirmation of the entire Bible: God will not violate his own covenant of love for his people? Adam and Eve driven from the garden, and God made them clothes; Cain put under a curse, and God put a mark upon him to protect him; the world to be destroyed by a flood, and an ark full of people and animals survive; Nineveh to be destroyed in forty days, and God "repents"; Israel cut down like a fruitless tree because of her unbelief, and there comes a shoot from the stock of Jesse. "And you shall call his name Jesus for he shall save his people from their sins."

Second Lesson: Heb. 4:2-10. Two words about the Epistle to the Hebrews might help the preacher appropriate with more confidence the message of the book. First, the style of the writer is to discuss a person or an event from Israel's history and then to draw lessons or exhortations. This pattern is repeated throughout the book, and the reading for today is an example of it. Second, the author regards Christianity as both superior to and the fulfillment of Judaism. The superiority is argued by means of a shadow-substance schema: Judaism is the shadow on earth of the substantial or real, which is Christianity. The tabernacle was the shadow of the real place of worship; the high priest was the shadow of the true high priest; Zion was the shadow of the eternal Mt. Zion above, etc. Judaism therefore has its completion or fulfillment in Christianity.

Our passage for today explores one dimension of this development. According to Psalm 95 there is a "rest of God" available to his people according to God's promise but Israel never entered into it. How so? Under Moses, Israel never entered, living in the wilderness forty years, complaining, falling into idolatry, and doubting. Under Joshua she entered into the land. Therein lay the bitter disappointment, for the land did not satisfy those whose search was for God. There was no rest. In fact, early prophets called the people back to the wilderness because the land had become a false security and an idol. The quest for God was abandoned by many; only a few continued to look for the city whose builder and maker is God.

The rest of God; that is, the offer of God's own presence to his creature after the work of creation was done, (Gen. 2:2) remains available. But it remains unclaimed, says the writer, because of lack of trust. He warns his Christian readers lest the error of Israel be repeated. And what is that error? *The illusion of the trip*: once we are there and have this and that, and our problems are over, and we are secure, and our children do not have to go through what we did, and the future is bright, *then* we shall be at rest. *The illusion of the destination*: now that we are here we want to make sure we do not lose it, sure that our borders are protected, sure that enemies among us are controlled, sure that proper recognition is given to our achievement, sure that the future is secure, *then* we shall be at rest.

In the meantime, who enters into this rest? He or she who, wherever and in whatever circumstances, trusts and delights in God. Our hearts are restless till they find rest in thee.

Gospel: Mark 10:46-52. All three readings for today speak of promise and hope: the return of the remnant (Jeremiah 31), the promise of a Sabbath rest for God's people (Hebrews 4), and now in this pre-triumphal entry story that introduces the reader to the hope and excitement of Jesus' entering Jerusalem.

More than one commentator on Mark has spoken of its likeness to a drama. The cast of characters include Jesus who seems all alone in knowing the direction and purpose of his life; the twelve, unclear and afraid, calling Jesus the Christ but misinterpreting its meaning; the Pharisees and their scribes, threatened, disturbed, critical; and the crowds, ever present in curiosity but never quite believing. In the scene before us, Jesus, his disciples, and a swelling crowd move closer to the Holy City. Jesus has spoken three times of his death in the city and now the distance of time and space between him and the cross rapidly closes. Already he can taste death at the corners of his mouth. The twelve should be three warnings wiser than the crowd but still apparently are not. The crowd is at the high noon of its excitement. If Jesus' entry was, as many believe, at the time of the Feast of Tents rather than Passover, then the songs of ascent, the cutting and waving of branches, the festival mood are much in evidence.

This parade Mark the dramatist interrupts with a shout, "Jesus, Son of David, have mercy," and then with the one who is shouting, a blind beggar. He *is* an interruption and some in the crowd rebuke and try to silence him. (Remember the disciples' reaction to the interrupting presence of children in Jesus' audience?) The parade must go on. As often before (Remember the woman with an issue of blood whom Jesus alone noticed in the crowd?) Jesus alone stops, listens, responds, helps. The beggar follows Jesus and amid an anonymous crowd, only his name is remembered.

What is Mark telling the church by the way he locates and tells this story? It is referred to as a pre-triumphal entry narrative to introduce the cry, "Jesus, Son of David," a Messianic image. It is that, and more. Since it follows immediately the James and John debacle, maybe by contrast this story is to show real faith in Jesus. Maybe. But who can resist the feeling that Mark is offering a judgment upon the church. Parading after Jesus with no notion of the cross ahead and the cost of discipleship, it refuses to be interrupted nor is it willing to include the disqualified, a blind beggar, who is, after all, the only one really qualified to follow Jesus. He trusts. He alone can see.

The Twenty-fourth Sunday after Pentecost

Lutheran	*Roman Catholic*	*Episcopal*	*Pres./UCC/Chr.*	*Methodist/COCU*
Deut. 6:1-9	Deut. 6:2-6	Deut. 6:1-6	Deut. 6:1-9	Deut. 6:1-9
Heb. 7:23-28	Heb. 7:23-28	Heb. 7:23-28	Heb. 7:23-28	Heb. 7:23-28
Mark 12:28-34 (35-37)	Mark 12:28b-34	Mark 12:28b-34	Mark 12:28-34	Mark 12:28-34

EXEGESIS

First Lesson: Deut. 6:1-9. The lesson easily divides into two parts, 6:1-3 and 6:4-9. The first points back into chap. 5, while the second provides the "text" for a series of sermonic expositions which follow.

To see our passage in its immediate literary context, we must begin reading at 4:44, which begins the core of the book (4:44–30:20). After providing the speech with a precise time and place(4:44-49), the author has Moses remind the people of the events at Sinai (here called Horeb); he reformulates the Decalogue (compare Exodus 20), and reports the remarkable response of the people: "To our amazement, we heard God and saw his glory and did not die. Let's not risk this again. Rather, you (Moses) listen to whatever else God may say, and report it to us; we will do what you report." According to 5:28-31, God agreed. In 5:32–6:3 the author has Moses insist on the importance of Israel's doing what he is about to report. 6:4-9 is the first, and primary command, whose concrete meaning is then unfolded.

Deut. 6:1-3 strikes notes which pervade Deuteronomy. First, the content of the book is what God commanded through Moses. Since the same point is made concerning the Decalogue (5:5), even though the people themselves heard and saw God (Deut. 5:5), this new material has the same authority. Second, these commands are to be observed after Israel crosses the Jordan to possess the "promised land." Obedience is to be Israel's way of keeping the covenant. Third, this covenant and the commandments are not merely past events but are of perpetual import. Deut. 5:3 is explicit: the covenant is with all the living. This is the Deuteronomist's way of giving Israel's sacred history contemporary meaning in the seventh century B.C. This is also why 6:2 speaks of succeeding generations. No generation is permitted to exclude itself from obedience by saying, "that was for our forefathers." Fourth, the prosperity of the people is contingent on obedience. The Deuteronomist never wearies of repeating this theme (e.g., 5:33; 6:18; 7:12-15; 8:1).

Deut. 6:4-9 begins with the Shema', which became the "credo" of Judaism (*shema'* = hear). Its precise meaning is unclear, as the translation variants show. It is not simply a matter of monotheism—the belief that only one God exists, for the statement is not really an answer to the question, how many gods are there? Rather, the point is that Israel is to confess that Yahweh, its God (the God to whom it is committed by covenant, and vice versa) is one—that Israel will have but one God because he is the One who cannot be fragmented into functions of culture (war), agriculture (fertility, rain, sun), etc. To the One, Israel is to respond with a single-minded love (v. 6), and the commandments are to be internalized so that they are the ever present factor in shaping the will (the heart) and the whole of life (vv. 7-9). V. 8 became the basis of the phylacteries (small boxes containing the Shema' as a token of the whole law) worn on the forearm and forehead, even to this day. V. 9 became the warrant for the *mazuzzah* a small capsule containing the Shema', fastened at the door, also to this day. The point of vv. 7-9 is perpetual remembrance—a theme developed at length in chap. 8. Historically, of course, the Deuteronomist bore down on this point precisely because he wanted to overcome Israel's amnesia.

Second Lesson: Heb. 7:23-28. Part of this passage concludes the exposition (vv. 23-25) of the contention that it is Christ who is the "high priest forever after the order of Melchizedek" (Ps. 110:4) and part of it sums up the argument (vv. 24-28). Therefore it would be helpful to review the argument in 7:1-22 before engaging the text of this lection.

Heb. 7:23-25, the first part of today's lesson, ends the exposition by calling attention to the fact that Levitical priests served only for a period of time because they died. Christ, however, holds office in perpetuity. Vv. 23-24 state but another aspect of vv. 20-22.

The second part of today's lesson (7:26-28) sums up the matter and points ahead as well. First, that Christ should be described as "holy, blameless, unstained" comes as no surprise in view of 4:15. That he is "separated from sinners" does not nullify the earlier point that the incarnation established solidarity with sinners (2:10-18); rather it alludes to his heavenly position at God's right hand (Ps. 110:1 is in the background), as "exalted above the heavens" makes clear (see also 8:1-2). Second, v. 27 combines several themes: (a) from v. 26 the author infers that a sinless high priest is exempt from those for whom he makes sacrifices; (b) whereas the Levitical high priests offer sacrifices daily, Christ did this "once for all"—a note struck also in 9:12, 24-28; especially 10:11-14. In a way, the whole book is an exposition of this definitive, permanent, significance of Christ. (c) Finally, the author signals a theme developed in chaps. 9-10—that Christ is also the sacrifice as well as the high priest. Third, v. 28 returns to the theme of chap. 7, and notes that the oath (Ps. 110:4, from David's time) comes later than the Mosaic law, and so supersedes it.

Three things need to be said about this theologian's criticism of the law. First, his focus is the cultic law which required animal sacrifice. He is convinced that animal blood cannot cleanse human conscience (9:9b-10). The OT law requires it, however; therefore the superior salvation which Christ brought must displace the old. Second, neither Jesus' own attitude toward the law (see today's Gospel) nor Paul's problem with the law as that which exposes human guilt (Rom. 3:20) crosses the horizon of Hebrews. What interests him is the inherent failure of sacrifice, on the one hand, and the inherent superiority of Christ, on the other. Third, this elaborate argument is not developed in order to demonstrate ingenuity but to bolster the faith of the church (10:19-25). It is pastoral concern that induced this author to write theology.

Gospel: Mark 12:28-34 (35-37). Mark introduces his account of Jesus' Jerusalem ministry with a series of incidents in which Jesus' authority is not only manifest but his judgment on Judaism is expressed. After the entry, the cursing of the fig tree frames the action in the temple so as to interpret the temple incident as a sign of judgment, not a "cleansing" (11:1-26). Then follows a series of scenes, introduced by the question of Jesus' authority, in which Jesus teaches in the temple (11:27–12:44), and this in turn is followed by the "little apocalypse" in chap. 13. The way Mark put these materials together, everything from 11:27 to 13:36–the entire body of teaching material–occurs on the same day. Actually, since the individual items had circulated independently before Mark, we can no longer discern when or where each incident occurred. Our story ends the cycle in which Jesus responds to questions; from now on Jesus takes the initiative. By assembling these stories and teachings as he did, Mark brings to an impressive climax the public ministry of Jesus.

Our pericope is presented as Jesus' response to a question put by a scribe who has been impressed by Jesus' astuteness in biblical interpretation. The question itself is not to be construed as a trap, since it is consonant with rabbinic teaching which also formulated the heart of the whole law.

Jesus responds by juxtaposing two passages, one from Deut. 6:4-5, the other from Lev. 19:18b; the first half of v. 18 forbids vengeance against fellow Israelites (indicating the original scope of "neighbor"). In the Markan version, love of God is the first command, love of neighbor the second; in Matt. 22:39, the second is "like" the first, and Jesus adds that "on these two commandments depend the entire law and prophets" (=Scripture). In Luke, the whole story is transformed: (a) the story occurs in an entirely different setting (Luke 10:25-28); (b) a lawyer who asks Jesus what he must do to inherit eternal life himself quotes these commandments when Jesus replies, "What is written in the law?"; (c) the two commandments are fused into one. In Mark, however, by giving a twofold command as a response to the request to identify the one which is most important, Jesus emphatically makes inseparable love for God and love for neighbor, while at the same time he makes it impossible to reverse the order. In doing so, Jesus was not breaking new ground, since the same point can be documented from Jewish sources.

The scribe continues to be impressed; in fact, he is the only teacher to agree with Jesus in all of Mark. Moreover, he deduces from Jesus' reply that loving God and neighbor surpass "all whole burnt offerings and sacrifices," though he does not say how; the Jerusalem Bible says they are "far more important," though it may also mean "far more efficacious" in rightly relating man to God. In any case, now Jesus agrees with the scribe. Anyone who understands God's will in this way is on the threshold of the kingdom. Why is he not "in" it? Because proper understanding, however important, is not yet doing.

Several observations are in order. First, neither scribe nor Jesus reject the sacrificial system; neither does the story advocate inner disposition in place of external deeds. It is rather a matter of identifying what is most important. Second, by using this story to bring to a head Jesus' encounters with the religious leaders in Jerusalem, Mark shows what Matthew has Jesus say—that he did not come to destroy the law but to fulfill it (Matt. 5:17). For Mark Jesus opposes the scribes because they distort what the law is all about (12:38-40), and predicts that the place of sacrifice will be destroyed (13:1-2) because it has been made into a "den of robbers" (11:17). It will not survive the coming catastrophe.

HOMILETICAL INTERPRETATION

First Lesson: Deut. 6:1-9. Many ministers, enjoying the liberty of the Christian faith, will be frightened by this text and may be inclined to tiptoe through it as through a mine field. In fact, it may prompt a sermon filled with warnings about dangers in religion. The text introduces the commands and statutes of the Lord. Beware the danger of legalism! The passage repeats the Shema, "Hear, O Israel, the Lord our God is one Lord, and you . . ." a creed to be recited morning and evening by every man in Israel. Beware the danger of empty ritualism! "You shall teach them to your children." Beware the danger of dead traditionalism! The readers are instructed to write God's laws on clothing, headbands, and doorposts. Beware the danger of hypocrisy and self-righteousness! If these laws are kept, says the Lord, you will prosper and multiply. Beware the danger of utilitarianism!

But when this attack is over, we probably will realize any unskilled laborer can clean off the lot; only the skilled can build. With this realization, the reader may hear anew the text. Deuteronomy was the basis for the national reform in the reign of Josiah. The recovery of tradition served with new relevance in keeping alive faith and moral seriousness in a time of corruption and decay. Central to that reform and to the passage before us was not legalistic demand for improved behavior. To be sure, the Torah makes demands, but first it announces the good news of God's election. The Torah commands, but first it recited the prior acts of God's deliverance, especially in the exodus. The commands begin, "Therefore." The Torah instructs, but first reveals. The revelation of God precedes all instruction because all the "thou shalts" grow out of the "I am."

As Deuteronomy represents a recovery of the moral and ethical earnestness of Israel's tradition, so the Gospel of Matthew sought to serve the early church. The reappropriation of Judaism and the ethical teachings of Jesus are very apparent in Matthew. Note the Jewishness, the refusal to destroy the law and the prophets, but rather the insistence in the Sermon on the Mount that we build firmly upon the law. And why? Because the church in Matthew's day was beset by those who said "Lord, Lord" but did not obey (7:21). Many set a premium on prophecy, exorcisms, and miracles rather than moral responsibility (7:22-23). Private pursuits of salvation experiences blinded them to basic acts of Christian duty. "When did we see you hungry or naked or . . .?" (25:44-46).

Is it time in the church today for Deuteronomy or Matthew again?

Second Lesson: Heb. 7:23-28. If the first reading for today lays upon the reader the demands of God, then this passage from the Epistle discusses provisions made for human frailties in the process. The image of the priest stands as testimony to our need for continual repair and renewal in our relation to God. And this image is not just a visible reminder of God's judging and forgiving presence among us. It is that, as the priest is so often regarded as God's man, representing God's word, God's will, toward us. But just as importantly the priest is *our* man, our presence, our needs, our lives represented before God. The text for today stresses this latter dimension of the priest's function: he is in our behalf.

In summary fashion, the writer celebrates the total adequacy and finality of Christ's priestly work with the description, "Once for all."

Once for all! Roll the phrase around over the mind. Complete, finished, adequate, total, final—these are words used to praise Christ's priestly act of giving himself in our behalf. But there is something heavy and threatening about the phrase, "Once for all." If he in one act redeemed us and we in one act embraced his death by baptism, now what? Once is not enough. No wonder the implications of "once for all" raised the frightening issue of post-baptismal sins and introduced the practice of delayed (nearer to the time of death) baptism. Relief is offered by the text: Christ lives in God's presence in continual intercession on our behalf. In him, in one who shared our temptations, fears, suffering, death, we have continued sympathetic access to God. The writer of Hebrews has, in his own categories, affirmed what others have said in describing the work of the Holy Spirit; that is, our relation to God does not depend alone upon the memory of an act long ago, once for all, but is continually being renewed and nourished by a living Christ. Otherwise, the whole event of the incarnation would have been but one bright moment in history, now a dim and distant Camelot.

Hear a parable: A man having fallen into a pit and unable to get himself out, is noticed by four passersby. One scolds him for his carelessness and judges him deserving of his fate. Another plants shrubs and flowers around the unsightly pit that disgraces the community. Another posts a sign announcing a $25.00 fine upon all who fall in the pit. And another offers a strong hand, commenting that his own path by that pit had made him aware of its dangers. Regrettably, all four have at times been presented as the Christ. Which one do I preach?

Gospel: Mark 12:28-34. What one hears in this text and therefore what is preached from it depends on the motivation attributed to the lawyer who asked, "What is the greatest commandment?" The question itself was not an unfamiliar one; rabbis and students had long discussed it. But one question can be asked in different ways becoming many different questions.

What is the greatest commandment? Hear the question asked in a tense interview. The issue is orthodoxy and the resolution of that issue determines whether this minister is called as leader. That is one question.

What is the greatest commandment? Hear someone ask it to begin the thirty minutes set aside for discussion following refreshments at the Classics Literary Club. This week's meeting is on the Bible. That is another question.

What is the greatest commandment? Hear it in the midst of a debate. The audience is already divided and polarized. The answer will put the speaker in one camp or the other. That is still another question.

What is the greatest commandment? So asks someone who does not want to have to worry about Bible reading, study, thinking, and deciding, but who does not want to be irreligious and most assuredly does not want to go to hell. Give it to me in a nutshell, Reverend; I never was much on this religion business. Yet another question.

What is the greatest commandment? The enquirer is sincerely seeking God's will but has encountered a mountain of demands from many quarters. Leaders and interpreters disagree, each insisting his priority is ultimate. What is needed is a governing consideration. Even though one must improvise, still some guiding principle is needed lest life shatter into a thousand relativities and weightless options. Recall the old Yiddish poem, "Der Ikker" (*The Main Thing*) by Oscherovitch?

> If your outlook
> on things has changed-
> this is not the main thing.
>
> If you feel like laughing
> at old dreams-
> this is not the main thing.
>
> Even if you know
> that, what you are doing now
> you'll regret some other time-
> this is not the main thing either.
>
> But beware lightheartly
> to conclude from this
> that there is no such thing
> as a main thing-
> this is the main thing.

In our Gospel for today, unlike the parallels in Matthew and Luke, we have such an enquirer. Answer: "Love God totally and your neighbor as yourself."

What is the greatest commandment? First, tell me, why do you ask?

The Twenty-fifth Sunday after Pentecost

Lutheran	*Roman Catholic*	*Episcopal*	*Pres./UCC/Chr.*	*Methodist/COCU*
1 Kings 17:8-16	1 Kings 17:10-16	1 Kings 17:10-16	1 Kings 17:8-16	1 Kings 17:8-16
Heb. 9:24-28	Heb. 9:24-28	Heb. 9:24-28	Heb. 9:24-28	Heb. 9:24-28
Mark 12:41-44	Mark 12:38-44	Mark 12:38-44	Mark 12:38-44	Mark 12:38-44

EXEGESIS

First Lesson: 1 Kings 17:8(10)-16. This chapter begins the cycle of Elijah stories, set in the time of Ahab, who ruled the northern kingdom from Samaria in the ninth century B.C. The writer regards Ahab as worse than his predecessors, including Jeroboam who had reintroduced the worship of the golden calves (1 Kings 16:33; 12:25-30). Elijah, the protagonist in the drama, is introduced next (1 Kings 17:1-8); in the name of God he puts a curse on the land: "There will be neither dew nor rain until I say so." The drought lasted three years (18:1; the rain comes after the contest on Mt. Carmel, 18:41-45). At the beginning, Elijah hid near a brook, but in time it dried up. At this point in the story, our pericope begins. It is the first of two miracle stories about Elijah and the widow in Phoenicia. By putting these at the beginning of the present cycle, the reader is assured that Elijah is indeed a "man of God," as the widow says at the end (17:24).

The theme of our story, like the brief report which precedes it (17:2-7), is God's miraculous preservation of his prophet. In interpreting miracle stories, such as this, one should not replace the miraculous with natural causes; thus one should not invent reasons why Elijah travelled so far, nor guess why God could not have found a hospitable widow nearer by, nor how Elijah knew that the woman gathering fuel was the widow God had selected. The point of the story from beginning to end is that God provides wondrously for the preservation of his word by caring for his prophet.

The story manifests the art of good oral narration. The tension builds as the woman is asked for food, for she had resigned herself to die of starvation and is preparing the last bread for herself and her son. But the word of Yahweh, delivered by this holy man of another religion (note v. 12), persuades her to give it to him. Amazingly, even after Elijah moved in with her, there was always enough—just as the word of Yahweh had said.

According to Luke 4:25-26, Jesus' inaugural sermon used this incident to imply that the sending of Elijah to this Phoenician widow instead of to Israelite widows was judgment on Israel. For Luke the story signals a theme of Acts—Israel rejects the word, so it goes to gentiles (Acts 13:46).

Second Lesson: Heb. 9:24-28. To understand this theologian one must remember that he has been sufficiently influenced by Platonist thinking to assume that the "really real" is invisible on earth, not part of the phenomenal world at all, but "heavenly." Things on earth are copies of the "really real" and so derive whatever reality they have from what is invisible and heavenly. This mode of thinking he combines with a quite different one, grounded in Jewish apocalyptic—that "this age" (aeon, meaning both time and space) is to be contrasted with "the age to come." In other words, Hebrews combines the earthly-heavenly duality with a now-then duality. Thereby he can say that the Mosaic law is not only a shadow of the really real, but its foreshadow (10:1)—that is, it is a shadow of the real which is to become manifest. Likewise the event of Christ is the manifestation of the real and the perfect, and as such is an eschatological event as well, for it cannot be surpassed. The very fact that on earth, within history, we do not see Christ the high priest actually guarantees the reality of his eternal priesthood, for if it were presently visible he would be merely an historical earthling whose priesthood would be like that of any other.

Heb. 9:24 (see also 9:11) asserts, accordingly, that the sanctuary which Christ entered was not a man-made one but the "really real" one, where he now functions on our behalf in the presence of God. Second, vv. 25-6, alluding to the Jewish Day of Atonement, point out that Christ did not offer himself (for Hebrews, Christ is both priest and sacrifice, 9:11-12) annually, but "once for all at the end of the [this] age." Since Christ is the incarnation of the eternal Son through whom God created the world (1:2-3), his self-sacrifice is either an ever-repeated process in history or an unrepeatable eschatological event. This theologian does not probe these alternatives but excludes the former for reasons not stated. We, however, can see that logically his position also excludes understanding Jesus' death in terms of a Christ-figure who appears again and again in human experience. An event which repeats itself constantly is what we mean by myth. Hebrews, however, insists that the Christ-story is an unrepeatable historical event; paradoxically perhaps, it is precisely to make this clear that the author uses modes of thought which we call mythological. Christ is not an instance of a timeless or ever-repeated truth but the definitive disclosure of the "really real."

Third, this event "put away sin by the sacrifice of himself" (v. 26).

Since the thought of Hebrews moves within the framework of temple-priest-sacrifice, it consistently uses language from the cultus to interpret Christ's death. The author neither questions nor explains why it is that "without the shedding of blood there is no forgiveness of sins" (9:22b). Nor should we expect an explanation, for this was a common view in antiquity. Therefore, the author was free to concentrate on the surpassing power of Christ's blood to do so (9:13-14).

Finally, the author's appropriation of Christianized apocalyptic thought is evident in vv. 27-28. As after one's death comes judgment, so after Christ's unrepeatable death comes the judgment. The analogy is not perfect, since logically persons will be judged but Christ will judge; moreover, the text does not speak of the Last Judgment but of salvation. The author evidently assumes that the future judgment will bring salvation for the believer. The believer's conscience is purified now by faith (9:14; 10:22) but salvation proper is future. Consistently, the author understands faith as "the assurance of things hoped for, the conviction [of the reality] of things not seen" (11:1). Hence he repeatedly warns against forefeiting the promise and urges perseverance.

Gospel: Mark 12:38-44. The two units of tradition which comprise this lesson are related to each other in two ways. First, the word "widows" in 12:40 might have attracted the story of the widow by word association, as frequently happened. Second, the units reinforce one another thematically, for the self-serving demeanor of the scribes is the opposite of the self-giving of the widow.

This brief warning against scribes stimulated Matthew to rework the Markan material so that it could serve as an introduction to his collection of sevenfold woes against "scribes, Pharisees, hypocrites" (Matthew 23). In Mark 12:38-39 Jesus accuses the scribes, who were generally honored in that society, of manipulating situations in order to claim the honor. What people freely gave the scribes claimed as their right. In v. 40 different charges are made: hypocrisy and greed (they take advantage of widows). Because, being interpreters of Torah, they know that this is contrary to God's intent, the judgment will come more severely on them. The different accusations, as well as the awkward syntax by which v. 40 is linked to what precedes it, indicate that this saying once circulated independently.

Mark 12:41-44 (abbreviated in Luke 21:1-4 and omitted by Matthew) emphasizes the unreserved giving by the widow. Trumpet-shaped containers received gifts for the temple. The contrast between the many rich who gave much and the one widow who gave little is fundamental to the saying in vv. 43-44. The two *lepta* ("the widow's mite") were the smallest copper coins in circulation. One should not ask how Jesus knew this was all the money she had, for the point of the saying is that the value of the gift is not determined by its inherent cash value but by what it represents for the giver—a percentage of abundance or one's whole life.

HOMILETICAL INTERPRETATION

First Lesson: 1 Kings 17:8-16. Now and then a biblical passage is so rich with explicit and implicit meaning that the preacher has the pleasant but perplexing task of choosing from many thematic directions, all of which lie within the province of the text. An exegesis of the particular congregation addressed will serve as the magnet to draw out the appropriate meaning. Woe be to him who makes no decision and goes in all possible directions! This is such a text.

This passage is, of course, a chapter in the story of God's providence in the life of his servant Elijah. Elijah is the man of God par excellence, obedient to God's word, itinerant at the prompting of God's Spirit, ecstatic though at times despairing, always faithful. Through the famine of three and one half rainless years, God cared for Elijah, but always so as to test and strengthen Elijah's faith for the major tasks of his ministry yet to be performed. "I will send ravens to feed you." "I have put it in the heart of a poor starving widow of Sidon to provide for you." Provisions, to be sure, but only for the believing. Otherwise, absurdity and foolishness.

This story is also a drama of unusual faith found in an unlikely place. The dry and parched land of Israel was not nearly so barren as the hearts of the faithless people. The light of faith in God seemed almost totally extinguished by King Ahab and his idolatrous wife, Jezebel. But in those years of flickering faith and harsh judgment, the light refuses to be snuffed out by the darkness. For instance, in Sidon, that is, in Gentile territory, to the north of Israel lived a widow who had one meager meal between herself and starvation. In fact she faced also the grim prospect of death for her son whom she could not support. The news media have shown us the face of starvation in recent years; we get the picture. The man of God says to her as she prepares the last meal: "Feed me first and the God of Israel will provide you with oil and flour in abundance until the famine breaks." The small loaf that would have kept death at bay a few more hours is given to him. Now all that stands between her and death is God. She trusts him.

But this story is also one of judgment. So Jesus understood it, according to Luke 4:16-26. In a sermon in his home synagogue Jesus justified his ministry beyond the bounds of his home territory by pointing to Elijah's ministry to a Gentile woman, a widow of Zarephath. There were many widows in Israel during the famine but where was the faith to bring God's favor? In an unacceptable foreigner, an outsider, a woman from the very territory that produced Jezebel (1 Kings 16:31). How many times in Israel and in the church, ancient and modern, have such cases been the finger of God pointing in judgment at our prejudices and postured faith?

Second Lesson: Heb. 9:24-28. The pattern of thought which frames the argument of Hebrews should no longer detain us. Repeatedly we have met the writer's two worlds: the earthly, which is visible, transient, a shadow of the real, and the heavenly, which is the invisible, eternal, true. The rites and institutions of Judaism are put in the first category, those of Christianity in the second. Hence the writer can say that following his death, Jesus passed through the veil (heavens) into the true holy of holies (God's presence) in our behalf.

Even if the language and thought pattern seem strange to us, they should not deter our grasp of the central thesis of the passage. Christ gave himself a sacrifice for us. This controlling theme should explain why this text is appropriately placed in the lectionary between two passages, both of which tell of the act of total giving by poor widows. Giving sacrificially is the thought at the heart of all of today's readings. In fact, some readers may already have remembered two passages in the NT which speak of Christ's self-giving as poverty: 2 Cor. 8:9, "for our sakes became poor" and Phil. 2:7, "emptied (synonym for becoming poor) himself."

The church has always insisted Christ gave himself. His death was not simply murder, though his killers were responsible, nor was it suicide even though he "laid down his life." But by calling his death a sacrifice, pale and sickly models of piety have been generated. In order to stay healthy, the word "sacrifice" must be confined to the comments of those who interpret the act of giving by another. On the lips of the one giving, the word "sacrifice" smacks of self-righteousness. It seems generally true that those who give of means and self insist that it was a joy; observers may call it a sacrifice.

In T. S. Eliot's play, *Murder in the Cathedral*, the archbishop, when faced with a conflict with the king, is visited by three tempters: one tempts him to compromise, another to political intrigue, and another to sensual pleasure. He resists them. Then comes a fourth tempter. "Why don't you give your life as a sacrifice?" asks the tempter. The right thing for the wrong reason! Who among us is strong enough to resist? Or should we?

Gospel: Mark 12:41-44. The story of the poor widow who gave her last penny is the account which closes Mark's record of the public ministry of Jesus. It is both appropriate and prophetic that Jesus' public words end with "She gave all that she had." That the story has parallels in other religions should not detract from our hearing it. Reminiscent of the poor widow of Zarephath in Elijah's time, this poor woman gave all she had to live on.

In dealing with this text the preacher needs to avoid idealizing the poor. The church has at times fallen into this, even as early as the Gospel of Luke and the Epistle of James, both of which tend to make "poor" a synonym for saint. Such idealizing tends to produce many bad effects. Some of the affluent have guilt feelings which are eased, not by generosity, but by recalling poorly their own deprived and stark childhoods. Perhaps you have attended one of those nice parties where the plush gather around the punch bowl and "out poor" each other's past. Another bad effect is to blind the poor to their own very real problems of bitterness, resentment, and materialism. Those who do not have money can be as bedeviled by the love of it as those who have it. The French novelist Gustave Flaubert once wrote that "Of all the winds that blow on love, the demand for money is the coldest and most destructive." And a major ill effect of idealizing poverty is to oversimplify the whole complex issue of responsible stewardship of life and resources. Giving away everything and becoming poor could be a huge cop-out, a sin praised as virtue and blessed with a proper text.

What needs to be borne in mind is that the poor widow, like the blind beggar and the little child, is the biblical image of emptiness before God. To be empty is to have capacity, capacity to be filled. But that means *receiving*, not giving or doing, and the kingdom of God is received. Having been rid of everything, having stood empty and childlike and poor without claim before God, one is able to receive everything, even one's own life, as a gift. Such a person is rich even if she or he has just placed in the tray the last penny.

The Twenty-sixth Sunday after Pentecost

Lutheran	*Roman Catholic*	*Episcopal*	*Pres./UCC/Chr.*	*Methodist/COC*
Dan. 12:1-3	Dan. 12:1-3	Dan. 7:9-12	Dan. 12:1-4	Dan. 12:1-4
Heb. 10:11-18	Heb. 10:11-14, 18	Heb. 10:11-14, 18	Heb. 10:11-18	Heb. 10:11-18
Mark 13:1-13	Mark 13:24-32	Mark 13:14-23	Mark 13:24-32	Mark 13:14-23

EXEGESIS

First Lesson: Dan 12:1-3 (for Dan. 7:9-12, see Pentecost 27). This passage is the climax of the final vision of the book (11:2–12:3). The vision reviews ancient near eastern history from the Persian period onward (11:2-35), deals briefly with the immediate situation which produced the Book of Daniel (11:36-39), then predicts the imminent future as "the time of the end" of history (11:40-45), and follows this with a portrait of the transition to the time of salvation (12:1-3). The book has long been dated shortly before 165 B.C. because only up to 11:39 is the review of history accurate. This date is important for placing correctly our lesson's view of resurrection in the history of biblical thought.

The transition from history as we have known it to the time of salvation will not be gradual or easy but traumatic—a constitutive perspective of all apocalyptic. The climactic struggle between God and anti-God comes to be described in great detail in apocalypses, but Dan. 12:1

simply predicts unprecedented woe. Precisely then, however, God's people will be delivered because Michael, Israel's angelic guardian, will intervene ("stand up," as 12:1 puts it). The idea that peoples have heavenly counterparts is common in apocalyptic literature; (Michael is mentioned also in Dan. 10:13, 21; Jude 9; Rev. 12:7). To be among the saved, however, more is required than being a Jew genealogically—one's name must be in the book, a metaphor for being known by God as one of the faithful. The saved people of God will also include the righteous dead who will be separated from the unrighteous after the resurrection.

Even though Daniel is the latest book in the OT, this is the earliest unambiguous statement of the resurrection. From this time onward, however, it rapidly became a fundamental tenet of Pharisaism as well as of apocalyptic. Belief in resurrection emerged in intimate relation to the theme of retribution. The experience of persecution for the faithful, during the time in which Daniel was written, served as a catalyst for theological thinking because now the righteous faithful did not prosper (as Deuteronomy and Psalm 1 promise) but suffered. Resurrection for punishment or reward affirms that the inequity of this life is not the final verdict. (In some apocalypses, the wicked are not raised because resurrection itself is the divinely given reward.)

Daniel envisages resurrection only for some—perhaps the specially righteous or specially wicked. The precise meaning of "shame and everlasting contempt" (v. 2) is not clear; the later idea of eternal punishment in Gehenna should not be read into this text. The "wise" and "those who turn many to righteousness" may be those who are receptive to the Book of Daniel and so become apocalyptically-oriented leaders and interpreters of the resistance movement.

Second Lesson: Heb. 10:11-18. Heb. 10:5-18 argues that the one sacrifice of Christ's death brought to an end all animal sacrifice, as required by the old covenant and inaugurated the promised new covenant in which sacrifices are unnecessary. By regarding Ps. 40:6-8 (which he modifies) as being spoken by Christ to God, the author contends that the coming of Christ ended the old covenant and established the new (10:5-10).

Important aspects of the logic which underlies 10:11-14 have been discussed before (see espec. Pentecost 23-25). The repetition of sacrifices shows, according to this author, that they are not really effective (10:1-3). This point is now restated in order to highlight the once for all sacrifice of Christ (vv. 11-12, 14). Vv. 12-13 allude to Ps. 110:1 (as does 1:3b).

In 10:15-18 the author reflects on Jer. 31:33-34; in 8:8-12 he had already quoted the entire passage which promises a new covenant with Israel, and inferred (8:13) that a new covenant does not merely modify or update the old but displaces it. Since the old covenant relied on animal sacrifices to deal with sin, he reasons that since the new covenant replaces the old, it also does away with sacrifices (which were ineffective anyway except as "foreshadowing"). In using Jer. 31:33-34 this time, however, he replaces "covenant with the house of Israel" with "covenant . . . with them" because the new covenant is not only with Israel; the other changes in the quotation are not as important. Because here his interest is not in internalized knowledge of God, as was Jeremiah's, but in doing away with sin, he bypasses an important part of the Jeremiah passage in order to pick up the last line: "I will remember their sin no more," which he rightly understands as meaning forgiveness (as the preceding line, which he does not quote, actually says). The writer sees that the new covenant promises forgiveness but does not mention sacrifice. Therefore in the new covenant the sacrificial system is displaced by the one sacrifice of Christ.

Whatever one may think of the author's reasoning, in terms of history he has been vindicated, for two generations ago Harnack observed that wherever the gospel has taken root, there animal sacrifices cease.

Gospel: Mark 13:1-32. For over a century, this chapter has been called "the little apocalypse" and scholars have discussed whether it incorporates part of a Jewish or Christian apocalypse and the extent to which it contains genuine sayings of Jesus. Many questions are still unanswered, including whether the designation "apocalypse" is appropriate. One can also regard it as a farewell speech or "testament," since in Mark it is the last extended teaching by Jesus, and given only to his followers. John 13-17 and Acts 20:18-35 also are samples of the farewell discourse form. One thing has become clear, however–the chapter as it stands is the end-product of a long and complex history which includes reflection upon many OT passages, appropriation of motifs common to Jewish and early Christian apocalyptic, and interpretation of some genuine sayings of Jesus.

The double introduction (13:1-4) illumines important aspects of the chapter, especially if we are alert to several strata of tradition which the text incorporates: Mark's own editorial work, early Christian use of Jewish apocalyptic motifs, Jesus' own words. Mark 13:1-2 reports the total destruction of the temple; the likelihood that this is from Jesus himself is widely acknowledged. In 13:3-4 the hand of Mark is disclosed, because having Jesus give private explanation of what had just been said is a distinctive literary device of this Evangelist (4:10; 7:17; 10:10; Matthew and Luke feel free to make changes here). There is reason to believe that the question in v. 4 is really two questions, the first having in mind the time of the destruction, the second asking about the sign by which one will know that "all these things" are about to happen. For one thing, in the rest of the chapter not another word is said about the destruction of the temple; besides, "all these things" seems to point to what is about to be said rather than to the single event of the temple's fall. Mark 13:3-4, then, appears to be the Evangelist's way of connecting the material that follows with the prediction in v. 2. In his mind, the fate of the temple is an eschatological event, for its destruction is to be understood as part of God's judgment, which itself is part of the end-time chaos. Accordingly, he has the disciples ask only about the *time* of these things, as if the destruction of the temple were self-evident.

Mark's concern to answer the question about the time of "these things" reveals that in various ways this had become an issue in his church. Evidently those who were saturated with apocalyptic thought were interpreting current events as signs that the End is imminent; then, when the events were past and the End had still not occurred and the Lord tarried, others were inclined to minimize the hope of Christ's coming altogether. Some such situation may account for the fact that chap. 13 both teaches apocalyptic and warns against an overheated expectation of the End.

Several passages show how Mark uses apocalyptic motifs about the End in order to make it clear that his own time is not the End. (A) On the one hand, the saying that wars and war-talk must happen reflects the apocalyptic view of divinely-determined history; on the other hand, "the end is not yet" (v. 7). (B) Likewise earthquakes (v. 8) are common in apocalyptic expectation; yet their occurrence does not signal the End but the beginning of the eschatological sufferings. (C) Persecution too awaits the saints in apocalyptic thought (vv. 9-13); yet before the End the gospel must be preached to all nations (v. 10, generally recognized as Mark's own line). (D) A sequence of End-events is indicated: the sacrilege in the temple (v. 14), unprecedented affliction (v. 19), false Messiahs and prophets (v. 21); *after* this comes the collapse of cosmic order (vv. 24-25); and only then will the Son of man come to gather the elect (vv. 26-27). Nonetheless, God alone knows precisely the day of the Lord's coming (v. 32).

It is not clear whether the apocalyptic teachings in this chapter were currently being used by overly intense Christian apocalyptists or whether they had been used in earlier years (perhaps during the crisis in A.D. 40-41 when Caligula ordered a statue of himself erected in the temple—a threat which was interpreted in light of Dan. 9:27; 12:11). In any case, it is clear that Mark does not reject apocalyptic but corrects it by providing a proper ordering of the material. His pastoral concern is evident. Four times he writes, "watch out" ("take heed" in RSV, NEB, Jerusalem Bible) and in v. 14 singles out the "sacrilege" as needing special astuteness in interpretation. Moreover, he reassures the persecuted (v. 11, 13b), while at the same time insists that one must be on guard and not slacken one's expectation (vv. 33-37).

HOMILETICAL INTERPRETATION

First Lesson: Dan. 12:1-3. The Book of Daniel is a response to extreme times for the people of God. In the second century B.C. the Syrian oppressors of Israel reached their worst. Jews were hanged for keeping the Sabbath or being true to their kosher diet. Some were forcefed pork and others executed at the time of prayer. On the other hand, apostate and renegade Jews were given position, power, and wealth. Out of this dark hour came the Maccabean revolution, and the Book of Daniel. Extreme times call for a new casting of old hopes. Either that or the abandonment of the old hopes. Read again the old creeds and sing again the old songs. These speak and sing of a God who is Lord of history, who has a purpose for his people and for the world, who will not rest until his kingdom is established. Are these the words of our naive parents lulled by nostalgia in "the little brown church in the vale"? Or were the cynical and secular neighbors right: life is an ever-recurring cycle of repeated events with nothing new under the sun? Is the governing force of history blind chance or cruel fate? These alternatives are weighed again, and bought by many under the pressure of absurd and senseless inequities.

But not Daniel. He lifts his eyes above the bloody pages of observable events and envisions God's fulfillment of his purposes beyond history. We need to be careful here. Daniel is not other-worldly in any sense of rejecting the world and its history. His vision of the end-time is an affirmation of God's work in history. God has kept his promise. If history is too small an arena for God to complete his work in the lives of his people, then the final chapter will be at another time, another place.

Here then are the beginnings of a doctrine of resurrection. At this point only the exceptional participate: the exceptionally pious, the martyrs, and the exceptionally wicked. It touches only the extremes because the times are extreme. But the striking and abiding truth is in seeing the dynamic of trust in God. The shape of one's faith bears the contours of the times and conditions and issues one faces. A doctrine of resurrection is not just borrowed from another religion. Too easy, too casual, too academic. Neither does one accept "the way the world is" as a life stance. At the center is trust in God who is Creator, Sustainer, and End of all things. God being who he is, and things being what they are, resurrection arises not as a faint hope but an inescapable necessity. Ernst Renan once said, "The martyr is the real creator of the belief in a second life." In a sense, perhaps so. But the *real* creator is the irreducible core of our faith: the sovereignty of a gracious God.

Second Lesson: Heb. 10:11-18. One priest standing, one priest seated: in these two images the writer captures the sum of his argument. The priest standing is continually serving at the altar, negotiating the distance between God and man with sacrifices, rituals, prayers. He is the image of repeated efforts, recurring offerings, monotonously routine rituals. Always at it but never finished; beginning again but he is never really beginning again. He is a part of religious exercises but he is never the first nor the last. All this has been done, will be done. Too much like life itself are this priest's duties. Mow the grass again; go to work again; paint the house again; wash the dishes again; make the bed again; again; again. Stop the system, I want to get off.

The other priest seated. He has finished his office, the sacrifice is made, access to God is open, God's assuring word is heard, worship is complete, we go down to our house justified. With an image of sitting rather than standing, the writer expresses the adequacy and finality of Jesus' ministry in our behalf.

And then, with hesitation and without comment lest he weaken the point he has made, the author completes the line from Psalm 110: "until I make your enemies a footstool for your feet." Let's face it: that "until" has to be there. On the one hand Christ is seated; all that is necessary to persuade us of God's love and grace has been done. The act by which the world's mind and heart and hand will be turned is done. He gave himself for us. But while he is seated, we are still standing because the announcements and countless expressions of that Good News are incomplete. Our limited self-understanding, our frayed relationships, our observations all around shout too loudly the fact that the report has not been heard, or believed.

Already, and not yet. Already, and so we are at peace. Not yet, and so we stir ourselves to bring to pass what already is. The kingdom is both gift and task. Is it possible for those of us who preach to make clear the paradox—the victory is won but the enemies are still very much alive?

Gospel: Mark 13:1-13. There is in our time a strong and apparently growing interest in eschatology, doctrines of the last things. This interest takes many forms—end of the world, second coming of Christ, rapture of the church, how are the dead raised, and signs of the times. Whether one reads sophisticated journals or bumper stickers, the subjects have been brought to our attention. It is difficult to know the sources of this particular appetite. Times of economic depression, war, and natural catastrophes nourish interest in the End, but so also do extended periods of prosperity. Among the leisure class, lectures, books, and discussion groups often focus on prophecies of the end and the coming of Christ. There may be among these a kind of spiritual depression when the magnificence of life's promise is lost in the poverty of its achievement. Some, of course, are bored and dip into eschatology to enjoy the tensing and relaxing that goes with pursuit of the subject. Then there are always those who treat the Bible as an almanac. And then some are serious seekers of truth in an area that has always been a part of Christian thought.

Materials similar to Revelation and Mark 13 were available to Christianity from Judaism. To understand the Christian era as the Messianic age was to activate much of the Jewish apocalyptic literature, especially when the church experienced persecutions similar to those which prompted some of the Jewish views of the end time.

Apparently Mark faces a problem that is arousing fanaticism. False prophets and messiahs are plaguing the church with their predictions. Vital Christian energies are being drained off by all types of calculating. Every near or distant war prompts new panic—this is it! Mark writes to offer some clear leadership when everyone in the church is whispering into the next ear—Do you think we are in the last days? Mark's message here is brief but strong: this is not the end; we have the mission still before us because the gospel has not reached every nation; stay faithfully at your task and in your witness. Any teaching or idea, however religious and banked by Bible verses, which pulls us away, in panic or in neglect, from the Christian mission in the world is from a false prophet.

Many Christians have found it more encouraging, more motivating, and more challenging to know that *God* is near than to wonder if the end is near.

The Twenty-seventh Sunday after Pentecost

Lutheran	*Roman Catholic*	*Episcopal*	*Pres./UCC/Chr.*	*Methodist/COCU*
Dan. 7:9-10	Dan. 7:13-14	Dan. 12:1-3	Dan. 7:13-14	Dan. 7:9-10
Heb. 13:20-21	Rev. 1:5-8	Heb. 10:31-33, 35-39	Rev. 1:4-8	Heb. 10:31-39
Mark 13:24-31	John 18:33-37	Mark 13:24-32	John 18:33-37	Mark 13:24-32

EXEGESIS

First Lesson: Dan. 7:9-14 (for Dan. 12:1-3 see Pentecost 26). These verses provide various lessons for the next Sunday as well. The whole of chap. 7 is devoted to the vision of the four beasts from the sea; after beasts resembling a lion, a bear, and a leopard comes an incomparably terrible one (7:1-8). The first three apparently represent, in turn, the Persian, Medean, and Greek empires, while the fourth is the Seleucid successor of Alexander's empire; the "little horn" who speaks "great things" is a contemptuous reference to Antiochus Epiphanes IV (*epiphanes*= [God] manifest). It was Antiochus's persecution of the Jews which evoked the Book of Daniel (ca. 165 B.C.), and the Maccabean Revolt. Dan. 7:19-31 shows that the author's real interest is in the fourth beast, and what will supplant it—the reign of the saints which is symbolized by a being from heaven (rather than a beast). See comments on "one like a son of man" in next Sunday's Lesson.

Dan. 7:9-10 appears to interrupt the account of the fourth beast (vv. 7-8, 11-12); moreover, these verses, like 7:13-14, 23-27 are poetry, whereas the rest of the chapter is prose. This suggests that the author has drawn together various traditions in order to compose the chapter. (The prose material may also be an expansion of earlier traditions.) The combining of diverse materials into a single text is characteristic of apocalypses. By inserting the vision of the heavenly court where he does, the author interprets the fate of the fourth beast as the judgment of God.

The imagery of the vision of God has numerous antecedents in various ancient near eastern texts, including the OT; moreover it reappears in later apocalypses. It serves to suggest majesty, power, and judgment; thereby Daniel's readers, the persecuted, were assured that despite their terrible experience with the beast, its fate is sealed by God. Moreover, the present is the immediate prelude to the coming of the final kingdom.

Second Lesson: Heb. 10:31-33, 35-39; 13:20-21. The lesson from Hebrews 10 fragments the text and its rationale. V. 31 belongs with the previous paragraph, which comments on the seriousness of forfeiting salvation (see 3:12). Vv. 32-34 remind the readers of their excellent record of faithfulness in adversity, and provide us with an important aperture into the actual experience of the readers. Evidently, however, the author is no longer confident that the readers will persevere, so vv. 35-39 urge them not to discard their hope.

Heb. 10:37-38 quote Hab. 2:3-4 in order to undergird the appeal. Hab. 2:4b had been an important line for Paul (Rom. 1:17; Gal. 3:11), whose understanding of it leads many to translate it "he who through faith is righteous shall live." Our author, on the other hand, interprets the text in a way that is closer to the original meaning—"the righteous shall live by faithfulness"—by the persistent trust in the invisible, eternal future, as chap. 11 goes on to develop. Clearly, our author is not dependent on Paul. The quotation itself is inexact; the opening line appears to come from Isa. 26:20, whose theme is also the coming judgment; the rest of the quotation (from Habakkuk 2) has also been modified. On the one hand, Hebrews speaks of "the coming one," although it is not clear whether it is God or Christ; on the other hand, the text now explicitly speaks of a future coming. These changes, as well as the "shall not tarry," imply that the author is responding to questions posed by the delay of the parousia. The passage concludes the exposition of the theme of the high priestly work of Christ, begun at 4:14. The pastoral concern which motivated this theologian to develop his Christology is clear once more.

Heb. 13:20-21 is often used as a benediction, but it is a doxology as well. It is not certain to whom the "glory" is ascribed; grammatically, it appears to be given to Christ, as the punctuation of the NEB and Jerusalem Bible implies; formally, however, it appears to be God, as the punctuation of the RSV suggests, for the whole sentence focuses attention on God's activity. The doxology draws on multiple traditions and allusions: Moses "brought up from death" (Isa. 63:11); traditional language about Jesus' resurrection (Rom. 10:7), Jesus as shepherd (John 10:1-18; 1 Pet. 2:25; 5:4), and the eternal covenant (Isa. 55:3; 61:8; Jer. 32:40). The second half of v. 21, apart from the closing line, is a benediction asking God to accomplish through Christ what is in accord with his will.

Gospel: Mark 13:24-31 (32); (see also Exegesis for previous Sunday). For John 18:33-37 see next lection. Several elements compose this lesson: instruction about the time of the coming of the Son of man (13:24-27); a parable of the fig tree (13:28-29); a double assurance (13:30-31); and a reminder that no one knows the precise time of the parousia (13:32).

The apocalyptic instruction makes clear a sequence: tribulation, collapse of the cosmic order, the coming of the Son of man, and finally the gathering of the elect. The language describing the return of chaos is shaped by Isa. 13:10 and 34:4, but the motif is much older. The description of the coming of the Son of man is a development of Dan. 7:13 (which speaks of a man-like being as a symbol of the saints), for now "Son of man" is a title and it is taken for granted that it is the exalted Christ who comes in this role. The gathering of the saints as part of God's promise is common in the OT (see, e.g., Deut. 30:4; Isa. 43:5-7; Jer. 32:37). Here, of course, Mark understands the elect to be the Christians scattered throughout the world. (Mark 13:10 had insisted that the gospel would be preached to all nations.) It must not be overlooked that although each of these elements in the apocalyptic instruction has its own antecedents, it is in our passage that they are brought together for the first time. 1 Thess. 4:13-17 also refers to the parousia, but not in an identical way. By bringing these traditions together into an explicit sequence our text clearly insists that the current experience of the church (Mark 13:9-23) is not yet the last hour.

The parable of the fig tree, in its present context, therefore means in effect, "not until you see these things happen is the Son of man at the door." ("These things" may refer back to the entire preceding material, just as the same phrase in v. 4 pointed ahead.)

The double assurance combines two sayings which have no inherent relation to each other. The first (v. 30) is an "amen" (RSV: truly) saying which appears to belong to the oldest stratum of the material, since it has Jesus pledge that his own generation would see all these things happen (see also Mark 9:1). The tension between this saying and Mark's own aims in writing this chapter is fairly clear. V. 31 is similar to Matt. 5:18, where it has to do with the permanence of the Torah. Putting this saying here reinforces not only v. 30 but the remainder in v. 32; only God knows precisely when the hour will strike—a clear rebuke to all who claim to know it.

HOMILETICAL INTERPRETATION

First Lesson: Dan. 7:9-10. Even if you are one of those preachers who avoids the strange shapes and sounds of the apocalyptic as presented in books like Daniel, Ezekiel, and Revelation, do pause before the vision in this reading. Here God is portrayed as a very old man—Ancient of Days. How unusual! We are so accustomed to God's praise being sung with lyrics such as infinite, holy, majestic, omniscient, eternal, lofty, unapproachable, divine, omnipotent. But as an old man? Have we not scolded, scorned, and corrected those poor souls who still have an image of God as an old man with a white beard? What comes to mind when you think of an old man? Feeble, forgetful, retired, sickly, poor hearing, poor eyesight, kind but senile. There he is, dozing amid prescriptions, walking canes, stainless steel trays, magnifying glass, large print Bible, and soft house slippers, storing up energy sufficient for shuffleboard on Friday.

But here Daniel presents God as an old man. The context makes the image even more unusual. Israel is in dire straits. The wicked Syrian ruler Antiochus Epiphanes is a cruel oppressor. His kingdom and the three preceding (Persian, Medean, Babylonian) are cast as four beasts. History agrees with the descriptions: ugly, powerful, ferocious. In their hands what is to become of poor little Israel? The scene changes to that of a courtroom. There is fire everywhere. Good—burn up the four beasts! Tens of thousands of angels fill the place. Good—let their chariots overrun the enemy! But there in the center, seated, is the Ancient of Days. Is there any hope or encouragement in this picture of God? Does it do anything for the faithful, overwhelmed, outnumbered, and at the rope's end, to be reminded that God is older than any of us?

Unlike our culture, that of the writer understood age to imply wisdom, authority, prestige, and power. Job, in his struggle with the ways of God, was reminded: "Behold, God is great, and we know him not; the number of his years is unsearchable" (Job 36:26). Before Babylon or Persia or Greece, God was. After Babylon, Persia, or Greece, God will be. Kings and lords and oppressors come and go, but God endures from generation to generation. His being presented as an old man is a way of saying that God himself forms a parenthesis around all our history. He is Alpha and Omega. We live our lives "from God—to God." And in spite of our sense of being victims in the world, he sits upon the throne.

"For what is man that he should live out the lifetime of his God?" (Herman Melville, *Moby Dick*)

Second Lesson: Heb. 13:20-21. This passage is one of the most familiar of the benedictions in the NT. Since it is most often quoted or read at the close of a service when everyone is more engaged in preparations for leaving than in listening, perhaps the preacher will want to take this occasion to share the content. Pausing to examine and hear exactly what is being said in a benediction could be most helpful. This benediction is pregnant with the grand themes of the Christian faith.

But it may also be an advantageous time to share what a benediction is. Why not *begin* your sermon with this benediction? You may want to have the congregation "stand for the benediction" and then be seated. Sometimes a relocation of a familiar portion of the service will bring it to our attention in a new way. Is it appropriate to *begin* with the benediction? Paul in his letters would place benedictions in the beginning, at the end, or within the flow of his discussion.

What, then, is a benediction? Notice it is not a prayer since it is addressed to the congregation. It is not "Goodbye; don't forget to check in the pew around you for all your belongings." It is not a summing up of all the announcements in a final reminder before leaving. ("Lord, help everyone to remember the fellowship dinner Wednesday evening.") It is not a wrap-up of the sermon in one last homiletical swing at them.

The benediction is rather a blessing. A blessing is the request for, or announcement of, God's favor. A blessing is not a word of approval upon all that has occurred. The word of exhortation to them still stands and no benediction pulls out its props. Nor does this blessing get its validity from the warm and pleasant relation of the speaker to the hearer. (Hebrews 13:18 implies some strain between the writer and the readers.) The benediction is an affirmation of the gospel which is there and which is true, though all men be liars. The church addressed in Hebrews is faltering, afraid, neglecting worship, giving up on the mission, and on the brink of falling away from the faith. The benediction affirms to such a church what God has done and is doing and will do in Jesus Christ. In other words, the benediction is a reminder of God's good favor and grace upon us in spite of us. A benediction is therefore appropriate at the beginning, in the middle, or at the end. After all, it is with God that we have to deal, here or elsewhere. And the final word about God is a "bene-diction," a good word.

Gospel: Mark 13:24-31. Have you ever been made aware of how much of the minister's time is spent making affirmative and negative statements on the same subjects? He calls for more Bible study and then has to battle the confusion and alarm created by a houseful of sudden scholars. He urges the congregation to pray and then tries to stir back into action the prayer groups that paralyze the program. He leads them to be open to the Spirit's presence and the spiritualists want a new minister who is more spiritual. He guides them in developing the inner life and then feels defeated by the psychological captivity of the church. But, we're in good company. Paul preached that the coming of Christ was at hand and then frantically wrote letters explaining "What I really meant." Mark, in our Gospel for today, affirms that the end is near but not as near as many are claiming. What a task!

Apparently the problem Mark faced was the theological interpretation of the destruction of Jerusalem. It was of profound significance for Christian and Jew. Historical events, events of social and political impact are not alien to the interpretive task of the minister. But to tie the whole of God's purpose to one event is to be overwhelmed and pressed into premature judgments about God's way in the world. False prophets were tying the end of the *world* to the end of Jerusalem. Not so, says Mark. No one tragedy means the end; no one triumph means victory. Those who jump on these bandwagons often have a lot of debris to clear up afterward. Those who follow are disillusioned and their hopes are bankrupt. "Where is the promise of his coming?" says the believer-turned-cynic. "All things have continued as they were from the beginning" (2 Pet. 3:4).

Of course, it is not enough to stand by and make learned comments about the parade of theological fads and new preachments of those who say, "Lo here, or lo there." The gospel must be proclaimed. That Jesus Christ is Lord of history we firmly believe in spite of the present hidden and ambiguous evidence of that claim. But in God's time he will be crowned with glory and power. In that grand enthronement all those faithful, gathered from every nation, will share. Of this we are confident, even on days when we seem to be assigned to the ocean with a teaspoon, or to be holding aloft a candle in a hurricane.

The Last Sunday after Pentecost, Christ the King

Lutheran	*Roman Catholic*	*Episcopal*	*Pres./UCC/Chr.*	*Methodist/COCU*
Dan. 7:13-14	Dan. 7:13-14	Dan. 7:13-14	Hosea 2:14-20	Dan. 7:13-14
Rev. 1:4b-8	Rev. 1:5-8	Rev. 1:4b-8	2 Cor. 3:17—4:2	Rev. 1:4b-8
John 18:33-37	John 18:33b-37	John 18:33b-37	Mark 2:18-22	John 18:33-37

EXEGESIS

First Lesson: Dan. 7:13-14. (For Daniel 7 as a whole, see Pentecost 27.) Whether the poetry in Dan. 7:9-11, 13-14 had an independent history of its own before being included in the present text is not clear. At any rate vv. 13-14 now climax the vision begun in 7:2, and the one who looked like a human in contrast with the four beasts is understood to be the God-given alternative to bestial history. Dan. 7:19-27 elaborates and interprets the fourth beast (representing Antiochus IV Epiphanes) and what will follow him; thus 7:27 interprets 7:13-14. The interpretation in v. 27 does not mention the "one like a son of man," who is a heavenly figure, but restricts its focus to the impending rule of God's saints on earth. This, in turn, suggests that the author reinterprets the figure to mean the heavenly counterpart of the saints, as is the archangel Michael in Dan. 12:1; Rev. 12:7. It must be admitted, however, that any reconstruction of the traditions and the author's use of them is burdened with serious limitations. This is because, on the one hand, although the motif of a heavenly Man (or primal Man) is widespread in antiquity, it is difficult to determine how all the evidence (e.g., the Man from the sea in 2 Esdras 13) coheres in an overall history of the motif; on the other hand, our text does not speak of *The* Son of man at all (as do the Book of Enoch and the

Gospels) but of one who is "like a son of man"—he is humaniform, one who appears to be a heavenly humanoid.

In our text, this man-like one comes with clouds (as does the Son of man in Mark 13:26), but he does not come to earth (as in Mark 13) but to God's throne. In other words, Dan. 7:13-14 speaks of his investiture with world-wide authority. Whereas the four preceding beasts had rapaciously seized power, this man-like one receives his dominion from God; moreover, whereas their power was transient (i.e., historical), his is permanent. He represents the divinely-ordained humane alternative to bestial history.

As the author understands the matter in v. 27, this figure represents the kingdom of God (although the term is not used), which on earth is manifested in the rule of the saints: the fate of those who are now victimized will be reversed.

Second Lesson: Rev. 1:4(5)-8. Rev. 1:4-8 juxtaposes four types of material: (a) vv. 4-5a generally follow the epistolary convention developed by Paul; (b) vv. 5b-6 are a doxology; (c) v. 7 may be called an eschatological announcement; (d) v. 8 is a divine self-proclamation. This diverse material is framed by the unusual reference to God as "(he) who is and who was and who is to come" (vv. 4, 8). The phrase amplifies the LXX of Exod. 3:14, where the LXX translates Yahweh's name as "He who is." Rev. 4:8 suggests that this formula was developed in Christian liturgy, where it was combined with Isa. 6:2. God as the "almighty" (*pantokrator*) is derived from the LXX, which used the term for "Yahweh Sabaoth" (Lord of hosts) in Amos 3:13; 4:13, for example. *Pantokrator* is a key word for Revelation (see also 11:17; 15:3; 16:7, 14; 19:6, 15; 21:22), perhaps because this term was also being used by the emperor cult.

Grace and peace come from three sources: God, the seven spirits (seven apparently suggests a court with a full staff of servants; see 5:6), and from Jesus Christ; Christ, in turn, is understood in three ways. First, he is the faithful witness. "Witness" is one translation of *martyrs*, which can also mean "martyr" (see also 3:14); the allusion is to Christ's fidelity in death. Second, he is "the first born of the dead" (used also in Col. 1:18), a phrase which means virtually the same as "first fruits of those who have fallen asleep" (1 Cor. 15:20). Third, he is ruler of earthly kings, an allusion to the exaltation of Christ. The latter two phrases may represent an adaptation of Ps. 89:27. The exalted Christ rules the kings of the earth, puts the power of the emperor into perspective, and asserts that the current ordeal of the faithful is not the last word.

The doxology to Christ calls attention to his love (note the present tense), his redemptive work, and to his making Christians both a kingdom and body of priests to God; the latter alludes to Exod. 19:1-6 (see also 1 Pet. 2:5). Again, the fact that these themes appear in hymnic material in Rev. 5:9-10 suggests that in our passage the author is using the language of Christian worship, which itself distills into poetic form a complex and sophisticated christological use of the OT.

The eschatological promise uses language about the coming of one like a son of man in Dan. 7:13, which long since had been understood by Christians to refer to the parousia of the Son of man (see Mark 13:26 par.). Zech. 12:10-14 also seems to have influenced this passage, though here it is the whole earth that shall wail, evidently because his coming signals the judgment. (NEB bypasses the question, while the Jerusalem Bible has "mourn for him.")

Although the passage begins and ends with a reference to God, the core content is Christocentric. It concentrates on the work of Christ, first in redeeming the saints, then on the consummation and public vindication.

Gospel: John 18:33-37. The differences among the reports of the trial of Jesus in the various Gospels are well known and important for reconstructing, insofar as possible, what happened. Our concern here, however, is to understand a segment of one account. Here as elsewhere, John is writing not primarily to report accurately what happened, but to disclose "what was really going on" in what happened. Just as the first twelve chapters show "what is really going on" when the Creator confronts "the Jews" (who usually represent the world, especially in its religious dimension), so here he shows "what is really going on" when Christ confronts political power, when kingdom confronts kingdom. Ostensibly Pilate is passing judgment on Jesus; actually, as John understands it, Pilate is condemning himself. (The same is true of the priests in 19:15; by pledging their loyalty they manifest their disloyalty to their king.) It may well be that the Synoptic accounts of the trial exonerate Pilate, but this is not the case in John.

The Johannine story puts Pilate between the Jews outside the praetorium (18:28) and Jesus who is inside. Part of the story's dynamic derives from Pilate's movement back and forth, unable to cope effectively either inside or out. The lesson amputates Pilate's closing line of this scene (v. 38)—evidently in order to end the lection with a word from Jesus rather than with Pilate's sneer.

The scene opens with Pilate's question (identical in all Gospels). "King of the Jews" is a political term. (Earlier, Jesus had rejected an effort to make him king; John 6:15.) The whole narrative (18:33—19:22) repeatedly comes back to the theme of Jesus the king of the Jews. Jesus does not answer the question but seizes the initiative with a counter question (v. 34), formulated to expose Pilate: either he is a tool of "others" or else he genuinely desires to know who Jesus really is. Pilate avoids the trap by implying that this is a question for Jews to decide—as if the procurator could avoid responsibility for investigating the charge and evaluating its source. (The question in v. 38 should be translated, "I'm not a Jew, am I?") Although it was only the priests who delivered Jesus to Pilate, the procurator includes the "nation" in the action. Then he asks an open-ended question by which Jesus could incriminate himself or deny his vocation by answering "Nothing."

Again Jesus dodges the question and seizes the initiative by clarifying his *basileia* (literally "kingdom," as in NEB and Jerusalem Bible; RSV has "kingship"). The clarification consists of an assertion and of supporting evidence. The assertion turns on the preposition "of." In Johannine theology, "of" means derived from, grounded in, determined by. Just as Jesus is not "of" this world, nor the disciples insofar as they belong to him (John 17:16), so his kingdom is not "of this world." This kingship is not "otherworldly" in the ordinary sense; rather it is totally other, just as what is "of the flesh" is contrasted with what is "of the Spirit" (John 3:6). For supporting evidence Jesus reasons from a negative point: if his kingship were of this world, his servants would struggle to prevent his being handed over to the Jews; but since they did not fight, and since he was handed over to them, it should be clear that his kingdom is of a wholly different order.

On the surface, Pilate rightly infers that Jesus has conceded that he is a "king"; actually, he missed the whole point because what he means by "king" and what Jesus implied are utterly different. But Jesus does not pursue the matter, for in John's view enough has been said for Pilate to expose his blindness. Those (only) who are "of the truth" respond rightly to Jesus (see John 8:47). The pervasive dualism in John appears here also: how one responds to Jesus reveals whether one is of truth, of God, of light, of Spirit, or of lies, of the devil, of darkness, of flesh. Pilate's contemptuous, "What is truth?" reveals what he is "of".

HOMILETICAL INTERPRETATION

(The writer is aware that the readings for today are entirely different in the Presbyterian and United Church of Christ lectionaries. The decision is to continue not just with the majority but with these texts which portray the eschatological triumph of Christ and his church, a fitting finale for this Pentecost series.)

First Lesson: Dan. 7:13-14. If the preacher is not careful this passage could easily lead to a seduction by the concordance. Son of man, clouds of heaven, glory, all nations: these are terms which can easily lead one to Matthew 25, Mark 13, Revelation, and other passages in which Jesus is presented in triumph as the coming Son of man. As vital and as powerful as those passages are, still Daniel has something significant to say in his own context.

In Daniel the scene is the heavenly court in which the Ancient of Days presides. The "coming" of the Son of man is not to earth but to God's presence. In fact, think of it as a human being coming from earth to heaven. (Later, of course, the image reversed to that of a heavenly figure coming to earth.) Son of man here means "man" in sharp contrast to the four beasts just described.

Now what does this say? The final victory is to the *human*. Man, male and female, created in God's image, is the figure present and approved in the final scene of God's fulfilled purpose. That ought to say something to us about ourselves. We are God's masterpiece of creation and his goal for us is not to be superhuman, supernatural, something other than what he made us to be. To be Christian is not to be an angel but to be human in the fullest sense of creation. When will we ever accept that and quit saying "only human," "to err is human," and quit explaining every failure by the word "human." A suggestion: every time you are commended or complimented for success, for a job well done, accept it with the words, "Well, after all, I'm human." See what happens.

In Daniel's vision, the Son of man, or Man, is a figure representing Israel, the people of God. A community represented as one person. This sense of the corporate, the whole community is the rich legacy Judaism gave to the church. We are members one of another. At the Lord's Table we are to wait on each other and fellowship with each other, discerning the body, his church. Christ has broken the wall between Jews and Gentiles and created one new man (the community imaged as one person). The problem of private religion and individual pursuits of salvation still plagues the community of faith; Daniel's image is still prophetic. Who would have ever dreamed that a time would come in the history of God's people when the idea of private salvation outside the church would be entertained as a possibility?

Second Lesson: Rev. 1:4b-8. The scene is after the last battle. God's victory over every evil is assured and the Lordship of Jesus Christ, so long victimized as a lamb bleeding, is beyond dispute. All who pierced him are now frightened by his re-appearance. The background music is about to begin: the drum speaks to the trumpet, the trumpet speaks to the cannon, and the cannon speaks to the sky. Tens of thousands of angels burst into the Hallelujah Chorus. And in this festival of victory, Jesus is called by the simple and humble term, "the faithful witness." Why?

Two reasons come quickly. First, the means whereby God's victory comes is in faithful witnessing. Second, as faithful witness Jesus Christ is model and pioneer for the Christians of Asia Minor facing persecution by Rome. To grasp the power of the image of the faithful witness, the term must be freed from current associations: leaflets circulated on street corners, two sober young men going from door to door, standing among friends in a cozy group telling personal experiences. When Revelation was written the term "witness" made its way among vulgar soldiers, noisy chariots, investigators at midnight, gavels of cynical judges, whispered information for thirty pieces of silver, dungeons, confused orphans crying, suspicions passed along narrow streets, stern edicts publicly posted, and the sign of the fish scratched in the dirt.

What was it these Christians were saying or doing that brought out the guard? What in the world was so threatening that it got Caesar's attention? We have all heard witnessing that would not stir the cat from the hearth.

Oh, the times are different now. True, thank God. But is that all? No, the place is different, because Christians today witness most often among Christians; they witnessed to the world. Is that all the difference? No, the content of the testimony is changed. Some witnessing today is about how I feel; I take you on a trip through my psyche. Early Christians witnessed to God's power and grace made known in Jesus Christ. God was at work, they said, and new value systems were brought to the marketplace, new understandings of marriage and home and social and political structures. The kingship of God is present among us. The vision of what will be spelled the end of what was.

The witness–it is here, not with the loud claims or counterclaims, that the case is won or lost. The faithful witness–it is here in quiet and humble strength, inescapable, that power resides to alter the world.

Gospel: John 18:33-37. In the comments above we have explored the reference to Jesus as the faithful witness. One early creed says that "Christ Jesus in his witness before Pontius Pilate made the good confession" (1 Tim. 6:13). In this passage from the Gospel for today Jesus tells Pilate he came to bear witness to the truth. The truth, according to John, is that God is the creator and sustainer of all things. Since they have their source in God, all things are good as long as they remain created and relative values. Institutions, customs, Sabbaths, the temple, even the Scriptures have their value as witnesses to God. Only God is giver of life. But if any created value, however good, is regarded as ultimate and as able to give life, that is idolatry, death, darkness. It is to be "of this world." John regards this as the error of the Jews: absolutizing created values such as the temple, customs, the Sabbath, etc. As a result they abide in death, having loved the darkness.

Having ended his witness to the Jews, Jesus now witnesses to Pilate, to the political structure of his day. In John the trial of Jesus almost totally focuses on Jesus before Pilate. To the witness of Jesus concerning God as the sole source of power and life, (1) Pilate may respond positively and accept the truth about the derived and relative power of the state. (2) He may, of course, deny the truth and assert his own power as absolute. (3) Or, he may remain neutral, without that much interest in the truth (Am I a Jew, a theologian, to be interested in this?). He makes an effort at neutrality but it is too feeble. Jesus is no direct political threat but he does raise the question of the limited authority of the state (You have only that power over me that God has given you). Where authority is uncertain, it is usually asserted all the more. The Jews have fled to the political powers to solve their problem and Pilate puts the power of the state at the disposal of the world. In this act Pilate and the state are "of the world," asserting themselves against the power of God. "The truth" is refused. "For God *and* country" becomes "For God *or* country."

"Crucified under Pontius Pilate." Who won? What was, what is, the truth?

Though the cause of evil prosper, yet 'tis truth alone is strong;
Though her portion be the scaffold, and upon the throne be wrong,
Yet that scaffold sways the future, And behind the dim unknown,
Standeth God within the shadow, keeping watch above his own.

(James Russell Lowell)

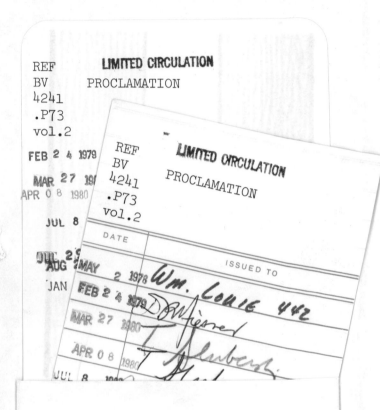